Continental Philosophy

BLACKWELL PHILOSOPHY ANTHOLOGIES

Each volume in this outstanding new series provides a comprehensive and author-itative collection of the essential primary readings from philosophy's main fields of study. Designed to complement the *Blackwell Companions to Philosophy* series, each volume represents an unparalleled resource in its own right, and will provide the ideal platform for course use.

Forthcoming

Continental Philosophy
An Anthology

Edited by

William McNeill and *Karen S. Feldman*
DePaul University, Chicago

First published 1998
2 4 6 8 10 9 7 5 3 1

Blackwell Publishers Inc.
350 Main Street
Malden, Massachusetts 02148
USA

Blackwell Publishers Ltd
108 Cowley Road
Oxford OX4 1JF
UK

Library of Congress Cataloging-in-Publication Data

Continental philosophy: an anthology / edited by William McNeill and Karen S. Feldman.
     p.   cm. – (Blackwell philosophy anthologies; 6)
  Includes bibliographical references and index.
  ISBN 1-55786-700-3 (alk. paper). – ISBN 1-55786-561-2 (pbk.: alk. paper)
  1. Philosophy, European. 2. Philosophy, Modern. I. McNeill, William (William A.) II. Feldman, Karen S. III. Series.
B791.C594 1998   97-37883
190–dc21   CIP

British Library Cataloguing in Publication Data

A CIP catalogue record for this book is available from the British Library.

Typeset in 9 on 11 pt Ehrhardt by Pure Tech India Ltd, Pondicherry
Printed in Great Britain by T. J. International, Padstow, Cornwall

This book is printed on acid-free paper

Contents

Contents

Contents

Introduction

This anthology seeks to bring together a representative cross-section of authors and texts commonly recognized as belonging to the broad field known today as Continental philosophy. It includes selections from key thinkers in the Continental tradition from Kant to the present day. The anthology is intended primarily as a sourcebook for students, teachers, and general readers who may be approaching Continental philosophy for the first time.

An obvious difficulty in editing a volume of this kind is deciding, even approximately, what Continental philosophy is. The term "Continental philosophy" is relatively new and more or less limited to Great Britain and North America. While it is difficult to say exactly when or where it appeared, the use of the term seems to have arisen with the increasing accessibility in translation of the texts of leading European (primarily French and German) philosophers from what the British refer to as "the Continent," meaning the mainland of Europe, excluding the British Isles. Continental philosophy is thus not defined by any particular doctrinal content or approach, but more by the texts that it chooses to read and by the way in which it reads them.

Although Continental philosophers read texts from throughout the history of philosophy, we have restricted the scope of this anthology to cover the period from Kant to the present day. This restriction is not only for reasons of length and practical feasibility, for, broadly speaking,

Kant's philosophy may legitimately be said to be the point at which so-called "Continental" thought begins to diverge from Anglo-American analytic philosophy. Whatever the historical and cultural reasons for this divergence, it seems apparent that while Kant was and continues to be widely read and taken seriously within the scholarship of analytic philosophy, the same can hardly be said of Fichte or Schelling, Hegel or Hölderlin. In a sense, then, the roots of Continental philosophy may be said to emerge from the debate between Kantian thought and the ensuing philosophies of German Idealism. This is also indicative of what has seemed to most clearly mark the divergence between subsequent analytic philosophy and the Continental tradition. For no matter how critical it may be of Hegelian thought, Continental philosophy broadly accepts and shares a fundamental insight of Hegel's thinking: namely, that reason, rationality, thought, i.e. *logos* in general, are constituted in an intrinsically historical manner; that their mode of being is the same as that of human existence itself, and in this sense guarantees no eternal truths or certainties. By contrast – again speaking very broadly, and without the necessary qualifications that could no doubt be multiplied *ad infinitum* – the "analytic" approach of modern Anglo-American philosophy tends (such at least is the Continental perception) to proceed *sub specie aeternitatis*, entrusting itself to the modern scientific quest for truth and certainty and its accompanying ideal of clarity and transparency of language. For Continental thought, on the other hand, the desire for scientific truth is no less historically contingent and questionable than any other purely "logical" truth, and offers no eternal or ultimate solutions to the fundamental questions of human existence. An awareness of the intrinsic historicality of its own undertaking thus tends to be a distinctive hallmark of Continental philosophy.

We do not intend here to enter into the argument about the relative merits of these two styles of philosophizing, both of which in any case share common roots that extend back at least to the beginnings of Western philosophy in ancient Greece. Nor do we claim that the observations just cited accurately reflect or depict the actual content and infinite richness found within each of these two styles. The anthology offered here intends only to reflect a contemporary and general perception, at least in Great Britain and North America, of what Continental philosophy is, or, perhaps better, of what it "does," of its practice and approach. We have sought to include a representative selection of texts and authors whose style of thinking (whatever their individual differences) may be broadly identified as Continental. This perception is of course very much a perception of the moment, one whose life is very likely to be limited to a few years. (This is especially likely in the case of the final section of the anthology, devoted to some of the most recent thinkers and texts to attain prominence within the field.) It is quite possible that the philosophical "scene" in Great Britain and North America will be very different in a decade's time. It is not inconceivable that the titles "analytic" and "Continental" may gradually cease to be used; indeed, there are some signs of increasing *rapprochement* and dialogue between analytic philosophy and Continental philosophy. However matters may turn out in this regard, we would simply ask our readers to take this anthology in the spirit of such a momentary perception or reflection – a kind of "sign of the times."

As the comments above indicate, "Continental philosophy" is not defined primarily in terms of geographical or nationalistic considerations, but philosophically, as a style of philosophizing in which the practitioners put their own traditions, cultures, histories, and languages into question and into dialogue with one another, beyond the perspective or objective of attaining eternal truths. Our hope is that the following selections will speak for themselves, and encourage dialogue and debate in the spirit of their authors, beyond the all too often closed or hostile boundaries of so-called "schools" of philosophy.

For the sake of convenience, the selections in this anthology have been ordered into five major sections: Part I: The Age of the System: Kant and German Idealism; Part II: Subjectivity in Question: Existentialism, Phenomenology, and Hermeneutics; Part III: Political Thought: Marxism and Critical Theory; Part IV: Structuralism and Psychoanalysis; and Part V: Deconstruction, Feminism, and Postmodernism. Again, these sections reflect both styles of approach and content or subject-matter. They should not be taken as fixed "categories" or classifications. Just as some of the philosophers presented might have been included in a number of different sections, so too other possible combinations and principles of ordering may be useful for pedagogical purposes. Within each section, texts are generally ordered chronologically according to date of publication, with one or two exceptions. A brief introduction is provided for each philosopher, intended only as a very rough sketch of the philosopher and his or her work. A bibliography following each selection offers some suggestions for further reading.

An anthology of this kind cannot be all things to all readers. As literary critic Paul de Man has pointedly noted, "Precisely because they have an appearance of impersonality about them, encyclopedias or anthologies can be among the most subjective of documents."[1] Thus, it is inevitable that some readers would have opted for different selections, while others will wonder why one philosopher rather than another has been included. In general, we have tried to balance centrality with accessibility: to select texts that are both representative of the thought of each philosopher and accessible to readers who may be approaching Continental philosophy for the first time. In our selection of texts for the last section in particular (on Deconstruction, Feminism, and Postmodernism), which by its very nature is no doubt the least coherently defined (reflecting as it does an ongoing and still emergent configuration of texts and thinkers), we have again used no hard-and-fast principles, but have taken certain risks. It is indeed debatable whether certain authors included in the anthology are philosophers strictly speaking; nevertheless, what "philosophy" itself is constitutes a central concern of Continental philosophizing as a style of thinking that puts its own activity in question. In general, the selections chosen reflect what we see as an increasingly interdisciplinary dimension of Continental philosophy today, which is not limited to philosophy departments, but finds audiences in such diverse fields as literature, sociology, political science, psychology, linguistics, and women's studies.

Such reservations notwithstanding, we hope that the present volume will nonetheless be a helpful resource for teachers and students in this field.

The editors wish to thank Michael Naas and Stephen Houlgate for their valuable suggestions.

In addition, our thanks are due to the many people who have offered assistance at various stages of this project, including Duncan Large, Bill Martin, Kas Saghafi, and Philippe van Haute, and our editors at Blackwell Publishers, Stephan Chambers and Steve Smith. Finally, special thanks to Jack Messenger for his diligent work on the proofs.

William McNeill
Karen S. Feldman
DePaul University

Note

1 Paul de Man, *Critical Writings, 1953–1978*, ed. L. Waters (Minneapolis: University of Minnesota Press, 1989), p. 139.

PART I

The Age of the System: Kant and German Idealism

1

Immanuel Kant

The critical philosophy of Immanuel Kant (1724–1804) represents the first attempt in the modern period to investigate and ground in a strictly systematic manner the legitimate limits of human knowledge. For Kant, "critique" means precisely such investigation and establishment of limits. In the *Critique of Pure Reason* (1781), Kant argues that our knowledge of sensible objects of nature must conform in advance to the structures of the human mind, and that we can therefore have legitimate knowledge only of objects as they appear for us, and not as they are in themselves. Such knowledge requires the givenness of its objects via the pure forms of sensibility (space and time as the forms of pure "intuition"), and the determination of such objects via the concepts of the understanding. The synthesis of intuition and empirical concept must occur in advance ("*a priori*") in accordance with the pure concepts or "categories" of the understanding (concepts such as unity, causality, negation). Pure *a priori* synthesis can thus be shown to underlie all legitimate human knowledge of external objects, and is the basis of all scientific and mathematical knowledge of the world. This view of human knowledge in which objects must conform in advance to the structures of the human mind Kant calls "transcendental idealism." The following selection presents some of the key sections from the *Critique of Pure Reason*.

Critique of Pure Reason

Introduction

I. *The Distinction between Pure and Empirical Knowledge*

There can be no doubt that all our knowledge begins with experience. For how should our faculty of knowledge be awakened into action did not

From *Critique of Pure Reason*, translated by Norman Kemp Smith (New York: St. Martin's Press, 1965), pp. 41–59. Copyright © 1965. Reprinted by permission of Macmillan Press Ltd.

objects affecting our senses partly of themselves produce representations, partly arouse the activity of our understanding to compare these representations, and, by combining or separating them, work up the raw material of the sensible impressions into that knowledge of objects which is entitled experience? In the order of time, therefore, we have no knowledge antecedent to experience, and with experience all our knowledge begins.

But though all our knowledge begins with experience, it does not follow that it all arises out of experience. For it may well be that even our empirical knowledge is made up of what we receive through impressions and of what our own faculty of knowledge (sensible impressions serving merely as the occasion) supplies from itself. If our faculty of knowledge makes any such addition, it may be that we are not in a position to distinguish it from the raw material, until with long practice of attention we have become skilled in separating it.

This, then, is a question which at least calls for closer examination, and does not allow of any off-hand answer: – whether there is any knowledge that is thus independent of experience and even of all impressions of the senses. Such knowledge is entitled *a priori*, and distinguished from the *empirical*, which has its sources *a posteriori*, that is, in experience.

The expression "*a priori*" does not, however, indicate with sufficient precision the full meaning of our question. For it has been customary to say, even of much knowledge that is derived from empirical sources, that we have it or are capable of having it *a priori*, meaning thereby that we do not derive it immediately from experience, but from a universal rule – a rule which is itself, how-ever, borrowed by us from experience. Thus we would say of a man who undermined the foundations of his house, that he might have known *a priori* that it would fall, that is, that he need not have waited for the experience of its actual falling. But still he could not know this completely *a priori*. For he had first to learn through experience that bodies are heavy, and therefore fall when their supports are withdrawn.

In what follows, therefore, we shall understand by *a priori* knowledge, not knowledge independent of this or that experience, but knowledge absolutely independent of all experience. Opposed to it is empirical knowledge, which is knowledge possible only *a posteriori*, that is, through experience. *A priori* modes of knowledge are entitled pure when there is no admixture of anything empirical. Thus, for instance, the proposition, "every alteration has its cause," while an *a priori* proposition, is not a pure proposition, because alteration is a concept which can be derived only from experience.

II. We are in Possession of certain Modes of a priori Knowledge, and even the Common Understanding is never without them

What we here require is a criterion by which to distinguish with certainty between pure and empirical knowledge. Experience teaches us that a thing is so and so, but not that it cannot be other-wise. First, then, if we have a proposition which in being thought is thought as *necessary*, it is an *a priori* judgment; and if, besides, it is not derived from any proposition except one which also has the validity of a necessary judgment, it is an absolutely *a priori* judgment. Secondly, experience never con-fers on its judgments true or strict, but only assumed and comparative *universality*, through induction. We can properly only say, therefore, that, so far as we have hitherto observed, there is no exception to this or that rule. If, then, a judg-ment is thought with strict universality, that is, in such manner that no exception is allowed as possi-ble, it is not derived from experience, but is valid absolutely *a priori*. Empirical universality is only an arbitrary extension of a validity holding in most cases to one which holds in all, for instance, in the proposition, "all bodies are heavy." When, on the other hand, strict universality is essential to a judg-ment, this indicates a special source of knowledge, namely, a faculty of *a priori* knowledge. Necessity and strict universality are thus sure criteria of *a priori* knowledge, and are inseparable from one another. But since in the employment of these criteria the contingency of judgments is sometimes more easily shown than their empirical limitation, or, as sometimes also happens, their unlimited universality can be more convincingly proved than their necessity, it is advisable to use the two criteria separately, each by itself being infallible.

Now it is easy to show that there actually are in human knowledge judgments which are necessary and in the strictest sense universal, and which are therefore pure *a priori* judgments. If an example from the sciences be desired, we have only to look to any of the propositions of mathematics; if we seek an example from the understanding in its quite ordinary employment, the proposition, "every alteration must have a cause," will serve our purpose. In the latter case, indeed, the very concept of a cause so manifestly contains the concept of a necessity of connection with an effect and of the strict universality of the rule, that the concept would be altogether lost if we attempted to derive it, as Hume has done, from a repeated association of that which happens with that which precedes, and from a custom of connecting representations, a custom originating in this repeated association, and constituting therefore a merely subjective neces-sity. Even without appealing to such examples, it is possible to show that pure *a priori* principles are indispensable for the possibility of experience, and so to prove their existence *a priori*. For whence could experience derive its certainty, if all the rules, according to which it proceeds, were always themselves empirical, and therefore contingent? Such rules could hardly be regarded as first principles. At present, however, we may be content to have established the fact that our faculty of knowledge does have a pure employment, and to have shown what are the criteria of such an employment....

III.   *Philosophy stands in Need of a Science which shall determine the Possibility, the Principles, and the Extent of all a priori Knowledge*

But what is still more extraordinary than all the preceding is this, that certain modes of knowledge leave the field of all possible experiences and have the appearance of extending the scope of our judgments beyond all limits of experience, and this by means of concepts to which no corresponding object can ever be given in experience.

It is precisely by means of the latter modes of knowledge, in a realm beyond the world of the senses, where experience can yield neither guidance nor correction, that our reason carries on those enquiries which owing to their importance we consider to be far more excellent, and in their purpose far more lofty, than all that the understanding can learn in the field of appearances. Indeed we prefer to run every risk of error rather than desist from such urgent enquiries, on the ground of their dubious character, or from disdain and indifference. These unavoidable problems set by pure reason itself are *God*, *freedom*, and *immortality*. The science which, with all its preparations, is in its final intention directed solely to their solution is metaphysics; and its procedure is at first dogmatic, that is, it confidently sets itself to this task without any previous examination of the capacity or incapacity of reason for so great an undertaking.

Now it does indeed seem natural that, as soon as we have left the ground of experience, we should, through careful enquiries, assure ourselves as to the foundations of any building that we propose to erect, not making use of any knowledge that we possess without first determining whence it has come, and not trusting to principles without knowing their origin. It is natural, that is to say, that the question should first be considered, how the understanding can arrive at all this knowledge *a*

priori, and what extent, validity, and worth it may have....

IV.   *The Distinction between Analytic and Synthetic Judgments*

In all judgments in which the relation of a subject to the predicate is thought (I take into consideration affirmative judgments only, the subsequent application to negative judgments being easily made), this relation is possible in two different ways. Either the predicate B belongs to the subject A, as something which is (covertly) contained in this concept A; or B lies outside the concept A, although it does indeed stand in connection with it. In the one case I entitle the judgment analytic, in the other synthetic. Analytic judgments (affirmative) are therefore those in which the connection of the predicate with the subject is thought through identity; those in which this connection is thought without identity should be entitled synthetic. The former, as adding nothing through the predicate to the concept of the subject, but merely breaking it up into those constituent concepts that have all along been thought in it, although confusedly, can also be entitled explicative. The latter, on the other hand, add to the concept of the subject a predicate which has not been in any wise thought in it, and which no analysis could possibly extract from it; and they may therefore be entitled ampliative. If I say, for instance, "All bodies are extended," this is an analytic judgment. For I do not require to go beyond the concept which I connect with "body" in order to find extension as bound up with it. To meet with this predicate, I have merely to analyse the concept, that is, to become conscious to myself of the manifold which I always think in that concept. The judgment is therefore analytic. But when I say, "All bodies are heavy," the predicate is something quite different from anything that I think in the mere concept of body in general; and the addition of such a predicate therefore yields a synthetic judgment.

Judgments of experience, as such, are one and all synthetic. For it would be absurd to found an analytic judgment on experience. Since, in framing the judgment, I must not go outside my concept, there is no need to appeal to the testimony of experience in its support. That a body is extended is a proposition that holds *a priori* and is not empirical. For, before appealing to experience, I have already in the concept of body all the conditions required for my judgment. I have only to extract from it, in accordance with the principle of contradiction, the required predicate, and in so doing can at the same time become conscious of the necessity of the judgment – and that is what experience could never have taught me. On the other hand, though I do not include in the concept of a body in general the predicate "weight," nonetheless this concept indicates an object of experience through one of its parts, and I can add to that part other parts of this same experience, as in this way belonging together with the concept. From the start I can apprehend the concept of body analytically through the characters of extension, impenetrability, figure, etc., all of which are thought in the concept. Now, however, looking back on the experience from which I have derived this concept of body, and finding weight to be invariably connected with the above characters, I attach it as a predicate to the concept; and in doing so I attach it synthetically, and am therefore extending my knowledge. The possibility of the synthesis of the predicate "weight" with the concept of "body" thus rests upon experience. While the one concept is not contained in the other, they yet belong to one another, though only contingently, as parts of a whole, namely, of an experience which is itself a synthetic combination of intuitions.

But in *a priori* synthetic judgments this help is entirely lacking. [I do not here have the advantage of looking around in the field of experience.] Upon what, then, am I to rely, when I seek to go beyond the concept A, and to know that another concept B is connected with it? Through what is the synthesis made possible? Let us take the proposition, "Everything which happens has its cause." In the concept of "something which happens," I do indeed think an existence which is preceded by a time, etc., and from this concept analytic judgments may be obtained. But the concept of a "cause" lies entirely outside the other concept, and signifies something different from "that which happens," and is not therefore in any way contained in this latter representation. How come I then to predicate of that which happens something quite different, and to apprehend that the concept of cause, though not contained in it, yet belongs, and indeed necessarily belongs, to it? What is here the unknown = X which gives support to the understanding when it believes that it can discover outside the concept A a predicate B foreign to this concept, which it yet at the same time considers to be connected with it? It cannot be experience, because the suggested prin-

ciple has connected the second representation with the first, not only with greater universality, but also with the character of necessity, and therefore completely *a priori* and on the basis of mere concepts. Upon such synthetic, that is, ampliative principles, all our *a priori* speculative knowledge must ultimately rest; analytic judgments are very important, and indeed necessary, but only for obtaining that clearness in the concepts which is requisite for such a sure and wide synthesis as will lead to a genuinely new addition to all previous knowledge.

V. In all Theoretical Sciences of Reason Synthetic a priori Judgments are contained as Principles

1 *All mathematical judgments, without exception, are synthetic*. This fact, though incontestably certain and in its consequences very important, has hitherto escaped the notice of those who are engaged in the analysis of human reason, and is, indeed, directly opposed to all their conjectures. For as it was found that all mathematical inferences proceed in accordance with the principle of contradiction (which the nature of all apodeictic certainty requires), it was supposed that the fundamental propositions of the science can themselves be known to be true through that principle. This is an erroneous view. For though a synthetic proposition can indeed be discerned in accordance with the principle of contradiction, this can only be if another synthetic proposition is presupposed, and if it can then be apprehended as following from this other proposition; it can never be so discerned in and by itself.

First of all, it has to be noted that mathematical propositions, strictly so called, are always judgments *a priori*, not empirical; because they carry with them necessity, which cannot be derived from experience. If this be demurred to, I am willing to limit my statement to *pure* mathematics, the very concept of which implies that it does not contain empirical, but only pure *a priori* knowledge. . . .

2 *Natural science (physics) contains a priori synthetic judgments as principles*. I need cite only two such judgments: that in all changes of the material world the quantity of matter remains unchanged; and that in all communication of motion, action and reaction must always be equal. Both propositions, it is evident, are not only necessary, and therefore in their origin *a priori*, but also synthetic. For in the concept of matter I do not think its permanence, but only its presence in the space

which it occupies. I go outside and beyond the concept of matter, joining to it *a priori* in thought something which I have not thought *in* it. The proposition is not, therefore, analytic, but synthetic, and yet is thought *a priori*; and so likewise are the other propositions of the pure part of natural science.

3 *Metaphysics*, even if we look upon it as having hitherto failed in all its endeavors, is yet, owing to the nature of human reason, a quite indispensable science, and *ought to contain a priori synthetic knowledge*. For its business is not merely to analyse concepts which we make for ourselves *a priori* of things, and thereby to clarify them analytically, but to extend our *a priori* knowledge. And for this purpose we must employ principles which add to the given concept something that was not contained in it, and through *a priori* synthetic judgments venture out so far that experience is quite unable to follow us, as, for instance, in the proposition, that the world must have a first beginning, and such like. Thus metaphysics consists, at least *in intention*, entirely of *a priori* synthetic propositions.

VI. *The General Problem of Pure Reason*

Much is already gained if we can bring a number of investigations under the formula of a single problem. For we not only lighten our own task, by defining it accurately, but make it easier for others, who would test our results, to judge whether or not we have succeeded in what we set out to do. Now the proper problem of pure reason is contained in the question: How are *a priori* synthetic judgments possible?

That metaphysics has hitherto remained in so vacillating a state of uncertainty and contradiction, is entirely due to the fact that this problem, and perhaps even the distinction between analytic and synthetic judgments, has never previously been considered. Upon the solution of this problem, or upon a sufficient proof that the possibility which it desires to have explained does in fact not exist at all, depends the success or failure of metaphysics. Among philosophers, David Hume came nearest to envisaging this problem, but still was very far from conceiving it with sufficient definiteness and universality. He occupied himself exclusively with the synthetic proposition regarding the connection of an effect with its cause (*principium causalitatis*), and he believed himself to have shown that such an *a priori* proposition is entirely impossible. If we accept his conclusions, then all that we call meta-physics is a mere delusion whereby we fancy ourselves to have rational insight into what, in actual fact, is borrowed solely from experience, and under the influence of custom has taken the illusory semblance of necessity. If he had envisaged our problem in all its universality, he would never have been guilty of this statement, so destructive of all pure philosophy. For he would then have recognized that, according to his own argument, pure mathematics, as certainly containing *a priori* synthetic propositions, would also not be possible; and from such an assertion his good sense would have saved him.

In the solution of the above problem, we are at the same time deciding as to the possibility of the employment of pure reason in establishing and developing all those sciences which contain a theoretical *a priori* knowledge of objects, and have therefore to answer the questions:

How is pure mathematics possible?
How is pure science of nature possible?

Since these sciences actually exist, it is quite proper to ask *how* they are possible; for that they must be possible is proved by the fact that they exist. But the poor progress which has hitherto been made in metaphysics, and the fact that no system yet propounded can, in view of the essential purpose of metaphysics, be said really to exist, leaves everyone sufficient ground for doubting as to its possibility.

Yet, in a certain sense, this *kind of knowledge* is to be looked upon as given; that is to say, metaphysics actually exists, if not as a science, yet still as natural disposition (*metaphysica naturalis*). For human reason, without being moved merely by the idle desire for extent and variety of knowledge, proceeds impetuously, driven on by an inward need, to questions such as cannot be answered by any empirical employment of reason, or by principles thence derived. Thus in all men, as soon as their reason has become ripe for speculation, there has always existed and will always continue to exist some kind of metaphysics. And so we have the question:

How is metaphysics, as natural disposition, possible?

that is, how from the nature of universal human reason do those questions arise which pure reason propounds to itself, and which it is impelled by its own need to answer as best it can?

But since all attempts which have hitherto been made to answer these natural questions—for instance, whether the world has a beginning or is from eternity—have always met with unavoidable contradictions, we cannot rest satisfied with the mere natural disposition to metaphysics, that is, with the pure faculty of reason itself, from which, indeed, some sort of metaphysics (be it what it may) always arises. It must be possible for reason to attain to certainty whether we know or do not know the objects of metaphysics, that is, to come to a decision either in regard to the objects of its enquiries or in regard to the capacity or incapacity of reason to pass any judgment upon them, so that we may either with confidence extend our pure reason or set to it sure and determinate limits. This last question, which arises out of the previous general problem, may, rightly stated, take the form:

How is metaphysics, as science, possible?

Thus the critique of reason, in the end, necessarily leads to scientific knowledge; while its dogmatic employment, on the other hand, lands us in dogmatic assertions to which other assertions, equally specious, can always be opposed—that is, in *skepticism.* . . .

VII. The Idea and Division of a Special Science, under the Title "Critique of Pure Reason"

In view of all these considerations, we arrive at the idea of a special science which can be entitled the Critique of Pure Reason. For reason is the faculty which supplies the principles of *a priori* knowledge. Pure reason is, therefore, that which contains the principles whereby we know anything absolutely *a priori.* An organon of pure reason would be the sum-total of those principles according to which all modes of pure *a priori* knowledge can be acquired and actually brought into being. The exhaustive application of such an organon would give rise to a system of pure reason. But as this would be asking rather much, and as it is still doubtful whether, and in what cases, any extension of our knowledge be here possible, we can regard a science of the mere examination of pure reason, of its sources and limits, as the *propaedeutic* to the system of pure reason. As such, it should be called a critique, not a doctrine, of pure reason. Its utility, in speculation, ought properly to be only negative, not to extend, but only to clarify our reason, and

keep it free from errors—which is already a very great gain. I entitle *transcendental* all knowledge which is occupied not so much with objects as with the mode of our knowledge of objects insofar as this mode of knowledge is to be possible *a priori.* A system of such concepts might be entitled transcendental philosophy. But that is still, at this stage, too large an undertaking. For since such a science must contain, with completeness, both kinds of *a priori* knowledge, the analytic no less than the synthetic, it is, so far as our present purpose is concerned, much too comprehensive. We have to carry the analysis so far only as is indispensably necessary in order to comprehend, in their whole extent, the principles of *a priori* synthesis, with which alone we are called upon to deal. It is upon this enquiry, which should be entitled not a doctrine, but only a transcendental critique, that we are now engaged. Its purpose is not to extend knowledge, but only to correct it, and to supply a touchstone of the value, or lack of value, of all *a priori* knowledge. . .

If we are to make a systematic division of the science which we are engaged in presenting, it must have first a *doctrine of the elements*, and secondly, a *doctrine of the method of pure reason.* Each of these chief divisions will have its subdivisions, but the grounds of these we are not yet in a position to explain. By way of introduction or anticipation we need only say that there are two stems of human knowledge, namely, *sensibility* and *understanding*, which perhaps spring from a common, but to us unknown, root. Through the former, objects are given to us; through the latter, they are thought. Now insofar as sensibility may be found to contain *a priori* representations constituting the condition under which objects are given to us, it will belong to transcendental philosophy. And since the conditions under which alone the objects of human knowledge are given must precede those under which they are thought, the transcendental doctrine of sensibility will constitute the first part of the science of the elements.

Transcendental Doctrine of Elements

First Part: Transcendental Aesthetic

Introduction
In whatever manner and by whatever means a mode of knowledge may relate to objects, *intuition* is that through which it is in immediate relation to them, and to which all thought as a means is

directed. But intuition takes place only in so far as the object is given to us. This again is only possible, to man at least, in so far as the mind is affected in a certain way. The capacity (receptivity) for receiving representations through the mode in which we are affected by objects, is entitled *sensibility*. Objects are *given* to us by means of sensibility, and it alone yields us *intuitions*; they are *thought* through the understanding, and from the understanding arise *concepts*. But all thought must, directly or indirectly, by way of certain characters, relate ultimately to intuitions, and therefore, with us, to sensibility, because in no other way can an object be given to us.

The effect of an object upon the faculty of representation, so far as we are affected by it, is *sensation*. That intuition which is in relation to the object through sensation, is entitled *empirical*. The undetermined object of an empirical intuition is entitled *appearance*.

That in the appearance which corresponds to sensation I term its *matter*; but that which so determines the manifold of appearance that it allows of being ordered in certain relations, I term the *form* of appearance. That in which alone the sensations can be posited and ordered in a certain form, cannot itself be sensation; and therefore, while the matter of all appearance is given to us *a posteriori* only, its form must lie ready for the sensations *a priori* in the mind, and so must allow of being considered apart from all sensation.

I term all representations *pure* (in the transcendental sense) in which there is nothing that belongs to sensation. The pure form of sensible intuitions in general, in which all the manifold of intuition is intuited in certain relations, must be found in the mind *a priori*. This pure form of sensibility may also itself be called *pure intuition*. Thus, if I take away from the representation of a body that which the understanding thinks in regard to it, substance, force, divisibility, etc., and likewise what belongs to sensation, impenetrability, hardness, color, etc., something still remains over from this empirical intuition, namely, extension and figure. These belong to pure intuition, which, even without any actual object of the senses or of sensation, exists in the mind *a priori* as a mere form of sensibility.

The science of all principles of *a priori* sensibility I call *transcendental aesthetic*. There must be such a science, forming the first part of the transcendental doctrine of elements, in distinction from that part which deals with the principles of pure thought, and which is called transcendental logic.

In the transcendental aesthetic we shall, therefore, first *isolate* sensibility, by taking away from it everything which the understanding thinks through its concepts, so that nothing may be left save empirical intuition. Secondly, we shall also separate off from it everything which belongs to sensation, so that nothing may remain save pure intuition and the mere form of appearances, which is all that sensibility can supply *a priori*. In the course of this investigation it will be found that there are two pure forms of sensible intuition, serving as principles of *a priori* knowledge, namely, space and time. To the consideration of these we shall now proceed.

Section I: Space

Metaphysical exposition of this concept

By means of outer sense, a property of our mind, we represent to ourselves objects as outside us, and all without exception in space. In space their shape, magnitude, and relation to one another are determined or determinable. Inner sense, by means of which the mind intuits itself or its inner state, yields indeed no intuition of the soul itself as an object; but there is nevertheless a determinate form [namely, time] in which alone the intuition of inner states is possible, and everything which belongs to inner determinations is therefore represented in relations of time. Time cannot be outwardly intuited, any more than space can be intuited as something in us. What, then, are space and time? Are they real existences? Are they only determinations or relations of things, yet such as would belong to things even if they were not intuited? Or are space and time such that they belong only to the form of intuition, and therefore to the subjective constitution of our mind, apart from which they could not be ascribed to anything whatsoever? In order to obtain light upon these questions, let us first give an exposition of the concept of space. By *exposition* (*expositio*) I mean the clear, though not necessarily exhaustive, representation of that which belongs to a concept: the exposition is *metaphysical* when it contains that which exhibits the concept *as given a priori*.

1 Space is not an empirical concept which has been derived from outer experiences. For in order that certain sensations be referred to something outside me (that is, to something in another region of space from that in which I find myself), and similarly in order that I may be able to represent them as outside and alongside one another, and accordingly as not only different but as in different

places, the representation of space must be presupposed. The representation of space cannot, therefore, be empirically obtained from the relations of outer appearance. On the contrary, this outer experience is itself possible at all only through that representation.

2   Space is a necessary *a priori* representation, which underlies all outer intuitions. We can never represent to ourselves the absence of space, though we can quite well think it as empty of objects. It must therefore be regarded as the condition of the possibility of appearances, and not as a determination dependent upon them. It is an *a priori* representation, which necessarily underlies outer appearances.

3   Space is not a discursive or, as we say, general concept of relations of things in general, but a pure intuition. For, in the first place, we can represent to ourselves only one space; and if we speak of diverse spaces, we mean thereby only parts of one and the same unique space. Secondly, these parts cannot precede the one all-embracing space, as being, as it were, constituents out of which it can be composed; on the contrary, they can be thought only as *in* it. Space is essentially one; the manifold in it, and therefore the general concept of spaces, depends solely on [the introduction of] limitations. Hence it follows that an *a priori*, and not an empirical, intuition underlies all concepts of space. For kindred reasons, geometrical propositions, that, for instance, in a triangle two sides together are greater than the third, can never be derived from the general concepts of line and triangle, but only from intuition, and this indeed *a priori*, with apodeictic certainty.

4   Space is represented as an infinite *given* magnitude. Now every concept must be thought as a representation which is contained in an infinite number of different possible representations (as their common character), and which therefore contains these *under* itself; but no concept, as such, can be thought as containing an infinite number of representations *within* itself. It is in this latter way, however, that space is thought; for all the parts of space coexist *ad infinitum*. Consequently, the original representation of space is an *a priori* intuition, not a concept. . . .

Section II: Time

Metaphysical exposition of the concept of time

1   Time is not an empirical concept that has been derived from any experience. For neither coexistence nor succession would ever come within our perception, if the representation of time were not presupposed as underlying them *a priori*. Only on the presupposition of time can we represent to ourselves a number of things as existing at one and the same time (simultaneously) or at different times (successively).

2   Time is a necessary representation that underlies all intuitions. We cannot, in respect of appearances in general, remove time itself, though we can quite well think time as void of appearances. Time is, therefore, given *a priori*. In it alone is actuality of appearances possible at all. Appearances may, one and all, vanish; but time (as the universal condition of their possibility) cannot itself be removed.

3   The possibility of apodeictic principles concerning the relations of time, or of axioms of time in general, is also grounded upon this *a priori* necessity. Time has only one dimension; different times are not simultaneous but successive (just as different spaces are not successive but simultaneous). These principles cannot be derived from experience, for experience would give neither strict universality nor apodeictic certainty. We should only be able to say that common experience teaches us that it is so; not that it must be so. These principles are valid as rules under which alone experiences are possible; and they instruct us in regard to the experiences, not by means of them.

4   Time is not a discursive, or what is called a general concept, but a pure form of sensible intuition. Different times are but parts of one and the same time; and the representation which can be given only through a single object is intuition. Moreover, the proposition that different times cannot be simultaneous is not to be derived from a general concept. The proposition is synthetic, and cannot have its origin in concepts alone. It is immediately contained in the intuition and representation of time.

5   The infinitude of time signifies nothing more than that every determinate magnitude of time is possible only through limitations of one single time that underlies it. The original representation, *time*, must therefore be given as unlimited. But when an object is so given that its parts, and every quantity of it, can be determinately represented only through limitation, the whole representation cannot be given through concepts, since they contain only partial representations; on the contrary, such concepts must themselves rest on immediate intuition. . . .

Conclusions from these concepts

(*a*) Time is not something which exists of itself, or which inheres in things as an objective determination, and it does not, therefore, remain when abstraction is made of all subjective conditions of its intuition. Were it self-subsistent, it would be something which would be actual and yet not an actual object. Were it a determination or order inhering in things themselves, it could not precede the objects as their condition, and be known and intuited *a priori* by means of synthetic propositions. But this last is quite possible if time is nothing but the subjective condition under which alone intuition can take place in us. For that being so, this form of inner intuition can be represented prior to the objects, and therefore *a priori*.

(*b*) Time is nothing but the form of inner sense, that is, of the intuition of ourselves and of our inner state. It cannot be a determination of outer appearances; it has to do neither with shape nor position, but with the relation of representations in our inner state. And just because this inner intuition yields no shape, we endeavor to make up for this want by analogies. We represent the time-sequence by a line progressing to infinity, in which the manifold constitutes a series of one dimension only; and we reason from the properties of this line to all the properties of time, with this one exception, that while the parts of the line are simultaneous the parts of time are always successive. From this fact also, that all the relations of time allow of being expressed in an outer intuition, it is evident that the representation is itself an intuition.

(*c*) Time is the formal *a priori* condition of all appearances whatsoever. Space, as the pure form of all *outer* intuition, is so far limited; it serves as the *a priori* condition only of outer appearances. But since all representations, whether they have for their objects outer things or not, belong, in themselves, as determinations of the mind, to our inner state; and since this inner state stands under the formal condition of inner intuition, and so belongs to time, time is an *a priori* condition of all appearance whatsoever. It is the immediate condition of inner appearances (of our souls), and thereby the mediate condition of outer appearances. Just as I can say *a priori* that all outer appearances are in space, and are determined *a priori* in conformity with the relations of space, I can also say, from the principle of inner sense, that all appearances whatsoever, that is, all objects of the senses, are in time, and necessarily stand in time-relations.

If we abstract from *our* mode of inwardly intuiting ourselves – the mode of intuition in terms of which we likewise take up into our faculty of representation all outer intuitions – and so take objects as they may be in themselves, then time is nothing. It has objective validity only in respect of appearances, these being things which we take *as objects of our senses*. It is no longer objective, if we abstract from the sensibility of our intuition, that is, from that mode of representation which is peculiar to us, and speak of *things in general*. Time is therefore a purely subjective condition of our (human) intuition (which is always sensible, that is, so far as we are affected by objects), and in itself, apart from the subject, is nothing. Nevertheless, in respect of all appearances, and therefore of all the things which can enter into our experience, it is necessarily objective. We cannot say that all things are in time, because in this concept of things in general we are abstracting from every mode of their intuition and therefore from that condition under which alone objects can be represented as being in time. If, however, the condition be added to the concept, and we say that all things as appearances, that is, as objects of sensible intuition, are in time, then the proposition has legitimate objective validity and universality *a priori*.

What we are maintaining is, therefore, the *empirical reality* of time, that is, its objective validity in respect of all objects which allow of ever being given to our senses. And since our intuition is always sensible, no object can ever be given to us in experience which does not conform to the condition of time. On the other hand, we deny to time all claim to absolute reality; that is to say, we deny that it belongs to things absolutely, as their condition or property, independently of any reference to the form of our sensible intuition; properties that belong to things in themselves can never be given to us through the senses. This, then, is what constitutes the *transcendental ideality* of time. What we mean by this phrase is that if we abstract from the subjective conditions of sensible intuition, time is nothing, and cannot be ascribed to the objects in themselves (apart from their relation to our intuition) in the way either of subsistence or of inherence. . . .

Conclusion of the transcendental aesthetic

Here, then, in pure *a priori* intuitions, space and time, we have one of the factors required for solution of the general problem of transcendental philosophy: *how are synthetic a priori judgments possible?*

When in *a priori* judgment we seek to go out beyond the given concept, we come in the *a priori* intuitions upon that which cannot be discovered in the concept but which is certainly found *a priori* in the intuition corresponding to the concept, and can be connected with it synthetically. Such judgments, however, thus based on intuition, can never extend beyond objects of the senses; they are valid only for objects of possible experience.

Transcendental Doctrine of Elements

Second Part: Transcendental Logic

Introduction: Idea of a Transcendental Logic

I. Logic in General

Our knowledge springs from two fundamental sources of the mind; the first is the capacity of receiving representations (receptivity for impressions), the second is the power of knowing an object through these representations (spontaneity [in the production] of concepts). Through the first an object is *given* to us, through the second the object is *thought* in relation to that [given] representation (which is a mere determination of the mind). Intuition and concepts constitute, therefore, the elements of all our knowledge, so that neither concepts without an intuition in some way corresponding to them, nor intuition without concepts, can yield knowledge. Both may be either pure or empirical. When they contain sensation (which presupposes the actual presence of the object), they are empirical. When there is no mingling of sensation with the representation, they are pure. Sensation may be entitled the material of sensible knowledge. Pure intuition, therefore, contains only the form under which something is intuited; the pure concept only the form of the thought of an object in general. Pure intuitions or pure concepts alone are possible *a priori*, empirical intuitions and empirical concepts only *a posteriori*.

If the *receptivity* of our mind, its power of receiving representations insofar as it is in any wise affected, is to be entitled sensibility, then the mind's power of producing representations from itself, the *spontaneity* of knowledge, should be called the understanding. Our nature is so constituted that our *intuition* can never be other than sensible; that is, it contains only the mode in which we are affected by objects. The faculty, on the other hand, which enables us to *think* the object of sensible intuition is the understanding. To

neither of these powers may a preference be given over the other. Without sensibility no object would be given to us, without understanding no object would be thought. Thoughts without content are empty, intuitions without concepts are blind. It is, therefore, just as necessary to make our concepts sensible, that is, to add the object to them in intuition, as to make our intuitions intelligible, that is, to bring them under concepts. These two powers or capacities cannot exchange their functions. The understanding can intuit nothing, the senses can think nothing. Only through their union can knowledge arise. But that is no reason for confounding the contribution of either with that of the other; rather is it a strong reason for carefully separating and distinguishing the one from the other. We therefore distinguish the science of the rules of sensibility in general, that is, aesthetic, from the science of the rules of the understanding in general, that is, logic. . . .

First Division: Transcendental Analytic
Book I: Analytic of Concepts

By "analytic of concepts" I do not understand their analysis, or the procedure usual in philosophical investigations, that of dissecting the content of such concepts as may present themselves, and so of rendering them more distinct; but the hitherto rarely attempted *dissection of the faculty of the understanding* itself, in order to investigate the possibility of concepts *a priori* by looking for them in the understanding alone, as their birthplace, and by analyzing the pure use of this faculty. This is the proper task of a transcendental philosophy; anything beyond this belongs to the logical treatment of concepts in philosophy in general. We shall therefore follow up the pure concepts to their first seeds and dispositions in the human understanding, in which they lie prepared, till at last, on the occasion of experience, they are developed, and by the same understanding are exhibited in their purity, freed from the empirical conditions attaching to them. . . .

Chapter I: The Transcendental Clue to the Discovery of All Pure Concepts of the Understanding
Section 1: The Logical Employment of the Understanding

The understanding has thus far been explained merely negatively, as a non-sensible faculty of knowledge. Now since without sensibility we cannot have any intuition, understanding cannot be a faculty of intuition. But besides intuition there is no other mode of knowledge except by means of concepts. The knowledge yielded by understanding, or at least by the human understanding, must therefore be by means of concepts, and so is not intuitive, but discursive. Whereas all intuitions, as sensible, rest on affections, concepts rest on functions. By "function" I mean the unity of the act of bringing various representations under one common representation. Concepts are based on the spontaneity of thought, sensible intuitions on the receptivity of impressions. Now the only use which the understanding can make of these concepts is to judge by means of them. Since no representation, save when it is an intuition, is in immediate relation to an object, no concept is ever related to an object immediately, but to some other representation of it, be that other representation an intuition, or itself a concept. Judgment is therefore the mediate knowledge of an object, that is, the representation of a representation of it. In every judgment there is a concept which holds of many representations, and among them of a given representation that is immediately related to an object. Thus in the judgment, "all bodies are divisible," the concept of the divisible applies to various other concepts, but is here applied in particular to the concept of body, and this concept again to certain appearances that present themselves to us. These objects, therefore, are mediately represented through the concept of divisibility. Accordingly, all judgments are functions of unity among our representations; instead of an immediate representation, a *higher* representation, which comprises the immediate representation and various others, is used in knowing the object, and thereby much possible knowledge is collected into one. Now we can reduce all acts of the understanding to judgments, and the *understanding* may therefore be represented as a *faculty of judgment*. For, as stated above, the understanding is a faculty of thought. Thought is knowledge by means of concepts. But concepts, as predicates of possible judgments, relate to some representation of a not *yet* determined object. Thus the concept of body means something, for instance, metal, which can be known by means of that concept. It is therefore a concept solely in virtue of its comprehending other representations, by means of which it can relate to objects. It is therefore the predicate of a possible judgment, for instance, "every metal is a body." The functions of the understanding

can, therefore, be discovered if we can give an exhaustive statement of the functions of unity in judgments. That this can quite easily be done will be shown in the next section.

Section 2: The Logical Function of the Understanding in Judgments

If we abstract from all content of a judgment, and consider only the mere form of understanding, we find that the function of thought in judgment can be brought under four heads, each of which contains three moments. They may be conveniently represented in the following table:

Table of Judgments

I		
	Quantity of Judgments	
	Universal	
	Particular	
II	Singular	III
Quality		*Relation*
Affirmative		Categorical
Negative		Hypothetical
Infinite		Disjunctive
	IV	
	Modality	
	Problematic	
	Assertoric	
	Apodeictic	

Section 3: The Pure Concepts of the Understanding, or Categories

General logic, as has been repeatedly said, abstracts from all content of knowledge, and looks to some other source, whatever that may be, for the representations which it is to transform into concepts by process of analysis. Transcendental logic, on the other hand, has lying before it a manifold of *a priori* sensibility, presented by transcendental aesthetic, as material for the concepts of pure understanding. In the absence of this material those concepts would be without any content, therefore entirely empty. Space and time contain a manifold of pure *a priori* intuition, but at the same time are conditions of the receptivity of our mind—conditions under which alone it can receive representations of objects, and which therefore must also always affect the concept of these objects. But if this manifold is to be known, the spontaneity of our thought requires that it be gone through in a certain way, taken up, and connected. This act I name *synthesis*.

By *synthesis*, in its most general sense, I understand the act of putting different representations together, and of grasping what is manifold in them in one [act of] knowledge. Such a synthesis is *pure*, if the manifold is not empirical but is given *a priori*, as is the manifold in space and time. Before we can analyze our representations, the representations must themselves be given, and therefore as regards *content* no concepts can first arise by way of analysis. Synthesis of a manifold (be it given empirically or *a priori*) is what first gives rise to knowledge. This knowledge may, indeed, at first, be crude and confused, and therefore in need of analysis. Still the synthesis is that which gathers the elements for knowledge, and unites them to [form] a certain content. It is to synthesis, therefore, that we must first direct our attention, if we would determine the first origin of our knowledge.

Synthesis in general, as we shall hereafter see, is the mere result of the power of imagination, a blind but indispensable function of the soul, without which we should have no knowledge whatsoever, but of which we are scarcely ever conscious. To bring this synthesis *to concepts* is a function which belongs to the understanding, and it is through this function of the understanding that we first obtain knowledge properly so called.

Pure synthesis, *represented in its most general aspect*, gives us the pure concept of the understanding. By this pure synthesis I understand that which rests upon a basis of *a priori* synthetic unity. Thus our counting, as is easily seen in the case of larger numbers, is a synthesis according to concepts, because it is executed according to a common ground of unity, as, for instance, the decade. In terms of this concept, the unity of the synthesis of the manifold is rendered necessary.

By means of analysis different representations are brought under one concept—a procedure treated of in general logic. What transcendental logic, on the other hand, teaches, is how we bring to concepts, not representations, but the *pure synthesis* of representations. What must first be given—with a view to the *a priori* knowledge of all objects—is the *manifold* of pure intuition; the second factor involved is the *synthesis* of this manifold by means of the imagination. But even this does not yet yield knowledge. The concepts which give *unity* to this pure synthesis, and which consist solely in the representation of this necessary synthetic unity, furnish the third requisite for the knowledge of an object; and they rest on the understanding.

The same function which gives unity to the various representations *in a judgment* also gives unity to the mere synthesis of various representations *in an intuition*; and this unity, in its most general expression, we entitle the pure concept of the understanding. The same understanding, through the same operations by which in concepts, by means of analytical unity, it produced the logical form of a judgment, also introduces a transcendental content into its representations, by means of the synthetic unity of the manifold in intuition in general. On this account we are entitled to call these representations pure concepts of the understanding, and to regard them as applying *a priori* to objects—a conclusion which general logic is not in a position to establish.

In this manner there arise precisely the same number of pure concepts of the understanding which apply *a priori* to objects of intuition in general, as, in the preceding table, there have been found to be logical functions in all possible judgments. For these functions specify the understanding completely, and yield an exhaustive inventory of its powers. These concepts we shall, with Aristotle, call *categories*, for our primary purpose is the same as his, although widely diverging from it in manner of execution.

Table of Categories

I

Of Quantity
Unity
Plurality
Totality

II	III
Of Quality	*Of Relation*
Reality	Of Inherence and Subsistence
Negation	(*substantia et accidens*)
Limitation	Of Causality and Dependence
	(*cause and effect*)
	Of Community (reciprocity
	between agent and patient)

IV

Of Modality
Possibility—Impossibility
Existence—Nonexistence
Necessity—Contingency

This then is the list of all original pure concepts of synthesis that the understanding contains within itself *a priori*. . . .

*Transition to the transcendental deduction
of the categories*

There are only two possible ways in which synthetic representations and their objects can establish connection, obtain necessary relation to one another, and, as it were, meet one another. Either the object alone must make the representation possible, or the representation alone must make the object possible. In the former case, this relation is only empirical, and the representation is never possible *a priori*. This is true of appearances, as regards that [element] in them which belongs to sensation. In the latter case, representation in itself does not produce its object in so far as *existence* is concerned, for we are not here speaking of its causality by means of the will. Nonetheless the representation is *a priori* determinant of the object, if it be the case that only through the representation is it possible to *know* anything *as an object*. Now there are two conditions under which alone the knowledge of an object is possible, first, *intuition*, through which it is given, though only as appearance; secondly, *concept*, through which an object is thought corresponding to this intuition. It is evident from the above that the first condition, namely, that under which alone objects can be intuited, does actually lie *a priori* in the mind as the formal ground of the objects. All appearances necessarily agree with this formal condition of sensibility, since only through it can they appear, that is, be empirically intuited and given. The question now arises whether *a priori* concepts do not also serve as antecedent conditions under which alone anything can be, if not intuited, yet thought as object in general. In that case all empirical knowledge of objects would necessarily conform to such concepts, because only as thus presupposing them is anything possible as *object of experience*. Now all experience does indeed contain, in addition to the intuition of the senses through which something is given, a *concept* of an object as being thereby given, that is to say, as appearing. Concepts of objects in general thus underlie all empirical knowledge as its *a priori* conditions. The objective validity of the categories as *a priori* concepts rests, therefore, on the fact that, so far as the form of thought is concerned, through them alone does experience become possible. They relate of necessity and *a priori* to objects of experience, for the reason that only by means of them can any object whatsoever of experience be thought.

The transcendental deduction of all *a priori* concepts has thus a principle according to which the whole enquiry must be directed, namely, that they must be recognized as *a priori* conditions of the possibility of experience, whether of the intuition which is to be met with in it or of the thought. Concepts which yield the objective ground of the possibility of experience are for this very reason necessary. But the unfolding of the experience wherein they are encountered is not their deduction; it is only their illustration. For on any such exposition they would be merely accidental. Save through their original relation to possible experience, in which all objects of knowledge are found, their relation to any one object would be quite incomprehensible. . . .

*Chapter II: The Deduction of the Pure
Concepts of Understanding [as in 1st edition]*

*Section 2: The a priori Grounds of the
Possibility of Experience*

That a concept, although itself neither contained in the concept of possible experience nor consisting of elements of a possible experience, should be produced completely *a priori* and should relate to an object, is altogether contradictory and impossible. For it would then have no content, since no intuition corresponds to it; and intuitions in general, through which objects can be given to us, constitute the field, the whole object, of possible experience. An *a priori* concept which did not relate to experience would be only the logical form of a concept, not the concept itself through which something is thought.

Pure *a priori* concepts, if such exist, cannot indeed contain anything empirical; yet, nonetheless, they can serve solely as *a priori* conditions of a possible experience. Upon this ground alone can their objective reality rest.

If, therefore, we seek to discover how pure concepts of understanding are possible, we must enquire what are the *a priori* conditions upon which the possibility of experience rests, and which remain as its underlying grounds when everything empirical is abstracted from appearances. A concept which universally and adequately expresses such a formal and objective condition of experience would be entitled a pure concept of understanding. Certainly, once I am in possession of pure concepts of understanding, I can think objects which may be impossible, or which, though perhaps in themselves possible, cannot be given in any experience. For in the connecting of these concepts something may be omitted which yet necessarily belongs to the condition of a possible experience (as in the concept of a spirit). Or, it may be, pure concepts are extended further than experience can follow (as with the concept of God). But the *elements* of all modes of *a priori* knowledge, even of capricious and incongruous fictions, though they cannot, indeed, be derived from experience, since in that case they would not be knowledge *a priori*, must nonetheless always contain the pure *a priori* conditions of a possible experience and of an empirical object. Otherwise nothing would be thought through them, and they themselves, being without data, could never arise even in thought.

The concepts which thus contain *a priori* the pure thought involved in every experience, we find in the categories. If we can prove that by their means alone an object can be thought, this will be a sufficient deduction of them, and will justify their objective validity. But since in such a thought more than simply the faculty of thought, the understanding, is brought into play, and since this faculty itself, as a faculty of *knowledge* that is meant to relate to objects, calls for explanation in regard to the possibility of such relation, we must first of all consider, not in their empirical but in their transcendental constitution, the subjective sources which form the *a priori* foundation of the possibility of experience.

If each representation were completely foreign to every other, standing apart in isolation, no such thing as knowledge would ever arise. For knowledge is [essentially] a whole in which representations stand compared and connected. As sense contains a manifold in its intuition, I ascribe to it a synopsis. But to such synopsis a synthesis must always correspond; receptivity can make knowledge possible only when combined with spontaneity. Now this spontaneity is the ground of a threefold synthesis which must necessarily be found in all knowledge; namely, the *apprehension* of representations as modifications of the mind in intuition, their *reproduction* in imagination, and their *recognition* in a concept. These point to three subjective sources of knowledge which make possible the understanding itself – and consequently all experience as its empirical product. . . .

1   The synthesis of apprehension in intuition
Whatever the origin of our representations, whether they are due to the influence of outer things, or are produced through inner causes, whether they arise *a priori*, or being appearances have an empirical origin, they must all, as modifications of the mind, belong to inner sense. All our knowledge is thus finally subject to time, the formal condition of inner sense. In it they must all be ordered, connected, and brought into relation. This is a general observation which, throughout what follows, must be borne in mind as being quite fundamental.

Every intuition contains in itself a manifold which can be represented as a manifold only insofar as the mind distinguishes the time in the sequence of one impression upon another; for each representation, *insofar as it is contained in a single moment*, can never be anything but absolute unity. In order that unity of intuition may arise out of this manifold (as is required in the representation of space) it must first be run through, and held together. This act I name the *synthesis of apprehension*, because it is directed immediately upon intuition, which does indeed offer a manifold, but a manifold which can never be represented as a manifold, and as contained *in a single representation*, save in virtue of such a synthesis.

This synthesis of apprehension must also be exercised *a priori*, that is, in respect of representations which are not empirical. For without it we should never have *a priori* the representations either of space or of time. They can be produced only through the synthesis of the manifold which sensibility presents in its original receptivity. We have thus a pure synthesis of apprehension.

2   The synthesis of reproduction in imagination
It is a merely empirical law, that representations which have often followed or accompanied one another finally become associated, and so are set in a relation whereby, even in the absence of the object, one of these representations can, in accordance with a fixed rule, bring about a transition of the mind to the other. But this law of reproduction presupposes that appearances are themselves actually subject to such a rule, and that in the manifold of these representations a coexistence or sequence takes place in conformity with certain rules. Otherwise our empirical imagination would never find opportunity for exercise appropriate to its powers, and so would remain concealed within the mind as a dead and to us unknown faculty. If cinnabar were sometimes red, sometimes black, sometimes light, sometimes heavy, if a man changed sometimes into this and sometimes into that animal form, if the

country on the longest day were sometimes covered with fruit, sometimes with ice and snow, my empirical imagination would never find opportunity when representing red color to bring to mind heavy cinnabar. Nor could there be an empirical synthesis of reproduction, if a certain name were sometimes given to this, sometimes to that object, or were one and the same thing named sometimes in one way, sometimes in another, independently of any rule to which appearances are in themselves subject.

There must then be something which, as the *a priori* ground of a necessary synthetic unity of appearances, makes their reproduction possible. What that something is we soon discover, when we reflect that appearances are not things in themselves, but are the mere play of our representations, and in the end reduce to determinations of inner sense. For if we can show that even our purest *a priori* intuitions yield no knowledge, save insofar as they contain a combination of the manifold such as renders a thoroughgoing synthesis of reproduction possible, then this synthesis of imagination is likewise grounded, antecedently to all experience, upon *a priori* principles; and we must assume a pure transcendental synthesis of imagination as conditioning the very possibility of all experience. For experience as such necessarily presupposes the reproducibility of appearances. When I seek to draw a line in thought, or to think of the time from one noon to another, or even to represent to myself some particular number, obviously the various manifold representations that are involved must be apprehended by me in thought one after the other. But if I were always to drop out of thought the preceding representations (the first parts of the line, the antecedent parts of the time period, or the units in the order represented), and did not reproduce them while advancing to those that follow, a complete representation would never be obtained: none of the above-mentioned thoughts, not even the purest and most elementary representations of space and time, could arise.

The synthesis of apprehension is thus inseparably bound up with the synthesis of reproduction. And as the former constitutes the transcendental ground of the possibility of all modes of knowledge whatsoever – of those that are pure *a priori* no less than of those that are empirical – the reproductive synthesis of the imagination is to be counted among the transcendental acts of the mind. We shall therefore entitle this faculty the transcendental faculty of imagination.

3 The synthesis of recognition in a concept

If we were not conscious that what we think is the same as what we thought a moment before, all reproduction in the series of representations would be useless. For it would in its present state be a new representation which would not in any way belong to the act whereby it was to be gradually generated. The manifold of the representation would never, therefore, form a whole, since it would lack that unity which only consciousness can impart to it. If, in counting, I forget that the units, which now hover before me, have been added to one another in succession, I should never know that a total is being produced through this successive addition of unit to unit, and so would remain ignorant of the number. For the concept of the number is nothing but the consciousness of this unity of synthesis.

The word "concept" might of itself suggest this remark. For this unitary consciousness is what combines the manifold, successively intuited, and thereupon also reproduced, into one representation. This consciousness may often be only faint, so that we do not connect it with the act itself, that is, not in any direct manner with the *generation* of the representation, but only with the outcome [that which is thereby represented]. But notwithstanding these variations, such consciousness, however indistinct, must always be present; without it, concepts, and therewith knowledge of objects, are altogether impossible.

At this point we must make clear to ourselves what we mean by the expression "an object of representations." We have stated above that appearances are themselves nothing but sensible representations, which, as such and in themselves, must not be taken as objects capable of existing outside our power of representation. What, then, is to be understood when we speak of an object corresponding to, and consequently also distinct from, our knowledge? It is easily seen that this object must be thought only as something in general $= x$, since outside our knowledge we have nothing which we could set over against this knowledge as corresponding to it.

Now we find that our thought of the relation of all knowledge to its object carries with it an element of necessity; the object is viewed as that which prevents our modes of knowledge from being haphazard or arbitrary, and which determines them *a priori* in some definite fashion. For insofar as they are to relate to an object, they must necessarily agree with one another, that is, must possess that unity which constitutes the concept of an object.

But it is clear that, since we have to deal only with the manifold of our representations, and since that x (the object) which corresponds to them is nothing to us – being, as it is, something that has to be distinct from all our representations – the unity which the object makes necessary can be nothing else than the formal unity of consciousness in the synthesis of the manifold of representations. It is only when we have thus produced synthetic unity in the manifold of intuition that we are in a position to say that we know the object. But this unity is impossible if the intuition cannot be generated in accordance with a rule by means of such a function of synthesis as makes the reproduction of the manifold *a priori* necessary, and renders possible a concept in which it is united. Thus we think a triangle as an object, in that we are conscious of the combination of three straight lines according to a rule by which such an intuition can always be represented. This *unity of rule* determines all the manifold, and limits it to conditions which make unity of apperception possible. The concept of this unity is the representation of the object $= x$, which I think through the predicates, above mentioned, of a triangle.

All knowledge demands a concept, though that concept may, indeed, be quite imperfect or obscure. But a concept is always, as regards its form, something universal which serves as a rule. The concept of body, for instance, as the unity of the manifold which is thought through it, serves as a rule in our knowledge of outer appearances. But it can be a rule for intuitions only insofar as it represents in any given appearances the necessary reproduction of their manifold, and thereby the synthetic unity in our consciousness of them. The concept of body, in the perception of something outside us, necessitates the representation of extension, and therewith representations of impenetrability, shape, etc.

All necessity, without exception, is grounded in a transcendental condition. There must, therefore, be a transcendental ground of the unity of consciousness in the synthesis of the manifold of all our intuitions, and consequently also of the concepts of objects in general, and so of all objects of experience, a ground without which it would be impossible to think any object for our intuitions; for this object is no more than that something, the concept of which expresses such a necessity of synthesis.

This original and transcendental condition is no other than *transcendental apperception*. Consciousness of self according to the determinations of our state in inner perception is merely empirical, and always changing. No fixed and abiding self can present itself in this flux of inner appearances. Such consciousness is usually named *inner sense*, or *empirical apperception*. What has *necessarily* to be represented as numerically identical cannot be thought as such through empirical data. To render such a transcendental presupposition valid, there must be a condition which precedes all experience, and which makes experience itself possible.

There can be in us no modes of knowledge, no connection or unity of one mode of knowledge with another, without that unity of consciousness which precedes all data of intuitions, and by relation to which representation of objects is alone possible. This pure original unchangeable consciousness I shall name *transcendental apperception*. That it deserves this name is clear from the fact that even the purest objective unity, namely, that of the *a priori* concepts (space and time), is only possible through relation of the intuitions to such unity of consciousness. The numerical unity of this apperception is thus the *a priori* ground of all concepts, just as the manifoldness of space and time is the *a priori* ground of the intuitions of sensibility.

This transcendental unity of apperception forms out of all possible appearances, which can stand alongside one another in one experience, a connection of all these representations according to laws. For this unity of consciousness would be impossible if the mind in knowledge of the manifold could not become conscious of the identity of function whereby it synthetically combines it in one knowledge. The original and necessary consciousness of the identity of the self is thus at the same time a consciousness of an equally necessary unity of the synthesis of all appearances according to concepts, that is, according to rules, which not only make them necessarily reproducible but also in so doing determine an object for their intuition, that is, the concept of something wherein they are necessarily interconnected. For the mind could never think its identity in the manifoldness of its representations, and indeed think this identity *a priori*, if it did not have before its eyes the identity of its act, whereby it subordinates all synthesis of apprehension (which is empirical) to a transcendental unity, thereby rendering possible their interconnection according to *a priori* rules.

Now, also, we are in a position to determine more adequately our concept of an *object* in general. All representations have, as representations, their object, and can themselves in turn become objects of other representations. Appearances are the sole objects which can be given to us immediately, and that in them which relates immediately to the object is called intuition. But these appearances are not things in themselves; they are only representations, which in turn have their object – an object which cannot itself be intuited by us, and which may, therefore, be named the non-empirical, that is, transcendental object = *x*.

The pure concept of this transcendental object, which in reality throughout all our knowledge is always one and the same, is what can alone confer upon all our empirical concepts in general relation to an object, that is, objective reality. This concept cannot contain any determinate intuition, and therefore refers only to that unity which must be met with in any manifold of knowledge which stands in relation to an object. This relation is nothing but the necessary unity of consciousness, and therefore also of the synthesis of the manifold, through a common function of the mind, which combines it in one representation. Since this unity must be regarded as necessary *a priori* – otherwise knowledge would be without an object – the relation to a transcendental object, that is, the objective reality of our empirical knowledge, rests on the transcendental law, that all appearances, insofar as through them objects are to be given to us, must stand under those *a priori* rules of synthetical unity whereby the interrelating of these appearances in empirical intuition is alone possible. In other words, appearances in experience must stand under the conditions of the necessary unity of apperception, just as in mere intuition they must be subject to the formal conditions of space and of time. Only thus can any knowledge become possible at all.

Select Bibliography

Anthropology from a Pragmatic Point of View. Edited by Hans H. Rudnick. Translated by Victor Lyle Dowdell. Carbondale: Southern Illinois University Press, 1996.

The Conflict of the Faculties/Der Streit der Fakultäten. Translated by Mary J. Gregor. Lincoln: University of Nebraska Press, 1992.

Critique of Judgment. Translated by Werner S. Pluhar. Indianapolis: Hackett Publishing, 1987.

Critique of Practical Reason. Translated by Lewis White Beck. New York: Macmillan, 1993.

Critique of Pure Reason. Translated by Norman Kemp Smith. London: Macmillan, 1976.

The Essential Kant. Edited by Arnulf Zweig. New York: New American Library, 1970.

Foundations of the Metaphysics of Morals, and What is Enlightenment? Translated by Lewis White Beck. New York: Macmillan, 1990.

Kant: Selections. Edited by Lewis White Beck. New York: Macmillan, 1988.

The Metaphysics of Morals. Translated by Mary Gregor. Cambridge: Cambridge University Press, 1996.

The One Possible Basis for a Demonstration of the Existence of God. Translated by Gordon Treash. Lincoln: University of Nebraska Press, 1994.

Perpetual Peace, and Other Essays on Politics, History, and Morals. Translated by Ted Humphrey. Indianapolis: Hackett Publishing, 1983.

Prolegomena to Any Future Metaphysics. New York: Macmillan, 1987.

Religion Within the Limits of Reason Alone. Translated by Theodore M. Greene and Hoyt H. Hudson. LaSalle, Ill.: Open Court, 1960.

2

Johann Gottlieb Fichte

Johann Gottlieb Fichte (1762–1814) was a student of Kant and subsequently professor of philosophy at Jena. In his *Foundation of the Science of Knowledge*, published in 1794, Fichte attempts, beyond the limits of the Kantian system, to develop Kant's insight from the *Critique of Practical Reason* that the "I" is not an object of theoretical observation, but has its primary being as free, practical activity. For Kant, the practical "I" remains a "thing in itself," of which no intuition – and thus no essential knowledge – is possible. According to Kant, we cannot ultimately know *what* the acting self is as such. In the following selections from 1797/98, which attempt to clarify his "science of knowledge" (*Wissenschaftslehre*), Fichte tries instead to show that the practical activity of self-consciousness can be apprehended in a pure act of intellectual intuition that accomplishes itself as a self-positing. For Fichte, the acting self simply *is* this self-positing activity of self-consciousness that can indeed come to know itself as such.

An Attempt at a New Presentation of the *Wissenschaftslehre*

Introduction

Attend to yourself; turn your gaze from everything surrounding you and look within yourself: this is the first demand philosophy makes upon anyone who studies it. Here you will not be concerned with

From *Introductions to the Wissenschaftslehre, and Other Writings (1797–1800)*, edited and translated by Daniel Breazeale (Indianapolis: Hackett Publishing, 1994), pp. 7–9, 106–18. Copyright © 1994. Reprinted by permission of Hackett Publishing Company.

anything that lies outside of you, but only with yourself.

Even on the most cursory self-observation, everyone will perceive a remarkable difference between the various ways in which his consciousness is immediately determined, and one could call these immediate determinations of consciousness "representations."[1] Some of these determinations appear to us to depend entirely upon our own freedom, and it is impossible for us to believe that anything outside of us, i.e. something that exists independently of our own efforts, corresponds to representations of this sort. Our imagination and our will appear to us to be free. We also possess representations of another sort. We refer representations of this second type to a truth that is supposed to be firmly established independently of us and is supposed to serve as the model for these representations. When a representation of ours is supposed to correspond to this truth, we discover that we are constrained in determining this representation. In the case of cognition, we do not consider ourselves to be free with respect to the content of our cognitions. In short, we could say that some of our representations are accompanied by a feeling of freedom and others are accompanied by a feeling of necessity.

We cannot reasonably ask why the representations that depend upon our freedom are determined in just the way they are determined and not in some other way. For when we posit them to be dependent upon freedom, we deny that the concept of a "basis" (or "foundation" or "reason" or "ground")[2] has any applicability in this case. These representations are what they are for the simple reason that I have determined them to be like this. If I had determined them differently, then they would be different.

But what is the basis of the system of those representations accompanied by a feeling of necessity, and what is the basis of this feeling of necessity itself? This is a question well worth pondering. It is the task of philosophy to answer this question; indeed, to my mind, nothing is philosophy except that science that discharges this task. Another name for the system of representations accompanied by a feeling of necessity is "experience" – whether inner or outer. We thus could express the task of philosophy in different words as follows: Philosophy has to display the basis or foundation of all experience.

Only three objections can be raised against this conception of philosophy's task. On the one hand, one might deny that consciousness contains any representations that are accompanied by a feeling of necessity and that refer to a truth determined without any help from us. A person who denies this would either do so against his own better knowledge, or else he would have to be constituted differently than other human beings. If so, then in this case nothing would exist for him which he could deny, and thus there would be no denial. Consequently, we could dismiss his objection without any further ado. Or else, someone might contend that the question we have raised is completely

unanswerable and that we are and must remain in a state of invincible ignorance on this point. It is superfluous to engage in reasoned debate with someone who makes this objection. The best way to refute him is by actually answering the question, in which case there will be nothing left for him to do but to examine our effort and to indicate where and why it seems to him to be insufficient. Finally, someone might lay a rival claim to the name "philosophy" and maintain that philosophy is something completely different or something more than what we have claimed. It would be easy to prove to anyone who raises this objection that this is precisely what all of the experts have at all times considered philosophy to be, that all the other things he might like to pass off as philosophy already possess other names of their own, and therefore, that if the word "philosophy" is to have any definite meaning at all, it has to designate precisely the science we have indicated.

We have no desire, however, to engage in a fruitless dispute over a word; and this is why we have long ceased to lay any claim to the name "philosophy" and have given the name *Wissenschaftslehre*, or "Theory of Scientific Knowledge," to the science that actually has to carry out the task indicated....

Chapter One: All Consciousness is Conditioned by Our Immediate Consciousness of Ourselves

I

With the permission of the reader, with whom it is our task to reach agreement, I will address him informally in the second person.

(1) You are undoubtedly able to think "I"; and insofar as you do this you will discover that your consciousness is internally *determined* in a specific manner and that you are thinking of *only* one thing: viz. precisely what you comprehend under the concept "I." It is this of which you are conscious, and when you think "I" you are not thinking of any of the other things of which you could otherwise well be thinking and of which you may have previously been thinking. – For the moment, I am unconcerned with whether you may have included more or less in the concept "I" than I have. Your concept certainly includes what I am concerned with, and this is enough for me.

(2) Instead of thinking of this particular, determinate [concept], you could also have thought of something else: of your table, for example, or of your walls or your window; moreover, you actually do think of these objects if I summon you to do so. You do this in response to a summons and in accordance with a concept of what you are supposed to think of (which, as you suppose, might just as easily have been some other object, or so I submit). Accordingly, while engaged in this act of thinking, in this movement of transition from thinking of the I to thinking of the table, the walls, etc., you take note of the activity and freedom that are involved therein. Your thinking is, for you, an *acting*. Have no fear that by admitting this you may be conceding to me anything you may later come to regret. I am speaking of nothing but the activity of which you become immediately conscious when you are in this state – and only insofar as you are conscious of this activity. If, however, you should find yourself to be conscious of no activity at all in this case (and many celebrated philosophers of our own day find themselves in just this situation), then let us part from each other in peace at this point, for you will be unable to understand anything I say from now on.

I am addressing myself to those of you who understand what I am saying concerning this point. Your thinking is an acting; and hence, when you are thinking of some specific thing, you are acting in some specific manner. In other words, the reason you are thinking of precisely this is because, in thinking, you have acted in precisely this way; and if, in engaging in this act of thinking, you had acted differently (if you had thought *differently*), then what you are thinking of would be something different (you would be thinking of *something different*).

(3) You should now be thinking of something quite specific: namely, "I." This is a particular thought, and thus, according to the principle just enunciated, you must necessarily think in a particular manner in order to produce this thought. My task for you, intelligent reader, is this: You must now become truly and most sincerely conscious of *how* you proceed when you think "I." Since our concepts of the "I" may not be exactly the same, I must assist you in doing this.

While you were thinking of your table or your wall, you were, for yourself, the *thinking subject* engaged in this act of thinking, since you, as an intelligent reader, are of course aware of the activity involved in your own act of thinking. On the other hand, what *was thought of* in this act of thinking was, for you, not you yourself, but rather something that has to be distinguished from you. In short, in every concept of this type [i.e. in every concept of an object], the thinking subject and what is thought of are two distinct things, as you will certainly discover within your own consciousness. In contrast, when you think of *yourself*, then you are, for yourself, not only the thinking subject; you are also at the same time that of which you are thinking. In this case the subject and the object of thinking are supposed to be one and the same. The sort of acting in which you are engaged when you are thinking of yourself is supposed to turn back upon or "revert into" yourself, the thinking subject.[3]

It follows from this that *the concept of the I or the act of thinking of the I consists in the I's acting upon itself*, and conversely, *such an acting upon itself yields an act of thinking of the I and no other thinking whatsoever.* You have just discovered within yourself the truth of the first of these claims and have conceded this to me. If you balk at the second claim and have any doubts about whether we are warranted in affirming the converse of our first assertion, then I will leave it up to you to make the following experiment: When your thinking turns back upon yourself, as the thinking subject, does this ever produce any concept other than that of yourself? Can you even think the possibility that some other concept could be produced in this way? – The concept of a self-reverting act of thinking and the concept of the I thus have exactly the same content.[4] The I is what posits itself,[5] and it is nothing more than this. What posits itself is the I and nothing more. Nothing else but the I is produced by the act we have just described; and the I can be produced by no other possible act except the one described.

You can also now appreciate the sense in which you were asked to think of the I. Linguistic signs have passed through the hands of thoughtlessness and have acquired some of its indeterminacy; one is therefore unable to make oneself sufficiently well understood simply by employing such signs. The only way in which a concept can be completely specified or determined is by indicating the act through which it comes into being: If you do what I say then you will think what I am thinking. This is the method that, without exception, we will be following in the course of our inquiry. – Though you may have included many things in your concept of the I which I have not (e.g. the concept of your own individuality, for this too is signified by the word "I"), you may henceforth put all of this aside. The only "I" that I am concerned with here is the one that comes into being through the sheer self-reverting act of your own thinking.

(4) The propositions that have been advanced *are the immediate expression of the observation we have just made*, and these propositions could arouse doubts only if one were to consider them to be anything more than the immediate expression of the same. I maintain that the I comes into being only through a self-reverting act of thinking, and when I say this I am not talking about anything except what can come into being purely by means of an act of thinking. All I am talking about here is what immediately appears within my consciousness whenever I think in the manner indicated, and if you too think in this manner, then this will immediately appear within your consciousness as well. In short, I am talking only about the concept of the I. Here I am not yet in the least concerned with any "being" the I may have apart from this concept. At the appropriate time we will see whether and to what extent one can talk about any being of this sort at all. In order to shield the reader against any possible doubts that might arise, and in order to protect him against the danger of seeing, in the course of this inquiry, a previously conceded proposition subsequently employed in some sense that he did not wish to concede, I will amend the propositions just established (viz. "the I is an act of self-positing" and other similar propositions) by adding the phrase "for the I."

At the same time I can also explain the reason for the reader's concern about perhaps having conceded too much. But I will do so only if the reader will promise not to allow himself to become distracted thereby, for this entire remark is a merely incidental one which really does not belong here, and I add it merely in order to avoid leaving any point obscure, even for a moment. – It was asserted that your I comes into being only through the reversion of your own act of thinking back upon itself. You probably harbor in some small corner of your soul the following objection to this claim: Either, "I am supposed *to think*, but before I can think I have *to exist*"; or, "I am supposed to think *of myself*, to direct my thinking back upon myself, but whatever I am supposed to think of or to turn my attention back upon must first exist before it can be

thought of or become the object of an act of reverting." In both of these cases, you postulate an *existence* of yourself that is independent of and presupposed by the thinking and being-thought-of of yourself.[6] In the former case, you postulate the independent existence of yourself as the *thinking subject*; in the latter, the independent existence of yourself as *what is to be thought of*. In connection with this objection, first simply answer for me the following question: Who is it that claims that you must have existed prior to your own act of thinking? It is undoubtedly you yourself who make this claim, and when you make such a claim you are undoubtedly engaging in an act of thinking. Furthermore, as you will also claim, and as I am only too ready to concede, this is a necessary act of thinking, one that forces itself upon you in this context. One nevertheless trusts that it is only insofar as and only inasmuch as you think about this existence that has to be presupposed that you possess any knowledge of it. It follows that this existence of the I is also nothing more than a posited being of yourself, that is, a being that you yourself have posited. If we examine it closely enough, therefore, we will find that the fact with which you have confronted us amounts to no more than this: *In addition to the act of self-positing which you have at present raised to clear consciousness, you must also think of this act as preceded by another act of self-positing, one that is not accompanied by any clear consciousness, but to which the former act refers and by means of which it is conditioned*. Until such time as I have had a chance to explain to you the fecund law in accordance with which this occurs, you can avoid becoming misled by the fact to which you have called attention if you will keep in mind that it asserts no more than what has just been stated.

II

Let us now shift to a higher speculative standpoint.

(1) "Think of yourself, and pay attention to how you do this": This was my first request. You had to attend to yourself in order to understand what I was saying (since I was discussing something that could exist only within yourself) and in order to discover within your own experience the truth of what I said to you. This *attentiveness* to ourselves in this act was the *subjective* element common to us both. *What* you paid attention *to* was the manner in which you went about thinking of yourself, which did not differ from the manner I went about

thinking of myself; and this was the object of our investigation, the *objective* element common to us both.

Now, however, I say to you: pay attention to *your own act of attending to* your act of self-positing. Attend to what you yourself did in the inquiry you have just completed and note how you managed to pay attention to yourself. What constituted the subjective element in the previous inquiry must be made into the object of the new inquiry we are now beginning.[7]

(2) The point that concerns me here is not all that easy to grasp. Yet if one fails to grasp it, then one will fail to grasp anything, since my entire theory is based upon this. Perhaps, therefore, the reader will allow me to guide him through the entrance and to place him just as close as possible to what he is supposed to observe.

When you are conscious of any object whatsoever – of the wall over there, let us say – then, as you just conceded, what you are really conscious of is your own act of thinking of this wall, and only insofar as you are conscious of this act of thinking is any consciousness of this wall possible. In order for you to be conscious of your own thinking, however, you must be conscious of yourself. – You say that *you* are conscious of *yourself*; in saying this, you necessarily distinguish your *thinking* I from the I that is *thought of* in the act of thinking the I. In order for you to be able to do this, however, the thinking subject within this act of thinking must, in turn, be the *object* of a higher act of thinking, for otherwise it could not be an object of consciousness. At the same time, you also obtain thereby a new *subject*, one that is conscious of what was previously the *being* of self-consciousness.[8] I now repeat this same argument over and over again, as before, and once we have embarked upon such a series of inferences you will never be able to point to a place where we should stop. Accordingly, we will always require, for every consciousness, another consciousness, one that takes the former as its object, and so on, forever. In this way, therefore, we will never arrive at a point where we will be able to assume the existence of any actual consciousness. – You are conscious of yourself as an object of consciousness only insofar as you are conscious of yourself as the conscious subject; but then this conscious subject becomes, in turn, an object of consciousness, and you must then, once again, become conscious of yourself as the subject who is conscious of this object of consciousness –

and so on, *ad infinitum*. How could you ever arrive at any original consciousness in this way?

In short, consciousness simply cannot be accounted for in this way. Once again, what was the gist of the line of reasoning we just pursued, and what is the real reason why the nature of consciousness could not be grasped in this way? The gist of the argument was as follows: I can be conscious of any object only on the condition that I am also conscious of myself, that is, of the conscious subject. This proposition is incontrovertible. – It was, however, further claimed that, within my self-consciousness, I am an object for myself and that what held true in the previous case also holds true of the subject that is conscious of this object: this subject too becomes an object, and thus a new subject is required, and so on *ad infinitum*. In every consciousness, therefore, the subject and the object were separated from each other and each was treated as distinct. This is why it proved impossible for us to comprehend consciousness in the above manner.

Yet consciousness does exist. Hence, what was just claimed concerning it must be false, and this means that the opposite of this claim is true; that is to say, there is a type of consciousness in which what is subjective and what is objective cannot be separated from each other at all, but are absolutely one and the same. This, accordingly, would be the type of consciousness that is required in order to explain consciousness at all. Let us now, without any further elaboration of this point, return straightaway to our inquiry.

(3) When you did as we asked and thought, first of objects that are supposed to lie outside of you, and then of yourself, you undoubtedly knew that you were thinking, what you were thinking, and how you were thinking. You must have known these things, for we were able to discuss this with one another, as indeed we have just done.

How then did you manage to obtain this consciousness of your own thinking? "I knew it immediately," you will reply. "My consciousness of my own thinking is not, as it were, an accidental feature of my thinking, an additional something that is posited only afterwards and subsequently connected with my thinking; instead, such consciousness is inseparable from thinking." – You will and must answer my question in this way, since you are quite unable to think of your thinking without having any consciousness of it.

Thus, from the very start, we could have discovered the type of consciousness we were just seeking, a consciousness in which what is subjective and what is objective are immediately united. The consciousness in question is our consciousness of our own thinking. – Hence you are immediately conscious of your own thinking. But how do you represent this to yourself? Evidently, you can do this only in the following way: Your inner activity, which is directed at something outside of you (viz. at the object you are thinking about), is, at the same time, directed within and at itself. According to what was said above, however, self-reverting activity is what generates the I. Accordingly, you were conscious of yourself in your own act of thinking, and this self-consciousness was precisely the same as your immediate consciousness of your own thinking; and this is true whether you were thinking of some object or were thinking of yourself. – Self-consciousness is therefore immediate; what is subjective and what is objective are inseparably united within self-consciousness and are absolutely one and the same.

The scientific name for such an immediate consciousness is "intuition,"[9] which is the name by which we wish to designate it as well. The intuition we are now discussing in an *act of self-positing as positing* (that is, as positing anything "objective" whatsoever, which can also be I myself, considered as a mere object); by no means, however, is it a mere *act of positing*, for then we would find ourselves once again entangled in the previously indicated impossibility of explaining consciousness. As far as I am concerned, everything depends upon one's understanding and being convinced of this point, which constitutes the very foundation of the entire system to be presented here.

All possible consciousness, as something objective for a subject, presupposes an immediate consciousness in which what is subjective and what is objective are simply one and the same. Otherwise, consciousness is simply incomprehensible. Unless one has grasped the subject and the object in their unity right from the start, one will forever seek in vain to discover any bond between them. For this reason, any philosophy that does not begin at the point where the subject and the object are united will necessarily be superficial and incomplete; it will be unable to explain what it is supposed to explain, and hence it will be no philosophy at all.

This immediate consciousness is the intuition of the I just described. The I necessarily posits itself within this intuition and is thus at once what is subjective and what is objective. All other consciousness is connected to and mediated by this immediate consciousness, and only through this connection with immediate consciousness does it become consciousness at all. Immediate consciousness alone is unmediated and unconditioned by anything else. It is absolutely possible and is quite simply necessary if any other consciousness is to occur. – The I should not be considered as a mere subject, which is how it has nearly always been considered until now; instead, it should be considered as a subject–object in the sense indicated.

The sole type of being of the I with which we are here concerned is the being it possesses within the self-intuition we have now described; or, more rigorously expressed, the being of the I with which we are concerned is the being of this intuition itself. I am this intuition and nothing more whatsoever, and this intuition itself is I. This act of self-positing is not supposed to produce an I that, so to speak, exists as a thing in itself and continues to exist independently of consciousness: Such a claim would undoubtedly be the greatest of all absurdities. Nor does this intuition presuppose an existence of the I as an (intuiting) thing, independent of consciousness. Indeed, in my opinion, such a claim would be no less absurd than the previous one; though, of course, one should not say this, since the most famous philosophers of our philosophical century subscribe to this opinion. The reason I maintain that no such existence [of the I] has to be presupposed is as follows: If you cannot talk about anything *of which you are not conscious*, and if, however, everything of which you are conscious *is conditioned by the self-consciousness here indicated, then you cannot turn around and allow this self-consciousness to be conditioned by some determinate object* of which you are conscious: viz. the alleged existence of the I apart from all intuiting and thinking. Either you must admit that you are here speaking of something without knowing anything about it (which you are hardly likely to do), or else you must deny that all other consciousness is conditioned by the self-consciousness in question (which, if you have understood me at all, you will be quite unable to do). – At this point, therefore, it also becomes obvious that, through our very first proposition, one has unavoidably adopted the standpoint of transcendental idealism – not just for the case in question, but for all possible cases – and that understanding this proposition is exactly the same as being convinced of the truth of transcendental idealism.

The intellect thus intuits itself only as an intellect, or as a pure intellect; and it is precisely this self-intuition that constitutes its essential nature. Accordingly, in the event that there might turn out to be some other type of intuition as well, we are entitled to designate the type of intuition we have been discussing here "*intellectual* intuition," in order to distinguish it from any other type of intuition. – Instead of "intellect," I prefer to use the term "I-hood," because, for anyone capable of the least bit of attentiveness, this term indicates, in the most direct way, the self-reverting of activity.[10]

III

Let us now direct our attention to yet another circumstance involved in observing the activity we have been asked to perform. What follows, however, should be treated as no more than a provisional remark from which nothing will be immediately inferred and the implications of which will become apparent only later. Nevertheless, we cannot let this opportunity pass without adding the following remark.

You discovered yourself to be active both in the act of representing an object and in the act of representing yourself. Now look again very carefully at what occurred within you when you entertained the representation of this activity. Activity is "agility" or inner movement; the mind here tears itself away from something absolutely opposed [to activity] – a description that is by no means intended, as it were, to make comprehensible what is incomprehensible,[11] but is instead designed to call attention more forcibly to an intuition that is necessarily present within everyone. – This agility is intuited as a *process by means of which the active force wrenches itself away from a state of repose*, and it can be intuited in no other way. And if you actually accomplished what we asked you to do, this is in fact how you intuited this agility.

In compliance with my summons, you thought of your table, your wall, etc.; and after you had succeeded in actively producing within yourself the thoughts of these objects, you then remained caught up in a state of peaceful and unchanging contemplation of them (*obtutu haerebas fixus in illo*,[12] as the poet says). Next I asked you to think of yourself and to take special note of the fact that this act of thinking is a kind of doing. In order to do this, you had to tear yourself away from your state of contemplative repose; that is to say, you had to tear yourself away from that determinacy of your thinking and determine your thinking differently. Moreover, you were able to notice that you were active only insofar as you took note of this act of wrenching yourself away and this act of altering the determinacy in question. I can do no more here than appeal to your own inner intuition; I cannot externally demonstrate to you something that can exist only within you.

The result of attending to oneself in the requested manner would be this: One discovers oneself to be active only insofar as one opposes to this activity a state of repose (in which the inner force is arrested and becomes fixed). (We should mention in passing that the converse of this proposition is true as well: One cannot become conscious of a state of repose unless one posits an activity. Activity is nothing apart from repose, and vice versa. Indeed, this proposition is universally true and will later be established in its universal validity: viz. that no matter what is being determined, all determination occurs by means of opposition. Here, however, we are concerned only with the individual case before us.)

What then was the particular determinacy of your thinking which, as a state of repose, immediately preceded that activity by virtue of which you thought of yourself? Or, more precisely, what determinacy was immediately united with that activity, in such a way that you could not perceive the one without perceiving the other? – In order to indicate the action you were supposed to perform, I asked you to think of *yourself*, and you were able to understand me without any further ado. Accordingly, you knew the meaning of the term "I." But you did not have to know, and I assume that you did not know, that the thought of the I is a thought that comes into being by means of a reversion of activity upon itself. This is something you first had to learn. Yet, according to what we have already said, the I is nothing but a self-reverting acting, and a self-reverting acting is the I. How then could you have been acquainted with the I without also being acquainted with the activity by means of which the I arises? This is possible only as follows: When you understood the word "I," you discovered *yourself* (*i.e. your acting as an intellect*) to be determined in a particular manner, yet you did not explicitly recognize what was determinate in this case *as an acting*. Instead, you recognized it only as a *determinacy* or a *state of repose*, without actually knowing or even inquiring into the origin of this determinacy of your consciousness. In short, when you understood me, this determinacy was immediately present. This is why you understood me and were able to give an appropriate direction to the activity that I summoned you to perform. The determinacy of your thinking produced through thinking of your-self[13] therefore was and necessarily had to be that state of repose from which you wrenched yourself into activity.

This may be expressed more clearly as follows: I asked you to "think of yourself," and when you understood this last word you also engaged – *in the very act of understanding it* – in that self-reverting activity that produces the thought of the I. But you accomplished this without realizing what you were doing, for you were not paying any special attention to this. And this was the origin of what you discovered within your own consciousness. I then asked you to pay attention to how you were able to accomplish this. You then engaged once again in the same activity in which you had engaged previously, but this time you did so with attentiveness and consciousness.

Inner activity, grasped in its state of repose, is generally called a "concept." Consequently, what was necessarily united with the intuition of the I was the concept of the I; and without this concept any consciousness of the I would have remained impossible, for it is this concept that first completes and comprises consciousness.

A concept is never anything other than the very activity of intuiting – simply grasped, not as agility, but as a state of repose and determinacy. This is true of the concept of the I as well. The concept of the I is the self-reverting activity, grasped as something stable and enduring; thus it is in this way that the I as active and the I as the object of my activity coincide.

Nothing is present within ordinary consciousness but concepts; by no means are intuitions as such ever encountered there, despite the fact that concepts arise only by means of intuitions (though this occurs without any consciousness on our part). Only through freedom can one lift oneself to a consciousness of intuition, as has just been done in the case of the I. Every conscious intuition, moreover, is related to a concept, which indicates the particular direction freedom has to take. This explains how, in every case, as in the particular case we have been examining, the object of intuition can be said to exist prior to the intuition itself. The object in question is precisely the concept. From this discussion, one can see that the concept is nothing but the intuition itself, grasped as a state of repose and not as such, i.e. not as an activity.[14]

Notes

1 *Vorstellungen.* Throughout this translation, the noun *Vorstellung* is translated as "representation" whenever it occurs in an even vaguely technical context. In many ordinary expressions, however, the word has no special technical meaning at all, but is merely a vague term designating whatever one "has in mind," similar to the informal sense of words like "notion" and "idea" in contemporary English usage. Fichte's technical employment of this term is derived from Kant and Reinhold, for whom it is the most general term that can be employed to designate all the objects of our consciousness (viz. "intuitions," "concepts," "Ideas," etc.) *as* objects of consciousness. A "representation" is, quite literally, whatever is *vorgestellt*, or "placed before," the mind. It is important to remember that "representations" need not be thought of as copying (or "representing") anything outside of themselves, though this is certainly the way in which they are frequently thought of within ordinary consciousness. (In this technical sense, "representation" plays a role in the writings of the early transcendental idealists similar to that played by the term "idea" in the writings of Descartes, Locke, Leibniz, and Berkeley and the expression "perceptions of the mind" in the writings of Hume.) Similarly, the verb *vorstellen*, which is here somewhat awkwardly rendered as "to represent" or "to entertain representations," is the term that designates the activity of representing. (Trans.)

2 "des Begriffs vom Grunde." The term *Grund* is variously translated here as "foundation," "ground," "basis," and "reason." (Trans.)

3 "dein Handeln im Denken soll auf dich selbst, das Denkende, zurückgehen." (Trans.)

4 "erschöpfen sich gegenseitig." Literally: "mutually exhaust one another." (Trans.)

5 "Das Ich ist das sich selbst Setzende." The verb *setzen* ("to posit") is a basic term in Fichte's technical vocabulary. It is the most general term one can employ to refer to the *act of consciousness* itself. Any object of consciousness – whether real or imaginary, whether an external object or the I itself – is therefore "posited by the I." Taken by itself, the verb *setzen* does not necessarily imply any "constitution" or

"creation" of the object of consciousness; it simply signifies that the conscious subject – whether freely or under compulsion – "puts" or "places" something within its field of awareness. "To posit" something is thus an essential condition for "being conscious" at all (though it does not follow that we are, in fact, always explicitly aware of all of the acts of positing involved in, for example, our everyday consciousness of objects; on the contrary, Fichte contends that we are typically unaware of many of these acts of positing – which can thus be described as occurring "unconsciously" – and become aware of them only through philosophical reflection). (Trans.)

6 "postulirst du ein von dem Denken und Gedachtseyn deiner selbst unabhängiges, und demselben vorauszusetzendes, *Daseyn* deiner selbst." (Trans.)

7 As a comparison with section 1 of Fichte's lectures on "Foundations of Transcendental Philosophy (*Wissenschaftslehre*) *nova methodo*" reveals, Fichte is here simply repeating the classroom instructions he was accustomed to give to his own students. Hendrik Steffens, who was present as a student for some of Fichte's lectures during the winter semester of 1798/99, included in his memoirs the following account of the listeners' puzzled reaction to these same instructions: "I cannot deny that I was awed by my first glimpse of this short, stocky man with a sharp, commanding tongue. Even his manner of speaking was sharp and cutting. Well aware of his listeners' weaknesses, he tried in every way to make himself understood by them. He made every effort to provide proofs for everything he said; but his speech still seemed commanding, as if he wanted to dispel any possible doubts by means of an unconditional order. 'Gentlemen,' he would say, 'collect your thoughts and enter into yourselves. We are not at all concerned now with anything external, but only with ourselves.' And, just as he requested, his listeners really seemed to be concentrating upon themselves. Some of them shifted their position and sat up straight, while others slumped with downcast eyes. But it was obvious that they were all waiting with great suspense for what was supposed to come next. Then Fichte would continue: 'Gentlemen, think about the wall.' And as I saw, they really did think about the wall, and everyone seemed able to do so with success. 'Have you thought about the wall?' Fichte would ask. 'Now, gentlemen, think about whoever it was that thought about the wall.' The obvious confusion and embarrassment provoked by this request was extraordinary. In fact, many of the listeners seemed quite unable to discover anywhere whoever it was that had thought about the wall. I now understood how young men who had stumbled in such a memorable manner over their first attempt at speculation might have fallen into a very dangerous frame of mind as a result of their further efforts in this direction. Fichte's delivery was excellent: precise and clear. I was completely swept away by the topic, and I had to admit that I had never before heard a lecture like that one." Quoted in Erich Fuchs, ed., *Fichte im Gespräch*, vol. 2 (Stuttgart-Bad Cannstatt: Frommann-Holzboog, 1980), p. 8. (Trans.)

8 "das vorhin das Selbstbewusst*seyn* war." I.e. one's previous self-consciousness now becomes the object of a new higher-level act of reflection, which thus requires the positing of a new subject. (Trans.)

9 See Kant's definition of "intuition" as the mode of cognition [*Erkenntnis*] in which "a cognition is immediately related to its object" (*Critique of Pure Reason*, A19/B33). (Trans.)

10 The word "self" has frequently been employed of late to designate this same concept. If my derivation is correct, all the words in the family to which the word "self" belongs (e.g. "self-same," "the same," etc.) signify a relationship to something that has already been posited, though only insofar as it has been posited *through its mere concept*. If what has been posited is I, then the word "self" is formed. Hence the word "self" presupposes the concept of the I, and everything that is thought to be absolute within the former is borrowed from the concept of the latter. Perhaps in a popular exposition the term "self" is more convenient, because it adds a special emphasis to the concept of the I as such, which – after all – is always obscurely thought of along with the word "self." Such an emphasis may well be required by the ordinary reader, but it seems to me that in a scientific exposition one should employ the term that designates this concept in the most immediate and proper way. – In a recently published work intended for the public at large, however, the concept of the self is distinguished from and opposed to that of the I, and a sublime theory is derived from the former and a detestable one is derived from the latter, even though the author of the work in question must know, at least as a historical fact, that the word "I" has also been taken in a quite different sense and that a system in which there is no place at all for the detestable theory in question is currently being erected upon the concept to which the word "I" (taken in this latter sense) refers. It is simply incomprehensible what purpose is supposed to be served by this – so long, that is, as one neither wishes nor is able to assume any hostile intent on the part of the author in question.

11 "Thätigkeit ist Agilität, innere Bewegung; der Geist reisst sich selbst über absolut entgegengesetzte hinweg; – durch welche Beschreibung keinesweges etwa das unbegreifliche begreiflich gemacht." (Note: *unbegreifliche* = "incomprehensible," in the sense of "incapable of being discursively grasped by means of concepts.") (Trans.)

12 "You were clinging transfixed in that gaze." Freely quoted from Virgil, *Aeneid*, I, 495. (Trans.)

13 "Die Bestimmtheit deines Denkens durch das Denken deiner selbst." (Trans.)

14   With the (unfulfilled) promise "(To be continued in future issues)," the fourth and final published installment of *An Attempt at a New Presentation of* *the Wissenschaftslehre* concludes at this point. (Trans.)

Select Bibliography

Addresses to the German Nation. Translated by R. F. Jones and G. H. Turnbull. Westport, Conn.: Greenwood Press, 1979.

Attempt at a Critique of All Revelation. Translated by Garrett Green. Cambridge: Cambridge University Press, 1978.

Fichte: Early Philosophical Writings. Edited and translated by Daniel Breazeale. Ithaca: Cornell University Press, 1993.

Foundations of Transcendental Philosophy (Wissenschaftslehre) Nova Methodo (1796/1799). Edited and translated by Daniel Breazeale. Ithaca: Cornell University Press, 1992.

Introductions to the Wissenschaftslehre and Other Writings (1797–1800). Edited and translated by Daniel Breazeale. Indianapolis: Hackett Publishing, 1994.

The Purpose of Higher Education, Also Known as the Vocation of the Scholar. Translated by Jorn K. Bramann. Mount Savage, Md.: Nightsun Books, 1988.

Science of Knowledge with the First and Second Introductions. Edited and translated by Peter Heath and John Lachs. Cambridge: Cambridge University Press, 1982.

The Science of Rights. Translated by A. E. Kroeger. London: Routledge and Kegan Paul, 1970.

The Vocation of Man. Translated by Peter Preuss. Indianapolis: Hackett Publishing, 1987.

3

Friedrich Hölderlin

Friedrich Hölderlin (1770–1843) was a friend of Hegel and Schelling during their student years in Tübingen. Whereas both Hegel and Schelling developed the project of Kantian philosophy in the direction of speculative idealism, Hölderlin soon turned to poetry in the conviction that only the poetic word could express the profound harmony between spirit and nature. In addition to a substantial number of poems, culminating in the well-known hymns of his later period, Hölderlin's work includes a novel called *Hyperion*, translations of Greek tragedy, and a number of theoretical writings and fragments. The following fragment, from 1795, documents Hölderlin's resistance to Fichte's conception of the being of the I as identity, emphasizing by contrast the primordiality of original or "arche-" separation of subject and object in speculative identity.

Judgment and Being[1]

Judgment, in the highest and strictest sense, is the original separation of object and subject which are most deeply united in intellectual intuition, that separation through which alone object and subject become possible, the arche-separation. In the concept of separation, there lies already the concept of the reciprocity of object and subject and the necessary presupposition of a whole of which object and subject form the parts. "I am I" is the most fitting

From *Friedrich Hölderlin: Essays and Letters on Theory*, translated and edited by Thomas Pfau (Albany: State University of New York Press, 1988), pp. 37–8. Permission of the State University of New York Press © 1988.

example for this concept of arche-separation as *theoretical* separation, for in the practical arche-separation it [the "I"] opposes the *non-I, not itself*.

Reality and potentiality are distinguished like mediate and immediate consciousness. If I think an object as potentiality, I only repeat the preceding consciousness by virtue of which it really is. There is no potentiality conceivable for us that was not reality. Hence the concept of potentiality does not apply to objects of reason, for they never occur in consciousness as what they are supposed to be, but only the concept of necessity ["... applies to such objects of reason."].[2] The concept of potentiality applies to objects of the intellect, that of reality [applies] to perception and intuition [...]

Being – expresses the connection between subject and object. Where subject and object are united altogether and not only in part, that is, united in such a manner that no separation can be performed without violating the essence of what is to be separated, there and nowhere else can be spoken of *Being proper*, as is the case with intellectual intuition.

Yet this Being must not be confused with identity. If I say: I am I, the subject ("I") and the object ("I") are not united in such a way that no separation could be performed without violating the essence of what is to be separated; on the contrary, the I is only possible by means of this separation of the I from the I. How can I say: "I"! without self-consciousness? Yet how is self-consciousness possible? In opposing myself to myself, separating myself from myself, yet in recognizing myself as the same in the opposed regardless of this separation. Yet to what extent as the same? I can, I must ask in this manner; for in another respect it [the "I"] is opposed to itself. Hence identity is not a union of object and subject which simply occurred, hence identity is not = to absolute Being.

Notes

1 The text appears to have been written early in 1795. For a long interpretative and philological assessment of this, perhaps most significant, fragment of the "early" Hölderlin, see: Dieter Henrich, "Hölderlin über 'Urteil und Sein'." – Hölderlin stresses the etymology of the German *Urteil* ("Ur-theil") by pointing to its implication of an "arche-separation." (Trans.)

2 The syntax in the MS is somewhat cryptic, however, the completion of the phrase appears quite unambiguous. (Trans.)

Select Bibliography

Friedrich Hölderlin: Essays and Letters on Theory. Translated by Thomas Pfau. Albany: State University of New York Press, 1988.

Hölderlin: Selected Verse. Edited and translated by Michael Hamburger. London: Anvil Press Poetry, 1986.

Hymns and Fragments. Translated by Richard Sieburth. Princeton: Princeton University Press, 1984.

Hyperion and Selected Poems. Edited by Eric L. Santner. New York: Continuum, 1990.

Poems and Fragments. Translated by Michael Hamburger. London: Anvil Poetry Press, 1994.

Selected Poems. Translated by David Constantine. Newcastle upon Tyne: Bloodaxe, 1996.

The Oldest Program Towards a System in German Idealism

This famous fragment, although preserved in Hegel's handwriting, is of disputed origin. Both Schelling and Hölderlin have been proposed as the original author; at any rate, it can be seen as showing the influences of all three philosophers. The piece appears to date from mid-1796, and projects a new "philosophy of spirit" that will systematically unify the realms of freedom, nature, and art, in the form of a new "mythology of reason." The fragment thus undertakes to ground the systematic unity of the three domains of Kant's critical philosophy, a grounding that Kant's *Critique of Judgment* (at least according to Schelling, Hölderlin, and Hegel) accomplished in a problematic fashion at best.

... an ethics. Inasmuch as the whole of metaphysics will in future be subsumed under *moral philosophy* – a matter in which Kant, with his two practical postulates, has merely provided an *example*, and has *exhausted* nothing) – this ethics will be nothing else than a complete system of all ideas, or, what comes to the same, of all practical postulates. The first idea is of course the representation *of me myself* as an absolutely free creature. At the same time, along with the free, self-conscious creature, a whole *world* comes to the fore – out of nothing – the sole true and conceivable *creation out of nothing*.

Translated by David Farrell Krell, in *The Owl of Minerva*, Volume 17, Number 1 (1985), pp. 8–13. Reprinted with the permission of *The Owl of Minerva*, Journal of the Hegel Society of America.

– Here I shall alight on the fields of physics; the question is: How must a world be fashioned for a moral creature? To our sluggish physics, advancing laboriously with its experiments, I would like to lend wings once more.

Thus – if philosophy provides the ideas, while experience supplies the data, we can finally get at least in general outline the physics I expect from later epochs. It does not seem as though current physics could satisfy a creative spirit, such as ours is, or ought to be.

From nature I shall advance to the *works of mankind*. First of all, the idea of humanity – I want to show that there is no idea of the *state*, because the state is something *mechanical*; just as little is there an idea of a *machine*. Only that which is an object of *freedom* is called an *idea*. Thus we must also proceed beyond the state! – For every state has to treat free human beings like mechanical cog-wheels; and it should not do so; hence it should *cease*. You yourselves see that here all ideas of eternal peace, etc. are only *subordinate* ideas with regard to a higher idea. At the same time I want to lay down the principles for a *history of humanity* here, and to strip bare, down to the skin, the whole wretched human apparatus of state, constitution, government, and legislation. Finally come the ideas of a moral world, divinity, immortality – the over-throw of all belief in a hinterhaven, the prosecution by reason itself of that hypocritical priesthood that has recently begun to ape reason. – The absolute freedom of all spirits who bear the intellectual world within themselves and who dare seek neither God nor immortality *outside themselves*.

At the close, the idea that unifies all, the idea of *beauty*, the word taken in its higher, Platonic sense. For I am convinced that the supreme act of reason, because it embraces all ideas, is an aesthetic act; and that only in *beauty* are *truth and goodness* of the same flesh. – The philosopher must possess as much aesthetic force as the poet. Those human beings who are devoid of aesthetic sense are our pedantic philosophers. The philosophy of spirit is an aesthetic philosophy. One can in no way be inspired – one cannot even ruminate on historical matters in an inspired way – without aesthetic sense. Here it should become obvious to us pre-cisely what is defective in those human beings who understand no ideas, – and who concede forth-rightly enough that everything becomes obscure to them the moment it involves more than tables and indices.

Poesy will thereby attain a higher dignity; in the end she will again become what she was in the beginning – *the instructress of humanity*; for there will no longer be any philosophy, any history; the poetic art alone will survive all the other sciences and arts.

At the same time, we so often hear that the great mass of men must have a *sensuous religion*. Not only the great mass of men, but the philosopher too, needs it. Monotheism of reason and of the heart, polytheism of the imagination and of art, that is what we need!

First, I shall speak here of an idea which, as far as I know, no human mind has ever entertained – we must have a new mythology; but this mythology must remain in service to the ideas, it must become a mythology of *reason*.

Until we make the ideas aesthetic, i.e. mytholo-gical, they will have no interest for the *people*; and, conversely, until the mythology is rational, the philosopher will perforce be ashamed of it. Thus the enlightened and unenlightened must at long last clasp hands; mythology must become philoso-phical, and the people rational, while philosophy must become mythological, in order to make the philosophers sensuous. Then eternal unity will prevail among us. No more the contemptuous glance, no more the blind quaking of the people before their sages and priests. Only then can we expect the *equal* formation of *all* forces, in particu-lar persons as well as in all individuals. No longer will any force be suppressed; then universal free-dom and equality of spirits will prevail! – A higher spirit, sent from heaven, will have to found this new religion among us; it will be the very last and the grandest of humanity's works.

5

Friedrich Wilhelm Joseph von Schelling

German idealist philosopher Friedrich Wilhelm Joseph von Schelling (1775–1854) was a student of Fichte and a friend of Hegel and Hölderlin. In 1798, at the age of 23, he became professor of philosophy at Jena. Schelling's early work is concerned with integrating a philosophy of nature into Fichte's system of idealism, which opposes the absolute, subjective identity of the I to the realm of the non-I, the realm of objective nature. As in Kant's *Critique of Judgment* (1790), the realm of art is conceived by Schelling as playing a pivotal role in the task of the reconciliation of nature and freedom into a unified whole. The following selections from Schelling's *System of Transcendental Idealism* (1800) provide an outline of this early attempt at a system that seeks to reconcile subjective and objective being in the thinking of absolute or speculative identity first broached by Fichte.

System of Transcendental Idealism

Foreword

That a system which completely alters and even overthrows the whole view of things prevailing, not merely in common life, but also in the greater part of the sciences, should encounter, despite the rigorous demonstration of its principles, a continuing opposition even among those in a position to feel or really to discern the force of its arguments, is a circumstance that can be due only to an incapacity for abstracting from the multitude of individual problems, which, on such an altered view, the busy imagination at once conjures up from the whole wealth of experience, so that the judgment is in consequence distracted and disturbed. We cannot deny the strength of the arguments, nor do we know of anything certain and assured to put in place of the principles; but we are afraid of the supposedly monstrous consequences that are foreseen to follow from them, and despair of resolving all those difficulties which the principles, in their application, must inevitably encounter. Nevertheless one may legitimately demand of anyone who takes any part whatever in philosophical enquiries, that he be capable of this abstraction, and know how to grasp the principles in the highest

From *System of Transcendental Idealism (1800)*, translated by Peter Heath (Charlottesville: University Press of Virginia, 1978), pp. 1–12, 231–3. Copyright © 1978. Reprinted with permission of the University Press of Virginia.

degree of generality, wherein details disappear entirely, and wherein, if it be only the highest, the solution of all possible problems is assuredly also contained in advance; and it is therefore natural that in first setting up the system, all enquiries descending into detail should be set aside, and only the first thing needful be done, namely to bring the principles into the open, and to put them beyond all doubt. And by this, indeed, such a system finds the surest touchstone of its truth, that it not only provides a ready solution to problems hitherto insoluble, but actually generates entirely new problems, never before considered, and by a general shattering of received opinion gives rise to a new sort of truth. But this is precisely characteristic of transcendental idealism, that as soon as it is once admitted, it puts us under the necessity of generating all knowledge afresh, as it were, of once more putting to the test what has long since passed as established truth, and, assuming that it stands the test, of at least compelling it to emerge therefrom in a wholly novel shape and form.

Now the purpose of the present work is simply this, to enlarge transcendental idealism into what it really should be, namely a system of all knowledge. The aim, then, is to provide proof of the system, not merely in general, but in actual fact, that is, through the real extension of its principles to all possible problems in regard to the main objects of knowledge, whether these have already been raised earlier, but not resolved, or have only now been rendered possible and have newly come into existence through the system itself. It follows accordingly that this work must treat of topics and questions that have simply never been agitated or articulated among a great many of those who now presume nonetheless to have an opinion in philosophical matters; inasmuch as they still halt at the first rudiments of the system, and cannot get beyond them, either because of an initial incapacity even to understand what the first principles of all knowledge require, or because of prejudice, or for whatever other reason. Now although the enquiry does of course revert to elementary first principles, the above class of persons has little to hope for from the present work, since in regard to basic enquiries nothing can be found herein that has not already been said long since, either in the writings of the originator of the Science of Knowledge, or in those of the present author; save that in the present treatment, the exposition in regard to certain points may perhaps have achieved a greater clarity than it previously possessed – though even this can

never, at any rate, make up for a fundamental want of understanding. The means, furthermore, whereby the author has sought to achieve his aim of setting forth idealism in its full extent, consist in presenting every part of philosophy in a single continuum, and the whole of philosophy as what in fact it is, namely a progressive history of self-consciousness, for which what is laid down in experience serves merely, so to speak, as a memorial and a document. In order to trace this history with precision and completeness, it was chiefly a matter, not only of separating exactly the individual stages thereof, and within these again the individual moments, but also of presenting them in a sequence, whereby one can be certain, thanks to the very method employed in its discovery, that no necessary intervening step has been omitted; the result being to confer upon the whole an internal coherence which time cannot touch, and which in all subsequent development remains, as it were, the unalterable framework, to which everything must be related. The author's chief motive for devoting particular care to the depiction of this coherence, which is really a *graduated sequence* of intuitions, whereby the self raises itself to the highest power of consciousness, was the parallelism of nature with intelligence; to this he has long since been led, and to depict it completely, neither transcendental philosophy nor the philosophy of nature is adequate by itself; *both sciences* together are alone able to do it, though on that very account the two must forever be opposed to one another, and can never merge into one. The conclusive proof of the perfectly equal reality of the two sciences from a theoretical standpoint, which the author has hitherto merely asserted, is thus to be sought in transcendental philosophy, and especially in that presentation of it which is contained in the present work; and the latter must therefore be considered as a necessary counterpart to his writings on the philosophy of nature. For in this work it will become apparent, that the same powers of intuition which reside in the self can also be exhibited up to a certain point in nature; and, since the boundary in question is itself that of theoretical and practical philosophy, that it is therefore indifferent, from a purely theoretical standpoint, whether objective or subjective be made primary, since this is a matter that practical philosophy (though it has no voice at all in this connection) is alone able to decide; whence it will also appear that even idealism has no purely theoretical basis, and to that extent, if theoretical evidence alone be accepted, can never have the evidential cogency of which natural science is capable, whose basis and proof alike are theoretical through and through. Readers acquainted with the *philosophy of nature* will, indeed, conclude from these observations, that there is a reason, lying pretty deep in the subject itself, why the author has opposed this science to transcendental philosophy and completely separated it therefrom, whereas, to be sure, if our whole enterprise were merely that of explaining nature, we should never have been driven into idealism.

But now as to the deductions which are effected in the present work from the primary objects of nature, from matter as such and its general functions, from the organism, etc., there are certainly idealistic, though not on that account teleological derivations (albeit many regard them as equivalent), which are as little capable of giving satisfaction in idealism as in any other system. For supposing I prove, for example, that it is necessary for the sake of freedom, or for practical purposes, that there should be matter having such and such properties, or that the intellect intuit its dealings with the external world as mediated through an organism, this demonstration continues to leave unanswered for me the question as to how and by what *mechanism* the intellect actually intuits precisely that which is necessary for this purpose. On the contrary, all proofs that the idealist offers for the existence of determinate external things must be derived from the primordial mechanism of intuition itself, that is, by a genuine *construction* of objects. Since the proofs are idealistic, the merely teleological application of them would not in fact advance true knowledge a single step, since notoriously the teleological explanation of an object can teach me nothing whatever as to its real origin.

In a system of transcendental idealism as such, the truths of *practical* philosophy can themselves emerge only as intervening links, and that part of practical philosophy actually pertaining to the system consists only of what is objective therein, and this, in its broadest generality, is history; a topic that, in a system of idealism, requires to be deduced transcendentally no less than does the objective of first order, namely nature. This deduction of history leads directly to the proof that what we have to regard as the ultimate ground of harmony between the subjective and the objective in action must in fact be conceived as an absolute identity; though to think of this latter as a substantial or personal entity would in no way be better

than to posit it in a pure abstraction – an opinion that could be imputed to idealism only through the grossest of misunderstandings.

So far as concerns the basic principles of *teleology*, the reader will doubtless recognize for himself that they point to the only way of explaining the coexistence of mechanism with purposiveness in nature in an intelligible manner. – And finally, with reference to the precepts concerning the *philosophy of art*, whereby the whole is concluded, the author begs those who may have some special interest in this subject to remember that the whole enquiry, which considered in itself is an infinite one, is here instituted merely in regard to the system of philosophy, whereby a multitude of aspects of this immense topic has had to be excluded from consideration in advance.

The author observes in conclusion that one of his subsidiary aims has been to provide an account of transcendental idealism that shall be, so far as possible, generally readable and intelligible; and that the possibility of some success in this, in virtue of the very method that he has chosen, is something of which he is already convinced by a twofold experience in publicly presenting the system.

This brief foreword will be sufficient, nonetheless, to arouse some interest in the book among those who share the author's standpoint and seek with him a solution of the same problems, and to attract those who wish for information and instruction; while those who are neither acquainted with the one, nor genuinely desirous of the other, will be scared away from it at the outset; and all its objects will be thereby achieved.

Jena, End of March, 1800

Introduction

§1   Concept of Transcendental Philosophy

1   All knowledge is founded upon the coincidence of an objective with a subjective. – For we *know* only what is true; but truth is generally taken to consist in the coincidence of presentations with their objects.

2   The intrinsic notion of everything merely *objective* in our knowledge, we may speak of as *nature*. The notion of everything *subjective* is called, on the contrary, the *self*, or the *intelligence*. The two concepts are mutually opposed. The intelligence is

initially conceived of as the purely presentative, nature purely as what can be presented; the one as the conscious, the other as the nonconscious. But now in every *knowing* a reciprocal concurrence of the two (the conscious and the intrinsically nonconscious) is necessary; the problem is to explain this concurrence.

3   In knowing as such – *in the fact of* my knowing – objective and subjective are so united that one cannot say which of the two has priority. Here there is no first and second; both are simultaneous and one. – Insofar as I *wish to explain* this identity, I must already have *done away with* it. To explain it, inasmuch as nothing else is given me (as explanatory principle) beyond these two factors of knowledge, I must necessarily *give priority* to one over the other, *set out* from the one, in order thence to arrive at the other; from *which* of the two I start, the problem does not specify.

4   Hence there are only two possibilities.

A   *Either the objective is made primary, and the question is: how a subjective is annexed thereto, which coincides with it?*

The concept of the subjective is not *contained* in that of the objective; on the contrary, they exclude one another. The subjective must therefore *be annexed* to the objective. – The concept *of nature* does not entail that there should also be an intelligence that is aware of it. Nature, it seems, would exist, even if there were nothing that was aware of it. Hence the problem can also be formulated *thus*: how does intelligence come to be added to nature, or how does nature come to be presented?

The problem assumes nature or the *objective* to be *primary*. Hence the problem is undoubtedly that of *natural science*, which does just this. – That natural science in fact – and without knowing it – at least *comes close* to the solution of this problem can be shown only briefly here.

If all *knowing* has, as it were, two poles, which mutually presuppose and demand one another, they must seek each other in all the sciences; hence there must necessarily be *two* basic sciences, and it must be impossible to set out from the one pole without being driven toward the other. The necessary tendency of all *natural science* is thus to move from nature to intelligence. This and nothing else is at the bottom of the urge to bring *theory* into the phenomena of nature. – The highest consummation of natural science would be the complete spiritualizing of all natural laws into laws of intui-

tion and thought. The phenomena (the matter) must wholly disappear, and only the laws (the form) remain. Hence it is, that the more lawfulness emerges in nature itself, the more the husk disappears, the phenomena themselves become more mental, and at length vanish entirely. The phenomena of optics are nothing but a geometry whose lines are drawn by light, and this light itself is already of doubtful materiality. In the phenomena of magnetism all material traces are already disappearing, and in those of gravitation, which even scientists have thought it possible to conceive of merely as an immediate spiritual influence, nothing remains but its law, whose large-scale execution is the mechanism of the heavenly motions. – The completed theory of nature would be that whereby the whole of nature was resolved into an intelligence. – The dead and unconscious products of nature are merely abortive attempts that she makes to reflect herself; inanimate nature so-called is actually as such an immature intelligence, so that in her phenomena the still unwitting character of intelligence is already peeping through. – Nature's highest goal, to become wholly an object to herself, is achieved only through the last and highest order of reflection, which is none other than man; or, more generally, it is what we call reason, whereby nature first completely returns into herself, and by which it becomes apparent that nature is identical from the first with what we recognize in ourselves as the intelligent and the conscious.

This may be sufficient to show that natural science has a necessary tendency to render nature intelligent; through this very tendency it becomes *nature-philosophy*, which is one of the necessary basic sciences of philosophy.[1]

B   *Alternatively, the subjective is made primary, and the problem is: how an objective supervenes, which coincides with it?*

If all knowledge rests upon the coincidence of these *two (1)*, then the problem of explaining this coincidence is undoubtedly the supreme problem for all knowledge; and if, as is generally admitted, philosophy is the highest and foremost of all sciences, we have here undoubtedly the main problem of philosophy.

However, the problem only requires an explanation of the concurrence as such, and leaves it completely open as to where explanation starts from, as to which it should make primary and which secondary. – Yet since the two opposites are mutually necessary to each other, the result of the operation is bound to be the same, whichever point we set out from.

To make the *objective* primary, and to derive the subjective from that, is, as has just been shown, the problem of *nature-philosophy*.

If, then, there is a *transcendental philosophy*, there remains to it only the opposite direction, that of *proceeding from the subjective, as primary and absolute, and having the objective arise from this*. Thus nature-philosophy and transcendental philosophy have divided into the two directions possible to philosophy, and if *all* philosophy must go about *either* to make an intelligence out of nature, *or* a nature out of intelligence, then transcendental philosophy, which has the latter task, is thus *the other necessary basic science of philosophy*.

§2 Corollaries

In the course of the foregoing, we have not only deduced the concept of transcendental philosophy, but have also furnished the reader with a glimpse into the entire system of philosophy; this, as we see, is constituted of two basic sciences which, though opposed to each other in principle and direction, mutually seek and supplement one another. Here we shall not set forth the entire system of philosophy, but only one of the basic sciences, and the derived concept thereof will thus first receive a more exact characterization.[2]

1. If the *subjective* – the *first* and only ground of all reality – is for transcendental philosophy the sole principle of explanation for everything else (§1), then it necessarily begins with a general doubt as to the reality of the objective.

Just as the nature-philosopher, directed solely upon the objective, has nothing he more dearly wishes to prevent than an admixture of the subjective into knowledge, so the transcendental philosopher, by contrast, wishes nothing more dearly than to avoid an admixture of the objective into the purely subjective principle of knowledge. The means of separation lie in absolute skepticism – not the half-skepticism which merely contends against the common prejudices of mankind, while never looking to fundamentals, but rather that thoroughgoing skepticism which is directed, not against individual prejudices, but against the basic preconception, whose rejection leads automatically to the collapse of everything else. For in addition to the artificial prejudices implanted in mankind, there are others far more fundamental, laid down in us not by art or education, but by nature herself;

prejudices which, for everyone but philosophers, serve as the principles of all knowledge, and for the merely self-made thinker rank even as the touchstone of all truth.

The one basic prejudice, to which all others reduce, is no other than this: *that there are things outside us*. This is a conviction that rests neither on grounds nor on inferences (since there is not a single reputable proof of it) and yet cannot be extirpated by any argument to the contrary (*naturam furca expellas, tamen usque redibit*); it makes claim to *immediate* certainty, since it assuredly relates to something entirely different from us, and even opposed to us, of which we understand not at all how it enters into immediate consciousness; and hence it can be regarded as nothing more than a prejudice – innate and primary, to be sure – but no less a prejudice on that account.

The contradiction, that a principle which by nature cannot be immediately certain is yet accepted as blindly and groundlessly as one that is so, is incapable of resolution by the transcendental philosopher, save on the presupposition that this principle is not just covertly and as yet uncomprehendingly connected with, but is identical with, one and the same with, an immediate certainty, *and to demonstrate this identity will* in fact be the concern of transcendental philosophy.

2. But now even for the common use of reason, nothing is immediately certain save the proposition *I exist*; which, since it actually loses its meaning *outside* immediate consciousness, is the most individual of all truths, and the *absolute preconception*, which must *first* be accepted, if anything else is to be certain. – The proposition *There are things outside us* will therefore only be certain for the transcendental philosopher in virtue of its identity with the proposition *I exist*, and its certainty will likewise only be *equal* to the certainty of the proposition from which it borrows its own.

Transcendental cognition would thus differ from ordinary cognition on two counts.

First, that the certainty that external things exist is for it a mere prejudice, which it goes beyond, in order to discover the grounds thereof. (It can never be the transcendental philosopher's business to demonstrate the existence of things-in-themselves, but merely that it is a natural and necessary prejudice to assume that external objects are real.)

Second, that it separates the two propositions, *I exist*, and *There are things outside me*, which in ordinary consciousness are fused together; setting the one before the other, precisely in order to prove their identity, and so that it can really exhibit the immediate connection which is otherwise merely felt. By this very act of separation, if complete, it shifts into the transcendental mode of apprehension, which is in no way natural, but artificial.

3 If only the subjective has initial reality for the transcendental philosopher, he will also make only the subjective the immediate object of his cognition: the objective will become an object for him indirectly only, and whereas in ordinary cognition *the knowing itself* (the act of knowing) vanishes into the object, in transcendental cognition, on the contrary, the object *as* such vanishes into the act of knowing. Transcendental cognition is thus a knowing of knowing, insofar as it is purely subjective.

Thus in intuition, for example, only the objective element attains to ordinary consciousness, the intuiting itself being lost in the object; whereas the transcendental mode of apprehension merely glimpses the intuited through the act of intuiting. – Again, ordinary thinking is a mechanism governed by concepts, though they are not distinguished *as* concepts; whereas transcendental thinking suspends this mechanism, and in becoming aware of the concept as an act, attains to the *concept of a concept*. – In ordinary action, the *acting itself* is lost sight of in the object of action; philosophizing is likewise an *action*, yet not only an action but also at the same time a continuous *scrutiny of the self* so engaged.

The nature of the transcendental mode of apprehension must therefore consist essentially in this, *that even that which in all other thinking, knowing, or acting escapes consciousness and is absolutely non-objective, is therein brought to consciousness and becomes objective; it consists, in short, of a constant objectifying-to-itself of the subjective.*

The transcendental artifice will thus consist in the ability to maintain oneself constantly in this duality of acting and thinking.

§3 Preliminary Division of Transcendental Philosophy

This division is *preliminary*, because the principles of division can only be first derived in the science itself.

We revert to the concept of the science.

Transcendental philosophy has to explain how knowledge as such is possible, it being presupposed that the subjective element therein is to be taken as dominant or primary.

It therefore takes as its object, not an individual portion, nor a special object of knowledge, but *knowledge itself* and *knowledge as such*.

But now all knowledge reduces to certain primordial convictions or primordial prejudices; transcendental philosophy must trace these individual convictions back to one fundamental conviction; this one, from which all others are derived, is formulated in the *first principle of this philosophy*, and the task of finding such a principle is nothing other than that of finding the absolute certainty whereby all other certainty is mediated.

The division of transcendental philosophy itself is determined by those original convictions whose validity it vindicates. These convictions must first be sought in the common understanding. – And if we thus transport ourselves back to the standpoint of the common outlook, we find the following convictions deeply rooted in the human understanding.

A That there not only exists a world of things outside and independent of us, but also that our presentations are so far coincident with it that there is *nothing else* in things save what we attribute to them. This explains the constraint in our objective presentations, that things should be unalterably determined, and that our own presentations should also be mediately determined by this determinacy of things. This first and most fundamental conviction suffices to determine the first task of philosophy: to explain how our presentations can absolutely coincide with objects existing wholly independent of them. – The assumption that things are just what we take them to be, so that we are acquainted with them as they are *in themselves*, underlies the possibility of all experience (for what would experience be, and to what aberrations would physics, for example, be subject, without this presupposition of absolute identity between appearance and reality?). Hence, the solution of this problem is identical with *theoretical* philosophy, whose task is to investigate the possibility of experience.

B The second and no less basic conviction is this, that presentations, arising *freely and without necessity* in us, pass over from the world of thought into the real world, and can attain objective reality.

This conviction is in opposition to the first. The first assumes that objects are *unalterably determined*, and thereby also our own presentations; the second assumes that objects are *alterable*, and are so, in fact, through the causality of presentations in us. On the first view there is a passage from the real world into the world of presentation, or a determining of presentation by an objective; on the second, there is a passage from the world of presentation into the real world, or a determining of the objective by a presentation (freely generated) in ourselves.

This second conviction serves to determine a second problem, namely how an objective can be altered by a mere thought, so that it perfectly coincides therewith.

Upon this conviction the possibility of all free action depends, so that the solution of this problem is identical with *practical philosophy*.

C But with these two problems we find ourselves involved in a contradiction. – B calls for a dominance of thought (the ideal) over the world of sense; but how is this conceivable if (by A) the presentation is in origin already the mere slave of the objective? – Conversely, if the real world is a thing wholly independent of us, to which (as A tells us) our presentation must conform (as to its archetype), it is inconceivable how the real world, on the contrary, could (as B says) conform itself to presentations in us. – In a word, for certainty in theory we lose it in practice, and for certainty in practice we lose it in theory; it is impossible both that our knowledge should contain truth and our volition reality.

If there is to be any philosophy at all, this contradiction must be resolved – and the solution of this problem, or answer to the question: *how can we think both of presentations as conforming to objects, and objects as conforming to presentations?* is, not the first, but the *highest* task of transcendental philosophy.

It is easy to see that this problem can be solved neither in theoretical nor in practical philosophy, but only in a higher discipline, which is the link that combines them, and neither theoretical nor practical, but *both* at once.

How both the objective world accommodates to presentations in us, and presentations in us to the objective world, is unintelligible unless between the two worlds, the ideal and the real, there exists a *predetermined harmony*. But this latter is itself unthinkable unless the activity, whereby the objective world is produced, is at bottom identical with that which expresses itself in volition, and vice versa.

Now it is certainly a *productive* activity that finds expression in willing; all free action is productive, albeit *consciously* productive. If we now suppose, since the two activities have only to be one in

principle, that the same activity which is *consciously* productive in free action, is productive *without consciousness* in bringing about the world, then our predetermined harmony is real, and the contradiction resolved.

Supposing that all this is really the case, then this fundamental identity, of the activity concerned in producing the world with that which finds expression in willing, will display itself in the former's products, and these will have to appear as products of an activity at once *conscious and nonconscious*.

Nature, both as a whole, and in its individual products, will have to appear as a work both consciously engendered, and yet simultaneously a product of the blindest mechanism; *nature is purposive, without being purposively explicable.* – The philosophy of *natural purposes*, or teleology, is thus our point of union between theoretical and practical philosophy.

D All that has so far been postulated is simply an identity of the nonconscious activity that has brought forth nature, and the conscious activity expressed in willing, without it being decided where the principle of this activity belongs, whether in nature or in ourselves.

But now the system of knowledge can only be regarded as complete if it reverts back into its own principle. – Thus the transcendental philosophy would be completed only if it could demonstrate this *identity* – the highest solution of its whole problem – *in its own principle* (namely the self).

It is therefore postulated that this simultaneously conscious and nonconscious activity will be exhibited in the subjective, *in consciousness itself.*

There is but one such activity, namely the *aesthetic*, and every work of art can be conceived only as a product of such activity. The ideal world of art and the real world of objects are therefore products of one and the same activity; the concurrence of the two (the conscious and the nonconscious) *without* consciousness yields the real, and *with* consciousness the aesthetic world.

The objective world is simply the original, as yet unconscious, poetry of the spirit; the universal organon of philosophy – and the keystone of its entire arch – *is the philosophy of art....*

[From the last chapter:] If aesthetic intuition is merely transcendental[3] intuition become objective, it is self-evident that art is at once the only true and eternal organ and document of philosophy, which ever and again continues to speak to us of what philosophy cannot depict in external form, namely the unconscious element in acting and producing, and its original identity with the conscious. Art is paramount to the philosopher, precisely because it opens to him, as it were, the holy of holies, where burns in eternal and original unity, as if in a single flame, that which in nature and history is rent asunder, and in life and action, no less than in thought, must forever fly apart. The view of nature, which the philosopher frames artificially, is for art the original and natural one. What we speak of as nature is a poem lying pent in a mysterious and wonderful script. Yet the riddle could reveal itself, were we to recognize in it the odyssey of the spirit, which, marvelously deluded, seeks itself, and in seeking flies from itself; for through the world of sense there glimmers, as if through words the meaning, as if through dissolving mists the land of fantasy, of which we are in search. Each splendid painting owes, as it were, its genesis to a removal of the invisible barrier dividing the real from the ideal world, and is no more than the gateway, through which come forth completely the shapes and scenes of that world of fantasy which gleams but imperfectly through the real. Nature, to the artist, is nothing more than it is to the philosopher, being simply the ideal world appearing under permanent restrictions, or merely the imperfect reflection of a world existing, not outside him, but within.

But now what may be the source of this kinship of philosophy and art, despite the opposition between them, is a question already sufficiently answered in what has gone before.

We therefore close with the following observation. – A system is completed when it is led back to its starting point. But this is precisely the case with our own. The ultimate ground of all harmony between subjective and objective could be exhibited in its original identity only through intellectual intuition; and it is precisely this ground which, by means of the work of art, has been brought forth entirely from the subjective, and rendered wholly objective, in such wise, that we have gradually led our object, the self itself, up to the very point where we ourselves were standing when we began to philosophize.

But now if it is art alone which can succeed in objectifying with universal validity what the philosopher is able to present in a merely subjective fashion, there is one more conclusion yet to be drawn. Philosophy was born and nourished by poetry in the infancy of knowledge, and with it all those sciences it has guided toward perfection; we may thus expect them, on completion, to flow back like so many individual streams into the universal ocean of poetry from which they took their source. Nor is it in general difficult to say what the medium for this return of science to poetry will be; for in mythology such a medium existed, before the occurrence of a breach now seemingly beyond repair.[4] But how a new mythology is itself to arise, which shall be the creation, not of some individual author, but of a new race, personifying, as it were, one single poet – that is a problem whose solution can be looked for only in the future destinies of the world, and in the course of history to come.

Notes

1 The further elaboration of the concept of a nature-philosophy, and its necessary tendency, is to be found in the author's *Sketch for a System of Nature-Philosophy*, coupled with the *Introduction* to this sketch and the elucidations that are to appear in the first number of the *Journal for Speculative Physics*.
2 Only on completion of the system of transcendental philosophy will one come to recognize the necessity of a nature-philosophy, as a complementary science, and thereupon desist from making demands upon the former, which only a nature-philosophy can satisfy.
3 Intellectual (author's correction).
4 The further development of this idea is contained in a treatise *On Mythology*, already sketched out a number of years ago.

Select Bibliography

The Ages of the World. Translated by Frederick De Wolfe Bolman, Jr. *New York*: AMS Press, 1967.

Bruno, or On the Natural and the Divine Principle of Things. Edited and translated by Michael G. Vater. Albany: State University of New York Press, 1984.

Idealism and the Endgame of Theory: Three Essays. Translated and edited by Thomas Pfau. Albany: State University of New York Press, 1994.

Ideas for a Philosophy of Nature as Introduction to the Study of this Science (1797). Translated by Errol E. Harris and Peter Heath. Cambridge: Cambridge University Press, 1988.

Philosophical Inquiries into the Nature of Human Freedom. Translated by James Gutmann. Chicago: Open Court, 1936.

On the History of Modern Philosophy. Translated by Andrew Bowie. Cambridge: Cambridge University Press, 1994.

On University Studies. Translated by E. S. Morgan. Edited by Norbert Guterman. Athens: Ohio University Press, 1966.

The Philosophy of Art. Edited and translated by Douglas W. Stott. Minneapolis: University of Minnesota Press, 1989.

System of Transcendental Idealism (1800). Translated by Peter Heath. Charlottesville: University Press of Virginia, 1978.

The Unconditional in Human Knowledge: Four Early Essays (1794–1796). Translated by Fritz Marti. Lewisburg, Pa. Bucknell University Press, 1980.

6

Georg Wilhelm Friedrich Hegel

The most influential of the German Idealists, Georg Wilhelm Friedrich Hegel (1770–1831) was born in Stuttgart and educated at a theological seminary in Tübingen, where he befriended Schelling and Hölderlin. Like them, Hegel was deeply influenced by Kant and Fichte, and sought to overcome what he regarded as the one-sidedness and ahistoricality of Kant's subjective idealism. Hegel's best-known work, the *Phenomenology of Spirit*, appeared in 1807 and undertakes to describe the various developmental stages of consciousness as historical manifestations of Spirit, which first comes to know itself as the Absolute subject–object of history in and through the *Phenomenology*. The following selections reproduce Hegel's Introduction to the *Phenomenology of Spirit* as itself presenting the dialectical movement of self-consciousness toward absolute knowledge, followed by his analysis of sense-certainty as the immediate and most basic experience of consciousness.

Phenomenology of Spirit

Introduction

73 It is a natural assumption that in philosophy, before we start to deal with its proper subject-matter, viz. the actual cognition of what truly is, one must first of all come to an understanding about cognition, which is regarded either as the instrument to get hold of the Absolute, or as the medium through which one discovers it. A certain uneasiness seems justified, partly because there are different types of cognition, and one of them might be more appropriate than another for the attainment of this goal, so that we could make a bad choice of means; and partly because cognition is a faculty of a definite kind and scope, and thus, without a more precise definition of its nature and limits, we might grasp clouds of error instead of the heaven of truth. This feeling of uneasiness is surely bound to be transformed into the conviction that the whole project of securing for consciousness through cognition what exists in itself is absurd, and that there is a boundary between cognition and the Absolute that completely separates them. For, if cognition is the instrument for getting hold of

From *Phenomenology of Spirit*, translated by A. V. Miller (Oxford: Oxford University Press, 1977), pp. 6–65.

absolute being, it is obvious that the use of an instrument on a thing certainly does not let it be what it is for itself, but rather sets out to reshape and alter it. If, on the other hand, cognition is not an instrument of our activity but a more or less passive medium through which the light of truth reaches us, then again we do not receive the truth as it is in itself, but only as it exists through and in this medium. Either way we employ a means which immediately brings about the opposite of its own end; or rather, what is really absurd is that we should make use of a means at all.

It would seem, to be sure, that this evil could be remedied through an acquaintance with the way in which the *instrument* works; for this would enable us to eliminate from the representation of the Absolute which we have gained through it whatever is due to the instrument, and thus get the truth in its purity. But this "improvement" would in fact only bring us back to where we were before. If we remove from a reshaped thing what the instrument has done to it, then the thing – here the Absolute – becomes for us exactly what it was before this [accordingly] superfluous effort. On the other hand, if the Absolute is supposed merely to be brought nearer to us through this instrument, without anything in it being altered, like a bird caught by a lime-twig, it would surely laugh our little ruse to scorn, if it were not with us, in and for itself, all along, and of its own volition. For a ruse is just what cognition would be in such a case, since it would, with its manifold exertions, be giving itself the air of doing something quite different from creating a merely immediate and therefore effortless relationship. Or, if by testing cognition, which we conceive of as a *medium*, we get to know the law of its refraction, it is again useless to subtract this from the end result. For it is not the refraction of the ray, but the ray itself whereby truth reaches us, that is cognition; and if this were removed, all that would be indicated would be a pure direction or a blank space.

74   Meanwhile, if the fear of falling into error sets up a mistrust of Science, which in the absence of such scruples gets on with the work itself, and actually cognizes something, it is hard to see why we should not turn round and mistrust this very mistrust. Should we not be concerned as to whether this fear of error is not just the error itself? Indeed, this fear takes something – a great deal in fact – for granted as truth, supporting its scruples and inferences on what is itself in need of prior scrutiny to see if it is true. To be specific, it takes for granted certain ideas about cognition as an *instrument* and as a *medium*, and assumes that there is a *difference between ourselves and this cognition*. Above all, it presupposes that the Absolute stands on one side and cognition on the other, independent and separated from it, and yet is something real; or in other words, it presupposes that cognition which, since it is excluded from the Absolute, is surely outside of the truth as well, is nevertheless true, an assumption whereby what calls itself fear of error reveals itself rather as fear of the truth.

75   This conclusion stems from the fact that the Absolute alone is true, or the truth alone is absolute. One may set this aside on the grounds that there is a type of cognition which, though it does not cognize the Absolute as Science aims to, is still true, and that cognition in general, though it be incapable of grasping the Absolute, is still capable of grasping other kinds of truth. But we gradually come to see that this kind of talk which goes back and forth only leads to a hazy distinction between an absolute truth and some other kind of truth, and that words like "absolute," "cognition," etc. presuppose a meaning which has yet to be ascertained.

76   Instead of troubling ourselves with such useless ideas and locutions about cognition as "an instrument for getting hold of the Absolute," or as "a medium through which we view the truth" (relationships which surely, in the end, are what all these ideas of a cognition cut off from the Absolute, and an Absolute separated from cognition, amount to); instead of putting up with excuses which create the incapacity of Science by assuming relationships of this kind in order to be exempt from the hard work of Science, while at the same time giving the impression of working seriously and zealously; instead of bothering to refute all these ideas, we could reject them out of hand as adventitious and arbitrary, and the words associated with them like "absolute," "cognition," "objective," and "subjective," and countless others whose meaning is assumed to be generally familiar, could even be regarded as so much deception. For to give the impression that their meaning is generally well known, or that their Notion is comprehended, looks more like an attempt to avoid the main problem, which is precisely to provide this Notion. We could, with better justification, simply spare ourselves the trouble of paying any attention whatever to such ideas and locutions; for they are intended to ward off Science itself, and constitute merely an empty appearance of knowing, which vanishes immediately as soon as Science comes on the

scene. But Science, just because it comes on the scene, is itself an appearance: in coming on the scene it is not yet Science in its developed and unfolded truth. In this connection it makes no difference whether we think of Science as the appearance because it comes on the scene alongside another mode of knowledge, or whether we call that other untrue knowledge its manifestation. In any case Science must liberate itself from this semblance, and it can do so only by turning against it. For, when confronted with a knowledge that is without truth, Science can neither merely reject it as an ordinary way of looking at things, while assuring us that its Science is a quite different sort of cognition for which that ordinary knowledge is of no account whatever; nor can it appeal to the vulgar view for the intimations it gives us of something better to come. By the former *assurance*, Science would be declaring its power to lie simply in its *being*; but the untrue knowledge likewise appeals to the fact that *it is*, and *assures* us that for it Science is of no account. *One* bare assurance is worth just as much as another. Still less can Science appeal to whatever intimations of something better it may detect in the cognition that is without truth, to the signs which point in the direction of Science. For one thing, it would only be appealing again to what merely *is*; and for another, it would only be appealing to itself, and to itself in the mode in which it exists in the cognition that is without truth. In other words, it would be appealing to an inferior form of its being, to the way it appears, rather than to what it is in and for itself. It is for this reason that an exposition of how knowledge makes its appearance will here be undertaken.

77 Now, because it has only phenomenal knowledge for its object, this exposition seems not to be Science, free and self-moving in its own peculiar shape; yet from this standpoint it can be regarded as the path of the natural consciousness which presses forward to true knowledge; or as the way of the Soul which journeys through the series of its own configurations as though they were the stations appointed for it by its own nature, so that it may purify itself for the life of the Spirit, and achieve finally, through a completed experience of itself, the awareness of what it really is in itself.

78 Natural consciousness will show itself to be only the Notion of knowledge, or in other words, not to be real knowledge. But since it directly takes itself to be real knowledge, this path has a negative significance for it, and what is in fact the realization of the Notion, counts for it rather as the loss of its own self; for it does lose its truth on this path. The road can therefore be regarded as the pathway of *doubt*, or more precisely as the way of despair. For what happens on it is not what is ordinarily understood when the word "doubt" is used: shilly-shallying about this or that presumed truth, followed by a return to that truth again, after the doubt has been appropriately dispelled – so that at the end of the process the matter is taken to be what it was in the first place. On the contrary, this path is the conscious insight into the untruth of phenomenal knowledge, for which the supreme reality is what is in truth only the unrealized Notion. Therefore this thoroughgoing skepticism is also not the skepticism with which an earnest zeal for truth and Science fancies it has prepared and equipped itself in their service: the *resolve*, in Science, not to give oneself over to the thoughts of others, upon mere authority, but to examine everything for oneself and follow only one's own conviction, or better still, to produce everything oneself, and accept only one's own deed as what is true.

The series of configurations which consciousness goes through along this road is, in reality, the detailed history of the *education* of consciousness itself to the standpoint of Science. That zealous resolve represents this education simplistically as something directly over and done with in the making of the resolution; but the way of the Soul is the actual fulfilment of the resolution, in contrast to the untruth of that view. Now, following one's own conviction is, of course, more than giving oneself over to authority; but changing an opinion accepted on authority into an opinion held out of personal conviction, does not necessarily alter the content of the opinion, or replace error with truth. The only difference between being caught up in a system of opinions and prejudices based on personal conviction, and being caught up in one based on the authority of others, lies in the added conceit that is innate in the former position. The skepticism that is directed against the whole range of phenomenal consciousness, on the other hand, renders the Spirit for the first time competent to examine what truth is. For it brings about a state of despair about all the so-called natural ideas, thoughts, and opinions, regardless of whether they are called one's own or someone else's, ideas with which the consciousness that sets about the examination [of truth] *straight away* is still filled and hampered, so that it is, in fact, incapable of carrying out what it wants to undertake.

79   The necessary progression and interconnection of the forms of the unreal consciousness will by itself bring to pass the *completion* of the series. To make this more intelligible, it may be remarked, in a preliminary and general way, that the exposition of the untrue consciousness in its untruth is not a merely *negative* procedure. The natural consciousness itself normally takes this one-sided view of it; and a knowledge which makes this one-sidedness its very essence is itself one of the patterns of incomplete consciousness which occurs on the road itself, and will manifest itself in due course. This is just the skepticism which only ever sees pure nothingness in its result and abstracts from the fact that this nothingness is specifically the nothingness of that *from which it results*. For it is only when it is taken as the result of that from which it emerges, that it is, in fact, the true result; in that case it is itself a *determinate* nothingness, one which has a *content*. The skepticism that ends up with the bare abstraction of nothingness or emptiness cannot get any further from there, but must wait to see whether something new comes along and what it is, in order to throw it too into the same empty abyss. But when, on the other hand, the result is conceived as it is in truth, namely, as a *determinate* negation, a new form has thereby immediately arisen, and in the negation the transition is made through which the progress through the complete series of forms comes about of itself.

80   But the *goal* is as necessarily fixed for knowledge as the serial progression; it is the point where knowledge no longer needs to go beyond itself, where knowledge finds itself, where Notion corresponds to object and object to Notion. Hence the progress towards this goal is also unhalting, and short of it no satisfaction is to be found at any of the stations on the way. Whatever is confined within the limits of a natural life cannot by its own efforts go beyond its immediate existence; but it is driven beyond it by something else, and this uprooting entails its death. Consciousness, however, is explicitly the *Notion* of itself. Hence it is something that goes beyond limits, and since these limits are its own, it is something that goes beyond itself. With the positing of a single particular the beyond is also established for consciousness, even if it is only *alongside* the limited object as in the case of spatial intuition. Thus consciousness suffers this violence at its own hands: it spoils its own limited satisfaction. When consciousness feels this violence, its

anxiety may well make it retreat from the truth, and strive to hold on to what it is in danger of losing. But it can find no peace. If it wishes to remain in a state of unthinking inertia, then thought troubles its thoughtlessness, and its own unrest disturbs its inertia. Or, if it entrenches itself in sentimentality, which assures us that it finds everything to be *good in its kind*, then this assurance likewise suffers violence at the hands of Reason, for, precisely insofar as something is merely a kind, Reason finds it *not* to be good. Or, again, its fear of the truth may lead consciousness to hide, from itself and others, behind the pretension that its burning zeal for truth makes it difficult or even impossible to find any other truth but the unique truth of vanity – that of being at any rate cleverer than any thoughts that one gets by oneself or from others. This conceit which understands how to belittle every truth, in order to turn back into itself and gloat over its own understanding, which knows how to dissolve every thought and always find the same barren Ego instead of any content – this is a satisfaction which we must leave to itself, for it flees from the universal, and seeks only to be for itself.

81   In addition to these preliminary general remarks about the manner and the necessity of the progression, it may be useful to say something about the *method of carrying out the inquiry*. If this exposition is viewed as a way of *relating Science* to *phenomenal* knowledge, and as an investigation and *examination of the reality of cognition*, it would seem that it cannot take place without some presupposition which can serve as its underlying *criterion*. For an examination consists in applying an accepted standard and in determining whether something is right or wrong on the basis of the resulting agreement or disagreement of the thing examined; thus the standard as such (and Science likewise if it were the criterion) is accepted as the *essence* or as the *in-itself*. But here, where Science has just begun to come on the scene, neither Science nor anything else has yet justified itself as the essence or the in-itself; and without something of the sort it seems that no examination can take place.

82   This contradiction and its removal will become more definite if we call to mind the abstract determinations of truth and knowledge as they occur in consciousness. Consciousness simultaneously *distinguishes* itself from something, and at the same time *relates* itself to it, or, as it is said, this something exists *for* consciousness; and the determinate aspect of this *relating*, or of the *being* of

something for a consciousness, is *knowing*. But we distinguish this being-for-another from *being-in-itself*; whatever is related to knowledge or knowing is also distinguished from it, and posited as existing outside of this relationship; this *being-in-itself* is called *truth*. Just what might be involved in these determinations is of no further concern to us here. Since our object is phenomenal knowledge, its determinations too will at first be taken directly as they present themselves; and they do present themselves very much as we have already apprehended them.

83 Now, if we inquire into the truth of knowledge, it seems that we are asking what knowledge is *in itself*. Yet in this inquiry knowledge is *our* object, something that exists *for us*; and the *in-itself* that would supposedly result from it would rather be the being of knowledge *for us*. What we asserted to be its essence would be not so much its truth but rather just our knowledge of it. The essence or criterion would lie within ourselves, and that which was to be compared with it and about which a decision would be reached through this comparison would not necessarily have to recognize the validity of such a standard.

84 But the dissociation, or this semblance of dissociation and presupposition, is overcome by the nature of the object we are investigating. Consciousness provides its own criterion from within itself, so that the investigation becomes a comparison of consciousness with itself; for the distinction made above falls within it. In consciousness one thing exists *for* another, i.e. consciousness regularly contains the determinateness of the moment of knowledge; at the same time, this other is to consciousness not merely *for it*, but is also outside of this relationship, or exists *in itself*: the moment of truth. Thus in what consciousness affirms from within itself as *being-in-itself* or the *True* we have the standard which consciousness itself sets up by which to measure what it knows. If we designate *knowledge* as the Notion, but the essence or the *True* as what exists, or the *object*, then the examination consists in seeing whether the Notion corresponds to the object. But if we call the *essence* or in-itself of the *object* the *Notion*, and on the other hand understand by the *object* the Notion itself as *object*, viz. as it exists *for an other*, then the examination consists in seeing whether the object corresponds to its Notion. It is evident, of course, that the two procedures are the same. But the essential point to bear in mind throughout the whole investigation is that these two moments, "Notion" and "object,"

"being-for-another" and "being-in-itself," both fall *within* that knowledge which we are investigating. Consequently, we do not need to import criteria, or to make use of our own bright ideas and thoughts during the course of the inquiry; it is precisely when we leave these aside that we succeed in contemplating the matter in hand as it is *in and for itself*.

85 But not only is a contribution by us superfluous, since Notion and object, the criterion and what is to be tested, are present in consciousness itself, but we are also spared the trouble of comparing the two and really *testing* them, so that, since what consciousness examines is its own self, all that is left for us to do is simply to look on. For consciousness is, on the one hand, consciousness of the object, and on the other, consciousness of itself; consciousness of what for it is the True, and consciousness of its knowledge of the truth. Since both are *for* the same consciousness, this consciousness is itself their comparison; it is for this same consciousness to know whether its knowledge of the object corresponds to the object or not. The object, it is true, seems only to be for consciousness in the way that consciousness knows it; it seems that consciousness cannot, as it were, get behind the object as it exists for consciousness so as to examine what the object is *in itself*, and hence, too, cannot test its own knowledge by that standard. But the distinction between the in-itself and knowledge is already present in the very fact that consciousness knows an object at all. Something is *for it* the *in-itself*; and knowledge, or the being of the object for consciousness, is, *for it*, another moment. Upon this distinction, which is present as a fact, the examination rests. If the comparison shows that these two moments do not correspond to one another, it would seem that consciousness must alter its knowledge to make it conform to the object. But, in fact, in the alteration of the knowledge, the object itself alters for it too, for the knowledge that was present was essentially a knowledge of the object: as the knowledge changes, so too does the object, for it essentially belonged to this knowledge. Hence it comes to pass for consciousness that what it previously took to be the *in-itself* is not an *in-itself*, or that it was only an in-itself *for consciousness*. Since consciousness thus finds that its knowledge does not correspond to its object, the object itself does not stand the test; in other words, the criterion for testing is altered when that for which it was to have been the criterion fails to pass the test; and the testing is not only a

testing of what we know, but also a testing of the criterion of what knowing is.

86 *Inasmuch as the new true object issues from it*, this *dialectical* movement which consciousness exercises on itself and which affects both its knowledge and its object, is precisely what is called *experience* [*Erfahrung*]. In this connection there is a moment in the process just mentioned which must be brought out more clearly, for through it a new light will be thrown on the exposition which follows. Consciousness knows *something*; this object is the essence or the *in-itself*; but it is also for consciousness the in-itself. This is where the ambiguity of this truth enters. We see that consciousness now has two objects: one is the first *in-itself*, the second is the *being-for-consciousness of this in-itself*. The latter appears at first sight to be merely the reflection of consciousness into itself, i.e. what consciousness has in mind is not an object, but only its knowledge of that first object. But, as was shown previously, the first object, in being known, is altered for consciousness; it ceases to be the in-itself, and becomes something that is the *in-itself* only *for consciousness*. And this then is the True: the being-for-consciousness of this in-itself. Or, in other words, this is the *essence*, or the *object* of consciousness. This new object contains the nothingness of the first, it is what experience has made of it.

87 This exposition of the course of experience contains a moment in virtue of which it does not seem to agree with what is ordinarily understood by experience. This is the moment of transition from the first object and the knowledge of it, to the other object, which experience is said to be about. Our account implied that our knowledge of the first object, or the being-*for*-consciousness of the first in-itself, itself becomes the second object. It usually seems to be the case, on the contrary, that our experience of the untruth of our first notion comes by way of a second object which we come upon by chance and externally, so that our part in all this is simply the pure *apprehension* of what is in and for itself. From the present viewpoint, however, the new object shows itself to have come about through a *reversal of consciousness itself*. This way of looking at the matter is something contributed by *us*, by means of which the succession of experiences through which consciousness passes is raised into a scientific progression – but it is not known to the consciousness that we are observing. But, as a matter of fact, we have here the same situation as the one discussed in regard to the

relation between our exposition and skepticism, viz. that in every case the result of an untrue mode of knowledge must not be allowed to run away into an empty nothing, but must necessarily be grasped as the nothing *of that from which it results* – a result which contains what was true in the preceding knowledge. It shows up here like this: since what first appeared as the object sinks for consciousness to the level of its way of knowing it, and since the in-itself becomes a *being-for-consciousness* of the in-itself, the latter is now the new object. Herewith a new pattern of consciousness comes on the scene as well, for which the essence is something different from what it was at the preceding stage. It is this fact that guides the entire series of the patterns of consciousness in their necessary sequence. But it is just this necessity itself, or the *origination* of the new object, that presents itself to consciousness without its understanding how this happens, which proceeds for us, as it were, behind the back of consciousness. Thus in the movement of consciousness there occurs a moment of *being-in-itself* or *being-for-us* which is not present to the consciousness comprehended in the experience itself. The *content*, however, of what presents itself to us does exist *for it*; we comprehend only the formal aspect of that content, or its pure origination. *For it*, what has thus arisen exists only as an object; *for us*, it appears at the same time as movement and a process of becoming.

88 Because of this necessity, the way to Science is itself already *Science*, and hence, in virtue of its content, is the Science of the *experience of consciousness*.

89 The experience of itself which consciousness goes through can, in accordance with its Notion, comprehend nothing less than the entire system of consciousness, or the entire realm of the truth of Spirit. For this reason, the moments of this truth are exhibited in their own proper determinateness, viz. as being not abstract moments, but as they are for consciousness, or as consciousness itself stands forth in its relation to them. Thus the moments of the whole are *patterns of consciousness*. In pressing forward to its true existence, consciousness will arrive at a point at which it gets rid of its semblance of being burdened with something alien, with what is only for it, and some sort of "other," at a point where appearance becomes identical with essence, so that its exposition will coincide at just this point with the authentic Science of Spirit. And finally, when consciousness itself grasps this its own

essence, it will signify the nature of absolute knowledge itself.

A. Consciousness

I. Sense-certainty: or the "this" and "meaning" [meinen]

90 The knowledge or knowing which is at the start or is immediately our object cannot be anything else but immediate knowledge itself, a knowledge of the immediate or of what simply *is*. Our approach to the object must also be *immediate* or *receptive*; we must alter nothing in the object as it presents itself. In *ap*prehending it, we must refrain from trying to *com*prehend it.

91 Because of its concrete content, sense-certainty immediately appears as the *richest* kind of knowledge, indeed a knowledge of infinite wealth for which no bounds can be found, either when we *reach out* into space and time in which it is dispersed, or when we take a bit of this wealth, and by division *enter into* it. Moreover, sense-certainty appears to be the *truest* knowledge; for it has not as yet omitted anything from the object, but has the object before it in its perfect entirety. But, in the event, this very *certainty* proves itself to be the most abstract and poorest *truth*. All that it says about what it knows is just that it *is*; and its truth contains nothing but the sheer *being* of the thing [*Sache*]. Consciousness, for its part, is in this certainty only as a pure "I"; or I am in it only as a pure "This," and the object similarly only as a pure "This." I, *this* particular I, am certain of *this* particular thing, not because I, *qua* consciousness, in knowing it have developed myself or thought about it in various ways; and also not because *the thing* of which I am certain, in virtue of a host of distinct qualities, would be in its own self a rich complex of connections, or related in various ways to other things. Neither of these has anything to do with the truth of sense-certainty: here neither I nor the thing has the significance of a complex process of mediation; the "I" does not have the significance of a manifold imagining or thinking; nor does the "thing" signify something that has a host of qualities. On the contrary, the thing *is*, and it *is*, merely because it *is*. It *is*; this is the essential point for sense-knowledge, and this pure *being*, or this simple immediacy, constitutes its *truth*. Similarly, certainty as a *connection* is an *immediate* pure connection: consciousness is "*I*," nothing more, a

pure "This"; the singular consciousness knows a pure "This," or the single item.

92 But when we look carefully at this *pure being* which constitutes the essence of this certainty, and which this certainty pronounces to be its truth, we see that much more is involved. An actual sense-certainty is not merely this pure immediacy, but an *instance* of it. Among the countless differences cropping up here we find in every case that the crucial one is that, in sense-certainty, pure being at once splits up into what we have called the two "Thises," one "This" as "I," and the other "This" as object. When *we* reflect on this difference, we find that neither one nor the other is only *immediately* present in sense-certainty, but each is at the same time *mediated*: I have this certainty *through* something else, viz. the thing; and it, similarly, is in sense-certainty *through* something else, viz. through the "I."

93 It is not just we who make this distinction between essence and instance, between immediacy and mediation; on the contrary, we find it within sense-certainty itself, and it is to be taken up in the form in which it is present there, not as we have just defined it. One of the terms is posited in sense-certainty in the form of a simple, immediate being, or as the essence, the *object*; the other, however, is posited as what is unessential and mediated, something which in sense-certainty is not *in itself* but through [the mediation of] an other, the "I," a *knowing* which knows the object only because the *object* is, while the knowing may either be or not be. But the object *is*: it is what is true, or it is the essence. It is, regardless of whether it is known or not; and it remains, even if it is not known, whereas there is no knowledge if the object is not there.

94 The question must therefore be considered whether in sense-certainty itself the object is in fact the kind of essence that sense-certainty proclaims it to be; whether this notion of it as the essence corresponds to the way it is present in sense-certainty. To this end, we have not to reflect on it and ponder what it might be in truth, but only to consider the way in which it is present in sense-certainty.

95 It is, then, sense-certainty itself that must be asked: "What is the *This*?" If we take the "This" in the twofold shape of its being, as "Now" and as "Here," the dialectic it has in it will receive a form as intelligible as the "This" itself is. To the question: "What is Now?", let us answer, e.g. "Now is Night." In order to test the truth of this

sense-certainty a simple experiment will suffice. We write down this truth; a truth cannot lose anything by being written down, any more than it can lose anything through our preserving it. If *now*, *this noon*, we look again at the written truth we shall have to say that it has become stale.

96 The Now that is Night is *preserved*, i.e. it is treated as what it professes to be, as something that *is*; but it proves itself to be, on the contrary, something that is *not*. The Now does indeed preserve itself, but as something that is *not* Night; equally, it preserves itself in face of the Day that it now is, as something that also is not Day, in other words, as a *negative* in general. This self-preserving Now is, therefore, not immediate but mediated; for it is determined as a permanent and self-preserving Now *through* the fact that something else, viz. Day and Night, is *not*. As so determined, it is still just as simply Now as before, and in this simplicity is indifferent to what happens in it; just as little as Night and Day are its being, just as much also is it Day and Night; it is not in the least affected by this its other-being. A simple thing of this kind which *is* through negation, which is neither This nor That, a *not-This*, and is with equal indifference This as well as That – such a thing we call a *universal*. So it is in fact the universal that is the true [content] of sense-certainty.

97 It is as a universal too that we *utter* what the sensuous [content] is. What we say is: "This," i.e. the *universal* This; or, "it is," i.e. *Being in general*. Of course, we do not *envisage* the universal This or Being in general, but we *utter* the universal; in other words, we do not strictly say what in this sense-certainty we *mean* to say. But language, as we see, is the more truthful; in it, we ourselves directly refute what we *mean* to say, and since the universal is the true [content] of sense-certainty and language expresses this true [content] alone, it is just not possible for us ever to say, or express in words, a sensuous being that we *mean*.

98 The same will be the case with the other form of the "This," with "Here." "Here" is, e.g., the tree. If I turn round, this truth has vanished and is converted into its opposite: "No tree is here, but a house instead." "Here" itself does not vanish; on the contrary, it abides constant in the vanishing of the house, the tree, etc., and is indifferently house or tree. Again, therefore, the "This" shows itself to be a *mediated simplicity*, or a *universality*.

99 *Pure being* remains, therefore, as the essence of this sense-certainty since sense-certainty has demonstrated in its own self that the truth of its

object is the universal. But this pure being is not an immediacy, but something to which negation and mediation are essential; consequently, it is not what we *mean* by "being," but is "being" defined as an abstraction, or as the pure universal; and our "meaning," for which the true [content] of sense-certainty is *not* the universal, is all that is left over in face of this empty or indifferent Now and Here.

100 When we compare the relation in which knowing and the object first came on the scene, with the relation in which they now stand in this result, we find that it is reversed. The object, which was supposed to be the essential element in sense-certainty, is now the unessential element; for the universal which the object has come to be is no longer what the object was supposed essentially to be for sense-certainty. On the contrary, the certainty is now to be found in the opposite element, viz. in knowing, which previously was the unessential element. Its truth is in the object as *my* object, or in its being *mine* [*Meinen*]; it is, because *I* know it. Sense-certainty, then, though indeed expelled from the object, is not yet thereby overcome, but only driven back into the "I." We have now to see what experience shows us about its reality in the "I."

101 The force of its truth thus lies now in the "I," in the immediacy of my *seeing*, *hearing*, and so on; the vanishing of the single Now and Here that we mean is prevented by the fact that *I* hold them fast. "Now" is day because I see it; "Here" is a tree for the same reason. But in this relationship sense-certainty experiences the same dialectic acting upon itself as in the previous one. I, *this* "I," see the tree and assert that "Here" is a tree; but another "I" sees the house and maintains that "Here" is not a tree but a house instead. Both truths have the same authentication, viz. the immediacy of seeing, and the certainty and assurance that both have about their knowing; but the one truth vanishes in the other.

102 What does not disappear in all this is the "I" as *universal*, whose seeing is neither a seeing of the tree nor of this house, but is a simple seeing which, though mediated by the negation of this house, etc., is all the same simple and indifferent to whatever happens in it, to the house, the tree, etc. The "I" is merely universal like "Now," "Here," or "This" in general; I do indeed *mean* a single "I," but I can no more say what I *mean* in the case of "I" than I can in the case of "Now" and "Here." When I say "this Here," "this Now," or a "single item," I am saying all Thises, Heres, Nows, all single items.

Similarly, when I say "I," this singular "I," I say in general all "I"s; everyone is what I say, everyone is "I," this singular "I." When Science is faced with the demand – as if it were an acid test it could not pass – that it should deduce, construct, find *a priori*, or however it is put, something called "this thing" or "this one man," it is reasonable that the demand should *say* which "this thing," or which "this particular man" is *meant*; but it is impossible to say this.

103 Sense-certainty thus comes to know by experience that its essence is neither in the object nor in the "I," and that its immediacy is neither an immediacy of the one nor of the other; for in both, what I *mean* is rather something unessential, and the object and the "I" are universals in which that "Now" and "Here" and "I" which I *mean* do not have a continuing being, or *are* not. Thus we reach the stage where we have to posit the *whole* of sense-certainty itself as its *essence*, and no longer only one of its moments, as happened in the two cases where first the object confronting the "I," and then the "I," were supposed to be its reality. Thus it is only sense-certainty as a *whole* which stands firm within itself as *immediacy* and by so doing excludes from itself all the opposition which has hitherto obtained.

104 This pure immediacy, therefore, no longer has any concern with the otherness of the "Here," as a tree which passes over into a "Here" that is not a tree, or with the otherness of the "Now" as day which changes into a "Now" that is night, or with another "I" for which something else is object. Its truth preserves itself as a relation that remains self-identical, and which makes no distinction of what is essential and what is unessential, between the "I" and the object, a relation therefore into which also no distinction whatever can penetrate. I, *this* "I," assert then the "Here" as a tree, and do not turn round so that the Here would become for me *not* a tree; also, I take no notice of the fact that another "I" sees the Here as *not* a tree, or that I myself at another time take the Here as not-tree, the Now as not-day. On the contrary, I am a pure [act of] intuiting; I, for my part, stick to the fact that the Now is day, or that the Here is a tree; also I do not compare Here and Now themselves with one another, but stick firmly to *one* immediate relation: the Now is day.

105 Since, then, this certainty will no longer come forth to *us* when we direct its attention to a Now that is night, or to an "I" to whom it is night, we will approach *it* and point to the Now that is

asserted. We must let ourselves *point to it*; for the truth of this immediate relation is the truth of *this* "I" which confines itself to one "Now" or one "Here." Were we to examine this truth *afterwards*, or stand *at a distance* from it, it would lose its significance entirely; for that would do away with the immediacy which is essential to it. We must therefore enter the same point of time or space, point them out to ourselves, i.e. make ourselves into the same singular "I" which is the one who knows with certainty. Let us, then, see how that immediate is constituted that is pointed out to us.

106 The Now is pointed to, *this* Now. "Now"; it has already ceased to be in the act of pointing to it. The Now that *is*, is another Now than the one pointed to, and we see that the Now is just this: to be no more just when it is. The Now, as it is pointed out to us, is Now that *has been*, and this is its truth; it has not the truth of *being*. Yet this much is true, that it has been. But what essentially *has been* [*gewesen ist*] is, in fact, not an essence that *is* [*kein Wesen*]; *it is not*, and it was with *being* that we were concerned.

107 In this pointing-out, then, we see merely a movement which takes the following course: (1) I point out the "Now," and it is asserted to be the truth. I point it out, however, as something that *has been*, or as something that has been superseded; I set aside the first truth. (2) I now assert as the second truth that it *has been*, that it is superseded. (3) But what has been, *is not*; I set aside the second truth, its *having been*, its supersession, and thereby negate the negation of the "Now," and thus return to the first assertion, that the "*Now*" *is*. The "Now," and pointing out the "Now," are thus so constituted that neither the one nor the other is something immediate and simple, but a movement which contains various moments. A *This* is posited: but it is rather an *other* that is posited, or the This is superseded: and this *otherness*, or the setting-aside of the first, is itself *in turn set aside*, and so has returned into the first. However, this first, thus reflected into itself, is not exactly the same as it was to begin with, viz. something *immediate*; on the contrary, it is *something that is reflected into itself*, or a *simple* entity which, in its otherness, remains what it is: a Now which is an absolute plurality of Nows. And this is the true, the genuine Now, the Now as a simple day which contains within it many Nows – hours. A Now of this sort, an hour, similarly is many minutes, and this Now is likewise many Nows, and so on. The pointing-out of the Now is thus itself the movement which expresses

what the Now is in truth, viz. a result, or a plurality of Nows all taken together; and the pointing-out is the experience of learning that Now is a *universal*.

108 The *Here pointed out*, to which I hold fast, is similarly a *this* Here which, in fact, is *not* this Here, but a Before and Behind, an Above and Below, a Right and Left. The Above is itself similarly this manifold otherness of above, below, etc. The Here, which was supposed to have been pointed out, vanishes in other Heres, but these likewise vanish. What is pointed out, held fast, and abides, is a *negative* This, which *is* negative only when the Heres are taken as they should be, but, in being so taken, they supersede themselves; what abides is a simple complex of many Heres. The Here that is *meant* would be the point; but it *is* not: on the contrary, when it is pointed out as something that *is*, the pointing-out shows itself to be not an immediate knowing [of the point], but a movement from the Here that is *meant* through many Heres into the universal Here which is a simple plurality of Heres, just as the day is a simple plurality of Nows.

109 It is clear that the dialectic of sense-certainty is nothing else but the simple history of its movement or of its experience, and sense-certainty itself is nothing else but just this history. That is why the natural consciousness, too, is always reaching this result, learning from experience what is true in it; but equally it is always forgetting it and starting the movement all over again. It is therefore astonishing when, in face of this experience, it is asserted as universal experience and put forward, too, as a philosophical proposition, even as the outcome of Skepticism, that the reality or being of external things taken as Thises or sense-objects has absolute truth for consciousness. To make such an assertion is not to know what one is saying, to be unaware that one is saying the opposite of what one wants to say. The truth for consciousness of a This of sense is supposed to be universal experience; but the very opposite is universal experience. Every consciousness itself supersedes such a truth, as e.g. Here is a tree, or, Now is noon, and proclaims the opposite: Here is *not* a tree, but a house; and similarly, it immediately again supersedes the assertion which set aside the first so far as it is also just such an assertion of a sensuous This. And what consciousness will learn from experience in all sense-certainty is, in truth, only what we have seen viz. the This as a *universal*, the very opposite of what that assertion affirmed to be universal experience. . . .

Select Bibliography

Aesthetics: Lectures on Fine Art, 2 vols. Translated by T. M. Knox. Oxford: Clarendon Press, 1975.

The Difference between Fichte's and Schelling's System of Philosophy. Translated by H. S. Harris and Walter Cerf. Albany: State University of New York Press, 1977.

Early Theological Writings. Translated by T. M. Knox. Philadelphia: University of Pennsylvania Press, 1988.

Hegel's Philosophy of Mind. Translated by William Wallace and A. V. Miller. Oxford: Clarendon Press, 1971.

Hegel's Philosophy of Nature. Translated by A. V. Miller and William Wallace. Oxford: Clarendon Press, 1970.

The Hegel Reader. Edited by Stephen Houlgate. Oxford: Blackwell Publishers, 1998.

Hegel's Science of Logic. Translated by A. V. Miller. Atlantic Highlands, NJ: Humanities Press International, 1989.

Hegel: Selections. Edited by M. J. Inwood. New York: Macmillan, 1989.

Lectures on the History of Philosophy, 3 vols. Translated by E. S. Haldane and Frances H. Simson. Lincoln: University of Nebraska Press, 1995.

Lectures on the Philosophy of Religion, 3 vols. Edited by Peter C. Hodgson. Translated by R. F. Brown, P. C. Hodgson, and J. M. Stewart, with the assistance of J. P. Fitzer and H. S. Harris. Berkeley: University of California Press, 1984–7.

On Art, Religion, and the History of Philosophy: Introductory Lectures. Edited by J. Glen Gray. Indianapolis: Hackett, 1997.

Phenomenology of Spirit. Translated by A. V. Miller. Oxford: Oxford University Press, 1977.

The Philosophy of History. Translated by J. Sibree. Buffalo, NY: Prometheus Books, 1991.

PART II

Subjectivity in Question: Existentialism, Phenomenology, and Hermeneutics

1

Arthur Schopenhauer

German philosopher Arthur Schopenhauer (1788–1860) was a contemporary of Fichte, Schelling, and Hegel, and for a period taught alongside Hegel at the University of Berlin. Schopenhauer vehemently opposed the German idealist project, developing a theory of the will profoundly indebted to Kant and later to influence the early Nietzsche. In the following excerpt from his best-known work, *The World as Will and Representation*, first published in 1818, Schopenhauer analyzes the will as an unfathomable "will-to-live," a "thing in itself" whose "mirror" is our objective representation of the phenomenal world and whose only form is the present. In this perspective, the individual appears as merely a phenomenon, individuated through space, time, and causality.

The World As Will and Representation

The first three books will, it is hoped, have produced the distinct and certain knowledge that the mirror of the will has appeared to it in the world as representation. In this mirror the will knows itself in increasing degrees of distinctness and completeness, the highest of which is man. Man's inner nature, however, receives its complete expression above all through the connected series of his actions. The self-conscious connexion of these actions is rendered possible by the faculty of reason, which enables him to survey the whole in the abstract.

The will, considered purely in itself, is devoid of knowledge, and is only a blind, irresistible urge, as we see it appear in inorganic and vegetable nature and in their laws, and also in the vegetative part of our own life. Through the addition of the world as representation, developed for its service, the will obtains knowledge of its own willing and what it wills, namely that this is nothing but this world, life, precisely as it exists. We have therefore called the phenomenal world the mirror, the objectivity, of the will; and as what the will wills is always life, just because this is nothing but the presentation of that willing for the representation, it is immaterial and a mere pleonasm if,

From *The World As Will and Representation*, translated by E. F. J. Payne (Indian Hills, Colorado: The Falcon's Wing Press, 1958), §54, pp. 274–82. Copyright © 1966. Reprinted by permission of Dover Publications, Inc.

instead of simply saying "the will," we say "the will-to-live."

As the will is the thing-in-itself, the inner content, the essence of the world, but life, the visible world, the phenomenon, is only the mirror of the will, this world will accompany the will as inseparably as a body is accompanied by its shadow; and if will exists, then life, the world, will exist. Therefore life is certain to the will-to-live, and as long as we are filled with the will-to-live we need not be apprehensive for our existence, even at the sight of death. It is true that we see the individual come into being and pass away; but the individual is only phenomenon, exists only for knowledge involved in the principle of sufficient reason, in the *principium individuationis*. Naturally, for this knowledge, the individual receives his life as a gift, rises out of nothing, and then suffers the loss of this gift through death, and returns to nothing. We, however, wish to consider life philosophically, that is to say, according to its Ideas, and then we shall find that neither the will, the thing-in-itself in all phenomena, nor the subject of knowing, the spectator of all phenomena, is in any way affected by birth and death. Birth and death belong only to the phenomenon of the will, and hence to life; and it is essential to this that it manifest itself in individuals that come into being and pass away, as fleeting phenomena, appearing in the form of time, of that which in itself knows no time, but must be manifested precisely in the way aforesaid in order to objectify its real nature. Birth and death belong equally to life, and hold the balance as mutual conditions of each other, or, if the expression be preferred, as poles of the whole phenomenon of life. The wisest of all mythologies, the Indian, expresses this by giving to the very god who symbolizes destruction and death (just as Brahma, the most sinful and lowest god of the Trimurti, symbolizes generation, origination, and Vishnu preservation), by giving, I say, to Shiva as an attribute not only the necklace of skulls, but also the lingam, that symbol of generation which appears as the counterpart of death. In this way it is intimated that generation and death are essential correlatives which reciprocally neutralize and eliminate each other. It was precisely the same sentiment that prompted the Greeks and Romans to adorn the costly sarcophagi, just as we still see them, with feasts, dances, marriages, hunts, fights between wild beasts, bacchanalia, that is with presentations of life's most powerful urge. This they present to us not only through such diversions and merriments, but even

in sensual groups, to the point of showing us the sexual intercourse between satyrs and goats. The object was obviously to indicate with the greatest emphasis from the death of the mourned individual the immortal life of nature, and thus to intimate, although without abstract knowledge, that the whole of nature is the phenomenon, and also the fulfilment, of the will-to-live. The form of this phenomenon is time, space, and causality, and through these individuation, which requires that the individual must come into being and pass away. But this no more disturbs the will-to-live – the individual being only a particular example or specimen, so to speak, of the phenomenon of this will – than does the death of an individual injure the whole of nature. For it is not the individual that nature cares for, but only the species; and in all seriousness she urges the preservation of the species, since she provides for this so lavishly through the immense surplus of the seed and the great strength of the fructifying impulse. The individual, on the contrary, has no value for nature, and can have none, for infinite time, infinite space, and the infinite number of possible individuals therein are her kingdom. Therefore nature is always ready to let the individual fall, and the individual is accordingly not only exposed to destruction in a thousand ways from the most insignificant accidents, but is even destined for this and is led towards it by nature herself, from the moment that individual has served the maintenance of the species. In this way, nature quite openly expresses the great truth that only the Ideas, not individuals, have reality proper, in other words are a complete objectivity of the will. Now man is nature herself, and indeed nature at the highest grade of her self-consciousness, but nature is only the objectified will-to-live; the person who has grasped and retained this point of view may certainly and justly console himself for his own death and for that of his friends by looking back on the immortal life of nature, which he himself is. Consequently, Shiva with the lingam is to be understood in this way, and so are those ancient sarcophagi that with their pictures of glowing life exclaim to the lamenting beholder: *Natura non contristatur.*[1]

That generation and death are to be regarded as something belonging to life, and essential to this phenomenon of the will, arises also from the fact that they both exhibit themselves merely as the higher powers of expression of that in which all the rest of life consists. This is everywhere nothing but a constant change of matter under a fixed permanence of form; and this is precisely the transitoriness of the individuals with the imperishableness of the species. Constant nourishment and renewal differ from generation only in degree, and only in degree does constant excretion differ from death. The former shows itself most simply and distinctly in the plant, which is throughout only the constant repetition of the same impulse of its simplest fiber grouping itself into leaf and branch. It is a systematic aggregate of homogeneous plants supporting one another, and their constant reproduction is its simple impulse. It ascends to the complete satisfaction of this impulse by means of the gradation of metamorphosis, finally to the blossom and the fruit, that compendium of its existence and effort in which it attains in a shorter way what is its sole aim. It now produces at one stroke a thousandfold what till then it effected in the particular case, namely the repetition of itself. Its growth up to the fruit is related to that fruit as writing is to printing. In the case of the animal, it is obviously exactly the same. The process of nourishment is a constant generation; the process of generation is a higher power of nourishment. The pleasure that accompanies procreation is a higher power of the agreeableness of the feeling of life. On the other hand, excretion, the constant exhalation and throwing off of matter, is the same as what at a higher power is death, namely the opposite of procreation. Now, if here we are always content to retain the form without lamenting the discarded matter, we must behave in the same way when in death the same thing happens at a higher potential and to the whole, as occurs every day and hour in a partial way with excretion. Just as we are indifferent to the one, so we should not recoil at the other. Therefore, from this point of view, it seems just as absurd to desire the continuance of our individuality, which is replaced by other individuals, as to desire the permanence of the matter of our body, which is constantly replaced by fresh matter. It appears just as foolish to embalm corpses as it would be carefully to preserve our excreta. As for the individual consciousness bound to the individual body, it is completely interrupted every day by sleep. Deep sleep, while it lasts, is in no way different from death, into which it constantly passes, for example in the case of freezing to death, differing only as to the future, namely with regard to the awakening. Death is a sleep in which individuality is forgotten; everything else awakens again, or rather has remained awake.[2]

Above all, we must clearly recognize that the form of the phenomenon of the will, and hence the form of life or of reality, is really only the *present*, not the future or the past. Future and past are only in the concept, exist only in the connexion and continuity of knowledge insofar as this follows the principle of sufficient reason. No man has lived in the past, and none will ever live in the future; the *present* alone is the form of all life, but it is also life's sure possession which can never be torn from it. The present always exists together with its content; both stand firm without wavering, like the rainbow over the waterfall. For life is sure and certain to the will, and the present is sure and certain to life. Of course, if we think back to the thousands of years that have passed, to the millions of men and women who lived in them, we ask, What were they? What has become of them? But, on the other hand, we need recall only the past of our own life, and vividly renew its scenes in our imagination, and then ask again, What was all this? What has become of it? As it is with our life, so is it with the life of those millions. Or should we suppose that the past took on a new existence by its being sealed through death? Our own past, even the most recent, even the previous day, is only an empty dream of the imagination, and the past of all those millions is the same. What was? What is? The will, whose mirror is life, and will-free knowledge beholding the will clearly in that mirror. He who has not already recognized this, or will not recognize it, must add to the above question as to the fate of past generations this question as well: Why precisely is he, the questioner, so lucky as to possess this precious, perishable, and only real present, while those hundreds of generations of men, even the heroes and sages of former times, have sunk into the night of the past, and have thus become nothing, while he, his insignificant ego, actually exists? Or, more briefly, although strangely: Why is this now, his now, precisely now and *was* not long ago? Since he asks such strange questions, he regards his existence and his time as independent of each other, and the former as projected into the latter. He really assumes two nows, one belonging to the object and the other to the subject, and marvels at the happy accident of their coincidence. Actually, however, only the point of contact of the object, the form of which is time, with the subject that has no mode of the principle of sufficient reason as its form, constitutes the present (as is shown in the essay *On the Principle of Sufficient Reason*). But all object is the will, insofar as the will has become representation, and the subject is the necessary correlative of all object; only in the present, however, are there real objects. Past and future contain mere concepts and phantasms; hence the present is the essential form of the phenomenon of the will, and is inseparable from that form. The present alone is that which always exists and stands firm and immovable. That which, empirically apprehended, is the most fleeting of all, manifests itself to the metaphysical glance that sees beyond the forms of empirical perception as that which alone endures, as the *nunc stans* of the scholastics. The source and supporter of its content is the will-to-live, or the thing-in-itself – which we are. That which constantly becomes and passes away, in that it either has been already or is still to come, belongs to the phenomenon as such by virtue of its forms which render coming into being and passing away possible. Accordingly, let us think: *Quid fuit? Quod est. Quid erit? Quod fuit,*[3] and take it in the strict sense of the words, understanding not *simile* but *idem*. For life is certain to the will, and the present is certain to life. Therefore everyone can also say: "I am once for all lord and master of the present, and through all eternity it will accompany me as my shadow; accordingly, I do not wonder where it comes from, and how it is that it is precisely now." We can compare time to an endlessly revolving sphere; the half that is always sinking would be the past, and the half that is always rising would be the future; but at the top, the indivisible point that touches the tangent would be the extensionless present. Just as the tangent does not continue rolling with the sphere, so also the present, the point of contact of the object whose form is time, does not roll on with the subject that has no form, since it does not belong to the knowable, but is the condition of all that is knowable. Or time is like an irresistible stream, and the present like a rock on which the stream breaks, but which it does not carry away. The will, as thing-in-itself, is as little subordinate to the principle of sufficient reason as is the subject of knowledge which is ultimately in a certain regard the will itself or its manifestation; and just as life, the will's own phenomenon, is certain to the will, so also is the present, the sole form of actual life. Accordingly, we have not to investigate the past before life or the future after death; rather have we to know the *present* as the only form in which the will manifests itself.[4] It will not run away from the will, nor the will from it. Therefore whoever is satisfied with life as it is, whoever affirms it in

every way, can confidently regard it as endless, and can banish the fear of death as a delusion. This delusion inspires him with the foolish dread that he can ever be deprived of the present, and deceives him about a time without a present in it. This is a delusion which in regard to time is like that other in regard to space, in virtue of which everyone imagines the precise position occupied by him on the globe as above, and all the rest as below. In just the same way, everyone connects the present with his own individuality, and imagines that all present becomes extinguished therewith; that past and future are then without a present. But just as on the globe everywhere is above, so the form of all life is the *present*; and to fear death because it robs us of the present is no wiser than to fear that we can slip down from the round globe on the top of which we are now fortunately standing. The form of the present is essential to the objectification of the will. As an extensionless point, it cuts time which extends infinitely in both directions, and stands firm and immovable, like an everlasting midday without a cool evening, just as the actual sun burns without intermission, while only apparently does it sink into the bosom of the night. If, therefore, a person fears death as his annihilation, it is just as if he were to think that the sun can lament in the evening and say: "Woe is me! I am going down into eternal night."[5] Conversely, whoever is oppressed by the burdens of life, whoever loves life and affirms it, but abhors its torments, and in particular can no longer endure the hard lot that has fallen to just him, cannot hope for deliverance from death, and cannot save himself through suicide. Only by a false illusion does the cool shade of Orcus allure him as a haven of rest. The earth rolls on from day into night; the individual dies; but the sun itself burns without intermission, an eternal noon. Life is certain to the will-to-live; the form of life is the endless present; it matters not how individuals, the phenomena of the Idea, arise and pass away in time, like fleeting dreams. Therefore suicide already appears to us to be a vain and therefore foolish action; when we have gone farther in our discussion, it will appear to us in an even less favorable light.

Dogmas change and our knowledge is deceptive, but nature does not err; her action is sure and certain, and she does not conceal it. Everything is entirely in nature, and she is entirely in everything. She has her center in every animal; the animal has certainly found its way into existence just as it will certainly find its way out of it. Meanwhile, it lives fearlessly and heedlessly in the presence of annihilation, supported by the consciousness that it is nature herself and is as imperishable as she. Man alone carries about with him in abstract concepts the certainty of his own death, yet this can frighten him only very rarely and at particular moments, when some occasion calls it up to the imagination. Against the mighty voice of nature reflection can do little. In man, as in the animal that does not think, there prevails as a lasting state of mind the certainty, springing from innermost consciousness, that he is nature, the world itself. By virtue of this, no one is noticeably disturbed by the thought of certain and never-distant death, but everyone lives on as though he is bound to live for ever. Indeed, this is true to the extent that it might be said that no one has a really lively conviction of the certainty of his death, as otherwise there could not be a very great difference between his frame of mind and that of the condemned criminal. Everyone recognizes that certainty in the abstract and theoretically, but lays it on one side, like other theoretical truths that are not applicable in practice, without taking it into his vivid consciousness. Whoever carefully considers this peculiarity of the human way of thinking, will see that the psychological methods of explaining it from habit and acquiescence in the inevitable are by no means sufficient, but that the reason for it is the deeper one that we state. The same thing can also explain why at all times and among all peoples dogmas of some kind, dealing with the individual's continued existence after death, exist and are highly esteemed, although the proofs in support of them must always be extremely inadequate, whereas those which support the contrary are bound to be powerful and numerous. This is really in no need of any proof, but is recognized by the healthy understanding as a fact; it is confirmed as such by the confidence that nature no more lies than errs, but openly exhibits her action and her essence, and even expresses these naively. It is only we ourselves who obscure these by erroneous views, in order to explain from them what is agreeable to our limited view. . . .

Notes

1 "Nature is not grieved." (Trans.)
2 The following remark can also help the person for whom it is not too subtle to understand clearly that the individual is only the phenomenon, not the thing-in-itself. On the one hand, every individual is the subject of knowing, in other words, the supplementary condition of the possibility of the whole objective world, and, on the other, a particular phenomenon of the will, of that will which objectifies itself in each thing. But this double character of our inner being does not rest on a self-existent unity, otherwise it would be possible for us to be conscious of ourselves *in ourselves and independently of the objects of knowing and willing.* Now we simply cannot do this, but as soon as we enter into ourselves in order to attempt it, and wish for once to know ourselves fully by directing our knowledge inwards, we lose ourselves in a bottomless void; we find ourselves like a hollow glass globe, from the emptiness of which a voice speaks. But the cause of this voice is not to be found in the globe, and since we want to comprehend ourselves, we grasp with a shudder nothing but a wavering and unstable phantom.
3 "What was? That which is. What will be? That which was." (Trans.)
4 *Scholastici docuerunt quod aeternitas non sit temporis sine fine aut principio successio, sed NUNC STANS; i.e. idem nobis NUNC esse, quod erat NUNC Adamo: i.e. inter NUNC et TUNC nullam esse differentiam.* Hobbes, *Leviathan* [Latin ed, 1841], c. 46.
   ["The scholastics taught that eternity is not a succession without beginning and end, but a permanent *Now*; in other words, that we possess the same *Now* which existed for Adam; that is to say, that there is no difference between the *Now* and the *Then*." (Trans.)]
5 In Eckermann's *Gespräche mit Goethe* (second edition, Vol. I, p. 154), Goethe says: "Our spirit is a being of a quite indestructible nature; it acts continuously from eternity to eternity. It is similar to the sun which seems to set only to our earthly eyes, but which really never sets; it shines on incessantly." Goethe took the simile from me, not I from him. He undoubtedly uses it in this conversation of 1824 in consequence of a (possibly unconscious) reminiscence of the above passage, for it appears in the first edition, p. 401, in the same words as here, and also occurs there again on p. 528, and here at the end of § 65. The first edition was sent to him in December 1818, and in March 1819 he sent me in Naples, where I then was, a letter of congratulation through my sister. He had enclosed a piece of paper on which he had noted the numbers of some pages that had specially pleased him. So he had read my book.

Select Bibliography

Counsels and Maxims, Being the Second Part of Arthur Schopenhauer's Aphorismen zur Lebensweisheit. Translated by Thomas Bailey Saunders. St Clair Shores, Mich.: Scholarly Press, 1970.

On the Basis of Morality. Translated by E. F. J. Payne. Providence: Berghahn Books, 1995.

On the Fourfold Root of the Principle of Sufficient Reason. Translated by E. F. J. Payne. La Salle, Ill.: Open Court, 1974.

On the Freedom of the Will. Translated by Konstantin Kolenda. Oxford: Blackwell Publishers, 1985.

On Human Nature: Essays, Partly Posthumous, In Ethics and Politics. Translated by Thomas Bailey Saunders. London: Allen and Unwin, 1957.

On the Will in Nature: A Discussion of the Corroboration from the Empirical Sciences that the Author's Philosophy Has Received Since its First Appearance. New York: Berg, 1992.

Parerga and Paralipomena: Short Philosophical Essays, 2 vols. Translated by E. F. J. Payne. Oxford: Clarendon Press, 1974.

Philosophical Writings. Edited by Wolfgang Schirmacher. New York: Continuum, 1994.

Religion: A Dialogue, and Other Essays. Selected and translated by T. Bailey Saunders. Westport, Conn.: Greenwood Press, 1973.

The Will to Live: Selected Writings of Arthur Schopenhauer. Edited by Richard Taylor. New York: Continuum, 1988.

The Wisdom of Life, Being the First Part of Arthur Schopenhauer's Aphorismen zur Lebensweisheit. Translated by Thomas Bailey Saunders. Freeport, NY: Books for Libraries Press, 1972.

The World as Will and Representation, 2 vols. Translated by E. F. J. Payne. Indian Hills, Col.: The Falcon's Wing Press, 1958.

2

Søren Kierkegaard

Danish philosopher Søren Kierkegaard (1813–55) was a powerful early opponent of German idealist thought, particularly in its Hegelian form. Kierkegaard argued against what he regarded in Hegel as the excessive idealization of the Absolute in service of the speculative identity of being and thinking. This identity, he objected, exists merely in thought, but never in reality, which is always the lived existence of eminently finite individuals. The existence of the living individual always exceeds the order of absolute being; for the individual, existence is not something to be known objectively, but something that is lived "subjectively," that is, chosen in the concrete engagement of one's freedom. Thus, Kierkegaard placed emphasis on the ethical moment of decision in which one freely chooses one's existence through action and through the passion of commitment. The individual chooses his or her existence in the inwardness of a passionate leap of faith in the face of the infinite, which is objectively unknowable. For Kierkegaard, the only authentic relation to the infinite is that of ethical and ethico–religious existence – a relation he saw as the original meaning of Christianity. The following excerpt, from the pseudonymous *Either / Or* (1843), opposes both the aesthetic ideal of finding pleasure in external objects and the contemplative ideal of "knowing oneself" to the ethical task of "choosing oneself."

Either/Or

The Balance Between the Aesthetic and the Ethical in the Development of the Personality

A human being's eternal dignity lies precisely in this, that he can gain a history. The divine in him

From *Either/Or, Part II*, edited and translated by Howard V. Hong and Edna H. Hong (Princeton: Princeton University Press, 1987) pp. 250–66. Copyright © 1987 by Postscript, Inc. Reprinted by permission of Princeton University Press.

lies in this, that he himself, if he so chooses, can give this history continuity, because it gains that, not when it is a summary of what has taken place or has happened to me, but only when it is my personal deed in such a way that even that which has happened to me is transformed and transferred from necessity to freedom. What is enviable about human life is that one can assist God, can understand him, and in turn the only worthy way for a human being to understand God is to appropriate in freedom everything that comes to him, both the happy and the sad. Or do you not think so? This is the way it appears to me – indeed, I think that to say this aloud to a person is all one needs to do to make him envy himself.

The two positions touched on here could be regarded as attempts to actualize an ethical life-view. The reason that they do not succeed is that the individual has chosen himself in his isolation or has chosen himself abstractly. To say it in other words, the individual has not chosen himself ethically. He therefore has no connection with actuality, and when that is the case no ethical view of life can be put into practice. But the person who chooses himself ethically chooses himself concretely as this specific individual, and he achieves this concretion because this choice is identical with the repentance, which ratifies the choice. The individual, then, becomes conscious as this specific individual with these capacities, these inclinations, these drives, these passions, influenced by this specific social milieu, as this specific product of a specific environment. But as he becomes aware of all this, he takes upon himself responsibility for it all. He does not hesitate over whether he will take this particular thing or not, for he knows that if he does not do it something much more important will be lost. In the moment of choice, he is in complete isolation, for he withdraws from his social milieu, and yet at the same moment he is in absolute continuity, for he chooses himself as a product. And this choice is freedom's choice in such a way that in choosing himself as product he can just as well be said to produce himself. At the moment of choice, he is at the point of consummation, for his personality is consummating itself, and yet at the same moment he is at the very beginning, because he is choosing himself according to his freedom. As a product he is squeezed into the forms of actuality; in the choice he makes himself elastic, transforms everything exterior into interiority. He has his place in the world; in freedom he himself chooses his place – that is, he chooses this place. He is a specific individual; in the choice he makes himself into a specific individual: namely, into the same one, because he chooses himself.

An individual thus chooses himself as a complex specific concretion and therefore chooses himself in his continuity. This concretion is the individual's actuality, but since he chooses it according to his freedom, it may also be said that it is his possibility or, in order not to use such an aesthetic expression, it is his task. In other words, the person who lives aesthetically sees only possibilities everywhere; for him these make up the content of future time, whereas the person who lives ethically sees tasks everywhere. Then the individual sees this, his actual concretion, as task, as goal, as objective. But in seeing his possibility as his task, the individual expresses precisely his sovereignty over himself, something he never surrenders, even though on the other hand he does not relish the very unconstrained sovereignty that a king without a country always has. This gives the ethical individual a security that the person who lives only aesthetically lacks altogether. The person who lives aesthetically expects everything from the outside. This accounts for the sickly anxiety with which many people speak of the dreadfulness of not having found their place in the world. Who will deny the joy in having made a good catch in this respect, but such an anxiety always indicates that the individual expects everything from the place, nothing from himself. The person who lives ethically will also be careful about choosing his place properly, but if he detects that he has made a mistake, or if obstacles are raised that are beyond his control, he does not lose heart, for he does not surrender sovereignty over himself. He promptly sees his task and therefore is in action without delay.

We frequently see men who fear that when they fall in love someday they will not find a girl who is precisely the ideal, who is just right for them. Who will deny the joy in finding a girl like that, but on the other hand it is indeed a superstition to think that something that lies outside a person is what can make him happy. The person who lives ethically also wishes to be happy in his choice, but if the choice proves to be not entirely according to his wish, he does not lose heart; he immediately sees his task and that the art is not to wish but to will.

Many who still have a conception of what human life is wish to be contemporary with great events, to be involved in meaningful life situations. Who will deny that such things have their validity, but on the other hand it is indeed a superstition to think that events and life situations as such make a person amount to something. The person who lives ethically knows that what counts is what one sees in each situation, and the energy with which he considers it, and that the one who thus disciplines himself in the most insignificant life situations can experience more than the one who has been a witness to – indeed, been a participant in – the most noteworthy events. He knows that there is a dancing place everywhere, that even the lowliest of men has his, and that if he himself so wills his dancing can be just as beautiful, just as gracious, just as mimetic, just as dramatic as the dancing of those to whom a place has been assigned in history. This is the fencer's skill, this litheness that is really the immortal life in the ethical. The old saying "to be – or not to be"[1] holds for the person who lives aesthetically, and the more aesthetically he is allowed to live, the more conditions his life requires, and if only the least of them is not satisfied, he is dead. The person who lives ethically always has a way out when everything goes against him; when the darkness of the storm clouds so envelops him that his neighbor cannot see him, he still has not perished, there is always a point to which he holds fast, and that point is – himself.

There is only one thing I do not want to fail to stress, that as soon as the ethical person's gymnastics become an imaginary constructing he has ceased to live ethically. All such imaginary gymnastic constructing is equivalent to sophistry in the realm of knowledge.

Here I now want to call to mind the definition of the ethical I gave before – that it is that whereby a person becomes what he becomes. It does not want to make the individual into someone else but into the individual himself; it does not want to destroy the aesthetic but to transfigure it. For a person to live ethically it is necessary that he become conscious of himself, so thoroughly that no accidental element escapes him. The ethical does not want to wipe out this concretion but sees in it its task, sees the material with which it is to build and that which it is to build. Ordinarily we view the ethical altogether abstractly and therefore have a secret horror of it. In that case the ethical is viewed as something alien to the personality, and we shrink from devoting ourselves to it, since we cannot be really sure what it will lead to in the course of time. In the same way, many people fear death, because they harbor obscure and confused notions that the soul in death has to cross over into another order of things where the established laws and conventions are completely different from the ones they have learned to know in this world. The reason for such a fear of death is the individual's aversion to becoming transparent to himself, for if he is willing to do this, he readily perceives the unreasonableness of this fear. So it is with the ethical also; if a person fears transparency, he always avoids the ethical, because the ethical really does not want anything else.

In contrast to an aesthetic life-view, which wants to enjoy life, we often hear about another life-view that places the meaning of life in living for the performance of one's duties. This is supposed to signify an ethical view of life. But the formulation falls far short, and one could almost believe that it was devised to discredit the ethical. One thing is sure, that in our day we often see it used in such a way that it almost makes us smile, for example, when Scribe has this thesis recited with a certain farcical solemnity that makes a very disparaging contrast to the joy and mirth of enjoyment.[2] The mistake is that the individual is placed in an external relation to duty. The ethical is defined as duty, and duty in turn as a multiplicity of particular rules, but the individual and duty stand outside each other. Of course, a life of duty such as that is very unlovely and boring, and if the ethical did not have a much deeper connection with the personality it would always be very difficult to champion it against the aesthetic. That there are many people who do not advance beyond this, I shall not deny, but that is not owing to duty but to the people themselves.

It is curious that the word "duty" can prompt one to think of an external relation, since the very derivation of the word[3] suggests an internal one; for that which is incumbent upon [*paaligge*] me, not as this individual with accidental characteristics but in accordance with my true being, certainly has the most intimate relation with myself. That is, duty is not something laid upon [*Paalæg*] but something that lies upon [*paaligge*]. When duty is regarded in this way, it is a sign that the individual is oriented within himself. Then duty will not split up for him into a multiplicity of particular stipulations, for this always indicates that he has only an external relation to duty. He has put on duty; for him it is the expression of his innermost being. When he is thus oriented within himself, he has immersed himself in the ethical, and he will not run himself ragged performing his duties. Therefore, the truly ethical person has an inner serenity and sense of security, for he does not have duty outside himself but within himself. The more deeply a man has structured his life ethically, the less he will feel compelled to talk about duty every moment, to worry every moment whether he is performing it, every moment to seek the advice of others about what his duty is. When the ethical is viewed properly, it makes the individual infinitely secure within himself; when it is viewed improperly, it makes the individual utterly insecure, and I cannot imagine an unhappier or more tormented life than when a person has his duty outside himself and yet continually wants to carry it out.

If the ethical is regarded as outside the personality and in an external relation to it, then one has given up everything, then one has despaired. The aesthetic as such is despair; the ethical is the abstract and as such is without the means for accomplishing the least thing. That is why it is both comic and tragic to see at times people with a kind of honest zeal working their fingers to the bone in order to carry out the ethical, which like a shadow continually evades them as soon as they try to grasp it.

The ethical is the universal and thus the abstract. That is why in its perfect abstraction the ethical is always interdictory. Thus the ethical takes the form of law. As soon as the ethical is prescriptive, it already has something of the aesthetic. The Jews were the people of the law. Therefore they understood most of the commandments in the Mosaic law splendidly, but the commandment they did not seem to have understood was the commandment to which Christianity attached itself most of all: You shall love God with all your heart. This commandment is neither negative nor abstract; it is highly positive and highly concrete. When the ethical becomes more concrete, it crosses over into the category of morals. But in this respect the reality of it lies in the reality of a national individuality, and here the ethical has already assimilated an aesthetic element.

But the ethical is still abstract and cannot be fully actualized because it lies outside the individual. Not until the individual himself is the universal, not until then can the ethical be actualized. This is the secret that lies in the conscience; this is the secret the individual life has with itself – that simultaneously it is an individual life and also the universal, if as such not immediately, then nevertheless according to its possibility. The person who views life ethically sees the universal, and the person who lives ethically expresses the universal in his life. He makes himself the universal human being, not by taking off his concretion, for then he becomes a complete non-entity, but by putting it on and interpenetrating it with the universal. The universal human being is not a phantom, but every human being is the universal human being – that is, every human being is shown the way by

which he becomes the universal human being. The person who lives aesthetically is an accidental human being; he believes he is the perfect human being by being the one and only human being. The person who lives ethically works toward becoming the universal human being. When, for example, a person is aesthetically in love, the accidental aspects play an enormous role, and it is important to him that no one has loved this way, with the nuances that are his; when the person who lives ethically marries, he actualizes the universal. That is why he is no hater of the concrete, but he has one expression in addition, deeper than every aesthetic expression, inasmuch as he sees in love a revelation of the universally human. Thus he who lives ethically has himself as his task. His self in its immediacy is defined by accidental characteristics; the task is to work the accidental and the universal together into a whole.

The ethical individual, then, does not have duty outside himself but within himself. This comes to light at the moment of despair and now works itself forward through the aesthetic in and with this. Of the ethical individual it may be said that he is like the still waters that have a deep source, whereas the one who lives aesthetically is only superficially moved. Therefore, when the ethical individual has completed his task, has fought the good fight,[4] he has come to the point where he has become the unique human being – that is, there is no other human being like him – and he has also become the universal human being. To be the unique human being is not so great in and by itself, for every human being shares this with every product of nature, but to be that in such a way that he is thereby also the universal – that is the true art of living.

So the personality does not have the ethical outside itself but within itself and it bursts forth from this depth. It is not, as said before, a matter of exterminating the concrete in an abstract and contentless assault but of assimilating it. Since the ethical lies so deep in the soul, it is not always visible, and the person who lives ethically may do exactly the same as one who lives aesthetically, and thus it may deceive for a long time, but eventually there comes a moment when it becomes manifest that the person who lives ethically has a boundary that the other does not know. The individual rests with confident security in the assurance that his life is ethically structured, and therefore he does not torment himself and others with quibbling anxiety about this or that.

I find it quite in order that the person who lives ethically has a whole territory for inconsequentials, and being unwilling to force it into every triviality is precisely a veneration for the ethical. Any effort to do so, which always fails, is made only by those who do not have the courage to believe in the ethical and who in a deeper sense lack inner security. There are people whose pusillanimity is known simply by their never being able to finish with the totality because for them this is a multiplicity. But these people lie outside the ethical, for no other reason, of course, than weakness of will, which like any other psychical weakness can be regarded as a kind of madness. The lives of such people are given to straining at gnats.[5] They have no notion either of the beautiful and pure earnestness of the ethical or of the carefree joy of the inconsequential. But, of course, for the ethical individual the inconsequential is dethroned, and he can set the limit at any moment. Thus one also believes that there is a providence, and the soul rests confidently in this conviction, and yet one would never think of venturing to interpenetrate every contingency with this thought or to be conscious of this faith every minute. To will the ethical without being disturbed by inconsequentials, to believe in a providence without being disturbed by contingency, is a healthiness that can be acquired and preserved if a person himself wills it. Here, too, it is a matter of seeing the task, that this, insofar as one has an inclination to be diverted this way, is to offer resistance, to hold fast to the infinite, and not run off on a wild goose chase.

The person who chooses himself ethically has himself as his task, not as a possibility, not as a plaything for the play of his arbitrariness. Ethically he can choose himself only if he chooses himself in continuity, and then he has himself as a multiply defined task. He does not try to blot out or evaporate this multiplicity; on the contrary, he repents himself firmly in it, because this multiplicity is himself, and only by penitently immersing himself in it can he come to himself, since he does not assume that the world begins with him or that he creates himself. The latter has been branded with contempt by language itself, for we always speak contemptuously of a man when we say: He is putting on airs. But in choosing himself penitently he is acting – not in the direction of isolation but in the direction of continuity.

Let us now compare an ethical and an aesthetic individual. The primary difference, the crux of the matter, is that the ethical individual is transparent to himself and does not live *ins Blaue hinein* [in the wild blue yonder], as does the aesthetic individual. This difference encompasses everything. The person who lives ethically has seen himself, knows himself, penetrates his whole concretion with his consciousness, does not allow vague thoughts to rustle around inside him or let tempting possibilities distract him with their juggling; he is not like a "magic" picture[6] that shifts from one thing to another, all depending on how one shifts and turns it. He knows himself. The phrase $\gamma\nu\tilde{\omega}\theta\iota$ $\sigma\epsilon\alpha\upsilon\tau\acute{o}\nu$ [know yourself][7] is a stock phrase, and in it has been perceived the goal of all a person's striving. And this is entirely proper, but yet it is just as certain that it cannot be the goal if it is not also the beginning. The ethical individual knows himself, but this knowing is not simply contemplation, for then the individual comes to be defined according to his necessity. It is a collecting of oneself, which itself is an action, and this is why I have with aforethought used the expression "to choose oneself" instead of "to know oneself."

When the individual knows himself, he is not finished; but this knowing is very productive, and from this knowing emerges the authentic individual. If I wanted to be clever, I could say here that the individual knows himself in a way similar to the way Adam knew Eve, as it says in the Old Testament.[8] Through the individual's intercourse with himself the individual is made pregnant by himself and gives birth to himself. The self the individual knows is simultaneously the actual self and the ideal self, which the individual has outside himself as the image in whose likeness he is to form himself, and which on the other hand he has within himself, since it is he himself. Only within himself does the individual have the objective toward which he is to strive, and yet he has this objective outside himself as he strives toward it. That is, if the individual believes that the universal human being lies outside him, so that it will come to him from the outside, then he is disoriented, then he has an abstract conception, and his method will always be an abstract annihilating of the original self. Only within himself can the individual become enlightened about himself. That is why the ethical life has this duplexity, in which the individual has himself outside himself within himself. Meanwhile the exemplary self is an imperfect self, for it is only a prophecy and thus is not the actual self. But it escorts him at all times; yet the more he actualizes it, the more it vanishes within him, until at last, instead of appearing before him, it is behind him as a faded possibility. This image is like a person's shadow. In the forenoon he casts his shadow before him; at noon it walks almost unnoticed beside him; in the afternoon it falls behind him. When the individual has known himself and has chosen himself, he is in the process of actualizing himself, but since he is supposed to do that freely, he must know what it is he wants to actualize. What he wants to actualize is certainly himself, but it is his ideal self, which he cannot acquire anywhere but within himself. If he does not hold firmly to the truth that the individual has the ideal self within himself, all of his aspiring and striving becomes abstract. Both the one who wants to copy another person and the one who wants to copy the normative person become equally affected, although in different ways.

The aesthetic individual considers himself in his concretion and makes distinctions *inter et inter* [between the one and the other].[9] He sees something as belonging to him in an accidental way, something else as belonging essentially. Yet this distinction is very relative, for as long as a person lives only aesthetically, everything really belongs to him equally accidentally, and when an aesthetic individual maintains this distinction, it merely shows a lack of energy.

The ethical individual has learned this in despair and thus has another distinction, for he also makes a distinction between the essential and the accidental. Everything that is posited in his freedom belongs to him essentially, however accidental it may seem to be; everything that is not posited in his freedom is accidental, however essential it may seem to be. But for the ethical individual this distinction is not a product of his arbitrariness so that he might seem to have absolute power to make himself into what it pleased him to be. To be sure, the ethical individual dares to employ the expression that he is his own editor, but he is also fully aware that he is responsible, responsible for himself personally, inasmuch as what he chooses will have a decisive influence on himself, responsible to the order of things in which he lives, responsible to God. Regarded in this way, the distinction is correct, I believe, for essentially only that belongs to me which I ethically take on as a task. If I refuse to take it on, then my having refused it essentially belongs to me.

When a person considers himself aesthetically, he may make distinctions as follows. He says: I have a talent for painting – this I regard as an accidental trait; but I have a keen wit and a keen mind – this I regard as the essential that cannot be taken away from me without my becoming somebody else. To that I would answer: This whole distinction is an illusion, for if you do not take on this keen wit and keen mind ethically, as a task, as something for which you are responsible, then it does not belong to you essentially, and primarily because as long as you live merely aesthetically your life is totally inessential. To a certain degree, the person who lives ethically cancels the distinction between the accidental and the essential, for he takes responsibility for all of himself as equally essential; but it comes back again, for after he has done that, he makes a distinction, but in such a manner that he takes an essential responsibility for excluding what he excludes as accidental.

Insofar as the aesthetic individual, with "aesthetic earnestness," sets a task for his life, it is really the task of becoming absorbed in his own accidental traits, of becoming an individual whose equal in paradoxicality and irregularity has never been seen, of becoming a caricature of a human being. The reason we rarely meet such characters in life is that we rarely meet people who have a notion of what it is to live. But since many people have a decided penchant for chattering, we encounter on the street, at parties, and in books a great amount of chatter that has the unmistakable stamp of the *Originalitets-Wuth* [mania for originality] that, carried over into life, would enrich the world with a host of artificial products, one more ridiculous than the other.

The task the ethical individual sets for himself is to transform himself into the universal individual. Only the ethical individual gives himself an account of himself in earnest and is therefore honest with himself; only he has the paradigmatic decorum and propriety that are more beautiful than anything else. But to transform himself into the universal human being is possible only if I already have it within myself $\kappa\alpha\tau\alpha$ $\delta\acute{v}\nu\alpha\mu\iota\nu$ [potentially]. In other words, the universal can very well continue in and with the specific without consuming it; it is like that fire that burned without consuming the bush.[10] If the universal human being is outside me, there is only one possible method, and that is to take off my entire concretion. This striving out in the unconstraint of abstraction is frequently seen. There was a sect of Hussites who thought that in order to become a normal human being one had to go around naked like Adam and Eve in Paradise.[11] In our day we not infrequently encounter people who in the spiritual sense teach the same thing – that one becomes a normal human being by going stark naked, which can be done by taking off one's entire concretion. But that is not the way it is. In the act of despair, the universal human being came forth and now is behind the concretion and emerges through it. There are many more paradigmatic verbs in a language than the one presented as the paradigm in the grammar book. It is accidental that this one is presented; all the other regular verbs could serve just as well – so also with human beings. Every person, if he so wills, can become a paradigmatic human being, not by brushing off his accidental qualities, but by remaining in them and ennobling them. But he ennobles them by choosing them.

By now you have easily seen that in his life the ethical individual goes through the stages we previously set forth as separate stages. He is going to develop in his life the personal, the civic, the religious virtues, and his life advances through his continually translating himself from one stage to another. As soon as a person thinks that one of these stages is adequate and that he dares to concentrate on it one-sidedly, he has not chosen himself ethically but has failed to see the significance of either isolation or continuity and above all has not grasped that the truth lies in the identity of these two.

The person who has ethically chosen and found himself possesses himself defined in his entire concretion. He then possesses himself as an individual who has these capacities, these passions, these inclinations, these habits, who is subject to these external influences, who is influenced in one direction thus and in another thus. Here he then possesses himself as a task in such a way that it is chiefly to order, shape, temper, inflame, control – in short, to produce an evenness in the soul, a harmony, which is the fruit of the personal virtues. Here the objective for his activity is himself, but nevertheless not arbitrarily determined, for he possesses himself as a task that has been assigned him, even though it became his by his own choosing. But although he himself is his objective, this objective is nevertheless something else also, for the self that is the objective is not an abstract self that fits everywhere and therefore nowhere but is a concrete self in living interaction with these specific surroundings, these life conditions, this order of things.

The self that is the objective is not only a personal self but a social, a civic self. He then possesses himself as a task in an activity whereby he engages in the affairs of life as this specific personality. Here his task is not to form himself but to act, and yet he forms himself at the same time, because, as I noted above, the ethical individual lives in such a way that he is continually transferring himself from one stage to another. If the individual has not originally conceived of himself as a concrete personality in continuity, he will not gain this next continuity either. If he thinks that the art is to begin like a Robinson Crusoe, he remains an adventurer all his life. If, however, he realizes that if he does not begin concretely he will never make a beginning, and that if he never makes a beginning he will never finish, he will then be simultaneously in continuity with the past and the future. He transfers himself from personal life to civic life, from this to personal life. Personal life as such was an isolation and therefore imperfect, but when he turns back into his personality through the civic life, the personal life appears in a higher form. The personality appears as the absolute that has its teleology in itself. When living for the fulfillment of duty is made a person's task in life, what is often pointed out is the skepticism that duty itself is unstable, that laws can be changed. You easily see that this last remark concerns the fluctuations to which civic virtues are always exposed.

This skepticism, however, does not apply to the negative aspect of morality, for that continues unchanged. But there is another skepticism that applies to every duty; it is the skepticism that I cannot discharge the duty at all. The duty is the universal. What is required of me is the universal; what I am able to do is the particular. Yet this skepticism has great significance, inasmuch as it shows that the personality itself is the absolute. But this must be defined more closely. Curiously enough, language itself points up this skepticism. I never say of a man: He is doing duty or duties; but I say: He is doing *his* duty; I say: I am doing *my* duty, do *your* duty. This shows that the individual is simultaneously the universal and the particular. Duty is the universal; it is required of me. Consequently, if I am not the universal, I cannot discharge the duty either. On the other hand, my duty is the particular, something for me alone, and yet it is duty and consequently the universal. Here personality appears in its highest validity. It is not lawless; neither does it itself establish its law, for the category of duty continues, but the personality takes the form of the unity of the universal and the particular. That this is so is clear; it can be made understandable to a child – for I can discharge the duty and yet not do *my* duty, and I can do *my* duty and yet not discharge the duty.

I am by no means of the opinion that the world would therefore sink into skepticism, because the difference between good and evil always remains, responsibility and duty likewise, even if it becomes impossible for someone else to say what *my* duty is, whereas it will always be possible for him to say what *his* duty is, which would not be the case if the unity of the universal and the particular were not posited. All skepticism may seem to be removed if duty is made into something external, fixed, and specific, something of which it can be said: This is duty. This, however, is a misunderstanding, for the doubt does not reside in the external but in the internal, in my relation to the universal. As a particular individual, I am not the universal, and to require it of me is unreasonable; consequently, if I am to be capable of performing the universal, I must be the universal at the same time as I am the particular, but then the dialectic of duty resides within me. As already stated, this position does not pose any threat to the ethical; on the contrary, it vindicates it. If this is not assumed, the personality becomes abstract, its relation to duty abstract, its immortality abstract. The difference between good and evil is not canceled either, for I doubt that there has ever been anyone who has claimed that it is a duty to do evil. That he did evil is something else, but he also tried to delude himself and others into thinking that it was good. That he would be able to persist in this delusion is unthinkable, since he himself is the universal; thus his enemy is not something external but within himself. If, however, I assume that duty is something external, then the difference between good and evil is canceled, for if I myself am not the universal, I can form only an abstract relation to it; but the difference between good and evil is incompatible with an abstract relation.

The very moment it is perceived that the personality is the absolute, is its own objective, is the unity of the universal and the particular, that very moment every skepticism that makes the historical its point of departure will be vanquished. Too often freethinkers have tried to confuse the concepts by pointing out how at times a people has pronounced something to be sacred and lawful that in the eyes of another people was abominable and evil. Here they have let themselves be blinded by the external, but with the ethical there is never a question of the external but of the internal. But however much the external is changed, the moral value of the action remains the same. Thus there has never been a nation that believed that children should hate their parents. In order to add fuel to doubt, however, it has been pointed out that whereas all civilized nations made it the children's duty to care for their parents, savages practiced the custom of putting their aged parents to death. This may very well be so, but still no headway is made thereby, because the question remains whether the savages intend to do something evil by this. The ethical always resides in this consciousness, whereas it is another question whether or not insufficient comprehension is responsible.

The atheist perceives very well that the way by which the ethical is most easily evaporated is to open the door to the historical infinity. And yet there is something legitimate in his behavior, for if, when all is said and done, the individual is not the absolute, then the empirical is the only road allotted to him, and the end of this road is just like the source of the Niger River – no one knows where it is.[12] If I am assigned to the finite, it is arbitrary to remain standing at any particular point. Therefore, along this road one never makes a beginning, for in order to start one must have come to the end, but this is an impossibility. When the personality is the absolute, then it is itself the Archimedean point from which one can lift the world. It is easy to see that this consciousness cannot inveigle the individual to discard his actuality, for if he wants to be the absolute in that way, he is a nonentity, an abstraction. Only as the single individual is he the absolute, and this consciousness will save him from all revolutionary radicalism.

Here I shall cease my theorizing; I am well aware that I am not cut out for it, nor is that my ambition, but I shall be perfectly contented if I might be assumed to be a passable practitioner. Then, too, theorizing takes so much time; any act I can do in a moment or embark upon promptly involves a great deal of trouble and difficulty before it can be put into words or into writing. Now, it is not my intention to give you a lecture on a doctrine of duty or to speak according to custom about duties to God, oneself, and one's neighbor. Not that I would spurn this grouping or that what I would have to teach would be too profound to be joined to Balle's catechism[13] or would presuppose much more previous knowledge than this catechism presupposes – not at all for those reasons, but because believe that with the ethical it is not a matter of the multiplicity of duty but of its intensity.

When a person has felt the intensity of duty with all his energy, then he is ethically matured, and then duty will break forth within him. The fundamental point, therefore, is not whether a person can count on his fingers how many duties he has, but that he has once and for all felt the intensity of duty in such a way that the consciousness of it is for him the assurance of the eternal validity of his being. That is why I by no means praise being a

man of duty, no more than I recommend being a bookworm, and yet I am sure that the person for whom the meaning of duty has never become manifest in all its infinitude is just as second-rate a human being as someone is a scholar who *ad modum* [in the fashion of] "the Grenaa-men"[14] thinks he will find wisdom *mir nichts und dir nichts* [without further ado]. Let the casuist immerse himself in finding out the complexity of duty; the primary question, the only salutary thing, is always that a person with respect to his own life is not his uncle but his father.

Notes

1 See Shakespeare, *Hamlet*, III, 1, 56. (Original ed.)
2 See Eugène Scribe, *Aurelia*, I, 2; II, 7, *Repertoire* (1834), 65, pp. 2, 18–19. (Original ed.)
3 Danish: *Pligt*; the verb, *pligte*, to bind, is related to the English verb "plight." The text proceeds to give another etymology with the same emphasis upon inner orientation and commitment. (Original ed.)
4 See II Timothy 4:7. (Original ed.)
5 See Matthew 23:24. (Original ed.)
6 Danish: *Hexebrev*, literally "witch's letter," which is a "magic" set of picture segments of people and animals that recombine when unfolded and turned. (Original ed.)
7 The inscription on the temple of the Delphic oracle. (Original ed.)
8 See Genesis 4:1. (Original ed.)
9 The Latin phrase was used by Kierkegaard in 1848 as a pseudonym for the author of *The Crisis and a Crisis in the Life of an Actress*. (Original ed.)

10 See Exodus 3:2. (Original ed.)
11 The Adamites, such as an Anabaptist sect in Holland in mid-sixteenth century and an Austrian sect in mid-nineteenth century. See *JP* II 1234 (*Pap*. II A 280). (Original ed.)
12 The source of the Niger River was not discovered until 1879 by M. Moustier and J. Zweifel. (Original ed.)
13 Nicolai Edinger Balle, *Lærebog i den Evangelisk-christelige Religion indrettet til Brug i de danske Skoler* (Copenhagen: 1824; *ASKB* 183). First published in 1791, the religious instruction book for use in the schools was frequently reprinted for over fifty years. (Original ed.)
14 A reference to the Molboer (inhabitants of the island of Mols, near the town of Grenaa in northeast Jylland), the butt of stories similar to those about the Wise Men of Gotham. (Original ed.)

Select Bibliography

The Concept of Irony, with Continual Reference to Socrates. Edited and translated by Howard V. Hong and Edna H. Hong. Princeton: Princeton University Press, 1989.
Concluding Unscientific Postscript to Philosophical Fragments, 2 vols. Edited and translated by Howard V. Hong and Edna H. Hong. Princeton: Princeton University Press, 1992.
Early Polemical Writings. Edited and translated by Julia Watkin. Princeton: Princeton University Press, 1990.
Either/Or, 2 vols. Edited and translated by Howard V. Hong and Edna H. Hong. Princeton: Princeton University Press, 1987.
Fear and Trembling, and Repetition. Edited and translated by Howard V. Hong and Edna H. Hong. Princeton: Princeton University Press, 1983.

For Self-Examination and Judge For Yourself! Edited and translated by Howard V. Hong and Edna H. Hong. Princeton: Princeton University Press.
Kierkegaard's Writings. Edited and translated by Howard V. Hong and Edna H. Hong. Princeton: Princeton University Press, 1978.
Philosophical Fragments and Johannes Climacus. Edited and translated by Howard V. Hong and Edna H. Hong. Princeton: Princeton University Press, 1985.
Practice in Christianity. Edited and translated by Howard V. Hong and Edna H. Hong. Princeton: Princeton University Press, 1991.
The Sickness Unto Death: A Christian Psychological Exposition for Upbuilding and Awakening. Edited and translated by Howard V. Hong and Edna H. Hong. Princeton: Princeton University Press, 1980.

Søren Kierkegaard

Stages on Life's Way: Studies by Various Persons. Edited and translated by Howard V. Hong and Edna H. Hong. Princeton: Princeton University Press, 1988.

Upbuilding Discourses in Various Spirits. Edited and translated by Howard V. Hong and Edna H. Hong. Princeton: Princeton University Press, 1993.

Works of Love. Edited and translated by Howard V. Hong and Edna H. Hong. Princeton: Princeton University Press, 1995.

3

Friedrich Nietzsche

The German philosopher Friedrich Nietzsche (1844–1900) began his academic career as a classical philologist, although his interest soon turned to philosophical inquiry concerning the beginnings and nature of Greek and Western civilization. Influenced early on by Schopenhauer, then increasingly by Wagner, whom he befriended, Nietzsche gradually came to distance himself from both and developed a radical critique of Western culture which he diagnosed as intrinsically nihilistic. For Nietzsche, contemporary culture approaches extreme nihilism when the highest values hitherto become devalued, when we no longer believe in "the True" or "the Good." The roots of such nihilism are philosophical and scientific (Plato's positing of a "true world" opposed to the world of "appearances") and theological (the Christian worldview that posits the true world as a world beyond our earthly existence). The ensuing devaluation of the sensuous reaches its crisis with "the death of God," that is, with the collapse of all belief in a transcendent truth. Nietzsche's mature thought attempts to understand this crisis in terms of his two central thoughts of "the will to power" and "the eternal recurrence of the same." The following aphorisms, from several different works, present a range of key reflections on these themes.

The Gay Science

Book Three

§125

The madman. – Have you not heard of that madman who lit a lantern in the bright morning hours, ran to the market place, and cried incessantly: "I seek

From *The Gay Science*, translated by Walter Kaufmann (New York: Random House, 1974), pp. 181–2, 273–4. Copyright © 1974 by Random House, Inc. Reprinted by permission of Random House, Inc.

God! I seek God!" – As many of those who did not believe in God were standing around just then, he provoked much laughter. Has he got lost? asked one. Did he lose his way like a child? asked another. Or is he hiding? Is he afraid of us? Has he gone on a voyage? emigrated? – Thus they yelled and laughed.

The madman jumped into their midst and pierced them with his eyes. "Whither is God?" he cried; "I will tell you. *We have killed him* – you and I. All of us are his murderers. But how did we do this? How could we drink up the sea? Who gave us the sponge to wipe away the entire horizon? What were we doing when we unchained this earth from its sun? Whither is it moving now? Whither are we moving? Away from all suns? Are we not plunging continually? Backward, sideward, forward, in all directions? Is there still any up or down? Are we not straying as through an infinite nothing? Do we not feel the breath of empty space? Has it not become colder? Is not night continually closing in on us? Do we not need to light lanterns in the morning? Do we hear nothing as yet of the noise of the gravediggers who are burying God? Do we smell nothing as yet of the divine decomposition? Gods, too, decompose. God is dead. God remains dead. And we have killed him.

"How shall we comfort ourselves, the murderers of all murderers? What was holiest and mightiest of all that the world has yet owned has bled to death under our knives: who will wipe this blood off us? What water is there for us to clean ourselves? What festivals of atonement, what sacred games shall we have to invent? Is not the greatness of this deed too great for us? Must we ourselves not become gods simply to appear worthy of it? There has never been a greater deed; and whoever is born after us – for the sake of this deed he will belong to a higher history than all history hitherto."

Here the madman fell silent and looked again at his listeners; and they, too, were silent and stared at him in astonishment. At last he threw his lantern on the ground, and it broke into pieces and went out. "I have come too early," he said then; "my time is not yet. This tremendous event is still on its way, still wandering; it has not yet reached the ears of men. Lightning and thunder require time; the light of the stars requires time; deeds, though done, still require time to be seen and heard. This deed is still more distant from them than the most distant stars – *and yet they have done it themselves.*"

It has been related further that on the same day the madman forced his way into several churches and there struck up his *requiem aeternam deo*. Led out and called to account, he is said always to have replied nothing but: "What after all are these churches now if they are not the tombs and sepulchers of God?" . . .

Book Four

§341

The greatest weight. – What, if some day or night a demon were to steal after you into your loneliest loneliness and say to you: "This life as you now live it and have lived it, you will have to live once more and innumerable times more; and there will be nothing new in it, but every pain and every joy and every thought and sigh and everything unutterably small or great in your life will have to return to you, all in the same succession and sequence – even this spider and this moonlight between the trees, and even this moment and I myself. The eternal hourglass of existence is turned upside down again and again, and you with it, speck of dust!"

Would you not throw yourself down and gnash your teeth and curse the demon who spoke thus? Or have you once experienced a tremendous moment when you would have answered him: "You are a god and never have I heard anything more divine." If this thought gained possession of you, it would change you as you are or perhaps crush you. The question in each and every thing, "Do you desire this once more and innumerable times more?" would lie upon your actions as the greatest weight. Or how well disposed would you have to become to yourself and to life *to crave nothing more fervently* than this ultimate eternal confirmation and seal?

Twilight of the Idols

"Reason" in Philosophy

§1

You ask me about the idiosyncrasies of philosophers? . . . There is their lack of historical sense, their hatred of even the idea of becoming, their Egyptianism. They think they are doing a thing *honor* when they dehistoricize it, *sub specie aeterni*[1] – when they make a mummy of it. All that philosophers have handled for millennia has been conceptual mummies; nothing actual has escaped from their hands alive. They kill, they stuff, when they worship, these conceptual idolaters – they become a mortal danger to everything when they worship. Death, change, age, as well as procreation and growth, are for them objections – refutations even. What is, does not *become*; what becomes, *is* not. . . . Now they all believe, even to the point of despair, in that which is. But since they cannot get hold of it, they look for reasons why it is being withheld from them. "It must be an illusion, a deception which prevents us from perceiving that which is: where is the deceiver to be found?" – "We've got it," they cry in delight, "it is the senses! These senses, *which are so immoral as well*, it is they which deceive us about the *real* world. Moral: escape from sense-deception, from becoming, from history, from falsehood – history is nothing but belief in the senses, belief in falsehood. Moral: denial of all that believes in the senses, of all the rest of mankind: all of that is mere 'people.' Be a philosopher, be a mummy, represent monotono–theism by a gravedigger-mimicry! – And away, above all, with the *body*, that pitiable *idée fixe* of the senses! infected with every error of logic there is, refuted, impossible even, notwithstanding it is impudent enough to behave as if it actually existed!" . . .

§2

I set apart with high reverence the name of *Heraclitus*. When the rest of the philosopher crowd

From *Twilight of the Idols and The Anti-Christ*, translated by R. J. Hollingdale (London: Penguin Books, 1990), pp. 45–51.

rejected the evidence of the senses because these showed plurality and change, he rejected their evidence because they showed things as if they possessed duration and unity. Heraclitus too was unjust to the senses, which lie neither in the way the Eleatics[2] believe nor as he believed – they do not lie at all. It is what we *make* of their evidence that first introduces a lie into it, for example the lie of unity, the lie of materiality, of substance, of duration. . . . "Reason" is the cause of our falsification of the evidence of the senses. Insofar as the senses show becoming, passing away, change, they do not lie. . . . But Heraclitus will always be right in this, that being is an empty fiction. The "apparent" world is the only one: the "real" world has only been *lyingly added* . . .

§3

– And what subtle instruments for observation we possess in our senses! This nose, for example, of which no philosopher has hitherto spoken with respect and gratitude, is nonetheless the most delicate tool we have at our command: it can detect minimal differences in movement which even the spectroscope cannot detect. We possess scientific knowledge today to precisely the extent that we have decided to *accept* the evidence of the senses – to the extent that we have learned to sharpen and arm them and to think them through to their conclusions. The rest is abortion and not-yet-science: which is to say metaphysics, theology, psychology, epistemology. *Or* science of formulae, sign-systems: such as logic and that applied logic, mathematics. In these reality does not appear at all, not even as a problem; just as little as does the question what value a system of conventional signs such as constitutes logic can possibly possess.

§4

The *other* idiosyncrasy of philosophers is no less perilous: it consists in mistaking the last for the first. They put that which comes at the end – unfortunately! for it ought not to come at all! – the "highest concepts," that is to say the most

general, the emptiest concepts, the last fumes of
evaporating reality, at the beginning *as* the beginning. It is again only the expression of their way of
doing reverence: the higher must not be *allowed* to
grow out of the lower, must not be *allowed* to have
grown at all.... Moral: everything of the first rank
must be *causa sui*.[3] Origin in something else counts
as an objection, as casting a doubt on value. All
supreme values are of the first rank, all the supreme
concepts – that which is, the unconditioned, the
good, the true, the perfect – all that cannot have
become, *must* therefore be *causa sui*. But neither can
these supreme concepts be incommensurate with
one another, be incompatible with one
another.... Thus they acquired their stupendous
concept "God".... The last, thinnest, emptiest is
placed as the first, as cause in itself, as *ens realissi-
mum*.[4]... That mankind should have taken
seriously the brain-sick fancies of morbid cobweb-
spinners! – And it has paid dearly for doing so!...

§5

– Let us, in conclusion, set against this the very
different way in which *we* (– I say "we" out of
politeness...) view the problem of error and
appearance. Change, mutation, becoming in general were formerly taken as proof of appearance, as
a sign of the presence of something which led us
astray. Today, on the contrary, we see ourselves as
it were entangled in error, *necessitated* to error, to
precisely the extent that our prejudice in favor of
reason compels us to posit unity, identity, duration, substance, cause, materiality, being; however
sure we may be, on the basis of a strict reckoning,
that error is to be found here. The situation is the
same as with the motions of the sun: in that case
error has our eyes, in the present case our *language*
as a perpetual advocate. Language belongs in its
origin to the age of the most rudimentary form of
psychology: we find ourselves in the midst of a
rude fetishism when we call to mind the basic
presuppositions of the metaphysics of language –
which is to say, of *reason*. It is *this* which sees
everywhere deed and doer; this which believes in
will as cause in general; this which believes in the
"ego," in the ego as being, in the ego as substance,
and which *projects* its belief in the ego-substance on
to all things – only thus does it *create* the concept
"thing".... Being is everywhere thought in, *foisted
on*, as cause; it is only from the conception "ego"
that there follows, derivatively, the concept
"being".... At the beginning stands the great fate-

ful error that the will is something which *produces
an effect* – that will is a *faculty*.... Today we know
it is merely a world.... Very much later, in a world
a thousand times more enlightened, the *security*,
the subjective *certainty* with which the categories of
reason could be employed came all of a sudden into
philosophers' heads: they concluded that these
could not have originated in the empirical world –
indeed, the entire empirical world was incompatible with them. *Where then do they originate?* – And
in India as in Greece they committed the same
blunder: "We must once have dwelt in a higher
world" – instead of *in a very much lower one*, which
would have been the truth! – "we must have been
divine, *for* we possess reason!"... Nothing, in fact,
has hitherto had a more direct power of persuasion
than the error of being as it was formulated by, for
example, the Eleatics: for every word, every sentence we utter speaks in its favor! – Even the
opponents of the Eleatics were still subject to the
seductive influence of their concept of being:
Democritus, among others, when he invented his
atom.... "Reason" in language: oh what a deceitful
old woman! I fear we are not getting rid of God
because we still believe in grammar...

§6

It will be a matter for gratitude if I now compress
so fundamental and new an insight into four theses:
I shall thereby make it easier to understand, I shall
thereby challenge contradiction.

First proposition. The grounds upon which
"this" world has been designated as apparent
establish rather its reality – *another* kind of reality
is absolutely undemonstrable.

Second proposition. The characteristics which
have been assigned to the "real being" of things
are the characteristics of non-being, of *nothingness* –
the "real world" has been constructed out of the
contradiction to the actual world: an apparent
world indeed, insofar as it is no more than a
moral–optical illusion.

Third proposition. To talk about "another" world
than this is quite pointless, provided that an
instinct for slandering, disparaging and accusing
life is not strong within us: in the latter case we
revenge ourselves on life by means of the phantas-
magoria of "another," a "better" life.

Fourth proposition. To divide the world into a
"real" and an "apparent" world, whether in the
manner of Christianity or in the manner of Kant
(which is, after all, that of a *cunning* Christian –) is

only a suggestion of *décadence* – a symptom of *declining* life.... That the artist places a higher value on appearance than on reality constitutes no objection to this proposition. For "appearance" here signifies reality *once more*, only selected, strengthened, corrected.... The tragic artist is *not* a pessimist – it is precisely he who *affirms* all that is questionable and terrible in existence, he is *Dionysian*...

How the "Real World" at last Became a Myth

History of an error

1 The real world, attainable to the wise, the pious, the virtuous man – he dwells in it, *he is it*.
    (Oldest form of the idea, relatively sensible, simple, convincing. Transcription of the proposition "I, Plato, *am* the truth.")[5]
2 The real world, unattainable for the moment, but promised to the wise, the pious, the virtuous man ("to the sinner who repents").
    (Progress of the idea: it grows more refined, more enticing, more incomprehensible – *it becomes a woman*, it becomes Christian...)

3 The real world, unattainable, undemonstrable, cannot be promised, but even when merely thought of a consolation, a duty, an imperative.
    (Fundamentally the same old sun, but shining through mist and skepticism; the idea grown sublime, pale, northerly, Königsbergian.)[6]
4 The real world – unattainable? Unattained, at any rate. And if unattained also *unknown*. Consequently also no consolation, no redemption, no duty: how could we have a duty towards something unknown?
    (The gray of dawn. First yawnings of reason. Cock–crow of positivism.)[7]
5 The "real world" – an idea no longer of any use, not even a duty any longer – an idea grown useless, superfluous, *consequently* a refuted idea: let us abolish it!
    (Broad daylight; breakfast; return of cheerfulness and *bons sens*; Plato blushes for shame; all free spirits run riot.)
6 We have abolished the real world: what world is left? the apparent world perhaps?...But no! *with the real world we have also abolished the apparent world!*
    (Mid-day; moment of the shortest shadow; end of the longest error; zenith of mankind; INCIPIT ZARATHUSTRA)[8]

The Will to Power

Book One: European Nihilism

§1 (1885–1886) Toward an outline

1 Nihilism stands at the door: whence comes this uncanniest of all guests? Point of departure: it is an error to consider "social distress" or "physiological degeneration" or, worse, corruption, as the *cause* of nihilism. Ours is the most decent and compassionate age. Distress, whether of the soul, body, or intellect, cannot of itself give birth to nihilism

From *The Will to Power*, translated by Walter Kaufmann and R. J. Hollingdale (New York: Random House, 1968), pp. 7–10, 12–15, 262–4, 267–72, 293–9. Copyright © 1967 by Walter Kaufmann. Reprinted by permission of Random House, Inc.

(i.e. the radical repudiation of value, meaning, and desirability). Such distress always permits a variety of interpretations. Rather: it is in one particular interpretation, the Christian-moral one, that nihilism is rooted.
2 The end of Christianity – at the hands of its own morality (which cannot be replaced), which turns against the Christian God (the sense of truthfulness, developed highly by Christianity, is nauseated by the falseness and mendaciousness of all Christian interpretations of the world and of history; rebound from "God is truth" to the fanatical faith "All is false"; Buddhism of *action* –).
3 Skepticism regarding morality is what is decisive. The end of the moral interpretation of the world, which no longer has any sanction after it has tried to escape into some beyond, leads to

nihilism. "Everything lacks meaning" (the untenability of one interpretation of the world, upon which a tremendous amount of energy has been lavished, awakens the suspicion that *all* interpretations of the world are false). Buddhistic tendency, yearning for Nothing. (Indian Buddhism is *not* the culmination of a thoroughly moralistic development; its nihilism is therefore full of morality that is not overcome: existence as punishment, existence construed as error, error thus as a punishment – a moral valuation.) Philosophical attempts to overcome the "moral God" (Hegel, pantheism). Overcoming popular ideals: the sage; the saint; the poet. The antagonism of "true" and "beautiful" and "good" –

4   Against "meaninglessness" on the one hand, against moral value judgments on the other: to what extent has all science and philosophy so far been influenced by moral judgments? and won't this net us the hostility of science? Or an antiscientific mentality? Critique of Spinozism. Residues of Christian value judgments are found everywhere in socialistic and positivistic systems. A *critique of Christian morality* is still lacking.

5   The nihilistic consequences of contemporary natural science (together with its attempts to escape into some beyond). The industry of its pursuit eventually leads to self-disintegration, opposition, an antiscientific mentality. Since Copernicus man has been rolling from the center toward *X*.

6   The nihilistic consequences of the ways of thinking in politics and economics, where all "principles" are practically histrionic: the air of mediocrity, wretchedness, dishonesty, etc. Nationalism. Anarchism, etc. Punishment. The *redeeming* class and human being are lacking – the justifiers –

7   The nihilistic consequences of historiography and of the "*practical* historians," i.e. the romantics. The position of art: its position in the modern world absolutely lacking in originality. Its decline into gloom. Goethe's allegedly Olympian stance.

8   Art and the preparation of nihilism: romanticism (the conclusion of Wagner's *Nibelungen*).

1   Nihilism

§2 (Spring–Fall 1887)

What does nihilism mean? *That the highest values devaluate themselves.* The aim is lacking; "why?" finds no answer.

§3 (Spring–Fall 1887)

Radical nihilism is the conviction of an absolute untenability of existence when it comes to the highest values one recognizes; plus the realization that we lack the least right to posit a beyond or an in-itself of things that might be "divine" or morality incarnate.

This realization is a consequence of the cultivation of "truthfulness" – thus itself a consequence of the faith in morality.

§4 (June 10, 1887)

What were the advantages of the Christian moral hypothesis?

1   It granted man an absolute value, as opposed to his smallness and accidental occurrence in the flux of becoming and passing away.

2   It served the advocates of God insofar as it conceded to the world, in spite of suffering and evil, the character of perfection – including "freedom": evil appeared full of meaning.

3   It posited that man had a *knowledge* of absolute values and thus *adequate knowledge* precisely regarding what is most important.

4   It prevented man from despising himself as man, from taking sides against life; from despairing of knowledge: it was a *means of preservation*.

In sum: morality was the great *antidote* against practical and theoretical *nihilism*. . . .

§12 (Nov. 1887–March 1888) Decline of cosmological values

(A)

Nihilism as a psychological state will have to be reached, *first*, when we have sought a "meaning" in all events that is not there: so the seeker eventually becomes discouraged. Nihilism, then, is the recognition of the long *waste* of strength, the agony of the "in vain," insecurity, the lack of any opportunity to recover and to regain composure – being ashamed in front of oneself, as if one had *deceived* oneself all too long. – This meaning could have been: the "fulfillment" of some highest ethical canon in all events, the moral world order; or the growth of love and harmony in the intercourse of beings; or the gradual approximation of a state of universal happiness; or even the development toward a state of universal annihilation – any goal at least constitutes some meaning. What all these notions have in common is that something is to be *achieved* through the process – and now one realizes that becoming aims at *nothing* and achieves *nothing*. – Thus, disappointment regarding an alleged aim of becoming as a cause of nihilism: whether regarding a specific aim or, universalized, the realization that all previous hypotheses about aims that concern the whole "evolution" are inadequate (man no longer the collaborator, let alone the center, of becoming).

Nihilism as a psychological state is reached, *secondly*, when one has posited a totality, a systematization, indeed any organization in all events, and underneath all events, and a soul that longs to admire and revere has wallowed in the idea of some supreme form of domination and administration (– if the soul be that of a logician, complete consistency and real dialectic are quite sufficient to reconcile it to everything). Some sort of unity, some form of "monism": this faith suffices to give man a deep feeling of standing in the context of, and being dependent on, some whole that is infinitely superior to him, and he sees himself as a mode of the deity. – "The well-being of the universal demands the devotion of the individual" – but behold, there is no such universal! At bottom, man has lost the faith in his own value when no infinitely valuable whole works through him; i.e. he conceived such a whole in order *to be able to believe in his own value.*

Nihilism as psychological state has yet a *third* and *last* form. Given these two insights, that becoming has no goal and that underneath all becoming there is no grand unity in which the individual could immerse himself completely as in an element of supreme value, an escape remains: to pass sentence on this whole world of becoming as a deception and to invent a world beyond it, a *true* world. But as soon as man finds out how that world is fabricated solely from psychological needs, and how he has absolutely no right to it, the last form of nihilism comes into being: it includes disbelief in any metaphysical world and forbids itself any belief in a *true* world. Having reached this standpoint, one grants the reality of becoming as the *only* reality, forbids oneself every kind of clandestine access to afterworlds and false divinities – but *cannot endure this world though one does not want to deny it.*

What has happened, at bottom? The feeling of valuelessness was reached with the realization that the overall character of existence may not be interpreted by means of the concept of "aim," the concept of "unity," or the concept of "truth." Existence has no goal or end; any comprehensive unity in the plurality of events is lacking: the character of existence is not "true," is *false*. One simply lacks any reason for convincing oneself that there is a *true* world. Briefly: the categories "aim," "unity," "being" which we used to project some value into the world – we *pull out* again; so the world looks *valueless*.

(B)

Suppose we realize how the world may no longer be interpreted in terms of these three categories, and that the world begins to become valueless for us after this insight: then we have to ask about the sources of our faith in these three categories. Let us try if it is not possible to give up our faith in them. Once we have devalued these three categories, the demonstration that they cannot be applied to the universe is no longer any reason for devaluating the universe.

Conclusion: The faith in the categories of reason is the cause of nihilism. We have measured the value of the world according to categories *that refer to a purely fictitious world.*

Final conclusion: All the values by means of which we have tried so far to render the world estimable for ourselves and which then proved inapplicable and therefore devaluated the world – all these values are, psychologically considered, the results of certain perspectives of utility, designed to maintain and increase human constructs of domination – and they have been falsely *projected* into the essence of things. What we find here is still the *hyperbolic naiveté* of man: positing himself as the meaning and measure of the value of things....

§15 (Spring–Fall 1887)

What is a *belief*? How does it originate? Every belief is a considering-something-true.

The most extreme form of nihilism would be the view that *every* belief, every considering-something-true, is necessarily false because there simply is no *true world*. Thus: a *perspectival appearance* whose origin lies in us (insofar as we continually *need* a narrower, abbreviated, simplified world).

– That it is the measure of strength to what extent we can admit to ourselves, without perishing, the merely *apparent* character, the necessity of lies.

To this extent, nihilism, as the denial of a truthful world, of being, might be *a divine way of thinking*....

Book Three: Principles of a New Evaluation

I. The Will to Power as Knowledge

2   The Epistemological Starting Point

§470 (1885–1886)

Profound aversion to reposing once and for all in any one total view of the world. Fascination of the opposing point of view: refusal to be deprived of the stimulus of the enigmatic.

§471 (1885–1886)

The presupposition that things are, at bottom, ordered so morally that human reason must be justified – is an ingenuous presupposition and a piece of *naiveté*, the after-effect of belief in God's veracity – God understood as the creator of things. – These concepts an inheritance from a former existence in a beyond –

§472 (1883–1888)

Contradiction of the alleged "facts of consciousness." Observation is a thousand times more difficult, error perhaps a condition of observation in general.

§473 (1886–1887)

The intellect cannot criticize itself, simply because it cannot be compared with other species of intellect and because its capacity to know would be revealed only in the presence of "true reality," i.e. because in order to criticize the intellect we should have to be a higher being with "absolute knowledge." This presupposes that, distinct from every perspective kind of outlook or sensual–spiritual appropriation, something exists, an "in-itself." – But the psychological derivation of the belief in things forbids us to speak of "things-in-themselves."

§474 (Nov. 1887–March 1888)

That a sort of adequate relationship subsists between subject and object, that the object is something that if seen from within would be a subject, is a well-meant invention which, I think, has had its day. The measure of that of which we are in any way conscious is totally dependent upon the coarse utility of its becoming-conscious: how could this nook-perspective of consciousness permit us to assert anything of "subject" and "object" that touched reality! –

§475 (1885–1886)

Critique of modern philosophy: erroneous starting point, as if there existed "facts of consciousness" – and no phenomenalism in introspection.

§476 (1884)

"Consciousness" – to what extent the idea of an idea, the idea of will, the idea of a feeling (known to ourselves alone) are totally superficial! Our inner world, too, "appearance"!

§477 (Nov. 1887–March 1888)

I maintain the phenomenality of the inner world, too: everything of which we become conscious is arranged, simplified, schematized, interpreted through and through – the actual process of inner "perception," the causal connection between thoughts, feelings, desires, between subject and object, are absolutely hidden from us – and are perhaps purely imaginary. The "apparent *inner world*" is governed by just the same forms and procedures as the "outer" world. We never encounter "facts": pleasure and displeasure are subsequent and derivative intellectual phenomena –

"Causality" eludes us; to suppose a direct causal link between thoughts, as logic does – that is the consequence of the crudest and clumsiest observation. Between two thoughts all kinds of affects play their game: but their motions are too fast, therefore we fail to recognize them, we deny them –

"Thinking," as epistemologists conceive it, simply does not occur: it is a quite arbitrary fiction, arrived at by selecting one element from the process and eliminating all the rest, an artificial arrangement for the purpose of intelligibility –

The "spirit," something that thinks: where possible even "absolute, pure spirit" – this conception is a second derivative of that false introspection which believes in "thinking": first an act is imagined which simply does not occur, "thinking," and secondly a subject-substratum in which every act of thinking, and nothing else, has its origin: that is to say, both the deed and the doer are fictions. . . .

3 Belief in the "Ego." The Subject

§481 (1883–1888)

Against positivism, which halts at phenomena – "There are only *facts*" – I would say: No, facts is precisely what there is not, only interpretations. We cannot establish any fact "in itself": perhaps it is folly to want to do such a thing.

"Everything is subjective," you say; but even this is interpretation. The "subject" is not something given, it is something added and invented and projected behind what there is. – Finally, is it necessary to posit an interpreter behind the interpretation? Even this is invention, hypothesis.

Insofar as the word "knowledge" has any meaning, the world is knowable; but it is *interpretable* otherwise, it has no meaning behind it, but countless meanings. – "Perspectivism."

It is our needs that interpret the world; our drives and their For and Against. Every drive is a kind of lust to rule; each one has its perspective that it would like to compel all the other drives to accept as a norm.

§482 (1886–1887)

We set up a word at the point at which our ignorance begins, at which we can see no further, e.g. the word "I," the word "do," the word "suffer": – these are perhaps the horizon of our knowledge, but not "truths."

§483 (1885)

Through thought the ego is posited; but hitherto one believed as ordinary people do, that in "I think" there was something of immediate certainty, and that this "I" was the given *cause* of thought, from which by analogy we understood all other causal relationships. However habitual and indispensable this fiction may have become by now – that in itself proves nothing against its imaginary origin: a belief can be a condition of life and nonetheless be false.

§484 (Spring–Fall 1887)

"There is thinking: therefore there is something that thinks": this is the upshot of all Descartes' argumentation. But that means positing as "true *a priori*" our belief in the concept of substance – that when there is thought there has to be something

"that thinks" is simply a formulation of our grammatical custom that adds a doer to every deed. In short, this is not merely the substantiation of a fact but a logical–metaphysical postulate – Along the lines followed by Descartes one does not come upon something absolutely certain but only upon the fact of a very strong belief.

If one reduces the proposition to "There is thinking, therefore there are thoughts," one has produced a mere tautology: and precisely that which is in question, the "reality of thought," is not touched upon – that is, in this form the "apparent reality" of thought cannot be denied. But what Descartes desired was that thought should have, not an *apparent* reality, but a reality *in itself*.

§485 (Spring–Fall 1887)

The concept of substance is a consequence of the concept of the subject: not the reverse! If we relinquish the soul, "the subject," the precondition for "substance" in general disappears. One acquires degrees of being, one loses that which *has* being.

Critique of "reality": where does the "more or less real," the gradation of being in which we believe, lead to? –

The degree to which we feel life and power (logic and coherence of experience) gives us our measure of "being," "reality," not-appearance.

The subject: this is the term for our belief in a unity underlying all the different impulses of the highest feeling of reality: we understand this belief as the *effect* of one cause – we believe so firmly in our belief that for its sake we imagine "truth," "reality," "substantiality" in general. – "The subject" is the fiction that many similar states in us are the effect of one substratum: but it is we who first created the "similarity" of these states; our adjusting them and making them similar is the fact, not their similarity (– which ought rather to be denied –).

§486 (1885–1886)

One would have to know what *being* is, in order to decide whether this or that is real (e.g. "the facts of consciousness"); in the same way, what *certainty* is, what *knowledge* is, and the like. – But since we do not know this, a critique of the faculty of knowledge is senseless: how should a tool be able to criticize itself when it can use only itself for the critique? It cannot even define itself!

§487 (1883–1886)

Must all philosophy not ultimately bring to light the preconditions upon which the process of reason depends? – our belief in the "ego" as a substance, as the sole reality from which we ascribe reality to things in general? The oldest "realism" at last comes to light: at the same time that the entire religious history of mankind is recognized as the history of the soul superstition. Here we come to a limit: our thinking itself involves this belief (with its distinction of substance, accident; deed, doer, etc.); to let it go means: being no longer able to think.

But that a belief, however necessary it may be for the preservation of a species, has nothing to do with truth, one knows from the fact that, e.g., we have to believe in time, space, and motion, without feeling compelled to grant them absolute reality.

§488 (Spring–Fall 1887)

Psychological derivation of our belief in reason. – The concept "reality," "being," is taken from our feeling of the "subject."

"The subject": interpreted from within ourselves, so that the ego counts as a substance, as the cause of all deeds, as a doer.

The logical–metaphysical postulates, the belief in substance, accident, attribute, etc., derive their convincing force from our habit of regarding all our deeds as consequences of our will – so that the ego, as substance, does not vanish in the multiplicity of change. – But there is no such thing as will. –

We have no categories at all that permit us to distinguish a "world in itself" from a "world of appearance." All our categories of reason are of sensual origin: derived from the empirical world. "The soul," "the ego" – the history of these concepts shows that here, too, the oldest distinction ("breath," "life") –

If there is nothing material, there is also nothing immaterial. The concept no longer contains anything.

No subject "atoms." The sphere of a subject constantly growing or decreasing, the center of the system constantly shifting; in cases where it cannot organize the appropriate mass, it breaks into two parts. On the other hand, it can transform a weaker subject into its functionary without

destroying it, and to a certain degree form a new unity with it. No "substance," rather something that in itself strives after greater strength, and that wants to "preserve" itself only indirectly (it wants to *surpass* itself –).

§489 (1886–1887)

Everything that enters consciousness as "unity" is already tremendously complex: we always have only a semblance of unity.

The phenomenon of the body is the richer, clearer, more tangible phenomenon: to be discussed first, methodologically, without coming to any decision about its ultimate significance.

§490 (1885)

The assumption of one single subject is perhaps unnecessary; perhaps it is just as permissible to assume a multiplicity of subjects, whose interaction and struggle is the basis of our thought and our consciousness in general? A kind of aristocracy of "cells" in which dominion resides? To be sure, an aristocracy of equals, used to ruling jointly and understanding how to command?

My hypotheses: The subject as multiplicity.

Pain intellectual and dependent upon the judgment "harmful": projected.

The effect always "unconscious": the inferred and imagined cause is projected, *follows* in time.

Pleasure is a kind of pain.

The only force that exists is of the same kind as that of the will: a commanding of other subjects, which thereupon change.

The continual transitoriness and fleetingness of the subject. "Mortal soul."

Number as perspective form.

§491 (1885–1886)

Belief in the body is more fundamental than belief in the soul: the latter arose from unscientific reflection on [the agonies of] the body (something that leaves it. Belief in the truth of dreams –).

§492 (1885)

The body and physiology the starting point: why? – We gain the correct idea of the nature of our subject-unity, namely as regents at the head of a communality (not as "souls" or "life forces"), also of the dependence of these regents upon the ruled and of an order of rank and division of labor as the conditions that make possible the whole and its parts. In the same way, how living unities continually arise and die and how the "subject" is not eternal; in the same way, that the struggle expresses itself in obeying and commanding, and that a fluctuating assessment of the limits of power is part of life. The relative ignorance in which the regent is kept concerning individual activities and even disturbances within the communality is among the conditions under which rule can be exercised. In short, we also gain a valuation of *not-knowing*, of seeing things on a broad scale, of simplification and falsification, of perspectivity. The most important thing, however, is: that we understand that the ruler and his subjects are of the same kind, all feeling, willing, thinking – and that, wherever we see or divine movement in a body, we learn to conclude that there is a subjective, invisible life appertaining to it. Movement is symbolism for the eye; it indicates that something has been felt, willed, thought.

The danger of the direct questioning of the subject *about* the subject and of all self-reflection of the spirit lies in this, that it could be useful and important for one's activity to interpret oneself *falsely*. That is why we question the body and reject the evidence of the sharpened senses: we try, if you like, to see whether the inferior parts themselves cannot enter into communication with us....

Against Causalism

§545 (1885)

I believe in absolute space as the substratum of force: the latter limits and forms. Time eternal. But space and time do not exist in themselves. "Changes" are only appearances (or sense processes for us); if we posit the recurrence of these, however regular, nothing is established thereby except this simple fact, that it has always happened thus. The feeling that *post hoc* is *propter hoc* can easily be shown to be a misunderstanding; it is comprehensible. But appearances cannot be "causes"!

§546 (1885–1886)

The interpretation of an event as either an act or the suffering of an act (– thus every act a suffering) says: every change, every becoming-other, presupposes an author and someone upon whom "change" is effected.

§547 (1885–1886)

Psychological history of the concept "subject." The body, the thing, the "whole" construed by the eye, awaken the distinction between a deed and a doer; the doer, the cause of the deed, conceived ever more subtly, finally left behind the "subject."

§548 (1885–1886)

Our bad habit of taking a mnemonic, an abbreviative formula, to be an entity, finally as a cause, e.g. to say of lightning "it flashes." Or the little word "I." To make a kind of perspective in seeing the cause of seeing: that was what happened in the invention of the "subject," the "I"!

§549 (1885)

"Subject," "object," "attribute" – these distinctions are fabricated and are now imposed as a schematism upon all the apparent facts. The fundamental false observation is that I believe it is *I* who do something, suffer something, "have" something, "have" a quality.

§550 (1885–1886)

In every judgment there resides the entire, full, profound belief in subject and attribute, or in cause and effect (that is, as the assertion that every effect is an activity and that every activity presupposes an agent); and this latter belief is only a special case of the former, so there remains as the fundamental belief the belief that there are subjects, that everything that happens is related attributively to some subject.

I notice something and seek a reason for it; this means originally: I seek an intention in it, and above all someone who has intentions, a subject, a doer: every event a deed – formerly one saw intentions in all events, this is our oldest habit. Do animals also possess it? As living beings, must they not also rely on interpretations based on *themselves*? –

The question "why?" is always a question after the *causa finalis*,[9] after the "what for?" We have no "sense for the *causa efficiens*":[10] here Hume was right; habit (but not only that of the individual!) makes us expect that a certain often–observed occurrence will follow another: nothing more! That which gives the extraordinary firmness to our belief in causality is not the great habit of seeing one occurrence following another but our inability to interpret events otherwise than as events caused by intentions. It is belief in the living and thinking as the only effective force – in will, in intention – it is belief that every event is a deed, that every deed presupposes a doer, it is belief in the "subject." Is this belief in the concept of subject and attribute not a great stupidity?

Question: is intention the cause of an event? Or is that also illusion?

Is it not the event itself?

§551 (March–June 1888)

Critique of the concept "cause." – We have absolutely no experience of a cause; psychologically considered, we derive the entire concept from the subjective conviction that *we* are causes, namely, that the arm moves – But that is an error. We separate ourselves, the doers, from the deed, and we make use of this pattern everywhere – we seek a doer for every event. What is it we have done? We have misunderstood the feeling of strength, tension, resistance, a muscular feeling that is already the beginning of the act, as the cause, or we have taken the will to do this or that for a cause because the action follows upon it – cause, i.e. –

There is no such thing as "cause"; some cases in which it seemed to be given us, and in which we have projected it out of ourselves in order to understand an event, have been shown to be self-deceptions. Our "understanding of an event" has consisted in our inventing a subject which was made responsible for something that happens and for how it happens. We have combined our feeling of will, our feeling of "freedom," our feeling of responsibility and our intention to perform an act, into the concept "cause": *causa efficiens* and *causa finalis* are fundamentally one.

We believed that an effect was explained when a condition was detected in which the effect was already inherent. In fact, we invent all causes after the schema of the effect: the latter is known to us – Conversely, we are not in a position to predict of any thing what it will "effect." The thing, the subject, will, intention – all inherent in the conception "cause." We search for things in order to explain why something has changed. Even the atom is this kind of super-added "thing" and "primitive subject" –

At length we grasp that things – consequently atoms, too – effect nothing: because they do not exist at all – that the concept of causality is completely useless. – A necessary sequence of states does not imply a causal relationship between them (– that would mean making their effective capacity leap from 1 to 2, to 3, to 4, to 5). There are neither causes nor effects: Linguistically we do not know how to rid ourselves of them. But that does not matter. If I think of the muscle apart from its "effects," I negate it –

In summa: an event is neither effected nor does it effect. *Causa* is a capacity to produce effects that has been super-added to the events –

Interpretation by causality a deception – A "thing" is the sum of its effects, synthetically united by a concept, an image. In fact, science has emptied the concept causality of its content and retained it as a formula of an equation, in which it has become at bottom a matter of indifference on which side cause is placed and on which side effect. It is asserted that in two complex states (constellations of force) the quanta of force remain constant.

The *calculability of an event* does not reside in the fact that a rule is adhered to, or that a necessity is obeyed, or that a law of causality has been projected by us into every event: it resides in the *recurrence of "identical cases."*

There is no such thing as a sense of causality, as Kant thinks. One is surprised, one is disturbed, one desires something familiar to hold on to – As soon as we are shown something old in the new, we are calmed. The supposed instinct for causality is only fear of the unfamiliar and the attempt to discover something familiar in it – a search, not for causes, but for the familiar.

§552 (Spring–Fall 1887)

Against determinism and teleology. – From the fact that something ensues regularly and ensues calculably, it does not follow that it ensues *necessarily*. That a quantum of force determines and conducts itself in every particular case in one way and manner does not make it into an "unfree will." "Mechanical necessity" is not a fact: it is we who first interpreted it into events. We have interpreted the formulatable character of events as the consequence of a necessity that rules over events. But from the fact that I do a certain thing, it by no means follows that I am compelled to do it. Compulsion in things certainly cannot be demonstrated: the rule proves only that one and the same event is not another event as well. Only because we have introduced subjects, "doers," into things does it appear that all events are the consequences of compulsion exerted upon subjects – exerted by whom? again by a "doer." Cause and effect – a dangerous concept so long as one thinks of something that causes and something upon which an effect is produced.

a. Necessity is not a fact but an interpretation.

b. When one has grasped that the "subject" is not something that creates effects, but only a fiction, much follows.

It is only after the model of the subject that we have invented the reality of things and projected them into the medley of sensations. If we no longer believe in the effective subject, then belief also disappears in effective things, in reciprocation, cause and effect between those phenomena that we call things.

There also disappears, of course, the world of effective atoms: the assumption of which always depended on the supposition that one needed subjects.

At last, the "thing-in-itself" also disappears, because this is fundamentally the conception of a "subject-in-itself." But we have grasped that the subject is a fiction. The antithesis "thing-in-itself" and "appearance" is untenable; with that, however, the concept "appearance" also disappears.

c. If we give up the effective subject, we also give up the object upon which effects are produced. Duration, identity with itself, being are inherent neither in that which is called subject nor in that which is called object: they are complexes of events apparently durable in comparison with other complexes – e.g. through the difference in tempo of the event (rest – motion, firm – loose: opposites that do not exist in themselves and that actually express

only variations in degree that from a certain perspective appear to be opposites. There are no opposites: only from those of logic do we derive the concept of opposites – and falsely transfer it to things).

d. If we give up the concept "subject" and "object," then also the concept "substance" – and as a consequence also the various modifications of it, e.g. "matter," "spirit," and other hypothetical entities, "the eternity and immutability of matter," etc. We have got rid of *materiality*.

From the standpoint of morality, the world is false. But to the extent that morality itself is a part of this world, morality is false.

Will to truth is a making firm, a making true and durable, an abolition of the false character of things, a reinterpretation of it into beings. "Truth" is therefore not something there, that might be found or discovered – but something that must be created and that gives a name to a process, or rather to a will to overcome that has in itself no end – introducing truth, as a *processus in infinitum*, an active determining – not a becoming-conscious of something that is in itself firm and determined. It is a word for the "will to power."

Life is founded upon the premise of a belief in enduring and regularly recurring things; the more powerful life is, the wider must be the knowable world to which we, as it were, attribute being. Logicizing, rationalizing, systematizing as expedients of life.

Man projects his drive to truth, his "goal" in a certain sense, outside himself as a world that has being, as a metaphysical world, as a "thing-in-itself," as a world already in existence. His needs as creator invent the world upon which he works, anticipate it; this anticipation (this "belief" in truth) is his support.

Notes

1 From the viewpoint of eternity. (Trans.)

2 The school of Parmenides of Elea (fifth century BC), who denied the logical possibility of change and motion and argued that the only logical possibility was unchanging being. (Trans.)

3 The cause of itself. (Trans.)

4 The most real being. (Trans.)

5 The truth = *Wahrheit*, corresponding to *wahre Welt* = real world. (Trans.)

6 I.e. Kantian, from the northerly German city in which Kant was born and in which he lived and died. (Trans.)

7 Here meaning empiricism, philosophy founded on observation and experiment. (Trans.)

8 Zarathustra begins. (Trans.)

9 Final cause or purpose. (Trans.)

10 Efficient cause. (Trans.)

Friedrich Nietzsche

Select Bibliography

Basic Writings of Nietzsche. Translated and edited by Walter Kaufmann. New York: Modern Library, 1992.

Beyond Good and Evil: Prelude to a Philosophy of the Future. Translated by R. J. Hollingdale. London: Penguin Books, 1990.

The Birth of Tragedy; and The Case of Wagner. Translated by Walter Kaufmann. New York: Vintage Books, 1967.

The Gay Science, with a Prelude in Rhymes and an Appendix of Songs. Translated by Walter Kaufmann. New York: Random House, 1974.

Human, All Too Human: A Book for Free Spirits. Translated by R. J. Hollingdale. Cambridge: Cambridge University Press, 1996.

A Nietzsche Reader. Translated by R. J. Hollingdale. Harmondsworth: Penguin Books, 1977.

On the Genealogy of Morals. Translated by Walter Kaufmann and R. J. Hollingdale. New York: Vintage Books, 1989.

Philosophy and Truth: Selections from Nietzsche's Notebooks of the Early 1870s. Translated and edited by Daniel Breazeale. Atlantic Highlands, NJ: Humanities Press, 1979.

The Portable Nietzsche. Translated by Walter Kaufmann. New York: Penguin Books, 1986.

Thus Spoke Zarathustra: A Book for Everyone and No One. Translated by R. J. Hollingdale. Harmondsworth: Penguin Books, 1975.

Twilight of the Idols and The Anti-Christ. Translated by R. J. Hollingdale. London: Penguin Books, 1990.

The Will to Power. Translated by Walter Kaufmann and R. J. Hollingdale. Edited by Walter Kaufmann. New York: Random House, 1968.

4

Henri Bergson

French philosopher Henri Bergson (1859–1941) was a professor at the Collège de France from 1900–21, and received the Nobel Prize for literature in 1927. Bergson was interested in the intrinsic dynamism of life, and was opposed to mechanistic schemas of explanation which, he argued, reify and abstract the concrete vitality of existence. His philosophical studies were directed largely toward the phenomena of time, freedom, and evolution, and led him to posit a nonmaterial *élan vital* or "vital impetus" as the basic force of all life. The following piece, the second of two lectures on the nature of change and duration, exhibits Bergson's characteristic nontechnical style. Here, Bergson argues that the habits of our perception tend to break up change into "states," and it is in terms of these spatialized images that we ordinarily understand time. Against this, Bergson proposes the seemingly paradoxical theses that there is change, but no underlying things that change, and that "real duration is what we have always called time."

The Perception of Change

. . . I am going to ask you to make a strenuous effort to put aside some of the artificial schema we interpose unknowingly between reality and us. What is required is that we should break with certain habits of thinking and perceiving that have become natural to us. We must return to the direct perception of change and mobility. Here is an immediate result of this effort. *We shall think of all change, all movement, as being absolutely indivisible.*

From *An Introduction to Metaphysics* (Totowa, NJ: Littlefield, Adams, 1975). Copyright © 1975. Reprinted by permission of Littlefield Publishers.

Let us begin with movement. I have my hand at point *A*. I move it over to point *B*, traversing the interval *AB*. I say that this movement from *A* to *B* is by nature simple.

But of this each one of us has the immediate sensation. No doubt while we are moving our hand from *A* to *B* we say to ourselves that we could stop it at an intermediary point, but in that case we should not have to do with the same movement. There would no longer be a single movement from *A* to *B*; there would be, by hypothesis, two movements, with an interval. Neither from within, through the muscular sense, nor from without through sight, should we still have the same perception. If I leave my movement from A to B as it is, I feel it undivided and must declare it to be indivisible.

It is true that, when I watch my hand going from A to B and describing the interval AB, I say: "The interval AB can be divided into as many parts as I wish, therefore the movement from A to B can be divided into as many parts as I like, since this movement is applied exactly upon this interval." Or again: "At each instant of its trajection, the mobile passes through a certain point, therefore one can distinguish in the movement as many stages as one likes, therefore the movement is infinitely divisible." But let us reflect for a moment. How could the movement *be applied upon* the space it traverses? How can something moving coincide with something immobile? How could the moving object *be* in a point of its trajectory passage? It *passes through*, or in other terms, it *could be there*. It would be there if it stopped; but if it should stop there, it would no longer be the same movement we were dealing with. It is always by a single bound that a passing is completed, when there is no break in the passage. The bound may last a few seconds, or days, months, years: it matters little. The moment it is one single bound, it is indecomposable. Only, once the passage is effected, as the trajectory is space and space is indefinitely divisible, we imagine that movement itself is indefinitely divisible. We like to imagine it because, in a movement, it is not the change of position which interests us, it is the positions themselves, the one the movement has left, the one it will take, the one it would take if it stopped on the way. We need immobility, and the more we succeed in imagining movement as coinciding with the immobilities of the points of space through which it passes, the better we think we understand it. To tell the truth, there never is real immobility, if we understand by that an absence of movement. Movement is reality itself, and what we call immobility is a certain state of things analogous to that produced when two trains move at the same speed, in the same direction, on parallel tracks: each of the two trains is then immovable to the travelers seated in the other. But a situation of this kind which, after all, is exceptional, seems to us to be the regular and normal situation, because it is what permits us to act upon things and also permits things to act upon us: the travelers in the two trains can hold out their hands to one another through the door and talk to one another only if they are "immobile," that is to say, if they are going in the

same direction at the same speed. "Immobility" being the prerequisite for our action, we set it up as a reality, we make of it an absolute, and we see in movement something which is superimposed. Nothing is more legitimate in practice. But when we transport this habit of mind into the domain of speculation, we fail to recognize the true reality, we deliberately create insoluble problems, we close our eyes to what is most living in the real.

I need not recall the arguments of Zeno of Elea. They all involve the confusion of movement with the space covered, or at least the conviction that one can treat movement as one treats space, divide it without taking account of its articulations. Achilles, they say, will never overtake the tortoise he is pursuing, for when he arrives at the point where the tortoise was the latter will have had time to go further, and so on indefinitely. Philosophers have refuted this argument in numerous ways, and ways so difficult that each of these refutations deprives the others of the right to be considered definitive. There would have been, nevertheless, a very simple means of making short work of the difficulty: that would have been to question Achilles. For since Achilles finally catches up to the tortoise and even passes it, he must know better than anyone else how he goes about it. The ancient philosopher who demonstrated the possibility of movement by walking was right: his only mistake was to make the gesture without adding a commentary. Suppose then we ask Achilles to comment on his race: here, doubtless, is what he will answer: "Zeno insists that I go from the point where I am to the point the tortoise has left, from that point to the next point it has left, etc., etc.; that is his procedure for making me run. But I go about it otherwise. I take a first step, then a second, and so on: finally, after a certain number of steps, I take a last one by which I skip ahead of the tortoise. I thus accomplish a series of indivisible acts. My course is the series of these acts. You can distinguish its parts by the number of steps it involves. But you have not the right to disarticulate it according to another law, or to suppose it articulated in another way. To proceed as Zeno does is to admit that the race can be arbitrarily broken up like the space which has been covered; it is to believe that the passage is in reality applied to the trajectory; it is making movement and immobility coincide and consequently confusing one with the other."

But that is precisely what our usual method consists in. We argue about movement as though it were made of immobilities and, when we look at it, it is with immobilities that we reconstitute it. Movement for us is a position, then another position, and so on indefinitely. We say, it is true, that there must be something else, and that from one position to another there is the *passage* by which the interval is cleared. But as soon as we fix our attention on this passage, we immediately make of it a series of positions, even though we still admit that between two successive positions one must indeed assume a passage. We put this passage off indefinitely the moment we have to consider it. We admit that it exists, we give it a name; that is enough for us: once that point has been satisfactorily settled we turn to the positions preferring to deal with them alone. We have an instinctive fear of those difficulties which the vision of movement as movement would arouse in our thought; and quite rightly, once we have loaded movement down with immobilities. If movement is not everything, it is nothing; and if to begin with we have supposed that immobility can be a reality, movement will slip through our fingers when we think we have it.

I have spoken of movement; but I could say the same for any change whatever. All real change is an indivisible change. We like to treat it as a series of distinct states which form, as it were, a line in time. That is perfectly natural. If change is continuous in us and also in things, on the other hand, in order that the uninterrupted change which each of us calls "me" may act upon the uninterrupted change that we call a "thing," these two changes must find themselves, with regard to one another, in a situation like that of the two trains referred to above. We say, for example, that an object changes color, and that change here consists in a series of shades which would be the constitutive elements of change and which, themselves, would not change. But in the first place, if each shade has any objective existence at all, it is an infinitely rapid oscillation, it is change. And in the second place, the perception we have of it, to the extent that it is subjective, is only an isolated, abstract aspect of the general state of our person, and this state as a whole is constantly changing and causing this so-called invariable perception to participate in its change; in fact, there is no perception which is not constantly being modified. So that color, outside of us, is mobility itself, and our own person is also mobility. But the whole mechanism of our perception of things, like the mechanism of our action upon things has been regulated in such a way as to bring about, between the external and the internal mobility, a situation comparable to that of our two trains – more complicated, perhaps, but of the same kind: when the two changes, that of the object and that of the subject, take place under particular conditions, they produce the particular appearance that we call a "state." And once in possession of "states," our mind recomposes change with them. I repeat, there is nothing more natural: the breaking up of change into states enables us to act upon things, and it is useful in a practical sense to be interested in the states rather than in the change itself. But what is favorable to action in this case would be fatal to speculation. If you imagine a change as being really composed of states, you at once cause insoluble metaphysical problems to arise. They deal only with appearances. You have closed your eyes to true reality.

I shall not press the point. Let each of us undertake the experiment, let him give himself the direct vision of a change, of a movement: he will have a feeling of absolute indivisibility. I come then to the second point, closely allied to the first. *There are changes, but there are underneath the change no things which change: change has no need of a support. There are movements, but there is no inert or invariable object which moves: movement does not imply a mobile.*

It is difficult to picture things in this way, because the sense *par excellence* is the sense of sight, and because the eye has developed the habit of separating, in the visual field, the relatively invariable figures which are then supposed to change place without changing form, movement is taken as super-added to the mobile as an accident. It is, in fact, useful to have to deal in daily life with objects which are stable and, as it were, responsible, to which one can address oneself as to persons. The sense of sight contrives to take things in this way: as an advance-guard for the sense of touch, it prepares our action upon the external world. But we already have less difficulty in perceiving movement and change as independent realities if we appeal to the sense of hearing. Let us listen to a melody, allowing ourselves to be lulled by it: do we not have the clear perception of a movement which is not attached to a mobile, of a change without anything changing? This change is enough, it is the thing itself. And even if it takes time, it is still indivisible; if the melody stopped sooner it would no longer be the same sonorous whole, it would be another, equally indivisible. We have, no doubt, a tendency to divide it and to picture, instead of the uninterrupted continuity of melody, a juxtaposition of distinct notes. But why?

Because we are thinking of the discontinuous series of efforts we should be making to recompose approximately the sound heard if we were doing the singing, and also because our auditory perception has acquired the habit of absorbing visual images. We therefore listen to the melody through the vision which an orchestra-leader would have of it as he watched its score. We picture notes placed next to one another upon an imaginary piece of paper. We think of a keyboard upon which some one is playing, of the bow going up and down, of the musicians, each one playing his part along with the others. If we do not dwell on these spatial images, pure change remains, sufficient unto itself, in no way divided, in no way attached to a "thing" which changes.

Let us come back, then, to the sense of sight. In further concentrating our attention upon it we perceive that even here movement does not demand a vehicle nor change a substance in the ordinary meaning of the word. A suggestion of this vision of material things already comes to us from physical science. The more it progresses the more it resolves matter into actions moving through space, into movements dashing back and forth in a constant vibration so that mobility becomes reality itself. No doubt science begins by assigning a support to this mobility. But as it advances, the support recedes; masses are pulverized into molecules, molecules into atoms, atoms into electrons or corpuscles: finally, the support assigned to movement appears merely as a convenient schema – a simple concession on the part of the scholar to the habits of our visual imagination. But there is no need to go so far. What is the "mobile" to which our eye attaches movement as to a vehicle? Simply a colored spot which we know perfectly well amounts, in itself, to a series of extremely rapid vibrations. This alleged movement of a thing is in reality only a movement of movements.

But nowhere is the *substantiality* of change so visible, so palpable as in the domain of the inner life. Difficulties and contradictions of every kind to which the theories of personality have led come from our having imagined, on the one hand, a series of distinct psychological states, each one invariable, which would produce the variations of the ego by their very succession, and on the other hand an ego, no less invariable, which would serve as support for them. How could this unity and this multiplicity meet? How, without either of them having duration – the first because change is something super-added, the second because it is made

up of elements which do not change – how could they constitute an ego which endures? But the truth is that there is neither a rigid, immovable substratum nor distinct states passing over it like actors on a stage. There is simply the continuous melody of our inner life – a melody which is going on and will go on, indivisible, from the beginning to the end of our conscious existence. Our personality is precisely that.

This indivisible continuity of change is precisely what constitutes true duration. I cannot here enter into the detailed examination of a question I have dealt with elsewhere. I shall confine myself therefore to saying, in reply to those for whom this "real duration" is something inexpressible and mysterious, that it is the clearest thing in the world: *real duration* is what we have always called *time*, but time perceived as indivisible. That time implies succession I do not deny. But that succession is first presented to our consciousness, like the distinction of a "before" and "after" set side by side, is what I cannot admit. When we listen to a melody we have the purest impression of succession we could possibly have – an impression as far removed as possible from that of simultaneity – and yet it is the very continuity of the melody and the impossibility of breaking it up which make that impression upon us. If we cut it up into distinct notes, into so many "befores" and "afters," we are bringing spatial images into it and impregnating the succession with simultaneity: in space, and only in space, is there a clear-cut distinction of parts external to one another. I recognize moreover that it is in spatialized time that we ordinarily place ourselves. We have no interest in listening to the uninterrupted humming of life's depths. And yet, that is where real duration is. Thanks to it, the more or less lengthy changes we witness within us and in the external world, take place in a single identical time.

Thus, whether it is a question of the internal or the external, of ourselves or of things, reality is mobility itself. That is what I was expressing when I said that there is change, but that there are not things which change.

Before the spectacle of this universal mobility there may be some who will be seized with dizziness. They are accustomed to terra firma; they cannot get used to the rolling and pitching. They must have "fixed" points to which they can attach thought and existence. They think that if everything passes, nothing exists; and that if reality is mobility, it has already ceased to exist at the moment one thinks it – it eludes thought. The material world, they say, is going to disintegrate, and the mind will drown in the torrent-like flow of things. – Let them be reassured! Change, if they consent to look directly at it without an interposed veil, will very quickly appear to them to be the most substantial and durable thing possible. Its solidity is infinitely superior to that of a fixity which is only an ephemeral arrangement between mobilities. I have come, in fact, to the third point to which I should like to draw your attention.

It is this: if change is real and even constitutive of reality, we must envisage the past quite differently from what we have been accustomed to doing through philosophy and language. We are inclined to think of our past as inexistent, and philosophers encourage this natural tendency in us. For them and for us the present alone exists by itself: if something of the past does survive it can only be because of help given it by the present, because of some act of charity on the part of the present, in short – to get away from metaphor – by the intervention of a certain particular function called memory, whose role is presumed to be to preserve certain parts of the past, for which exception is made, by storing them away in a kind of box. – This is a profound mistake! A useful one, I admit, perhaps necessary to action, but fatal to speculation. One could find in it, "in a nutshell" as you say, most of the illusions capable of vitiating philosophical thought.

Let us reflect for a moment on this "present" which alone is considered to have existence. What precisely is the present? If it is a question of the present instant – I mean, of a mathematical instant which would be to time what the mathematical point is to the line – it is clear that such an instant is a pure abstraction, an aspect of the mind; it cannot have real existence. You could never create time out of such instants any more than you could make a line out of mathematical points. Even if it does exist, how could there be an instant anterior to it? The two instants could not be separated by an interval of time since, by hypothesis, you reduce time to a juxtaposition of instants. Therefore they would not be separated by anything, and consequently they would be only one: two mathematical points which touch are identical. But let us put such subtleties aside. Our consciousness tells us that when we speak of our present we are thinking of a certain interval of duration. What duration? It is impossible to fix it exactly, as it is something rather elusive. My present, at this moment, is the sentence

I am pronouncing. But it is so because I want to limit the field of my attention to my sentence. This attention is something that can be made longer or shorter, like the interval between the two points of a compass. For the moment, the points are just far enough apart to reach from the beginning to the end of my sentence; but if the fancy took me to spread them further my present would embrace, in addition to my last sentence, the one that preceded it: all I should have had to do is to adopt another punctuation. Let us go further: an attention which could be extended indefinitely would embrace, along with the preceding sentence, all the anterior phrases of the lecture and the events which preceded the lecture, and as large a portion of what we call our past as desired. The distinction we make between our present and past is therefore, if not arbitrary, at least relative to the extent of the field which our attention to life can embrace. The "present" occupies exactly as much space as this effort. As soon as this particular attention drops any part of what it held beneath its gaze, immediately that portion of the present thus dropped becomes *ipso facto* a part of the past. In a word, our present falls back into the past when we cease to attribute to it an immediate interest. What holds good for the present of individuals holds also for the present of nations: an event belongs to the past, and enters into history when it is no longer of any direct interest to the politics of the day and can be neglected without the affairs of the country being affected by it. As long as its action makes itself felt, it adheres to the life of a nation and remains present to it.

Consequently nothing prevents us from carrying back as far as possible the line of separation between our present and our past. An attention to life, sufficiently powerful and sufficiently separated from all practical interest, would thus include in an undivided present the entire past history of the conscious person – not as instantaneity, not like a cluster of simultaneous parts, but as something continually present which would also be something continually moving: such, I repeat, is the melody which one perceives as indivisible, and which constitutes, from one end to the other – if we wish to extend the meaning of the word – a perpetual present, although this perpetuity has nothing in common with immutability, or this indivisibility with instantaneity. What we have is a present which endures.

That is not a hypothesis. It happens in exceptional cases that the attention suddenly loses the interest it had in life: immediately, as though by magic, the past once more becomes present. In people who see the threat of sudden death unexpectedly before them, in the mountain climber falling down a precipice, in drowning men, in men being hanged, it seems that a sharp conversion of the attention can take place – something like a change of orientation of the consciousness which, up until then turned toward the future and absorbed by the necessities of action, suddenly loses all interest in them. That is enough to call to mind a thousand different "forgotten" details and to unroll the whole history of the person before him in a moving panorama.

Memory therefore has no need of explanation. Or rather, there is no special faculty whose role is to retain quantities of past in order to pour it into the present. The past preserves itself automatically. Of course, if we shut our eyes to the indivisibility of change, to the fact that our most distant past adheres to our present and constitutes with it a single and identical uninterrupted change, it seems that the past is normally what is abolished and that there is something extraordinary about the preservation of the past: we think ourselves obliged to conjure up an apparatus whose function would be to record the parts of the past capable of reappearing in our consciousness.

But if we take into consideration the continuity of the inner life and consequently of its indivisibility, we no longer have to explain the preservation of the past, but rather its apparent abolition. We shall no longer have to account for remembering, but for forgetting. The explanation moreover will be found in the structure of the brain. Nature has invented a mechanism for canalizing our attention in the direction of the future, in order to turn it away from the past – I mean of that part of our history which does not concern our present actions – in order to bring to it at most, in the form of "memories," one simplification or another of anterior experience, destined to complete the experience of the moment; it is in this that the function of the brain consists. We cannot here undertake the discussion of that theory which claims that the brain is useful for the preservation of the past, that it stores up memories like so many photographic plates from which we afterward develop proofs, or like so many phonograms destined to become sounds again. We have examined this thesis elsewhere. This doctrine was largely inspired by a certain metaphysics with which contemporary psychology and psycho–physiology are imbued,

and which one accepts naturally: this accounts for its apparent clarity. But as we consider it more closely, we see what difficulties and impossibilities accumulate in it. Let us take the case most favorable to the thesis, that of a material object making an impression on the eye and leaving a visual memory in the mind. What can this memory possibly be, if it is really the result of the fixation in the brain of the impression received by the eye? The slightest movement on the part of the object or the eye and there would be not one image but ten, a hundred, a thousand images, as many and more than on a cinematographic film. Were the object merely considered for a certain time, or seen at various moments, the different images of that object could be counted by millions. And we have taken the simplest example! Let us suppose all those images are stored up; what good will they serve? which one shall we use? Let us grant that we have our reasons for choosing one of them, why, and how, shall we throw it back into the past when we perceive it? But to pass over these difficulties, how shall we explain the diseases of the memory? In those diseases which correspond to local lesions of the brain, that is in the various forms of aphasia, the psychological lesion consists less in an abolition of the memories than in an ability to recall them. An effort, an emotion, can bring suddenly to consciousness words believed definitely lost. These facts, with many others, unite to prove that in such cases the brain's function is to choose from the past, to diminish it, to simplify it, to utilize it, but not to preserve it. We should have no trouble in looking upon things from this angle if we had not acquired the habit of believing that the past is abolished. Then its partial reappearance creates the effect of an extraordinary event which demands an explanation. And that is why we imagine here and there in the brain, memory "pigeon-holes" for preserving fragments of the past – the brain moreover, being self-preserving. As though that were not postponing the difficulty and simply putting off the problem! As though, by positing that cerebral matter is preserved through time, or more generally that all matter endures, one did not attribute to it precisely the memory one claimed to explain by it! Whatever we do, even if we imagine that the brain stores up memories, we do not escape the conclusion that the past can preserve itself automatically.

This holds not only for our own past, but also for the past of any change whatsoever, always providing that it is a question of a single and therefore indivisible change: the preservation of the past in the present is nothing else than the indivisibility of change. It is true that, with regard to the changes which take place outside of us we almost never know whether we are dealing with a single change or one composed of several movements interspersed with stops (the stop never being anything but relative). We would have to be inside beings and things as we are inside ourselves before we could express our opinion on this point. But that is not where the importance lies. It is enough to be convinced once and for all that reality is change, that change is indivisible, and that in an indivisible change the past is one with the present.

Let us imbibe this truth and we shall see a good many philosophical enigmas melt away and evaporate. Certain great problems such as that of substance, of change, and of their relation to one another, will no longer arise. All the difficulties raised around these points – difficulties which caused substance to recede little by little to the regions of the unknowable – came from the fact that we shut our eyes to the indivisibility of change. If change, which is evidently constitutive of all our experience, is the fleeting thing most philosophers have spoken of, if we see in it only a multiplicity of states replacing other states, we are obliged to re-establish the continuity between these states by an artificial bond; but this immobile substratum of immobility, being incapable of possessing any of the attributes we know – since all are changes – recedes as we try to approach it: it is as elusive as the phantom of change it was called upon to fix. Let us, on the contrary, endeavor to perceive change as it is in its natural indivisibility: we see that it is the very substance of things, and neither does movement appear to us any longer under the vanishing form which rendered it elusive to thought, nor substance with the immutability which made it inaccessible to our experience. Radical instability and absolute immutability are therefore mere abstract views taken from outside of the continuity of real change, abstractions which the mind then hypostasizes into multiple *states* on the one hand, into *thing* or substance on the other. The difficulties raised by the ancients around the question of movement and by the moderns around the question of substance disappear, the former because movement and change are substantial, the latter because substance is movement and change.

At the same time that theoretical obscurities disappear we get a glimpse of the possible solution of more than one reputedly unsolvable problem.

The discussions on the subject of free will would come to an end if we saw ourselves where we are really, in a concrete duration where the idea of necessary determination loses all significance, since in it the past becomes identical with the present and continuously creates with it – if only by the fact of being added to it – something absolutely new. And we could gradually acquire a deeper appreciation of the relation of man to the universe if we took into account the true nature of *states*, of *qualities*, in fact of everything which presents itself to us with the appearance of stability. In such a case the object and the subject should be, with regard to one another, in a situation analogous to that of the two trains we spoke of at the beginning: it is a certain regulating of mobility on mobility which produces the effect of immobility. Let us then become imbued with this idea, let us never lose sight of the particular relation of the object to the subject translated by a static vision of things: everything that experience teaches us of the one will increase the knowledge we had of the other, and the light the latter receives will in turn be able, by reflection, to illuminate the former.

But as I said in the beginning, pure speculation will not be the only thing to benefit by this vision of universal becoming. We shall be able to make it penetrate into our everyday life, and through it, obtain from philosophy satisfactions similar to those we receive from art, but more frequent, more continual and more accessible to the majority of men. Art enables us, no doubt, to discover in things more qualities and more shades than we naturally perceive. It dilates our perception, but on the surface rather than in depth. It enriches our present, but it scarcely enables us to go beyond it. Through philosophy we can accustom ourselves never to isolate the present from the past which it pulls along with it. Thanks to philosophy, all things acquire depth – more than depth, something like a fourth dimension which permits anterior perceptions to remain bound up with present perceptions, and the immediate future itself to become partly outlined in the present. Reality no longer appears then in the static state, in its manner of being; it affirms itself dynamically, in the continuity and variability of its tendency. What was immobile and frozen in our perception is warmed and set in motion. Everything comes to life around us, everything is revivified in us. A great impulse carries beings and things along. We feel ourselves uplifted, carried away, borne along by it. We are more fully alive and this increase of life brings with it the conviction that grave philosophical enigmas can be resolved or even perhaps that they need not be raised, since they arise from a frozen vision of the real and are only the translation, in terms of thought, of a certain artificial weakening of our vitality. In fact, the more we accustom ourselves to think and to perceive all things *sub specie dur-* *ationis*, the more we plunge into real duration. And the more we immerse ourselves in it, the more we set ourselves back in the direction of the principle, though it be transcendent, in which we participate and whose eternity is not to be an eternity of immutability, but an eternity of life: how, otherwise, could we live and move in it? *In ea vivimus et movemur et sumus.*

Select Bibliography

An Introduction to Metaphysics. Totowa, NJ: Littlefield, Adams, 1975.

Creative Evolution. Translated by Arthur Mitchell. Lanham, Md.: University Press of America, 1984.

The Creative Mind. Translated by Mabelle L. Andison. New York: Greenwood Press, 1968.

Laughter. Baltimore: Johns Hopkins University Press, 1980.

Matter and Memory. Translated by Nancy Margaret Paul and W. Scott Palmer. New York: Zone Books, 1988.

Mind-Energy: Lectures and Essays. Translated by H. Wildon Carr. Westport, Conn.: Greenwood Press, 1975.

Time and Free Will: An Essay on the Immediate Data of Consciousness. Translated by F. L. Pogson. New York: Humanities Press, 1971.

The Two Sources of Morality and Religion. Translated by R. Ashley Audra and Cloudesley Brereton, with W. Horsfall Carter. Notre Dame, Ind.: University of Notre Dame Press, 1977.

The World of Dreams. Translated by Wade Baskin. New York: Philosophical Library, 1958.

5

Edmund Husserl

Regarded as the founder of modern phenomenology, Edmund Husserl (1859–1938) was a pupil of Franz Brentano (1838–1917) and adopted the latter's thesis that all consciousness is by its very nature intentional, that is, directed toward some object. Husserl's phenomenology is concerned with phenomena as they appear to consciousness; it may study the intentional acts of consciousness, or the content of such acts. In each case, phenomenology – which for Husserl is conceived as a pure and rigorous science – directs its study toward consciousness, and suspends our natural attitude toward the world. Whereas the natural attitude is directed toward things and states of affairs, the phenomenologist brackets questions concerning the ultimate reality or intrinsic truth of objects and shifts his or her view solely to the way things appear to consciousness. In the following reflections from *Cartesian Meditations* (an elaboration of two lectures from 1929 intended as an introduction to transcendental phenomenology), Husserl argues that Descartes' *ego cogito*, when conceived in its full phenomenological import, must be understood as the epoch-making discovery of transcendental subjectivity.

Cartesian Meditations

Introduction

§1 Descartes' Meditations *as the prototype of philosophical reflection*

I have particular reason for being glad that I may talk about transcendental phenomenology in this,

From *Cartesian Meditations*, translated by Dorion Cairns (The Hague: Martinus Nijhoff, 1960), pp. 1–26. Copyright 1960 by Martinus Nijhoff, The Hague, Netherlands. Reprinted with kind permission from Kluwer Academic Publishers.

the most venerable abode of French science.[1] France's greatest thinker, René Descartes, gave transcendental phenomenology new impulses through his *Meditations*; their study acted quite directly on the transformation of an already developing phenomenology into a new kind of transcendental philosophy. Accordingly one might almost call transcendental phenomenology a neo-Cartesianism, even though it is obliged – and precisely by its radical development of Cartesian motifs – to reject nearly all the well-known doctrinal content of the Cartesian philosophy.

That being the situation, I can already be assured of your interest if I start with those motifs in the *Meditationes de prima philosophia* that have, so I believe, an eternal significance and go on to characterize the transformations, and the novel formations, in which the method and problems of transcendental phenomenology originate.

Every beginner in philosophy knows the remarkable train of thoughts contained in the *Meditations*. Let us recall its guiding idea. The aim of the *Meditations* is a complete reforming of philosophy into a science grounded on an absolute foundation. That implies for Descartes a corresponding reformation of all the sciences, because in his opinion they are only non-selfsufficient members of the one all-inclusive science, and this is philosophy. Only within the systematic unity of philosophy can they develop into genuine sciences. As they have developed historically, on the other hand, they lack that scientific genuineness which would consist in their complete and ultimate grounding on the basis of absolute insights, insights behind which one cannot go back any further. Hence the need for a radical rebuilding that satisfies the idea of philosophy as the all-inclusive unity of the sciences, within the unity of such an absolutely rational grounding. With Descartes this demand gives rise to a philosophy turned toward the subject himself. The turn to the subject is made at two significant levels.

First, anyone who seriously intends to become a philosopher must "once in his life" withdraw into himself and attempt, within himself, to overthrow and build anew all the sciences that, up to then, he has been accepting. Philosophy – wisdom (*sagesse*) – is the philosophizer's quite personal affair. It must arise as *his* wisdom, as his self-acquired knowledge tending toward universality, a knowledge for which he can answer from the beginning, and at each step, by virtue of his own absolute insights. If I have decided to live with this as my aim – the decision that alone can start me on the course of a philosophical development – I have thereby chosen to begin in absolute poverty, with an absolute lack of knowledge. Beginning thus, obviously one of the first things I ought to do is reflect on how I might find a method for going on, a method that promises to lead to genuine knowing. Accordingly the Cartesian *Meditations* are not intended to be a merely private concern of the philosopher Descartes, to say nothing of their being merely an impressive literary form in which

to present the foundations of his philosophy. Rather they draw the prototype for any beginning philosopher's necessary meditations, the meditations out of which alone a philosophy can grow originally.[2]

When we turn to the content of the *Meditations*, so strange to us men of today, we find a regress to the philosophizing ego[3] in a second and deeper sense: the ego as subject of his pure *cogitationes*. The meditator executes this regress by the famous and very remarkable method of doubt. Aiming with radical consistency at absolute knowledge, he refuses to let himself accept anything as existent unless it is secured against every conceivable possibility of becoming doubtful. Everything that is certain, in his natural experiencing and thinking life, he therefore subjects to methodical criticism with respect to the conceivability of a doubt about it; and, by excluding everything that leaves open any possibility of doubt, he seeks to obtain a stock of things that are absolutely evident. When this method is followed, the certainty of sensuous experience, the certainty with which the world is given in natural living, does not withstand criticism; accordingly the being of the world must remain unaccepted at this initial stage. The meditator keeps only himself, *qua* pure ego of his *cogitationes*, as having an absolutely indubitable existence, as something that cannot be done away with, something that would exist even though this world were nonexistent. Thus reduced, the ego carries on a kind of solipsistic philosophizing. He seeks apodictically certain ways by which, within his own pure inwardness, an Objective[4] outwardness can be deduced. The course of the argument is well known: First God's existence and veracity are deduced and then, by means of them, Objective Nature, the duality of finite substances – in short, the Objective field of metaphysics and the positive sciences, and these disciplines themselves. All the various inferences proceed, as they must, according to guiding principles that are immanent, or "innate," in the pure ego....

First Meditation: The Way to the Transcendental Ego

§3 *The Cartesian overthrow and the guiding final idea of an absolute grounding of science*

And so we make a new beginning, each for himself and in himself, with the decision of philosophers who begin radically: that at first we shall put out of action all the convictions we have been accepting up to now, including all our sciences. Let the idea guiding our meditations be at first the Cartesian idea of a science that shall be established as radically genuine, ultimately an all-embracing science.

But, now that we no longer have at our disposal any already-given science as an example of radically genuine science (after all, we are not accepting any given science), what about the indubitability of that idea itself, the idea namely of a science that shall be grounded absolutely? Is it a legitimate final idea, the possible aim of some possible practice? Obviously that too is something we must not presuppose, to say nothing of taking any norms as already established for testing such possibilities – or perchance a whole system of norms in which the style proper to genuine science is allegedly prescribed. That would mean presupposing a whole logic as a theory of science; whereas logic must be included among the sciences overthrown in overthrowing all science. Descartes himself presupposed an ideal of science, the ideal approximated by geometry and mathematical natural science. As a fateful prejudice this ideal determines philosophies for centuries and hiddenly determines the *Meditations* themselves. Obviously it was, for Descartes, a truism from the start that the all-embracing science must have the form of a deductive system, in which the whole structure rests, *ordine geometrico*, on an axiomatic foundation that grounds the deduction absolutely. For him a role similar to that of geometrical axioms in geometry is played in the all-embracing science by the axiom of the ego's absolute certainty of himself, along with the axiomatic principles innate in the ego – only this axiomatic foundation lies even deeper than that of geometry and is called on to participate in the ultimate grounding even of geometrical knowledge.

None of that shall determine our thinking. As beginning philosophers we do not as yet accept any normative ideal of science; and only so far as we produce one newly for ourselves can we ever have such an ideal.

But this does not imply that we renounce the general aim of grounding science absolutely. That aim shall indeed continually motivate the course of our meditations, as it motivated the course of the Cartesian meditations; and gradually, in our meditations, it shall become determined concretely. Only we must be careful about how we make an absolute grounding of science our aim. At first we

must not presuppose even its possibility. How then are we to find the legitimate manner in which to make it our aim? How are we to make our aim perfectly assured, and thus assured as a practical possibility? How are we then to differentiate the possibility, into which at first we have a general insight, and thereby mark out the determinate methodical course of a genuine philosophy, a radical philosophy that begins with what is intrinsically first?

Naturally we get the general idea of science from the sciences that are factually given. If they have become for us, in our radical critical attitude, merely alleged sciences, then, according to what has already been said, their general final idea has become, in a like sense, a mere supposition. Thus we do not yet know whether that idea is at all capable of becoming actualized. Nevertheless we do have it in this form, and in a state of indeterminate fluid generality; accordingly we have also the idea of philosophy: as an idea about which we do not know whether or how it can be actualized. We take the general idea of science, therefore, as a precursory presumption, which we allow ourselves tentatively, by which we tentatively allow ourselves to be guided in our meditations. We consider how it might be thought out as a possibility and then consider whether and how it might be given determinate actualization. To be sure, we get into what are, at first, rather strange circumstantialities – but how can they be avoided, if our radicalness is not to remain an empty gesture but is to become an actual deed? Let us go on then with patience.

§4 *Uncovering the final sense of science by becoming immersed in science qua noematic phenomenon*

Obviously one of the first things we must do now is make distinct the guiding idea that, at the beginning, floats before us as a vague generality. The genuine concept of science, naturally, is not to be fashioned by a process of abstraction based on comparing the de facto sciences, i.e. the Objectively documented theoretical structures (propositions, theories) that are in fact generally accepted as sciences. The sense of our whole meditation implies that sciences, as these facts of Objective culture, and sciences "in the true and genuine sense" need not be identical and that the former, over and above being cultural facts, involve a claim, which ought to be established as one they already satisfy. Science as an idea – as the idea, genuine science – "lies," still undisclosed, precisely in this claim.

How can this idea be uncovered and apprehended? Even though we must not take any position with respect to the *validity* of the de facto sciences (the ones "claiming" validity) – i.e. with respect to the genuineness of their theories and, correlatively, the competence of their methods of theorizing – there is nothing to keep us from "immersing ourselves" in the scientific striving and doing that pertain to them, in order to see clearly and distinctly what is really being aimed at. If we do so, if we immerse ourselves progressively in the characteristic intention of scientific endeavor, the constituent parts of the general final idea, genuine science, become explicated for us, though at first the differentiation is itself general ....

§5 Evidence and the idea of genuine science

As we go on meditating in this manner and along this line, we beginning philosophers recognize that the Cartesian idea of a science (ultimately an all-embracing science) grounded on an absolute foundation, and absolutely justified, is none other than the idea that constantly furnishes guidance in all sciences and in their striving toward universality – whatever may be the situation with respect to a de facto actualization of that idea.

Evidence is, in an *extremely broad sense*, an "*experiencing*" of something that is, and is thus: it is precisely a mental seeing of something itself. Conflict with what evidence shows, with what "experience" shows, yields the negative of evidence (or negative evidence) – put in the form of a judgment: positive evidence of the affair's nonbeing. In other words, negative evidence has as its content evident falsity. Evidence, which in fact includes all experiencing in the usual and narrower sense, can be more or less perfect. *Perfect evidence* and its correlate, *pure and genuine truth*, are given as ideas lodged in the striving for knowledge, for fulfillment of one's meaning intention. By immersing ourselves in such a striving, we can extract those ideas from it. Truth and falsity, criticism and critical comparison with evident data, are an everyday theme, playing their incessant part even in prescientific life. For this everyday life, with its changing and relative purposes, relative evidences and truths suffice. But science looks for truths that are valid, and remain so, *once for all and for everyone*; accordingly it seeks verifications of a new kind,

verifications carried through to the end. Though de facto, as science itself must ultimately see, it does not attain actualization of a system of absolute truths, but rather is obliged to modify its "truths" again and again, it nevertheless follows the idea of absolute or scientifically genuine truth; and accordingly it reconciles itself to an infinite horizon of approximations, tending toward that idea. By them, science believes, it can surpass *in infinitum* not only everyday knowing but also itself; likewise however by its aim at systematic universality of knowledge, whether that aim concern a particular closed scientific province or a presupposed all-embracing unity of whatever exists – as it does if a "philosophy" is possible and in question. According to intention, therefore, the idea of science and philosophy involves an *order of cognition, proceeding from intrinsically earlier to intrinsically later cognitions*; ultimately, then, *a beginning and a line of advance* that are not to be chosen arbitrarily but have their basis "in the nature of things themselves."

Thus, by immersing ourselves meditatively in the general intentions of scientific endeavor, we discover fundamental parts of the final idea, genuine science, which, though vague at first, governs that striving. Meanwhile we have made no advance judgment in favor of the possibility of those components or in favor of a supposedly unquestionable scientific ideal ....

By this preliminary work, here roughly indicated rather than done explicitly, we have gained a measure of clarity sufficient to let us fix, for our whole further procedure, a *first methodological principle*. It is plain that I, as someone beginning philosophically, since I am striving toward the presumptive end, genuine science, must neither make nor go on accepting any judgment as scientific *that I have not derived from evidence*, from "experiences" in which the affairs and affair-complexes in question are present to me as "*they themselves*." Indeed, even then I must at all times reflect on the pertinent evidence; I must examine its "range" and make evident to myself *how far* that evidence, how far its "perfection," *the actual giving of the affairs themselves*, extends. Where this is still wanting, I must not claim any final validity, but must account my judgment as, at best, a possible intermediate stage on the way to final validity.

Because the sciences aim at predications that express completely and with evident fitness what is beheld pre-predicatively, it is obvious that I must be careful also about this aspect of scientific evidence. Owing to the instability and ambiguity of common language and its much too great complacency about completeness of expression, we require, even where we use its means of expression, a new legitimation of significations by orienting them according to accrued insights, and a fixing of words as expressing the significations thus legitimated. That too we account as part of our normative principle of evidence, which we shall apply consistently from now on.

But how would this principle, or all our meditation up to now, help us, if it gave us no hold for making an actual beginning, that is, for starting to actualize the idea of genuine science? Since the form belonging to a systematic order of cognitions – genuine cognitions – is part of this idea, there emerges, as the *question of the beginning*, the inquiry for those cognitions that are first in themselves and can support the whole storied edifice of universal knowledge. Consequently, if our presumptive aim is to be capable of becoming a practically possible one, we meditators, while completely destitute of all scientific knowledge, must have access to evidences that already bear the stamp of fitness for such a function, in that they are recognizable as preceding all other imaginable evidences. Moreover, in respect of this evidence of preceding, they must have a certain perfection, they must carry with them an absolute certainty, if advancing from them and constructing on their basis a science governed by the idea of a definitive system of knowledge – considering the infinity presumed to be part of this idea – is to be capable of having any sense.

§6 Differentiations of evidence. The philosophical demand for an evidence that is apodictic and first in itself

But here, at this decisive point in the process of beginning, we must penetrate deeper with our meditations. The phrase *absolute certainty* and the equivalent phrase *absolute indubitability* need clarifying. They call our attention to the fact that, on more precise explication, the ideally demanded *perfection of evidence becomes differentiated*. At the present introductory stage of philosophical meditation we have the boundless infinity of prescientific experiences, evidences: more or less perfect. With reference to them *imperfection*, as a rule, signifies *incompleteness*, a one-sidedness and at the same time a relative obscurity and indistinctness that qualify the givenness of the affairs themselves

or the affair-complexes themselves: i.e. an infectedness of the "experience" with *unfulfilled components*, with *expectant* and *attendant meanings*. Perfecting then takes place as a synthetic course of further harmonious experiences in which these attendant meanings become fulfilled in actual experience. The corresponding idea of perfection would be that of "*adequate evidence*" – and the question whether adequate evidence does not necessarily lie at infinity may be left open.

Though this idea continuously guides the scientist's intent, *a different perfection* of evidence has for him (as we see by the aforesaid process of "immersing ourselves" in his intent) a higher dignity. This perfection is "*apodicticity*"; and it can occur even in evidences that are inadequate. It is *absolute indubitability* in a quite definite and peculiar sense, the absolute indubitability that the scientist demands of all "*principles*"; and its superior value is evinced in his endeavor, where groundings already evident in and by themselves are concerned, to ground them further and at a higher level by going back to principles, and thereby to obtain for them the highest dignity, that of apodicticity. The fundamental nature of apodicticity can be characterized in the following manner:

Any evidence is a grasping of something itself that is, or is thus, a grasping in the mode "it itself," with full certainty of its being, a certainty that accordingly excludes every doubt. But it does not follow that full certainty excludes the conceivability that what is evident could subsequently become doubtful, or the conceivability that being could prove to be illusion – indeed, sensuous experience furnishes us with cases where that happens. Moreover, this open possibility of becoming doubtful, or of nonbeing, *in spite of evidence*, can always be recognized in advance by critical reflection on what the evidence in question does. An *apodictic* evidence, however, is not merely certainty of the affairs or affair-complexes (states-of-affairs) evident in it; rather it discloses itself, to a critical reflection, as having the signal peculiarity of being *at the same time the absolute unimaginableness* (inconceivability) of their *nonbeing*, and thus excluding in advance every doubt as "objectless," empty. Furthermore the evidence of that critical reflection likewise has the dignity of being apodictic, as does therefore the evidence of the unimaginableness of what is presented with apodictically evident certainty. And the same is true of every critical reflection at a higher level....

§7 The evidence for the factual existence of the world not apodictic; its inclusion in the Cartesian overthrow

The question of evidences that are first in themselves can apparently be answered without any trouble. Does not the *existence of the world* present itself forthwith as such an evidence? The life of everyday action relates to the world. All the sciences relate to it: the sciences of matters of fact relate to it immediately; the *a priori* sciences, mediately, as instruments of scientific method. More than anything else the being of the world is obvious. It is so very obvious that no one would think of asserting it expressly in a proposition. After all, we have our continuous experience in which this world incessantly stands before our eyes, as existing without question. But, however much this evidence is prior in itself to all the other evidences of life (as turned toward the world) and to all the evidences of all the world sciences (since it is the basis that continually supports them), we soon become doubtful about the extent to which, in this capacity, it can lay claim to being apodictic. And, if we follow up this doubt, it becomes manifest that our experiential evidence of the world lacks also the superiority of being the absolutely primary evidence. Concerning the first point, we note that the universal sensuous experience in whose evidence the world is continuously given to us beforehand is obviously not to be taken forthwith as an apodictic evidence, which, as such, would absolutely exclude both the possibility of eventual doubt whether the world is actual and the possibility of its nonbeing. Not only can a particular experienced thing suffer devaluation as an illusion of the senses; the whole unitarily surveyable nexus, experienced throughout a period of time, can prove to be an illusion, a coherent dream. We need not take the indicating of these possible and sometimes actual reversals of evidence as a sufficient criticism of the evidence in question and see in it a full proof that, in spite of the continual experiencedness of the world, a nonbeing of the world is conceivable. We shall retain only this much: that the evidence of world-experience would, at all events, need to be criticized with regard to its validity and range, before it could be used for the purposes of a radical grounding of science, and that therefore we must not take that evidence to be, without question, immediately apodictic. It follows that denying acceptance to all the sciences given us beforehand, treating them as, for us, inadmissible prejudices, is not enough. Their universal basis, the experienced world, must also be deprived of its naive acceptance. The being of the world, by reason of the evidence of natural experience, must no longer be for us an obvious matter of fact; it too must be for us, henceforth, only an acceptance-phenomenon.

If we maintain this attitude, is any being whatever left us as a basis for judgments, let alone for evidences on which we could establish an all-embracing philosophy and, furthermore, do so apodictically? Is not "the world" the name for the universe of whatever exists? If so, how can we avoid starting *in extenso*, and as our first task, that criticism of world-experience which, a moment ago, we merely indicated? Then, if criticism were to yield the result considered likely in advance, would not our whole philosophical aim be frustrated? But what if the world were, in the end, not at all the absolutely first basis for judgments and a being that is intrinsically prior to the world were the already presupposed basis for the existence of the world?

§8 The ego cogito *as transcendental subjectivity*

At this point, following Descartes, we make the great reversal that, if made in the right manner, leads to transcendental subjectivity: the turn to the *ego cogito* as the ultimate and apodictically certain basis for judgments, the basis on which any radical philosophy must be grounded.

Let us consider. As radically meditating philosophers, we now have neither a science that we accept nor a world that exists for us. Instead of simply existing for us – that is, being accepted naturally by us in our experiential believing in its existence – the world is for us only something that claims being. Moreover, that affects the intramundane existence of all other Egos, so that rightly we should no longer speak communicatively, in the plural. Other men than I, and brute animals, are data of experience for me only by virtue of my sensuous experience of their bodily organisms; and, since the validity of this experience too is called in question, I must not use it. Along with other Egos, naturally, I lose all the formations pertaining to sociality and culture. In short, not just corporeal Nature but the whole concrete surrounding life-world is for me, from now on, only a phenomenon of being, instead of something that is.

But, no matter what the status of this phenomenon's claim to actuality and no matter whether, at some future time, I decide critically that the world exists or that it is an illusion, still this phenomenon itself, as mine, is not nothing but is precisely what makes such critical decisions at all possible and accordingly makes possible whatever has for me sense and validity as "true" being – definitively decided or definitively decideable being. And besides: If I abstained – as I was free to do and as I did – and still abstain from every believing involved in or founded on sensuous experiencing, so that the being of the experienced world remains unaccepted by me, still this abstaining is what it is; and it exists, together with the whole stream of my experiencing life. Moreover, this life is continually there *for me*. Continually, in respect of a field of the present, it is given to consciousness perceptually, with the most originary originality, as it itself; memorially, now these and now those pasts thereof are "again" given to consciousness, and that implies: as the "pasts themselves." Reflecting, I can at any time look at this original living and note particulars; I can grasp what is present as present, what is past as past, each as itself. I do so now, as the Ego who philosophizes and exercises the aforesaid abstention.

Meanwhile the world experienced in this reflectively grasped life goes on being for me (in a certain manner) "experienced" as before, and with just the content it has at any particular time. It goes on appearing, as it appeared before; the only difference is that I, as reflecting philosophically, no longer keep in effect (no longer accept) the natural believing in existence involved in experiencing the world – though that believing too is still there and grasped by my noticing regard. The same is true of all the processes of meaning that, in addition to the world-experiencing ones, belong to my lifestream: the nonintuitive processes of meaning objects, the judgings, valuings, and decidings, the processess of setting ends and willing means, and all the rest, in particular the position-takings necessarily involved in them all when I am in the natural and nonreflective attitude – since precisely these position-takings always presuppose the world, i.e. involve believing in its existence. Here too the philosophically reflective Ego's abstention from position-takings, his depriving them of acceptance, does not signify their disappearance from his field of experience. The concrete subjective processes, let us repeat, are indeed the things to which his attentive regard is directed: but the attentive Ego, *qua* philosophizing Ego, practices abstention with respect to what he intuits. Likewise everything *meant* in such

accepting or positing processes of consciousness (the meant judgment, theory, value, end, or whatever it is) is still retained completely – but with the acceptance-modification, "mere phenomenon."

This universal depriving of acceptance, this "inhibiting" or "putting out of play" of all positions taken toward the already-given Objective world and, in the first place, all existential positions (those concerning being, illusion, possible being, being likely, probable, etc.), – or, as it is also called, this "phenomenological epoché" and "parenthesizing" of the Objective world – therefore does not leave us confronting nothing. On the contrary we gain possession of something by it; and what we (or, to speak more precisely, what I, the one who is meditating) acquire by it is my pure living, with all the pure subjective processes making this up, and everything meant in them, *purely as* meant in them: the universe of "phenomena" in the (particular and also the wider) phenomenological sense. The epoché can also be said to be the radical and universal method by which I apprehend myself purely; as Ego, and with my own pure conscious life, in and by which the entire Objective world exists for me and is precisely as it is for me. Anything belonging to the world, any spatiotemporal being, exists for me – that is to say, is accepted by me – in that I experience it, perceive it, remember it, think of it somehow, judge about it, value it, desire it, or the like. Descartes, as we know, indicated all that by the name *cogito*. The world is for me absolutely nothing else but the world existing for and accepted by me in such a conscious *cogito*. It gets its whole sense, universal and specific, and its acceptance as existing, exclusively from such *cogitationes*. In these my whole world-life goes on, including my scientifically inquiring and grounding life. By my living, by my experiencing, thinking, valuing, and acting, I can enter no world other than the one that gets its sense and acceptance or status [*Sinn und Geltung*] in and from me, myself. If I put myself above all this life and refrain from doing any believing that takes "the" world straightforwardly as existing – if I direct my regard exclusively to this life itself, as consciousness *of* "the" world – I thereby acquire myself as the pure ego, with the pure stream of my *cogitationes*.

Thus the being of the pure ego and his *cogitationes*, as a being that is prior in itself, is antecedent to the natural being of the world – the world of which I always speak, the one of which I *can* speak. Natural being is a realm whose existential status [*Seinsgeltung*] is secondary; it continually presupposes the realm of transcendental being. The fundamental phenomenological method of transcendental epoché, because it leads back to this realm, is called transcendental–phenomenological reduction.

§9 The range covered by apodictic evidence of the "I am"

The next question is whether this reduction makes possible an *apodictic* evidence of the being of transcendental subjectivity. Only if my experiencing of my transcendental self is apodictic can it serve as ground and basis for apodictic judgments; only then is there accordingly the prospect of a philosophy, a systematic structure made up of apodictic cognitions, starting with the intrinsically first field of experience and judgment. The *ego sum* or *sum cogitans* must be pronounced apodictic, and that accordingly we get a first apodictically existing basis to stand on, was already seen by Descartes. As we all know, he emphasizes the indubitability of that proposition and stresses the fact that "I doubt" would itself presuppose "I am." For Descartes too it is a matter of that Ego who grasps himself after he has deprived the experienced world of acceptance, because it might be doubtful. After our differentiations, it is clear that the sense of the indubitability with which the ego becomes given by transcendental reduction actually conforms to the concept of apodicticity we explicated earlier. To be sure, the problem of apodicticity – and consequently the problem of the primary basis on which to ground a philosophy – is not thereby removed. In fact, doubt arises immediately. For example: Does not transcendental subjectivity at any given moment include its past as an inseparable part, which is accessible only by way of memory? But can apodictic evidence be claimed for memory? Assuredly it would be wrong to deny the apodicticity of "I am," on the ground that the evidence of memory is not apodictic; such a denial is possible only if one confines oneself to arguing about that apodicticity – that is to say, if one shuts one's eyes to it. Nevertheless, in view of such questions, the problem of the range covered by our apodictic evidence becomes urgent.

We remember in this connexion an earlier remark: that *adequacy and apodicticity* of evidence *need not go hand in hand*. Perhaps this remark was made precisely with the case of transcendental self-experience in mind. In such experience the ego is accessible to himself *originaliter*. But at any parti-

cular time this experience offers only a core that is experienced "with strict adequacy," namely the ego's living present (which the grammatical sense of the sentence, *ego cogito*, expresses); while, beyond that, only an indeterminately general presumptive horizon extends, comprising what is strictly non–experienced but necessarily also meant. To it belongs not only the ego's past, most of which is completely obscure, but also his transcendental abilities and his habitual peculiarities at the time. External perception too (though not apodictic) is an experiencing of something itself, the physical thing itself: "it itself is there." But, in being there itself, the physical thing has for the experiencer an open, infinite, indeterminately general horizon, comprising what is itself not strictly perceived – a horizon (this is implicit as a presumption) that can be opened up by possible experiences. Something similar is true about the apodictic certainty characterizing transcendental experience of my transcendental I-am, with the indeterminate generality of the latter as having an open horizon. Accordingly the actual being of the intrinsically first field of knowledge is indeed assured absolutely, though not as yet what determines its being more particularly and is still not itself given, but only presumed, during the living evidence of the I-am. This presumption implicit in the apodictic evidence is subject therefore to criticism, regarding the possibilities of its fulfillment and their range (which may be apodictically determinable). How far can the transcendental ego be deceived about himself? And how far do those components extend that are absolutely indubitable, in spite of such possible deception?

When making certain of the transcendental ego, we are standing at an altogether dangerous point, even if at first we leave out of consideration the difficult question of apodicticity.

§10 Digression: Descartes' failure to make the transcendental turn

It seems so easy, following Descartes, to lay hold of the pure Ego and his *cogitationes*. And yet it is as though we were on the brink of a precipice, where advancing calmly and surely is a matter of philosophical life and death. Descartes had the serious will to free himself radically from prejudice. But we know from recent inquiries, in particular the fine and profound researches of Mr Gilson and Mr Koyré,[5] how much scholasticism lies hidden, as unclarified prejudice, in Descartes' *Meditations*.

Not only that. In the first place we must stay clear of the previously mentioned prejudice, arising from admiration of mathematical natural science and, as an old heritage, exercising a determining influence even on us: the prejudice that, under the name *ego cogito*, one is dealing with an apodictic "axiom," which, in conjunction with other axioms and, perhaps, inductively grounded hypotheses, is to serve as the foundation for a deductively "explanatory" world-science, a "nomological" science, a science *ordine geometrico*, similar indeed to mathematical natural science. In this connexion, furthermore, it must by no means be accepted as a matter of course that, with our apodictic pure ego, we have rescued a little *tag-end of the world*, as the sole unquestionable part of it for the philosophizing Ego, and that now the problem is to infer the rest of the world by rightly conducted arguments, according to principles innate in the ego.

Unfortunately these prejudices were at work when Descartes introduced the apparently insignificant but actually fateful change whereby the ego becomes a *substantia cogitans*, a separate human "*mens sive animus*," and the point of departure for inferences according to the principle of causality – in short, the change by virtue of which Descartes became the father of transcendental realism, an absurd position, though its absurdity cannot be made apparent at this point. We remain aloof from all that, if we remain true to the radicalness of our meditative self-examination and therefore to the principle of pure "intuition" or evidence – that is to say, if we accept nothing here but what we find actually given (and, at first, quite immediately) in the field of the *ego cogito*, which has been opened up to us by epoché, and if accordingly we assert nothing we ourselves do not "see." Descartes erred in this respect. Consequently he stands on the threshold of the greatest of all discoveries – in a certain manner, has already made it – yet he does not grasp its proper sense, the sense namely of transcendental subjectivity, and so he does not pass through the gateway that leads into genuine transcendental philosophy.

§11 *The psychological and the transcendental Ego. The transcendency of the world*

If I keep purely what comes into view – for me, the one who is meditating – by virtue of my free epoché with respect to the being of the experienced world, the momentous fact is that I, with my life, remain untouched in my existential status, regardless of whether or not the world exists and regardless of what my eventual decision concerning its being or nonbeing might be. This Ego, with his Ego-life, who necessarily remains for me, by virtue of such epoché, is not a piece of the world; and if he says, "I exist, *ego cogito*," that no longer signifies, "I, this man, exist." No longer am I the man who, in natural self-experience, finds himself *as* a man and who, with the abstractive restriction to the pure contents of "internal" or purely psychological self-experience, finds his own pure "*mens sive animus sive intellectus*"; nor am I the separately considered psyche itself. Apperceived in this "natural" manner, I and all other men are themes of sciences that are Objective, or positive, in the usual sense: biology, anthropology, and also (as included in these) *psychology*. The psychic life that psychology talks about has in fact always been, and still is, meant as psychic life in the world. Obviously the same is true also of one's own psychic life, which is grasped and considered in *purely internal experience*. But phenomenological epoché (which the course of our purified Cartesian meditations demands of him who is philosophizing) inhibits acceptance of the Objective world as existent, and thereby excludes this world completely from the field of judgment. In so doing, it likewise inhibits acceptance of any Objectively apperceived facts, including those of internal experience. Consequently for me, the meditating Ego who, standing and remaining in the attitude of epoché, posits exclusively himself as the *acceptance-basis* of all Objective acceptances and bases [*als Geltungsgrund aller objektiven Geltungen und Gründe*], there is no psychological Ego and there are no psychic phenomena in the sense proper to psychology, i.e. as components of psychophysical men.

By phenomenological epoché I reduce my natural human Ego and my psychic life – the realm of my *psychological self-experience* – to my transcendental–phenomenological Ego, the realm of *transcendental–phenomenological self-experience*. The Objective world, the world that exists for me, that always has and always will exist for me, the only world that ever can exist for me – this world, with all its Objects, I said, derives its whole sense and its existential status, which it has for me, from me myself, *from me as the transcendental Ego*, the Ego who comes to the fore only with transcendental–phenomenological epoché.

This concept of the transcendental and its correlate, the concept of the transcendent, must be derived exclusively from *our* philosophically meditative situation. The following should be noted in this connexion: Just as the reduced Ego is not a piece of the world, so, conversely, neither the world nor any worldly Object is a piece of my Ego, to be found in my conscious life as a really inherent part of it, as a complex of data of sensation or a complex of acts. This "*transcendence*" is part of the intrinsic sense of anything worldly, *despite* the fact that anything worldly necessarily acquires all the sense determining it, along with its existential status, exclusively from my experiencing, my objectivating, thinking, valuing, or doing, at particular times – notably the status of an evidently valid being is one it can acquire only from my own evidences, my grounding acts. If this "transcendence," which consists in being non-really included, is part of the intrinsic sense of the world, then, by way of contrast, the Ego himself, who bears within him the world as an accepted sense and who, in turn, is necessarily presupposed by this sense, is legitimately called *transcendental*, in the phenomenological sense. Accordingly the philosophical problems arising from this correlation are called transcendental–philosophical.

Notes

1 The *Meditations* are an elaboration of two lectures, entitled "*Einleitung in die transzendentale Phänomeno-logie*" (Introduction to Transcendental Phenomenology) that Husserl delivered at the Sorbonne on February 23 and February 25, 1929. See Strasser's introduction, *Husserliana*, Vol. I, p. XXIII. (Trans.)

2 For confirmation of this interpretation see *Lettre de l'auteur* to the translator of the *Principia* (Descartes, *Oeuvres*, Adam and Tannery edition, Vol. IX, 1904, Part 2, pp. 1–20). (Trans.)

3 Sometimes Husserl uses *Ego* and *Ich* to express different senses. Since the homophony of *I* and *eye* makes the English noun *I* intolerable, *Ich* has been translated as *Ego* (spelled with a capital) and *Ego* has been translated as *ego* (spelled with a small letter). (Trans.)

4 Husserl frequently uses the words *Gegenstand* and *Objekt* to express importantly different senses. Having found no acceptable alternative to translating them both as *object*, I differentiate by spelling this word with a small letter when it represents *Gegenstand* and with a capital when it represents *Objekt*. All this applies, *mutatis mutandis*, in the case of any word derived from *Gegenstand* or *Objekt*. If the English word *object*, or a word derived from it, stands first in a sentence, the German word is given in brackets. (Trans.)

5 Etienne Gilson, *Études sur la rôle de la pensée médiévale dans la formation du système cartésien* (Paris, 1930), and Alexandre Koyré, *Essai sur l'idée de dieu et sur les preuves de son existence chez Descartes* (Paris, 1922). (Trans.)

Select Bibliography

Cartesian Meditations: An Introduction to Phenomenology. Translated by Dorion Cairns. The Hague: Martinus Nijhoff, 1965.

The Crisis of European Sciences and Transcendental Phenomenology: An Introduction to Phenomenological Philosophy. Translated by David Carr. Evanston, Ill.: Northwestern University Press, 1970.

Experience and Judgment: Investigations in a Genealogy of Logic. Edited by Ludwig Landgrebe. Translated by James S. Churchill and Karl Ameriks. Evanston, Ill.: Northwestern University Press, 1973.

Formal and Transcendental Logic. Translated by Dorion Cairns. The Hague: Martinus Nijhoff, 1969.

Husserl: Shorter Works. Edited by Peter McCormick and Frederick A. Elliston. Notre Dame, Ind.: University of Notre Dame Press, 1981.

Ideas: General Introduction to Pure Phenomenology. Translated by W. R. Boyce Gibson. London: Allen and Unwin, 1969.

The Idea of Phenomenology. Translated by William P. Alston and George Nakhnikian. Dordrecht: Kluwer Academic Publishers, 1990.

Logical Investigations, 2 vols. Translated by J. N. Findlay. London: Routledge and Kegan Paul, 1970.

On the Phenomenology of the Consciousness of Internal Time (1893–1917). Translated by John Barnett Brough. Dordrecht: Kluwer Academic Publishers, 1991.

The Paris Lectures. Translated by Peter Koestenbaum. The Hague: Martinus Nijhoff, 1967.

Phenomenological Psychology: Lectures, Summer Semester, 1925. Translated by John Scanlon. The Hague: Martinus Nijhoff, 1977.

Phenomenology and the Crisis of Philosophy. New York: Harper and Row, 1965.

Phenomenology and the Foundations of the Sciences. Translated by Ted E. Klein and William E. Pohl. The Hague: Martinus Nijhoff, 1980.

6

Martin Heidegger

The German philosopher Martin Heidegger (1889–1976), who began his philosophical career as a student of Franz Brentano (1838–1917) and Edmund Husserl, quickly rose to fame during the 1920s, first as a teacher and then as author of the influential book *Being and Time* (1927). The guiding and central question throughout Heidegger's work is "the question of being," that is, of the meaning of "being" in the philosophical tradition. In *Being and Time*, Heidegger argues that philosophy has traditionally and problematically understood "being" to mean presence – a meaning that has not been explicitly pondered by philosophy, but implicitly presupposed in an unquestioned manner. This primary meaning, which has dominated philosophy since Plato, tends to oppose being as permanence to becoming or transitoriness. In *Being and Time*, Heidegger aims to show that being is not to be opposed to time conceived as becoming, but rather itself *is* time, since presence is a temporal determination. His investigation unfolds via an analysis of the kind of being proper to *Dasein*, his designation for the entity that we ourselves are, and whose existence is shown to be radically temporal. The following selections, from the Introduction to *Being and Time*, provide an outline of Heidegger's early project.

Martin Heidegger

Being and Time

Introduction: The Exposition of the Question of the Meaning of Being

Chapter One: The Necessity, Structure, and Priority of the Question of Being

§1 The necessity of an explicit recovery of the question of Being

This question has today been forgotten – although our time considers itself progressive in again affirming "metaphysics." All the same we believe that we are spared the exertion of rekindling a *gigantomachia peri tēs ousias* ["a Battle of Giants concerning Being," Plato, *Sophist* 245e 6–246e 1]. But the question touched upon here is hardly an arbitrary one. It sustained the avid research of Plato and Aristotle but from then on ceased to be heard *as a thematic question of actual investigation*. What these two thinkers gained has been preserved in various distorted and "camouflaged" forms down to Hegel's *Logic*. And what then was wrested from phenomena by the highest exertion of thinking, albeit in fragments and first beginnings, has long since been trivialized.

Not only that. On the foundation of the Greek point of departure for the interpretation of Being a dogmatic attitude has taken shape which not only declares the question of the meaning of Being to be superfluous but sanctions its neglect. It is said that "Being" is the most universal and the emptiest concept. As such it resists every attempt at definition. Nor does this most universal and thus undefinable concept need any definition. Everybody uses it constantly and also already understands what they mean by it. Thus what made ancient

From *Martin Heidegger: Basic Writings*, edited by David Farrell Krell (New York: HarperCollins, 1993), pp. 41–87. Introduction to *Being and Time* translated by Joan Stambaugh in collaboration with J. Glenn Gray and David Farrell Krell. English translation copyright © 1977 by Harper & Row, Publishers, Inc. General Introduction and introductions to each selection copyright © 1977 by David Farrell Krell. Reprinted by permission of HarperCollins Publishers, Inc.

philosophizing uneasy and kept it so by virtue of its obscurity has become obvious, clear as day; and this to the point that whoever pursues it is accused of an error of method.

At the beginning of this inquiry the prejudices that implant and nurture ever anew the superfluousness of a questioning of Being cannot be discussed in detail. They are rooted in ancient ontology itself. That ontology in turn can only be interpreted adequately under the guidance of the question of Being which has been clarified and answered beforehand. One must procced with regard to the soil from which the fundamental ontological concepts grew and with reference to the suitable demonstration of the categories and their completeness. We therefore wish to discuss these prejudices only to the extent that the necessity of a recovery[1] of the question of the meaning of Being becomes clear. There are three such prejudices.

1 "Being" is the most "universal" concept: *to on esti katholou malista pantōn,*[2] *Illud quod primo cadit sub apprehensione est ens, cuius intellectus includitur in omnibus, quaecumque quis apprehendit.* "An understanding of Being is always already contained in everything we apprehend in beings."[3] But the "universality" of "Being" is not that of *genus*. "Being" does not delimit the highest region of beings so far as they are conceptually articulated according to genus and species: *oute to on genos* ["Being is not a genus"].[4] The "universality" of Being *"surpasses"* the universality of genus. According to the designation of medieval ontology, "Being" is a *transcendens*. Aristotle himself understood the unity of this transcendental "universal," as opposed to the manifold of the highest generic concepts with material content, as the *unity of analogy*. Despite his dependence upon Plato's ontological position, Aristotle placed the problem of Being on a fundamentally new basis with this discovery. To be sure, he too did not clarify the obscurity of these categorical connections. Medieval ontology discussed this problem in many ways, above all in the Thomist and Scotist schools, without gaining fundamental clarity. And when Hegel

finally defines "Being" as the "indeterminate Immediate," and makes this definition the foundation of all the further categorial explications of his *Logic*, he remains within the perspective of ancient ontology – except that he does give up the problem, raised early on by Aristotle, of the unity of Being in contrast to the manifold of "categories" with material content. If one says accordingly that "Being" is the most universal concept, that cannot mean that it is the clearest and that it needs no further discussion. The concept of "Being" is rather the most obscure of all.

2   The concept of "Being" is undefinable. This conclusion was drawn from its highest universality.[5] And correctly so – if *definitio fit per genus proximum et differentiam specificam* [if "definition is achieved through the nearest genus and the specific difference"]. Indeed, "Being" cannot be understood as a being. *Enti non additur aliqua natura*: "Being" cannot be defined by attributing beings to it. Being cannot be derived from higher concepts by way of definition and cannot be represented by lower ones. But does it follow from this that "Being" can no longer constitute a problem? By no means. We can conclude only that "Being" is not something like a being. Thus the manner of definition of beings which has its justification within limits – the "definition" of traditional logic which is itself rooted in ancient ontology – cannot be applied to Being. The undefinability of Being does not dispense with the question of its meaning but compels that question.

3   "Being" is the self-evident concept. "Being" is used in all knowing and predicating, in every relation to beings and in every relation to oneself, and the expression is understandable "without further ado." Everybody understands, "The sky *is* blue," "I *am* happy," and similar statements. But this average comprehensibility only demonstrates the incomprehensibility. It shows that an enigma lies *a priori* in every relation and being toward beings as beings. The fact that we live already in an understanding of Being and that the meaning of Being is at the same time shrouded in darkness proves the fundamental necessity of recovering the question of the meaning of "Being."

If what is "self-evident" and this alone – "the covert judgments of common reason" (Kant) – is to become and remain the explicit theme of our analysis (as "the business of philosophers"), then the appeal to self-evidence in the realm of basic philosophical concepts, and indeed with

regard to the concept "Being," is a dubious procedure.

But consideration of the prejudices has made it clear at the same time that not only is the *answer* to the question of Being lacking but even the question itself is obscure and without direction. Thus to recover the question of Being means first of all to develop adequately the *formulation* of the question.

§2   *The formal structure of the question of Being*

The question of the meaning of Being must be *formulated*. If it is a – or even *the* – fundamental question, such questioning needs the suitable perspicuity. Thus we must briefly discuss what belongs to a question in general in order to be able to make clear that the question of Being is a *distinctive* one.

Every questioning is a seeking. Every seeking takes its direction beforehand from what is sought. Questioning is a knowing search for beings in their thatness and whatness. The knowing search can become an "investigation," as the revealing determination of what the question aims at. As questioning about . . . questioning has *what it asks*. All asking about . . . is in some way an inquiring of . . . . Besides what is asked, what is *interrogated* also belongs to questioning. What is questioned is to be defined and conceptualized in the investigative or specifically theoretical question. As what is really intended, what is to be *ascertained* lies in what is questioned; here questioning arrives at its goal. As an attitude adopted by a being, the questioner, questioning has its own character of Being. Questioning can come about as mere "asking around" or as an explicitly formulated question. What is peculiar to the latter is the fact that questioning becomes lucid in advance with regard to all the above-named constitutive characteristics of the question.

The meaning of Being is the question to be *formulated*. Thus we are confronted with the necessity of explicating the question of Being with regard to the structural moments cited.

As a seeking, questioning needs previous guidance from what it seeks. The meaning of Being must therefore already be available to us in a certain way. We intimated that we are always already involved in an understanding of Being. From this grows the explicit question of the meaning of Being and the tendency toward its concept. We do not *know* what "Being" means. But already when we ask, "What *is* 'Being'?" we stand in an understanding of the "is" without being able to determine conceptually what the "is" means. We do not even know the horizon upon which we are supposed to grasp and pin down the meaning. *This average and vague understanding of Being is a fact.*

No matter how much this understanding of Being wavers and fades and borders on mere verbal knowledge, this indefiniteness of the understanding of Being that is always already available is itself a positive phenomenon which needs elucidation. However, an investigation of the meaning of Being will not wish to provide this at the outset. The interpretation of the average understanding of Being attains its necessary guideline only with the developed concept of Being. From the clarity of that concept and the appropriate manner of its explicit understanding we shall be able to discern what the obscure or not yet elucidated understanding of Being means, what kinds of obscuration or hindrance of an explicit elucidation of the meaning of Being are possible and necessary.

Furthermore, the average, vague understanding of Being can be permeated by traditional theories and opinions about Being in such a way that these theories, as the sources of the prevailing understanding, remain hidden. What is sought in the question of Being is not something completely unfamiliar, although it is at first totally ungraspable.

What is *asked about* in the question to be elaborated is Being, that which determines beings as beings, that in terms of which beings have always been understood no matter how they are discussed. The Being of beings "is" itself not a being. The first philosophical step in understanding the problem of Being consists in avoiding the *mython tina diēgeisthai*,[6] in not "telling a story," i.e. not determining beings as beings by tracing them back in their origins to another being – as if Being had the character of a possible being. As what is asked about, Being thus requires its own kind of demonstration which is essentially different from discovery of beings. Hence what is to be *ascertained*, the meaning of Being, will require its own conceptualization, which again is essentially distinct from the concepts in which beings receive their meaningful determination.

Insofar as Being constitutes what is asked about, and insofar as Being means the Being of beings, beings themselves turn out to be what is *interrogated* in the question of Being. Beings are, so to speak, interrogated with regard to their Being. But if they are to exhibit the characteristics of their Being without falsification they must for their part have become accessible in advance as they are in themselves. The question of Being demands that the right access to beings be gained and secured in advance with regard to what it interrogates. But we call many things "in being" [*seiend*], and in different senses. Everything we talk about, mean, and are related to in such and such a way is in being. What and how we ourselves are is also in being. Being is found in thatness and whatness, reality, the being at hand of things [*Vorhandenheit*], subsistence, validity, existence [*Dasein*], and in the "there is" [*es gibt*]. In *which* being is the meaning of Being to be found; from which being is the disclosure of Being to get its start? Is the starting point arbitrary, or does a certain being have priority in the elaboration of the question of Being? Which is this exemplary being and in what sense does it have priority?

If the question of Being is to be explicitly formulated and brought to complete clarity concerning itself, then the elaboration of this question requires, in accord with what has been elucidated up to now, explication of the ways of regarding Being and of understanding and conceptually grasping its meaning, preparation of the possibility of the right choice of the exemplary being, and elaboration of the genuine mode of access to this being. Regarding, understanding and grasping, choosing, and gaining access to, are constitutive attitudes of inquiry and are thus themselves modes of being of a definite being, of *the* being we inquirers ourselves in each case are. Thus to work out the question of Being means to make a being – he who questions – perspicuous in his Being. Asking this question, as a mode of *being* of a being, is itself essentially determined by what is asked about in it – Being. This being which we ourselves in each case are and which includes inquiry among the possibilities of its Being we formulate terminologically as *Dasein*. The explicit and lucid formulation of the question of the meaning of Being requires a prior suitable explication of a being (Dasein) with regard to its Being....[7]

§3   The ontological priority of the question of Being
...Fundamental concepts are determinations in which the area of knowledge underlying all the thematic objects of a science attain an understanding that precedes and guides all positive investigation. Accordingly these concepts first receive their genuine evidence and "grounding" in a correspondingly preliminary research into the area of knowledge itself. But since each of these areas

arises from the domain of beings themselves, this preliminary research that creates the fundamental concepts amounts to nothing else than interpreting these beings in terms of the basic constitution of their Being. This kind of investigation must precede the positive sciences – and it *can* do so. The work of Plato and Aristotle is proof of this. Laying the foundations of the sciences in this way is different in principle from "logic" limping along behind, investigating here and there the status of a science in terms of its "method." Such laying of foundations is productive logic in the sense that it leaps ahead, so to speak, into a definite realm of Being, discloses it for the first time in its constitutive Being, and makes the acquired structures available to the positive sciences as lucid directives for inquiry. Thus, for example, what is philosophically primary is not a theory of concept-formation in historiology, nor the theory of historical knowledge, nor even the theory of history as the object of historiology; what is primary is rather the interpretation of properly historical beings with regard to their historicity. Similarly, the positive result of Kant's *Critique of Pure Reason* consists in its beginning to work out what belongs to any nature whatsoever, and not in a "theory" of knowledge. His transcendental logic is an *a priori* logic of the realm of Being called nature.

But such inquiry – ontology taken in its broadest sense without reference to specific ontological directions and tendencies – itself still needs a guideline. It is true that ontological inquiry is more original than the ontic inquiry of the positive sciences. But it remains naive and opaque if its investigations into the Being of beings leave the meaning of Being in general undiscussed. And precisely the ontological task of a genealogy of the different possible ways of Being (which is not to be construed deductively) requires a preliminary understanding of "what we properly mean by this expression 'Being.'"

The question of Being thus aims at an *a priori* condition of the possibility not only of the sciences which investigate beings of such and such a type – and are thereby already involved in an understanding of Being; but it aims also at the condition of the possibility of the ontologies which precede the ontic sciences and found them. *All ontology, no matter how rich and tightly knit a system of categories it has at its disposal, remains fundamentally blind and perverts its most proper intent if it has not previously clarified the meaning of Being sufficiently and grasped this clarification as its fundamental task.*

Ontological research itself, correctly understood, gives the question of Being its ontological priority over and above merely resuming an honored tradition and making progress on a problem until now opaque. But this scholarly, scientific priority is not the only one.

§4 The ontic[8] priority of the question of Being

Science in general can be defined as the totality of fundamentally coherent true propositions. This definition is not complete, nor does it get at the meaning of science. As ways in which man behaves, sciences have this being's (man's) kind of Being. We are defining this being terminologically as *Dasein*. Scientific research is neither the sole nor the primary kind of possible Being of this being. Moreover, Dasein itself is distinctly different from other beings. We must make this distinct difference visible in a preliminary way. Here the discussion must anticipate subsequent analyses, which only later will become properly demonstrative.

Dasein is a being that does not simply occur among other beings. Rather it is ontically distinguished by the fact that in its Being this being is concerned *about* its very Being. Thus it is constitutive of the Being of Dasein to have, in its very Being, a relation of Being to this Being. And this in turn means that Dasein understands itself in its Being in some way and with some explicitness. It is proper to this being that it be disclosed to itself with and through its Being. *Understanding of Being is itself a determination of the Being of Dasein.* The ontic distinction of Dasein lies in the fact that it *is* ontological.

To be ontological does not yet mean to develop ontology. Thus if we reserve the term ontology for the explicit, theoretical question of the meaning of beings, the intended ontological character of Dasein is to be designated as preontological. That does not signify being simply ontical, but rather being in the manner of an understanding of Being.

We shall call the very Being to which Dasein can relate in one way or another, and somehow always does relate, existence [*Existenz.*] And because the essential definition of this being cannot be accomplished by ascribing to it a "what" that specifies its material content, because its essence lies rather in the fact that it has always to be its Being as its own, the term Dasein, as a pure expression of Being, has been chosen to designate this being.

Dasein always understands itself in terms of its existence, in terms of its possibility to be itself or not to be itself. Dasein has either chosen these possibilities itself, stumbled upon them, or already grown up in them. Existence is decided only by each Dasein itself in the manner of seizing upon or neglecting such possibilities. We come to terms with the question of existence always only through existence itself. We shall call *this* kind of understanding of itself *existentiell* understanding. The question of existence is an ontic "affair" of Dasein. For this the theoretical perspicuity of the ontological structure of existence is not necessary. The question of structure aims at the analysis of what constitutes existence. We shall call the coherence of these structures *existentiality*. Its analysis does not have the character of an existentiell understanding but rather an *existential* one. The task of an existential analysis of Dasein is prescribed with regard to its possibility and necessity in the ontic constitution of Dasein.[9]

But since existence defines Dasein, the ontological analysis of this being always requires a previous glimpse of existentiality. However, we understand existentiality as the constitution-of-Being of the being that exists. But the idea of Being already lies in the idea of such a constitution of Being. And thus the possibility of carrying out the analysis of Dasein depends upon the prior elaboration of the question of the meaning of Being in general.

Sciences and disciplines are ways of being of Dasein in which Dasein relates also to beings that it need not itself be. But *being in a world* belongs essentially to Dasein. Thus the understanding of Being that belongs to Dasein just as originally implies the understanding of something like "world" and the understanding of the Being of beings accessible within the world. Ontologies that have beings unlike Dasein as their theme are accordingly founded and motivated in the ontic structure of Dasein itself. This structure includes in itself the determination of a preontological understanding of Being.

Thus *fundamental ontology*, from which alone all other ontologies can originate, must be sought in the *existential analysis of Dasein*.

Dasein accordingly takes priority in several ways over all other beings. The first priority is an *ontic* one: this being is defined in its Being by existence. The second priority is an *ontological* one: on the basis of its determination as existence Dasein is in itself "ontological." But just as originally Dasein possesses – in a manner constitutive of its understanding of existence – an understanding of the Being of all beings unlike itself. Dasein therefore has its third priority as the ontic–ontological condition of the possibility of all ontologies. Dasein has proven to be what, before all other beings, is ontologically the primary being to be interrogated.

However, the roots of the existential analysis, for their part, are ultimately *existentiell* – they are *ontic*. Only when philosophical research and inquiry themselves are grasped in an existentiell way – as a possibility of being of each existing Dasein – does it become possible at all to disclose the existentiality of existence and therewith to get hold of a sufficiently grounded set of ontological problems. But with this the ontic priority of the question of Being as well has become clear. . . .

If the interpretation of the meaning of Being is to become a task, Dasein is not only the primary being to be interrogated; in addition to this it is the being that always already in its Being is related to *what is sought* in this question. But then the question of Being is nothing else than the radicalization of an essential tendency of Being that belongs to Dasein itself, namely, of the preontological understanding of Being.

Chapter Two: The Double Task in Working Out the Question of Being. The Method of the Investigation and Its Outline

§5 The ontological analysis of Dasein as exposure of the horizon for an interpretation of the meaning of Being in general

In designating the tasks that lie in "formulating" the question of Being, we showed that not only must we pinpoint the particular being that is to function as the primary object of interrogation but also that an explicit appropriation and securing of correct access to this being is required. We discussed which being it is that takes over the major role within the question of Being. But how should this being, Dasein, become accessible and, so to speak, be envisaged in a perceptive interpretation?

The ontic–ontological priority that has been demonstrated for Dasein could lead to the mistaken opinion that this being would have to be what is primarily given also ontically–ontologically, not only in the sense that such a being could be grasped immediately but also that the prior givenness of its manner of being would be just as "immediate." True, Dasein is ontically not only what is near or even nearest – we ourselves *are* it in each case. Nevertheless, or precisely for this reason, it is ontologically what is farthest away. True, it belongs to its most proper Being to have an understanding of this Being and to sustain a certain interpretation of it. But this does not at all mean that the most readily available preontological interpretation of its own Being could be adopted as an adequate guideline, as though this understanding of Being perforce stemmed from a thematic ontological reflection on the most proper constitution of its Being. Rather, in accordance with the manner of being belonging to it, Dasein tends to understand its own Being in terms of that being to which it is essentially, continually, and most closely related – the "world." In Dasein itself and therewith in its own understanding of Being, as we shall show, the way the world is understood is ontologically reflected back upon the interpretation of Dasein.

The ontic–ontological priority of Dasein is therefore the reason why the specific constitution of the Being of Dasein – understood in the sense of the "categorial" structure that belongs to it – remains hidden from it. Dasein is ontically "closest" to itself, while ontologically farthest away; but preontologically it is surely not foreign to itself.

For the time being we have only indicated that an interpretation of this being is confronted with peculiar difficulties rooted in the mode of being of the thematic object and the way it is thematized. These difficulties do not result from some shortcoming of our powers of knowledge or lack of a suitable way of conceiving – a lack seemingly easy to remedy.

Not only does an understanding of Being belong to Dasein, but this understanding also develops or decays according to the actual manner of being of Dasein at any given time; for this reason it has a wealth of interpretations at its disposal. Philosophical psychology, anthropology, ethics, "politics," poetry, biography, and the discipline of history pursue in different ways and to varying extents the behavior, faculties, powers, possibilities, and vicissitudes of Dasein. But the question remains whether these interpretations were carried out in as original an existential manner as their existentiell originality perhaps merited. The two do not necessarily go together, but they also do not exclude one another. Existentiell interpretation can require existential analysis, provided philosophical knowledge is understood in its possibility and necessity. Only when the fundamental structures of Dasein are adequately worked out with explicit orientation toward the problem of Being will the previous results of the interpretation of Dasein receive their existential justification.

Hence the first concern in the question of Being must be an analysis of Dasein. But then the problem of gaining and securing the access that leads to Dasein becomes really crucial. Expressed negatively, no arbitrary idea of Being and reality, no matter how "self-evident" it is, may be brought to bear on this being in a dogmatically constructed way; no "categories" prescribed by such ideas may be forced upon Dasein without ontological deliberation. The manner of access and interpretation must instead be chosen in such a way that this being can show itself to itself on its own terms. Furthermore, this manner should show that being as it is *at first and for the most part* – in its average *everydayness*. Not arbitrary and accidental structures but essential ones are to be demonstrated in this everydayness, structures that remain determinative in every mode of being of factual Dasein. By looking at the fundamental constitution of the everydayness of Dasein we shall bring out in a preparatory way the Being of this being.

The analysis of Dasein thus understood is wholly oriented toward the guiding task of working out the question of Being. Its limits are thereby determined. It cannot hope to provide a complete ontology of Dasein, which of course must be supplied if something like a "philosophical" anthropology is to rest on a philosophically adequate basis. With a view to a possible anthropology or its ontological foundation, the following interpretation will provide only a few "parts," although not unessential ones. However, the analysis of Dasein is not only incomplete but at first also *preliminary*. It only brings out the Being of this being, without interpreting its meaning. Its aim is rather to expose the horizon for the most original interpretation of Being. Once we have reached that horizon the preparatory analysis of Dasein requires recovery on a higher, properly ontological basis.

The meaning of the Being of that being we call Dasein proves to be *temporality [Zeitlichkeit]*. In order to demonstrate this we must recover our interpretation of those structures of Dasein that shall have been indicated in a preliminary way – this time as modes of temporality. While it is true that with this interpretation of Dasein as temporality the answer to the guiding question about the meaning of Being in general is not given as such, the soil from which we may reap it will nevertheless be prepared.

We intimated that a preontological Being belongs to Dasein as its ontic constitution. Dasein *is* in such a way that, by being, it understands something like Being. Remembering this connection, we must show that *time* is that from which Dasein tacitly understands and interprets something like Being at all. Time must be brought to light and genuinely grasped as the horizon of every understanding and interpretation of Being. For this to become clear we need an *original explication of time as the horizon of the understanding of Being, in terms of temporality as the Being of Dasein which understands Being.* This task as a whole requires that the concept of time thus gained be distinguished from the common understanding of it. The latter has become explicit in an interpretation of time which reflects the traditional concept that has persisted since Aristotle and beyond Bergson. We must thereby make clear that and in what way this concept of time and the common understanding of time in general originate from temporality. In this way the common concept of time receives again its rightful autonomy – contrary to Bergson's thesis that time understood in the common way is really space.

For a long while, "time" has served as the ontological – or rather ontic – criterion for naively distinguishing the different regions of beings. "Temporal" beings (natural processes and historical events) are separated from "atemporal" beings (spatial and numerical relationships). We are accustomed to distinguishing the "timeless" meaning of propositions from the "temporal" course of propositional statements. Further, a "gap" between "temporal" being and "supratemporal" eternal being is found, and the attempt made to bridge the gap. "Temporal" here means as much as being "in time," an obscure enough definition to be sure. The fact remains that time in the sense of "being in time" serves as a criterion for separating the regions of Being. How time comes to have this distinctive ontological function, and even with what right precisely something like time serves as such a criterion, and most of all whether in this naive ontological application of time its genuinely possible ontological relevance is expressed, has neither been asked nor investigated up to now. "Time," especially on the horizon of the common understanding of it, has chanced to acquire this "obvious" ontological function "of itself," as it were, and has retained it to the present day.

In contrast we must show, on the basis of the question of the meaning of Being which shall have been worked out, *that – and in what way – the central range of problems of all ontology is rooted in the phenomenon of time correctly viewed and correctly explained.*

If Being is to be conceived in terms of time, and if the various modes and derivatives of Being, in their modifications and derivations, are in fact to become intelligible through consideration of time, then Being itself – and not only beings that are "in time" – is made visible in its "temporal" ["*zeitlich*"] character. But then "temporal" can no longer mean only "being in time." The "atemporal" and the "supratemporal" are also "temporal" with respect to their Being; this not only by way of privation when compared to "temporal" beings which are "in time," but in a *positive* way which, of course, must first be clarified. Because the expression "temporal" belongs to both prephilosophical and philosophical usage, and because that expression will be used in a different sense in the following investigations, we shall call the original determination of the meaning of Being and its characters and modes which devolve from time its *Temporal* [temporale] determination. The fundamental ontological task of the interpretation of Being as such thus includes the elaboration of the *Temporality of Being* [*Temporalität des Seins.*] In the exposition of the problem of Temporality the concrete answer to the question of the meaning of Being is first given.

Because Being is comprehensible only on the basis of the consideration of time, the answer to the question of Being cannot lie in an isolated and blind proposition. The answer is not grasped by repeating what is stated propositionally, especially when it is transmitted as a free-floating result, so that we merely take notice of a standpoint which perhaps deviates from the way the matter has been previously treated. Whether the answer is "novel" is of no importance and remains extrinsic. What is positive about the answer must lie in the fact that it is *old* enough to enable us to learn to comprehend possibilities prepared by the "ancients." In conformity to its most proper sense, the answer provides a directive for concrete ontological research, that is, a directive to begin its investigative inquiry within the horizon exhibited – and that is all it provides.

If the answer to the question of Being thus becomes the guiding directive for research, then it is sufficiently given only if the specific mode of being of previous ontology – the vicissitudes of its questioning, its findings, and its failures – becomes visible as necessary to the very character of Dasein.

§6   *The task of a destructuring of the history of ontology*[10]

All research – especially when it moves in the sphere of the central question of Being – is an ontic possibility of Dasein. The Being of Dasein finds its meaning in temporality. But temporality is at the same time the condition of the possibility of historicity as a temporal mode of being of Dasein itself, regardless of whether and how it is a being "in time." As a determination, historicity is prior to what is called history (world-historical occurrences). Historicity means the constitution of Being of the "occurrence" of Dasein as such; it is the ground for the fact that something like the discipline of "world history" is at all possible and historically belongs to world history. In its factual Being Dasein always is as and "what" it already was. Whether explicitly or not, it *is* its past. It is its own past not only in such a way that its past, as it were, pushes itself along "behind" it, and that it possesses what is past as a property that is still at hand and occasionally has an effect on it. Dasein "is" its past in the manner of *its* Being which, roughly expressed, actually "occurs" out of its future. In its manner of being at any given time, and accordingly also with the understanding of Being that belongs to it, Dasein grows into a customary interpretation of itself and grows up in that interpretation. It understands itself in terms of this interpretation at first, and within a certain range, constantly. This understanding discloses the possibilities of its Being and regulates them. Its own past – and that always means that of its "generation" – does not *follow after* Dasein but rather always goes already ahead of it.

This elemental historicity of Dasein can remain concealed from it. But it can also be discovered in a certain way and be properly cultivated. Dasein can discover, preserve, and explicitly pursue tradition. The discovery of tradition and the disclosure of what it "transmits," and how it does this, can be undertaken as an independent task. In this way Dasein advances to the mode of being of historical inquiry and research. But the discipline of history – more precisely, the historicality underlying it – as the manner of being of inquiring Dasein, is possible only because Dasein is determined by historicity in the ground of its Being. If historicity remains concealed from Dasein, and so long as it does so, the possibility of historical inquiry and discovery of history is denied it. If the discipline of history is lacking, that is no evidence *against* the historicity of Dasein; rather it is evidence for this constitution-of-Being in a deficient mode. Only because it is "historic" in the first place can an age lack the discipline of history.

On the other hand, if Dasein has seized upon its inherent possibility not only of making its existence perspicuous but also of inquiring into the meaning of existentiality itself, that is to say, of provisionally inquiring into the meaning of Being in general; and if insight into the essential historicity of Dasein has opened up in such inquiry; then it is inevitable that inquiry into Being, which was designated with regard to its ontic–ontological necessity, is itself characterized by historicity. The elaboration of the question of Being must therefore receive its directive to inquire into its own history from the most proper ontological sense of the inquiry itself, as a historical one; that means to become historical in order to come to the positive appropriation of the past, to come into full possession of its most proper possibilities of inquiry. The question of the meaning of Being is led to understand itself as historical in accordance with its own way of proceeding, i.e. as the provisional explication of Dasein in its temporality and historicity.

However, the preparatory interpretation of the fundamental structures of Dasein with regard to its usual and average way of being – in which it is also first of all historical – will make the following clear: Dasein not only has the inclination to be ensnared in the world in which it is and to interpret itself in terms of that world by its reflected light; at the same time Dasein is also ensnared in a tradition which it more or less explicitly grasps. This tradition deprives Dasein of its own leadership in questioning and choosing. This is especially true of *that* understanding (and its possible development) which is rooted in the most proper Being of Dasein – the ontological understanding.

The tradition that hereby gains dominance makes what it "transmits" so little accessible that at first and for the most part it covers it over instead. What has been handed down it hands over to obviousness; it bars access to those original "wellsprings" out of which the traditional categories and concepts were in part genuinely drawn. The tradition even makes us forget such a provenance altogether. Indeed it makes us wholly incapable of even understanding that such a return is necessary. The tradition uproots the historicity of Dasein to such a degree that it only takes an interest in the manifold forms of possible types, directions, and standpoints of philosophizing in the most remote and strangest cultures, and with this interest tries to veil its own lack of foundation. Consequently, in spite of all historical interest and zeal for a philologically "viable" interpretation, Dasein no longer understands the most elementary conditions which alone make a positive return to the past possible – in the sense of its productive appropriation.

At the outset (section 1) we showed that the question of the meaning of Being was not only unresolved, not only inadequately formulated, but in spite of all interest in "metaphysics" has even been forgotten. Greek ontology and its history, which through many twists and turns still determine the conceptual character of philosophy today, are proof of the fact that Dasein understands itself and Being in general in terms of the "world." The ontology that thus arises is ensnared by the tradition, which allows it to sink to the level of the obvious and become mere material for reworking (as it was for Hegel). Greek ontology thus uprooted becomes a fixed body of doctrine in the Middle Ages. But its systematics is not at all a mere joining together of traditional elements into a single structure. Within the limits of its dogmatic adoption of the fundamental Greek interpretations of Being, this systematics contains a great deal of unpretentious work which does make advances. In its *scholastic* mold, Greek ontology makes the essential transition via the *Disputationes metaphysicae* of Suarez into the "metaphysics" and transcendental philosophy of the modern period; it still determines the foundations and goals of Hegel's *Logic*. Insofar as certain distinctive domains of Being become visible in the course of this history and henceforth chiefly dominate the range of problems (Descartes' *ego cogito*, subject, the "I," reason, spirit, person), the beings just cited remain unquestioned with respect to the Being and structure of their being, this corresponding to the thorough neglect of the question of Being. But the categorial content of traditional ontology is transferred to these beings with corresponding formalizations and purely negative restrictions, or else dialectic is called upon to help with an ontological interpretation of the substantiality of the subject.

If the question of Being is to achieve clarity regarding its own history, a loosening of the sclerotic tradition and a dissolving of the concealments produced by it are necessary. We understand this task as the *destructuring* of the traditional content of ancient ontology, which is to be carried out along the *guidelines of the question of Being*. This destructuring is based on the original experiences in which the first and subsequently guiding determinations of Being were gained.

This demonstration of the provenance of the fundamental ontological concepts, as the investigation that displays their "birth certificate," has nothing to do with a pernicious relativizing of ontological standpoints. The destructuring has just as little the *negative* sense of disburdening ourselves of the ontological tradition. On the contrary, it should stake out the positive possibilities of the tradition, and that always means to fix its *boundaries*. These are factually given with the specific formulation of the question and the prescribed demarcation of the possible field of investigation. The destructuring is not related negatively to the past: its criticism concerns "today" and the dominant way we treat the history of ontology, whether it be conceived as the history of opinions, ideas, or problems. However, the destructuring does not wish to bury the past in nullity; it has a *positive* intent. Its negative function remains tacit and indirect.

The destructuring of the history of ontology essentially belongs to the formulation of the question of Being and is possible solely within such a formulation. Within the scope of this treatise, which has as its goal a fundamental elaboration of the question of Being, the destructuring can be carried out only with regard to the fundamentally decisive stages of that history . . . .

§7 The phenomenological method of the investigation

With the preliminary characterization of the thematic object of the investigation (the Being of beings, or the meaning of Being in general) its method would appear to be already prescribed. The task of ontology is to set in relief the Being of beings and to explicate Being. And the method of ontology remains questionable in the highest degree as long as we wish merely to consult historically transmitted ontologies or similar efforts. Since the term "ontology" is used in a formally broad sense for this investigation, the approach of clarifying its method by pursuing the history of that method is automatically precluded.

In using the term "ontology" we do not specify any definite philosophical discipline standing in relation to others. It should not at all be our task to satisfy the demands of any established discipline. On the contrary, such a discipline can be developed only from the compelling necessity of definite questions and procedures demanded by the "things themselves."

With the guiding question of the meaning of Being the investigation arrives at the fundamental question of philosophy in general. The treatment of this question is *phenomenological*. With this term the treatise dictates for itself neither a "standpoint" nor a "direction," because phenomenology is neither of these and can never be as long as it understands itself. The expression "phenomenology" signifies primarily a *concept of method*. It does not characterize the "what" of the objects of philosophical research in terms of their content but the "how" of such research. The more genuinely effective a concept of method is and the more comprehensively it determines the fundamental conduct of a science, the more originally is it rooted in confrontation with the things themselves and the farther away it moves from what we call a technical device – of which there are many in the theoretical disciplines.

The term "phenomenology" expresses a maxim that can be formulated: "To the things themselves!" It is opposed to all freefloating constructions and accidental findings; it is also opposed to taking over concepts only seemingly demonstrated; and likewise to pseudo–questions which often are spread abroad as "problems" for generations. But one might object that this maxim is, after all, abundantly self-evident and, moreover, an expression of the principle of all scientific knowledge. It is not clear why this commonplace should be explicitly put in the title of our research. In fact we are dealing with "something self-evident" which we want to get closer to, insofar as that is important for clarification of the procedure in our treatise. We shall explicate only the preliminary concept of phenomenology.

The expression has two components, phenomenon and logos. These go back to the Greek terms *phainomenon* and *logos*. Viewed extrinsically, the word "phenomenology" is formed like the terms theology, biology, sociology, translated as the science of God, of life, of the community. Accordingly, phenomenology would be the *science of phenomena*. The preliminary concept of phenomenology is to be exhibited by characterizing what is meant by the two components, phenomenon and logos, and by establishing the meaning of the *combined* word. The history of the word itself, which originated presumably with the Wolffian school, is not important here.

A   THE CONCEPT OF PHENOMENON

The Greek expression *phainomenon*, from which the term "phenomenon" derives, comes from the verb *phainesthai*, meaning "to show itself." Thus *phainomenon* means what shows itself, the self-showing, the manifest. *Phainesthai* itself is a "middle voice" construction of *phainō*, to bring into daylight, to place in brightness. *Phainō* belongs to the root *pha-*, like *phōs*, light or brightness, i.e. that within which something can become manifest, visible in itself. Thus the meaning of the expression "phenomenon" is *established* as *what shows itself in itself*, what is manifest. The *phainomena*, "phenomena," are thus the totality of what lies in the light of day or can be brought to light. Sometimes the Greeks simply identified this with *ta onta* (beings). Beings can show themselves from themselves in various ways, depending on the mode of access to them. The possibility even exists that they can show themselves as they are *not* in themselves. In this self-showing beings "look like...." Such self-showing we call *seeming* [Scheinen]. And so the expression *phainomenon*, phenomenon, means in Greek: what looks like something, what "seems," "semblance." *Phainomenon agathon* means a good that looks like – but "in reality" is not what it gives itself out to be. It is extremely important for further understanding of the concept of phenomenon to see how what is named in both meanings of *phainomenon* ("phenomenon" as self-showing and "phenomenon" as semblance) are structurally connected. Only because something claims to show itself in accordance with its meaning at all, that is, claims to be a phenomenon, *can* it show itself *as* something it is *not*, or *can* it "only look like...." The original meaning (phenomenon, what is manifest) already contains and is the basis of *phainomenon* ("semblance"). We attribute to the term "phenomenon" the positive and original meaning of *phainomenon* terminologically, and separate the phenomenon of semblance from it as a privative modification. But what *both* terms express has at first nothing at all to do with what is called "appearance" or even "mere appearance."...

B   THE CONCEPT OF LOGOS

The concept of *logos* has many meanings in Plato and Aristotle, indeed in such a way that these meanings diverge, without a basic meaning positively taking the lead. This is in fact only an illusion which lasts so long as an interpretation is not able to grasp adequately the basic meaning in its primary content. If we say that the basic meaning of *logos* is speech, this literal translation becomes valid only when we define what speech itself means. The later history of the word *logos*, and especially the manifold and arbitrary interpretations of subsequent philosophy, conceal constantly the proper meaning of speech – which is manifest enough. *Logos* is "translated," and that always means interpreted, as reason, judgment, concept, definition, ground, relation. But how can "speech" be so susceptible of modification that *logos* means all the things mentioned, indeed in scholarly usage? Even if *logos* is understood in the sense of a statement, and statement as "judgment," this apparently correct translation can still miss the fundamental meaning – especially if judgment is understood in the sense of some contemporary "theory of judgment." *Logos* does not mean judgment, in any case not primarily, if by judgment we understand "connecting two things" or "taking a position" either by endorsing or rejecting.

Rather, *logos* as speech really means *dēloun*, to make manifest "what is being talked about" in speech. Aristotle explicates this function of speech more precisely as *apophainesthai*.[11] *Logos* lets something be seen (*phainesthai*), namely what is being talked about, and indeed *for* the speaker (who serves as the medium) or for those who speak with each other. Speech "lets us see," from itself, *apo* . . ., what is being talked about. In speech (*apophansis*), insofar as it is genuine, *what* is said should be derived *from* what is being talked about. In this way spoken communication, in what it says, makes manifest what it is talking about and thus makes it accessible to another. Such is the structure of *logos* as *apophansis*. Not every "speech" suits *this* mode of making manifest, in the sense of letting something be seen by indicating it. For example, requesting (*euchē*) also makes something manifest, but in a different way.

When fully concrete, speech (letting something be seen) has the character of speaking or vocalization in words. *Logos* is *phonē*, indeed *phonē meta phantasias* – vocalization in which something always is sighted.

Only *because* the function of *logos* as *apophansis* lies in letting something be seen by indicating it can *logos* have the structure of *synthesis*. Here synthesis does not mean to connect and conjoin representations, to manipulate psychical occurrences, which then gives rise to the "problem" of how these connections, as internal, correspond to what is external and physical. The *syn* [of *synthesis*] here

has a purely apophantical meaning: to let something be seen in its *togetherness* with something, to let something be seen *as* something.

Furthermore, because *logos* lets something be seen, it can *therefore* be true or false. But everything depends on staying clear of any concept of truth construed in the sense of "correspondence" or "accordance" [*Übereinstimmung*]. This idea is by no means the primary one in the concept of *alētheia*. The "being true" of *logos* as *alētheuein* means: to take beings that are being talked *about* in *legein* as *apophainesthai* out of their concealment; to let them be seen as something unconcealed (*alēthes*); to *discover* them. Similarly "being false," *pseudesthai*, is tantamount to deceiving in the sense of covering up: putting something in front of something else (by way of letting it be seen) and thereby proffering it *as* something it is *not*.

But because "truth" has this meaning, and because *logos* is a specific mode of letting something be seen, *logos* simply may *not* be acclaimed as the primary "place" of truth. If one defines truth as what "properly" pertains to judgment, which is quite customary today, and if one invokes Aristotle in support of this thesis, such invocation is without justification and the Greek concept of truth thoroughly misunderstood. In the Greek sense what is "true" – indeed more originally true than the *logos* we have been discussing – is *aisthēsis*, the straightforward sensuous apprehending of something. To the extent that an *aisthēsis* aims at its *idia* [what is its own] – the beings genuinely accessible only *through* it and *for* it, for example, *looking* at colors – apprehending is always true. This means that looking always discovers colors, hearing always discovers tones. What is in the purest and most original sense "true" – that is, what only discovers in such a way that it can never cover up anything – is pure *noein*, straightforwardly observant apprehension of the simplest determinations of the Being of beings as such. This *noein* can never cover up, can never be false; at worst it can be a nonapprehending, *agnoein*, not sufficing for straightforward, appropriate access.

What no longer takes the form of a pure letting be seen, but rather in its indicating always has recourse to something else and so always lets something be seen *as* something, acquires a structure of synthesis and therewith the possibility of covering up. However, "truth of judgment" is only the opposite of this covering up; it is a *multiply founded* phenomenon of truth. Realism and idealism alike thoroughly miss the meaning of the Greek concept of truth from which alone the possibility of something like a "theory of Ideas" can be understood at all as philosophical *knowledge*. And because the function of *logos* lies in letting something be seen straightforwardly, in *letting* beings be *apprehended*, *logos* can mean *reason*. Moreover, because *logos* is used in the sense not only of *legein* but also of *legomenon* – what is pointed to as such; and because the latter is nothing other than the *hypokeimenon* – what always already is at hand at the *basis* of every discourse and discussion in progress; for these reasons *logos qua legomenon* means ground, *ratio*. Finally, because *logos* as *legomenon* can also mean what is addressed, as something that has become visible in its relation to something else, in its "relatedness," *logos* acquires the meaning of a *relationship with* and a *relating to* something.

This interpretation of "apophantic speech" may suffice to clarify the primary function of *logos*.

C   THE PRELIMINARY CONCEPT OF PHENOMENOLOGY
When we bring to mind concretely what has been exhibited in the interpretation of "phenomenon" and "logos" we are struck by an inner relation between what is meant by these terms. The expression "phenomenology" can be formulated in Greek as *legein ta phainomena*. But *legein* means *apophainesthai*. Hence phenomenology means: *apophainesthai ta phainomena* – to let what shows itself be seen from itself, just as it shows itself from itself. That is the formal meaning of the type of research that calls itself "phenomenology." But this expresses nothing other than the maxim formulated above: "To the things themselves!"

Accordingly, the term "phenomenology" differs in meaning from such expressions as "theology" and the like. Such titles designate the objects of the respective disciplines in terms of their content. "Phenomenology" neither designates the object of its researches nor is it a title that describes their content. The word only tells us something about the *how* of the demonstration and treatment of *what* this discipline considers. Science "of" the phenomena means that it grasps its objects in *such* a way that everything about them to be discussed must be directly indicated and directly demonstrated. The basically tautological expression "descriptive phenomenology" has the same sense. Here description does not mean a procedure like that of, say, botanical morphology. The term rather has the sense of a prohibition, insisting that we avoid all nondemonstrative determinations. The character of description itself, the specific sense

of the *logos*, can be established only from the "compelling nature" ["*Sachheit*"] of what is "described," i.e. of what is to be brought to scientific determinateness in the way phenomena are encountered. The meaning of the formal and common concepts of the phenomenon formally justifies our calling every way of indicating beings as they show themselves in themselves "phenomenology."

Now, what must be taken into account if the formal concept of the phenomenon is to be deformalized to the phenomenological one, and how does this differ from the common concept? What is it that phenomenology is to "let be seen"? What is it that is to be called "phenomenon" in a distinctive sense? What is it that by its very essence becomes the *necessary* theme when we indicate something *explicitly*? Manifestly it is something that does *not* show itself at first and for the most part, something that is *concealed*, in contrast to what at first and for the most part does show itself. But at the same time it is something that essentially belongs to what at first and for the most part shows itself, indeed in such a way that it constitutes its meaning and ground.

But what remains *concealed* in an exceptional sense, or what falls back and is *covered up* again, or shows itself only in a *distorted* way, is not this or that being but rather, as we have shown in our foregoing observations, the *Being* of beings. It can be covered up to such a degree that it is forgotten and the question about it and its meaning is in default. Thus what demands to become a phenomenon in a distinctive sense, in terms of its most proper content, phenomenology has taken into its "grasp" thematically as its object.

Phenomenology is the way of access to, and the demonstrative manner of determination of, what is to become the theme of ontology. *Ontology is possible only as phenomenology*. The phenomenological concept of phenomenon, as self-showing, means the Being of beings – its meaning, modifications, and derivatives. This self-showing is nothing arbitrary, nor is it something like an appearing. The Being of beings can least of all be something "behind which" something else stands, something that "does not appear."

Essentially, nothing else stands "behind" the phenomena of phenomenology. Nevertheless, what is to become a phenomenon can be concealed. And precisely because phenomena are at first and for the most part *not* given phenomenology is needed. Being covered up is the counterconcept to "phenomenon." . . .

On the basis of the preliminary concept of phenomenology just delimited, the terms "phenomenal" and "phenomenological" can now be given fixed meanings. What is given and is explicable in the way we encounter the phenomenon is called "phenomenal." In this sense we speak of phenomenal structures. Everything that belongs to the manner of indication and explication, and constitutes the conceptual tools this research requires, is called "phenomenological."

Because phenomenon in the phenomenological understanding is always just what constitutes Being, and furthermore because Being is always the Being of beings, we must first of all bring beings themselves forward in the right way if we are to have any prospect of exposing Being. These beings must likewise show themselves in the way of access that genuinely belongs to them. Thus the common concept of phenomenon becomes phenomenologically relevant. The preliminary task of a "phenomenological" securing of that being which is to serve as our example, as the point of departure for the analysis proper, is always already prescribed by the goal of this analysis.

As far as content goes, phenomenology is the science of the Being of beings – ontology. In our elucidation of the tasks of ontology the necessity arose of a fundamental ontology which would have as its theme that being which is ontologically and ontically distinctive, namely, Dasein. This must be done in such a way that our ontology confronts the cardinal problem, the question of the meaning of Being in general. From the investigation itself we shall see that the methodological meaning of phenomenological description is *interpretation*. The *logos* of the phenomenology of Dasein has the character of *hermēneuein*, through which the proper meaning of Being and the basic structures of the very Being of Dasein are *made known* to the understanding of Being that belongs to Dasein itself. Phenomenology of Dasein is *hermeneutics* in the original signification of that word, which designates the work of interpretation. But since discovery of the meaning of Being and of the basic structures of Dasein in general exhibits the horizon for every further ontological research into beings unlike Dasein, the present hermeneutic is at the same time "hermeneutics" in the sense that it works out the conditions of the possibility of every ontological investigation. Finally, since Dasein has ontological priority over all other beings – as a being that has the possibility of existence [*Existenz*] – hermeneutics, as the interpretation of the Being of Dasein, receives a specific third and, philosophically understood, *primary* meaning of an analysis of the existentiality of existence. To the extent that this hermeneutic elaborates the historicity of Dasein ontologically as the ontic condition of the possibility of the discipline of history, it contains the roots of what can be called "hermeneutics" only in a derivative sense: the methodology of the historical humanistic disciplines.

As the fundamental theme of philosophy, Being is no sort of genus of beings; yet it pertains to every being. Its "universality" must be sought in a higher sphere. Being and its structure transcend every being and every determination of beings there might be. *Being is the transcendens pure and simple*. The transcendence of the Being of Dasein is a distinctive one since in it lies the possibility and necessity of the most radical *individuation*. Every disclosure of Being as the *transcendens* is *transcendental* knowledge. *Phenomenological truth (disclosedness of Being)* is *veritas transcendentalis*.

Ontology and phenomenology are not two different disciplines that among others belong to philosophy. Both terms characterize philosophy itself, its object and procedure. Philosophy is universal, phenomenological ontology, taking its departure from the hermeneutic of Dasein, which as an analysis of *existence* has fastened the end of the guideline of all philosophical inquiry at the point from which it *arises* and to which it *returns*.

The following investigations would not have been possible without the foundation laid by Edmund Husserl; with his *Logical Investigations* phenomenology achieved a breakthrough. Our elucidations of the preliminary concept of phenomenology show that what is essential to it does not consist in its *actuality* as a philosophical "movement." Higher than actuality stands *possibility*. We can understand phenomenology solely by seizing upon it as a possibility.[12]

Notes

1 The German word *Wiederholung* means literally "repetition." Heidegger uses it not in the sense of a mere reiteration of what preceded, but rather in the sense of fetching something back as a new beginning.

Perhaps his use is close to the musical term *recapitulation*, which implies a new beginning incorporating and transforming what preceded. Alternative translations might be "retrieval" or "reprise." (Original trans./ed.)

2 Aristotle, *Metaphysics* III, 4, 1001a 21.

3 Thomas Aquinas, *Summa theologiae* II, 1, Qu. 94, a. 2.

4 Aristotle, *Metaphysics* III, 3, 998b 22.

5 See Pascal, *Pensées et Opuscules* (ed. Brunschvicg), Paris: Hachette, 1912, p. 169: "One cannot undertake to define *being* without falling into this absurdity. For one cannot define a word without beginning in this way: 'It is...' This beginning may be expressed or implied. Thus, in order to define *being* one must say, 'It is...' and hence employ the word to be defined in its definition."

6 Plato, *Sophist* 242 c.

7 Since the "rationalist school" of Christian Wolff (1679–1754), *Dasein* has been widely used in German philosophy to mean the "existence" (or *Dass-sein*, "that it is"), as opposed to the "essence" (or *Wassein*, "what it is") of a thing, state of affairs, person, or God. The word connotes especially the existence of living creatures – around 1860 Darwin's "struggle for life" was translated as *Kampf ums Dasein* – and most notably of human beings. Heidegger thus stresses the word's primary nuance: for him Dasein is that kind of existence that is always involved in an understanding of its Being. It must never be confused with the existence of things that lie before us and are on hand or at hand as natural or cultural objects (*Vorhandenheit, Zuhandenheit*). In order to stress the special meaning Dasein has for him, Heidegger often hyphenates the word (Da-sein), suggesting "there being," which is to say, the openness to Being characteristic of human existence, which is "there" in the world. (The hyphenated form appears in chapter five of *Being and Time* and in many of the later writings.) We will follow tradition and let the German word *Dasein* or *Da-sein* stand, translating the former as "existence" or "human being" only when the usage seems to be nonterminological. Finally, in light of Heidegger's interpretation of Being as presence, we note that *Dasein* originally (around 1700) meant nothing more or less than such presence, *Anwesenheit*. (Original ed.)

8 Throughout *Being and Time* Heidegger contrasts the "ontic" to the "ontological." As we have seen, "ontological" refers to the Being of beings (*onta*) or to any account (*logos*) of the same; hence it refers to a particular discipline (traditionally belonging to metaphysics) or to the content or method of this discipline. On the contrary, "ontic" refers to any manner of dealing with beings that does *not* raise the ontological question. Most disciplines and sciences remain "ontic" in their treatment of beings. What it means to speak of the "ontic priority" of the question of the meaning of Being – a paradox that should give us pause – the present section elucidates. Compare the parallel but not identical opposition of "existentiell" and "existential" in this same section, below. (Original ed.)

9 Heidegger coins the term *existentiell* (here translated as "existentiell") to designate the way Dasein in any given case actually exists by realizing or ignoring its various possibilities – in other words, by living its life. *One* of those possibilities is to inquire into the *structure* of its life and possibilities; the kind of understanding thereby gained Heidegger calls *existenzial* (here translated as "existential"). The nexus of such structures he calls *Existentialität* (here translated as "existentiality"). (Original ed.)

10 Heidegger's word *Destruktion* does not mean "destruction" in the usual sense – which the German word *Zerstörung* expresses. The word *destructuring* should serve to keep the negative connotations at a distance and to bring out the neutral, ultimately constructive, sense of the original. (Original trans./ed.)

11 See *De interpretatione*, ch 1–6. See further, *Metaphysics* VII, 4 and *Nicomachean Ethics*, Bk VI.

12 If the following investigation takes any steps forward in disclosing "the things themselves" the author must above all thank E. Husserl, who by providing his own incisive personal guidance and by very generously sharing his unpublished investigations familiarized the author during his student years in Freiburg with the most diverse areas of phenomenological research.

Select Bibliography

An Introduction to Metaphysics. Translated by Ralph Manheim. Garden City, NY: Doubleday, 1961.

The Basic Problems of Phenomenology. Translated by Albert Hofstadter. Bloomington: Indiana University Press, 1988.

Being and Time. Translated by John Macquarrie and Edward Robinson. Oxford: Blackwell Publishers, 1987.

The Concept of Time. Translated by William McNeill. Oxford: Blackwell Publishers, 1992.

Discourse on Thinking. Translated by John M. Anderson and E. Hans Freund. New York: Harper and Row, 1966.

History of the Concept of Time: Prolegomena. Translated by Theodore Kisiel. Bloomington: Indiana University Press, 1992.

Martin Heidegger

Identity and Difference. Translated by Joan Stambaugh. New York: Harper and Row, 1969.

Martin Heidegger: Basic Writings. Edited by David Farrell Krell. New York: Harper San Francisco, 1993.

On the Way to Language. Translated by Peter D. Hertz. San Francisco: Harper and Row, 1982.

On Time and Being. Translated by Joan Stambaugh. New York: Harper and Row, 1972.

Pathmarks. Edited by William McNeill. Cambridge: Cambridge University Press, 1998.

Poetry, Language, Thought. Translated by Albert Hofstadter. New York: Harper and Row, 1975.

The Question Concerning Technology, and Other Essays. Translated by William Lovitt. New York: Harper and Row, 1977.

What is Called Thinking? Translated by J. Glenn Gray. New York: Harper and Row, 1972.

What is Philosophy? Translated by William Kluback and Jean T. Wilde. London: Vision, 1989.

7

Max Scheler

Man's Place in Nature

German philosopher Max Scheler (1874–1928) was born in Munich. He taught at the University of Jena, and later at the University of Munich, where he developed an enduring interest in phenomenology under the influence of Franz Brentano (1838–1917) and Edmund Husserl. His major work of this period, written from 1913–16, discusses formalism in ethics and material ethics of values. After World War I, Scheler's interest turned briefly to Catholicism, leading to a book on "the eternal in man." Scheler subsequently became chair of philosophy and sociology at the University of Cologne, devoting himself to the study of sociology and worldviews. The final phase of his work turned to anthropology and the study of man as a living being in relation to other forms of life. The following excerpt, which comprises the second chapter of his last book *Man's Place in Nature* (1928), presents Scheler's attempt to understand "spirit" as what distinguishes the human being from the animal organism.

The Essence of Spirit

We have now come to the problem that is crucial for our inquiry. If the animal has intelligence, does this mean there is only a difference in degree between man and animal – or is there still an essential difference? Is there still in man, beyond the stages of life discussed heretofore, something

From *Man's Place in Nature*, translated by Hans Meyerhoff (Boston: Beacon Press, 1961), pp. 35–55. © 1961 by Beacon Press. Reprinted by permission of Beacon Press, Boston.

that is quite different and unique, something that is not yet defined by, or included in, the capacity for choice and intelligence?

Here the paths divide sharply. One side would reserve intelligence and choice for man and deny them to the animal. This view, in fact, affirms that there is an essential, qualitative difference, but locates it at a point where in my opinion it does not exist. The other side, especially the evolutionists of the Darwinian–Lamarckian school, deny that there is an essential difference between man and animal precisely because the animal does have intelligence. These writers adhere, in one way or another, to a unified conception of man which I have called the theory of "*Homo faber*." Accordingly, they do not recognize any distinctive metaphysical or ontological status of man.

For my own part, I reject both views. I assert that the nature of man, or that which may be called his unique place in nature, goes far beyond the capacity for choice and intelligence and would not be reached even if we were to enlarge these powers, in a quantitative sense, to infinity.[1] But it would also be a mistake to think that the new element which gives man his unique characteristics is nothing but a new essential form of being added to the previous stages of psychic life – the vital impulse, instinct, associative memory, intelligence and choice; in other words, an element which still belongs to the psychic and vital functions and capacities, and which falls into the province of psychology and biology.

The new principle transcends what we call "life" in the most general sense. It is not a stage of life, especially not a stage of the particular mode of life called psyche, but a principle opposed to life as such, even to life in man. Thus it is a genuinely new phenomenon which cannot be derived from the natural evolution of life, but which, if reducible to anything, leads back to the ultimate Ground of Being of which "life" is a particular manifestation.

The Greeks affirmed the existence of such a principle and called it reason.[2] We will use a more inclusive term and call it "spirit" – a term which includes the concept of reason, but which, in addition to conceptual thought, also includes the intuition of essences and a class of voluntary and emotional acts such as kindness, love, remorse, reverence, wonder, bliss, despair, and free decision. The center of action in which spirit appears within a finite mode of being we call "person" in sharp contrast to all functional vital centers which, from an inner perspective, may be called "psychic centers."

What, then, is this spirit, this new crucial principle? Seldom has a word been more abused so that it hardly has a clear meaning for anybody. If we put at the head of this concept of spirit a special function of knowledge which it alone can provide, then the essential characteristic of the spiritual being, regardless of its psychological make-up, is its existential liberation from the organic world – its freedom and detachability from the bondage and pressure of life, from its dependence upon all that belongs to life, including its own drive-motivated intelligence.

The spiritual being, then, is no longer subject to its drives and its environment. Instead, it is "free from the environment" or, as we shall say, "open to the world." Such a being has a "world." Moreover, such a being is capable of transforming the primary centers of resistance and reaction into "objects." (The animal remains immersed in them "ecstatically.") Such a being is capable of grasping the qualities of objects without the restriction imposed upon this thing-world by the system of vital drives and the mediating functions and organs of the sensory apparatus.

Thus, spirit is objectivity, or the determination of the objective nature of things. Spirit only belongs to a being capable of strict objectivity. More precisely: in order to be a bearer of spirit, the being must have *reversed*, dynamically and in principle, its relationship both to external reality and to itself as compared with the animal, including its intelligence. What is this reversal?

In the case of the animal, whether it is highly organized or not, every action and reaction, even that which is "intelligent," proceeds from a physiological condition of the nervous system with which are coordinated, on the psychic side, certain instincts, drives, and sensory perceptions. What does not interest the instinct or drive is not given. What is given is given only as a center of resistance to attraction and repulsion, that is, to the animal as a biological unit. Thus the impetus from a physiological–psychological condition is always the first act in the drama of an animal's behavior toward the environment. The structure of the environment is precisely adapted to the physiological peculiarities of the animal, and indirectly to its morphological characteristics as well, and to its instincts and sensory structure, which form a strictly functional unity. Animals only notice and grasp those things which fall into the secure boundaries of their environmental structure. The second act of the drama of animal behavior consists in making some actual changes in the environment as a result of the animal's free action with respect to a dominant goal set by its drives. The third act consists in a concomitant change of its physiological–psychological condition. The course of animal behavior therefore always has this form:

$$A \text{ (animal)} \rightleftharpoons E \text{ (environment)}$$

The situation is altogether different in the case of a being that has spirit. Such a being is capable of behavior (at least insofar as it makes use of spirit) that runs a diametrically opposed course. The first act of this new and human drama is this: Its behavior is "motivated" by a complex of sensations and ideas raised to the status of an object. It is, in principle, independent of the drives and the sensuous surfaces in the environment conditioned by the system of drives that appear in the visual and auditory fields. The second act of the drama consists in the voluntary inhibition, or release, of a drive and of the corresponding reaction. The third act consists of a final and intrinsic change with regard to the objective nature of a thing. The course of such behavior is "world-openness," and such behavior, once it appears, is capable of unlimited expansion – as far as the "world" of existing things extends.

$$M \text{ (man)} \rightleftarrows W \text{ (world)} \rightarrow \rightarrow$$

Man, then, is a being that can exhibit, to an unlimited degree, behavior which is open to the world. To become human is to acquire this openness to the world by virtue of the spirit.

The animal has no "object." It lives, as it were, ecstatically immersed in its environment which it carries along as a snail carries its shell. It cannot transform the environment into an object. It cannot perform the peculiar act of detachment and distance by which man transforms an "environment" into the "world," or into a symbol of the world. It cannot perform the act by which man transforms the centers of resistance determined by drives and affects into "objects."

Objective being or objectification, therefore, is the most formal category of the logical aspect of spirit. I might say the animal is involved too deeply in the actualities of life which correspond to its organic needs and conditions ever to experience and grasp them as objects. The animal, to be sure, no longer lives in quite the same ecstatic state as the plant does, that is to say, subject to nothing but the vital impulse without sensation, representation, consciousness, and without any reporting back of the particular states of the organism to an inner center. Owing to the separation of the sensory and the motor system, and owing to its continuously holding back of specific sensory contents, the animal, as it were, owns itself. It does have a "body schema." But in relation to the environment, the animal still behaves "ecstatically" – even when it acts "intelligently." Its intelligence remains strictly within the bounds of organic drives and practical needs. The spiritual act in man, in contrast to the simple reporting back of the animal's body schema and its contents, is essentially linked with the second dimension stage of the reflexive act. We call this act "concentration," and if we bring the act together with the goal at which concentration aims, we have "self-consciousness," by which is meant the consciousness that the spiritual center of action has of itself. The animal has consciousness as distinguished from the plant, but, as Leibniz knew, it has no self-consciousness. It does not "own itself," it is not its own master; hence, it is not conscious of itself.

Concentration, self-consciousness and the capacity to objectify the original centers of resistance encountered by the drives – these characteristics form a single indivisible structure which, as such, is peculiar only to man. Self-consciousness, or the new act of centering its existence, is the second essential characteristic of man. By virtue of the spirit, man is capable of expanding the environment into the dimension of a world and of objectifying resistance. He is also capable – and this is most remarkable – of objectifying his own physiological and psychological states, every psychic experience and every vital function. It is for this reason that this being can also throw his life away freely.

The animal hears and sees – without knowing that it does so. The psyche of the animal functions and works, but the animal is not a potential psychologist or physiologist. We must single out very exceptional ecstatic states in man; for example, the state of emerging from hypnosis or the state induced by drugs – techniques that in certain cases, as in orgiastic cults of all kinds, render the spirit inactive – in order to imagine the normal condition of the animal. The animal does not even experience its drives as its own, but as dynamic pushes and pulls that emanate from the things in the environment. Primitive man, who in certain psychic characteristics is still close to the animal, does not say, "I avoid this thing," but "This thing is taboo." For the animal there are only those factors in the environment that are determined by attraction and repulsion. The monkey who jumps hither and yonder lives, as it were, in successive states of ecstasy (comparable to the pathological flights of ideas in man). It does not have a "will" that outlasts the drives and their changing states, and that preserves a kind of continuity in the variations of the psychophysical conditions. An animal always arrives, as it were, elsewhere than at the destination at which it originally aimed. Nietzsche made a profound and correct remark when he said, "Man is an animal that can make promises."

There are four essential stages in which all existence manifests itself with regard to inner being. *Inorganic* forms have no such inner state or self-being whatsoever. They have no center that is their own; hence, no medium, no environment in which they live. What we designate as unities in this world, down to the world of molecules, atoms, and electrons depends entirely upon our power to divide bodies, whether we do so in actual practice or in conceptual thought. Every inorganic body is a unity only within a specific context of causal action relative to other bodies. The nonspatial centers of energy, which give the appearance of extension through time and which we attribute to the images of bodies on metaphysical grounds, are mutually interacting points of energy in which the lines of an energy field run together.

An organism, on the other hand, is always an ontic center. It invariably forms "its own" spatio-temporal unity and individuality. These are not produced, as in the case of inorganic unities, by virtue of our capacity to synthesize, which is itself conditioned biologically. An organism is self-limiting. It has individuality. To dissect it means to murder it, that is, to destroy its essence and being. To the vital impulse of the plant there corresponds a center and a medium into which the plant, relatively open in its growth, is placed without any reporting back of its varying states to its center. Yet the plant does have an "inner being" or a kind of soul. In the animal, however, we find both sensation and consciousness and, together with them, a central organization for the reporting back of changing conditions in the organism and the capacity of modifying the central organization on the basis of these reports. It is thus given to itself a second time. Man, however, by virtue of his spirit, is given to himself a third time: in self-consciousness and in the capacity to objectify psychic states and his sensory and motor system. "Person," as applied to man, therefore, must be envisaged as the center of acts raised beyond the interaction and contrast between organism and environment. Does this hierarchy of forms not appear as if there were different levels in the structure of being in which the ultimate Ground of Being bends back more and more upon itself to become more and more conscious of itself on higher levels and new dimensions – until it comes to possess and grasp itself completely in man?

The structure of man – his self-consciousness and his capacity to objectify both the environment and his own physiological and psychic states and the causal relations existing in both – helps to explain a number of specific human characteristics. I shall mention a few of them.

Only in man do we find the fully developed categories of thing and substance. The animal does not have them. The spider waiting for prey will rush immediately after an insect that is caught in its web and whose presence is probably communicated through the tactile sense by a faint pull. But if the insect is put into such proximity that the spider can see it, the spider will run away. Thus the thing that is seen is quite different from the thing that is felt by touch. The spider is incapable of coordinating visual space with kinaesthetic space, or the respective objects disclosed in each. Even the highest animals do not have a fully developed thing-category. The ape that is handed a half-peeled banana will again run away from it, whereas he will eat it if it is completely peeled, and he will peel and eat it if it is not peeled at all. The thing called "banana" has not changed for the animal; rather, the thing has changed into something else. The animal lacks a center which would relate all the psychophysical functions of seeing, hearing, smelling, and grasping, and the different things coordinated with them, into a unity belonging to one and the same concrete object.

Next, man has, from the start, a unified space. For example, a person born blind whose sight is restored through an operation does not learn to synthesize different spaces – such as tactile space, visual space, auditory space, and kinaesthetic space – into a unified intuition of space. What he learns is only how to identify sensory data as symbols and qualities of the same thing occupying one place. The animal again lacks the central function which provides a unified space as a fixed form prior to the particular things and their perception in it. More importantly, it lacks the capacity of self-reference to a center by means of which man combines all sensory data, and the drives coordinated with them, and relates them to a single world as an ordered field composed of different substances. The animal lacks a "world space" which persists as a stable background independent of the animal's movements. It also lacks the empty forms of space and time into which man is placed and in which he originally encounters things and events. These forms are possible only for a being in whom the frustration of drives always exceeds their gratification. For "empty" means, to begin with, an expectation that is not satisfied. The original "emptiness" is, as it were, the emptiness of our hearts.

The basis for the human intuitions of space and time preceding all external sensations is the capacity for spontaneous movement and action according to a definite order. The fact (apparent in certain pathological deficiencies) that tactile space is not directly coordinated with visual space, but that this coordination is possible only through the mediation of kinaesthetic sensations, also indicates that the empty form of space, at least in the sense of an unformed "spatiality," is experienced prior to any conscious sensations. In other words, it is first experienced merely on the basis of motor impulses and the capacity to produce such impulses, for it is these very motor impulses that are followed by kinaesthetic sensations. This primitive "movement-space," this "consciousness-of-being-around-and/or-surrounded," remains with us even when visual space in which the uniform manifold of extension is given, is completely removed.

Although the higher animals do have spatial manifolds (in the most primitive animals we probably find only temporal impressions) these spaces are not homogeneous. There is no fixed, prior ordering system of places in the visual sphere from which the qualities and movements of things in the environment are sharply separated. Only the highest visual organization in man (with erect posture!) has such a system, but he can lose it in pathological cases so that only the primitive space remains. The animal can no more separate the empty forms of space and time from specific objects in the environment than it can isolate the concept of "number" from the notion of plurality, the notion of more or less inherent in the things outside. It lives wholly in the concrete actuality of its immediate present. Only in man do we find the strange phenomenon that both spatial and temporal emptiness appears prior to, and is the basis of, all possible perceptions in the world of objects. This is possible only because the drive expectations converted into motor impulses outweigh the actual gratification of drives in sensation. Thus, without suspecting it, man takes his own emptiness of heart for the "infinite emptiness" of space and time – as if the latter could exist without objects. Science has corrected the serious illusion of the natural world-view only very late by showing that space and time are nothing but forms of ordering things, possibilities for relations and successions among things, and that they have no independent reality apart from these things.

The animal, as I said, has no world space. A dog may have lived for years in a garden, and may have frequently visited every place in it, yet he will not be able to form an overall picture of the garden, no matter how large or small it may be, or of the arrangements of the trees and bushes independent of his own position. He has only "environmental spaces" that vary with his movements, and he is not able to coordinate these with the garden space that is independent of the position of his own body. The reason is that he cannot objectify his own body and its movements so as to include them as variable features in his intuition of space and to reckon instinctively, as it were, with the accident of his own position as man is able to do even without science.

This achievement is but the beginning of what man continues in science. For the greatness of science is this: by means of science, man learns to reckon on a more and more comprehensive scale with his own accidental position in the universe, and with himself or his whole physical and psychical apparatus, as if it were an external object linked in strict causal relations with other things. In this way, he gradually constructs a picture of the world, the objects and laws of which are completely independent of his own psychophysical organism, of his senses, their thresholds, of his needs and their interests in things. Thus the objective world and its laws remain constant throughout the changing conditions of man's place in the universe.[3]

Man alone – insofar as he is a person – is able to go beyond himself as an organism and to transform, from a center beyond the spatiotemporal world, everything (himself included) into an object of knowledge. Thus man as a spiritual being is a being that surpasses himself in the world. As such he is also capable of irony and humor which always indicate the transcendence of actual existence (*Dasein*). The center, however, from which man performs the acts by means of which he objectifies body, psyche, and world in its spatial and temporal abundance cannot itself be part of this world. It cannot be located in space or in time: it can only be located in the highest Ground of Being itself. In his profound theory of the transcendental apperception, Kant clarified this new unity of the *cogito* as the "condition of all possible experience and, therefore, also of all objects in experience," both outer and inner, by which our own inner life

127

becomes accessible to us. He was thus the first to raise "spirit" above "psyche" and expressly denied that spirit was nothing but a group of functions belonging to a so-called mental substance, or soul, which owes its fictitious status merely to an unjustified reification of the actual unity of the spirit.

Thus, we have come to a third important characteristic of spirit. Spirit is the only being incapable of becoming an object. It is pure actuality. It has its being only in and through the execution of its acts. The center of spirit, the person, is not an object or a substantial kind of being, but a continuously self-executing, ordered structure of acts. The person is only in and through his acts. The psychic act is not self-contained. It is an event "in" time which, in principle, we can observe from the center of spirit and which we can objectify through introspection. Psychic acts are capable of objectification, but not the spiritual act – the intentionality itself which makes the psychic process visible. We can only "collect" ourselves with regard to our being as a person: we can concentrate upon it; we cannot objectify it. Other people, too, as *persons* cannot become objects. (In this sense Goethe said of Lili Schönemann that he "loved her too much" to be able to "observe" her.) We can come to "know" them only by participating in, or by entering into, their free acts, through the kind of "understanding" possible in an attitude of empathetic love, the very opposite of objectification – in short, by "identifying," as we say, with the will and love of another person and thereby with himself.

In the acts of a superindividual spirit, too, we can participate only by some kind of identification. We postulate such a spirit on the basis of the essential bond between fact and idea insofar as we assume that there is a self-realizing order of ideas independent of human consciousness, and insofar as we ascribe this order to the ultimate Ground of Being as one of its attributes. We participate in such an order in three respects: in an order of essences, insofar as the spirit is intellect; in an objective order of values insofar as the spirit expresses itself in love, and in a teleological order of the world insofar as the spirit expresses itself in action. The traditional type of philosophical idealism, prevailing since St Augustine, held that "ideas were prior to things" (*ideae ante res*), that there was providence and a *plan* of creation before the *act* of creation. But ideas do not exist "before," "in," or "after" things, but *with* them. They are created by the eternal spirit in the act of continuous world realization (*creatio continua*). Therefore our own participation in these acts is not simply a matter of discovering or of disclosing some being or essence that exists independently of us. It is, rather, a genuine cocreation of the essences, ideas, values, and goals coordinated with the eternal logos, the eternal love, and the eternal will.

If we wish to clarify the special and unique quality of what we call "spirit," it is best to begin with a special spiritual act – the act of ideation. This is an act completely different from all technical intelligence and from the inferential kind of thinking, the beginnings of which we find in animals. Practical intelligence would set itself a problem such as this: I now have a pain in my arm. What caused it? How can it be removed? This would be a task for such sciences as physiology, psychology, or medicine. But I can also take the same experience in a more detached and contemplative attitude, as a "case" disclosing the strange and surprising essential condition that this world is polluted by pain, evil, and sorrow. Then I would ask another question: What is "pain itself" apart from the fact that I experience it here and now? What must be the nature of things that such a thing as "pain itself" is possible?

A striking example of such an act of ideation is the well-known conversion of the Buddha. The prince encounters one poor man, one sick person, one dead man after having been protected from such experiences for years in his father's palace. But he immediately grasps these three chance occurrences as signs for an essential condition of the world. Descartes tried to grasp the essence or essential structure of bodies, by examining a piece of wax – which is quite different from the chemist who analyzes the ingredients of a certain substance. The whole field of mathematics provides impressive evidence for essences of this kind. The animal has a vague conception of plurality which is completely attached to things perceived in their shapes and arrangements. Man alone is able to separate the concept or class of "threeness," as a "collection" of three things from these things themselves, and to operate with the "number" 3 as an independent object according to formal rules for producing a series of such objects. Yet, what mathematics discovers about the relations of nonsensible entities in an axiomatic system is, strange to say, capable of being applied, if not today, then tomorrow with great precision to the world of real things. These are the achievements of the spirit, not of a practical, inferential intelligence. The animal cannot do anything like this.

Ideation, therefore, means to grasp the essential modes and formal structures of the world through a single case only, independent of the number of observations and inductive inferences which belong to intelligence. The knowledge so gained is then universally valid for all possible cases of the same essential nature, and for all possible subjects who think about the same case, quite independent of the accidents of the senses and the manner and degree of their stimulation. Insights so gained, therefore, are valid beyond the limits of sensory experience. They are valid not only for this world, but for all possible worlds. In technical language, we call them *a priori*.

This knowledge of essences fulfills two different functions. On the one hand, it provides the presuppositions, or fundamental axioms, for the positive sciences whose field of research is strictly delimited by methods of proof through observation and measurement. There are different groups of such axioms in different areas within the general system of logic, and they give direction to fruitful observation and inferences, both inductive and deductive. For metaphysics, on the other hand, whose goal is the knowledge of absolute being, the essences are, as Hegel said appropriately, "windows into the absolute." For each genuine essence which reason discovers in the world cannot be reduced to causes of a finite kind, nor can the existence of "something" characterized by such an essence be so reduced. It can only be ascribed *qua* essence to a superindividual spirit as an attribute of the superindividual being in itself (*ens a se*). And the existence of such an essence can only be understood as a secondary attribute inherent in the nature of the eternal vital impulse.

The capacity to distinguish between essence and existence is a basic characteristic of the human spirit. Not that man's capability of knowledge in general is his essential characteristic, as Leibniz observed, but that he is capable of *a priori* knowledge. This does not mean that there is a constant, permanent structure of reason, as Kant believed. On the contrary, this structure is always subject to historical change. What is constant is reason as a diposition and capacity to create and to shape, through the actualization of new essential insights, new forms of thought, intuition, love, and value. (These forms first take shape in the minds of the leading pioneers and then are shared by the rest of mankind through participation.)

If we wish to probe more deeply into the nature of man, we must try to deal with the structure of processes which lead to the act of ideation. Whether consciously or unconsciously, man employs a technique which may be described as a tentative experimental suspension of reality. In this experimental technique the essence is peeled off, as it were, from the concrete sensory object. The animal, as we saw, still lives entirely within the domain of concrete reality. The notion of reality involves, partly, a place in space and time, a here and now and, partly, an adventitious quality as it is disclosed through sense perception from a particular perspective.

To be human means to oppose this reality with an emphatic "No." Buddha knew this when he said that it is wonderful to look upon the things of this world and terrible to be them, and when he developed his technique of deactualizing the world and the self. Plato knew this when he envisaged the intuition of forms as a turning away of the soul from the sensory world, and the return of the soul to itself, in order to go back to the original nature and source of things. And Husserl meant the same thing when he based the intuition of essences upon a phenomenological reduction, a "canceling" or "bracketing" of the accidental coefficients of things in the world in order to bring out their essences. While I do not go along with Husserl's theory of reduction in its details, I do believe that it refers to the essential act by which the human spirit must be defined.

If we wish to know how this act of reduction takes place, we must first ask what our experience of reality is. There is no specific sensory experience that conveys the impression of reality, nor do the senses in general do so, or memory or thought. They can convey some quality (*Sosein*) of things, not their existence (*Dasein*). Existence, or a sense of reality, is derived from the experience of resistance in a world already present as given, and this experience of resistance is inherent in the vital drive, in the central life impulse of our being.[4] The reality of the external world (which is present even in dreams) is not a matter of inference, is not a perceptual experience, is not associated with an experience of objects (which occurs even in fantasy) or with a fixed position in space, arresting our attention. Reality is always a sense of resistance experienced on the lowest and most primitive stage of psychic life, or in the very center of our vital drives constantly active even in sleep and in a state of unconsciousness. In the strict organization of the characteristics of a physical thing, including color, shape, and extension – an organization which we can study in pathological deficiencies of perception – there is nothing more immediate than the sense of reality. Suppose we let all colors and sensory qualities, all forms and relations of a physical thing dissolve in our consciousness, what remains naked, as it were, and without qualitative characteristics, is the powerful impression of reality itself, the impression of the reality of the world.

This original experience of reality as an experience of resistance precedes any consciousness, conception, and perception. Even the strongest sensory experience is never a function of the stimulus and the normal processes of the nervous system only. A drive-attitude, whether attraction or repulsion, must also be present if there is to be even the simplest perception. A drive-attitude is an indispensable accessory condition for all possible perceptions. This explains why the resistances which the centers and fields of forces behind the physical images in the environment exercise upon the vital impulse – the images themselves are ineffective – can be experienced at a point in the temporal process of an incipient perception when it has not yet become a conscious image. Experience of reality, therefore, does not come after, but before any representation of the world.

What, then, is meant by this radical "No" of which I just spoke? What does it mean to "de-actualize" the world or to "ideate" it? It does not mean, as Husserl believed, to suspend the existential judgment which is inherent in every natural act of perception. The judgment "A is real" presupposes, as far as the predicate is concerned, the content of experience, if "real" is not to be an empty word. No, what it means is to suspend, at least tentatively, the experience of reality itself, or to annihilate the entire, indivisible, powerful impression of reality together with its affective corollates. What it means is to remove the "anguish of earthly existence" which, as Schiller wrote, is overcome only "in those regions where the pure forms dwell." For all reality, because it is reality, and regardless of what it is, is a kind of inhibiting, constraining pressure for every living being. Its corollate is "pure" anxiety, an anxiety without an object. If reality means resistance, the canceling of reality can only be the kind of ascetic act by which we suspend the operation of the vital impulse in relation to which the world appears as resistance, and which is the precondition for all sensory experience and its accidental qualities. Drives and

senses belong together. This is the reason why Plato said that philosophy is a process of "dying" (to the body), and this is the reason why every type of extreme rationalism is ultimately founded upon an "ascetic ideal."

This act of deactualization, or derealizing the world, can be performed only by a being which we have called "spirit." Only spirit in its form as pure will can, by an act of will – an act of inhibition – put out of action that center of vital impulses which we recognized as the key to reality.

Man is the kind of being who, by means of the spirit, can take an ascetic attitude toward life. He can suppress and repress his own vital drives and deny them the nourishment of perceptual images and representations. Compared with the animal that always says "Yes," to reality, even when it avoids it and flees from it, man is the being who can say "No," the "ascetic of life," the protestant *par excellence*, against mere reality. This has nothing to do with any question of value or *Weltanschauung*. It does not matter whether we follow Buddha and say that this ascent of the spirit into the unreal sphere of essence is the ultimate goal and good of man because reality is inherently evil (*omne ens est malum*) or whether, as I believe, we must try to return from the sphere of essences to the reality of the world in order to improve it (in this case existence is, to begin with, neutral with respect to good and evil) and whether we envisage the true life and destiny of man in terms of an eternal rhythmic movement between idea and reality, spirit and instinct – and in the reconciliation of this constant tension.

At any rate, as compared with the animal whose existence is, as it were, Philistinism incarnate, man is the eternal Faust, the creature always seeking and desiring (*bestia cupidissima rerum novarum*), never at peace with his environment, always anxious to break through the barriers of his life here and now, always striving to transcend his environment, including his own state of being. For Freud, too, man is the being who represses his instincts.[5]

Only because man has this capacity for repression, not now and then, but as a permanent capacity, does he accomplish two things. First, he erects a superstructure of ideas above the world of sensory experience. Secondly, by this very means, he makes accessible to his spirit the latent energy of the repressed drives. In other words, man is capable of sublimating his instinctual energy into spiritual activity.

Notes

1 Between the clever chimpanzee and an Edison, taking the latter only as a technician, there is only a difference *in degree* – though a great one to be sure.
2 Cf. Julius Stenzel, "Der Ursprung des Geistbegriffes bei den Griechen," in *Die Antike*.
3 Treated more thoroughly in the essay, "Idealismus– Realismus" (*Philosophischer Anzeiger* (Bonn, 1927) II, 3 – Ed.)
4 Cf. "Erkenntnis und Arbeit" in *Die Wissensformen und die Gesellschaft* (Leipzig, 1926), and "Idealismus-Realismus" [*ibid.*].
5 Cf. Sigmund Freud, *Beyond the Pleasure Principle*.

Select Bibliography

Formalism in Ethics and Non-Formal Ethics of Values: A New Attempt Toward the Foundation of an Ethical Personalism. Translated by Manfred S. Frings and Roger L. Funk. Evanston, Ill.: Northwestern University Press, 1973.

Man's Place in Nature. Translated by Hans Meyerhoff. Boston: Beacon Press, 1961.

The Nature of Sympathy. Translated by Peter Heath. London: Routledge and Kegan Paul, 1979.

On the Eternal in Man. Translated by Bernard Noble. Hamden, Conn.: Archon Books, 1972.

On Feeling, Knowing, and Valuing: Selected Writings. Edited by Harold J. Bershady. Chicago: University of Chicago Press, 1992.

Person and Self-Value: Three Essays. Edited by Manfred S. Frings. Dordrecht: Martinus Nijhoff, 1987.

Philosophical Perspectives. Translated by Oscar A. Haac. Boston: Beacon Press, 1958.

Problems of a Sociology of Knowledge. Edited by Kenneth W. Stikkers. Translated by Manfred S. Frings. London: Routledge and Kegan Paul, 1980.

Ressentiment. Translated by Lewis B. Coser and William W. Holdheim. Milwaukee: Marquette University Press, 1994.

Selected Philosophical Essays. Translated by David R. Lachterman. Evanston, Ill.: Northwestern University Press, 1973.

8

Karl Jaspers

Karl Jaspers (1883–1969), considered one of the founders of German "existentialist" philosophy or "philosophy of existence," was professor at the University of Heidelberg and later at the University of Basel. With its roots in psychiatry and psychology, Jaspers' thinking revolves around the predicament of the free and unique individual situated in a particular historical context, and whose existence is subject to certain "limit situations" (such as death, anxiety, guilt, and contingency) that mark the finitude of the individual within the "encompassing" horizon of the world. Like Kierkegaard and Nietzsche before him, Jaspers places emphasis on the primacy of individual engagement with existence, and shared with them a suspicion of all universalizing and abstract philosophy. As the following excerpt from *Philosophy of Existence* (1938) clarifies, philosophy for Jaspers should be undertaken as a living philosophizing, and not as the development of or adherence to philosophical theories.

Philosophy of Existence

Introduction

I have been invited to speak about the philosophy of existence.[1] Part of philosophy today goes by this name. The distinguishing term "existence" is meant to emphasize that it is of the present.

From *Philosophy of Existence*, translated by Richard F. Grabau (Philadelphia: University of Pennsylvania Press, 1971), pp. 3–29. Copyright 1971 in the English translation by the Trustees of the University of Pennsylvania. Reprinted with permission of the publisher.

What is called philosophy of existence is really only a form of the one, primordial philosophy. It is no accident, however, that for the moment the word "existence" became the distinguishing term. It emphasized the task of philosophy that for a time had been almost forgotten: *to catch sight of reality at its origin and to grasp it through the way in which I, in thought, deal with myself — in inner action*. From mere knowledge of something, from ways of speaking, from conventions and role-playing — from all kinds of foreground phenomena — philosophizing wanted to find its way back to reality. *Existenz* is one of the words for reality, with the accent Kierkegaard gave it: everything essentially real is for me only by virtue of the fact that I am I myself. We do not merely exist; rather, our existence is entrusted to us as the arena and the body for the realization of our origin.

Already in the nineteenth century, movements with this turn of mind kept recurring. People wanted "life," wanted "really to live." They demanded "realism." Instead of wanting merely to know, they wanted to experience for themselves. Everywhere, they wanted the "genuine," searched for "origins," and wanted to press on to *man* himself. Superior men became more clearly visible; at the same time, it became possible to discover the true and the real in the smallest particle.

If for a century now the tenor of the age has been entirely different – namely, one of leveling, mechanization, the development of a mass mentality and universal interchangeability of everything and everyone where no one seemed to exist any longer as himself, it was also a stimulating background. Men who could be themselves woke up in this pitiless atmosphere in which every individual was sacrificed as individual. They wanted to take themselves seriously; they searched for the hidden reality; they wanted to know what was knowable; and they thought that by understanding themselves they could arrive at the foundation of their being.

But even this thinking frequently degenerated into the frivolous veiling of reality that is characteristic of the leveling process, by perversion into a tumultuous and pathetic philosophy of feeling and life. The will to experience being for oneself could be perverted into a contentment with the merely vital; the will to find the origin into a mania for primitivism; the sense of rank into a betrayal of the genuine orders of value.

We do not propose to consider in its totality this loss of reality in an age of apparently heightened realism – an age out of whose growing awareness developed the soul's distress, and philosophizing. Instead, we shall attempt to recall by an historical account the tortuous route taken by this return to reality – a return that took many shapes – using as an example *our relation to the sciences*, an example that is inherently essential to our theme.

At the turn of the century, philosophy was for the most part conceived as one science among others. It was a field of academic study, and was approached by young people as an educational possibility.

Sparkling lectures offered vast surveys of its history, its doctrines, problems, and systems. Vague feelings of a freedom and truth often devoid of content (because rarely effective in actual life) combined with a faith in the progress of philosophical knowledge. The thinker "advanced further" and was convinced that with each step he stood at the summit of knowledge attained up to that time.

This philosophy, however, seemed to lack self-confidence. The boundless respect of the age for the exact empirical sciences made them the great exemplar. Philosophy wanted to regain its lost reputation before the judgment seat of the sciences by means of equal exactness. To be sure, all objects of inquiry had been parcelled out to the special sciences. But philosophy wanted to legitimize itself alongside of them by making the whole into a scientific object; the whole of knowledge, for example, by means of epistemology (since the fact of science in general was after all not the object of any particular science); the whole of the universe by means of a metaphysics constructed by analogy with scientific theories, and with their aid; the totality of human ideals by means of a doctrine of universally valid values. These seemed to be objects that did not belong to any special science and yet ought to be open to investigation by scientific methods. Nevertheless, the basic tenor of all this thinking was ambiguous. For it was at once scientific-objective and moral-normative. Men could think they were establishing a harmonious union between the "needs of the mind" and the "results of the sciences." Finally, they could say that they merely wanted objectively to understand the possible worldviews and values, and yet again could claim at the same time to be giving the one true worldview: the scientific . . .

But when the sciences were taken up as though they themselves already contained true philosophy, that is, when they were supposed to give what had been sought to no avail in philosophy, typical errors became possible. Men wanted a science that would tell them what goals to pursue in life – an evaluating science. They deduced from science the right ways of conduct, and pretended to know by means of science what in fact were articles of faith – albeit about things immanent in this world. Or, conversely, they despaired of science because it did not yield what is important in life and, worse, because scientific reflection seemed to paralyze life. Thus attitudes wavered between a superstitious faith in science that makes an absolute starting point out of presumed results, and an antagonism to science that rejects it as meaningless and attacks it as destructive. But these aberrations were only incidental. In fact, powers arose in the sciences themselves that defeated both aberrations, in that knowledge, as knowledge purified itself.

For, when in the sciences too much was asserted for which there was no proof, when comprehensive theories were all too confidently put forward as absolute knowledge of reality, when too much was accepted as self-evident without examination (for example, the basic idea of nature as a mechanism, or many question-begging theories such as the doctrine that the necessity of historical events can be known, and so on), bad philosophy reappeared in the sciences in even worse form. But – and this was magnificent and exalting – *criticism* still existed and was still at work in science itself: not the endless round of philosophical polemic that never leads to any agreement, but the effective, step-by-step criticism that determines the truth for everyone. This criticism destroyed illusions in order to grasp the really knowable in greater purity.

Also, there were great *scientific events* that broke through all dogmatism. At the turn of the century, with the discovery of radioactivity and the beginnings of quantum theory, began the intellectual relativizing of the rigid shell of the mechanistic view of nature. There began the development which has continued to this day, of ideas of discovery that no longer led into the cul-de-sac of a nature existing and known in itself. The earlier alternative, of either assuming that we know the reality of nature in itself, or else believing that we operate with mere fictions in order to be able to describe natural phenomena in the simplest way, collapsed. Precisely by breaking through every absolute, one was in touch with every reality open to investigation.

Analogous though less magnificent phenomena occurred everywhere in the special sciences. Every *absolute presupposition collapsed*. For example, the nineteenth-century dogma of psychiatry that diseases of the mind are diseases of the brain, was called into question. With the surrender of this confining dogma, the expansion of *factual* knowledge replaced an almost mythological construing of mental disturbances in terms of entirely unknown brain-changes. Researchers endeavored to discover *to what extent* mental illnesses are diseases of the brain, and learned to abstain from anticipatory general judgments: while they enormously extended the realistic knowledge of man, they still did not capture man.

Great, awe-inspiring investigators emerged – figures as merciless in their self-criticism as they were fertile in their discoveries.

Max Weber exposed the error in the assumption that science – e.g. economics and sociology – could discover and prove what ought to be done. The scientific method discloses facts and possibilities. To know them objectively and truly, the scientist must suspend his own value judgments in the cognitive act itself, particularly his wishes, sympathies, and antipathies, although these provide fruitful stimuli and sharpen our vision on the way to cognition. Only in this way can he cancel out the obfuscation and onesidedness caused by his value judgments. Science has integrity only as *value-free science*. But, as Max Weber showed, this value-free science is in its turn always guided in its selection of problems and objects by valuations which it, science itself, is capable of recognizing. The passion for evaluation, predominant for life and indeed the basic reason why science should exist at all, and the self-conquest it takes to suspend value-judgments in the pursuit of knowledge, together comprise the power of scientific inquiry.

Such scientific experiences demonstrated the possibility of possessing a wholly determined and concrete knowledge at any given time, as well as the impossibility of finding in science what had been expected in vain from the philosophy of that time. Those who had searched in science for the basis of their own lives, for a guide to their actions, or for being itself, were bound to be disappointed.

The way *to philosophy* had to be found once again.

Our contemporary philosophizing is conditioned by this experience with science. The route from the disillusionment with *decayed philosophy* to the *real sciences*, and from these again to *authentic philosophy*, is such that it must have a decisive role in shaping the kind of philosophizing that is possible today. Therefore, before giving a rough sketch of the way back to philosophy, we must define the far from unambiguous relation between present-day philosophizing and science.

First, the *limits of science* become clear. They may be briefly indicated:

(a) Scientific *cognition of things* is not *cognition of being*. Scientific cognition is particular, concerned with determinate objects, not with being itself. The philosophical relevance of science, therefore, is that, precisely by means of knowledge, it produces the most decisive knowledge of our lack of knowledge, namely our lack of knowledge of what being itself is.

(b) Scientific cognition can provide *no goals whatever* for life. It establishes no valid values. Therefore it cannot lead. By its clarity and decisiveness it points to another source of our lives.

(c) Science can give no answer to the question of its *own meaning*. The existence of science rests upon impulses for which there is no scientific proof that they are true and legitimate.

At the same time as the limits of science became clear, the positive significance and *indispensability of science for philosophy* also became clear.

First, science, having in recent centuries achieved methodological and critical purification (although this had rarely been fully realized by scientists), offered for the first time, by its *contrast* with philosophy, the possibility of recognizing and overcoming the muddy *confusion* of philosophy and science.

The road of science is indispensable for philosophy, since only a knowledge of that road prevents philosophizing from again making unsound and subjective claims to factual knowledge that really belongs to methodologically exact research.

Conversely, philosophical clarity is indispensable to the life and purity of genuine science. Without philosophy, science does not understand itself, and even scientific investigators, though for a time capable of extending specialized knowledge by building on foundations laid by the great scientists, abandon science completely as soon as they are without the counsel of philosophy.

If on the one hand philosophy and science are impossible without each other, and on the other hand the muddy confusion can no longer endure, the present task is to establish their true unity following their separation. Philosophizing can neither be identical with nor opposed to scientific thought.

Second, only the sciences, which engage in research and thereby produce compelling knowledge of objects, bring us face to face with the factual content of appearances. Only the sciences teach me to know clearly the *way things are*. If the philosopher had no current knowledge of the sciences, he would remain without clear knowledge of the world, like a blind man.

Third, philosophizing that is a pursuit of truth rather than enthusiasm must incorporate the *scientific attitude* or *approach*. The scientific attitude is characterized by a continual discrimination of its compelling knowledge – between knowledge accompanied on the one hand by knowledge of the methods that have led to it, and, on the other hand, knowledge accompanied by knowledge of the limits of its validity. The scientific attitude further requires that the scientist be prepared to entertain every criticism of his assertions. For the scientist, criticism is a vital necessity. He cannot be questioned enough in order to test his insights. The genuine scientist profits even from unjustified criticism. If he shrinks from criticism he has no genuine will to know. – Loss of the scientific attitude and approach is loss also of truthfulness in philosophizing. –

Everything works together *to bind philosophy to science*. Philosophy deals with the sciences in such a way that their own meaning is brought out and set forth. By remaining in living touch with the sciences philosophy dissolves the dogmatism (that unclear pseudo-philosophy) which tends to spring up in them again and again. Above all, however, philosophy becomes the conscious witness for the scientific endeavor against the enemies of science. To live philosophically is inseparable from the attitude of mind that will affirm science without reservations.

Together with this clarification of the limits and the meaning of science, there emerged the *independence of philosophy's origin*. Only as each premature assertion was exposed to the sharp light of criticism in the bright realm of science, did men become aware of that independence, and the *one primordial philosophy* begin to speak again through its great representatives. It was as if long-familiar texts had returned from oblivion to the light of day, and as if men learned only now to read them truly, with new eyes. Kant, Hegel, Schelling, Nicolas of Cusa, Anselm, Plotinus, Plato, and a few others became so freshly relevant that one experienced the truth of Schelling's remark that philosophy is an "open secret." One may *know* texts, and be able to trace their thought constructions with precision – and yet not *understand* them.

From this origin we may learn something no science teaches us. For philosophy cannot arise from scientific ways of thinking and scientific knowledge alone. Philosophy demands a *different thinking*, a thinking that, in knowing, reminds me, awakens me, brings me to myself, transforms me.

But the new discovery of philosophy's origin in the old tradition immediately demonstrated the *impossibility of finding the true philosophy ready-made in the past.* The old philosophy in its past forms cannot be ours.

Although we see the historical starting point of our philosophizing in the old philosophy, and develop our own thinking by studying it because only in dialogue with it can we gain clarity, philosophical thinking is nevertheless *always original* and must express itself historically under new conditions in every age.

Most striking among the new conditions is the development of the pure sciences we have just discussed. Philosophy can *no longer be both naive* and truthful. The naive union of philosophy and science was an incomparably forceful and in its cultural situation true cipher. But today such a union is possible only as a muddy confusion that must be radically overcome. As both science and philosophy come to understand themselves, awareness is enhanced. Philosophy, together with science, must create the philosophical thinking that stems from an origin other than science.

Present-day philosophy may, therefore, understand the sublime greatness of the pre-Socratics, but while it derives irreplaceable incentives from them, it cannot follow them. Nor can it any longer remain in the deep naïveté of the questions of its childhood. In order to preserve the depth which children for the most part likewise lose as they mature, philosophy must find paths of inquiry and verification that lie within reality as it is conceived today in all its manifestations. This reality, however, can in no instance be genuine and wholly present without science.

Although the origin speaks to us from the ancient texts, we cannot simply adopt their doctrines. Historical understanding of past doctrines must be distinguished from the appropriation of what is present in all philosophy at all times. For only this appropriation becomes in turn the ground of the possibility of an historical understanding of the distant and the strange.

Present-day philosophizing consciously proceeds from its own source, neither discoverable nor attainable by science alone:

It carries out the quest for *reality* by means of *thinking* as *inner action*. This thinking is involved in all things, in order to transcend them to its authentic fulfillment.

This reality *cannot* be discovered once again, as in the sciences, to be a *determinate content of know-* *ledge*. Philosophy can no longer present a doctrine of the whole of being in objective unity.

Neither can mere lived *feeling* be relied upon to make this reality present. Reality can be attained with and through feeling only in thinking.

Philosophizing presses on reflectively to the point where *thinking becomes the experience of reality itself*. To reach that point, however, I must think constantly, though without attaining reality in such thinking alone. By way of a *provisional, preparatory* thinking I experience something *more* than thought.

Philosophy is *the methodical objectification of this thinking*. I cannot provide a concept of it by giving a synopsis either of the achievements currently going by the name of the philosophy of existence, or of my own philosophy. I can only point *by way of example* to a few *basic ideas* with which it is concerned. I put the following questions:

In the first lecture: the question of *being*, in the sense of the widest *realm* of the encompassing, in which we encounter whatever being is for us.

In the second lecture: the question of *truth*, in the sense of the *way* to the being that we encounter.

In the third lecture: the question of *reality*, in the sense of being as the *goal* and *source* in which all our thought and life find rest.

The Being of the Encompassing

The first answer to the question of *being* arises from the following *basic experience*:

Whatever becomes an object for me is always a *determinate* being among others, and only a *mode* of being. When I think of being as matter, energy, spirit, life, and so on – every conceivable category has been tried – in the end I always discover that I have absolutized a mode of determinate being, which appears within the totality of being, into being itself. No known being is *being itself*.

We always live, as it were, within a horizon of our knowledge. We strive to get beyond every horizon which still surrounds us and obstructs our view. But we never attain a standpoint where the limiting horizon disappears and from where we could survey the whole, now complete and without horizon, and therefore no longer pointing to anything beyond itself. Nor do we attain a series of standpoints constituting a totality in which we arrive at absolute being by moving through the horizons – as in circumnavigating the earth. For us, being remains open. On all sides it draws us into the unlimited. Over and over again it is always causing some new determinate being to confront us.

Such is the course of our progressing knowledge. By reflecting upon that course we ask about *being itself*, which always seems to *recede* from us, in the very manifestation of all the appearances we encounter. This being we call the *encompassing*. But the encompassing is not the horizon of our knowledge at any particular moment. Rather, it is the source from which all new horizons emerge, without itself ever being visible even as a horizon.

The encompassing always merely announces itself – in present objects and within the horizons – but it *never* becomes an *object*. Never appearing to us itself, it is that wherein everything else appears. It is also that due to which all things not merely are what they immediately seem to be, but remain transparent.

With this first thought we carry out *a basic philosophical operation*. With it we desire to free our sense of being from its connection with knowledge (a connection that returns in ever different form). It is a simple thought, yet seemingly impossible to perform just as it opens up the greatest prospect.

The structure of our thought forces us to make whatever we want to know into a determinate object. If we want to think about the encompassing, we must immediately make even it into something objective, such as: the encompassing is the world, is our own existence, is consciousness in general. When we think clearly about the encompassing, we thus do precisely what thinking about the encompassing is supposed to transcend. If we seek the ground of everything in the encompassing, we may no longer take any object for the encompassing; but in thinking about it we cannot avoid using determinate concepts of being. These should disappear in the execution of the thought, when we become aware of that being itself which is no longer a determinate being. Every proposition referring to the encompassing thus contains a paradox. And if it were possible to conceive something nonobjective in objective form – in fact this is the basic accomplishment of philosophizing – every proposition would at the same time be unavoidably open to misunderstandings. Instead of becoming aware of the encompassing in a dynamic movement of thought, we would, in the literal meaning of isolated propositions, possess a spurious knowledge of the whole of the encompassing.

What is logically impossible to accomplish in the usual sense of knowledge is nonetheless philoso-phically possible as *increasing lucidity of a sense of being* totally different from all determinate knowledge. We enter the *widest realm of possibility*. Everything that has being for us in being known acquires a depth from its relation to this realm, from which it comes to meet us, announcing being without being identical to it. . . .

Let us reflect upon the significance of what we have discussed so far. When the elucidation of the encompassing and its modes is successful, its effect permeates the meaning of every cognition. For it clarifies *philosophical decisions* that touch every aspect of our being.

1 The basic philosophical operation *alters my sense of being*. No longer can the totality of being be known in *ontological* concepts; in the last analysis it can be illuminated only as the encompassing realm, and as the realms in which we encounter all being. While ontology involved thinking of being as an order of objects or sense-unities, now – since Kant – every ontology must be rejected. What remains are the realms within which we must first discover what being is. For ontology, everything was only what thought conceives it to be; for philosophizing, everything is simultaneously permeated by the encompassing, or else it is as good as lost. Ontology clarified the meaning of statements about being by referring back to a first being; philosophizing clarifies the encompassing in which everything that can be met in statements has its source and ground. Ontology attempted an objective clarification – that is, it pointed to something immediately evident in immanent thinking; philosophizing encounters being indirectly in transcending thinking. The model for the meaning of ontology is an ordered table of static categories, whereas the model for the meaning of the elucidation of the encompassing is an interlacing band of clarifying lines that move as though in suspension.

In the illumination of the modes of the encompassing a series of pseudo-ontologies inevitably arises upon which we seize. For the conceptual structure of these ontologies provides us with language. But the movement of philosophizing immediately dissolves their ontological meaning, and instead of a knowledge of a mere something causes the presence of an in each instance peculiarly colorful and open realm to emerge.

2 On the one hand, the interlacement in which being stands for us allows for an unlimited extension of cognition into everything that becomes an object. But on the other hand, in the encompassing

it sets an impassable limit which at the same time gives wings to the meaning of cognition.

This has far-reaching implications, especially for our *knowledge of the reality of man*. The encompassing that I am as existence and spirit is objectified and thus becomes an object of research, as the empirical reality of human existence and spirit that comes to my attention. But scientific knowledge about existence and spirit is not knowledge of the encompassing. Rather, it is knowledge of an appearance whose being is what we ourselves are or can be, and to which we have two approaches, mutually bound to each other: through knowledge of it as appearance, and through inner awareness.

All modes of the encompassing virtually collapse when they become objects of investigation and are supposed to be no more than that. They expire in what is left when they become visible and knowable objects of research. The kind of reality possessed by a given object of scientific knowledge is a question that must be asked in any case. Negatively, it is easy to say:

No *anthropology* knows the real, living existence of man. That living encompassing existence which we ourselves are possesses biological knowledge of itself only as a perspective or uses it only as means. In our research we move about within the encompassing that we are by making our existence into an object for ourselves, acting upon it and manipulating it; but as we do this it must at the same time let us know that we never have it in hand – except for our ability to destroy this uncomprehended existence in its entirety.

No *aesthetic theory* can scientifically understand the intrinsic reality of art – that is, the truth that was experienced and created in art. What, for example, objective thinking calls "expression" and relates to a "sense of life" or character, is really a communication from the origin to a possible origin, and is encompassing reality.

No *science of religion* (history, psychology, or sociology of religion) understands the reality of religion. Science can know and understand religions without the investigator's belonging to or having faith in any of them. Real faith is not knowable.

The encompassing preserves my freedom against knowability. But if I take the content of knowledge already to be reality itself, that which is known leads me, so to speak, along a detour bypassing reality. The philosophical task within every science is positively to develop what comes to be known. All practice on the basis of knowledge must rely on the unseen encompassing: medical treatment must rely on un-understood life; planned alteration of human existence on real, un-understood faith and on the encompassing nature in the ranks of man. All true practice is therefore guided also by the encompassing, which, however, nowhere displaces knowledge. For awareness of the encompassing never cancels out the knowledge that is possible for us. Rather, this knowledge, together with its relativization, is grasped with a new profundity; for its limitless movement is incorporated within a realm, which, though it is nowhere known, becomes present as that which illuminates, as it were, all known objects.

No known being is being itself. As that which I know of myself, I am never truly myself. What I know of being is never being itself. Whatever is known has become known; it is thus a particular that we have grasped, but also something that conceals and restricts. One must continually break out of the confinement of knowledge, but one can find the content of knowledge only by unreserved and concrete mastery of cognition, which is always of particulars.

3   Whether or not I keep the *totality* of the modes of the encompassing in mind as I philosophize is a basic decision. It seems possible to grasp true being in *single* modes – in the world, consciousness in general, existence or spirit, or in a combination of these. But characteristic falsehoods and loss of reality arise in every case.

The most profoundly effective among these decisions, however, is whether I reject the *leap* from the totality of *immanence* to *transcendence*, or make the performance of this leap the starting point of philosophizing.

It is the leap from everything that can be experienced in time and can be known timelessly (and therefore always remains mere appearance) to real and eternal being itself (which therefore is not knowable in temporal existence even though it comes to expression for us only in temporal existence).

It is the leap from the encompassing that *we are* as existence, consciousness, spirit, to the encompassing that *we can be*, or authentically are, as *Existenz*. And it is thus also the leap from the encompassing that we know as world to the encompassing that being in itself is.

This leap is decisive for my freedom. For freedom exists only with and by transcendence.

No doubt there is something that seems akin to *freedom* even *at the level of immanence*, provided I do not identify the encompassing that I am as existence and spirit with its knowability. But this is only the relative freedom to remain open to the encompassing of existence and spirit.

No doubt there is also the *freedom of thought* that rises to the absolute freedom of the ability to disregard everything – the freedom of negativity. But positive freedom has another origin than has thought. It arises only for the *Existenz* that is reached by a leap. And this freedom is obliterated if the ability of thought to disregard is extended to freedom itself and to transcendence. I cannot disregard myself as possible *Existenz* – and therefore also disregard transcendence – without betraying myself and sinking into a void.

For the *freedom of Existenz* exists only as identity with the origin on which thought founders. This freedom is lost to me the moment I rescind the leap and slide back into immanence – for example into the deceptive idea of a universal, necessary and knowable totality of events (of the world, of existence, of spirit) in the face of which I surrender my freedom.

Here, in this leap to transcendence, I grasp in thought the basic decisions about my own being, and about its reality.

Philosophizing in the modes of the encompassing is a matter of a *resolution* – the resolution of the will-to-being to detach itself from all determinate knowledge of being, after I have appropriated its full portent, so that being itself may truly come to me.

It is the resolution in which I determine whether I relax in a satisfying knowledge of being, or whether, instead, in an open, horizonless realm encompassing all horizons, I hear what speaks to me and perceive the flashing signals that point, warn, tempt – and perhaps reveal what is;

– whether in the reflections of being, all of which appear as representations of being, I make sure myself, and never try to avoid this route of immanence accessible to me alone, as though without it I could straightway gain access to the ground of being;

– whether I persevere until I become aware that the sole basis at the foundation of the possible *Existenz* which I am is the transcendence that supports me;

– whether, instead of gaining a deceptive toehold in a doctrine of being, I as an historic phenomenon become myself with the other Self within the encompassing that remains open.

The modes of the encompassing illuminate a basic feature of *man's* possibility.

We would like to see the *human ideal*. We would like to recognize in our thoughts what we ought to be, and what we can be on the basis of our obscure ground. It is as if in the represented image we were to find a certainty of our essence through the clarity of the idea of ideal humanity.

But every conceptual and every visible form of being human lacks universal validity. The form is only one aspect of historic *Existenz*, not *Existenz* itself. And every form of possible human perfection proves upon reflection to be defective and unachievable in reality.

Therefore, ideals serve well as guides. They are like beacons on a journey; but they do not permit us to tarry, as though our goal and rest were already contained in them.

Like everything objectively known, ideals are fused with the encompassing. Philosophizing points beyond all ideals – though only by way of and in constant touch with them – to the abiding realm of the encompassing. It is of the essence of being human to attain *consciousness of this breadth*, because the encompassing keeps us alert *to our own possibility*.

We are indeed truly human only to the extent that we always grasp what is nearest at hand, according to the standard of the ideals that have become lucid up to that moment. But thinking of the encompassing, in extending this realm, opens the soul to the perception of the origin.

For the essence of man consists not in the ideal that can be fixed, but only in his unlimited task, by the accomplishment of which he penetrates to the origin from whence he came and to which he gives himself back.

Man's essence is still less contained in the anthropological knowledge he can gain of himself as a living being in the world. Nor is it exhausted in the context of his existence, in his consciousness or his spirit. Man is all of these, and he vanishes or is stunted if one of these essentials is lost.

But although as finite temporal existence we remain veiled, and must uneasily make do from moment to moment with preliminaries, yet there is within us a hidden depth that we can feel in exalted moments, something that permeates all modes of the encompassing and that becomes certain for us precisely through them. Schelling said that we are "privy to creation" – as if in our ground we had been present at the origin of all things and then had lost this awareness in the confines of our world. In philosophizing, we are engaged in awakening the memory through which we will return to our ground. The realization of the encompassing is the first, so far still negative, step in breaking out of this confinement.

Thus far we have pointed to a *breadth* and a *depth* only in the *abstract*. Do they remain *empty*, or do we really encounter *being* in them? Consciousness of the breadth gives as such only an incentive, but not yet fulfillment. After breaking through into the realm of the encompassing, therefore, we encounter a double possibility:

Either I sink into the bottomless of the infinite: I stand in *Nothingness*, in the face of which I am what I can be *through myself alone*. If this idea does not volatilize my essence which is so problematic to itself, so that in the end I lose all sense of being, then it fanaticizes it in order to rescue me into something grasped by force, some determinate particular – blind before the encompassing and face to face with Nothingness.

Or, the awareness of the breadth engenders unlimited capacity of vision and unlimited readiness. In the encompassing, *being itself* comes out of all origins to meet me. I myself am given to myself.

Both alternatives are possible. In losing the substance of myself I sense Nothingness. In being given to myself I sense the fullness of the encompassing.

I can force neither of these two. Intentionally I can only maintain my integrity, can prepare, and can remember.

If nothing comes to meet me, if I do not love, if what is does not come to me through my love and I do not become myself in it, then I remain in the end as an existence that can be used only like raw material. But because man is never only a means, but is always also an ultimate end, the philosopher, confronting that double possibility, and constantly threatened by Nothingness, wills fulfillment out of the origin.

Note

1 Throughout, "philosophy of existence" is a translation of "Existenzphilosophie," "existence" the translation of "Dasein," and "Exist-enz," where it occurs alone, is left untranslated. (Trans.)

Select Bibliography

The Atom Bomb and the Future of Man, translated by E. B. Ashton. Chicago: University of Chicago Press, 1963.

Basic Psychopathology. Translated by J. Hoening and Marian W. Hamilton. Baltimore: Johns Hopkins University Press, 1997.

Existentialism and Humanism: Three Essays. Edited by Hanns E. Fischer. Translated by E. B. Ashton. New York: R. F. Moore, 1952.

The Idea of the University. Edited by Karl W. Deutsch. Translated by H. A. T. Reiche and H. F. Vanderschmidt. Boston: Beacon Press, 1959.

Karl Jaspers: Basic Philosophical Writings. Edited and translated by Edith Ehrlich, Leonard Ehrlich, and George B. Pepper. Atlantic Highlands, NJ: Humanities Press, 1994.

Man in the Modern Age. Translated by Eden Paul and Cedar Paul. New York: AMS Press, 1978.

Nietzsche: An Introduction to the Understanding of his Philosophical Activity. Translated by Charles F. Wallraff and Frederick J. Schmitz. Baltimore: Johns Hopkins University Press, 1997.

The Origin and Goal of History. Translated by Michael Bullock. New Haven: Yale University Press, 1965.

Philosophy and the World: Selected Essays and Lectures. Translated by E. B. Ashton. Chicago: Regnery, 1963.

Philosophy Is for Everyman: A Short Course in Philosophical Thinking. Translated by R. F. C. Hull and Grete Wels. London: Hutchinson, 1969.

Philosophy of Existence. Translated by Richard F. Grabau. Philadelphia: University of Pennsylvania Press, 1971.

Reason and Anti-Reason in Our Time. Translated by Stanley Godman. Hamden, Conn.: Archon Books, 1971.

9

Alexandre Kojève

Marxist Hegelian philosopher Alexandre Kojève (1902–68) was born in Russia and studied in Berlin before settling in Paris where, from 1933–9, he delivered a series of lectures on Hegel's *Phenomenology of Spirit* at the École des Hautes Études. Although not published until 1947, Kojève's penetrating readings of Hegel influenced an entire generation of French philosophers, including Sartre, Merleau-Ponty, Bataille, and Lacan. Particularly important is the following commentary on Section A of Chapter IV of Hegel's *Phenomenology of Spirit*, entitled "Autonomy and Dependence of Self-consciousness: Mastery and Slavery." This selection reproduces and translates part of Hegel's text; Kojève's commentary is in square brackets.

Introduction to the Reading of Hegel

Hegel . . . erfasst die Arbeit *als das* Wesen, als das sich bewährende Wesen des Menschen.

Karl Marx

[Man is Self-Consciousness. He is conscious of himself, conscious of his human reality and dignity; and it is in this that he is essentially different from animals, which do not go beyond the level of

From *Introduction to the Reading of Hegel*, edited by Allan Bloom, translated by James H. Nichols, Jr (Ithaca: Cornell University Press, 1986), pp. 3–30. Copyright © 1947 by Editions Gallimard, and copyright © 1969 by Basic Books, Inc. Reprinted by permission of Basic Books, a division of HarperCollins Publishers, Inc., and Editions Gallimard.

simple Sentiment of self. Man becomes conscious of himself at the moment when – for the "first" time – he says "I." To understand man by understanding his "origin" is, therefore, to understand the origin of the I revealed by speech.

[Now, the analysis of "thought," "reason," "understanding," and so on – in general, of the cognitive, contemplative, passive behavior of a being or a "knowing subject" – never reveals the why or the how of the birth of the word "I," and consequently of self-consciousness – that is, of the human reality. The man who contemplates is "absorbed" by what he contemplates; the "knowing subject" "loses" himself in the object that is known. Contemplation reveals the object, not the subject. The object, and not the subject, is what shows itself to him in and by – or better, as – the act of knowing. The man who is "absorbed" by the object that he is contemplating can be "brought back to himself" only by a Desire; by the desire to eat, for example. The (conscious) Desire of a being is what constitutes that being as I and reveals it as such by moving it to say "I..." Desire is what transforms Being, revealed to itself by itself in (true) knowledge, into an "object" revealed to a "subject" by a subject different from the object and "opposed" to it. It is in and by – or better still, as – "his" Desire that man is formed and is revealed – to himself and to others – as an I, as the I that is essentially different from, and radically opposed to, the non-I. The (human) I is the I of a Desire or of Desire.

[The very being of man, the self-conscious being, therefore, implies and presupposes Desire. Consequently, the human reality can be formed and maintained only within a biological reality, an animal life. But, if animal Desire is the necessary condition of Self-Consciousness, it is not the sufficient condition. By itself, this Desire constitutes only the Sentiment of self.

.[In contrast to the knowledge that keeps man in a passive quietude, Desire dis-quiets him and moves him to action. Born of Desire, action tends to satisfy it, and can do so only by the "negation," the destruction, or at least the transformation, of the desired object: to satisfy hunger, for example, the food must be destroyed or, in any case, transformed. Thus, all action is "negating." Far from leaving the given as it is, action destroys it; if not in its being, at least in its given form. And all "negating-negativity" with respect to the given is necessarily active. But negating action is not purely destructive, for if action destroys an objective reality, for the sake of satisfying the Desire from which it is born, it creates in its place, in and by that very destruction, a subjective reality. The being that eats, for example, creates and preserves its own reality by the overcoming of a reality other than its own, by the "transformation" of an alien reality into its own reality, by the "assimilation," the "internalization" of a "foreign," "external" reality. Generally speaking, the I of Desire is an emptiness that receives a real positive content only by negating action that satisfies Desire in destroying, transforming, and "assimilating" the desired non-I. And the positive content of the I, constituted by negation, is a function of the positive content of the negated non-I. If, then, the Desire is directed toward a "natural" non-I, the I, too, will

be "natural." The I created by the active satisfaction of such a Desire will have the same nature as the things toward which that Desire is directed: it will be a "thingish" I, a merely living I, an animal I. And this natural I, a function of the natural object, can be revealed to itself and to others only as Sentiment of self. It will never attain Self-Consciousness.

[For there to be Self-Consciousness, Desire must therefore be directed toward a non-natural object, toward something that goes beyond the given reality. Now, the only thing that goes beyond the given reality is Desire itself. For Desire taken as Desire – i.e. before its satisfaction – is but a revealed nothingness, an unreal emptiness. Desire, being the revelation of an emptiness, the presence of the absence of a reality, is something essentially different from the desired thing, something other than a thing, than a static and given real being that stays eternally identical to itself. Therefore, Desire directed toward another Desire, taken as Desire, will create, by the negating and assimilating action that satisfies it, an I essentially different from the animal "I." This I, which "feeds" on Desires, will itself be Desire in its very being, created in and by the satisfaction of its Desire. And since Desire is realized as action negating the given, the very being of this I will be action. This I will not, like the animal "I," be "identity" or equality to itself, but "negating-negativity." In other words, the very being of this I will be becoming, and the universal form of this being will not be space, but time. Therefore, its continuation in existence will signify for this I: "not to be what it is (as static and given being, as natural being, as 'innate character') and to be (that is, to become) what it is not." Thus, this I will be its own product: it will be (in the future) what it has become by negation (in the present) of what it was (in the past), this negation being accomplished with a view to what it will become. In its very being this I is intentional becoming, deliberate evolution, conscious and voluntary progress; it is the act of transcending the given that is given to it and that it itself is. This I is a (human) individual, free (with respect to the given real) and historical (in relation to itself). And it is this I, and only this I, that reveals itself to itself and to others as Self-Consciousness.

[Human Desire must be directed toward another Desire. For there to be human Desire, then, there must first be a multiplicity of (animal) Desires. In other words, in order that Self-Consciousness be born from the Sentiment of self, in order that the human reality come into being within the animal reality, this reality must be essentially manifold. Therefore, man can appear on earth only within a herd. That is why the human reality can only be social. But for the herd to become a society, multiplicity of Desires is not sufficient by itself; in addition, the Desires of each member of the herd must be directed – or potentially directed – toward the Desires of the other members. If the human reality is a social reality, society is human only as a set of Desires mutually desiring one another as Desires. Human Desire, or better still, anthropogenetic Desire, produces a free and historical individual, conscious of his individuality, his freedom, his history, and finally, his historicity. Hence, anthropogenetic Desire is different from animal Desire (which produces a natural being, merely living and having only a sentiment of its life) in that it is directed, not toward a real, "positive," given object, but toward another Desire. Thus, in the relationship between man and woman, for example, Desire is human only if the one desires, not the body, but the Desire of the other; if he wants "to possess" or "to assimilate" the Desire taken as Desire – that is to say, if he wants to be "desired" or "loved," or, rather, "recognized" in his human value, in his reality as a human individual. Likewise, Desire directed toward a natural object is human only to the extent that it is "mediated" by the Desire of another directed toward the same object: it is human to desire what others desire, because they desire it. Thus, an object perfectly useless from the biological point of view (such as a medal, or the enemy's flag) can be desired because it is the object of other desires. Such a Desire can only be a human Desire, and human reality, as distinguished from animal reality, is created only by action that satisfies such Desires: human history is the history of desired Desires.

[But, apart from this difference – which is essential – human Desire is analogous to animal Desire. Human Desire, too, tends to satisfy itself by a negating – or better, a transforming and assimilating – action. Man "feeds" on Desires as an animal feeds on real things. And the human I, realized by the active satisfaction of its human Desires, is as much a function of its "food" as the body of an animal is of its food.

[For man to be truly human, for him to be essentially and really different from an animal, his human Desire must actually win out over his animal Desire. Now, all Desire is desire for a value.

The supreme value for an animal is its animal life. All the Desires of an animal are in the final analysis a function of its desire to preserve its life. Human Desire, therefore, must win out over this desire for preservation. In other words, man's humanity "comes to light" only if he risks his (animal) life for the sake of his human Desire. It is in and by this risk that the human reality is created and revealed as reality; it is in and by this risk that it "comes to light," i.e. is shown, demonstrated, verified, and gives proofs of being essentially different from the animal, natural reality. And that is why to speak of the "origin" of Self-Consciousness is necessarily to speak of the risk of life (for an essentially nonvital end).

[Man's humanity "comes to light" only in risking his life to satisfy his human Desire – that is, his Desire directed toward another Desire. Now, to desire a Desire is to want to substitute oneself for the value desired by this Desire. For without this substitution, one would desire the value, the desired object, and not the Desire itself. Therefore, to desire the Desire of another is in the final analysis to desire that the value that I am or that I "represent" be the value desired by the other: I want him to "recognize" my value as his value. I want him to "recognize" me as an autonomous value. In other words, all human, anthropogenetic Desire – the Desire that generates Self-Consciousness, the human reality – is, finally, a function of the desire for "recognition." And the risk of life by which the human reality "comes to light" is a risk for the sake of such a Desire. Therefore, to speak of the "origin" of Self-Consciousness is necessarily to speak of a fight to the death for "recognition."

[Without this fight to the death for pure prestige, there would never have been human beings on earth. Indeed, the human being is formed only in terms of a Desire directed toward another Desire, that is – finally – in terms of a desire for recognition. Therefore, the human being can be formed only if at least two of these Desires confront one another. Each of the two beings endowed with such a Desire is ready to go all the way in pursuit of its satisfaction; that is, is ready to risk its life – and, consequently, to put the life of the other in danger – in order to be "recognized" by the other, to impose itself on the other as the supreme value; accordingly, their meeting can only be a fight to the death. And it is only in and by such a fight that the human reality is begotten, formed, realized, and revealed to itself and to others.

Therefore, it is realized and revealed only as "recognized" reality.

[However, if all men – or, more exactly, all beings in the process of becoming human beings – behaved in the same manner, the fight would necessarily end in the death of one of the adversaries, or of both. It would not be possible for one to give way to the other, to give up the fight before the death of the other, to "recognize" the other instead of being "recognized" by him. But if this were the case, the realization and the revelation of the human being would be impossible. This is obvious in the case of the death of both adversaries, since the human reality – being essentially Desire and action in terms of Desire – can be born and maintained only within an animal life. But it is equally impossible when only one of the adversaries is killed. For with him disappears that other Desire toward which Desire must be directed in order to be a human Desire. The survivor, unable to be "recognized" by the dead adversary, cannot realize and reveal his humanity. In order that the human being be realized and revealed as Self-Consciousness, therefore, it is not sufficient that the nascent human reality be manifold. This multiplicity, this "society," must in addition imply two essentially different human or anthropogenetic behaviors.

[In order that the human reality come into being as "recognized" reality, both adversaries must remain alive after the fight. Now, this is possible only on the condition that they behave differently in this fight. By irreducible, or better, by unforeseeable or "undeducible" acts of liberty, they must constitute themselves as unequals in and by this very fight. Without being predestined to it in any way, the one must fear the other, must give in to the other, must refuse to risk his life for the satisfaction of his desire for "recognition." He must give up his desire and satisfy the desire of the other: he must "recognize" the other without being "recognized" by him. Now, "to recognize" him thus is "to recognize" him as his Master and to recognize himself and to be recognized as the Master's Slave.

[In other words, in his nascent state, man is never simply man. He is always, necessarily, and essentially, either Master or Slave. If the human reality can come into being only as a social reality, society is human – at least in its origin – only on the basis of its implying an element of Mastery and an element of Slavery, of "autonomous" existences and "dependent" existences. And that is why to speak of the origin of Self-Consciousness is necessarily to

speak of "the autonomy and dependence of Self-Consciousness, of Mastery and Slavery."

[If the human being is begotten only in and by the fight that ends in the relation between Master and Slave, the progressive realization and revelation of this being can themselves be effected only in terms of this fundamental social relation. If man is nothing but his becoming, if his human existence in space is his existence in time or as time, if the revealed human reality is nothing but universal history, that history must be the history of the interaction between Mastery and Slavery: the historical "dialectic" is the "dialectic" of Master and Slave. But if the opposition of "thesis" and "antithesis" is meaningful only in the context of their reconciliation by "synthesis," if history (in the full sense of the word) necessarily has a final term, if man who becomes must culminate in man who has become, if Desire must end in satisfaction, if the science of man must possess the quality of a definitively and universally valid truth – the interaction of Master and Slave must finally end in the "dialectical overcoming" of both of them.

[However that may be, the human reality can be begotten and preserved only as "recognized" reality. It is only by being "recognized" by another, by many others, or – in the extreme – by all others, that a human being is really human, for himself as well as for others. And only in speaking of a "recognized" human reality can the term *human* be used to state a truth in the strict and full sense of the term. For only in this case can one reveal a reality in speech. That is why it is necessary to say this of Self-Consciousness, of self-conscious man:] Self-Consciousness exists *in* and *for itself* in and by the fact that it exists (in and for itself) for another Self-Consciousness; i.e. it exists only as an entity that is recognized.

This pure concept of recognition, of the doubling of Self-Consciousness within its unity, must now be considered as its evolution appears to Self-Consciousness [i.e. not to the philosopher who speaks of it, but to the self-conscious man who recognizes another man or is recognized by him.]

In the first place, this evolution will make manifest the aspect of the inequality between the two Self-Consciousnesses [i.e. between the two men who confront one another for the sake of recognition], or the expansion of the middle-term [which is the mutual and reciprocal recognition] into the two extremes [which are the two who confront one another]; these are opposed to one another as extremes, the one only recognized, the other only recognizing. [To begin with, the man who wants to be recognized by another in no sense wants to recognize him in turn. If he succeeds, then, the recognition will not be mutual and reciprocal: he will be recognized but will not recognize the one who recognizes him.]

To begin with, Self-Consciousness is simple-or-undivided Being-for-itself: it is identical-to-itself by excluding from *itself* everything *other* [than itself]. Its essential-reality and its absolute object are, for it, *I* [I isolated from everything and opposed to everything that is not I]. And, in this *immediacy*, in this *given-being* [i.e. being that is not produced by an active, creative process] of its Being-for-itself, Self-Consciousness is *particular-and-isolated*. What is other for it exists as an object without essential-reality, as an object marked with the character of a negative-entity.

But [in the case we are studying] the other-entity, too, is a Self-Consciousness; a human-individual comes face to face with a human-individual. Meeting thus *immediately*, these individuals exist for one another as common objects. They are *autonomous* concrete-forms, Consciousnesses submerged in the *given-being* of *animal-life*. For it is as animal-life that the merely existing object has here presented itself. They are Consciousnesses that have not yet accomplished *for one another* the [dialectical] movement of absolute abstraction, which consists in the uprooting of all immediate given-being and in being nothing but the purely negative-or-negating given-being of the consciousness that is identical-to-itself.

Or in other words, these are entities that have not yet manifested themselves to one another as pure *Being-for-itself* – i.e. as *Self*-Consciousness. [When the "first" two men confront one another for the first time, the one sees in the other only an animal (and a dangerous and hostile one at that) that is to be destroyed, and not a self-conscious being representing an autonomous value.] Each of these two human-individuals is, to be sure, subjectively-certain of himself; but he is not certain of the other. And that is why his own subjective-certainty of himself does not yet possess truth [i.e. it does not yet reveal a reality – or, in other words, an entity that is objectively, intersubjectively, i.e. universally, recognized, and hence existing and valid]. For the truth of his subjective-certainty [of the idea that he has of himself, of the value that he attributes to himself] could have been nothing but the fact that his own Being-for-itself was mani-

fested to him as an autonomous object; or again, to say the same thing: the fact that the object was manifested to him as this pure subjective-certainty of himself; [therefore, he must find the private idea that he has of himself in the external, objective reality.] But according to the concept of recognition, this is possible only if he accomplishes for the other (just as the other does for him) the pure abstraction of Being-for-itself; each accomplishing it in himself both by his own activity and also by the other's activity.

[The "first" man who meets another man for the first time already attributes an autonomous, absolute reality and an autonomous, absolute value to himself: we can say that he believes himself to be a man, that he has the "subjective certainty" of being a man. But his certainty is not yet knowledge. The value that he attributes to himself could be illusory; the idea that he has of himself could be false or mad. For that idea to be a truth, it must reveal an objective reality – i.e. an entity that is valid and exists not only for itself, but also for realities other than itself. In the case in question, man, to be really, truly "man," and to know that he is such, must, therefore, impose the idea that he has of himself on beings other than himself: he must be recognized by the others (in the ideal, extreme case, by all the others). Or again, he must transform the (natural and human) world in which he is not recognized into a world in which this recognition takes place. This transformation of the world that is hostile to a human project into a world in harmony with this project is called "action," "activity." This action – essentially human, because humanizing and anthropogenetic – will begin with the act of imposing oneself on the "first" other man one meets. And since this other, if he is (or more exactly, if he wants to be, and believes himself to be) a human being, must himself do the same thing, the "first" anthropogenetic action necessarily takes the form of a fight: a fight to the death between two beings that claim to be men, a fight for pure prestige carried on for the sake of "recognition" by the adversary. Indeed:]

The *manifestation* of the human-individual taken as pure abstraction of Being-for-itself consists in showing itself as being the pure negation of its objective-or-thingish mode-of-being – or, in other words, in showing that to be for oneself, or to be a man, is not to be bound to any determined *existence*, not to be bound to the universal isolated-particularity of existence as such, not to be bound to life. This manifestation is a *double* activity: activity of the other and activity by oneself. To the extent that this activity is activity *of the other*, each of the two men seeks the death of the other. But in that activity of the other is also found the second aspect, namely, the *activity by oneself*: for the activity in question implies in it the risk of the life of him who acts. The relation of the two Self-Consciousnesses, therefore, is determined in such a way that they come to light – each for itself and one for the other – through the fight for life and death.

[They "come to light" – that is, they prove themselves, they transform the purely subjective certainty that each has of his own value into objective, or universally valid and recognized, truth. Truth is the revelation of a reality. Now, the human reality is created, is constituted, only in the fight for recognition and by the risk of life that it implies. The truth of man, or the revelation of his reality, therefore, presupposes the fight to the death. And that is why] human-individuals are obliged to start this fight. For each must raise his subjective-certainty of *existing for self* to the level of truth, both in the other and in himself. And it is only through the risk of life that freedom comes to light, that it becomes clear that the essential-reality of Self-Consciousness is not *given-being* [being that is not created by conscious, voluntary action], nor the *immediate* [natural, not mediated by action (that negates the given)] mode in which it first comes to sight [in the given world], nor submersion in the extension of animal-life; but that there is, on the contrary, nothing given in Self-Consciousness that is anything but a passing constituent-element for it. In other words, only by the risk of life does it come to light that Self-Consciousness is nothing but pure *Being-for-itself*. The human-individual that *has* not dared-to-risk his life can, to be sure, be recognized as a *human-person*; but he has not attained the truth of this fact of being recognized as an autonomous Self-Consciousness. Hence, each of the two human-individuals must have the death of the other as his goal, just as he risks his own life. For the other-entity is worth no more to him than himself. His essential-reality [which is his recognized, human reality and dignity] manifests itself to him as an other-entity [or another man, who does not recognize him and is therefore independent of him]. He is outside of himself [insofar as the other has not "given him back" to himself by recognizing him, by revealing that he has recognized him, and by showing him that he (the other) depends on him, and is not absolutely other than he]. He must overcome his being-outside-of-himself. The other-entity [than he] is here a Self-Consciousness existing as a given-being and involved [in the natural world] in a manifold and diverse way. Now, he must look upon his other-being as pure Being-for-itself, i.e. as absolute negating-negativity. [This means that man is human only to the extent that he wants to impose himself on another man, to be recognized by him. In the beginning, as long as he is not yet actually recognized by the other, it is the other that is the end of his action; it is on this other, it is on recognition by this other, that his human value and reality depend; it is in this other that the meaning of his life is condensed. Therefore, he is "outside of himself." But his own value and his own reality are what are important to him, and he wants to have them in himself. Hence, he must overcome his "other-being." This is to say that he must make himself recognized by the other, he must have in himself the certainty of being recognized by another. But for that recognition to satisfy him, he has to know that the other is a human being. Now, in the beginning, he sees in the other only the aspect of an animal. To know that this aspect reveals a human reality, he must see that the other also wants to be recognized, and that he, too, is ready to risk, "to deny," his animal life in a fight for the recognition of his human being-for-itself. He must, therefore, "provoke" the other, force him to start a fight to the death for pure prestige. And having done this, he is obliged to kill the other in order not to be killed himself. In these circumstances, then, the fight for recognition can end only in the death of one of the adversaries – or of both together.] But this proving oneself by death does away with the truth [or revealed objective reality] that was supposed to come from it; and, for that very reason, it also does away with the subjective-certainty of oneself as such. For just as animal-life is the *natural* position of Consciousness, i.e. autonomy without absolute negating-negativity, so is death the *natural* negation of Consciousness, i.e. negation without autonomy, which negation, therefore, continues to lack the significance required by recognition. [That is to say: if both adversaries perish in the fight, "consciousness" is completely done away with, for man is nothing more than an inanimate body after his death. And if one of the adversaries remains alive but kills the other, he can no longer be recognized by the other; the man who has been defeated and killed does not recognize the victory of the conqueror. Therefore, the victor's certainty of his being and of his value remains subjective, and thus has no "truth."] Through death, it is true, the subjective-certainty of the fact that both risked their lives and that each despised his own and the other's life has been established. But this certainty has not been established for those who underwent this struggle. Through death, they do away with their consciousness, which resides in that foreign entity, natural existence. That is to say, they do away with themselves. [For man is real only to the extent that he lives in a natural world. This world is, to be sure, "foreign" to him; he must "deny" it, transform it, fight it, in order to realize himself in it. But without this world, outside of this world, man is nothing.] And they are done away with as *extremes* that want to exist for self [i.e. consciously, and independently of the rest of the universe]. But, thereby, the essential constituent-element – i.e. the splitting up into extremes of opposed determinate things – disappears from the play of change. And the middle-term collapses in a dead unity, broken up into dead extremes, which merely exist as given-beings and are not opposed [to one another in, by, and for an action in which one tries "to do away with" the other by "establishing" himself and to establish himself by doing away with the other.] And the two do not give themselves reciprocally to one another, nor do they get themselves back in return from one another through consciousness. On the contrary, they merely leave one another free, indifferently, as things. [For the dead man is no longer anything more than an unconscious thing, from which the living man turns away in indifference, since he can no longer expect anything from it for himself.] Their murderous action is abstract negation. It is not negation [carried out] by consciousness, which overcomes in such a way that it *keeps* and *preserves* the overcome-entity and, for that very reason, survives the fact of being overcome. [This "overcoming" is "dialectical." "To overcome dialectically" means to overcome while preserving what is overcome; it is sublimated in and by that overcoming which preserves or that preservation which overcomes. The dialectically overcome-entity is annulled in its contingent (stripped of sense, "senseless") aspect of natural, given ("immediate") entity, but it is preserved in its essential (and meaningful, significant) aspect; thus mediated by negation, it is sublimated or raised up to a more "comprehensive" and comprehensible mode of being than that of its immediate reality of pure and simple, positive and static given, which is not the result of creative action (i.e. of action that negates the given).

[Therefore, it does the man of the Fight no good to kill his adversary. He must overcome him "dialectically." That is, he must leave him life and consciousness, and destroy only his autonomy. He must overcome the adversary only insofar as the adversary is opposed to him and acts against him. In other words, he must enslave him.]

In that experience [of the murderous fight] it becomes clear to Self-Consciousness that animal-life is just as important to it as pure self-consciousness. In the immediate Self-Consciousness [i.e. in the "first" man, who is not yet "mediated" by this contact with the other that the fight creates], the simple-or-undivided I [of isolated man] is the absolute object. But for us or in itself [i.e. for the author and the reader of this passage, who see man as he has been definitively formed at the end of history by the accomplished social inter-action] this object, i.e. the I, is absolute mediation, and its essential constituent-element is abiding autonomy. [That is to say, real and true man is the result of his inter-action with others; his I and the idea he has of himself are "mediated" by recognition obtained as a result of his action. And his true autonomy is the autonomy that he *maintains* in the social reality by the effort of that action.] The dissolution of that simple-or-undivided unity [which is the isolated I] is the result of the first experience [which man has at the time of his "first" (murderous) fight]. By this experience are established: a pure Self-Consciousness [or an "abstract" one, since it has made the "abstraction" of its animal life by the risk of the fight – the victor], and a Consciousness that [being in fact a living corpse – the man who has been defeated and spared] does not exist purely for itself, but rather for another Consciousness [namely, for that of the victor]: i.e., a Consciousness that exists as a *given-being*, or in other words, a Consciousness that exists in the concrete-form of *thingness*. Both constituent-elements are essential – since in the beginning they are unequal and opposed to one another and their reflection into unity has not yet resulted [from their action], they exist as two opposed concrete-forms of Consciousness. The one is autonomous Consciousness, for which the essential-reality is Being-for-itself. The other is dependent Consciousness, for which the essential-reality is animal-life, i.e. given-being for an other-entity. The former is the *Master*, the latter – the *Slave*. [This Slave is the defeated adversary, who has not gone all the way in risking his life, who has not adopted the principle of the Masters: to conquer or to die. He has accepted life granted him by another. Hence, he depends on that other. He has preferred slavery to death, and that is why, by remaining alive, he lives as a Slave.]

The Master is Consciousness existing *for itself*. And he is no longer merely the [abstract] concept of Consciousness, but a [real] Consciousness existing for itself, which is mediated with itself by *another* Consciousness, namely, by a Consciousness to whose essential-reality it belongs to be synthesized with *given-being*, i.e. with thingness as such. [This "Consciousness" is the Slave who, in binding himself completely to his animal-life, is merely one with the natural world of things. By refusing to risk his life in a fight for pure prestige, he does not rise above the level of animals. Hence he considers himself as such, and as such is he considered by the Master. But the Slave, for his part, recognizes the Master in his human dignity and reality, and the Slave behaves accordingly. The Master's "certainty" is therefore not purely subjective and "immediate," but objectivized and "mediated" by another's, the Slave's, recognition. While the Slave still remains an "immediate," natural, "bestial" being, the Master – as a result of his fight – is already human, "mediated." And consequently, his behavior is also "mediated" or human, both with regard to things and with regard to other men; moreover, these other men, for him, are only slaves.] The Master is related to the following two constituent-elements: on the one hand, to a *thing* taken as such, i.e. the object of Desire; and, on the other hand, to the Consciousness for which thingness is the essential-entity [i.e. to the Slave, who, by refusing the risk, binds himself completely to the things on which he depends. The Master, on the other hand, sees in these things only a simple means of satisfying his desire; and, in satisfying it, he destroys them]. Given that: (1) the Master, taken as concept of self-consciousness, is the immediate relation of *Being-for-itself*, and that (2) he now [i.e. after his victory over the Slave] exists at the same time as mediation, i.e. as a Being-for-itself that exists for itself only through an other-entity [since the Master is Master only by the fact of having a Slave who recognizes him as Master]; the Master is related (1) immediately to both [i.e. to the thing and to the Slave], and (2) in a mediated way to each of the two through the other. The Master is related *in a mediated way to the Slave*, viz. by *autonomous given-being*; for it is precisely to this given-being that the Slave is tied. This given-being is his chain, from which he could not abstract in the fight, in which fight he was revealed –

because of that fact – as dependent, as having his autonomy in thingness. The Master, on the other hand, is the power that rules over this given-being; for he revealed in the fight that this given-being is worth nothing to him except as a negative-entity. Given that the Master is the power that rules over this given-being and that this given-being is the power that rules over the Other [i.e. over the Slave], the Master holds – in this [real or active] syllogism – that Other under his domination. Likewise, the Master is related *in a mediated way to the thing*, viz. *by the Slave*. Taken as Self-Consciousness as such, the Slave, too, is related to the thing in a negative or negating way, and he overcomes it [dialectically]. But – for him – the thing is autonomous at the same time. For that reason, he cannot, by his act-of-negating, finish it off to the point of the [complete] annihilation [of the thing, as does the Master who "consumes" it]. That is, he merely *transforms it by work* [i.e. he prepares it for consumption, but does not consume it himself]. For the Master, on the other hand, the *immediate* relation [to the thing] comes into being, through that mediation [i.e. through the work of the Slave who transforms the natural thing, the "raw material," with a view to its consumption (by the Master)], as pure negation of the object, that is, as *Enjoyment*. [Since all the effort is made by the Slave, the Master has only to enjoy the thing that the Slave has prepared for him, and to enjoy "negating" it, destroying it, by "consuming" it. (For example, he eats food that is completely prepared)]. What Desire [i.e. isolated man "before" the Fight, who was alone with Nature and whose desires were directed without detour toward that Nature] did not achieve, the Master [whose desires are directed toward things that have been transformed by the Slave] does achieve. The Master can finish off the thing completely and satisfy himself in Enjoyment. [Therefore, it is solely thanks to the work of another (his Slave) that the Master is free with respect to Nature, and consequently, satisfied with himself. But, he is Master of the Slave only because he previously freed himself from Nature (and from his own nature) by risking his life in a fight for pure prestige, which – as such – is not at all "natural."] Desire cannot achieve this because of the autonomy of the thing. The Master, on the other hand, who introduced the Slave between the thing and himself, is consequently joined only to the aspect of the thing's dependence, and has pure enjoyment from it. As for the aspect of the thing's autonomy, he leaves it to the Slave, who transforms the thing by work.

In these two constituent-elements the Master gets his recognition through another Consciousness; for in them the latter affirms itself as unessential, both by the act of working on the thing and by the fact of being dependent on a determinate existence. In neither case can this [slavish] Consciousness become master of the given-being and achieve absolute negation. Hence it is given in this constituent-element of recognition that the other Consciousness overcomes itself as Being-for-itself and thereby does itself what the other Consciousness does to it. [That is to say, the Master is not the only one to regard the Other as his Slave; this Other also considers himself as such.] The other constituent-element of recognition is equally implied in the relation under consideration; this other constituent-element is the fact that this activity of the second Consciousness [the slavish Consciousness] is the activity proper of the first Consciousness [i.e. the Master's]. For everything that the Slave does is, properly speaking, an activity of the Master. [Since the Slave works only for the Master, only to satisfy the Master's desire and not his own, it is the Master's desire that acts in and through the Slave.] For the Master, only Being-for-itself is the essential-reality. He is pure negative-or-negating power, for which the thing is nothing; and consequently, in this relation of Master and Slave, he is the pure essential activity. The Slave, on the other hand, is not pure activity, but nonessential activity. Now, for there to be an authentic recognition, there must also be the third constituent-element, which consists in the Master's doing with respect to himself what he does with respect to the other, and in the Slave's doing with respect to the Other what he [the Slave] does with respect to himself. It is, therefore, an unequal and one-sided recognition that has been born from this relation of Master and Slave. [For although the Master treats the Other as Slave, he does not behave as Slave himself; and although the Slave treats the Other as Master, he does not behave as Master himself. The Slave does not risk his life, and the Master is idle.

[The relation between Master and Slave, therefore, is not recognition properly so-called. To see this, let us analyze the relation from the Master's point of view. The Master is not the only one to consider himself Master. The Slave, also, considers him as such. Hence, he is recognized in his human reality and dignity. But this recognition is one-sided, for he does not recognize in turn the Slave's human reality and dignity. Hence, he is recognized by someone whom he does not recognize. And this is what is insufficient – what is tragic – in his situation. The Master has fought and risked his life for a recognition without value for him. For he can be satisfied only by recognition from one whom he recognizes as worthy of recognizing him. The Master's attitude, therefore, is an existential impasse. On the one hand, the Master is Master only because his Desire was directed not toward a thing, but toward another desire – thus, it was a desire for recognition. On the other, when he has consequently become Master, it is as Master that he must desire to be recognized; and he can be recognized as such only by making the Other his Slave. But the Slave is for him an animal or a thing. He is, therefore, "recognized" by a thing. Thus, finally, his Desire is directed toward a thing, and not – as it seemed at first – toward a (human) Desire. The Master, therefore, was on the wrong track. After the fight that made him a Master, he is not what he wanted to be in starting that fight: a man recognized by another man. Therefore: if man can be satisfied only by recognition, the man who behaves as a Master will never be satisfied. And since – in the beginning – man is either Master or Slave, the satisfied man will necessarily be a Slave; or more exactly, the man who has been a Slave, who has passed through Slavery, who has "dialectically overcome" his slavery. Indeed:]

Thus, the nonessential [or slavish] Consciousness is – for the Master – the object that forms the *truth* [or revealed reality] of the subjective-certainty he has of himself [since he can "know" he is Master only by being recognized as such by the Slave]. But it is obvious that this object does not correspond to its concept. For in the Master's fulfilling himself, something entirely different from an autonomous Consciousness has come into being [since he is faced with a Slave]. It is not such an autonomous Consciousness, but all to the contrary, a dependent Consciousness, that exists for him. Therefore, he is not subjectively certain of his *Being-for-itself* as of a truth [or of a revealed objective reality]. His truth, all to the contrary, is nonessential Consciousness, and the nonessential activity of that Consciousness. [That is to say, the Master's "truth" is the Slave and the Slave's Work. Actually, others recognize the Master as Master only because he has a Slave; and the Master's life consists in consuming the products of slavish Work, and in living on and by this Work.]

Consequently, the *truth* of autonomous Consciousness is *slavish Consciousness*. This latter first appears, it is true, as existing *outside* of itself and not as the truth of Self-Consciousness [since the Slave recognizes human dignity not in himself, but in the Master, on whom his very existence depends]. But, just as Mastery showed that its essential-reality is the reverse or perversion of what it wants to be, so much the more will Slavery, in its fulfillment, probably become the opposite of what it is immediately; as *repressed* Consciousness it will go within itself and reverse and transform itself into true autonomy.

[The complete, absolutely free man, definitively and completely satisfied by what he is, the man who is perfected and completed in and by this satisfaction, will be the Slave who has "overcome" his Slavery. If idle Mastery is an impasse, laborious Slavery, in contrast, is the source of all human, social, historical progress. History is the history of the working Slave. To see this, one need only consider the relationship between Master and Slave (that is, the first result of the "first" human, social, historical contact), no longer from the Master's point of view, but from the Slave's.]

We have seen only what Slavery is in its relation to Mastery. But Slavery is also Self-Consciousness. What it is as such, in and for itself, must now be considered. In the first place, it is the Master that is the essential-reality for Slavery. The *autonomous Consciousness existing for itself* is hence, for it, *the truth* [or a revealed reality], which, however, *for it*, does not yet exist *in it*. [The Slave is subordinated to the Master. Hence the Slave esteems, recognizes, the value and the reality of "autonomy," of human freedom. However, he does not find it realized in himself; he finds it only in the Other. And this is his advantage. The Master, unable to recognize the Other who recognizes him, finds himself in an impasse. The Slave, on the other hand, recognizes the Other (the Master) from the beginning. In order that mutual and reciprocal recognition, which alone can fully and definitively realize and satisfy man, be established, it suffices for the Slave to impose himself on the Master and be recognized by him. To be sure, for this to take place, the Slave must cease to be Slave: he must transcend himself, "overcome" himself, as Slave. But if the Master has no desire to "overcome" – and hence no possibility of "overcoming" – himself as Master (since this would mean, for him, to become a Slave), the Slave has every reason to cease to be a Slave. Moreover, the experience of

the fight that made him a Slave predisposes him to that act of self-overcoming, of negation of himself (negation of his given I, which is a slavish I). To be sure, in the beginning, the Slave who binds himself to his given (slavish) I does not have this "negativity" in himself. He sees it only in the Master, who realized pure "negating-negativity" by risking his life in the fight for recognition.] However, Slavery *in fact* has *in itself* this truth [or revealed reality] of pure negating-negativity and of *Being-for-itself*. For it has *experienced* this essential-reality within itself. This slavish Consciousness was afraid not for this or that, not for this moment or that, but for its [own] entire essential-reality: it underwent the fear of death, the fear of the absolute Master. By this fear, the slavish Consciousness melted internally; it shuddered deeply and everything fixed-or-stable trembled in it. Now, this pure universal [dialectical] movement, this absolute liquefaction of every stable-support, is the simple-or-undivided essential-reality of Self-Consciousness, absolute negating-negativity, *pure Being-for-itself*. Thus, this Being-for-itself exists *in* the slavish Consciousness. [The Master is fixed in his Mastery. He cannot go beyond himself, change, progress. He must conquer – and become Master or preserve himself as such – or die. He can be killed; he cannot be transformed, educated. He has risked his life to be Master. Therefore, Mastery is the supreme given value for him, beyond which he cannot go. The Slave, on the other hand, did not want to be a Slave. He became a Slave because he did not want to risk his life to become a Master. In his mortal terror he understood (without noticing it) that a given, fixed, and stable condition, even though it be the Master's, cannot exhaust the possibilities of human existence. He "understood" the "vanity" of the given conditions of existence. He did not want to bind himself to the Master's condition, nor does he bind himself to his condition as a Slave. There is nothing fixed in him. He is ready for change; in his very being, he is change, transcendence, transformation, "education"; he is historical becoming at his origin, in his essence, in his very existence. On the one hand, he does not bind himself to what he is; he wants to transcend himself by negation of his given state. On the other hand, he has a positive ideal to attain; the ideal of autonomy, of Being-for-itself, of which he finds the incarnation, at the very origin of his Slavery, in the Master.] This constituent-element of Being-for-itself also exists *for slavish Consciousness*. For in the Master, Being-for-itself is, for it [the slavish Consciousness], its object. [An object that it knows to be external, opposed, to it, and that it tends to appropriate for itself. The Slave knows what it is to be free. He also knows that he is not free, and that he wants to become free. And if the experience of the Fight and its result predispose the Slave to transcendence, to progress, to History, his life as a Slave working in the Master's service realizes this predisposition.] In addition, slavish Consciousness is not only this universal dissolution [of everything fixed, stable, and given], taken *as such*; in the Master's service, it accomplishes this dissolution *in an objectively real way* [i.e. concretely]. In service [in the forced work done in the service of another (the Master)], slavish Consciousness [dialectically] overcomes its attachment to natural existence in all the *particular-and-isolated* constituent-elements, and it eliminates this existence by work. [The Master forces the Slave to work. And by working, the Slave becomes master of Nature. Now, he became the Master's Slave only because – in the beginning – he was a slave of Nature, joining with it and subordinating himself to its laws by accepting the instinct of preservation. In becoming master of Nature by work, then, the Slave frees himself from his own nature, from his own instinct that tied him to Nature and made him the Master's Slave. Therefore, by freeing the Slave from Nature, work frees him from himself as well, from his Slave's nature: it frees him from the Master. In the raw, natural, given World, the Slave is slave of the Master. In the technical world transformed by his work, he rules – or, at least, will one day rule – as absolute Master. And this Mastery that arises from work, from the progressive transformation of the given World and of man given in this World, will be an entirely different thing from the "immediate" Mastery of the Master. The future and History hence belong not to the warlike Master, who either dies or preserves himself indefinitely in identity to himself, but to the working Slave. The Slave, in transforming the given World by his work, transcends the given and what is given by that given in himself; hence, he goes beyond himself, and also goes beyond the Master who is tied to the given which, not working, he leaves intact. If the fear of death, incarnated for the Slave in the person of the warlike Master, is the *sine qua non* of historical progress, it is solely the Slave's work that realizes and perfects it.]

However, the feeling of absolute power that the Slave experienced as such in the fight and also experiences in the particularities of service [for the Master whom he fears] is as yet only dissolution effected *in itself*. [Without this sense of power – i.e. without the terror and dread inspired by the Master – man would never be Slave and consequently could not attain the final perfection. But this condition "in itself" – i.e. this objectively real and necessary condition – is not sufficient. Perfection (which is always conscious of itself) can be attained only in and by work. For only in and by work does man finally become aware of the significance, the value, and the necessity of his experience of fearing absolute power, incarnated for him in the Master. Only after having worked for the Master does he understand the necessity of the fight between Master and Slave and the value of the risk and terror that it implies.] Thus, although the terror inspired by the Master is the beginning of wisdom, it can only be said that in this terror Consciousness exists *for itself*, but is not yet *Being-for-itself*. [In mortal terror man becomes aware of his reality, of the value that the simple fact of living has for him; only thus does he take account of the "seriousness" of existence. But he is not yet aware of his autonomy, of the value and the "seriousness" of his liberty, of his human dignity.] But through work Consciousness comes to itself. [In work, i.e.] in the constituent-element that corresponds to Desire in the Master's consciousness, it seemed, it is true, that the nonessential relation to the thing was what fell to the lot of the slavish Consciousness; this is because the thing preserves its autonomy. [It seemed that, in and by work, the Slave is enslaved to Nature, to the thing, to "raw material"; while the Master, who is content to consume the thing prepared by the Slave and to enjoy it, is perfectly free with respect to it. But this is not the case. To be sure] the [Master's] Desire has reserved for itself the pure act-of-negating the object [by consuming it] and has thereby reserved for itself the unmixed sentiment-of-self-and-of-one's-dignity [experienced in enjoyment]. But for the same reason this satisfaction itself is but a passing phase, for it lacks the *objective* aspect – i.e. the *stable support*. [The Master, who does not work, produces nothing stable outside of himself. He merely destroys the products of the Slave's work. Thus his enjoyment and his satisfaction remain purely subjective: they are of interest only to him and therefore can be recognized only by him; they have no "truth," no objective reality revealed to all. Accordingly, this "consumption," this idle enjoyment of the Master's, which results from the "immediate" satisfaction of desire, can at the most procure some pleasure for man; it can never give him complete and definitive satisfaction.] Work, on the other hand, is *repressed* Desire, an *arrested* passing phase; or, in other words, it forms-and-educates. [Work transforms the World and civilizes, educates, Man. The man who wants to work – or who must work – must repress the instinct that drives him "to consume" "immediately" the "raw" object. And the Slave can work for the Master – that is, for another than himself – only by repressing his own desires. Hence, he transcends himself by working – or, perhaps better, he educates himself, he "cultivates" and "sublimates" his instincts by repressing them. On the other hand, he does not destroy the thing as it is given. He postpones the destruction of the thing by first transforming it through work: he prepares it for consumption – that is to say, he "forms" it. In his work, he trans-forms things and trans-forms himself at the same time: he forms things and the World by transforming himself, by educating himself; and he educates himself, he forms himself, by transforming things and the World. Thus,] the negative-or-negating relation to the object becomes a *form* of this object and gains *permanence*, precisely because, for the worker, the object has autonomy. At the same time, the *negative-or-negating* middle-term – i.e. the forming *activity* [of work] – is the *isolated-particularity* or the pure Being-for-itself of the Consciousness. And this Being-for-itself, through work, now passes into what is outside of the Consciousness, into the element of permanence. The working Consciousness thereby attains a contemplation of autonomous given-being such that it contemplates *itself* in it. [The product of work is the worker's production. It is the realization of his project, of his idea; hence, it is he that is realized in and by this product, and consequently he contemplates himself when he contemplates it. Now, this artificial product is at the same time just as "autonomous," just as objective, just as inde-

pendent of man, as is the natural thing. Therefore, it is by work, and only by work, that man *realizes* himself *objectively* as man. Only after producing an artificial object is man himself really and objectively more than and different from a natural being; and only in this real and objective product does he become truly conscious of his subjective human reality. Therefore, it is only by work that man is a supernatural being that is conscious of its reality; by working, he is "incarnated" Spirit, he is historical "World," he is "objectivized" History.

[Work, then, is what "forms-or-educates" man beyond the animal. The "formed-or-educated" man, the completed man who is satisfied by his completion, is hence necessarily not Master, but Slave; or, at least, he who has passed through Slavery. Now, there is no Slave without a Master. The Master, then, is the catalyst of the historical, anthropogenetic process. He himself does not participate actively in this process; but without him, without his presence, this process would not be possible. For, if the history of man is the history of his work, and if this work is historical, social, human, only on the condition that it is carried out against the worker's instinct or "immediate interest," the work must be carried out in the service of another, and must be a forced work, stimulated by fear of death. It is this work, and only this work, that frees – i.e. humanizes – man (the Slave). On the one hand, this work creates a real objective World, which is a non-natural World, a cultural, historical, human World. And it is only in this World that man lives an essentially different life from that of animals (and "primitive" man) in the bosom of Nature. On the other hand, this work liberates the Slave from the terror that tied him to given Nature and to his own innate animal nature. It is by work in the Master's service performed in terror that the Slave frees himself from the terror that enslaved him to the Master.]

Select Bibliography

Introduction to the Reading of Hegel. Edited by Allan Bloom. Translated by James H. Nichols, Jr. Ithaca: Cornell University Press, 1986.

10

Jean-Paul Sartre

The most famous of the French existentialists, Jean-Paul Sartre (1905–80) was not only a philosopher, but also a playwright, novelist, political activist, and social critic whose work was probably the single most important force shaping the intellectual climate of a generation of French thinkers. Influenced by post-Kantian German philosophy, most prominently Hegel, Marx, Husserl (under whom he studied), and Heidegger, Sartre held a professorship at the Lycée Condorçet in Paris from 1935–42. Together with Simone de Beauvoir and Maurice Merleau-Ponty, he founded *Les Temps modernes*, an influential journal dealing with philosophical, political, and literary issues of the time. Sartre's existentialism places a premium on human freedom and responsibility, emphasizing our inevitable entanglements in the concrete world and issues of our times. Human beings not only choose their existence, according to Sartre, but are "condemned" to do so; freedom, which distinguishes human self-consciousness, is also a fatality. The following selection, from Sartre's central philosophical work *Being and Nothingness* (1943), describes this freedom as a nothingness experienced in "anguish," which we attempt to flee in an attitude of "bad faith."

Being and Nothingness

The Problem of Nothingness

Being can generate only being and if man is enclosed in this process of generation, only being will come out of him. If we are to assume that man

From *Being and Nothingness*, translated by Hazel E. Barnes (New York: Washington Square Press, 1992), pp. 59–60, 72–8, 82–3, 101–7, 109–12. Copyright © 1956. Published by Philosophical Library, New York. Reprinted by permission of Regeen Najar.

is able to question this process – i.e. to make it the object of interrogation – he must be able to hold it up to view as a totality. He must be able to put himself *outside of* being and by the same stroke weaken the structure of the being of being. Yet it is not given to "human reality" to annihilate even provisionally the mass of being which it posits before itself. Man's *relation* with being is that he can modify it. For man to put a particular existent out of circuit is to put himself out of circuit in relation to that existent. In this case he is not subject to it; he is out of reach; it can not act on him, for he has retired *beyond a nothingness*. Descartes following the Stoics has given a name to this possibility which human reality has to secrete a nothingness which isolates it – it is *freedom*. But freedom here is only a name. If we wish to penetrate further into the question, we must not be content with this reply and we ought to ask now, What is human freedom if through it nothingness comes into the world?

It is not yet possible to deal with the problem of freedom in all its fullness. In fact the steps which we have completed up to now show clearly that freedom is not a faculty of the human soul to be envisaged and described in isolation. What we have been trying to define is the being of man insofar as he conditions the appearance of nothingness, and this being has appeared to us as freedom. Thus freedom as the requisite condition for the nihilation of nothingness is not a *property* which belongs among others to the essence of the human being. We have already noticed furthermore that with man the relation of existence to essence is not comparable to what it is for the things of the world. Human freedom precedes essence in man and makes it possible; the essence of the human being is suspended in his freedom. What we call freedom is impossible to distinguish from the *being* of "human reality." Man does not exist *first* in order to be free *subsequently*; there is no difference between the being of man and his *being-free*. This is not the time to make a frontal attack on a question which can be treated exhaustively only in the light of a rigorous elucidation of the human being. Here we are dealing with freedom in connection with the problem of nothingness and only to the extent that it conditions the appearance of nothingness. . . .

What we should note at present is that freedom, which manifests itself through anguish, is characterized by a constantly renewed obligation to remake the *Self* which designates the free being. As a matter of fact when we showed earlier that my possibilities were filled with anguish because it depended on *me* alone to sustain them in their existence, that did not mean that they derived from a *Me* which, to itself at least, would first be given and would then pass in the temporal flux from one consciousness to another consciousness. The gambler who must realize anew the synthetic apperception of a *situation* which would forbid him to play, must rediscover at the same time the *self* which can appreciate that situation, which "is in

situation." This *self* with its *a priori* and historical content is the *essence* of man. Anguish as the manifestation of freedom in the face of self means that man is always separated by a nothingness from his essence. We should refer here to Hegel's statement: "*Wesen ist was gewesen ist*." Essence is what has been. Essence is everything in the human being which we can indicate by the words – that *is*. Due to this fact it is the totality of characteristics which *explain* the act. But the act is always beyond that essence; it is a human act only insofar as it surpasses every explanation which we can give of it, precisely because the very application of the formula "that is" to man causes all that is designated, *to have-been*. Man continually carries with him a pre-judicative comprehension of his essence, but due to this very fact he is separated from it by a nothingness. Essence is all that human reality apprehends in itself as *having been*. It is here that anguish appears as an apprehension of self inasmuch as it exists in the perpetual mode of detachment from what is; better yet, insofar as it makes itself exist as such. For we can never apprehend an *Erlebnis* as a living consequence of that *nature* which is ours. The overflow of our consciousness progressively constitutes that nature, but it remains always behind us and it dwells in us as the permanent object of our retrospective comprehension. It is insofar as this nature is a demand without being a recourse that it is apprehended in anguish.

In anguish freedom is anguished before itself inasmuch as it is instigated and bound by nothing. Someone will say, freedom has just been defined as a permanent structure of the human being; if anguish manifests it, then anguish ought to be a permanent state of my affectivity. But, on the contrary, it is completely exceptional. How can we explain the rarity of the phenomenon of anguish?

We must note first of all that the most common situations of our life, those in which we apprehend our possibilities as such by means of actively realizing them, do not manifest themselves to us through anguish because their very structure excludes anguished apprehension. Anguish in fact is the recognition of a possibility as *my* possibility; that is, it is constituted when consciousness sees itself cut from its essence by nothingness or separated from the future by its very freedom. This means that a nihilating nothing removes from me all excuse and that at the same time what I project as my future being is always nihilated and reduced to the rank of simple possibility because the future which I am remains out of my reach. . . .

Now at each instant we are thrust into the world and engaged there. This means that we act before positing our possibilities and that these possibilities which are disclosed as realized or in process of being realized refer to meanings which necessitate special acts in order to be put into question. The alarm which rings in the morning refers to the possibility of my going to work, which is *my* possibility. But to apprehend the summons of the alarm as a summons is to get up. Therefore the very act of getting up is reassuring, for it eludes the question, "Is work *my* possibility?" Consequently it does not put me in a position to apprehend the possibility of quietism, of refusing to work, and finally the possibility of refusing the world and the possibility of death. In short, to the extent that I apprehend the meaning of the ringing, I am already up at its summons; this apprehension guarantees me against the anguished intuition that it is I who confer on the alarm clock its exigency – I and I alone.

In the same way, what we might call everyday morality is exclusive of ethical anguish. There is ethical anguish when I consider myself in my original relation to values. Values in actuality are demands which lay claim to a foundation. But this foundation can in no way be *being*, for every value which would base its ideal nature on its being would thereby cease even to be a value and would realize the heteronomy of my will. Value derives its being from its exigency and not its exigency from its being. It does not deliver itself to a contemplative intuition which would apprehend it as *being* value and thereby would remove from it its right over my freedom. On the contrary, it can be revealed only to an active freedom which makes it exist as value by the sole fact of recognizing it as such. It follows that my freedom is the unique foundation of values and that *nothing*, absolutely nothing, justifies me in adopting this or that particular value, this or that particular scale of values. As a being by whom values exist, I am unjustifiable. My freedom is anguished at being the foundation of values while itself without foundation. It is anguished in addition because values, due to the fact that they are essentially revealed to a freedom, cannot disclose themselves without being at the same time "put into question," for the possibility of overturning the scale of values appears complementarily as *my* possibility. It is anguish before

values which is the recognition of the ideality of values.

Ordinarily, however, my attitude with respect to values is eminently reassuring. In fact I am engaged in a world of values. The anguished apperception of values as sustained in being by my freedom is a secondary and mediated phenomenon. The immediate is the world with its urgency; and in this world where I engage myself, my acts cause values to spring up like partridges. My indignation has given to me the negative value "baseness," my admiration has given the positive value "grandeur." Above all my obedience to a multitude of taboos, which is real, reveals these taboos to me as existing in fact. The bourgeois who call themselves "respectable citizens" do not become respectable as the result of contemplating moral values. Rather from the moment of their arising in the world they are thrown into a pattern of behaviour the meaning of which is respectability. Thus respectability acquires a being; it is not put into question. Values are sown on my path as thousands of little real demands, like the signs which order us to keep off the grass.

Thus in what we shall call the world of the immediate, which delivers itself to our unreflective consciousness, we do not first appear to ourselves, to be thrown subsequently into enterprises. Our being is immediately "in situation"; that is, it arises in enterprises and knows itself first insofar as it is reflected in those enterprises. We discover ourselves then in a world peopled with demands, in the heart of projects "in the course of realization." I write. I am going to smoke. I have an appointment this evening with Pierre. I must not forget to reply to Simon. I do not have the right to conceal the truth any longer from Claude. All these trivial passive expectations of the real, all these commonplace, everyday values, derive their meaning from an original projection of myself which stands as my choice of myself in the world. But to be exact, this projection of myself toward an original possibility, which causes the existence of values, appeals, expectations, and in general a world, appears to me only beyond the world as the meaning and the abstract, logical signification of my enterprises. For the rest, there exist concretely alarm clocks, signboards, tax forms, policemen, so many guard rails against anguish. But as soon as the enterprise is held at a distance from me, as soon as I am referred to myself because I must await myself in the future, then I discover myself suddenly as the one who gives its meaning to the alarm clock, the one who by a signboard forbids himself to walk on a flower bed or on the lawn, the one from whom the boss's order borrows its urgency, the one who decides the interest of the book which he is writing, the one finally who makes the values exist in order to determine his action by their demands. I emerge alone and in anguish confronting the unique and original project which constitutes my being; all the barriers, all the guard rails collapse, nihilated by the consciousness of my freedom. I do not have nor can I have recourse to any value against the fact that it is I who sustain values in being. Nothing can insure me against myself, cut off from the world and from my essence by this nothingness which I *am*. I have to realize the meaning of the world and of my essence; I make my decision concerning them – without justification and without excuse.

Anguish then is the reflective apprehension of freedom by itself. In this sense it is mediation, for although it is immediate consciousness of itself, it arises from the negation of the appeals of the world. It appears at the moment that I disengage myself from the world where I had been engaged – in order to apprehend myself as a consciousness which possesses a preontological comprehension of its essence and a prejudicative sense of its possibilities. Anguish is opposed to the mind of the serious man who apprehends values in terms of the world and who resides in the reassuring, materialistic substantiation of values. In the serious mood I define myself in terms of the object by pushing aside *a priori* as impossible all enterprises in which I am not engaged at the moment; the meaning which my freedom has given to the world, I apprehend as coming from the world and constituting my obligations. In anguish I apprehend myself at once as totally free and as not being able to derive the meaning of the world except as coming from myself.

We should not however conclude that being brought on to the reflective plane and envisaging one's distant or immediate possibilities suffice to apprehend oneself in *pure* anguish. In each instance of reflection anguish is born as a structure of the reflective consciousness insofar as the latter considers consciousness as an object of reflection; but it still remains possible for me to maintain various types of conduct with respect to my own anguish – in particular, patterns of flight. Everything takes place, in fact, as if our essential and immediate behavior with respect to anguish is flight. ...

Thus we flee from anguish by attempting to apprehend ourselves from without as an Other or as *a thing*. What we are accustomed to call a revelation of the inner sense or an original intuition of our freedom contains nothing original; it is an already constructed process, expressly designed to hide from ourselves anguish, the veritable "immediate given" of our freedom.

Do these various constructions succeed in stifling or hiding our anguish? It is certain that we cannot overcome anguish, for we *are* anguish. As for veiling it, aside from the fact that the very nature of consciousness and its translucency forbid us to take the expression literally, we must note the particular type of behavior which it indicates. We can hide an external object because it exists independently of us. For the same reason we can turn our look or our attention away from it – that is, very simply, fix our eyes on some other object; henceforth each reality – mine and that of the object – resumes its own life, and the accidental relation which united consciousness to the thing disappears without thereby altering either existence. But if I *am* what I wish to veil, the question takes on quite another aspect. I can in fact wish "not to see" a certain aspect of my being only if I am acquainted with the aspect which I do not wish to see. This means that in my being I must indicate this aspect in order to be able to turn myself away from it; better yet, I must think of it constantly in order to take care not to think of it. In this connection it must be understood not only that I must of necessity perpetually carry within me what I wish to flee but also that I must aim at the object of my flight in order to flee it. This means that anguish, the intentional aim of anguish, and a flight from anguish toward reassuring myths must all be given in the unity of the same consciousness. In a word, I flee in order not to know, but I cannot avoid knowing that I am fleeing; and the flight from anguish is only a mode of becoming conscious of anguish. Thus anguish, properly speaking, can be neither hidden nor avoided.

Yet to flee anguish and to be anguish cannot be exactly the same thing. If I am my anguish in order to flee it, that presupposes that I can decenter myself in relation to what I am, that I can be anguish in the form of "not-being it," that I can dispose of a nihilating power at the heart of anguish itself. This nihilating power nihilates anguish insofar as I flee it and nihilates itself in so far as *I am anguish in order to flee it*. This attitude is what we call *bad faith*. There is then no question of expelling anguish from consciousness nor of constituting it in an unconscious psychic phenomenon; very simply I can make myself guilty of bad faith while apprehending the anguish which I am, and this bad faith, intended to fill up the nothingness which I *am* in my relation to myself, precisely implies the nothingness which it suppresses....

If man is what he is, bad faith is forever impossible and candor ceases to be his ideal and becomes instead his being. But is man what he is? And more generally, how can he *be* what he is when he exists as consciousness of being? If candor or sincerity is a universal value, it is evident that the maxim "one must be what one is" does not serve solely as a regulating principle for judgments and concepts by which I express what I am. It posits not merely an ideal of knowing but an ideal of *being*; it proposes for us an absolute equivalence of being with itself as a prototype of being. In this sense it is necessary that we *make ourselves* what we are. But what *are we* then if we have the constant obligation to make ourselves what we are, if our mode of being is having the obligation to be what we are?

Let us consider this waiter in the café. His movement is quick and forward, a little too precise, a little too rapid. He comes toward the patrons with a step a little too quick. He bends forward a little too eagerly; his voice, his eyes express an interest a little too solicitous for the order of the customer. Finally there he returns, trying to imitate in his walk the inflexible stiffness of some kind of automaton while carrying his tray with the recklessness of a tight-rope-walker by putting it in a perpetually unstable, perpetually broken equilibrium which he perpetually re-establishes by a light movement of the arm and hand. All his behaviour seems to us a game. He applies himself to chaining his movements as if they were mechanisms, the one regulating the other; his gestures and even his voice seem to be mechanisms; he gives himself the quickness and pitiless rapidity of things. He is playing, he is amusing himself. But what is he playing? We need not watch long before we can explain it: he is playing at *being* a waiter in a café. There is nothing there to surprise us. The game is a kind of marking out and investigation. The child plays with his body in order to explore it, to take inventory of it; the waiter in the café plays with his condition in order to *realize* it. This obligation is not different from that which is imposed on all tradesmen. Their condition is wholly one of ceremony. The public demands of them that they realize it as a ceremony; there is the dance of the grocer, of the tailor, of the auctioneer, by which they endeavor to persuade their clientele that they are nothing but a grocer, an auctioneer, a tailor. A grocer who dreams is offensive to the buyer, because such a grocer is not wholly a grocer. Society demands that he limit himself to his function as a grocer, just as the soldier at attention makes himself into a soldier-thing with a direct regard which does not see at all, which is no longer meant to see, since it is the rule and not the interest of the moment which determines the point he must fix his eyes on (the sight "fixed at ten paces"). There are indeed many precautions to imprison a man in what he is, as if we lived in perpetual fear that he might escape from it, that he might break away and suddenly elude his condition.

In a parallel situation, from within, the waiter in the café cannot be immediately a café waiter in the sense that this inkwell *is* an inkwell, or the glass is a glass. It is by no means that he cannot form reflective judgments or concepts concerning his condition. He knows well what it "means": the obligation of getting up at five o'clock, of sweeping the floor of the shop before the restaurant opens, of starting the coffee pot going, etc. He knows the rights which it allows: the right to the tips, the right to belong to a union, etc. But all these concepts, all these judgments refer to the transcendent. It is a matter of abstract possibilities, of rights and duties conferred on a "person possessing rights." And it is precisely this person *who I have to be* (if I am the waiter in question) and who I am not. It is not that I do not wish to be this person or that I want this person to be different. But rather there is no common measure between his being and mine. It is a "representation" for others and for myself, which means that I can be he only in *representation*. But if I represent myself as him, I am not he; I am separated from him as the object from the subject, separated *by nothing*, but this nothing isolates me from him. I can not be he, I can only play *at being* him; that is, imagine to myself that I am he. And thereby I affect him with nothingness. In vain do I fulfill the functions of a café waiter. I can be he only in the neutralized mode, as the actor is Hamlet, by mechanically making the *typical gestures* of my state and by aiming at myself as an imaginary café waiter through those gestures taken as an "analogue."[1] What I attempt to realize is a being-in-itself of the café waiter, as if it were not just in my power to confer their value and their urgency upon my duties and the rights of my position, as if it were not my free choice to get up each morning at five o'clock or to remain in bed, even though it meant getting fired. As if from the very fact that I sustain this role in existence I did not transcend it on every side, as if I did not constitute myself as one *beyond* my condition. Yet there is no doubt that I *am* in a sense a café waiter – otherwise could I not just as well call myself a diplomat or a reporter? But if I am one, this cannot be in the mode of being in-itself. I am a waiter in the mode of *being what I am not*.

Furthermore we are dealing with more than mere social positions; I am never any one of my attitudes, any one of my actions. The good speaker is the one who *plays* at speaking, because he cannot *be speaking*. The attentive pupil who wishes to *be* attentive, his eyes riveted on the teacher, his ears wide open, so exhausts himself in playing the attentive role that he ends up by no longer hearing anything. Perpetually absent to my body, to my acts, I am despite myself that "divine absence" of which Valéry speaks. I cannot say either that I *am* here or that I *am* not here, in the sense that we say "that box of matches *is* on the table"; this would be to confuse my "being-in-the-world" with a "being-in-the-midst-of-the-world." Nor that I *am* standing, nor that I *am* seated; this would be to confuse my body with the idiosyncratic totality of which it is only one of the structures. On all sides I escape being and yet – I am. . . .

Under these conditions what can be the significance of the ideal of sincerity except as a task impossible to achieve, of which the very meaning is in contradiction with the structure of my consciousness. To be sincere, we said, is to be what one is. That supposes that I am not originally what I am. But here naturally Kant's "You ought, therefore you can" is implicitly understood. I can *become* sincere; this is what my duty and my effort to achieve sincerity imply. But we definitely establish that the original structure of "not being what one is" renders impossible in advance all movement toward being in itself or "being what one is." And this impossibility is not hidden from consciousness; on the contrary, it is the very stuff of consciousness; it is the embarrassing constraint which we constantly experience; it is our very incapacity to recognize ourselves, to constitute ourselves as being what we are. It is this necessity which means that, as soon as we posit ourselves as a certain being, by a legitimate judgment, based on inner experience or correctly deduced from *a priori* or empirical premises, then by that very positing we surpass this being – and that not toward another being but toward emptiness, toward *nothing*.

How then can we blame another for not being sincere or rejoice in our own sincerity since this sincerity appears to us at the same time to be impossible? How can we in conversation, in confession, in introspection, even attempt sincerity since the effort will by its very nature be doomed to failure and since at the very time when we announce it we have a prejudicative comprehension of its futility? In introspection I try to determine exactly what I am, to make up my mind to be my true self without delay – even though it means consequently to set about searching for ways to change myself. But what does this mean if not that I am constituting myself as a thing? Shall I determine the ensemble of purposes and motivations which have pushed me to do this or that action? But this is already to postulate a causal determinism which constitutes the flow of my states of consciousness as a succession of physical states. Shall I uncover in myself "drives," even though it be to affirm them in shame? But is this not deliberately to forget that these drives are realized with my consent, that they are not forces of nature but that I lend them their efficacy by a perpetually renewed decision concerning their value? Shall I pass judgment on my character, on my nature? Is this not to veil from myself at that moment what I know only too well, that I thus judge a past to which by definition my present is not subject? The proof of this is that the same man who in sincerity posits that he is what in actuality he was, is indignant at the reproach of another and tries to disarm it by asserting that he can no longer be what he was. We are readily astonished and upset when the penalties of the court affect a man who in his new freedom *is no longer* the guilty person he was. But at the same time we require of this man that he recognize himself as *being* this guilty one. What then is sincerity except precisely a phenomenon of bad faith? Have we not shown indeed that in bad faith human reality is constituted as a being which is what it is not and which is not what it is? . . .

Thus the essential structure of sincerity does not differ from that of bad faith since the sincere man constitutes himself as what he is *in order not to be it*. This explains the truth recognized by all that one can fall into bad faith through being sincere. As Valéry pointed out, this is the case with Stendhal. Total, constant sincerity as a constant effort to adhere to oneself is by nature a constant effort to dissociate oneself from oneself. A person frees himself from himself by the very act by which he makes himself an object for himself. To draw up a perpetual inventory of what one is means constantly to redeny oneself and to take refuge in a sphere where one is no longer anything but a pure, free regard. The goal of bad faith, as we said, is to put oneself out of reach; it is an escape. Now we see that we must use the same terms to define sincerity. What does this mean?

In the final analysis the goal of sincerity and the goal of bad faith are not so different. To be sure, there is a sincerity which bears on the past and which does not concern us here; I am sincere if I confess *having had* this pleasure or that intention. We shall see that if this sincerity is possible, it is because in his fall into the past, the being of man is constituted as a being-in-itself. But here our concern is only with the sincerity which aims at itself in present immanence. What is its goal? To bring me to confess to myself what I am in order that I may finally coincide with my being; in a word, to cause myself to be, in the mode of the in-itself, what I am in the mode of "not being what I am." Its assumption is that fundamentally I am already, in the mode of the in-itself, what I have to be. Thus we find at the base of sincerity a continual game of mirror and reflection, a perpetual passage from the being which is what it is to the being which is not what it is and inversely from the being which is not what it is to the being which is what it is. And what is the goal of bad faith? To cause me to be what I am, in the mode of "not being what one is," or not to be what I am in the mode of "being what one is." We find here the same game of mirrors. In fact in order for me to have an intention of sincerity, I must at the outset simultaneously be and not be what I am. Sincerity does not assign to me a mode of being or a particular quality, but in relation to that quality it aims at making me pass from one mode of being to another mode of being. This second mode of being, the ideal of sincerity, I am prevented by nature from attaining; and at the very moment when I struggle to attain it, I have a vague prejudicative comprehension that I shall not attain it. But all the same, in order for me to be able to conceive an intention in bad faith, I must have such a nature that within my being I escape from my being. If I were sad or cowardly in the way in which this inkwell is an inkwell, the possibility of bad faith could not even be conceived. Not only should I be unable to escape from my being; I could not even imagine that I could escape from it. But if bad faith is possible by virtue of a simple project, it is because so far as my being is concerned, there is no difference between being and nonbeing if I am cut off from my project.

Bad faith is possible only because sincerity is conscious of missing its goal inevitably, due to its very nature. I can try to apprehend myself as "*not being cowardly*," when I *am* so, only on condition that the "being cowardly" is itself "in question" at the very moment when it exists, on condition that it is itself *one* question, that at the very moment when I wish to apprehend it, it escapes me on all sides and annihilates itself. The condition under which I can attempt an effort in bad faith is that in one sense, I *am not* this coward which I do not wish to be. But if I *were not* cowardly in the simple mode of not-being-what-one-is-not, I would be "in good faith" by declaring that I am not cowardly. Thus this inapprehensible coward is evanescent; in order for me not to be cowardly, I must in some way also be cowardly. That does not mean that I must be "a little" cowardly, in the sense that "a little" signifies "to a certain degree cowardly – and not cowardly to a certain degree." No. I must at once both be and not be totally and in all respects a coward. Thus in this case bad faith requires that I should not be what I am; that is, that there be an imponderable difference separating being from nonbeing in the mode of being of human reality.

But bad faith is not restricted to denying the qualities which I possess, to not seeing the being which I am. It attempts also to constitute myself as being what I am not. It apprehends me positively as courageous when I am not so. And that is possible, once again, only if I am what I am not; that is, if nonbeing in me does not have being even as nonbeing. Of course necessarily I *am not* courageous; otherwise bad faith would not be *had* faith. But in addition my effort in bad faith must include the ontological comprehension that even in my usual being what I *am*, I am not it really and that there is no such difference between the being of "being-sad," for example – which I *am* in the mode of not being what I am – and the "nonbeing" of not-being-courageous which I wish to hide from myself. Moreover it is particularly requisite that the very negation of being should be itself the object of a perpetual nihilation, that the very meaning of "nonbeing" be perpetually in question in human reality. If I *were not* courageous in the way in which this inkwell is not a table; that is, if I were isolated in my cowardice, propped firmly against it, incapable of putting it in relation to its opposite, if I were not capable of *determining* myself as cowardly – that is, to deny courage to myself and thereby to escape my cowardice in the very moment that I posit it – if it were not on principle *impossible* for me to coincide with my *not-being-courageous* as well as with my being-courageous – then any project of bad faith would be prohibited me. Thus in order for bad faith to be possible, sincerity itself must be in bad faith. The condition of the possibility for bad faith is that human reality, in its most immediate being, in the intrastructure of the prereflective *cogito*, must be what it is not and not be what it is.

Note

1 Cf. *L'Imaginaire, psychologie phénoménologique de l'imagination* (Paris: Gallimard, 1940); *The Psychology of Imagination* (New York: Philosophical Library, 1948).

Select Bibliography

The Age of Reason. Translated by Eric Sutton. New York: Vintage Books, 1992.

Being and Nothingness. Translated by Hazel E. Barnes. New York: Washington Square Press, 1992.

Between Existentialism and Marxism: Sartre on Philosophy, Politics, Psychology and the Arts. Translated by John Mathews. New York: Pantheon Books, 1983.

Critique of Dialectical Reason: Theory of Practical Ensembles. Edited by Jonathan Ree. Translated by Alan Sheridan-Smith. London: NLB, 1976.

Existentialism and Humanism. Translated by Philip Mairet. Brooklyn: Haskell House, 1977.

Life/Situations: Essays Written and Spoken. Translated by Paul Auster and Lydia Davis. New York: Pantheon Books, 1977.

Nausea. Translated by Lloyd Alexander. New York: New Directions Publishing, 1969.

No Exit, and Three Other Plays. New York: Vintage Books, 1989.

Notebooks for an Ethics. Translated by David Pellauer. Chicago: University of Chicago Press, 1992.

Of Human Freedom. Edited by Wade Baskin. New York: Philosophical Library, 1967.

Saint Genet, Actor and Martyr. Translated by Bernard Frechtman. New York: Pantheon Books, 1983.

Search for a Method. Translated by Hazel E. Barnes. New York: Vintage Books, 1968.

"What is Literature?" and Other Essays. Cambridge, Mass.: Harvard University Press, 1988.

The Words. Translated by Bernard Frechtman. New York: Vintage Books, 1981.

11

Simone de Beauvoir

French philosopher Simone de Beauvoir (1908–86), one of the leading authors of twentieth-century feminism, wrote philosophical texts, novels, travel books, essays, and memoirs. Her political commitment to socialism and her philosophical commitment to existentialism are reflected in the emphasis her writings place on freedom, action, and self-creation. In the following excerpt from the Introduction to *The Second Sex* (1949), de Beauvoir attempts to debunk the notion of an "eternal feminine," which defines woman as having a particular feminine essence and thereby limits women's freedom to define themselves. De Beauvoir attempts to show the extent to which woman continues to be defined as "the Other" to man and as a result is denied her own subjectivity and autonomy.

The Second Sex

Introduction

For a long time I have hesitated to write a book on woman. The subject is irritating, especially to women; and it is not new. Enough ink has been spilled in the quarreling over feminism, now practically over, and perhaps we should say no more about it. It is still talked about, however, for the voluminous nonsense uttered during the last century seems to have done little to illuminate the problem. After all, is there a problem? And if so, what is it? Are there women, really? Most assuredly the theory of the eternal feminine still has its adherents who will whisper in your ear: "Even in Russia women still are *women*"; and other erudite persons – sometimes the very same – say with a sigh: "Woman is losing her way, woman is lost." One wonders if women still exist, if they will always exist, whether or not it is desirable that they should, what place they occupy in this world, what their place should be. "What has become of women?" was asked recently in an ephemeral magazine.[1]

But first we must ask: what is a woman? "*Tota mulier in utero*," says one, "woman is a womb." But in speaking of certain women, connoisseurs declare

From *The Second Sex*, translated and edited by H. M Parshley (New York: Vintage Books, 1974), pp. xv – xxiv. Copyright © 1952 and renewed 1980 by Alfred A. Knopf Inc. Reprinted by permission of the publishers, Alfred A. Knopf and Jonathan Cape.

that they are not women, although they are equipped with a uterus like the rest. All agree in recognizing the fact that females exist in the human species; today as always they make up about one half of humanity. And yet we are told that femininity is in danger; we are exhorted to be women, remain women, become women. It would appear, then, that every female human being is not necessarily a woman; to be so considered she must share in that mysterious and threatened reality known as femininity. Is this attribute something secreted by the ovaries? Or is it a Platonic essence, a product of the philosophic imagination? Is a rustling petticoat enough to bring it down to earth? Although some women try zealously to incarnate this essence, it is hardly patentable. It is frequently described in vague and dazzling terms that seem to have been borrowed from the vocabulary of the seers, and indeed in the times of St Thomas it was considered an essence as certainly defined as the somniferous virtue of the poppy.

But conceptualism has lost ground. The biological and social sciences no longer admit the existence of unchangeably fixed entities that determine given characteristics, such as those ascribed to woman, the Jew, or the Negro. Science regards any characteristic as a reaction dependent in part upon a *situation*. If today femininity no longer exists, then it never existed. But does the word *woman*, then, have no specific content? . . . In truth, to go for a walk with one's eyes open is enough to demonstrate that humanity is divided into two classes of individuals whose clothes, faces, bodies, smiles, gaits, interests, and occupations are manifestly different. Perhaps these differences are superficial, perhaps they are destined to disappear. What is certain is that right now they do most obviously exist.

If her functioning as a female is not enough to define woman, if we decline also to explain her through "the eternal feminine," and if nevertheless we admit, provisionally, that women do exist, then we must face the question: what is a woman?

To state the question is, to me, to suggest, at once, a preliminary answer. The fact that I ask it is in itself significant. A man would never get the notion of writing a book on the peculiar situation of the human male.[2] But if I wish to define myself, I must first of all say: "I am a woman"; on this truth must be based all further discussion. A man never begins by presenting himself as an individual of a certain sex; it goes without saying that he is a man. The terms *masculine* and *feminine* are used symmetrically only as a matter of form, as on legal papers. In actuality the relation of the two sexes is not quite like that of two electrical poles, for man represents both the positive and the neutral, as is indicated by the common use of *man* to designate human beings in general; whereas woman represents only the negative, defined by limiting criteria, without reciprocity. In the midst of an abstract discussion it is vexing to hear a man say: "You think thus and so because you are a woman"; but I know that my only defense is to reply: "I think thus and so because it is true," thereby removing my subjective self from the argument. It would be out of the question to reply: "And you think the contrary because you are a man," for it is understood that the fact of being a man is no peculiarity. A man is in the right in being a man; it is the woman who is in the wrong. It amounts to this: just as for the ancients there was an absolute vertical with reference to which the oblique was defined, so there is an absolute human type, the masculine. Woman has ovaries, a uterus; these peculiarities imprison her in her subjectivity, circumscribe her within the limits of her own nature. It is often said that she thinks with her glands. Man superbly ignores the fact that his anatomy also includes glands, such as the testicles, and that they secrete hormones. He thinks of his body as a direct and normal connection with the world, which he believes he apprehends objectively, whereas he regards the body of woman as a hindrance, a prison, weighed down by everything peculiar to it. "The female is a female by virtue of a certain *lack* of qualities," said Aristotle; "we should regard the female nature as afflicted with a natural defectiveness." And St Thomas for his part pronounced woman to be an "imperfect man," an "incidental" being. This is symbolized in Genesis where Eve is depicted as made from what Bossuet called "a supernumerary bone" of Adam.

Thus humanity is male and man defines woman not in herself but as relative to him; she is not regarded as an autonomous being. Michelet writes: "Woman, the relative being. . . ." And Benda is most positive in his *Rapport d' Uriel:* "The body of man makes sense in itself quite apart from that of woman, whereas the latter seems wanting in significance by itself. . . . Man can think of himself without woman. She cannot think of herself without man." And she is simply what man decrees; thus she is called "the sex," by which is meant that she appears essentially to the male as a sexual being. For him she is sex – absolute sex, no less. She is defined and differentiated with reference to

162

man and not he with reference to her; she is the incidental, the inessential as opposed to the essential. He is the Subject, he is the Absolute – she is the Other.[3]

The category of the *Other* is as primordial as consciousness itself. In the most primitive societies, in the most ancient mythologies, one finds the expression of a duality – that of the Self and the Other. This duality was not originally attached to the division of the sexes; it was not dependent upon any empirical facts. It is revealed in such works as that of Granet on Chinese thought and those of Dumézil on the East Indies and Rome. The feminine element was at first no more involved in such pairs as Varuna–Mitra, Uranus–Zeus, Sun–Moon, and Day–Night than it was in the contrasts between Good and Evil, lucky and unlucky auspices, right and left, God and Lucifer. Otherness is a fundamental category of human thought.

Thus it is that no group ever sets itself up as the One without at once setting up the Other over against itself. If three travelers chance to occupy the same compartment, that is enough to make vaguely hostile "others" out of all the rest of the passengers on the train. In small-town eyes all persons not belonging to the village are "strangers" and suspect; to the native of a country all who inhabit other countries are "foreigners"; Jews are "different" for the anti-Semite, Negroes are "inferior" for American racists, aborigines are "natives" for colonists, proletarians are the "lower class" for the privileged.

Lévi-Strauss, at the end of a profound work on the various forms of primitive societies, reaches the following conclusion: "Passage from the state of Nature to the state of Culture is marked by man's ability to view biological relations as a series of contrasts; duality, alternation, opposition, and symmetry, whether under definite or vague forms, constitute not so much phenomena to be explained as fundamental and immediately given data of social reality."[4] These phenomena would be incomprehensible if in fact human society were simply a *Mitsein* or fellowship based on solidarity and friendliness. Things become clear, on the contrary, if, following Hegel, we find in consciousness itself a fundamental hostility toward every other consciousness; the subject can be posed only in being opposed – he sets himself up as the essential, as opposed to the other, the inessential, the object.

But the other consciousness, the other ego, sets up a reciprocal claim. The native traveling abroad is shocked to find himself in turn regarded as a "stranger" by the natives of neighboring countries. As a matter of fact, wars, festivals, trading, treaties, and contests among tribes, nations, and classes tend to deprive the concept *Other* of its absolute sense and to make manifest its relativity; willy-nilly, individuals and groups are forced to realize the reciprocity of their relations. How is it, then, that this reciprocity has not been recognized between the sexes, that one of the contrasting terms is set up as the sole essential, denying any relativity in regard to its correlative and defining the latter as pure otherness? Why is it that women do not dispute male sovereignty? No subject will readily volunteer to become the object, the inessential; it is not the Other who, in defining himself as the Other, establishes the One. The Other is posed as such by the One in defining himself as the One. But if the Other is not to regain the status of being the One, he must be submissive enough to accept this alien point of view. Whence comes this submission in the case of woman?

There are, to be sure, other cases in which a certain category has been able to dominate another completely for a time. Very often this privilege depends upon inequality of numbers – the majority imposes its rule upon the minority or persecutes it. But women are not a minority, like the American Negroes or the Jews; there are as many women as men on earth. Again, the two groups concerned have often been originally independent; they may have been formerly unaware of each other's existence, or perhaps they recognized each other's autonomy. But a historical event has resulted in the subjugation of the weaker by the stronger. The scattering of the Jews, the introduction of slavery into America, the conquests of imperialism are examples in point. In these cases the oppressed retained at least the memory of former days; they possessed in common a past, a tradition, sometimes a religion or a culture.

The parallel drawn by Bebel between women and the proletariat is valid in that neither ever formed a minority or a separate collective unit of mankind. And instead of a single historical event it is in both cases a historical development that explains their status as a class and accounts for the membership of *particular individuals* in that class. But proletarians have not always existed, whereas there have always been women. They are women in virtue of their anatomy and physiology. Throughout history they have always been subordinated to men, and hence their dependency is not the result of a historical event or a social change – it was not something that *occurred*. The reason why otherness in this case seems to be an absolute is in part that it lacks the contingent or incidental nature of historical facts. A condition brought about at a certain time can be abolished at some other time, as the Negroes of Haiti and others have proved; but it might seem that a natural condition is beyond the possibility of change. In truth, however, the nature of things is no more immutably given, once for all, than is historical reality. If woman seems to be the inessential which never becomes the essential, it is because she herself fails to bring about this change. Proletarians say "We"; Negroes also. Regarding themselves as subjects, they transform the bourgeois, the whites, into "others." But women do not say "We," except at some congress of feminists or similar formal demonstration; men say "women," and women use the same word in referring to themselves. They do not authentically assume a subjective attitude. The proletarians have accomplished the revolution in Russia, the Negroes in Haiti, the Indo-Chinese are battling for it in Indo-China; but the women's effort has never been anything more than a symbolic agitation. They have gained only what men have been willing to grant; they have taken nothing, they have only received.

The reason for this is that women lack concrete means for organizing themselves into a unit which can stand face to face with the correlative unit. They have no past, no history, no religion of their own; and they have no such solidarity of work and interest as that of the proletariat. They are not even promiscuously herded together in the way that creates community feeling among the American Negroes, the ghetto Jews, the workers of Saint-Denis, or the factory hands of Renault. They live dispersed among the males, attached through residence, housework, economic condition, and social standing to certain men – fathers or husbands – more firmly than they are to other women. If they belong to the bourgeoisie, they feel solidarity with men of that class, not with proletarian women; if they are white, their allegiance is to white men, not to Negro women. The proletariat can propose to massacre the ruling class, and a sufficiently fanatical Jew or Negro might dream of getting sole possession of the atomic bomb and making humanity wholly Jewish or black; but woman cannot even dream of exterminating the males. The bond that unites her to her oppressors is not comparable to any other. The division of the sexes is a biological fact, not an event in human history. Male and female stand opposed within a primordial *Mitsein*,

and woman has not broken it. The couple is a fundamental unity with its two halves riveted together, and the cleavage of society along the line of sex is impossible. Here is to be found the basic trait of woman: she is the Other in a totality of which the two components are necessary to one another.

One could suppose that this reciprocity might have facilitated the liberation of woman. When Hercules sat at the feet of Omphale and helped with her spinning, his desire for her held him captive; but why did she fail to gain a lasting power? To revenge herself on Jason, Medea killed their children; and this grim legend would seem to suggest that she might have obtained a formidable influence over him through his love for his offspring. In *Lysistrata* Aristophanes gaily depicts a band of women who joined forces to gain social ends through the sexual needs of their men; but this is only a play. In the legend of the Sabine women, the latter soon abandoned their plan of remaining sterile to punish their ravishers. In truth woman has not been socially emancipated through man's need – sexual desire and the desire for offspring – which makes the male dependent for satisfaction upon the female.

Master and slave, also, are united by a reciprocal need, in this case economic, which does not liberate the slave. In the relation of master to slave the master does not make a point of the need that he has for the other; he has in his grasp the power of satisfying this need through his own action; whereas the slave, in his dependent condition, his hope and fear, is quite conscious of the need he has for his master. Even if the need is at bottom equally urgent for both, it always works in favor of the oppressor and against the oppressed. That is why the liberation of the working class, for example, has been slow. . . .

At the present time, when women are beginning to take part in the affairs of the world, it is still a world that belongs to men – they have no doubt of it at all and women have scarcely any. To decline to be the Other, to refuse to be a party to the deal – this would be for women to renounce all the advantages conferred upon them by their alliance with the superior caste. Man-the-sovereign will provide woman-the-liege with material protection and will undertake the moral justification of her existence; thus she can evade at once both economic risk and the metaphysical risk of a liberty in which ends and aims must be contrived without assistance. Indeed, along with the ethical urge of each individual to affirm his subjective existence, there is also the temptation to forgo liberty and become a thing. This is an inauspicious road, for he who takes it – passive, lost, ruined – becomes henceforth the creature of another's will, frustrated in his transcendence and deprived of every value. But it is an easy road; on it one avoids the strain involved in undertaking an authentic existence. When man makes of woman the *Other*, he may, then, expect her to manifest deep-seated tendencies toward complicity. Thus, woman may fail to lay claim to the status of subject because she lacks definite resources, because she feels the necessary bond that ties her to man regardless of reciprocity, and because she is often very well pleased with her role as the *Other*.

But it will be asked at once: how did all this begin? It is easy to see that the duality of the sexes, like any duality, gives rise to conflict. And doubtless the winner will assume the status of absolute. But why should man have won from the start? It seems possible that women could have won the victory; or that the outcome of the conflict might never have been decided. How is it that this world has always belonged to the men and that things have begun to change only recently? Is this change a good thing? Will it bring about an equal sharing of the world between men and women?

These questions are not new, and they have often been answered. But the very fact that woman *is the Other* tends to cast suspicion upon all the justifications that men have ever been able to provide for it. These have all too evidently been dictated by men's interest....

But it is doubtless impossible to approach any human problem with a mind free from bias. The way in which questions are put, the points of view assumed, presuppose a relativity of interest; all characteristics imply values, and every objective description, so called, implies an ethical background. Rather than attempt to conceal principles more or less definitely implied, it is better to state them openly at the beginning. This will make it unnecessary to specify on every page in just what sense one uses such words as *superior*, *inferior*, *better*, *worse*, *progress*, *reaction*, and the like. If we survey some of the works on woman, we note that one of the points of view most frequently adopted is that of the public good, the general interest; and one always means by this the benefit of society as one wishes it to be maintained or established. For our part, we hold that the only public good is that which assures the private good of the citizens; we shall pass judgment on institutions according to their effectiveness in giving concrete opportunities to individuals. But we do not confuse the idea of private interest with that of happiness, although that is another common point of view. Are not women of the harem more happy than women voters? Is not the housekeeper happier than the working woman? It is not too clear just what the word *happy* really means and still less what true values it may mask. There is no possibility of measuring the happiness of others, and it is always easy to describe as happy the situation in which one wishes to place them.

In particular those who are condemned to stagnation are often pronounced happy on the pretext that happiness consists in being at rest. This notion we reject, for our perspective is that of existentialist ethics. Every subject plays his part as such specifically through exploits or projects that serve as a mode of transcendence; he achieves liberty only through a continual reaching out toward other liberties. There is no justification for present existence other than its expansion into an indefinitely open future. Every time transcendence falls back into immanence, stagnation, there is a degradation of existence into the "*en-soi*" – the brutish life of subjection to given conditions – and of liberty into constraint and contingence. This downfall represents a moral fault if the subject consents to it; if it is inflicted upon him, it spells frustration and oppression. In both cases it is an absolute evil. Every individual concerned to justify his existence feels that his existence involves an undefined need to transcend himself, to engage in freely chosen projects.

Now, what peculiarly signalizes the situation of woman is that she – a free and autonomous being like all human creatures – nevertheless finds herself living in a world where men compel her to assume the status of the Other. They propose to stabilize her as object and to doom her to immanence since her transcendence is to be overshadowed and forever transcended by another ego (*conscience*) which is essential and sovereign. The drama of woman lies in this conflict between the fundamental aspirations of every subject (ego) – who always regards the self as the essential – and the compulsions of a situation in which she is the inessential. How can a human being in woman's situation attain fulfillment? What roads are open to her? Which are blocked? How can independence be recovered in a state of dependency? What circumstances limit woman's liberty and how can they be overcome? These are the fundamental questions on which I would fain throw some light. This means that I am interested in the fortunes of the individual as defined not in terms of happiness but in terms of liberty.

Quite evidently this problem would be without significance if we were to believe that woman's destiny is inevitably determined by physiological, psychological, or economic forces. Hence I shall discuss first of all the light in which woman is viewed by biology, psychoanalysis, and historical materialism. Next I shall try to show exactly how the concept of the "truly feminine" has been fashioned – why woman has been defined as the Other – and what have been the consequences from man's point of view. Then from woman's point of view I shall describe the world in which women must live; and thus we shall be able to envisage the difficulties in their way as, endeavoring to make their escape from the sphere hitherto assigned them, they aspire to full membership in the human race.

Notes

1 *Franchise*, dead today.
2 The Kinsey Report [Alfred C. Kinsey and others: *Sexual Behavior in the Human Male* (W. B. Saunders, 1948)] is no exception, for it is limited to describing the sexual characteristics of American men, which is quite a different matter.
3 E. Lévinas expresses this idea most explicitly in his essay *Temps et l'Autre.* "Is there not a case in which otherness, alterity [*altérité*], unquestionably marks the nature of a being, as its essence, an instance of otherness not consisting purely and simply in the opposition of two species of the same genus? I think that the feminine represents the contrary in its absolute sense, this contrariness being in no wise affected by any relation between it and its correlative and thus remaining absolutely other. Sex is not a certain specific difference . . . no more is the sexual difference a mere contradiction. . . . Nor does this difference lie in the duality of two complementary terms, for two complementary terms imply a pre-existing whole. . . . Otherness reaches its full flowering in the feminine, a term of the same rank as consciousness but of opposite meaning."

I suppose that Lévinas does not forget that woman, too, is aware of her own consciousness, or ego. But it is striking that he deliberately takes a man's point of view, disregarding the reciprocity of subject and object. When he writes that woman is mystery, he implies that she is mystery for man. Thus his description, which is intended to be objective, is in fact an assertion of masculine privilege.
4 See C. Lévi-Strauss, *Les Structures élementaires de la parenté.* My thanks are due to C. Lévi-Strauss for his kindness in furnishing me with the proofs of his work, which, among others, I have used liberally in Part II.

Select Bibliography

Adieux: A Farewell to Sartre. Translated by Patrick O'Brian. New York: Pantheon Books, 1984.

All Men Are Mortal: A Novel. Translated by Leonard M. Friedman. New York: Norton, 1992.

All Said and Done. Translated by Patrick O'Brian. New York: Paragon House, 1993.

The Blood of Others. Translated by Roger Senhouse and Yvonne Moyse. New York: Pantheon Books, 1983.

Brigitte Bardot and the Lolita Syndrome. New York: Arno Press, 1972.

The Coming of Age. Translated by Patrick O'Brian. New York: Putnam, 1972.

The Ethics of Ambiguity. Translated by Bernard Frechtman. Secaucus, NY: Carol Publishing Group, 1994.

The Mandarins: A Novel. New York: W. W. Norton, 1991.

The Marquis de Sade: An Essay by Simone De Beauvoir. Translated by Annette Michelson. New York: Grove Press, 1953.

Memoirs of a Dutiful Daughter. Translated by James Kirkup. New York: Harper and Row, 1974.

The Second Sex. Translated and edited by H. M. Parshley. New York: Vintage Books, 1974.

12

Maurice Merleau-Ponty

French philosopher Maurice Merleau-Ponty (1908–61) is best known for his work on the "phenomenology of perception," a theme that furnished the title for one of his major works. Influenced by the phenomenological approaches of Husserl, Heidegger, and Sartre, Merleau-Ponty emphasizes the primacy of perception and of the lived body in our access to the world. This emphasis stands in marked contrast to Husserl's phenomenological reduction, which, Merleau-Ponty argues, tends to reduce the real world to an object of intentional consciousness. Merleau-Ponty seeks instead to understand the body as the primary locus of lived consciousness, providing us with access to a world which, for us, is marked by its physical opacity and discontinuity. The body as my lived and living body, he argues, is never simply another possible object for consciousness, but the very seat of my living relation to the world, a relation that I myself am. Perception, furthermore, is never an access to pure sense-data; rather, our sensations and perceptions are themselves always historically situated interpretations of the world we inhabit. In addition to his work on human perception, Merleau-Ponty's *oeuvre* also includes studies on Marxism, on aesthetics, and on philosophy of language. The following excerpt, from the posthumously published book *The Visible and the Invisible*, illustrates how our perceptual consciousness is always "intertwined" with the flesh of the living body.

The Visible and the Invisible

The Intertwining – The Chiasm

If it is true that as soon as philosophy declares itself to be reflection or coincidence it prejudges what it will find, then once again it must recommence everything, reject the instruments reflection and intuition had provided themselves, and install itself in a locus where they have not yet been distinguished, in experiences that have not yet been "worked over," that offer us all at once, pell-mell, both "subject" and "object," both existence and essence, and hence give philosophy resources to redefine them. Seeing, speaking, even thinking (with certain reservations, for as soon as we distinguish thought from speaking absolutely we are already in the order of reflection), are experiences of this kind, both irrecusable and enigmatic. They have a name in all languages, but a name which in all of them also conveys significations in tufts, thickets of proper meanings and figurative meanings, so that, unlike those of science, not one of these names clarifies by attributing to what is named a circumscribed signification. Rather, they are the repeated index, the insistent reminder of a mystery as familiar as it is unexplained, of a light which, illuminating the rest, remains at its source in obscurity. If we could rediscover within the exercise of seeing and speaking some of the living references that assign them such a destiny in a language, perhaps they would teach us how to form our new instruments, and first of all to understand our research, our interrogation, themselves.

The visible about us seems to rest in itself. It is as though our vision were formed in the heart of the visible, or as though there were between it and us an intimacy as close as between the sea and the strand. And yet it is not possible that we blend into

From *The Visible and the Invisible*, edited by Claude Lefort, translated by Alphonso Lingis (Evanston, Ill.: Northwestern University Press, 1987), pp. 130–45. Originally published in French under the title *Le Visible et L' invisible*, copyright © 1964, Editions Gallimard. Copyright © 1968 by Northwestern University Press. Reprinted by permission of the publisher.

it, nor that it passes into us, for then the vision would vanish at the moment of formation, by disappearance of the seer or of the visible. What there is then are not things first identical with themselves, which would then offer themselves to the seer, nor is there a seer who is first empty and who, afterward, would open himself to them – but something to which we could not be closer than by palpating it with our look, things we could not dream of seeing "all naked" because the gaze itself envelops them, clothes them with its own flesh. Whence does it happen that in so doing it leaves them in their place, that the vision we acquire of them seems to us to come from them, and that to be seen is for them but a degradation of their eminent being? What is this talisman of color, this singular virtue of the visible that makes it, held at the end of the gaze, nonetheless much more than a correlative of my vision, such that it imposes my vision upon me as a continuation of its own sovereign existence? How does it happen that my look, enveloping them, does not hide them, and, finally, that, veiling them, it unveils them?[1]

We must first understand that this red under my eyes is not, as is always said, a *quale*, a pellicle of being without thickness, a message at the same time indecipherable and evident, which one has or has not received, but of which, if one has received it, one knows all there is to know, and of which in the end there is nothing to say. It requires a focusing, however brief; it emerges from a less precise, more general redness, in which my gaze was caught, into which it sank, before – as we put it so aptly – *fixing* it. And, now that I have fixed it, if my eyes penetrate into it, into its fixed structure, or if they start to wander round about again, the *quale* resumes its atmospheric existence. Its precise form is bound up with a certain wooly, metallic, or porous [?] configuration or texture, and the *quale* itself counts for very little compared with these participations. Claudel has a phrase saying that a certain blue of the sea is so blue that only blood would be more red. The color is yet a variant in another dimension of variation, that of its relations with the surroundings: this red is what it is only by connecting up from its place with other reds about it, with which it forms a constellation, or with other colors it dominates or that dominate it, that it attracts or that attract it, that it repels or that repel it. In short, it is a certain node in the woof of the simultaneous and the successive. It is a concretion of visibility, it is not an atom. The red dress *a fortiori* holds with all its fibers onto the fabric of the visible, and thereby onto a fabric of invisible being. A punctuation in the field of red things, which includes the tiles of roof tops, the flags of gatekeepers and of the Revolution, certain terrains near Aix or in Madagascar, it is also a punctuation in the field of red garments, which includes, along with the dresses of women, robes of professors, bishops, and advocate generals, and also in the field of adornments and that of uniforms. And its red literally is not the same as it appears in one constellation or in the other, as the pure essence of the Revolution of 1917 precipitates in it, or that of the eternal feminine, or that of the public prosecutor, or that of the gypsies dressed like hussars who reigned twenty-five years ago over an inn on the Champs-Elysées. A certain red is also a fossil drawn up from the depths of imaginary worlds. If we took all these participations into account, we would recognize that a naked color, and in general a visible, is not a chunk of absolutely hard, indivisible being, offered all naked to a vision which could be only total or null, but is rather a sort of straits between exterior horizons and interior horizons ever gaping open, something that comes to touch lightly and makes diverse regions of the colored or visible world resound at the distances, a certain differentiation, an ephemeral modulation of this world – less a color or a thing, therefore, than a difference between things and colors, a momentary crystallization of colored being or of visibility. Between the alleged colors and visibles, we would find anew the tissue that lines them, sustains them, nourishes them, and which for its part is not a thing, but a possibility, a latency, and a *flesh* of things.

If we turn now to the seer, we will find that this is no analogy or vague comparison and must be taken literally. The look, we said, envelops, palpates, espouses the visible things. As though it were in a relation of pre-established harmony with them, as though it knew them before knowing them, it moves in its own way with its abrupt and imperious style, and yet the views taken are not desultory – I do not look at a chaos, but at things – so that finally one cannot say if it is the look or if it is the things that command. What is this prepossession of the visible, this art of interrogating it according to its own wishes, this inspired exegesis? We would perhaps find the answer in the tactile palpation where the questioner and the questioned are closer, and of which, after all, the palpation of the eye is a remarkable variant. How does it happen that I give to my hands, in particular, that degree, that rate, and that direction of movement that are capable of making me feel the textures of the sleek and the rough? Between the exploration and what it will teach me, between my movements and what I touch, there must exist some relationship by principle, some kinship, according to which they are not only, like the pseudopods of the amoeba, vague and ephemeral deformations of the corporeal space, but the initiation to and the opening upon a tactile world. This can happen only if my hand, while it is felt from within, is also accessible from without, itself tangible, for my other hand, for example, if it takes its place among the things it touches, is in a sense one of them, opens finally upon a tangible being of which it is also a part. Through this crisscrossing within it of the touching and the tangible, its own movements incorporate themselves into the universe they interrogate, are recorded on the same map as it; the two systems are applied upon one another, as the two halves of an orange. It is no different for the vision – except, it is said, that here the exploration and the information it gathers do not belong "to the same sense." But this delimitation of the senses is crude. Already in the "touch" we have just found three distinct experiences which subtend one another, three dimensions which overlap but are distinct: a touching of the sleek and of the rough, a touching of the things – a passive sentiment of the body and of its space – and finally a veritable touching of the touch, when my right hand touches my left hand while it is palpating the things, where the "touching subject" passes over to the rank of the touched, descends into the things, such that the touch is formed in the midst of the world and as it were in the things. Between the massive sentiment I have of the sack in which I am enclosed, and the control from without that my hand exercises over my hand, there is as much difference as between the movements of my eyes and the changes they produce in the visible. And as, conversely, every experience of the visible has always been given to me within the context of the movements of the look, the visible spectacle belongs to the touch neither more nor less than do the "tactile qualities." We must habituate ourselves to think that every visible is cut out in the tangible, every tactile being in some manner promised to visibility, and that there is encroachment, infringement, not only between the touched and the touching, but also between the tangible and the visible, which is encrusted in it, as, conversely, the tangible itself is not a nothingness of visibility, is not without visual existence. Since the same body sees and touches, visible and tangible belong to the same world. It is a marvel too little noticed that every movement of my eyes – even more, every displacement of my body – has its place in the same visible universe that I itemize and explore with them, as, conversely, every vision takes place somewhere in the tactile space. There is double and crossed situating of the visible in the tangible and of the tangible in the visible; the two maps are complete, and yet they do not merge into one. The two parts are total parts and yet are not superposable.

Hence, without even entering into the implications proper to the seer and the visible, we know that, since vision is a palpation with the look, it must also be inscribed in the order of being that it discloses to us; he who looks must not himself be foreign to the world that he looks at. As soon as I see, it is necessary that the vision (as is so well indicated by the double meaning of the word) be doubled with a complementary vision or with another vision: myself seen from without, such as another would see me, installed in the midst of the visible, occupied in considering it from a certain spot. For the moment we shall not examine how far this identity of the seer and the visible goes, if we have a complete experience of it, or if there is something missing, and what it is. It suffices for us for the moment to note that he who sees cannot possess the visible unless he is possessed by it, unless he *is of it*,[2] unless, by principle, according to what is required by the articulation of the look with the things, he is one of the visibles, capable, by a singular reversal, of seeing them – he who is one of them.[3]

We understand then why we see the things themselves, in their places, where they are, according to their being which is indeed more than their being-perceived – and why at the same time we are separated from them by all the thickness of the look and of the body; it is that this distance is not the contrary of this proximity, it is deeply consonant with it, it is synonymous with it. It is that the thickness of flesh between the seer and the thing is constitutive for the thing of its visibility as for the

seer of his corporeity; it is not an obstacle between them, it is their means of communication. It is for the same reason that I am at the heart of the visible and that I am far from it: because it has thickness and is thereby naturally destined to be seen by a body. What is indefinable in the *quale*, in the color, is nothing else than a brief, peremptory manner of giving in one sole something, in one sole tone of being, visions past, visions to come, by whole clusters. I who see have my own depth also, being backed up by this same visible which I see and which, I know very well, closes in behind me. The thickness of the body, far from rivaling that of the world, is on the contrary the sole means I have to go unto the heart of the things, by making myself a world and by making them flesh.

The body interposed is not itself a thing, an interstitial matter, a connective tissue, but a *sensible for itself*, which means, not that absurdity: color that sees itself, surface that touches itself – but this paradox [?]: a set of colors and surfaces inhabited by a touch, a vision, hence an *exemplar sensible*, which offers to him who inhabits it and senses it the wherewithal to sense everything that resembles himself on the outside, such that, caught up in the tissue of the things, it draws it entirely to itself, incorporates it, and, with the same movement, communicates to the things upon which it closes over that identity without superposition, that difference without contradiction, that divergence between the within and the without that constitutes its natal secret.[4] The body unites us directly with the things through its own ontogenesis, by welding to one another the two outlines of which it is made, its two laps: the sensible mass it is and the mass of the sensible wherein it is born by segregation and upon which, as seer, it remains open. It is the body and it alone, because it is a two-dimensional being, that can bring us to the things themselves, which are themselves not flat beings but beings in depth, inaccessible to a subject that would survey them from above, open to him alone that, if it be possible, would coexist with them in the same world. When we speak of the flesh of the visible, we do not mean to do anthropology, to describe a world covered over with all our own projections, leaving aside what it can be under the human mask. Rather, we mean that carnal being, as a being of depths, of several leaves or several faces, a being in latency, and a presentation of a certain absence, is a prototype of Being, of which our body, the sensible sentient, is a very remarkable variant, but whose constitutive paradox already lies in every visible. For already the cube assembles within itself incompossible *visibilia*, as my body is at once phenomenal body and objective body, and if finally it is, it, like my body, is by a tour de force. What we call a visible is, we said, a quality pregnant with a texture, the surface of a depth, a cross section upon a massive being, a grain or corpuscle borne by a wave of Being. Since the total visible is always behind, or after, or between the aspects we see of it, there is access to it only through an experience which, like it, is wholly outside of itself. It is thus, and not as the bearer of a knowing subject, that our body commands the visible for us, but it does not explain it, does not clarify it, it only concentrates the mystery of its scattered visibility; and it is indeed a paradox of Being, not a paradox of man, that we are dealing with here. To be sure, one can reply that, between the two "sides" of our body, the body as sensible and the body as sentient (what in the past we called objective body and phenomenal body), rather than a spread, there is the abyss that separates the In Itself from the For Itself. It is a problem – and we will not avoid it – to determine how the sensible sentient can also be thought. But here, seeking to form our first concepts in such a way as to avoid the classical impasses, we do not have to honor the difficulties that they may present when confronted with a *cogito*, which itself has to be re-examined. Yes or no: do we have a body – that is, not a permanent object of thought, but a flesh that suffers when it is wounded, hands that touch? We know: hands do not suffice for touch – but to decide for this reason alone that our hands do not touch, and to relegate them to the world of objects or of instruments, would be, in acquiescing to the bifurcation of subject and object, to forego in advance the understanding of the sensible and to deprive ourselves of its lights. We propose on the contrary to take it literally to begin with. We say therefore that our body is a being of two leaves, from one side a thing among things and otherwise what sees them and touches them; we say, because it is evident, that it unites these two properties within itself, and its double belongingness to the order of the "object" and to the order of the "subject" reveals to us quite unexpected relations between the two orders. It cannot be by incomprehensible accident that the body has this double reference; it teaches us that each calls for the other. For if the body is a thing among things, it is so in a stronger and deeper sense than they: in the sense that, we said, it *is of them*, and this means that

it detaches itself upon them, and, accordingly, detaches itself from them. It is not simply a thing *seen* in fact (I do not see my back), it is visible by right, it falls under a vision that is both ineluctable and deferred. Conversely, if it touches and sees, this is not because it would have the visibles before itself as objects: they are about it, they even enter into its enclosure, they are within it, they line its looks and its hands inside and outside. If it touches them and sees them, this is only because, being of their family, itself visible and tangible, it uses its own being as a means to participate in theirs, because each of the two beings is an archetype for the other, because the body belongs to the order of the things as the world is universal flesh. One should not even say, as we did a moment ago, that the body is made up of two leaves, of which the one, that of the "sensible," is bound up with the rest of the world. There are not in it two leaves or two layers; fundamentally it is neither thing seen only nor seer only, it is Visibility sometimes wandering and sometimes reassembled. And as such it is not in the world, it does not detain its view of the world as within a private garden: it sees the world itself, the world of everybody, and without having to leave "itself," because it is wholly – because its hands, its eyes, are nothing else than – this reference of a visible, a tangible-standard to all those whose resemblance it bears and whose evidence it gathers, by a magic that is the vision, the touch themselves. To speak of leaves or of layers is still to flatten and to juxtapose, under the reflective gaze, what coexists in the living and upright body. If one wants metaphors, it would be better to say that the body sensed and the body sentient are as the obverse and the reverse, or again, as two segments of one sole circular course which goes above from left to right and below from right to left, but which is but one sole movement in its two phases. And everything said about the sensed body pertains to the whole of the sensible of which it is a part, and to the world. If the body is one sole body in its two phases, it incorporates into itself the whole of the sensible and with the same movement incorporates itself into a "Sensible in itself." We have to reject the age-old assumptions that put the body in the world and the seer in the body, or, conversely, the world and the body in the seer as in a box. Where are we to put the limit between the body and the world, since the world is flesh? Where in the body are we to put the seer, since evidently there is in the body only "shadows stuffed with organs," that is, more of the visible? The world seen is not "in" my body, and my body is not "in" the visible world ultimately: as flesh applied to a flesh, the world neither surrounds it nor is surrounded by it. A participation in and kinship with the visible, the vision neither envelops it nor is enveloped by it definitively. The superficial pellicle of the visible is only for my vision and for my body. But the depth beneath this surface contains my body and hence contains my vision. My body as a visible thing is contained within the full spectacle. But my seeing body subtends this visible body, and all the visibles with it. There is reciprocal insertion and intertwining of one in the other. Or rather, if, as once again we must, we eschew the thinking by planes and perspectives, there are two circles, or two vortexes, or two spheres, concentric when I live naively, and as soon as I question myself, the one slightly decentered with respect to the other....

We have to ask ourselves what exactly we have found with this strange adhesion of the seer and the visible. There is vision, touch, when a certain visible, a certain tangible, turns back upon the whole of the visible, the whole of the tangible, of which it is a part, or when suddenly it finds itself *surrounded* by them, or when between it and them, and through their commerce, is formed a Visibility, a Tangible in itself, which belong properly neither to the body *qua* fact nor to the world *qua* fact – as upon two mirrors facing one another where two indefinite series of images set in one another arise which belong really to neither of the two surfaces, since each is only the rejoinder of the other, and which therefore form a couple, a couple more real than either of them. Thus since the seer is caught up in what he sees, it is still himself he sees: there is a fundamental narcissism of all vision. And thus, for the same reason, the vision he exercises, he also undergoes from the things, such that, as many painters have said, I feel myself looked at by the things, my activity is equally passivity – which is the second and more profound sense of the narcissism: not to see in the outside, as the others see it, the contour of a body one inhabits, but especially to be seen by the outside, to exist within it, to emigrate into it, to be seduced, captivated, alienated by the phantom, so that the seer and the visible reciprocate one another and we no longer know which sees and which is seen. It is this Visibility, this generality of the Sensible in itself, this anonymity innate to Myself that we have previously called flesh, and one knows there is no name in traditional philosophy to designate it. The flesh is not matter, in the sense of corpuscles of being which would add

up or continue on one another to form beings. Nor is the visible (the things as well as my own body) some "psychic" material that would be – God knows how – brought into being by the things factually existing and acting on my factual body. In general, it is not a fact or a sum of facts "material" or "spiritual." Nor is it a representation for a mind: a mind could not be captured by its own representations; it would rebel against this insertion into the visible which is essential to the seer. The flesh is not matter, is not mind, is not substance. To designate it, we should need the old term "element," in the sense it was used to speak of water, air, earth, and fire, that is, in the sense of a *general thing*, midway between the spatiotemporal individual and the idea, a sort of incarnate principle that brings a style of being wherever there is a fragment of being. The flesh is in this sense an "element" of Being. Not a fact or a sum of facts, and yet adherent to *location* and to the *now*. Much more: the inauguration of the *where* and the *when*, the possibility and exigency for the fact; in a word: facticity, what makes the fact be a fact. And, at the same time, what makes the facts have meaning, makes the fragmentary facts dispose themselves about "something." For if there is flesh, that is, if the hidden face of the cube radiates forth somewhere as well as does the face I have under my eyes, and coexists with it, and if I who see the cube also belong to the visible, I am visible from elsewhere, and if I and the cube are together caught up in one same "element" (should we say of the seer, or of the visible?), this cohesion, this visibility by principle, prevails over every momentary discordance. In advance every vision or very partial visible that would here definitively come to naught is not nullified (which would leave a gap in its place), but, what is better, it is replaced by a more exact vision and a more exact visible, according to the principle of visibility, which, as though through a sort of abhorrence of a vacuum, already invokes the true vision and the true visible, not only as substitutes for their errors, but also as their explanation, their relative justification, so that they are, as Husserl says so aptly, not erased, but "crossed out."... Such are the extravagant consequences to which we are led when we take seriously, when we question, vision. And it is, to be sure, possible to refrain from doing so and to move on, but we would simply find again, confused, indistinct, nonclarified, scraps of this ontology of the visible mixed up with all our theories of knowledge, and in particular with those that serve, desultorily, as vehicles of science. We are, to be sure, not finished ruminating over them. Our concern in this preliminary outline was only to catch sight of this strange domain to which interrogation, properly so-called, gives access. . . .

But this domain, one rapidly realizes, is unlimited. If we can show that the flesh is an ultimate notion, that it is not the union or compound of two substances, but thinkable by itself, if there is a relation of the visible with itself that traverses me and constitutes me as a seer, this circle which I do not form, which forms me, this coiling over of the visible upon the visible, can traverse, animate other bodies as well as my own. And if I was able to understand how this wave arises within me, how the visible which is yonder is simultaneously my landscape, I can understand *a fortiori* that elsewhere it also closes over upon itself and that there are other landscapes besides my own. If it lets itself be captivated by one of its fragments, the principle of captation is established, the field open for other Narcissus, for an "intercorporeity." If my left hand can touch my right hand while it palpates the tangibles, can touch it touching, can turn its palpation back upon it, why, when touching the hand of another, would I not touch in it the same power to espouse the things that I have touched in my own? It is true that "the things" in question are my own, that the whole operation takes place (as we say) "in me," within my landscape, whereas the problem is to institute another landscape. When one of my hands touches the other, the world of each opens upon that of the other because the operation is reversible at will, because they both belong (as we say) to one sole space of consciousness, because one sole man touches one sole thing through both hands. But for my two hands to open upon one sole world, it does not suffice that they be given to one sole *consciousness* – or if that were the case the difficulty before us would disappear: since other bodies would be known by me in the same way as would be my own, they and I would still be dealing with the same world. No, my two hands touch the same things because they are the hands of one same body. And yet each of them has its own tactile experience. If nonetheless they have to do with one sole tangible, it is because there exists a very peculiar relation from one to the other, across the corporeal space – like that holding between my two eyes – making of my hands one sole organ of experience, as it makes of my two eyes the channels of one sole Cyclopean vision. A difficult relation to conceive – since one eye, one hand, are capable of vision, of touch, and since what has to be comprehended is that these visions, these touches, these little subjectivities, these "consciousnesses of . . . ," could be assembled like flowers into a bouquet, when each being "consciousness of," being For Itself, reduces the others into objects. We will get out of the difficulty only by renouncing the bifurcation of the "consciousness of " and the object, by admitting that my synergic body is not an object, that it assembles into a cluster the "consciousnesses" adherent to its hands, to its eyes, by an operation that is in relation to them lateral, transversal; that "my consciousness" is not the synthetic, uncreated, centrifugal unity of a multitude of "consciousnesses of . . ." which would be centrifugal like it is, that it is sustained, subtended, by the prereflective and preobjective unity of my body. This means that while each monocular vision, each touching with one sole hand has its own visible, its tactile, each is bound to every other vision, to every other touch; it is bound in such a way as to make up with them the experience of one sole body before one sole world, through a possibility for reversion, reconversion of its language into theirs, transfer, and reversal, according to which the little private world of each is not juxtaposed to the world of all the others, but surrounded by it, levied off from it, and all together are a Sentient in general before a Sensible in general. Now why would this generality, which constitutes the unity of my body, not open it to other bodies? The handshake too is reversible; I can feel myself touched as well and at the same time as touching, and surely there does not exist some huge animal whose organs our bodies would be, as, for each of our bodies, our hands, our eyes are the organs. Why would not the synergy exist among different organisms, if it is possible within each? Their landscapes interweave, their actions and their passions fit together exactly: this is possible as soon as we no longer make belongingness to one same "consciousness" the primordial definition of sensibility, and as soon as we rather understand it as the return of the visible upon itself, a carnal adherence of the sentient to the sensed and of the sensed to the sentient. For, as overlapping and fission, identity and difference, it brings to birth a ray of natural light that illuminates all flesh and not only my own. It is said that the colors, the tactile reliefs given to the other, are for me an absolute mystery, forever inaccessible. This is not completely true; for me to have not an idea, an image, nor a representation, but as it were the imminent experience of them, it suffices that I look at a landscape, that I speak of it with someone.

Then, through the concordant operation of his body and my own, what I see passes into him, this individual green of the meadow under my eyes invades his vision without quitting my own, I recognize in my green his green, as the customs officer recognizes suddenly in a traveler the man whose description he had been given. There is here no problem of the *alter ego* because it is not *I* who sees, not *he* who sees, because an anonymous visibility inhabits both of us, a vision in general, in virtue of that primordial property that belongs to the flesh, being here and now, of radiating everywhere and forever, being an individual, of being also a dimension and a universal.

What is open to us, therefore, with the reversibility of the visible and the tangible, is – if not yet the incorporeal – at least an intercorporeal being, a presumptive domain of the visible and the tangible, which extends further than the things I touch and see at present.

There is a circle of the touched and the touching, the touched takes hold of the touching; there is a circle of the visible and the seeing, the seeing is not without visible existence;[5] there is even an inscription of the touching in the visible, of the seeing in the tangible – and the converse; there is finally a propagation of these exchanges to all the bodies of the same type and of the same style which I see and touch – and this by virtue of the fundamental fission or segregation of the sentient and the sensible which, laterally, makes the organs of my body communicate and founds transitivity from one body to another.

As soon as we see other seers, we no longer have before us only the look without a pupil, the plate glass of the things with that feeble reflection, that phantom of ourselves they evoke by designating a place among themselves whence we see them: henceforth, through other eyes we are for ourselves fully visible; that lacuna where our eyes, our back, lie is filled, filled still by the visible, of which we are not the titulars. To believe that, to bring a vision that is not our own into account, it is to be sure inevitably, it is always from the unique treasury of our own vision that we draw, and experience therefore can teach us nothing that would not be outlined in our own vision. But what is proper to the visible is, we said, to be the surface of an inexhaustible depth: this is what makes it able to be open to visions other than our own. In being realized, they therefore bring out the limits of our factual vision, they betray the solipsist illusion that consists in thinking that every going beyond is a surpassing accomplished by one-self. For the first time, the seeing that I am is for me really visible; for the first time I appear to myself completely turned inside out under my own eyes. For the first time also, my movements no longer proceed unto the things to be seen, to be touched, or unto my own body occupied in seeing and touching them, but they address themselves to the body in general and for itself (whether it be my own or that of another), because for the first time, through the other body, I see that, in its coupling with the flesh of the world, the body contributes more than it receives, adding to the world that I see the treasure necessary for what the other body sees. For the first time, the body no longer couples itself up with the world, it clasps another body, applying [itself to it][6] carefully with its whole extension, forming tirelessly with its hands the strange statue which in its turn gives everything it receives; the body is lost outside of the world and its goals, fascinated by the unique occupation of floating in Being with another life, of making itself the outside of its inside and the inside of its outside. And henceforth movement, touch, vision, applying themselves to the other and to themselves, return toward their source and, in the patient and silent labor of desire, begin the paradox of expression.

Yet this flesh that one sees and touches is not all there is to flesh, nor this massive corporeity all there is to the body. The reversibility that defines the flesh exists in other fields; it is even incomparably more agile there and capable of weaving relations between bodies that this time will not only enlarge, but will pass definitively beyond the circle of the visible. Among my movements, there are some that go nowhere – that do not even go find in the other body their resemblance or their archetype: these are the facial movements, many gestures, and especially those strange movements of the throat and mouth that form the cry and the voice. Those movements end in sounds and I hear them. Like crystal, like metal and many other substances, I am a sonorous being, but I hear my own vibration from within; as Malraux said, I hear myself with my throat. In this, as he also has said, I am incomparable; my voice is bound to the mass of my own life as is the voice of no one else. But if I am close enough to the other who speaks to hear his breath and feel his effervescence and his fatigue, I almost witness, in him as in myself, the awesome birth of vociferation. As there is a reflexivity of the touch, of sight, and of the touch-vision system, there is a reflexivity of the movements of phonation and of hearing; they have their sonorous inscription, the vociferations have in me their motor echo. This new reversibility and the emergence of the flesh as expression are the point of insertion of speaking and thinking in the world of silence.[7] . . .

Notes

1 Here in the course of the text itself, these lines are inserted: "it is that the look is itself incorporation of the seer into the visible, quest for itself, which *is* of *it*, within the visible – it is that the visible of the world is not an envelope of *quale*, but what is between the qualia, a connective tissue of exterior and interior horizons – it is as flesh offered to flesh that the visible has its aseity, and that it is mine – The flesh as *Sichtigkeit* and generality. → whence vision is question and response. . . . The openness through flesh: the two leaves of my body and the leaves of the visible world. . . . It is between these intercalated leaves that there is visibility. . . . My body model of the things and the things model of my body: the body bound to the world through all its parts, up against it → all this means: the world, the flesh not as fact or sum of facts, but as the locus of an inscription of truth: the false crossed out, not nullified." (Original ed.)

2 The *Uerpräsentierbarkeit* is the flesh.

3 The visible is not a tangible zero, the tangible is not a zero of visibility (relation of encroachment).

4 Here, in the course of the text itself, between brackets, these lines are inserted: "One can say that we perceive the things themselves, that we are the world that thinks itself – or that the world is at the heart of our flesh. In any case, once a body-world relationship is recognized, there is a ramification of my body and a ramification of the world and a correspondence between its inside and my outside, between my inside and its outside." (Original ed.)

5 Here is inserted between brackets, in the course of the text itself, the note: "what are these adhesions compared with those of the voice and the hearing?" (Original ed.)

6 These words, which we reintroduce into the text, had been erased apparently by error. (Original ed.)

7 Inserted here between brackets: "in what sense we have not yet introduced thinking: to be sure, we are not in the in itself. From the moment we said *seeing*, *visible*, and described the dehiscence of the sensible, we were, if one likes, in the order of thought. We were not in it in the sense that the thinking we have introduced was *there is*, and not *it appears to me that* . . . (appearing that would make up the whole of being, self-appearing). Our thesis is that this *there is* by inherence is necessary, and our problem to show that thought, in the restrictive sense (pure signification, thought of seeing and of feeling), is comprehensible only as the accomplishment by other means of the will of the *there is*, by sublimation of the *there is* and realization of an invisible that is exactly the reverse of the visible, the power of the visible. Thus between sound and meaning, speech and what it means to say, there is still the relation of reversibility, and no question of priority, since the exchange of words is exactly the differentiation of which the thought is the integral." (Original ed.)

Select Bibliography

Adventures of the Dialectic. Translated by Joseph Bien. Evanston, Ill.: Northwestern University Press, 1973.

Consciousness and the Acquisition of Language. Translated by Hugh Silverman. Evanston, Ill.: Northwestern University Press, 1973.

The Essential Writings of Merleau-Ponty. Edited by Alden L. Fisher. New York: Harcourt, Brace and World, 1969.

Humanism and Terror: An Essay on the Communist Problem. Translated by John O'Neill. Boston: Beacon Press, 1985.

The Merleau-Ponty Aesthetics Reader: Philosophy and Painting. Edited by Galen A. Johnson. Evanston, Ill.: Northwestern University Press, 1993.

In Praise of Philosophy and Other Essays. Translated by John Wild and James Edie, and John O'Neill. Evanston, Ill.: Northwestern University Press, 1988.

Phenomenology of Perception. Translated by Colin Smith. New York: Humanities Press, 1962.

The Primacy of Perception, and Other Essays on Phenomenological Psychology, the Philosophy of Art, History, and Politics. Edited by James M. Edie. Evanston, Ill.: Northwestern University Press, 1964.

The Prose of the World. Edited by Claude Lefort. Translated by John O'Neill. Evanston, Ill.: Northwestern University Press, 1973.

Sense and Non-Sense. Translated by Hubert L. Dreyfus and Patricia Allen Dreyfus. Evanston, Ill.: Northwestern University Press, 1964.

Signs. Translated by Richard C. McCleary. Evanston, Ill.: Northwestern University Press, 1964.

Texts and Dialogues. Edited by Hugh J. Silverman and James Barry, Jr. Translated by Michael B. Smith, et al. Atlantic Highlands, NJ: Humanities Press, 1992.

The Visible and the Invisible, Followed by Working Notes. Edited by Claude Lefort. Translated by Alphonso Lingis. Evanston, Ill.: Northwestern University Press, 1987.

13

Emmanuel Levinas

French philosopher Emmanuel Levinas (1906–96) began his philosophical career as a student of phenomenology. Influenced especially by Husserl and Heidegger, and also by his Judaic heritage, Levinas soon came to criticize these thinkers, as well as the history of philosophy as metaphysics and ontology, for what he regarded as a fundamental neglect of the ethical and of the radical alterity of the other human being. His central work *Totality and Infinity* (1961) sets forth the philosophical and historical basis of this argument. Traditional ontology, according to Levinas, reduces the otherness of the other by grounding the ethical relation to the other in a theoretical or cognitive relation to self, whether this relation is understood ontologically, transcendentally, or historically. Against this, Levinas argues that the relation to the other is primarily an ethical (rather than ontological or epistemological) relation grounded in the "face to face" encounter. The following essay, "The Trace of the Other" (1963) presents a concise defense of Levinas's central thesis by trying to show that the ethical disclosure of the other entails an experience of infinity that radically exceeds appropriation by a system of totality or order of the same.

The Trace of the Other

1 Being and the Same

The I is identification in the strong sense; it is the origin of the very phenomenon of identity. The

From *Deconstruction in Context*, edited by Mark C. Taylor (Chicago: University of Chicago Press, 1986), pp. 345–59. Original excerpted from Emmanuel Levinas, "La Trace de l'autre," translated by A. Lingis, *Tijdschrift voor Philosophie* (Sept. 1963), pp. 605–23.

identity of the I is not the permanence of an unalterable quality; I am myself not because of some character trait which I first identify, and then find myself to be the same. It is because I am from the first the same – *me ipse*, an ipseity – that I can identify every object, every character trait, and every being.

This identification is not a simple "restating" of the self: The "A is A" that characterizes the I is an "A anxious for A," or an "A enjoying A," always an "A bent over A." The *outside of me* solicits it in need: the *outside of me* is *for me*. The tautology of ipseity is an egoism.

The true cognition where the I "leaves it to him" and lets an alien being shine forth does not interrupt this original identification, does not draw the I out of itself without return. The being *enters* into the sphere of true knowledge. In becoming a theme, it does indeed retain a foreignness with respect to the thinker that embraces it. But it at once ceases to strike up against thought. The alien being is as it were naturalized as soon as it commits itself with knowledge. In itself – and consequently *elsewhere* than in thought, *other* than it – it does not have the wild barbarian character of alterity. It has a meaning. The being is propagated in infinite images which emanate from it; it dilates in a kind of ubiquity and penetrates the inwardness of men. It shows itself and radiates, as though the very plenitude of its alterity overflowed the mystery that harbors it, and pro-duces itself. Though it surprised the I, a being that is in truth does not alter the identity of the I. The obscurity from which it comes is promised to research. It thus opens a future whose night is but the opacity produced by the density of the superimposed transparencies. Memory brings back the past itself and puts it into this future in which research and historical interpretation wander. The traces of the irreversible past are taken as signs that ensure the discovery and unity of a world. The priority of the future among the "ecstasies" of time constitutes knowledge as comprehension of being. This priority bears witness to the adequateness of being with thought. The idea of being with which philosophers interpret the irreducible alienness of the non-I is thus cut to the measure of the same. It is the idea that is of itself adequate.

The being of beings – difference in itself, and consequently alterity – enlightens, according to Heidegger, inasmuch as it is buried and always already forgotten. But the poets and philosophers force, for a moment, its inexpressible essence. For it is still in terms of light and obscurity, disclosure and veiling, truth and nontruth – that is, in the priority of the future – that the being of beings is approached.

The intentionality caught sight of, by the phenomenological movement, at the core of practice and affectivity confirms the fact that self-consciousness, or the identification of the self, is not incompatible with consciousness of . . ., that is, consciousness of being. And, conversely, the whole weight of being can be resolved into a play of inwardness and stand on the brink of illusion, so rigorous is the adequation. The apparition of being is possibly but appearance. The shadow is taken for a prey; the prey is let loose for the shadow. Descartes thought that I could have accounted for the heavens and the sun out of myself – despite all their magnificence. Every experience, however passive it be, however welcoming, is at once converted into a "constitution of being" which it receives, as though the *given* were drawn from oneself, as though the meaning it brings were ascribed to it by me. Being bears in itself the possibility of idealism.

Western philosophy coincides with the disclosure of the other where the other, in manifesting itself as a being, loses its alterity. From its infancy philosophy has been struck with a horror of the other that remains other – with an insurmountable allergy. It is for this reason that it is essentially a philosophy of being, that the comprehension of being is its last word, and the fundamental structure of man. It is for this reason that it becomes philosophy of immanence and of autonomy, or atheism. The God of the philosophers, from Aristotle to Leibniz, by way of the God of the scholastics, is a god adequate to reason, a comprehended god who could not trouble the autonomy of consciousness, which finds itself again in all its adventures, returning home to itself like Ulysses, who through all his peregrinations is only on the way to his native island.

The philosophy handed down to us reduces to this return not only theoretical thought, but every spontaneous movement of consciousness. Not only the world understood by reason ceases to be other, for consciousness finds itself in that world, but everything that is an *attitude* of consciousness, that is, valorization, feeling, action, labor, and, in general commitment, is in the last analysis self-consciousness, that is, identity and autonomy. Hegel's philosophy represents the logical outcome of this underlying allergy of philosophy. One of the most profound modern interpreters of Hegelianism, Eric Weil, has expressed this admirably in his *Logique de la philosophie*, showing how every attitude of the rational being turns into a category, that is, grasps itself in a new attitude. But, in conformity with philosophical tradition, he thinks that the outcome is a category reabsorbing all the attitudes.

Even if life precedes philosophy, even if contemporary philosophy, which wishes to be anti-intellectualist, insists on this antecedence of existence with respect to essence, of life with respect to understanding, even if Heidegger conceives the comprehension of being as gratitude and obedience, the complacency of modern philosophy for the multiplicity of cultural significations and for the games of art lightens being of its alterity and represents the form in which philosophy prefers expectation to action, remaining indifferent to the other and to others, refusing every movement without return. It mistrusts every inconsiderate gesture, as if a lucidity of old age had to repair all the imprudence of youth. Action recuperated in advance in the light that should guide it – is perhaps the very definition of philosophy.

2 Movement Without Return

Yet the transcendence of being which is described by immanence is not the only transcendence the philosophers themselves speak of. The philosophers bring us also the enigmatic message of the beyond being.

The transcendence of the Good with respect to being *epekeina tēs ousias* is a transcendence to the second degree, and we are not obliged to make it immediately re-enter into the Heideggerian interpretation of being that transcends beings. The One in Plotinus is posited beyond being, and also *epekeina nou*. The One of which Plato speaks in the first hypothesis of the Parmenides is foreign to definition and limit, place and time, self-identity and difference with respect to oneself, resemblance and dissemblance, foreign to being and to knowledge – for which all these attributes constitute the categories of knowledge. It is something else than all that, *other* absolutely and not with respect to some relative term. It is the Unrevealed, but not unrevealed because all knowledge would be too limited or too narrow to receive its light. It is unrevealed because it is *One*, and because making oneself known implies a duality which already clashes with the unity of the One. The One is not beyond being because it is buried and hidden; it is buried because it is beyond being, wholly other than being.

In what sense, then, does the *absolutely other* concern me? Must we with the – from the first unthinkable – contact with transcendence and alterity renounce philosophy? Would transcendence be possible only for a completely blind touch, or for a faith attached to nonsignification? Or, on the contrary, if the Platonic hypothesis

concerning the One, which is One above being and knowledge, is not the development of a sophism, is there not an experience of it, an experience different from that in which the other is transmuted into the same? It would be an experience, for it would be a movement toward the transcendent, but also because in this movement the same does not lose itself ecstatically in the other, and resists the sirens' song, does not dissolve into the rumble of an anonymous event. This experience would still remain a movement of the same, a movement of an I; it consequently approaches the transcendent in a signification which it will not have ascribed to it. Does there exist a signifyingness of signification which would not be equivalent to the transmutation of the other into the same? Can there be something as strange as an experience of the absolutely exterior, as contradictory in its terms as a heteronomous experience? In the affirmative case, we will, to be sure, not succumb to the temptation and the illusion that would consist in finding again by philosophy the empirical data of positive religions, but we will disengage a movement of transcendence that is ensured like the bridgehead of the "other shore," without which the simple coexistence of philosophy and religion in souls and even in civilizations is but an inadmissible weakness of the mind. We will also put into question the thesis according to which the ultimate essence of man and of truth is the *comprehension of the being of beings*, a thesis to which, we must agree, theory, experience, and discourse seem to lead.

The heteronomous experience we seek would be an attitude that cannot be converted into a category, and whose movement unto the other is not recuperated in identification, does not return to its point of departure. Is it not furnished us by what we call quite simply goodness, and works, without which goodness is but a dream without transcendence, a pure wish (*blosser Wunsch*), as Kant put it?

But then we must not conceive of a work as an apparent agitation of a ground which afterwards remains identical with itself, like an energy which, in all its transformations, remains equal to itself. Nor must we conceive it as a technical operation, which through its much-proclaimed negativity reduces an alien world to a world whose alterity is converted into my idea. Both conceptions continue to affirm being as identical with itself and reduce its fundamental event to thought which is (and this is the ineffaceable lesson of idealism) thought of itself, thought of thought. *A work conceived radically is a movement of the same unto the other which never returns to the same*. To the myth of Ulysses returning to Ithaca, we wish to oppose the story of Abraham who leaves his fatherland forever for a yet unknown land, and forbids his servant to even bring back his son to the point of departure.

A work conceived in its ultimate nature requires a radical generosity of the same who in the work goes unto the other. It then requires an *ingratitude* of the other. Gratitude would in fact be the *return* of the movement to its origin. On the other hand, a work differs from a game or pure expenditure. It is not realized in pure loss, and it is not enough for it to affirm the same in its identity circumvented with nothingness. A work is neither a pure acquiring of merits nor a pure nihilism. Beneath the apparent gratuity of his action, both he who chases after merits and the nihilist agent forthwith takes himself as the goal. A work is thus a relationship with the other who is reached without showing himself touched. It forms outside of the morose delectation of failure, and outside of the consolations with which Nietzsche defines religion.

The departure without return, which does not go forth into the void, would also lose its absolute goodness if the work sought for its recompense in the immediacy of its triumph, if it impatiently awaited the triumph of its cause. The one-way movement would be inverted into a reciprocity. The work, confronting its departure and its end, would be absorbed again in calculations of deficits and compensations, in accountable operations. It would be subordinated to thought. The one-way action is possible only in patience, which, pushed to the limit, means for the agent to renounce being the contemporary of its outcome, to act without entering the promised land.

The future for which the work is undertaken must be posited from the start as indifferent to my death. A work, distinguished from games and from calculation, is being-for-beyond-my-death. Patience does not consist in the agent belying his generosity by giving himself the time of a *personal immortality*. To renounce being the contemporary of the triumph of one's work is to have this triumph in a time *without me*, to aim at this world without me, to aim at a time beyond the horizon of my time. It works in an eschatology without hope for oneself, an eschatology of liberation from my own time.

To be for a time that would be without me, to be for a time after my time, for a future beyond the celebrated "being-for-death," to-be-for-after-my-death – "Let the future and the most far-off things

be the rule for all the present days" – is not a banal thought that extrapolates one's own duration; it is passage to the time of the other. Do we have to call what makes such a passage possible eternity? But perhaps the possibility of sacrifice goes unto the end of this passage, and discovers the non-inoffensive character of this extrapolation: to-be-for-death in order to be for-what-is-after-me.

I should like to fix the work of the same as a movement without return of the same to the other with a Greek term which in its primary meaning indicates the exercise of an office that is not only completely gratuitous, but that requires, on the part of him that exercises it, a putting out of funds at a loss. I would like to fix it with the term "liturgy." We must for the moment remove from this term every religious signification, even if a certain idea of God should become visible, as a trace, at the end of our analysis. Liturgy, as an absolutely patient action, does not take its place as a cult alongside of works and of ethics. It is ethics itself.

3 Need and Desire

The liturgical orientation of a work does not proceed from need. Need opens upon a world that is for-me; it returns to the self. Even when sublime, as the need for salvation, it is still nostalgia, homesickness. Need is the return itself, the anxiety of an ego for itself, the original form of identification which we have called egoism. It is an assimilation of the world in view of coincidence with oneself, or happiness.

In the "Canticle of the Columns," Valéry speaks of a "desire without lack." He refers, no doubt, to Plato, who, in his analysis of the pure pleasures, discovered an aspiration that is conditioned by no pre-existing lack. I shall take up this term desire. To a subject turned to himself, which according to the Stoic formula is characterized by *ornē* or the tendency to persist in his being, or for whom, according to Heidegger's formula, "in his existence this very existence is in question," to a subject that is thus defined by concern for himself and who in happiness fulfills his "for himself" – we oppose the desire for the other which proceeds from a being already replenished to overflowing and independent, and who does not desire for himself. Desire is the need of him who has no more needs. We can recognize it in the desire for an other who is another [*autrui*], neither my enemy (as he is in

Hobbes and in Hegel) nor my complement (as is still the case in Plato's *Republic*, which is constituted because something would be lacking for the subsistence of each individual). The desire for another is born in a being that lacks nothing, or, more exactly, it comes to birth on the other side of all that can be lacking him or can satisfy him. This desire for another, which is our very sociality, is not a simple relationship with a being where, according to our formulas at the beginning, the other is converted into the same.

In desire the ego is borne unto another in such a way as to compromise the sovereign identification of the I with itself, an identification of which need is but the nostalgia, and which the consciousness of need anticipates. The movement unto another, instead of completing and contenting me, implicates me in a situation which by one side should not concern me and should leave me indifferent: "What then was I looking for in this convict-ship?" Whence comes to me this shock when I pass, indifferent, under the gaze of another? The relationship with another puts me into question, empties me of myself, and does not let off emptying me – uncovering for me ever new resources. I did not know myself so rich, but I have no longer any right to keep anything. Is the desire for another an appetite or a generosity? The desirable does not fill up my desire but hollows it out, nourishing me as it were with new hungers. Desire is revealed to be goodness. There is a scene in Dostoyevski's *Crime and Punishment* where, apropos of Sonia Marmeladova who looks at Raskolnikov in his despair, Dostoyevski speaks of "insatiable compassion." He does not say "inexhaustible compassion." It is as though the compassion that goes from Sonia to Raskolnikov were a hunger which the presence of Raskolnikov nourished beyond all saturation, increasing this hunger *ad infinitum*.

The analysis of desire, which it was important to us to first distinguish from need, will be specified by the analysis of the other toward which desire bears.

The manifestation of the other is, to be sure, first produced in conformity with the way every signification is produced. The other is present in a cultural whole and is illuminated by this whole, like a text by its context. The manifestation of the whole ensures this presence and this present; they are illuminated by the light of the world. The comprehension of the other is thus a hermeneutics and an exegesis. The other is given in the concept

of the totality to which he is immanent, and which, in conformity with Merleau-Ponty's remarkable analyses, our own cultural initiative, the corporeal, linguistic, or artistic gesture, expresses and discloses.

But the epiphany of the other involves a signifyingness of its own, independently of this signification received from the world. The other does not only come to us out of a context, but comes without mediation; he signifies by himself. His cultural signification is revealed and reveals as it were *horizontally*, on the basis of the historical world to which it belongs. According to the phenomenological expression, it reveals the horizons of this world. But this mundane signification is found to be disturbed and shaken by another presence, abstract, not integrated into the world. His presence consists in coming unto us, *making an entry*. This can be stated in this way: the phenomenon which is the apparition of the other is also a *face*. Again, to show this entry at every moment into the immanence and historicity of the phenomenon, we can say: the epiphany of a face is alive. Its life consists in undoing the form in which every entity, when it enters into immanence, that is, when it exposes itself as a theme, is already dissimulated.

The other who manifests himself in the face as it were breaks through his own plastic essence, like someone who opens a window on which his figure is outlined. His presence consists in *divesting* himself of the form which, however, manifests him. His manifestation is a surplus over the inevitable paralysis of manifestation. This is what the formula "the face speaks" expresses. The manifestation of a face is the first discourse. To speak is before all this way of coming from behind one's appearance, behind one's form – an opening in the openness.

4 Diaconate

The visitation of a face is then not the disclosure of a world. In the concreteness of the world the face is abstract or naked. It is denuded of its own image. Through the nudity of the face nudity in itself is first possible in the world.

The nudity of the face is a destitution without any cultural ornament, an absolution – a detaching in the midst of its very production. A face *enters* our world from an absolutely alien sphere – that is, precisely out of an absoluteness, which in fact is the name for fundamental strangeness. The signification of a face in its abstractness is, in the literal sense of the term, extra-ordinary. How is such a production possible? How can the coming of the other out of the absolute, in the visitation of a face, be in no way convertible into a revelation – not even by a symbolism or a suggestion? How is a face not simply a true *representation*, in which the other renounces his alterity? To answer, we will have to study the exceptional signifyingness of a trace, and the personal order in which such a signifyingness is possible.

For the moment let us emphasize the sense involved in the abstractness or the nudity of a face which opens to us this order, and works the overwhelming of consciousness, which answers to this abstractness. Stripped of its very form, a face is benumbed in its nudity. It is a wretchedness. The nudity of a face is a denuding, and already a supplication in the uprightness that aims at me. But this supplication is an exigency; in it humbleness is joined with height. Here the ethical dimension of the visitation is announced. While a true representation remains the possibility of a mere appearance, while the world that strikes up against thought can do nothing against the free thought which is capable of refusing it inwardly, taking refuge in itself, remaining precisely a free thought before the true and existing as "there first," the origin of what it receives, mastering by memory what precedes it, while free thought remains "the same" – a face is imposed on me without my being able to be deaf to its appeal nor to forget it, that is, without my being able to cease to be held responsible for its wretchedness. Consciousness loses its first place.

The presence of a face thus signifies an irrecusable order, a command, which calls a halt to the availability of consciousness. Consciousness is put into question by a face. The putting into question is not reducible to becoming aware of this being put into question. The absolutely other is not reflected in consciousness. It resists it to the point that even its resistance is not converted into a content of consciousness. The visitation consists in overwhelming the very egoism of the I; a face disconcerts the intentionality that aims at it.

It is a matter of the putting into question of consciousness, and not of a consciousness of a being put into question. The I loses its sovereign coincidence with itself, its identification, in which consciousness returned triumphally to itself and rested on itself. Before the exigency of the other, the I is expelled from this rest, and is not the consciousness of this exile, already glorious.

Every complacency would destroy the uprightness of the ethical movement.

But the putting into question of this wild and naive freedom, sure of its refuge in itself, is not reducible to this negative movement. The putting into question of the self is precisely the welcome of the absolutely other. The epiphany of the absolutely other is a face in which the other calls to me and signifies an order to me by its nudity, its denuding. Its presence is a summation to respond. The I does not simply become conscious of this necessity to answer, as if it were a matter of an obligation or a duty which it would have to decide of. In its very position it is completely responsibility or diaconate, as said in Isaiah 53.

To be an I then signifies not to be able to slip away from responsibility. This surplus of being, this exaggeration which we call to be an I, this upsurgence of ipseity in being, is realized as a turgescence of responsibility. The putting into question of the I by the other makes me solidary with the other in an incomparable and unique way – not solidary as matter is solidary with the block which it is a part of, or as an organ is solidary with the organism in which it has its function. Solidarity here is responsibility – as though the whole edifice of creation rested on my shoulders. The unicity of the I is the fact that no one can answer in my place. Responsibility which empties the I of its imperialism and its egoism, be it the egoism of salvation, does not transform it into a moment of the universal order. It confirms it in its ipseity, in its function of being a support for the universe.

To discover in the I such an orientation is to identify the I and morality. The I before another is infinitely responsible. The other who provokes this ethical movement in consciousness, and who disorders the good conscience of the coinciding of the same with itself involves a surplus for which intentionality is inadequate. To desire is to burn with another fire than that of need which saturation puts out, to think beyond what one conceives. Because of this unassimilable surplus, this beyond, we have called the relationship which attaches the I to the other the idea of infinity.

The idea of infinity is desire. It consists, paradoxically, in thinking more than what is thought while conserving it still in its inordinateness relative to thought, entering into relationship with the ungraspable while certifying its status of being ungraspable. Infinity is then not the correlate of the idea of infinity, as though this idea were an intentionality that is fulfilled in its object. The marvel of infinity in the finite is the overwhelming of intentionality, the overwhelming of this appetite for light; unlike the saturation in which intentionality is appeased, infinity disconnects its idea. The I in relationship with infinity is an impossibility of stopping one's march forward, the impossibility, to say it with Plato's expression in the *Phaedo*, of deserting one's post; it is literally not to have time to turn back. *The attitude irreducible to a category* is not to be able to slip away from responsibility, not to have a hiding place in inwardness in which one can return into oneself, to go forward without regard for oneself. There is continual increase of demands put on one: the more I face my responsibilities the more I am responsible. Responsible is a power made of impotencies. Such is the putting into question of consciousness and its entry into a confluence of relationships which break with disclosure.

5 The Trace

But is the *beyond* from which a face comes an idea understood and disclosed in its turn? If the extraordinary experience of entry and visitation retains its signifyingness, it is because the *beyond* is not a simple background from which a face solicits us, is not "another world" behind the world. The *beyond* is precisely beyond the "world," that is, beyond every disclosure – like the One of the first hypothesis of the *Parmenides*, which transcends all cognition, be it symbolic or signified. The One is "neither similar nor dissimilar, neither identical nor nonidentical," Plato says, thus excluding it from every even indirect revelation. A symbol still brings the symbolized back to the world in which it appears.

What then can be this relationship with an absence radically withdrawn from disclosure and from dissimulation? And what is this absence that renders visitation possible, an absence not reducible to hiddenness, since it involves a signifyingness – a signifyingness in which the other is not converted into the same?

A face is abstract. This abstractness is not, to be sure, like the brute sensible datum of the empiricists. Nor is it an instantaneous cross-section of the world in which time would cross with eternity. It is an incision made in time that does not bleed. But the abstractness of a face is a visitation and a coming. It disturbs immanence without settling into the horizons of the world. Its abstractness is not

obtained by a logical process starting from the substance of beings and going from the particular to the general. On the contrary, it goes toward those beings, but does not compromise itself with them, withdraws from them, ab-solves itself. Its wonder is due to the elsewhere from which it comes and into which it already withdraws. This coming from elsewhere is not a symbolic reference to that elsewhere as to a term. A face presents itself in its nudity; it is not a form concealing, but thereby indicating, a ground, a phenomenon that hides, but thereby betrays a thing itself. Otherwise, a face would be one with a mask – but a mask presupposes a face. If *signifying* were equivalent to *indicating* a face would be insignificant. Sartre says that the other is a pure hole in the world – a most noteworthy insight, but he stops his analysis too soon. The other proceeds from the absolutely absent. His relationship with the absolutely absent from which he comes *does not indicate, does not reveal* this absent; and yet the absent has a meaning in a face. This signifyingness is not a way for the absent to be given in a blank in the presence of a face – which would again bring us back to a mode of disclosure. The relationship which goes from a face to the absent is outside every revelation and dissimulation, a third way excluded by these contradictories. How is this third way possible? But – are we not still seeking that from which a face proceeds as though it were a sphere, a place, a world? Have we been attentive enough to the interdiction against seeking the *beyond* as a world behind our world? The order of being would still seem to be presupposed, an order which contains no other status but that of the revealed and of the dissimulated. Within being, a transcendence revealed is inverted into immanence, the extraordinary is inserted into an order, the other is absorbed into the same. In the presence of the other do we not respond to an "order" in which signifyingness remains an irremissible disturbance, an utterly bygone past? Such is the signifyingness of a trace. The beyond from which a face comes signifies as a trace. A face is in the trace of the utterly bygone, utterly passed absent, withdrawn into what Paul Valéry calls "the deep yore, never long ago enough," which cannot be discovered in the self by an introspection. For a face is the unique openness in which the signifyingness of the transcendent does not nullify the transcendence and make it enter into an immanent *order*; here on the contrary transcendence refuses immanence precisely as the ever bygone transcendence of the transcendent. In a trace the relationship between the signified and the signification is not a correlation, but *unrightness* itself. The allegedly mediated and indirect relationship between a sign and the signified is thus still a rightness, for it is a disclosure which neutralizes transcendence. The signifyingness of a trace places us in a lateral relationship, unconvertible into rightness (something inconceivable in the order of disclosure and being), answering to an irreversible past. No memory could follow the traces of this past. It is an immemorial past – and this also is perhaps eternity, whose signifyingness is not foreign to the past. Eternity is the very irreversibility of time, the source and refuge of the past.

But if the signifyingness of a trace is not immediately transformed into the straightforwardness which still marks signs, which reveal the signified absent and bring it into immanence, it is because a trace signifies beyond being. The personal order to which a face obliges us is beyond being. *Beyond being is a third person*, which is not definable by the oneself, by ipseity. It is the possibility of this third direction of radical *unrightness* which escapes the bipolar play of immanence and transcendence proper to being, where immanence always wins against transcendence. Through a trace the irreversible past takes on the profile of a "He." The *beyond* from which a face comes is in the third person. The pronoun *He* expresses exactly its inexpressible irreversibility, already escaping every relation as well as every dissimulation, and in this sense absolutely unencompassable or absolute, a transcendence in an ab-solute past. The *illeity* of the third person is the condition for the irreversibility.

This third person who in a face has already withdrawn from every relation and every dissimulation, who has passed, this illeity, is not a "less than being" by comparison with the world in which a face enters; it is the whole enormity, the inordinateness, the infinity of the absolutely other, which eludes treatment by ontology. The supreme presence of a face is inseparable from this supreme and irreversible absence which founds the eminence of visitation.

6 Traces and "Illeity"

If the signifyingness of a trace consists in signifying without making appear, if it establishes a relationship with illeity, a relationship which is personal and ethical – is an obligation and does not disclose, and if, consequently, a trace does not belong to phenomenology, to the comprehension of the "appearing" and the "self-dissimulating," we can at least approach this signifyingness in another way by situating it with respect to the phenomenology it interrupts.

A trace is not a sign like any other. But every trace also plays the role of a sign; it can be taken for a sign. A detective examines everything in the area where a crime took place, as revealing signs which betoken the voluntary or involuntary work of the criminal; a hunter follows the traces of the game, which reflect the activity and movement of the animal the hunter is after; a historian discovers ancient civilizations which form the horizon of our world on the basis of the vestiges left by their existence. Everything is arranged in an order, in a world, where each thing reveals another or is revealed in function of another.

But when a trace is thus taken as a sign, it is exceptional with respect to other signs in that it signifies outside of every intention of signaling and outside of every project of which it would be the aim. When in transactions one "pays by check" so that there will be a trace of the payment, the trace is inscribed in the very order of the world. But a trace in the strict sense disturbs the order of the world. It occurs by overprinting. Its original signifyingness is sketched out in, for example, the fingerprints left by someone who wanted to wipe away his traces and commit a perfect crime. He who left traces in wiping out his traces did not mean to say or do anything by the traces he left. He disturbed the order in an irreparable way. He has passed absolutely. *To be qua leaving a trace* is to pass, to depart, to absolve oneself.

But in this sense every sign is a trace. In addition to what the sign signifies, it is the past of him who delivered the sign. The signifyingness of a trace doubles up this signifyingness proper to a sign issued in view of communication. A sign stands in this trace. This signifyingness lies in, for example, the writing and the style of a letter, in all that brings it about that during the emission of a message, which we capture on the basis of the letter's language and its sincerity, someone passes, purely and simply. This trace can be taken in its turn as a sign. A graphologist, an expert in writing styles, or a psychoanalyst could interpret a trace's singular signifyingness, and seek in it the sealed and unconscious, but real, intentions of him who delivered the message. But then what remains in the specific sense a trace in the writing and style of the letter does not signal any of these intentions, any of these qualities, reveals and hides nothing. In a trace has passed a past absolutely bygone. In a trace its irreversible lapse is sealed. Disclosure, which reinstates the world and leads back to the world, and is proper to a sign or a signification, is suppressed in traces.

But then is not a trace the weight of being itself outside of its acts and its language, weighing not through its presence, which fits it into the world, but by its very irreversibility, its ab-soluteness?

A trace would seem to be the very indelibility of being, its omnipotence before all negativity, its immensity incapable of being self-enclosed, somehow too great for discretion, inwardness, or a self. And it was indeed important for us to say that a trace does not effect a relationship with what would be less than being, but obliges with regard to the infinite, the absolutely other.

But this superiority of the superlative, this height, this constant elevation to power, this exaggeration, or this infinite overbidding – and, let us say the word, this divinity – are not deducible from the being of beings nor its revelation, even if it is contemporary with a concealment, nor deducible from "concrete duration." These signify something on the basis of a past which, in a trace, is neither *indicated* nor signaled, but yet disturbs order, while coinciding neither with revelation nor with dissimulation. A trace is the insertion of space in time, the point at which the world inclines toward a past and a time. This time is a withdrawal of the other, and, consequently, nowise a degradation of duration, which, in memory, is still complete. Superiority does not reside in a presence in the world, but in an irreversible transcendence. It is not a modulation of the being of entities. As He and third person it is somehow outside the distinction between being and entities. Only a being that transcends the world can leave a trace. A trace is a presence of that which properly speaking has never been there, of what is always past. Plotinus conceived the procession from the One as compromising neither the immutability nor the ab-solute separation of the One. It is in this situation, at first purely dialectical and quasi-verbal (and which is also the case for Intelligence and the Soul, which remain with their principle in their higher parts and are inclined only through their lower parts – a structure which still belongs to iconography), that the exceptional signifyingness of a trace delineates in the world. "Much more

then does the unit, The One, remain intact in the principle which is before all beings; especially since the entities produced in its likeness, while it thus remains intact, owe their existence to no other, but to its own all-sufficient power ... in the realm of Being, the trace of the One establishes reality; existence is a trace of The One ..." (Enneads 5.5).

That which preserves the specific signifyingness of a trace in each trace of an empirical passage, over and above the sign it can become, is possible only through its situation in the trace of this transcendence. This position in a trace, which we have called *illeity*, does not begin in things, which by themselves do not leave traces but produce effects, that is, remain in the world. When a stone has scratched another stone, the scratch can, to be sure, be taken as a trace, but in fact without the man who held the stone this scratch is but an effect. It is as little a trace as the forest fire is a trace of the lightning. A cause and an effect, even separated by time, belong to the same world. Everything in things is exposed, even what is unknown in them. The traces that mark them are part of this plenitude of presence; their history is without a past. A trace *qua* trace does not simply lead to the past, but is the very *passing* toward a past more remote than any past and any future which still are set in my time – the past of the other, in which eternity takes form, an absolute past which unites all times.

The absoluteness of the presence of the other, which has justified our interpreting the exceptional uprightness of thou-saying as an epiphany of this absoluteness, is not the simple presence in which in the last analysis things are also present. Their presence belongs to the present of *my* life. Everything that constitutes my life with its past and its future is assembled in the present in which things come to me. But it is in the trace of the other that a face shines; what is presented there is absolving itself from my life and visits me as already ab-solute. Someone has already passed. His trace does not *signify* his past, as it does not *signify* his labor or his enjoyment in the world; it is a disturbance imprinting itself (we are tempted to say *engraving* itself) with an unexceptionable gravity.

The illeity of this *He* is not the *it* of things which are at our disposal, and to which Buber and Gabriel Marcel rightly prefer the *thou* to describe a human encounter. The movement of an encounter is not something added to an immobile face; it is in the face itself. A face is of itself a visitation and transcendence. But a face, wholly open, can at the same time be in itself because it is in the trace of illeity.

Illeity is the origin of the alterity of being in which the in itself of objectivity participates, while also betraying it.

The God who passed is not the model of which the face would be an image. To be in the image of God does not mean to be an icon of God, but to find oneself in his trace. The revealed God of our Judeo-Christian spirituality maintains all the infinity of his absence, which is in the personal order itself. He shows himself only by his trace, as is said in Exodus 33. To go toward Him is not to follow this trace which is not a sign; it is to go toward the others who stand in the trace of illeity.

Select Bibliography

Beyond the Verse: Talmudic Readings and Lectures. Translated by Gary D. Mole. Bloomington: Indiana University Press, 1994.

Collected Philosophical Papers. Translated by Alphonso Lingis. Dordrecht: Martinus Nijhoff, 1987.

Difficult Freedom: Essays on Judaism. Translated by Sean Hand. Baltimore: Johns Hopkins University Press, 1990.

Emmanuel Levinas: Basic Philosophical Writings. Edited by Adrian T. Peperzak, Simon Critchley and Robert Bernasconi. Bloomington: Indiana University Press, 1996.

Ethics and Infinity. Translated by Richard A. Cohen. Pittsburgh: Duquesne University Press, 1985.

Existence and Existents. Translated by Alphonso Lingis. The Hague: Martinus Nijhoff, 1978.

The Levinas Reader. Edited by Sean Hand. Oxford: Blackwell Publishers, 1989.

Nine Talmudic Readings. Translated by Annette Aronowicz. Bloomington: Indiana University Press, 1990.

Otherwise Than Being, or Beyond Essence. Translated by Alphonso Lingis. The Hague: Martinus Nijhoff, 1981.

Outside the Subject. Translated by Michael B. Smith. Stanford: Stanford University Press, 1994.

The Theory of Intuition in Husserl's Phenomenology. Translated by Andre Orianne. Evanston, Ill. Northwestern University Press, 1995.

Time and the Other, and Additional Essays. Translated by Richard A. Cohen. Pittsburgh: Duquesne University Press, 1987.

Totality and Infinity: An Essay on Exteriority. Translated by Alphonso Lingis. Pittsburgh: Duquesne University Press, 1994.

14

Hans-Georg Gadamer

Hans-Georg Gadamer (1900–), professor of philosophy in Leipzig and subsequently at the University of Heidelberg, is one of the leading exponents of philosophical hermeneutics. A student of Heidegger, Gadamer sought to develop Heidegger's insights concerning the nature of interpretation and understanding into a general theory of how human understanding happens, with particular reference to the human sciences, aesthetics, and jurisprudence. Throughout his work, Gadamer emphasizes the significance of the inevitable presuppositions or "prejudices" at work in all interpretation. Such prejudices, historical and cultural in their import, are not merely something negative to be overcome or avoided, according to Gadamer. Rather, they are positive and constitutive; they make human understanding and communication possible in the first instance. Furthermore, the task of the hermeneutic endeavor is not to reach the "true meaning" or author's intention, but rather to become as clear as possible about the different prejudices at play in any interpretation. Thus interpretation, whether that of a text or of the spoken word, unfolds as a kind of dialogue in which one's own presuppositions, and those of others, become clarified to a greater or lesser extent. In the following essay from 1966, Gadamer emphasizes the universal and linguistic aspects of hermeneutics thus conceived.

The Universality of the Hermeneutical Problem

Why has the problem of language come to occupy the same central position in current philosophical discussions that the concept of thought, or

From *Philosophical Hermeneutics*, translated and edited by David E. Linge (Berkeley: University of California Press, 1977), pp. 3–17. Copyright © 1976 the Regents of the University of California. Reprinted by permission of the University of California Press.

"thought thinking itself," held in philosophy a century and a half ago? By answering this question, I shall try to give an answer indirectly to the central question of the modern age – a question posed for us by the existence of modern science. It is the question of how our natural view of the world – the experience of the world that we have as we simply live out our lives – is related to the unassailable and anonymous authority that confronts us in the pronouncements of science. Since the seventeenth century, the real task of philosophy has been to mediate this new employment of man's cognitive and constructive capacities with the totality of our experience of life. This task has found expression in a variety of ways, including our own generation's attempt to bring the topic of language to the center of philosophical concern. Language is the fundamental mode of operation of our being-in-the-world and the all-embracing form of the constitution of the world. Hence we always have in view the pronouncements of the sciences, which are fixed in nonverbal signs. And our task is to reconnect the objective world of technology, which the sciences place at our disposal and discretion, with those fundamental orders of our being that are neither arbitrary nor manipulable by us, but rather simply demand our respect.

I want to elucidate several phenomena in which the universality of this question becomes evident. I have called the point of view involved in this theme "hermeneutical," a term developed by Heidegger. Heidegger was continuing a perspective stemming originally from Protestant theology and transmitted into our own century by Wilhelm Dilthey.

What is hermeneutics? I would like to start from two experiences of alienation that we encounter in our concrete existence: the experience of alienation of the aesthetic consciousness and the experience of alienation of the historical consciousness. In both cases what I mean can be stated in a few words. The aesthetic consciousness realizes a possibility that as such we can neither deny nor diminish in its value, namely, that we relate ourselves, either negatively or affirmatively, to the quality of an artistic form. This statement means we are related in such a way that the judgment we make decides in the end regarding the expressive power and validity of what we judge. What we reject has nothing to say to us – or we reject it because it has nothing to say to us. This characterizes our relation to art in the broadest sense of the word, a sense that, as Hegel has shown, includes the entire religious world of the ancient Greeks, whose religion of beauty experienced the divine in concrete works of art that man creates in response to the gods. When it loses its original and unquestioned authority, this whole world of experience becomes alienated into an object of aesthetic judgment. At the same time, however, we must admit that the world of artistic tradition – the splendid contemporaneousness that we gain through art with so many human worlds – is more than a mere object of our free acceptance or

rejection. Is it not true that when a work of art has seized us it no longer leaves us the freedom to push it away from us once again and to accept or reject it on our own terms? And is it not also true that these artistic creations, which come down through the millennia, were not created for such aesthetic acceptance or rejection? No artist of the religiously vital cultures of the past ever produced his work of art with any other intention than that his creation should be received in terms of what it says and presents and that it should have its place in the world where men live together. The consciousness of art – the aesthetic consciousness – is always secondary to the immediate truth-claim that proceeds from the work of art itself. To this extent, when we judge a work of art on the basis of its aesthetic quality, something that is really much more intimately familiar to us is alienated. This alienation into aesthetic judgment always takes place when we have withdrawn ourselves and are no longer open to the immediate claim of that which grasps us. Thus one point of departure for my reflections in *Truth and Method* was that the aesthetic sovereignty that claims its rights in the experience of art represents an alienation when compared to the authentic experience that confronts us in the form of art itself.

About thirty years ago, this problem cropped up in a particularly distorted form when National Socialist politics of art, as a means to its own ends, tried to criticize formalism by arguing that art is bound to a people. Despite its misuse by the National Socialists, we cannot deny that the idea of art being bound to a people involves a real insight. A genuine artistic creation stands within a particular community, and such a community is always distinguishable from the cultured society that is informed and terrorized by art criticism.

The second mode of the experience of alienation is the historical consciousness – the noble and slowly perfected art of holding ourselves at a critical distance in dealing with witnesses to past life. Ranke's celebrated description of this idea as the extinguishing of the individual provided a popular formula for the ideal of historical thinking: the historical consciousness has the task of understanding all the witnesses of a past time out of the spirit of that time, of extricating them from the preoccupations of our own present life, and of knowing, without moral smugness, the past as a human phenomenon. In his well-known essay *The Use and Abuse of History*, Nietzsche formulated the contradiction between this historical distancing and the immediate will to shape things that always cleaves to the present. And at the same time he exposed many of the consequences of what he called the "Alexandrian," weakened form of the will, which is found in modern historical science. We might recall his indictment of the weakness of evaluation that has befallen the modern mind because it has become so accustomed to considering things in ever different and changing lights that it is blinded and incapable of arriving at an opinion of its own regarding the objects it studies. It is unable to determine its own position *vis-à-vis* what confronts it. Nietzsche traces the value-blindness of historical objectivism back to the conflict between the alienated historical world and the life-powers of the present.

To be sure, Nietzsche is an ecstatic witness. But our actual experience of the historical consciousness in the last one hundred years has taught us most emphatically that there are serious difficulties involved in its claim to historical objectivity. Even in those masterworks of historical scholarship that seem to be the very consummation of the extinguishing of the individual demanded by Ranke, it is still an unquestioned principle of our scientific experience that we can classify these works with unfailing accuracy in terms of the political tendencies of the time in which they were written. When we read Mommsen's *History of Rome*, we know who alone could have written it, that is, we can identify the political situation in which this historian organized the voices of the past in a meaningful way. We know it too in the case of Treitschke or of Sybel, to choose only a few prominent names from Prussian historiography. This clearly means, first of all, that the whole reality of historical experience does not find expression in the mastery of historical method. No one disputes the fact that controlling the prejudices of our own present to such an extent that we do not misunderstand the witnesses of the past is a valid aim, but obviously such control does not completely fulfill the task of understanding the past and its transmissions. Indeed, it could very well be that only *insignificant* things in historical scholarship permit us to approximate this ideal of totally extinguishing individuality, while the great productive achievements of scholarship always preserve something of the splendid magic of immediately mirroring the present in the past and the past in the present. Historical science, the second experience from which I begin, expresses only one part of our actual experience – our actual encounter with historical tradition – and

it knows only an alienated form of this historical tradition.

We can contrast the hermeneutical consciousness with these examples of alienation as a more comprehensive possibility that we must develop. But, in the case of this hermeneutical consciousness also, our initial task must be to overcome the epistemological truncation by which the traditional "science of hermeneutics" has been absorbed into the idea of modern science. If we consider Schleiermacher's hermeneutics, for instance, we find his view of this discipline peculiarly restricted by the modern idea of science. Schleiermacher's hermeneutics shows him to be a leading voice of historical romanticism. But at the same time, he kept the concern of the Christian theologian clearly in mind, intending his hermeneutics, as a general doctrine of the art of understanding, to be of value in the special work of interpreting Scripture. Schleiermacher defined hermeneutics as the art of avoiding misunderstanding. To exclude by controlled, methodical consideration whatever is alien and leads to misunderstanding – misunderstanding suggested to us by distance in time, change in linguistic usages, or in the meanings of words and modes of thinking – that is certainly far from an absurd description of the hermeneutical endeavor. But the question also arises as to whether the phenomenon of understanding is defined appropriately when we say that to understand is to avoid misunderstanding. Is it not, in fact, the case that every misunderstanding presupposes a "deep common accord"?

I am trying to call attention here to a common experience. We say, for instance, that understanding and misunderstanding take place between I and thou. But the formulation "I and thou" already betrays an enormous alienation. There is nothing like an "I and thou" at all – there is neither the I nor the thou as isolated, substantial realities. I may say "thou" and I may refer to myself over against a thou, but a common understanding [*Verständigung*] always precedes these situations. We all know that to say "thou" to someone presupposes a deep common accord [*tiefes Einverständnis*]. Something enduring is already present when this word is spoken. When we try to reach agreement on a matter on which we have different opinions, this deeper factor always comes into play, even if we are seldom aware of it. Now the science of hermeneutics would have us believe that the opinion we have to understand is something alien that seeks to lure us into misunderstanding, and our task is to exclude every element through which a misunderstanding can creep in. We accomplish this task by a controlled procedure of historical training, by historical criticism, and by a controllable method in connection with powers of psychological empathy. It seems to me that this description is valid in one respect, but yet it is only a partial description of a comprehensive life-phenomenon that constitutes the "we" that we all are. Our task, it seems to me, is to transcend the prejudices that underlie the aesthetic consciousness, the historical consciousness, and the hermeneutical consciousness that has been restricted to a technique for avoiding misunderstandings and to overcome the alienations present in them all.

What is it, then, in these three experiences that seemed to us to have been left out, and what makes us so sensitive to the distinctiveness of these experiences? What is the *aesthetic* consciousness when compared to the fullness of what has already addressed us – what we call "classical" in art? Is it not always already determined in this way what will be expressive for us and what we will find significant? Whenever we say with an instinctive, even if perhaps erroneous, certainty (but a certainty that is initially valid for our consciousness) "this is classical; it will endure," what we are speaking of has already preformed our possibility for aesthetic judgment. There are no purely formal criteria that can claim to judge and sanction the formative level simply on the basis of its artistic virtuosity. Rather, our sensitive-spiritual existence is an aesthetic resonance chamber that resonates with the voices that are constantly reaching us, preceding all explicit aesthetic judgment.

The situation is similar with the historical consciousness. Here, too, we must certainly admit that there are innumerable tasks of historical scholarship that have no relation to our own present and to the depths of its historical consciousness. But it seems to me there can be no doubt that the great horizon of the past, out of which our culture and our present live, influences us in everything we want, hope for, or fear in the future. History is only present to us in light of our futurity. Here we have all learned from Heidegger, for he exhibited precisely the primacy of futurity for our possible recollection and retention, and for the whole of our history.

Heidegger worked out this primacy in his doctrine of the productivity of the hermeneutical circle. I have given the following formulation to this insight: It is not so much our judgments as it is our prejudices that constitute our being.[1] This is a provocative formulation, for I am using it to restore to its rightful place a positive concept of prejudice that was driven out of our linguistic usage by the French and the English Enlightenment. It can be shown that the concept of prejudice did not originally have the meaning we have attached to it. Prejudices are not necessarily unjustified and erroneous, so that they inevitably distort the truth. In fact, the historicity of our existence entails that prejudices, in the literal sense of the word, constitute the initial directedness of our whole ability to experience. Prejudices are biases of our openness to the world. They are simply conditions whereby we experience something – whereby what we encounter says something to us. This formulation certainly does not mean that we are enclosed within a wall of prejudices and only let through the narrow portals those things that can produce a pass saying, "Nothing new will be said here." Instead we welcome just that guest who promises something new to our curiosity. But how do we know the guest whom we admit is one who has something *new* to say to us? Is not our expectation and our readiness to hear the new also necessarily determined by the old that has already taken possession of us? The concept of prejudice is closely connected to the concept of authority, and the above image makes it clear that it is in need of hermeneutical rehabilitation. Like every image, however, this one too is misleading. The nature of the hermeneutical experience is not that something is outside and desires admission. Rather, we are possessed by something and precisely by means of it we are opened up for the new, the different, the true. Plato made this clear in his beautiful comparison of bodily foods with spiritual nourishment: while we can refuse the former (e.g. on the advice of a physician), we have always taken the latter into ourselves already.

But now the question arises as to how we can legitimate this hermeneutical conditionedness of our being in the face of modern science, which stands or falls with the principle of being unbiased and prejudiceless. We will certainly not accomplish this legitimation by making prescriptions for science and recommending that it toe the line – quite aside from the fact that such pronouncements always have something comical about them. Science will not do us this favor. It will continue along its own path with an inner necessity beyond its control, and it will produce more and more breathtaking knowledge and controlling power. It can be no other way. It is senseless, for instance, to hinder a genetic researcher because such research threatens to breed a superman. Hence the problem cannot appear as one in which our human consciousness ranges itself over against the world of science and presumes to develop a kind of anti-science. Nevertheless, we cannot avoid the question of whether what we are aware of in such apparently harmless examples as the aesthetic consciousness and the historical consciousness does not represent a problem that is also present in modern natural science and our technological attitude toward the world. If modern science enables us to erect a new world of technological purposes that transforms everything around us, we are not thereby suggesting that the researcher who gained the knowledge decisive for this state of affairs even considered technical applications. The genuine researcher is motivated by a desire for knowledge and by nothing else. And yet, over against the whole of our civilization that is founded on modern science, we must ask repeatedly if something has not been omitted. If the presuppositions of these possibilities for knowing and making remain half in the dark, cannot the result be that the hand applying this knowledge will be destructive?

The problem is really universal. The hermeneutical question, as I have characterized it, is not restricted to the areas from which I began in my own investigations. My only concern there was to secure a theoretical basis that would enable us to deal with the basic factor of contemporary culture, namely, science and its industrial, technological utilization. Statistics provide us with a useful example of how the hermeneutical dimension encompasses the entire procedure of science. It is an extreme example, but it shows us that science always stands under definite conditions of methodological abstraction and that the successes of modern sciences rest on the fact that other possibilities for questioning are concealed by abstraction. This fact comes out clearly in the case of statistics, for the anticipatory character of the questions statistics answer make it particularly suitable for propaganda purposes. Indeed, effective propaganda must always try to influence initially the judgment of the person addressed and to restrict his possibilities of judgment. Thus what is established by statistics seems to be a language of facts, but which questions these facts answer and which facts would begin to speak if other questions were asked are hermeneutical questions. Only a hermeneutical inquiry would legitimate the meaning of

these facts and thus the consequences that follow from them.

But I am anticipating, and have inadvertently used the phrase, "which answers to which questions fit the facts." This phrase is in fact the hermeneutical *Urphänomen*: No assertion is possible that cannot be understood as an answer to a question, and assertions can only be understood in this way. It does not impair the impressive methodology of modern science in the least. Whoever wants to learn a science has to learn to master its methodology. But we also know that methodology as such does not guarantee in any way the productivity of its application. Any experience of life can confirm the fact that there is such a thing as methodological sterility, that is, the application of a method to something not really worth knowing, to something that has not been made an object of investigation on the basis of a genuine question.

The methodological self-consciousness of modern science certainly stands in opposition to this argument. A historian, for example, will say in reply: It is all very nice to talk about the historical tradition in which alone the voices of the past gain their meaning and through which the prejudices that determine the present are inspired. But the situation is completely different in questions of serious historical research. How could one seriously mean, for example, that the clarification of the taxation practices of fifteenth-century cities or of the marital customs of Eskimos somehow first receive their meaning from the consciousness of the present and its anticipations? These are questions of historical knowledge that we take up as tasks quite independently of any relation to the present.

In answering this objection, one can say that the extremity of this point of view would be similar to what we find in certain large industrial research facilities, above all in America and Russia. I mean the so-called random experiment in which one simply covers the material without concern for waste or cost, taking the chance that some day one measurement among the thousands of measurements will finally yield an interesting finding; that is, it will turn out to be the answer to a question from which someone can progress. No doubt modern research in the humanities also works this way to some extent. One thinks, for instance, of the great editions and especially of the ever more perfect indexes. It must remain an open question, of course, whether by such procedures modern historical research increases the chances of actually noticing the interesting fact and thus gaining from it the corresponding enrichment of our knowledge. But even if they do, one might ask: Is this an ideal, that countless research projects (i.e. determinations of the connection of facts) are extracted from a thousand historians, so that the 1,001st historian can find something interesting? Of course I am drawing a caricature of genuine scholarship. But in every caricature there is an element of truth, and this one contains an indirect answer to the question of what it is that really makes the productive scholar. That he has learned the methods? The person who never produces anything new has also done that. It is imagination [*Phantasie*] that is the decisive function of the scholar. Imagination naturally has a hermeneutical function and serves the sense for what is questionable. It serves the ability to expose real, productive questions, something in which, generally speaking, only he who masters all the methods of his science succeeds.

As a student of Plato, I particularly love those scenes in which Socrates gets into a dispute with the Sophist virtuosi and drives them to despair by his questions. Eventually they can endure his questions no longer and claim for themselves the apparently preferable role of the questioner. And what happens? They can think of nothing at all to ask. Nothing at all occurs to them that is worth while going into and trying to answer.

I draw the following inference from this observation. The real power of hermeneutical consciousness is our ability to see what is questionable. Now if what we have before our eyes is not only the artistic tradition of a people, or historical tradition, or the principle of modern science in its hermeneutical preconditions but rather the whole of our experience, then we have succeeded, I think, in joining the experience of science to our own universal and human experience of life. For we have now reached the fundamental level that we can call (with Johannes Lohmann) the "linguistic constitution of the world."[2] It presents itself as the consciousness that is effected by history [*wirkungsgeschichtliches Bewusstsein*] and that provides an initial schematization for all our possibilities of knowing. I leave out of account the fact that the scholar – even the natural scientist – is perhaps not completely free of custom and society and from all possible factors in his environment. What I mean is that precisely *within* his scientific experience it is not so much the "laws of ironclad inference" (Helmholz) that present fruitful ideas to him, but rather unforeseen constellations that kin-

dle the spark of scientific inspiration (e.g. Newton's falling apple or some other incidental observation).

The consciousness that is effected by history has its fulfillment in what is linguistic. We can learn from the sensitive student of language that language, in its life and occurrence, must not be thought of as merely changing, but rather as something that has a teleology operating within it. This means that the words that are formed, the means of expression that appear in a language in order to say certain things, are not accidentally fixed, since they do not once again fall altogether into disuse. Instead, a definite articulation of the world is built up – a process that works as if guided and one that we can always observe in children who are learning to speak.

We can illustrate this by considering a passage in Aristotle's *Posterior Analytics* that ingeniously describes one definite aspect of language formation.[3] The passage treats what Aristotle calls the *epagoge*, that is, the formation of the universal. How does one arrive at a universal? In philosophy we say: how do we arrive at a general concept, but even words in this sense are obviously general. How does it happen that they are "words," that is, that they have a general meaning? In his first apperception, a sensuously equipped being finds himself in a surging sea of stimuli, and finally one day he begins, as we say, to know something. Clearly we do not mean that he was previously blind. Rather, when we say "to know" [*erkennen*] we mean "to recognize" [*wiedererkennen*], that is, to pick something out [*herauserkennen*] of the stream of images flowing past as being identical. What is picked out in this fashion is clearly retained. But how? When does a child know its mother for the first time? When it sees her for the first time? No. Then when? How does it take place? Can we really say at all that there is a single event in which a first knowing extricates the child from the darkness of not knowing? It seems obvious to me that we cannot. Aristotle has described this wonderfully. He says it is the same as when an army is in flight, driven by panic, until at last someone stops and looks around to see whether the foe is still dangerously close behind. We cannot say that the army stops when one soldier has stopped. But then another stops. The army does not stop by virtue of the fact that two soldiers stop. When does it actually stop, then? Suddenly it stands its ground again. Suddenly it obeys the command once again. A subtle pun is involved in Aristotle's description, for in Greek "command" means *arche*, that is, *principium*. When is the principle present as a principle? Through what capacity? This question is in fact the question of the occurrence of the universal.

If I have not misunderstood Johannes Lohmann's exposition, precisely this same teleology operates constantly in the life of language. When Lohmann speaks of linguistic tendencies as the real agents of history in which specific forms expand, he knows of course that it occurs in these forms of realization, of "coming to a stand" [*Zum-Stehen-Kommen*], as the beautiful German word says. What is manifest here, I contend, is the real mode of operation of our whole human experience of the world. Learning to speak is surely a phase of special productivity, and in the course of time we have all transformed the genius of the three-year-old into a poor and meager talent. But in the utilization of the linguistic interpretation of the world that finally comes about, something of the productivity of our beginnings remains alive. We are all acquainted with this, for instance, in the attempt to translate, in practical life or in literature or wherever; that is, we are familiar with the strange, uncomfortable, and tortuous feeling we have as long as we do not have the right word. When we have found the right expression (it need not always be one word), when we are certain that we have it, then it "stands," then something has come to a "stand." Once again we have a halt in the midst of the rush of the foreign language, whose endless variation makes us lose our orientation. What I am describing is the mode of the whole human experience of the world. I call this experience hermeneutical, for the process we are describing is repeated continually throughout our familiar experience. There is always a world already interpreted, already organized in its basic relations, into which experience steps as something new, upsetting what has led our expectations and undergoing reorganization itself in the upheaval. Misunderstanding and strangeness are not the first factors, so that avoiding misunderstanding can be regarded as the specific task of hermeneutics. Just the reverse is the case. Only the support of familiar and common understanding makes possible the venture into the alien, the lifting up of something out of the alien, and thus the broadening and enrichment of our own experience of the world.

This discussion shows how the claim to universality that is appropriate to the hermeneutical dimension is to be understood. Understanding is language-bound. But this assertion does not lead us into any kind of linguistic relativism. It is indeed true that we live within a language, but language is not a system of signals that we send off with the aid of a telegraphic key when we enter the office or transmission station. That is not speaking, for it does not have the infinity of the act that is linguistically creative and world experiencing. While we live wholly within a language, the fact that we do so does not constitute linguistic relativism because there is absolutely no captivity within a language – not even within our native language. We all experience this when we learn a foreign language, especially on journeys insofar as we master the foreign language to some extent. To master the foreign language means precisely that when we engage in speaking it in the foreign land, we do not constantly consult inwardly our own world and its vocabulary. The better we know the language, the less such a side glance at our native language is perceptible, and only because we never know foreign languages well enough do we always have something of this feeling. But it is nevertheless already speaking, even if perhaps a stammering speaking, for stammering is the obstruction of a desire to speak and is thus opened into the infinite realm of possible expression. Any language in which we live is infinite in this sense, and it is completely mistaken to infer that reason is fragmented because there are various languages. Just the opposite is the case. Precisely through our finitude, the particularity of our being, which is evident even in the variety of languages, the infinite dialogue is opened in the direction of the truth that we are.

If this is correct, then the relation of our modern industrial world, founded by science, which we described at the outset, is mirrored above all on the level of language. We live in an epoch in which an increasing leveling of all life-forms is taking place – that is the rationally necessary requirement for maintaining life on our planet. The food problem of mankind, for example, can only be overcome by the surrender of the lavish wastefulness that has covered the earth. Unavoidably, the mechanical, industrial world is expanding within the life of the individual as a sort of sphere of technical perfection. When we hear modern lovers talking to each other, we often wonder if they are communicating with words or with advertising labels and technical terms from the sign language of the modern industrial world. It is inevitable that the leveled life-forms of the industrial age also affect language, and in fact the impoverishment of the vocabulary of language is making enormous progress, thus bringing about an approximation of language to a technical sign-system. Leveling tendencies of this kind are irresistible. Yet in spite of them the simultaneous building up of our own world in language still persists whenever we want to say something to each other. The result is the actual relationship of men to each other. Each one is at first a kind of linguistic circle, and these linguistic circles come into contact with each other, merging more and more. Language occurs once again, in vocabulary and grammar as always, and never without the inner infinity of the dialogue that is in progress between every speaker and his partner. That is the fundamental dimension of hermeneutics. Genuine speaking, which has something to say and hence does not give prearranged signals, but rather seeks words through which one reaches the other person, is the universal human task – but it is a special task for the theologian, to whom is commissioned the saying-further (*Weitersagen*) of a message that stands written.

Notes

1 Cf. *Wahrheit und Methode*, p. 261.
2 Cf. Johannes Lohmann, *Philosophie und Sprachwissenschaft* (Berlin: Duncker & Humbolt, 1963).
3 Aristotle, *Posterior Analytics*, 100a 11–13.

Select Bibliography

Dialogue and Dialectic: Eight Hermeneutical Studies on Plato. Translated by P. Christopher Smith. New Haven, Conn.: Yale University Press, 1980.

Hans-Georg Gadamer on Education, Poetry, and History: Applied Hermeneutics. Edited by Dieter Misgeld and Graeme Nicholson. Translated by Lawrence Schmidt and Monica Reuss. Albany: State University of New York Press, 1992.

Hegel's Dialectic: Five Hermeneutical Studies. Translated by P. Christopher Smith. New Haven, Conn.: Yale University Press, 1976.

Heidegger's Ways. Translated by John W. Stanley. Albany: State University of New York Press, 1994.

The Idea of the Good in Platonic–Aristotelian Philosophy. Translated by P. Christopher Smith. New Haven, Conn.: Yale University Press, 1986.

Literature and Philosophy in Dialogue: Essays in German Literary Theory. Translated by Robert H. Paslick. Albany: State University of New York Press, 1994.

Philosophical Apprenticeships. Translated by Robert R. Sullivan. Cambridge, Mass.: MIT Press, 1985.

Philosophical Hermeneutics. Edited and translated by David E. Linge. Berkeley: University of California Press, 1977.

Reason in the Age of Science. Translated by Frederick G. Lawrence. Cambridge, Mass.: MIT Press, 1996.

The Relevance of the Beautiful and Other Essays. Edited by Robert Bernasconi. Translated by Nicholas Walker. Cambridge: Cambridge University Press, 1986.

Truth and Method. Revisions translation by Joel Weinsheimer and Donald G. Marshall. New York: Crossroad, 1989.

15

Paul Ricoeur

French philosopher Paul Ricoeur (1913–) is widely known as a proponent of phenomenological hermeneutics. Influenced in his early work by Gabriel Marcel, Karl Jaspers, and Edmund Husserl, Ricoeur published studies on each of these thinkers before producing a major work of his own, published in English under the title *Freedom and Nature*. In this text Ricoeur opposes in particular Sartre's conception of human freedom as absolute, arguing that all human freedom is conditioned by various forms of worldly and historical finitude. In his later work, Ricoeur became increasingly interested in the ways in which our experiences of the world are mediated by narrative, symbol, and metaphor, while remaining true to the phenomenological emphasis on attentiveness to the self-showing of phenomena. The hermeneutic tasks of interpretation and mediation between different interpretations, none of which has an exclusive access to truth, come to the fore in Ricoeur's later studies of metaphor, symbol, and narrative in the philosophical tradition. In the following essay from 1972, Ricoeur connects the disclosure of meaning by metaphor to the hermeneutic task of interpretation by showing that both metaphor and text belong to the category of "discourse."

Metaphor and the Central Problem of Hermeneutics

It will be assumed here that the central problem of hermeneutics is that of interpretation. Not interpretation in any sense of the word, but interpretation determined in two ways: the first concerning

From "Metaphor and the Central Problem of Hermeneutics," in *Hermeneutics and the Human Sciences*, edited and translated by John B. Thompson (Cambridge: Cambridge University Press, 1989), pp. 165–81. © Maison des Sciences de l'Homme and Cambridge University Press, 1981. Reprinted with the permission of Cambridge University Press.

its field of application, the second its epistemological specificity. As regards the first point, I shall say that there is a problem of interpretation because there are texts, written texts, the autonomy of which creates specific difficulties. By "autonomy" I understand the independence of the text with respect to the intention of the author, the situation of the work and the original reader. The relevant problems are resolved in oral discourse by the kind of exchange or intercourse which we call dialogue or conversation. With written texts, discourse must speak by itself. Let us say, therefore, that there are problems of interpretation because the writing–reading relation is not a particular case of the speaking–hearing relation which we experience in the dialogical situation. Such is the most general feature of interpretation as regards its field of application.

Second, the concept of interpretation seems, at the epistemological level, to be opposed to the concept of explanation. Taken together, these concepts form a contrasting pair which has given rise to a great many disputes since the time of Schleiermacher and Dilthey. According to the tradition to which the latter authors belong, interpretation has certain subjective connotations, such as the implication of the reader in the processes of understanding and the reciprocity between interpretation of the text and self-interpretation. This reciprocity is known by the name of the hermeneutical circle; it entails a sharp opposition to the sort of objectivity and nonimplication which is supposed to characterize the scientific explanation of things. Later I shall say to what extent we may be able to amend, indeed to reconstruct on a new basis, the opposition between interpretation and explanation. Whatever the outcome of the subsequent discussion may be, this schematic description of the concept of interpretation suffices for a provisional circumscription of the central problem of hermeneutics: the status of written texts *versus* spoken language, the status of interpretation *versus* explanation.

Now for the metaphor! The aim of this essay is to link up the problems raised in hermeneutics by the interpretation of texts and the problems raised in rhetoric, semantics, stylistics – or whatever the discipline concerned may be – by metaphor.

1   The Text and Metaphor as Discourse

Our first task will be to find a common ground for the theory of the text and the theory of metaphor. This common ground has already received a name – discourse; it has yet to be given a status.

One thing is striking: the two sorts of entities that we are considering are of different lengths. In this respect, they can be compared to the sentence, which is the basic unit of discourse. A text can undoubtedly be reduced to a single sentence, as in proverbs or aphorisms; but texts have a maximum length which can extend from a paragraph to a chapter, a book, a collection of "selected works" or even the corpus of the "complete works" of an author. Let us use the term "work" to describe the closed sequence of discourse which can be considered as a text. Whereas texts can be identified on the basis of their maximal length, metaphors can be identified on the basis of their minimal length, that of the word. Even if the rest of this discussion seeks to show that there is no metaphor – in the sense of a word taken metaphorically – in the absence of certain contexts, and consequently even if we are constrained by what follows to replace the notion of metaphor by that of the metaphorical statement which implies at least the length of the sentence, nevertheless the "metaphorical twist" (to speak like Monroe Beardsley) is something which happens to the word....The word remains the "focus," even if the focus requires the "frame" of the sentence, to use the vocabulary of Max Black.

This first, altogether formal remark concerning the difference in length between the text and the metaphor, or better between the *work* and the *word*, is going to help us to elaborate our initial problem in a more precise way: to what extent can we treat the metaphor as a *work in miniature*? The answer to this question will then help us to pose the second: to what extent can the hermeneutical problems raised by the interpretation of texts be considered as a large-scale extension of the problems condensed in the explanation of a local metaphor in a given text?

Is a metaphor a work in miniature? Can a work, say a poem, be considered as a sustained or extended metaphor? The answer to this first question requires a prior elaboration of the general properties of discourse, if it is true that text and metaphor, work and word, fall within the same category of discourse. I shall not elaborate in detail the concept of discourse, restricting my analysis to the features which are necessary for the comparison between text and metaphor. It is remarkable that all of these features present themselves in the form of paradoxes, that is, apparent contradictions.

To begin with, all discourse is produced as an event; as such, it is the counterpart of language understood as code or system. Discourse *qua* event has a fleeting existence: it appears and disappears. But at the same time – and herein lies the paradox – it can be identified and reidentified as the same. This "sameness" is what we call, in a broad sense, its meaning. All discourse, we shall say, is realized as event but understood as meaning. Soon we shall see in what sense the metaphor concentrates this double character of event and meaning.

The second pair of contrasting features stems from the fact that meaning is supported by a specific structure, that of the proposition, which envelops an internal opposition between a pole of singular identification (this man, this table, Monsieur Dupont, Paris) and a pole of general predication (humanity as a class, brightness as a property, equality as a relation, running as an action). Metaphor, we shall also see, rests upon this "attribution" of characteristics to the "principal subject" of a sentence.

The third pair of opposing features is the polarity, which discourse primarily in sentential form implies, between sense and reference. That is, discourse implies the possibility of distinguishing between *what* is said by the sentence as a whole and by the words which compose it on the one hand, and *that about which* something is said on the other. To speak is to say something about something. This polarity will play a decisive role in the second and third parts of this essay, where I shall try to connect the problem of explanation to the dimension of "sense" or the immanent pattern of discourse, and the problems of interpretation to the dimension of "reference," understood as the power of discourse to apply itself to an extralinguistic reality about which it says what it says.

Fourth, discourse as an act can be considered from the viewpoint of the "contents" of the propositional act (it predicates a certain characteristic of a certain subject), or from the viewpoint of what Austin called the "force" of the complete act of discourse (the *speech-act* in his terminology). What is said of the subject is one thing; what I "do" *in* saying it is another: I can make a mere description, or give an order, or formulate a wish, or give a warning, etc. Hence the polarity between the locutionary act (the act *of* saying) and the illocutionary act (what I do *in* saying). This polarity may seem less useful than the preceding ones, at least at the structural level of the metaphorical statement. Nevertheless, it will play a decisive role when we have to place the metaphor back in the concrete setting of, for example, a poem, an essay, or a work of fiction.

Before developing the dichotomy of sense and reference as the basis of the opposition between explanation and interpretation, let us introduce a final polarity which will play a decisive role in hermeneutical theory. Discourse has not merely one sort of reference but two: it is related to an extralinguistic reality, to the world or a world; and it refers equally to its own speaker, by means of

specific procedures which function only in the sentence and hence in discourse – personal pronouns, verbal tenses, demonstratives, etc. In this way, language has both a reference to reality and a self-reference. It is the same entity – the sentence – which supports this double reference: intentional and reflexive, turned towards the thing and towards the self. In fact, we should speak of a triple reference, for discourse refers as much to the one to whom it is addressed as to its own speaker . . . As we shall see later, this connection between the two and even the three directions of reference will provide us with the key to the hermeneutical circle and the basis for our reinterpretation of this circle.

I shall list the basic polarities of discourse in the following condensed fashion: event and meaning, singular identification and general predication, propositional act and illocutionary act, sense and reference, reference to reality and reference to interlocutors. In what sense can we now say that the text and metaphor both rest upon the sort of entity which we have just called discourse?

It is easy to show that all texts are discourses, since they stem from the smallest unit of discourse, the sentence. A text is at least a series of sentences. We shall see that it must be something more in order to be a work; but it is at least a set of sentences, and consequently a discourse. The connection between metaphor and discourse requires a special justification, precisely because the definition of metaphor as a transposition affecting names or words seems to place it in a category of entities smaller than the sentence. But the semantics of the word demonstrates very clearly that words acquire an actual meaning only in a sentence and that lexical entities – the words of the dictionary – have merely potential meanings in virtue of their potential uses in typical contexts. In this respect, the theory of polysemy is a good preparation for the theory of metaphor. At the lexical level, words (if indeed they can already be called that) have more than one meaning; it is only by a specific contextual action of sifting that they realize, in a given sentence, a part of their potential semantics and acquire what we call a determinate meaning. The contextual action which enables univocal discourse to be produced with polysemic words is the model for that other contextual action whereby we draw genuinely novel metaphorical effects from words whose meaning is already codified in the vocabulary. We are thus prepared to allow that even if the meaningful effect which we call metaphor is inscribed in the word, nevertheless the origin of this effect lies in a contextual action which places the semantic fields of several words in interaction.

As regards the metaphor itself, semantics shows with the same force that the metaphorical meaning of a word is nothing which can be found in the dictionary. In this sense, we can continue to oppose metaphorical meaning to literal meaning, if by the latter we understand *any* of the meanings that can be found among the partial meanings codified by the vocabulary. By literal meaning, therefore, we do not understand the supposedly original, fundamental, primitive or proper meaning of a word on the lexical plane; rather, literal meaning is the totality of the semantic field, the set of possible contextual uses which constitutes the polysemy of a word. So even if metaphorical meaning is something more and other than the actualization of one of the possible meanings of a polysemic word (and all of the words in natural languages are polysemic), nevertheless this metaphorical use must be solely contextual, that is, a meaning which emerges as the unique and fleeting result of a certain contextual action. We are thus led to oppose contextual changes of meaning to the lexical changes which concern the diachronic aspect of language as code or system. Metaphor is one such contextual change of meaning.

In this respect, I am partially in agreement with the modern theory of metaphor, as elaborated in English by I. A. Richards, Max Black, Monroe Beardsley, Douglas Berggren, etc.[1] More precisely, I agree with these authors on the fundamental point: a word receives a metaphorical meaning in specific contexts, within which it is opposed to other words taken literally. The shift in meaning results primarily from a clash between literal meanings, which excludes the literal use of the word in question and provides clues for finding a new meaning capable of according with the context of the sentence and rendering the sentence meaningful therein. Consequently, I retain the following points from this recent history of the problem of metaphor: the replacement of the rhetorical theory of substitution by a properly semantic theory of the interaction between semantic fields; the decisive role of semantic clash leading to logical absurdity; the issuance of a particle of meaning which renders the sentence as a whole meaningful. We shall now see how this properly semantic theory – or the interaction theory – satisfies the principal characteristics which we have recognized in discourse.

To begin with, let us return to the contrast between event and meaning. In the metaphorical statement (we shall speak of metaphor as a sentence and no longer as a word), contextual action creates a new meaning which is indeed an event, since it exists only in this particular context; but at the same time, it can be repeated and hence identified as the same. Thus the innovation of an "emergent meaning" (Beardsley) may be regarded as a linguistic creation; but if it is adopted by an influential part of the language community, it may become an everyday meaning and add to the polysemy of lexical entities, contributing thereby to the history of language as code or system. At this final stage, when the meaningful effect that we call metaphor has rejoined the change of meaning which augments polysemy, the metaphor is no longer living but dead. Only authentic, living metaphors are at the same time "event" *and* "meaning."

Contextual action similarly requires our second polarity, that between singular identification and general predication. A metaphor is said of a "principal subject"; as "modifier" of this subject, it works like a kind of "attribution." All of the theories to which I have referred above rest upon this predicative structure, whether they oppose "vehicle" to "tenor" (Richards), "frame" to "focus" (Max Black), or "modifier" to "principal subject" (Beardsley).

To show that metaphor requires the polarity between sense and reference, we shall need a whole section of this essay; the same thing must be said of the polarity between reference to reality and reference to self....

2 From Metaphor to the Text: Explanation

I propose to explore a working hypothesis which, to begin with, I shall simply state. From one point of view, the understanding of metaphor can serve as a guide to the understanding of longer texts, such as a literary work. This point of view is that of explanation; it concerns only that aspect of meaning which we have called the "sense," that is, the immanent pattern of discourse. From another point of view, the understanding of a work taken as a whole gives the key to metaphor. This other point of view is that of interpretation proper; it develops the aspect of meaning which we have called "reference," that is, the intentional orientation towards a world and the reflexive orientation towards a self. So if we apply explanation to "sense," as the immanent pattern of the work, then we can reserve interpretation for the sort of inquiry concerned with the *power of a work* to project a world of its own and to set in motion the hermeneutical circle, which encompasses in its spiral both the apprehension of projected worlds and the advance of self-understanding in the presence of these new worlds. Our working hypothesis thus invites us to proceed from metaphor to text at the level of "sense" and the explanation of "sense," then from text to metaphor at the level of the reference of a work to a world and to a self, that is, at the level of interpretation proper.

What aspects of the explanation of metaphor can serve as a paradigm for the explanation of a text? These aspects are features of the explanatory process which could not appear so long as trivial examples of metaphor were considered, such as man is a wolf, a fox, a lion (if we read the best authors on metaphor, we observe interesting variations within the bestiary which provides them with examples!). With these examples, we elude the major difficulty, that of *identifying a meaning* which is *new*. The only way of achieving this identification is to construct a meaning which alone enables us to make sense of the sentence as a whole. For what do trivial metaphors rest upon? Max Black and Monroe Beardsley note that the meaning of a word does not depend merely on the semantic and syntactic rules which govern its literal use, but also on other rules (which are nevertheless rules) to which the members of a language community are "committed" and which determine what Black calls the "system of associated commonplaces" and Beardsley the "potential range of connotations." In the statement, "man is a wolf" (the example favored by Black!), the principal subject is qualified by one of the features of animal life which belongs to "the lupine system of associated commonplaces." The system of implications operates like a filter or screen; it does not merely select, but also accentuates new aspects of the principal subject.

What are we to think of this explanation in relation to our description of metaphor as a new meaning appearing in a new context? As I said above, I entirely agree with the "interaction view" implied by this explanation; metaphor is more than a simple substitution whereby one word would replace a literal word, which an exhaustive paraphrase could restore to the same place. The algebraic sum of these two operations – substitution by the speaker and restoration by the author or reader – is equal to zero. No new mean-

ing emerges and we learn nothing. As Black says, "'interaction-metaphors' are not expendable... This use of a 'subsidiary subject' to foster insight into a 'principal subject' is a distinctive intellectual operation." Hence interaction metaphors cannot be translated into direct language without "a loss in cognitive content."...[2]

Beardsley's theory of metaphor leads us a stage further in this direction. If, following him, we emphasize the role of logical absurdity or the clash between literal meanings within the same context, then we are ready to recognize the genuinely creative character of metaphorical meaning: "In poetry, the principal tactic for obtaining this result is logical absurdity".[3] Logical absurdity creates a situation in which we have the choice of either preserving the literal meaning of the subject and the modifier and hence concluding that the entire sentence is absurd, or attributing a new meaning to the modifier so that the sentence as a whole makes sense. We are now faced not only with "self-contradictory" attribution, but with a "meaningful self-contradictory" attribution. If I say "man is a fox" (the fox has chased away the wolf!), I must slide from a literal to a metaphorical attribution if I want to save the sentence. But from where do we draw this new meaning?

As long as we ask this type of question – "from where do we draw...?" – we return to the same type of ineffectual answer. The "potential range of connotations" says nothing more than the "system of associated commonplaces." Of course, we expand the notion of meaning by including "secondary meanings," as connotations, within the perimeter of full meaning; but we continue to bind the creative process of metaphor to a non-creative aspect of language.

Is it sufficient to supplement this "potential range of connotations," as Beardsley does in the "revised verbal-opposition theory,"[4] with the properties which do not yet belong to the range of connotations of my language? At first sight, this supplementation ameliorates the theory; as Beardsley forcefully says, "metaphor transforms a *property* (actual or attributed) into a *sense*."[5] This change is important, since it must now be said that metaphors do not merely actualize a potential connotation, but establish it "as a staple one"; and further, "some of [the object's] relevant properties can be given a new status as elements of verbal meaning."[6]

However, to speak of properties of *things* (or *objects*), which are supposed not yet to have been signified, is to admit that the new, emergent meaning is not drawn from anywhere, at least not from anywhere in language (the property is an implication of things, not of words). To say that a metaphor is not drawn from anywhere is to recognize it for what it is: namely, a momentary creation of language, a semantic innovation which does not have a status in the language as something already established, whether as a designation or as a connotation.

It may be asked how we can speak of a semantic innovation, a semantic event, as a meaning capable of being identified and reidentified (that was the first criterion of discourse stated above). Only one answer remains possible: it is necessary to take the viewpoint of the hearer or the reader and to treat the novelty of the emergent meaning as the counterpart, on the author's side, of a construction on the side of the reader. Thus the process of explanation is the only access to the process of creation....

The decisive moment of explanation is the construction of a network of interactions which constitutes the context as actual and unique. In so doing, we direct our attention towards the semantic event which is produced at the point of intersection between several semantic fields. This construction is the means by which all of the words taken together make sense. Then and only then, the "metaphorical twist" is both an event and a meaning, a meaningful event and an emergent meaning in language.

Such is the fundamental feature of explanation which makes metaphor a paradigm for the explanation of a literary work. We construct the meaning of a text in a manner similar to the way in which we make sense of all the terms of a metaphorical statement.

Why must we "construct" the meaning of a text? First, because it is written: in the asymmetrical relation between the text and the reader, one of the partners speaks for both. Bringing a text to language is always something other than hearing someone and listening to his speech. Reading resembles instead the performance of a musical piece regulated by the written notations of the score. For the text is an autonomous space of meaning which is no longer animated by the intention of its author; the autonomy of the text, deprived of this essential support, hands writing over to the sole interpretation of the reader.

A second reason is that the text is not only something written but is a work, that is, a singular totality. As a totality, the literary work cannot be reduced to a sequence of sentences which are individually intelligible; rather, it is an architecture of themes and purposes which can be constructed in several ways. The relation of part to whole is ineluctably circular. The presupposition of a certain whole precedes the discernment of a determinate arrangement of parts; and it is by constructing the details that we build up the whole....

What, then, can we say about this construction? Here understanding a text, at the level of its articulation of sense, is strictly homologous to understanding a metaphorical statement. In both cases, it is a question of "making sense," of producing the best overall intelligibility from an apparently discordant diversity. In both cases, the construction takes the form of a wager or guess. As Hirsch says in *Validity in Interpretation*, there are no rules for making good guesses, but there are methods for validating our guesses.[7] This dialectic between guessing and validating is the realization at the textual level of the microdialectic at work in the resolution of the local enigmas of a text. In both cases, the procedures of validation have more affinity with a logic of probability than with a logic of empirical verification – more affinity, let us say, with a logic of uncertainty and qualitative probability. Validation, in this sense, is the concern of an argumentative discipline akin to the juridical procedures of legal interpretation.

We can now summarize the corresponding features which underlie the analogy between the explanation of metaphorical statements and that of a literary work as a whole. In both cases, the construction rests upon "clues" contained in the text itself. A clue serves as a guide for a specific construction, in that it contains at once a permission and a prohibition; it excludes unsuitable constructions and allows those which give more meaning to the same words. Second, in both cases, one construction can be said to be more probable than another, but not more truthful. The more probable is that which, on the one hand, takes account of the greatest number of facts furnished by the text, including its potential connotations, and on the other hand, offers a qualitatively better convergence between the features which it takes into account. A mediocre explanation can be called narrow or forced.

Here I agree with Beardsley when he says that a good explanation satisfies two principles: the principle of congruence and that of plenitude. Until now, we have in fact spoken about the principle of congruence. The principle of plenitude will provide us with a transition to the third part of the essay. This principle may be stated as follows: "All of the connotations which are suitable must be attributed; the poem means all that it can mean." This principle leads us further than a mere concern with "sense"; it already says something about reference, since it takes as a measure of plenitude the requirements stemming from an experience which demands to be said and to be equalled by the semantic density of the text. I shall say that the principle of plenitude is the corollary, at the level of meaning, of a principle of full expression which draws our investigation in a quite different direction.

A quotation from Humboldt will lead us to the threshold of this new field of investigation: "Language as discourse (*Rede*) lies on the boundary between the expressible and the inexpressible. Its aim and its goal is to push back still further this boundary." Interpretation, in its proper sense, similarly lies on this frontier.

3 From the Text to Metaphor: Interpretation

At the level of interpretation proper, understanding the text provides the key to understanding metaphor. Why? Because certain features of discourse begin to play an explicit role only when discourse takes the form of a literary *work*. These features are the very ones which we have placed under the heading of reference and self-reference. It will be recalled that I opposed reference to sense, saying that sense is the "what" and reference the "about what" of discourse. Of course, these two features can be recognized in the smallest units of language as discourse, namely in sentences. The sentence is about a situation which it expresses, and it refers back to its speaker by means of the specific procedures that we have enumerated. But reference and self-reference do not give rise to perplexing problems so long as discourse has not become a text and has not taken the form of a work. What are these problems?

Let us begin once again from the difference between written and spoken languages. In spoken language, that to which a dialogue ultimately refers is the situation common to the interlocutors, that is, the aspects of reality which can be shown or pointed to; we then say that the reference is "ostensive." In written language, the reference is no longer ostensive; poems, essays, works of fiction speak of things, events, states of affairs and characters which are evoked but which are not there. And yet literary texts are about something. About what? I do not hesitate to say: about a world, which is the world of the work. Far from saying that the text is without a world, I shall say that only now does man have a world and not merely a situation, a *Welt* and not merely an *Umwelt*. In the same way that the text frees its meaning from the tutelage of mental intention, so too it frees its reference from the limits of ostensive reference. For us, the world is the totality of references opened up by texts. Thus we speak of the "world" of Greece, not to indicate what the situations were for those who experienced them, but to designate the nonsituational references which outlast the effacement of the first and which then offer themselves as possible modes of being, as possible symbolic dimensions of our being-in-the-world.

The nature of reference in the context of literary works has an important consequence for the concept of interpretation. It implies that the meaning of a text lies not behind the text but in front of it. The meaning is not something hidden but something disclosed. What gives rise to understanding is that which points towards a possible world, by means of the nonostensive references of the text. Texts speak of possible worlds and of possible ways of orientating oneself in these worlds. In this way, disclosure plays the equivalent role for written texts as ostensive reference plays in spoken language. Interpretation thus becomes the apprehension of the proposed worlds which are opened up by the nonostensive references of the text.

This concept of interpretation expresses a decisive shift of emphasis with respect to the Romantic tradition of hermeneutics. In that tradition, the emphasis was placed on the ability of the hearer or reader to transfer himself into the spiritual life of a speaker or writer. The emphasis, from now on, is less on the other as a spiritual entity than on the world which the work unfolds. To understand is to follow the dynamic of the work, its movement from what it says to that about which it speaks. Beyond my situation as reader, beyond the situation of the author, I offer myself to the possible mode of being-in-the-world which the text opens up and discloses to me. That is what Gadamer calls the "fusion of horizons" (*Horizontverschmelzung*) in historical knowledge.

The shift of emphasis from understanding the other to understanding the world of his work entails a corresponding shift in the conception of the "hermeneutical circle." For the thinkers of Romanticism, the latter term meant that the understanding of a text cannot be an objective procedure, in the sense of scientific objectivity, but that it necessarily implies a pre-understanding, expressing the way in which the reader already understands himself and his work. Hence a sort of circularity is produced between understanding the text and self-understanding. Such is, in condensed terms, the principle of the hermeneutical circle. It is easy to see how thinkers trained in the tradition of logical empiricism could only reject, as utterly scandalous, the mere idea of a hermeneutical circle and consider it to be an outrageous violation of all the canons of verifiability.

For my part, I do not wish to conceal the fact that the hermeneutical circle remains an unavoidable structure of interpretation. An interpretation is not authentic unless it culminates in some form of appropriation (*Aneignung*), if by that term we understand the process by which one makes one's own (*eigen*) what was initially other or alien (*fremd*). But I believe that the hermeneutical circle is not correctly understood when it is presented, first, as a circle between two subjectivities, that of the reader and that of the author; and second, as the projection of the subjectivity of the reader into the reading itself.

Let us correct each of these assumptions in turn. What we make our own, what we appropriate for ourselves, is not an alien experience or a distant intention, but the horizon of a world towards which a work directs itself. The appropriation of the reference is no longer modelled on the fusion of consciousnesses, on empathy or sympathy. The emergence of the sense and the reference of a text in language is the coming to language of a world and not the recognition of another person. The second correction of the Romantic concept of interpretation results from the first. If appropriation is the counterpart of disclosure, then the role of subjectivity must not be described in terms of projection. I should prefer to say that the reader understands himself in front of the text, in front of the world of the work. To understand oneself in front of a text is quite the contrary of projecting oneself and one's own beliefs and prejudices; it is to let the work and its world enlarge the horizon of the understanding which I have of myself.... Thus the hermeneutical circle is not repudiated but displaced from a subjectivistic level to an ontological plane. The circle is between my mode of being – the mode of being of the work as disclosed by the

beyond the knowledge which I may have of it – and the mode opened up and disclosed by the text as the world of the work.

Such is the model of interpretation which I now propose to transfer from texts, as long sequences of discourse, to the metaphor, understood as "a poem in miniature" (Beardsley). Of course, the metaphor is too short a discourse to unfold this dialectic between the disclosure of a world and the disclosure of oneself in front of that world. Nevertheless, this dialectic points to some features of metaphor which the modern theories cited so far do not seem to take into consideration, but which were not absent from the classical theory of metaphor....

Thus the theory of interpretation paves the way for an ultimate approximation to the power of the metaphor. The priority given to the interpretation of the text in this final stage of the analysis does not mean that the relation between the two is not reciprocal. The explanation of metaphor, as a local event in the text, contributes to the interpretation of the work as a whole. We could even say that if the interpretation of local metaphors is illuminated by the interpretation of the text as a whole and by the clarification of the kind of world which the work projects, then in turn the interpretation of the poem as a whole is controlled by the explanation of the metaphor as a local phenomenon of the text.

As an example of this reciprocal relation between the regional and local aspects of the text, I shall venture to mention a possible connection, implicit in Aristotle's *Poetics*, between what he says about *mimesis* on the one hand and metaphor on the other. *Mimesis*...makes human actions appear higher than they are in reality; and the function of metaphor is to transpose the meanings of ordinary language by way of unusual uses. Is there not a mutual and profound affinity between the project of making human actions appear better than they are and the special procedure of metaphor which raises language above itself?

Let us express this relation in more general terms. Why should we draw new meanings from our language if we have nothing new to say, no new world to project? The creations of language would be devoid of sense unless they served the general project of letting new worlds emerge by means of poetry....

Allow me to conclude in a way which would be consistent with a theory of interpretation which places the emphasis on "opening up a world." Our conclusion should also "open up" some new perspectives, but on what? Perhaps on the old problem of the imagination which I have carefully put aside. Are we not ready to recognize in the power of imagination, no longer the faculty of deriving "images" from our sensory experience, but the capacity for letting new worlds shape our understanding of ourselves? This power would not be conveyed by images, but by the emergent meanings in our language. Imagination would thus be treated as a dimension of language. In this way, a new link would appear between imagination and metaphor. We shall, for the time being, refrain from entering this half-open door.

Notes

1 On this subject, see I. A. Richards, *The Philosophy of Rhetoric* (New York: Oxford University Press, 1936); Max Black, *Models and Metaphors* (Ithaca: Cornell University Press, 1962); Monroe Beardsley, *Aesthetics* (New York: Harcourt, Brace and World, 1958), and "The Metaphorical Twist," *Philosophy and Phenomenological Research*, 20 (1962), pp. 293–307; Douglas Berggren, "The Use and Abuse of Metaphor, I and II," *Review of Metaphysics*, 16 (1962), pp. 237–58, and 16 (1963), pp. 450–72.

2 *Models and Metaphors*, p. 46.
3 *Aesthetics*, p. 138.
4 Cf. "The Metaphorical Twist."
5 Ibid., p. 302.
6 Ibid.
7 Cf. Eric D. Hirsch, Jr, *Validity in Interpretation* (New Haven, Conn.: Yale University Press, 1967), chapter 5.

Select Bibliography

The Conflict of Interpretations: Essays in Hermeneutics. Edited by Don Ihde. Translated by Kathleen McLaughlin. Evanston, Ill.: Northwestern University Press, 1974.

Freedom and Nature: The Voluntary and the Involuntary. Translated by Erazim V. Kohak. Evanston, Ill.: Northwestern University Press, 1966.

Freud and Philosophy: An Essay on Interpretation. Translated by Denis Savage. New Haven, Conn.: Yale University Press, 1970.

From Text to Action. Translated by Kathleen Blamey and John B. Thompson. Evanston, Ill.: Northwestern University Press, 1991.

Hermeneutics and the Human Sciences: Essays on Language, Action, and Interpretation. Edited and translated by John B. Thompson. Cambridge: Cambridge University Press, 1981.

Oneself as Another. Translated by Kathleen Blamey. Chicago: University of Chicago Press, 1992.

The Philosophy of Paul Ricoeur: An Anthology of His Work. Edited by Charles E. Reagan and David Stewart. Boston: Beacon Press, 1978.

Political and Social Essays. Edited by David Stewart and Joseph Bien. Athens: Ohio University Press, 1975.

A Ricoeur Reader: Reflection and Imagination. Edited by Mario J. Valdes. Toronto: University of Toronto Press, 1991.

The Rule of Metaphor: Multi-Disciplinary Studies of the Creation of Meaning in Language. Translated by Robert Czerny with Kathleen McLaughlin and John Costello. Toronto: University of Toronto Press, 1977.

The Symbolism of Evil. Translated by Emerson Buchanan. Boston: Beacon Press, 1969.

Time and Narrative, 3 vols. Translated by Kathleen McLaughlin and David Pellauer. Chicago: University of Chicago Press, 1984–8.

Part III

Political Thought: Marxism and Critical Theory

Georg Wilhelm Friedrich Hegel

Following the analysis of the self-unfolding of consciousness in the *Phenomenology of Spirit*, Hegel in *The Philosophy of Right* (first published in 1821) investigates the unfolding of the concept of right from abstract freedom into concrete structures of civil society and the state. *The Philosophy of Right*, a key text of modern political philosophy, therefore contains a discussion of ethics, morality, law, politics, and history. Hegel argues that the very concept of right gives rise dialectically to the notions of property, contract, wrong, and ultimately morality. However, he also argues that such structures do not actually exist apart from family, civil society, and the state, and the bulk of the text deals with these latter, more concrete structures. In the excerpts that follow, Hegel shows how the contradictions in civil society – generated by the drive to maximize production and consumption, and by the ensuing competition between members of society with innately different skills and talents – lead to systemic poverty. The estate, the corporation, and ultimately the state provide a resolution of these contradictions by providing the context within which both the particular needs of individuals and the universal needs of society as a whole can find satisfaction.

The Philosophy of Right

Civil Society

The system of needs

The nature of needs and their satisfaction

§ 190

The ways and means by which the *animal* can satisfy its needs are limited in scope, and its needs are likewise limited. Though sharing this dependence, the *human being* is at the same time able to transcend it and to show his universality, first by *multiplying* his needs and means [of satisfying them], and secondly by *dividing* and *differentiating* the concrete need into individual parts and aspects which then become different needs, *particularized* and hence *more abstract*....

§ 191

In the same way, the *means* employed by particularized needs, and in general the ways in which these are satisfied, are *divided* and *multiplied* so that they in turn become relative ends and abstract needs. It is an infinite process of multiplication which is in equal measure a *differentiation* of these determinations and a *judgment* on the suitability of the means to their ends – i.e. [a process of] *refinement*.

Addition (H).[1] What the English call "comfortable" is something utterly inexhaustible; its ramifications are infinite, for every comfort in turn reveals its less comfortable side, and the resulting inventions are endless. A need is therefore created not so much by those who experience it directly as by those who seek to profit from its emergence.

§ 192

Needs and means, as existing in reality, become a *being* for *others* by whose needs and work their

From *Elements of the Philosophy of Right*, edited by Allen W. Wood and translated by H. B. Nisbet (Cambridge: Cambridge University Press, 1991), pp. 228–348. © Cambridge University Press, 1991. Reprinted with the permission of Cambridge University Press.

satisfaction is mutually conditioned. That abstraction which becomes a quality of both needs and means (see § 191) also becomes a determination of the mutual relations between individuals. This universality, as the *quality of being recognized*, is the moment which makes isolated and abstract needs, means, and modes of satisfaction into *concrete*, i.e. *social* ones.

Addition (H). The fact that I have to fit in with other people brings the form of universality into play at this point. I acquire my means of satisfaction from others and must accordingly accept their opinions. But at the same time, I am compelled to produce means whereby others can be satisfied. Thus, the one plays into the hands of the other and is connected with it....

§ 193

This moment thus becomes a particular end-determinant for the means themselves and their ownership, and also for the way in which needs are satisfied. In addition, it immediately involves the requirement of *equality* in this respect with others. On the one hand, the need for this equality, together with *imitation* as the process whereby people make themselves like others, and on the other hand the need of *particularity* (which is likewise present here) to assert itself through some distinctive quality, themselves become an actual source of the multiplication and expansion of needs....

§ 195

... The tendency of the social condition towards an indeterminate multiplication and specification of needs, means, and pleasures – i.e. *luxury* – a tendency which, like the distinction between natural and educated needs, has no limits, involves an equally infinite increase in dependence and want. These are confronted with a material which offers infinite resistance, i.e. with external means whose particular character is that they are the property of the free will [of others] and are therefore absolutely unyielding....

The nature of work

§ 196

The mediation whereby appropriate and *particularized* means are acquired and prepared for similarly *particularized* needs is *work*. By the most diverse processes, work specifically applies to these numerous ends the material which is immediately provided by nature. This process of formation gives the means their value and appropriateness, so that man, as a consumer, is chiefly concerned with *human* products, and it is human effort which he consumes.

Addition (H). There are few immediate materials which do not need to be processed: even air has to be earned – inasmuch as it has to be heated – and perhaps water is unique in that it can be drunk as it is found. It is by the sweat and labor of human beings that man obtains the means to satisfy his needs.

§ 197

The variety of determinations and objects which are worthy of interest is the basis from which *theoretical education* develops. This involves not only a variety of representations and items of knowledge but also an ability to form such representations and pass from one to the other in a rapid and versatile manner, to grasp complex and general relations, etc. – it is the education of the understanding in general, and therefore also includes language. – *Practical education* through work consists in the self-perpetuating need and *habit of being occupied* in one way or another, in the *limitation of one's activity* to suit both the nature of the material in question and, in particular, the arbitrary will of others, and in a habit, acquired through this discipline, of *objective* activity and *universally applicable* skills. . . .

§ 198

The universal and objective aspect of work consists, however, in that [process of] *abstraction* which confers a specific character on means and needs and hence also on production, so giving rise to the *division of labor*. Through this division, the work of the individual becomes *simpler*, so that his skill at his abstract work becomes greater, as does the volume of his output. At the same time, this abstraction of skill and means makes the *dependence* and *reciprocity* of human beings in the satisfaction of their other needs complete and entirely neces-

sary. Furthermore, the abstraction of production makes work increasingly *mechanical*, so that the human being is eventually able to step aside and let a *machine* take his place.

Resources [and estates]

§ 199

In this dependence and reciprocity of work and the satisfaction of needs, *subjective selfishness* turns into a *contribution towards the satisfaction of the needs of everyone else*. By a dialectical movement, the particular is mediated by the universal so that each individual, in earning, producing, and enjoying on his own account thereby earns and produces for the enjoyment of others. This necessity which is inherent in the interlinked dependence of each on all now appears to each individual in the form of *universal and permanent resources* in which, through his education and skill, he has an opportunity to share; he is thereby assured of his livelihood, just as the universal resources are maintained and augmented by the income which he earns through his work.

§ 200

The *possibility of sharing* in the universal resources – i.e. of holding *particular* resources – is, however, *conditional* upon one's own immediate basic assets (i.e. capital) on the one hand, and upon one's skill on the other; the latter in turn is itself conditioned by the former, but also by contingent circumstances whose variety gives rise to *differences* in the *development* of natural physical and mental aptitudes which are already unequal in themselves. In this sphere of particularity, these differences manifest themselves in every direction and at every level, and, in conjunction with other contingent and arbitrary circumstances, necessarily result in *inequalities in the resources and skills* of individuals. . . .

§ 201

The infinitely varied means and their equally infinite and intertwined movements of reciprocal production and exchange *converge*, by virtue of the universality inherent in their content, and become *differentiated* into *universal masses*. In consequence, the whole complex evolves into *particular systems* of needs, with their corresponding means, varieties of work, modes of satisfaction, and theoretical and practical education – into systems to which individuals are separately assigned, i.e. into different *estates*. . . .

The police and the corporation

§ 230

In the *system of needs*, the livelihood and welfare of each individual are a *possibility* whose actualization is conditioned by the individual's own arbitrary will and particular nature, as well as by the objective system of needs. Through the administration of justice, *infringements* of property or personality are annulled. But the right *which is actually present in particularity* means not only that *contingencies* which interfere with this or that end should be *cancelled* and that the *undisturbed security* of *persons* and *property* should be guaranteed, but also that the livelihood and welfare of individuals should be *secured* – i.e. that *particular welfare* should be *treated as a right* and duly *actualized*.

The police[2]

§ 235

In the indeterminate multiplication and interdependence of daily needs, the *procurement* and *exchange of means* to satisfy these (a process on whose unimpeded continuance everyone relies) and the need to make the requisite inquiries and negotiations as short as possible give rise to aspects of common interest in which the business *of one* is at the same time carried out on behalf of *all*; they also give rise to means and arrangements which may be of use to the community. These *universal functions* and arrangements *of public utility* require oversight and advance provision on the part of the public authority.

§ 236

The differing interests of producers and consumers may come into collision with each other, and even if, *on the whole*, their correct relationship re-establishes itself automatically, its adjustment also needs to be consciously regulated by an agency which stands above both sides. The right to regulate individual matters in this way (e.g. by deciding the value of the commonest necessities of life) is based on the fact that, when commodities in completely universal everyday use are publicly marketed, they are offered not so much to a particular individual as such, as to the individual in a universal sense, i.e. to the public; and the task of upholding the public's right not to be cheated and of inspecting market commodities may, as a common concern, be entrusted to a public authority. – But the main reason why some universal provision and direction are necessary is that large branches of industry are dependent on external circumstances and remote combinations whose full implications cannot be grasped by the individuals who are tied to these spheres by their occupation.

At the opposite extreme to freedom of trade and commerce in civil society are public arrangements to provide for and determine the work of everyone. These included, for example, the building of the pyramids in ancient times, and other enormous works in Egypt and Asia which were undertaken for public ends, and in which the work of the individual was not mediated by his particular arbitrary will and particular interest. This interest invokes the freedom of trade and commerce against regulation from above; but the more blindly it immerses itself in its selfish ends, the more it requires such regulation to bring it back to the universal, and to moderate and shorten the duration of those dangerous convulsions to which its collisions give rise, and which should return to equilibrium by a process of unconscious necessity.

Addition (H). The aim of oversight and provisions on the part of the police is to mediate between the individual and the universal possibility which is available for the attainment of individual ends. The police should provide for street-lighting, bridge-building, the pricing of daily necessities, and public health. Two main views are prevalent on this subject. One maintains that the police should have oversight over everything, and the other maintains that the police should have no say in such matters, since everyone will be guided in his actions by the needs of others. The individual must certainly have a right to earn his living in this way or that; but on the other hand, the public also has a right to expect that necessary tasks will be performed in the proper manner. Both viewpoints must be satisfied, and the freedom of trade should not be such as to prejudice the general good.

§ 237

Now even if the possibility exists for individuals to share in the universal resources, and even if this possibility is guaranteed by the public authority, it remains – apart from the fact that such a guarantee must always be incomplete – open to contingencies of a subjective kind. This is increasingly the case the more it takes such conditions as skill, health, capital, etc. for granted.

§ 238

Initially, the family is the substantial whole whose task it is to provide for this particular aspect of the individual, both by giving him the means and skills he requires in order to earn his living from the universal resources, and by supplying his livelihood and maintenance in the event of his incapacity to look after himself. But civil society tears the individual away from family ties, alienates the members of the family from one another, and recognizes them as self-sufficient persons. Furthermore, it substitutes its own soil for the external inorganic nature and paternal soil from which the individual gained his livelihood, and subjects the existence of the whole family itself to dependence on civil society and to contingency. Thus, the individual becomes a *son of civil society*, which has as many claims upon him as he has rights in relation to it.

Addition (H). Admittedly, the family must provide food for its individual members, but in civil society, the family is subordinate and merely lays the foundations; its effectiveness is no longer so comprehensive. Civil society, on the other hand, is the immense power which draws people to itself and requires them to work for it, to owe everything to it, and to do everything by its means. Thus, if a human being is to be a member of civil society, he has rights and claims in relation to it, just as he had in relation to his family. Civil society must protect its members and defend their rights, just as the individual owes a duty to the rights of civil society.

§ 239

In this character as a *universal family*, civil society has the duty and right, in the face of *arbitrariness* and contingency on the part of *the parents*, to supervise and influence the *education* of children insofar as this has a bearing on their capacity to become members of society, and particularly if this education is to be completed not by the parents themselves, but by others. Insofar as communal arrangements can be made for this purpose, it is likewise incumbent upon civil society to make them....

§ 240

In the same way, society has the duty and right to act as guardian on behalf of those who destroy the security of their own and their family's livelihood by their extravagance, and to implement their end and that of society in their place.

Addition (G). In Athens, the law obliged every citizen to give an account of his means of support; the view nowadays is that this is a purely private matter. On the one hand, it is true that every individual has an independent existence; but on the other, the individual is also a member of the system of civil society, and just as every human being has a right to demand a livelihood from society, so also must society protect him against himself. It is not just starvation which is at stake here; the wider viewpoint is the need to prevent a rabble from emerging. Since civil society is obliged to feed its members, it also has the right to urge them to provide for their own livelihood.

§ 241

Not only arbitrariness, however, but also contingent physical factors and circumstances based on external conditions (see § 200) may reduce individuals to *poverty*. In this condition, they are left with the needs of civil society and yet – since society has at the same time taken from them the natural means of acquisition, and also dissolves the bond of the family in its wider sense as a kinship group – they are more or less deprived of all the advantages of society, such as the ability to acquire skills and education in general, as well as of the administration of justice, health care, and often even of the consolation of religion. For the *poor*, the universal authority takes over the role of the family with regard not only to their immediate deficiencies, but also to the disposition of laziness, viciousness, and the other vices to which their predicament and sense of wrong give rise....

§243

When the activity of civil society is unrestricted, it is occupied internally with *expanding its population and industry*. – On the one hand, as the association of human beings through their needs is *universalized*, and with it the ways in which means of satisfying these needs are devised and made available, the *accumulation of wealth* increases; for the greatest profit is derived from this twofold universality. But on the other hand, the *specialization* and *limitation* of particular work also increase, as do likewise the *dependence* and *want* of the class which is tied to such work; this in turn leads to an inability to feel and enjoy the wider freedoms, and particularly the spiritual advantages, of civil society.

§244

When a large mass of people sinks below the level of a certain standard of living – which automatically regulates itself at the level necessary for a member of the society in question – that feeling of right, integrity, and honor which comes from supporting oneself by one's own activity and work is lost. This leads to the creation of a *rabble*, which in turn makes it much easier for disproportionate wealth to be concentrated in a few hands.

Addition (G) ... Poverty in itself does not reduce people to a rabble; a rabble is created only by the disposition associated with poverty, by inward rebellion against the rich, against society, the government, etc. It also follows that those who are dependent on contingency become frivolous and lazy, like the *lazzaroni* of Naples, for example. This in turn gives rise to the evil that the rabble do not have sufficient honor to gain their livelihood through their own work, yet claim that they have a right to receive their livelihood. No one can assert a right against nature, but within the conditions of society hardship at once assumes the form of a wrong inflicted on this or that class. The important question of how poverty can be remedied is one which agitates and torments modern societies especially.

§245

If the direct burden [of support] were to fall on the wealthier class, or if direct means were available in other public institutions (such as wealthy hospitals, foundations, or monasteries) to maintain the increasingly impoverished mass at its normal standard of living, the livelihood of the needy would be ensured without the mediation of work; this would be contrary to the principle of civil society and the feeling of self-sufficiency and honor among its individual members. Alternatively, their livelihood might be mediated by work (i.e. by the opportunity to work) which would increase the volume of production; but it is precisely in overproduction and the lack of a proportionate number of consumers who are themselves productive that the evil consists, and this is merely exacerbated by the two expedients in question. This shows that, despite an *excess of wealth*, civil society is *not wealthy enough* – i.e. its own distinct resources are not sufficient – to prevent an excess of poverty and the formation of a rabble.

The example of *England* permits us to study these phenomena on a large scale, especially the results achieved by poor-rates, boundless donations, and equally limitless private charity, and above all by the abolition of the corporations. There (especially in Scotland), it has emerged that the most direct means of dealing with poverty, and particularly with the renunciation of shame and honor as the subjective bases of society and with the laziness and extravagance which give rise to a rabble, is to leave the poor to their fate and direct them to beg from the public.

§246

This inner dialectic of society drives it – or in the first instance *this specific society* – to go beyond its own confines and look for consumers, and hence the means it requires for subsistence, in other nations which lack those means of which it has a surplus or which generally lag behind it in creativity, etc. . . .

§248

This extended link also supplies the means necessary for *colonization* – whether sporadic or systematic – to which the fully developed civil society is driven, and by which it provides part of its population with a return to the family principle in a new country, and itself with a new market and sphere of industrial activity.

Addition (G). Civil society is driven to establish colonies. The increase of population alone has this effect; but a particular factor is the emergence of a mass of people who cannot gain satisfaction for their needs by their work when production exceeds the needs of consumers. Sporadic colonization is found particularly in Germany. The colonists move to America or Russia and retain no links with their home country, to which they are consequently of no service. The second variety of colonization, quite different from the first, is systematic. It is initiated by the state, which is aware of the proper way of carrying it out and regulates it accordingly. This mode of colonization was frequently employed by the ancients, especially the Greeks. Hard work was not the concern of the Greek citizen, whose activity was directed rather towards public affairs. Accordingly, whenever the population grew to a point at which it could become difficult to provide for it, the young people were sent off to a new region, which was either specifically chosen or left to be discovered by chance. In more recent times, colonies have not been granted the same rights as the inhabitants of the mother country, and this situation has resulted in wars and eventual independence as the history of the English and Spanish colonies shows. The liberation of colonies itself proves to be of the greatest advantage to the mother state, just as the emancipation of slaves is of the greatest advantage to the master....

The corporation

§251

The work performed by civil society is divided into different branches according to its particular nature. Since the inherent likeness of such particulars, as the quality *common* to them all, comes into existence in the *association*, the *selfish* end which pursues its own particular interest comprehends and expresses itself at the same time as a universal end; and the member of civil society, in accordance with his *particular skill*, is a member of a corporation whose universal end is therefore wholly *concrete*, and no wider in scope than the end inherent in the trade which is the corporation's proper business and interest.

§252

By this definition, the corporation has the right, under the supervision of the public authority, to look after its own interests within its enclosed sphere, to admit members in accordance with their objective qualification of skill and rectitude and in numbers determined by the universal context, to protect its members against particular contingencies, and to educate others so as to make them eligible for membership. In short, it has the right to assume the role of a *second* family for its members, a role which must remain more indeterminate in the case of civil society in general, which is more remote from individuals and their particular requirements....

§253

In the corporation, the family not only *has* its firm basis in that its livelihood is *guaranteed* – i.e. it has secure *resources* – on condition of its [possessing a certain] *capability*, but the two [i.e. livelihood and capability] are also *recognized*, so that the member of a corporation has no need to demonstrate his competence and his regular income and means of support – i.e. the fact that he *is somebody* – by any

further *external evidence*. In this way, it is also recognized that he belongs to a whole which is itself a member of society in general, and that he has an interest in, and endeavors to promote, the less selfish end of this whole. Thus, he has *his honor in his estate*....

If the individual is not a member of a legally recognized corporation (and it is only through legal recognition that a community becomes a corporation), he is without the *honor of belonging to an estate*, his isolation reduces him to the selfish aspect of his trade, and his livelihood and satisfaction lack *stability*. He will accordingly try to gain *recognition* through the external manifestations of success in his trade, and these are without limit, because it is impossible for him to live in a way appropriate to his estate if his estate does not exist; for a community can *exist* in civil society only if it is legally constituted and recognized. Hence no way of life of a more general kind appropriate to such an estate can be devised. – Within the corporation, the help which poverty receives loses its contingent and unjustly humiliating character, and wealth, in fulfilling the duty it owes to its association, loses the ability to provoke arrogance in its possessor and envy in others; rectitude also receives the true recognition and honor which are due to it.

§254

In the corporation, the so-called *natural right* to practice one's skill and thereby earn what there is to earn is limited only to the extent that, in this context, the skill is rationally determined. That is, it is freed from personal opinion and contingency, from its danger to oneself and others, and is recognized, guaranteed, and at the same time raised to a conscious activity for a common end.

§255

...*Addition* (H). When the corporations were abolished in recent times, it was with the intention that the individual should look after himself. But even if we accept this, the corporation does not affect the individual's obligation to earn his living. In our modern states, the citizens have only a limited share in the universal business of the state; but it is necessary to provide ethical man with a universal activity in addition to his private end. This universal [activity], which the modern state does not always offer him, can be found in the corporation. We saw earlier that, in providing for himself, the individual in civil society is also acting for others. But this unconscious necessity is not enough; only in the corporation does it become a knowing and thinking [part of] ethical life. The corporation, of course, must come under the higher supervision of the state, for it would otherwise become ossified and set in its ways, and decline into a miserable guild system. But the corporation in and for itself is not an enclosed guild; it is rather a means of giving the isolated trade an ethical status, and of admitting it to a circle in which it gains strength and honor. . . .

The State

§257

The state is the actuality of the ethical Idea – the ethical spirit as substantial will, *manifest* and clear to itself, which thinks and knows itself and implements what it knows insofar as it knows it. It has its immediate existence in *custom* and its mediate existence in the *self-consciousness* of the individual, in the individual's knowledge and activity, just as self-consciousness, by virtue of its disposition, has its *substantial freedom* in the state as its essence, its end, and the product of its activity. . . .

Constitutional law

§260

The state is the actuality of concrete freedom. But *concrete freedom* requires that personal individuality and its particular interests should reach their full *development* and gain *recognition of their right* for itself (within the system of the family and of civil society), and also that they should, on the one hand, *pass over* of their own accord into the interest of the universal, and on the other, knowingly and willingly acknowledge this universal interest even as their own *substantial spirit*, and *actively pursue it* as their *ultimate end*. The effect of this is that the universal does not attain validity or fulfillment without the interest, knowledge, and volition of the particular, and that individuals do not live as private persons merely for these particular interests without at the same time directing their will to a universal end and acting in conscious awareness of this end. The principle of modern states has enormous strength and depth because it allows the principle of subjectivity to attain fulfillment in the *self-sufficient extreme* of personal particularity, while at the same time *bringing it back to substantial unity* and so preserving this unity in the principle of subjectivity itself.

Addition (H, G). The Idea of the state in modern times has the distinctive characteristic that the state is the actualization of freedom not in accordance with subjective caprice, but in accordance with the concept of the will, i.e. in accordance with its universality and divinity. Imperfect states are those in which the Idea of the state is still invisible and where the particular determinations of this Idea have not yet reached free self-sufficiency. In the states of classical antiquity, universality was indeed already present, but particularity had not yet been released and set at liberty and brought back to universality, i.e. to the universal end of the whole. The essence of the modern state is that the universal should be linked with the complete freedom of particularity and the well-being of individuals, and hence that the interest of the family and of civil society must become focused on the state; but the universality of the end cannot make further progress without the personal knowledge and volition of the particular individuals who must retain their rights. Thus, the universal must be activated, but subjectivity on the other hand must be developed as a living whole. Only when both moments are present in full measure can the state be regarded as articulated and truly organized. . . .

§265

. . . *Addition* (G). It has already been noted that the sanctity of marriage and the institutions in which civil society takes on an ethical appearance constitute the stability of the whole – that is, the universal is simultaneously the concern of each [individual] as a particular [entity]. What matters most is that the law of reason should merge with the law of particular freedom, and that my particular end should become identical with the universal; otherwise, the state must hang in the air. It is the self-awareness of individuals which constitutes the actuality of the state, and its stability consists in the identity of the two aspects in question. It has often been said that the end of the state is the happiness of its citizens. This is certainly true, for if their welfare is deficient, if their subjective ends are not satisfied, and if they do not find that the state as such is the means to this satisfaction, the state itself stands on an insecure footing. . . .

§268

The political *disposition*, i.e. *patriotism* in general, is certainty based on *truth* (whereas merely subjective certainty does not originate in *truth*, but is only opinion) and a volition which has become *habitual*.

As such, it is merely a consequence of the institutions within the state, a consequence in which rationality is *actually* present, just as rationality receives its practical application through action in conformity with the state's institutions. – This disposition is in general one of *trust* (which may pass over into more or less educated insight), or the consciousness that my substantial and particular interest is preserved and contained in the interest and end of an other (in this case, the state), and in the latter's relation to me as an individual. As a result, this other immediately ceases to be an other for me, and in my consciousness of this, I am free.

Patriotism is frequently understood to mean only a willingness to perform *extraordinary* sacrifices and actions. But in essence, it is that disposition which, in the normal conditions and circumstances of life, habitually knows that the community is the substantial basis and end. It is this same consciousness, tried and tested in all circumstances of ordinary life, which underlies the willingness to make extraordinary efforts. But just as human beings often prefer to be guided by magnanimity instead of by right, so also do they readily convince themselves that they possess this extraordinary patriotism in order to exempt themselves from the genuine disposition, or to excuse their lack of it. – Furthermore, if we take this *disposition* to be something which can originate independently and arise out of subjective representations and thoughts, we are confusing it with opinion; for in this interpretation, it is deprived of its true ground, i.e. objective reality.

Addition (H). Uneducated people delight in argument and fault-finding, for it is easy to find fault, but difficult to recognize the good and its inner necessity. Education in its early stages always begins with fault-finding, but when it is complete, it sees the positive element in everything. In religion, it is equally easy to say that this or that is superstition, but it is infinitely more difficult to comprehend the truth which it contains. Thus people's apparent political disposition should be distinguished from what they genuinely will; for inwardly, they in fact will the thing, but they fasten on to details and delight in the vanity of claiming superior insight. They trust that the state will continue to exist and that particular interests can be fulfilled within it alone; but habit blinds us to the basis of our entire existence. It does not occur

to someone who walks the streets in safety at night that this might be otherwise, for this habit of [living in] safety has become second nature, and we scarcely stop to think that it is solely the effect of particular institutions. Representational thought often imagines that the state is held together by force; but what holds it together is simply the basic sense of order which everyone possesses. . . .

The legislative power

§308

. . . The idea that *all* individuals ought to participate in deliberations and decisions on the universal concerns of the state – on the grounds that they are all members of the state and that the concerns of the state are the concerns of *everyone*, so that everyone has a *right* to share in them with his own knowledge and volition – seeks to implant in the organism of the state a *democratic* element *devoid of rational form*, although it is only by virtue of its rational form that the state is an organism. This idea appears plausible precisely because it stops short at the *abstract* determination of membership of the state and because superficial thinking sticks to abstractions. Rational deliberation or the consciousness of the Idea is *concrete*, and it coincides to that extent with true *practical* sense, which is itself nothing other than rational sense or the sense of the Idea; it must not, however, be confused with the mere routine of business and the horizon of a limited sphere. The concrete state is *the whole, articulated into its particular circles*. Each member of the state is a *member* of an *estate* of this kind, and only in this objective determination can he be considered in relation to the state. His universal determination in general includes two moments, for he is a *private person* and at the same time a *thinking* being with consciousness and volition of the *universal*. But this consciousness and volition remain empty and lack *fulfillment* and actual *life* until they are filled with particularity, and this is [to be found in] a particular estate and determination. Otherwise, the individual remains a *generic category*, but only within the *next* generic category does he attain his *immanent* universal *actuality*. – Consequently, it is within the sphere of his corporation, community, etc. (see § 251) that the individual first attains his actual and living determination as *universal*, and it remains open to him to enter any sphere, including the universal estate, for which his aptitude qualifies him. The idea that *everyone* should participate in the concerns of the state entails the further assumption that *everyone is an expert on such matters*; this is also absurd, notwithstanding the frequency with which we hear it asserted. In public opinion, however, the way is open for everyone to express and give effect to his subjective opinions on the universal.

Notes

1 The book from which this excerpt is taken comprises Hegel's main text of the *Philosophy of Right*, which is made up of numbered sections; elucidatory "Remarks" (indented); and "Additions" compiled from the lecture notes of his students, K. G. von Griesheim (hence these additions are preceded by a "G") and H. G. Hotho (preceded by an "H"). (Eds)

2 What Hegel here calls the "police" are not primarily the keepers of law and order so much as the authorities that see to the public good. (Eds)

2

Karl Marx and Friedrich Engels

The collaboration of Karl Marx (1818–83) and Friedrich Engels (1820–95) resulted in the revolutionary philosophy known as Marxism, which synthesizes analyses of history, economics, and politics into a broad theory of the evolution of society and anticipates the overcoming of capitalism and eventual establishment of a communist society according to the famous dictum, "from each according to his ability, to each according to his needs!" ("Critique of the Gotha Programme," 1875). Marx began as a student of law, subsequently transferring to study philosophy at the University of Berlin, where he was influenced by the Young Hegelian movement. In 1844 he met Friedrich Engels in Paris, and together they wrote *The German Ideology* and (in 1848) *The Communist Manifesto*. Marx and Engels claimed to invert Hegel by interpreting the dialectic of history in a materialist (rather than idealist) fashion, ascribing concrete historical developments to material, rather than ideal forces. In "Alienated Labor" (from the *Economic and Philosophical Manuscripts of 1844*) Marx describes in detail the ways in which the capitalist organization of labor results in the alienation of workers. The selections from *The German Ideology* (written in 1845–6 and published in 1932) summarize Marx's and Engels' materialist view of history.

Alienated Labor

...So what we have to understand now is the essential connection of private property, selfishness, the separation of labor, capital, and landed property, of exchange and competition, of the value and degradation of man, of monopoly and competition, etc. – the connection of all this alienation with the money system.

From "Alienated Labour," in *Karl Marx: Selected Writings*, edited by David McLellan (Oxford: Oxford University Press, 1985), pp. 77–87.

Let us not be like the political economist who, when he wishes to explain something, puts himself in an imaginary original state of affairs. Such an original state of affairs explains nothing. He simply pushes the question back into a gray and nebulous distance. He presupposes as a fact and an event what he ought to be deducing, namely the necessary connection between the two things, for example, between the division of labor and exchange. Similarly, the theologian explains the origin of evil through the fall, i.e. he presupposes as an historical fact what he should be explaining.

We start with a contemporary fact of political economy:

The worker becomes poorer the richer is his production, the more it increases in power and scope. The worker becomes a commodity that is all the cheaper the more commodities he creates. The depreciation of the human world progresses in direct proportion to the increase in value of the world of things. Labor does not only produce commodities; it produces itself and the laborer as a commodity and that to the extent to which it produces commodities in general.

What this fact expresses is merely this: the object that labor produces, its product, confronts it as an alien being, as a power independent of the producer. The product of labor is labor that has solidified itself into an object, made itself into a thing, the objectification of labor. The realization of labor is its objectification. In political economy this realization of labor appears as a loss of reality for the worker, objectification as a loss of the object or slavery to it, and appropriation as alienation, as externalization.

The realization of labor appears as a loss of reality to an extent that the worker loses his reality by dying of starvation. Objectification appears as a loss of the object to such an extent that the worker is robbed not only of the objects necessary for his life but also of the objects of his work. Indeed, labor itself becomes an object he can only have in his power with the greatest of efforts and at irregular intervals. The appropriation of the object appears as alienation to such an extent that the more objects the worker produces, the less he can possess and the more he falls under the domination of his product, capital.

All these consequences follow from the fact that the worker relates to the product of his labor as to an alien object. For it is evident from this presupposition that the more the worker externalizes himself in his work, the more powerful becomes the alien, objective world that he creates opposite himself, the poorer he becomes himself in his inner life and the less he can call his own. It is just the same in religion. The more man puts into God, the less he retains in himself. The worker puts his life into the object and this means that it no longer belongs to him but to the object. So the greater this activity, the more the worker is without an object. What the product of his labor is, that he is not. So the greater this product the less he is himself. The externaliza-

tion of the worker in his product implies not only that his labor becomes an object, an exterior existence but also that it exists outside him, independent and alien, and becomes a self-sufficient power opposite him, that the life that he has lent to the object affronts him, hostile and alien.

Let us now deal in more detail with objectification, the production of the worker, and the alienation, the loss of the object, his product, which is involved in it.

The worker can create nothing without nature, the sensuous exterior world. It is the matter in which his labor realizes itself, in which it is active, out of which and through which it produces.

But as nature affords the means of life for labor in the sense that labor cannot live without objects on which it exercises itself, so it affords a means of life in the narrower sense, namely the means for the physical subsistence of the worker himself.

Thus the more the worker appropriates the exterior world of sensuous nature by his labor, the more he doubly deprives himself of the means of subsistence, firstly since the exterior sensuous world increasingly ceases to be an object belonging to his work, a means of subsistence for his labor; secondly, since it increasingly ceases to be a means of subsistence in the direct sense, a means for the physical subsistence of the worker.

Thus in these two ways the worker becomes a slave to his object: firstly he receives an object of labor, that is he receives labor, and secondly, he receives the means of subsistence. Thus it is his object that permits him to exist first as a worker and secondly as a physical subject. The climax of this slavery is that only as a worker can he maintain himself as a physical subject and it is only as a physical subject that he is a worker.

(According to the laws of political economy the alienation of the worker in his object is expressed as follows: the more the worker produces the less he has to consume, the more values he creates the more valueless and worthless he becomes, the more formed the product the more deformed the worker, the more civilized the product, the more barbaric the worker, the more powerful the work the more powerless becomes the worker, the more cultured the work the more philistine the worker becomes and more of a slave to nature.)

Political economy hides the alienation in the essence of labor by not considering the immediate relationship between the worker (labor) and production. Labor produces works of wonder for the rich, but nakedness for the worker. It produces palaces, but only hovels for the worker; it produces beauty, but cripples the worker; it replaces labor by machines but throws a part of the workers back to a barbaric labor and turns the other part into machines. It produces culture, but also imbecility and cretinism for the worker.

The immediate relationship of labor to its products is the relationship of the worker to the objects of his production. The relationship of the man of means to the objects of production and to production itself is only a consequence of this first relationship. And it confirms it. We shall examine this other aspect later.

So when we ask the question: what relationship is essential to labor, we are asking about the relationship of the worker to production.

Up to now we have considered only one aspect of the alienation or externalization of the worker, his relationship to the products of his labor. But alienation shows itself not only in the result; but also in the act of production, inside productive activity itself. How would the worker be able to affront the product of his work as an alien being if he did not alienate himself in the act of production itself? For the product is merely the summary of the activity of production. So if the product of labor is externalization, production itself must be active externalization, the externalization of activity, the activity of externalization. The alienation of the object of labor is only the résumé of the alienation, the externalization in the activity of labor itself.

What does the externalization of labor consist of then?

Firstly, that labor is exterior to the worker, that is, it does not belong to his essence. Therefore he does not confirm himself in his work, he denies himself, feels miserable instead of happy, deploys no free physical and intellectual energy, but mortifies his body and ruins his mind. Thus the worker only feels a stranger. He is at home when he is not working and when he works he is not at home. His labor is therefore not voluntary but compulsory, forced labor. It is therefore not the satisfaction of a need but only a means to satisfy needs outside itself. How alien it really is is very evident from the fact that when there is no physical or other compulsion, labor is avoided like the plague. External labor, labor in which man externalizes himself, is a labor of self-sacrifice and mortification. Finally, the external character of labor for the worker shows itself in the fact that it is not his own but someone else's, that it does not belong to him, that he does not belong to himself in his labor

but to someone else. As in religion the human imagination's own activity, the activity of man's head and his heart, reacts independently on the individual as an alien activity of gods or devils, so the activity of the worker is not his own spontaneous activity. It belongs to another and is the loss of himself.

The result we arrive at then is that man (the worker) only feels himself freely active in his animal functions of eating, drinking, and procreating, at most also in his dwelling and dress, and feels himself an animal in his human functions.

Eating, drinking, procreating, etc. are indeed truly human functions. But in the abstraction that separates them from the other round of human activity and makes them into final and exclusive ends they become animal.

We have treated the act of alienation of practical human activity, labor, from two aspects. (1) The relationship of the worker to the product of his labor as an alien object that has power over him. This relationship is at the same time the relationship to the sensuous exterior world and to natural objects as to an alien and hostile world opposed to him. (2) The relationship of labor to the act of production inside labor. This relationship is the relationship of the worker to his own activity as something that is alien and does not belong to him; it is activity that is passivity, power that is weakness, procreation that is castration, the worker's own physical and intellectual energy, his personal life (for what is life except activity?) as an activity directed against himself, independent of him and not belonging to him. It is self-alienation, as above it was the alienation of the object.

We now have to draw a third characteristic of alienated labor from the two previous ones.

Man is a species-being not only in that practically and theoretically he makes both his own and other species into his objects, but also, and this is only another way of putting the same thing, he relates to himself as to the present, living species, in that he relates to himself as to a universal and therefore free being.

Both with man and with animals the species-life consists physically in the fact that man (like animals) lives from inorganic nature, and the more universal man is than animals the more universal is the area of inorganic nature from which he lives. From the theoretical point of view, plants, animals, stones, air, light, etc. form part of human consciousness, partly as objects of natural science, partly as objects of art; they are his intellectual inorganic nature, his intellectual means of subsistence, which he must first prepare before he can enjoy and assimilate them. From the practical point of view, too, they form a part of human life and activity. Physically man lives solely from these products of nature, whether they appear as food, heating, clothing, habitation, etc. The universality of man appears in practice precisely in the universality that makes the whole of nature into his inorganic body in that it is both (i) his immediate means of subsistence and also (ii) the material object and tool of his vital activity. Nature is the inorganic body of a man, that is, insofar as it is not itself a human body. That man lives from nature means that nature is his body with which he must maintain a constant interchange so as not to die. That man's physical and intellectual life depends on nature merely means that nature depends on itself, for man is a part of nature.

While alienated labor alienates (1) nature from man, and (2) man from himself, his own active function, his vital activity, it also alienates the species from man; it turns his species-life into a means towards his individual life. Firstly it alienates species-life and individual life, and secondly in its abstraction it makes the latter into the aim of the former which is also conceived of in its abstract and alien form. For firstly, work, vital activity, and productive life itself appear to man only as a means to the satisfaction of a need, the need to preserve his physical existence. But productive life is species-life. It is life producing life. The whole character of a species, its generic character, is contained in its manner of vital activity, and free conscious activity is the species-characteristic of man. Life itself appears merely as a means to life.

The animal is immediately one with its vital activity. It is not distinct from it. They are identical. Man makes his vital activity itself into an object of his will and consciousness. He has a conscious vital activity. He is not immediately identical to any of his characterizations. Conscious vital activity differentiates man immediately from animal vital activity. It is this and this alone that makes man a species-being. He is only a conscious being, that is, his own life is an object to him, precisely because he is a species-being. This is the only reason for his activity being free activity. Alienated labor reverses the relationship so that, just because he is a conscious being, man makes his vital activity and essence a mere means to his existence.

The practical creation of an objective world, the working-over of inorganic nature, is the confirmation of man as a conscious species-being, that is, as a being that relates to the species as to himself and to himself as to the species. It is true that the animal, too, produces. It builds itself a nest, a dwelling, like the bee, the beaver, the ant, etc. But it only produces what it needs immediately for itself or its offspring; it produces one-sidedly whereas man produces universally; it produces only under the pressure of immediate physical need, whereas man produces freely from physical need and only truly produces when he is thus free; it produces only itself whereas man reproduces the whole of nature. Its product belongs immediately to its physical body whereas man can freely separate himself from his product. The animal only fashions things according to the standards and needs of the species it belongs to, whereas man knows how to produce according to the measure of every species and knows everywhere how to apply its inherent standard to the object; thus man also fashions things according to the laws of beauty.

Thus it is in the working over of the objective world that man first really affirms himself as a species-being. This production is his active species-life. Through it nature appears as his work and his reality. The object of work is therefore the objectification of the species-life of man; for he duplicates himself not only intellectually, in his mind, but also actively in reality and thus can look at his image in a world he has created. Therefore when alienated labor tears from man the object of his production, it also tears from him his species-life, the real objectivity of his species and turns the advantage he has over animals into a disadvantage in that his inorganic body, nature, is torn from him.

Similarly, in that alienated labor degrades man's own free activity to a means, it turns the species-life of man into a means for his physical existence.

Thus consciousness, which man derives from his species, changes itself through alienation so that species-life becomes a means for him.

Therefore alienated labor:

(3) makes the species-being of man, both nature and the intellectual faculties of his species, into a being that is alien to him, into a means for his individual existence. It alienates from man his own body, nature exterior to him, and his intellectual being, his human essence.

(4) An immediate consequence of man's alienation from the product of his work, his vital activity and his species-being, is the alienation of man from man. When man is opposed to himself, it is another

man that is opposed to him. What is valid for the relationship of a man to his work, of the product of his work and himself, is also valid for the relationship of man to other men and of their labor and the objects of their labor.

In general, the statement that man is alienated from his species–being, means that one man is alienated from another as each of them is alienated from the human essence.

The alienation of man and in general of every relationship in which man stands to himself is first realized and expressed in the relationship with which man stands to other men.

Thus in the situation of alienated labor each man measures his relationship to other men by the relationship in which he finds himself placed as a worker.

We began with a fact of political economy, the alienation of the worker and his production. We have expressed this fact in conceptual terms: alienated, externalized labor. We have analyzed this concept and thus analyzed a purely economic fact.

Let us now see further how the concept of alienated, externalized labor must express and represent itself in reality.

If the product of work is alien to me, opposes me as an alien power, whom does it belong to then?

If my own activity does not belong to me and is an alien, forced activity to whom does it belong then?

To another being than myself.

Who is this being?

The gods? Of course in the beginning of history the chief production, as for example, the building of temples etc. in Egypt, India, and Mexico was both in the service of the gods and also belonged to them. But the gods alone were never the masters of the work. And nature just as little. And what a paradox it would be if, the more man mastered nature through his work and the more the miracles of the gods were rendered superfluous by the miracles of industry, the more man had to give up his pleasure in producing and the enjoyment in his product for the sake of these powers.

The alien being to whom the labor and the product of the labor belongs, whom the labor serves and who enjoys its product, can only be man himself. If the product of labor does not belong to the worker but stands over against him as an alien power, this is only possible in that it belongs to another man apart from the worker.

If his activity torments him it must be a joy and a pleasure to someone else. This alien power above

man can be neither the gods nor nature, only man himself.

Consider further the above sentence that the relationship of man to himself first becomes objective and real to him through his relationship to other men. So if he relates to the product of his labor, his objectified labor, as to an object that is alien, hostile, powerful, and independent of him, this relationship implies that another man is the alien, hostile, powerful, and independent master of this object. If he relates to his own activity as to something unfree, it is a relationship to an activity that is under the domination, oppression, and yoke of another man.

Every self-alienation of man from himself and nature appears in the relationship in which he places himself and nature to other men distinct from himself. Therefore religious self-alienation necessarily appears in the relationship of layman to priest, or, because here we are dealing with a spiritual world, to a mediator, etc. In the practical, real world, the self-alienation can only appear through the practical, real relationship to other men. The means through which alienation makes progress are themselves practical. Through alienated labor, then, man creates not only his relationship to the object and act of production as to alien and hostile men; he creates too the relationship in which other men stand to his production and his product and the relationship in which he stands to these other men. Just as he turns his production into his own loss of reality and punishment and his own product into a loss, a product that does not belong to him, so he creates the domination of the man who does not produce over the production and the product. As he alienates his activity from himself, so he hands over to an alien person an activity that does not belong to him.

Up till now we have considered the relationship only from the side of the worker and we will later consider it from the side of the nonworker.

Thus through alienated, externalized labor the worker creates the relationship to this labor of a man who is alien to it and remains exterior to it. The relationship of the worker to his labor creates the relationship to it of the capitalist, or whatever else one wishes to call the master of the labor. Private property is thus the product, result, and necessary consequence of externalized labor, of the exterior relationship of the worker to nature and to himself.

Thus private property is the result of the analysis of the concept of externalized labor, i.e.

externalized man, alienated work, alienated life, alienated man.

We have, of course, obtained the concept of externalized labor (externalized life) from political economy as the result of the movement of private property. But it is evident from the analysis of this concept that, although private property appears to be the ground and reason for externalized labor, it is rather a consequence of it, just as the gods are originally not the cause but the effect of the aberration of the human mind, although later this relationship reverses itself.

It is only in the final culmination of the development of private property that these hidden characteristics come once more to the fore, in that firstly it is the product of externalized labor and secondly it is the means through which labor externalizes itself, the realization of this externalization....

We can therefore also see that wages and private property are identical: for wages, in which the product, the object of the labor, remunerates the labor itself, are just a necessary consequence of the alienation of labor. In the wage system the labor does not appear as the final aim but only as the servant of the wages. We will develop this later and for the moment only draw a few consequences.

An enforced raising of wages (quite apart from other difficulties, apart from the fact that, being an anomaly, it could only be maintained by force) would only mean a better payment of slaves and would not give this human meaning and worth either to the worker or to his labor....

Wages are an immediate consequence of alienated labor and alienated labor is the immediate cause of private property. Thus the disappearance of one entails also the disappearance of the other.

It is a further consequence of the relationship of alienated labor to private property that the emancipation of society from private property, etc., from slavery, is expressed in its political form by the emancipation of the workers. This is not because only their emancipation is at stake but because general human emancipation is contained in their emancipation. It is contained within it because the whole of human slavery is involved in the relationship of the worker to his product and all slave relationships are only modifications and consequences of this relationship....

The German Ideology

Preface

Hitherto men have constantly made up for themselves false conceptions about themselves, about what they are and what they ought to be. They have arranged their relationships according to their ideas of God, of normal man, etc. The phantoms of their brains have got out of their hands. They, the creators, have bowed down before their creations. Let us liberate them from the chimeras, the ideas, dogmas, imaginary beings under the yoke of which they are pining away. Let us revolt against the rule of thoughts. Let us teach men, says one, to exchange these imaginations for thoughts which correspond to the essence of man; says the second, to take up a critical attitude to them, says the third, to knock them out of their heads, and existing reality will collapse.

These innocent and childlike fancies are the kernel of the modern Young Hegelian philosophy, which not only is received by the German public with horror and awe, but is announced by our philosophic heroes with the solemn consciousness of its cataclysmic dangerousness and criminal ruthlessness. The first volume of the present publication has the aim of uncloaking these sheep, who take themselves and are taken for wolves; of showing how their bleating merely imitates in a philosophic form the conceptions of the German middle class; how the boasting of these philosophic commentators only mirrors the wretchedness of the real conditions in Germany. It is its aim to debunk and discredit the philosophic struggle with the shadows of reality, which appeals to the dreamy and muddled German nation.

Once upon a time a valiant fellow had the idea that men were drowned in water only because they

From "The German Ideology," in *Karl Marx: Selected Writings*, edited by David McLellan (Oxford: Oxford University Press, 1985) pp. 160–5, 168–71.

were possessed with the idea of gravity. If they were to knock this notion out of their heads, say by stating it to be a superstition, a religious concept, they would be sublimely proof against any danger from water. His whole life long he fought against the illusion of gravity, of whose harmful results all statistics brought him new and manifold evidence. This honest fellow was the type of the new revolutionary philosophers in Germany....

The Premisses of the Materialist Method

The premisses from which we begin are not arbitrary ones, not dogmas, but real premisses from which abstraction can only be made in the imagination. They are the real individuals, their activity and the material conditions under which they live, both those which they find already existing and those produced by their activity. These premisses can thus be verified in a purely empirical way.

The first premise of all human history is, of course, the existence of living human individuals. Thus the first fact to be established is the physical organization of these individuals and their consequent relation to the rest of nature. Of course, we cannot here go either into the actual physical nature of man, or into the natural conditions in which man finds himself – geological, oro-hydrographical, climatic, and so on. The writing of history must always set out from these natural bases and their modification in the course of history through the action of men.

Men can be distinguished from animals by consciousness, by religion, or anything else you like. They themselves begin to distinguish themselves from animals as soon as they begin to produce their means of subsistence, a step which is conditioned by their physical organization. By producing their means of subsistence men are indirectly producing their actual material life.

The way in which men produce their means of subsistence depends first of all on the nature of the actual means of subsistence they find in existence and have to reproduce. This mode of production must not be considered simply as being the production of the physical existence of the individuals. Rather it is a definite form of activity of these individuals, a definite form of expressing their life, a definite mode of life on their part. As individuals express their life, so they are. What they are, therefore, coincides with their production, both with *what* they produce and with *how* they produce.

The nature of individuals thus depends on the material conditions determining their production.

This production only makes its appearance with the increase of population. In its turn this presupposes the intercourse of individuals with one another. The form of this intercourse is again determined by production.... Not only the relation of one nation to others, but also the whole internal structure of the nation itself depends on the stage of development reached by its production and its internal and external intercourse. How far the productive forces of a nation are developed is shown most manifestly by the degree to which the division of labor has been carried. Each new productive force, insofar as it is not merely a quantitative extension of productive forces already known (for instance the bringing into cultivation of fresh land), causes a further development of the division of labor....

The various stages of development in the division of labor are just so many different forms of ownership, i.e. the existing stage in the division of labor determines also the relations of individuals to one another with reference to the material, instrument, and product of labor.

The first form of ownership is tribal ownership. It corresponds to the undeveloped stage of production, at which a people lives by hunting and fishing, by the rearing of beasts, or, in the highest stage, agriculture. In the latter case it presupposes a great mass of uncultivated stretches of land. The division of labor is at this stage still very elementary and is confined to a further extension of the natural division of labor existing in the family. The social structure is, therefore, limited to an extension of the family; patriarchal family chieftains, below them the members of the tribe, finally slaves. The slavery latent in the family only develops gradually with the increase of population, the growth of wants, and with the extension of external relations, both of war and of barter.

The second form is the ancient communal and state ownership which proceeds especially from the union of several tribes into a city by agreement or by conquest, and which is still accompanied by slavery....

The third form of ownership is feudal or estate property.... Like tribal and communal ownership, it is based again on a community; but the directly producing class standing over against it is not, as in the case of the ancient community, the slaves, but the enserfed small peasantry.... This feudal organization was, just as much as the ancient communal ownership, an association against a subjected producing class; but the form of association and the relation to the direct producers were different because of the different conditions of production.

This feudal system of landownership had its counterpart in the towns in the shape of corporative property, the feudal organization of trades. Here property consisted chiefly in the labor of each individual person.…

Thus the chief form of property during the feudal epoch consisted on the one hand of landed property with serf labor chained to it, and on the other of the labor of the individual with small capital commanding the labor of journeymen.…

The grouping of larger territories into feudal kingdoms was a necessity for the landed nobility as for the towns. The organization of the ruling class, the nobility, had, therefore, everywhere a monarch at its head.

The fact is, therefore, that definite individuals who are productively active in a definite way enter into these definite social and political relations. Empirical observation must in each separate instance bring out empirically, and without any mystification and speculation, the connection of the social and political structure with production. The social structure and the state are continually evolving out of the life-process of definite individuals, but of individuals, not as they may appear in their own or other people's imagination, but as they really are, i.e. as they operate, produce materially, and hence as they work under definite material limits, presuppositions, and conditions independent of their will.

The production of ideas, of conceptions, of consciousness, is at first directly interwoven with the material activity and the material intercourse of men, the language of real life. Conceiving, thinking, the mental intercourse of men, appear at this stage as the direct efflux of their material behavior. The same applies to mental production as expressed in the language of politics, laws, morality, religion, metaphysics, etc. of a people. Men are the producers of their conceptions, ideas, etc. – real, active men, as they are conditioned by a definite development of their productive forces and of the intercourse corresponding to these, up to its furthest forms. Consciousness can never be anything else than conscious existence, and the existence of men is their actual life-process. If in all ideology men and their circumstances appear upside-down as in a camera obscura, this phenomenon arises just as much from their historical life-process as the inversion of objects on the retina does from their physical life-process.

In direct contrast to German philosophy which descends from heaven to earth, here we ascend from earth to heaven. That is to say, we do not set out from what men say, imagine, conceive, nor from men as narrated, thought of, imagined, conceived, in order to arrive at men in the flesh. We set out from real, active men, and on the basis of their real life-process we demonstrate the development of the ideological reflexes and echoes of this life-process. The phantoms formed in the human brain are also, necessarily, sublimates of their material life-process, which is empirically verifiable and bound to material premises. Morality, religion, metaphysics, all the rest of ideology and their corresponding forms of consciousness, thus no longer retain the semblance of independence. They have no history, no development; but men, developing their material production and their material intercourse, alter, along with this their real existence, their thinking and the products of their thinking. Life is not determined by consciousness, but consciousness by life. In the first method of approach the starting point is consciousness taken as the living individual; in the second method, which conforms to real life, it is the real living individuals themselves, and consciousness is considered solely as their consciousness.

This method of approach is not devoid of premises. It starts out from the real premises and does not abandon them for a moment. Its premises are men, not in any fantastic isolation and rigidity, but in their actual, empirically perceptible process of development under definite conditions. As soon as this active life-process is described, history ceases to be a collection of dead facts as it is with the empiricists (themselves still abstract), or an imagined activity of imagined subjects, as with the idealists.

Where speculation ends – in real life – there real, positive science begins: the representation of the practical activity, of the practical process of development of men. Empty talk about consciousness ceases, and real knowledge has to take its place. When reality is depicted, philosophy as an independent branch of knowledge loses its medium of existence. At the best its place can only be taken by a summing-up of the most general results, abstractions which arise from the observation of the historical development of men. Viewed apart from real history, these abstractions have in themselves no value whatsoever. They can only serve to facilitate the arrangement of historical material, to indicate the sequence of its separate strata. But they by no means afford a recipe or schema, as does philosophy, for neatly trimming the epochs of history. On the contrary, our difficulties begin only when we set about the observation and the arrangement – the real depiction – of our historical material, whether of a past epoch or of the present. The removal of these difficulties is governed by premisses which it is quite impossible to state here, but which only the study of the actual life-process and the activity of the individuals of each epoch will make evident. . . .

Private Property and Communism

With the division of labor, in which all these contradictions are implicit, and which in its turn is based on the natural division of labor in the family and the separation of society into individual families opposed to one another, is given simultaneously the distribution, and indeed the unequal distribution, both quantitative and qualitative, of labor and its products, hence property: the nucleus, the first form of which lies in the family, where wife and children are the slaves of the husband. This latent slavery in the family, though still very crude, is the first property, but even at this early stage it corresponds perfectly to the definition of modern economists who call it the power of disposing of the labor-power of others. Division of labor and private property are, moreover, identical expressions: in the one the same thing is affirmed with reference to activity as is affirmed in the other with reference to the product of the activity.

Further, the division of labor implies the contradiction between the interest of the separate individual or the individual family and the communal interest of all individuals who have intercourse with one another. And indeed, this communal interest does not exist merely in the imagination, as the "general interest," but first of all in reality, as the mutual interdependence of the individuals among whom the labor is divided. And finally, the division of labor offers us the first example of how, as long as man remains in natural society, that is, as long as a cleavage exists between the particular and the common interest, as long, therefore, as activity is not voluntarily, but naturally, divided, man's own deed becomes an alien power opposed to

him, which enslaves him instead of being controlled by him. For as soon as the distribution of labor comes into being, each man has a particular, exclusive sphere of activity, which is forced upon him and from which he cannot escape. He is a hunter, a fisherman, a shepherd, or a critical critic, and must remain so if he does not want to lose his means of livelihood; while in communist society, where nobody was one exclusive sphere of activity but each can become accomplished in any branch he wishes, society regulates the general production and thus makes it possible for me to do one thing today and another tomorrow, to hunt in the morning, fish in the afternoon, rear cattle in the evening, criticize after dinner, just as I have a mind, without ever becoming hunter, fisherman, cowherd, or critic. This fixation of social activity, this consolidation of what we ourselves produce into an objective power above us, growing out of our control, thwarting our expectations, bringing to naught our calculations, is one of the chief factors in historical development up till now.

And out of this very contradiction between the interest of the individual and that of the community the latter takes an independent form as the state, divorced from the real interests of individual and community, and at the same time as an illusory communal life, always based, however, on the real ties existing in every family and tribal conglomeration – such as flesh and blood, language, division of labor on a larger scale, and other interests – and especially, as we shall enlarge upon later, on the classes, already determined by the division of labor, which in every such mass of men separate out, and of which one dominates all the others. It follows from this that all struggles within the state, the struggle between democracy, aristocracy, and monarchy, the struggle for the franchise, etc. etc. are merely the illusory forms in which the real struggles of the different classes are fought out among one another. Of this the German theoreticians have not the faintest inkling, although they have received a sufficient introduction to the subject in the *Deutsch–französische Jahrbücher* and *Die heilige Familie*. Further, it follows that every class which is struggling for mastery, even when its domination, as is the case with the proletariat, postulates the abolition of the old form of society in its entirety and of domination itself, must first conquer for itself political power in order to represent its interest in turn as the general interest, which immediately it is forced to do. Just because individuals seek only their particular interest, which for them does not coincide with their communal interest, the latter will be imposed on them as an interest "alien" to them, and "independent" of them, as in its turn a particular, peculiar "general" interest; or they themselves must remain within this discord, as in democracy. On the other hand, too, the practical struggle of these particular interests, which constantly really run counter to the communal and illusory communal interests, makes practical intervention and control necessary through the illusory "general" interest in the form of the state.

The social power, i.e. the multiplied productive force, which arises through the cooperation of different individuals as it is determined by the division of labor, appears to these individuals, since their cooperation is not voluntary but has come about naturally, not as their own united power, but as an alien force existing outside them, of the origin and goal of which they are ignorant, which they thus cannot control, which on the contrary passes through a peculiar series of phases and stages independent of the will and the action of man, nay even being the prime governor of these.

How otherwise could, for instance, property have had a history at all, have taken on different forms, and landed property, for example, according to the different premises given, have proceeded in France from parcellation to centralization in the hands of a few, in England from centralization in the hands of a few to parcellation, as is actually the case today? Or how does it happen that trade, which after all is nothing more than the exchange of products of various individuals and countries, rules the whole world through the relation of supply and demand – a relation which, as an English economist says, hovers over the earth like the Fates of the ancients, and with invisible hand allots fortune and misfortune to men, sets up empires and overthrows empires, causes nations to rise and to disappear – while with the abolition of the basis of private property, with the communistic regulation of production (and, implicit in this, the destruction of the alien relation between men and what they themselves produce), the power of the relation of supply and demand is dissolved into nothing, and men get exchange, production, the mode of their mutual relation, under their own control again?

This "alienation" (to use a term which will be comprehensible to the philosophers) can, of course, only be abolished given two practical premises. For it to become an "intolerable" power, i.e. a power against which men make a revolution, it must necessarily have rendered the great mass of humanity "propertyless," and produced, at the same time, the contradiction of an existing world of wealth and culture, both of which conditions presuppose a great increase in productive power, a high degree of its development. And, on the other hand, this development of productive forces (which itself implies the actual empirical existence of men in their world-historical, instead of local, being) is an absolutely necessary practical premise because without it want is merely made general, and with destitution the struggle for necessities and all the old filthy business would necessarily be reproduced; and furthermore, because only with this universal development of productive forces is a universal intercourse between men established, which produces in all nations simultaneously the phenomenon of the "propertyless" mass (universal competition), makes each nation dependent on the revolutions of the others, and finally has put world-historical, empirically universal individuals in place of local ones. Without this, (1) communism could only exist as a local event; (2) the forces of intercourse themselves could not have developed as universal, hence intolerable powers: they would have remained home-bred conditions surrounded by superstition; and (3) each extension of intercourse would abolish local communism. Empirically, communism is only possible as the act of the dominant peoples "all at once" and simultaneously, which presupposes the universal development of productive forces and the world intercourse bound up with communism. Moreover, the mass of propertyless workers – the utterly precarious position of labor-power on a mass scale cut off from capital or from even a limited satisfaction and, therefore, no longer merely temporarily deprived of work itself as a secure source of life – presupposes the world market through competition. The proletariat can thus only exist world-historically, just as communism, its activity, can only have a "world-historical" existence. World-historical existence of individuals means existence of individuals which is directly linked up with world history.

Communism is for us not a state of affairs which is to be established, an ideal to which reality will have to adjust itself. We call communism the real movement which abolishes the present state of things. The conditions of this movement result from the premises now in existence.

Select Bibliography

Basic Writings on Politics and Philosophy. (Marx and Engels.) Edited by Lewis S. Feuer. New York: Anchor Books, 1989.

Capital: A Critique of Political Economy, 3 vols. (Marx.) Translated by Samuel Moore and Edward Aveling. Edited by Friedrich Engels. New York: International Publishers, 1984.

The Communist Manifesto. (Marx and Engels.) Edited by Frederic L. Bender. New York: W. W. Norton, 1988.

Critique of Hegel's Philosophy of Right. (Marx.) Translated by Annette Jolin and Joseph O'Malley. Edited by Joseph O'Malley. Cambridge: Cambridge University Press, 1970.

Early Writings. (Marx.) Translated by Rodney Livingstone and Gregor Benton. London: Penguin Books, 1992.

Economic and Philosophic Manuscripts of 1844. (Marx.) Edited by Dirk J. Struik. Translated by Martin Milligan. New York: International Publishers, 1986.

The Essential Marx: The Non-Economic Writings, A Selection. (Marx.) Edited by Saul K. Padover. New York: New American Library, 1979.

Karl Marx: The Essential Writings. (Marx.) Edited by Frederic L. Bender. Boulder, Col.: Westview Press, 1986.

Karl Marx: Selected Writings. (Marx.) Edited by David McLellan. Oxford: Oxford University Press, 1985.

The Marx–Engels Reader. (Marx and Engels.) Edited by Robert C. Tucker. New York: Norton, 1978.

Marx: Later Political Writings. (Marx.) Edited and translated by Terrell Carver. Cambridge: Cambridge University Press, 1996.

Marx Selections. (Marx.) Edited by Allen W. Wood. New York: Macmillan, 1988.

The Origin of the Family, Private Property and the State. (Engels.) Harmondsworth: Penguin Books, 1985.

Political Writings. (Marx.) Edited by David Fernbach. London: Penguin Books, 1992.

The Poverty of Philosophy. (Marx and Engels.) New York: International Publishers, 1992.

3

Rosa Luxemburg

Rosa Luxemburg (1870–1919) was born in Poland and came to play a prominent role in the socialist movement in Germany. A theoretician in the German Communist Party, Luxemburg became a powerful left-wing advocate of democratic socialism and an opponent of an over-centralized or bureaucratic Party apparatus. As Luxemburg saw it, the proper role of the Party should not be to organize and control the revolution from above, but to emerge out of and serve the spontaneous uprisings of the workers. In the following excerpt from *The Russian Revolution* (1919), Luxemburg criticizes Lenin and Trotsky for imposing on the socialist state a dictatorship, conceived along bourgeois lines and opposed to democracy, at the expense of a genuinely socialist democracy conceived as a "dictatorship of the proletariat."

Democracy and Dictatorship

The basic error of the Lenin–Trotsky theory is that they too, just like Kautsky, oppose dictatorship to democracy. "Dictatorship *or* democracy" is the way the question is put by Bolsheviks and Kautsky alike. The latter naturally decides in favor of "democracy," that is, of bourgeois democracy, precisely because he opposes it to the alternative of the socialist revolution. Lenin and Trotsky, on the other hand, decide in favor of dictatorship in contradistinction to democracy, and thereby, in favor

From *The Russian Revolution and Leninism or Marxism?* (Ann Arbor: University of Michigan Press, 1962), pp. 76–80. Copyright © 1961 by the University of Michigan Press.

of the dictatorship of a handful of persons, that is, in favor of dictatorship on the bourgeois model. They are two opposite poles, both alike being far removed from a genuine socialist policy. The proletariat, when it seizes power, can never follow the good advice of Kautsky, given on the pretext of the "unripeness of the country," the advice being to renounce the socialist revolution and devote itself to democracy. It cannot follow this advice without betraying thereby itself, the International, and the revolution. It should and must at once undertake socialist measures in the most energetic, unyielding, and unhesitant fashion, in other words, exercise a dictatorship, but a dictatorship of the *class*, not of a party or of a clique – dictatorship of the class, that means in the broadest public form on the basis of the most active, unlimited participation of the mass of the people, of unlimited democracy.

"As Marxists," writes Trotsky, "we have never been idol worshippers of formal democracy." Surely, we have never been idol worshippers of formal democracy. Nor have we ever been idol worshippers of socialism or Marxism either. Does it follow from this that we may also throw socialism on the scrap-heap, *a la* Cunow, Lensch, and Parvus, if it becomes uncomfortable for us? Trotsky and Lenin are the living refutation of this answer.

"We have never been idol-worshippers of formal democracy." All that that really means is: We have always distinguished the social kernel from the political form of *bourgeois* democracy; we have always revealed the hard kernel of social inequality and lack of freedom hidden under the sweet shell of formal equality and freedom – not in order to reject the latter but to spur the working class into not being satisfied with the shell, but rather, by conquering political power, to create a socialist democracy to replace bourgeois democracy – not to eliminate democracy altogether.

But socialist democracy is not something which begins only in the promised land after the foundations of socialist economy are created; it does not come as some sort of Christmas present for the worthy people who, in the interim, have loyally supported a handful of socialist dictators. Socialist democracy begins simultaneously with the beginnings of the destruction of class rule and of the construction of socialism. It begins at the very moment of the seizure of power by the socialist party. It is the same thing as the dictatorship of the proletariat.

Yes, dictatorship! But this dictatorship consists in the *manner of applying democracy*, not in its *elimination*, in energetic, resolute attacks upon the well-entrenched rights and economic relationships of bourgeois society, without which a socialist transformation cannot be accomplished. But this dictatorship must be the work of the *class* and not of a little leading minority in the name of the class – that is, it must proceed step by step out of the active participation of the masses; it must be under their direct influence, subjected to the control of complete public activity; it must arise out of the growing political training of the mass of the people.

Doubtless the Bolsheviks would have proceeded in this very way were it not that they suffered under the frightful compulsion of the world war,

the German occupation and all the abnormal difficulties connected therewith, things which were inevitably bound to distort any socialist policy, however imbued it might be with the best intentions and the finest principles.

A crude proof of this is provided by the use of terror to so wide an extent by the Soviet government, especially in the most recent period just before the collapse of German imperialism, and just after the attempt on the life of the German ambassador. The commonplace to the effect that revolutions are not pink teas is in itself pretty inadequate.

Everything that happens in Russia is comprehensible and represents an inevitable chain of causes and effects, the starting point and end term of which are: the failure of the German proletariat and the occupation of Russia by German imperialism. It would be demanding something superhuman from Lenin and his comrades if we should expect of them that under such circumstances they should conjure forth the finest democracy, the most exemplary dictatorship of the proletariat, and a flourishing socialist economy. By their determined revolutionary stand, their exemplary strength in action, and their unbreakable loyalty to international socialism, they have contributed whatever could possibly be contributed under such devilishly hard conditions. The danger begins only when they make a virtue of necessity and want to freeze into a complete theoretical system all the tactics forced upon them by these fatal circumstances, and want to recommend them to the international proletariat as a model of socialist tactics. When they get in their own light in this way, and hide their genuine, unquestionable historical service under the bushel of false steps forced upon them by necessity, they render a poor service to international socialism for the sake of which they have fought and suffered; for they want to place in its storehouse as new discoveries all the distortions prescribed in Russia by necessity and compulsion – in the last analysis only byproducts of the bankruptcy of international socialism in the present world war.

Let the German Government Socialists cry that the rule of the Bolsheviks in Russia is a distorted expression of the dictatorship of the proletariat. If it was or is such, that is only because it is a product of the behavior of the German proletariat, in itself a distorted expression of the socialist class struggle. All of us are subject to the laws of history, and it is only internationally that the socialist order of society can be realized. The Bolsheviks have shown that they are capable of everything that a genuine revolutionary party can contribute within the limits of the historical possibilities. They are not supposed to perform miracles. For a model and faultless proletarian revolution in an isolated land, exhausted by world war, strangled by imperialism, betrayed by the international proletariat, would be a miracle.

What is in order is to distinguish the essential from the nonessential, the kernel from the accidental excrescences in the policies of the Bolsheviks. In the present period, when we face decisive final struggles in all the world, the most important problem of socialism was and is the burning question of our time. It is not a matter of this or that secondary question of tactics, but of the capacity for action of the proletariat, the strength to act, the will to power of socialism as such. In this, Lenin and Trotsky and their friends were the *first*, those who went ahead as an example to the proletariat of the world; they are still the *only ones* up to now who can cry with Hutten: "I have dared!"

This is the essential and *enduring* in Bolshevik policy. In *this* sense theirs is the immortal historical service of having marched at the head of the international proletariat with the conquest of political power and the practical placing of the problem of the realization of socialism, and of having advanced mightily the settlement of the score between capital and labor in the entire world. In Russia the problem could only be posed. It could not be solved in Russia. And in *this* sense, the future everywhere belongs to "Bolshevism."

Select Bibliography

The Accumulation of Capital. Translated by Agnes Schwarzchild. New York: Monthly Review Press, 1968.

The Crisis in the German Social-Democracy. New York: H. Fertig, 1969.

The Letters of Rosa Luxemburg. Edited by Stephen Eric Bronner. Atlantic Highlands, NJ: Humanities Press, 1993.

The Mass Strike: The Political Party and the Trade Unions, and the Junius Pamphlet. New York: Harper and Row, 1971.

The National Question: Selected Writings. Edited by Horace B. Davis. New York: Monthly Review Press, 1976.

Reform or Revolution. London: Bookmarks, 1989.

Rosa Luxemburg Speaks. Edited by Mary-Alice Waters. New York: Pathfinder Press, 1970.

The Russian Revolution, and Leninism or Marxism? Ann Arbor: University of Michigan Press, 1962.

Selected Political Writings. Edited by Robert Looker. Translated by William D. Graf. New York: Grove Press, 1974.

4

Georg Lukács

Hungarian Marxist philosopher Georg Lukács (1885–1971) was a leading figure in the Hungarian Communist Party and played an important role in Hungary's revolutionary government of 1919. His highly influential book *History and Class Consciousness*, written in 1922, is a collection of essays that develop a Marxist theory of consciousness around the pivotal concepts of reification and alienation. According to Lukács, human beings in capitalist society become alienated from themselves and from one another through the reification of consciousness, whereby human relations come to be regarded as purely objective relations between things, and not as historical-dialectical relations of human beings to one another. In addition to his political writings, Lukács published a great deal on literary and aesthetic theory, including an important study on the theory of the novel. The following excerpts from the essay "What is Orthodox Marxism?" (1919), taken from *History and Class Consciousness*, emphasize the importance of understanding the dialectical totality of social processes as the practical and historical basis of all Marxist theory.

History and Class Consciousness

What is Orthodox Marxism?

The philosophers have only interpreted *the world in various ways; the point, however, is to* change *it.*

Marx, *Theses on Feuerbach*

This question, simple as it is, has been the focus of much discussion in both proletarian and bourgeois

From *History and Class Consciousness: Studies in Marxist Dialectics*, translated by Rodney Livingstone (London: Merlin Press, 1971), pp. 1–10, 13–15, 18–24. Copyright © 1971. Reprinted by permission of the Merlin Press Ltd.

circles. But among intellectuals it has gradually become fashionable to greet any profession of faith in Marxism with ironical disdain. Great disunity has prevailed even in the "socialist" camp as to what constitutes the essence of Marxism, and which theses it is "permissible" to criticize and even reject without forfeiting the right to the title of "Marxist." In consequence it came to be thought increasingly "unscientific" to make scholastic exegeses of old texts with a quasi-biblical status, instead of fostering an "impartial" study of the "facts." These texts, it was argued, had long been "superseded" by modern criticism and they should no longer be regarded as the sole fount of truth.

If the question were really to be formulated in terms of such a crude antithesis it would deserve at best a pitying smile. But in fact it is not (and never has been) quite so straightforward. Let us assume for the sake of argument that recent research had disproved once and for all every one of Marx's individual theses. Even if this were to be proved, every serious "orthodox" Marxist would still be able to accept all such modern findings without reservation and hence dismiss all of Marx's theses *in toto* – without having to renounce his orthodoxy for a single moment. Orthodox Marxism, therefore, does not imply the uncritical acceptance of the results of Marx's investigations. It is not the "belief" in this or that thesis, nor the exegesis of a "sacred" book. On the contrary, orthodoxy refers exclusively to *method*. It is the scientific conviction that dialectical materialism is the road to truth and that its methods can be developed, expanded and deepened only along the lines laid down by its founders. It is the conviction, moreover, that all attempts to surpass or "improve" it have led and must lead to over-simplification, triviality, and eclecticism.

I

Materialist dialectic is a revolutionary dialectic. This definition is so important and altogether so crucial for an understanding of its nature that if the problem is to be approached in the right way this must be fully grasped before we venture upon a discussion of the dialectical method itself. The issue turns on the question of theory and practice. And this not merely in the sense given it by Marx when he says in his first critique of Hegel that "theory becomes a material force when it grips the masses."[1] Even more to the point is the need to discover those features and definitions both of the theory and the ways of gripping the masses which convert the theory, the dialectical method, into a vehicle of revolution. We must extract the practical essence of the theory from the method and its relation to its object. If this is not done that "gripping the masses" could well turn out to be a will o' the wisp. It might turn out that the masses were in the grip of quite different forces, that they were in pursuit of quite different ends. In that event, there would be no necessary connection between the theory and their activity, it would be

a form that enables the masses to become conscious of their socially necessary or fortuitous actions, without insuring a genuine and necessary bond between consciousness and action.

In the same essay[2] Marx clearly defined the conditions in which a relation between theory and practice becomes possible. "It is not enough that thought should seek to realise itself; reality must also strive towards thought." Or, as he expresses it in an earlier work:[3] "It will then be realized that the world has long since possessed something in the form of a dream which it need only take possession of consciously, in order to possess it in reality." Only when consciousness stands in such a relation to reality can theory and practice be united. But for this to happen the emergence of consciousness must become the *decisive step* which the historical process must take towards its proper end (an end constituted by the wills of men, but neither dependent on human whim, nor the product of human invention). The historical function of theory is to make this step a practical possibility. Only when a historical situation has arisen in which a class must understand society if it is to assert itself; only when the fact that a class understands itself means that it understands society as a whole and when, in consequence, the class becomes both the subject and the object of knowledge; in short, only when these conditions are all satisfied will the unity of theory and practice, the precondition of the revolutionary function of the theory, become possible.

Such a situation has in fact arisen with the entry of the proletariat into history. "When the proletariat proclaims the dissolution of the existing social order," Marx declares, "it does no more than disclose the secret of its own existence, for it is the effective dissolution of that order."[4] The links between the theory that affirms this and the revolution are not just arbitrary, nor are they particularly tortuous or open to misunderstanding. On the contrary, the theory is essentially the intellectual expression of the revolutionary process itself. In it every stage of the process becomes fixed so that it may be generalized, communicated, utilized, and developed. Because the theory does nothing but arrest and make conscious each necessary step, it becomes at the same time the necessary premise of the following one.

To be clear about the function of theory is also to understand its own basis, i.e. dialectical method. This point is absolutely crucial, and because it has been overlooked much confusion has been introduced into discussions of dialectics. Engels' arguments in the *Anti-Dühring* decisively influenced the later life of the theory. However we regard them, whether we grant them classical status or whether we criticize them, deem them to be incomplete or even flawed, we must still agree that this aspect is nowhere treated in them. That is to say, he contrasts the ways in which concepts are formed in dialectics as opposed to "metaphysics"; he stresses the fact that in dialectics the definite contours of concepts (and the objects they represent) are dissolved. Dialectics, he argues, is a continuous process of transition from one definition into the other. In consequence a one-sided and rigid causality must be replaced by interaction. But he does not even mention the most vital interaction, namely the *dialectical relation between subject and object in the historical process*, let alone give it the prominence it deserves. Yet without this factor dialectics ceases to be revolutionary, despite attempts (illusory in the last analysis) to retain "fluid" concepts. For it implies a failure to recognize that in all metaphysics the object remains untouched and unaltered so that thought remains contemplative and fails to become practical; while for the dialectical method the central problem is *to change reality*.

If this central function of the theory is disregarded, the virtues of forming "fluid" concepts become altogether problematic: a purely "scientific" matter. The theory might then be accepted or rejected in accordance with the prevailing state of science without any modification at all to one's basic attitudes, to the question of whether or not reality can be changed. Indeed, as the so-called Machists among Marx's supporters have demonstrated, it even reinforces the view that reality with its "obedience to laws," in the sense used by bourgeois, contemplative materialism and the classical economics with which it is so closely bound up, is impenetrable, fatalistic, and immutable. That Machism can also give birth to an equally bourgeois voluntarism does not contradict this. Fatalism and voluntarism are only mutually contradictory to an undialectical and unhistorical mind. In the dialectical view of history they prove to be necessarily complementary opposites, intellectual reflexes clearly expressing the antagonisms of capitalist society and the intractability of its problems when conceived in its own terms.

For this reason all attempts to deepen the dialectical method with the aid of "criticism" inevitably lead to a more superficial view. For "criticism" always starts with just this separation between method and reality, between thought and being. And it is just this separation that it holds to be an improvement deserving of every praise for its introduction of true scientific rigor into the crude, uncritical materialism of the Marxian method. Of course, no one denies the right of "criticism" to do this. But if it does so we must insist that it will be moving counter to the essential spirit of dialectics.

The statements of Marx and Engels on this point could hardly be more explicit. "Dialectics thereby reduced itself to the science of the general laws of motion – both in the external world and in the thought of man – two sets of laws which are identical *in substance*" (Engels).[5] Marx formulated it even more precisely. "In the study of economic categories, as in the case of every historical and social science, it must be borne in mind that ... *the categories are therefore but forms of being, conditions of existence* ..."[6] If this meaning of dialectical method is obscured, dialectics must inevitably begin to look like a superfluous additive, a mere ornament of Marxist "sociology" or "economics." Even worse, it will appear as an obstacle to the "sober," "impartial" study of the "facts," as an empty construct in whose name Marxism does violence to the facts.

This objection to dialectical method has been voiced most clearly and cogently by Bernstein, thanks in part to a "freedom from bias" unclouded by any philosophical knowledge. However, the very real political and economic conclusions he deduces from this desire to liberate method from the "dialectical snares" of Hegelianism, show clearly where this course leads. They show that it is precisely the dialectic that must be removed if one wishes to found a thoroughgoing opportunistic theory, a theory of "evolution" without revolution and of "natural development" into Socialism without any conflict.

II

We are now faced with the question of the methodological implications of these so-called facts that are idolized throughout the whole of Revisionist literature. To what extent may we look to them to provide guidelines for the actions of the revolutionary proletariat? It goes without saying that all knowledge starts from the facts. The only question is: which of the data of life are relevant to knowledge and in the context of which method?

The blinkered empiricist will of course deny that facts can only become facts within the framework of a system – which will vary with the knowledge desired. He believes that every piece of data from economic life, every statistic, every raw event already constitutes an important fact. In so doing he forgets that however simple an enumeration of "facts" may be, however lacking in commentary, it already implies an "interpretation." Already at this stage the facts have been comprehended by a theory, a method; they have been wrenched from their living context and fitted into a theory.

More sophisticated opportunists would readily grant this despite their profound and instinctive dislike of all theory. They seek refuge in the methods of natural science, in the way in which science distills "pure" facts and places them in the relevant contexts by means of observation, abstraction and experiment. They then oppose this ideal model of knowledge to the forced constructions of the dialectical method.

If such methods seem plausible at first this is because capitalism tends to produce a social structure that in great measure encourages such views. But for that very reason we need the dialectical method to puncture the social illusion so produced and help us to glimpse the reality underlying it. The "pure" facts of the natural sciences arise when a phenomenon of the real world is placed (in thought or in reality) into an environment where its laws can be inspected without outside interference. This process is reinforced by reducing the phenomena to their purely quantitative essence, to their expression in numbers and numerical relations. Opportunists always fail to recognize that it is in the nature of capitalism to process phenomena in this way. Marx gives an incisive account[7] of such a "process of abstraction" in the case of labor, but he does not omit to point out with equal vigor that he is dealing with a *historical* peculiarity of capitalist society. "Thus the most general abstractions commonly appear where there is the highest concrete development, where one feature appears to be shared by many, and to be common to all. Then it cannot be thought of any longer in one particular form."

But this tendency in capitalism goes even further. The fetishistic character of economic forms, the reification of all human relations, the constant expansion and extension of the division of labor which subjects the process of production to an abstract, rational analysis, without regard to the human potentialities and abilities of the immediate producers, all these things transform the phenomena of society and with them the way in which they are perceived. In this way arise the "isolated" facts, "isolated" complexes of facts, separate, specialist disciplines (economics, law, etc.) whose very appearance seems to have done much to pave the way for such scientific methods. It thus appears extraordinarily "scientific" to think out the tendencies implicit in the facts themselves and to promote this activity to the status of science.

By contrast, in the teeth of all these isolated and isolating facts and partial systems, dialectics insists on the concrete unity of the whole. Yet although it exposes these appearances for the illusions they are – albeit illusions necessarily engendered by capitalism – in this "scientific" atmosphere it still gives the impression of being an arbitrary construction.

The unscientific nature of this seemingly so scientific method consists, then, in its failure to see and take account of the *historical character* of the facts on which it is based. This is the source of more than one error (constantly overlooked by the practitioners of the method) to which Engels has explicitly drawn attention.[8] The nature of this source of error is that statistics and the "exact" economic theory based upon them always lag behind actual developments. "For this reason, it is only too often necessary in current history, to treat this, the most decisive factor, as constant, and the economic situation existing at the beginning of the period concerned as given and unalterable for the whole period, or else to take notice of only those changes in the situation as arise out of the patently manifest events themselves and are therefore, likewise, patently manifest."

Thus we perceive that there is something highly problematic in the fact that capitalist society is predisposed to harmonize with scientific method, to constitute indeed the social premises of its exactness. If the internal structure of the "facts" of their interconnections is essentially historical, if, that is to say, they are caught up in a process of continuous transformation, then we may indeed question when the greater scientific inaccuracy occurs. Is it when I conceive of the "facts" as existing in a form and as subject to laws concerning which I have a methodological certainty (or at least probability) that they no longer apply to these facts? Or is it when I consciously take this situation into account, cast a critical eye at the "exactitude" attainable by such a method and concentrate instead on those points where this *historical* aspect, this decisive fact of change really manifests itself?

The historical character of the "facts" which science seems to have grasped with such "purity" makes itself felt in an even more devastating manner. As the products of historical evolution they are involved in continuous change. But in addition they are also *precisely in their objective structure the products of a definite historical epoch, namely capitalism*. Thus when "science" maintains that the manner in which data immediately present themselves is an adequate foundation of scientific conceptualization and that the actual form of these data is the appropriate starting point for the formation of scientific concepts, it thereby takes its stand simply and dogmatically on the basis of capitalist society. It uncritically accepts the nature of the object as it is given and the laws of that society as the unalterable foundation of "science."

In order to progress from these "facts" to facts in the true meaning of the word it is necessary to perceive their historical conditioning as such and to abandon the point of view that would see them as immediately given: they must themselves be subjected to a historical and dialectical examination. For as Marx says:[9] "The finished pattern of economic relations as seen on the surface in their real existence and consequently in the ideas with which the agents and bearers of these relations seek to understand them, is very different from, and indeed quite the reverse of and antagonistic to their inner, essential but concealed core and the concepts corresponding to it."

If the facts are to be understood, this distinction between their real existence and their inner core must be grasped clearly and precisely. This distinction is the first premise of a truly scientific study which in Marx's words, "would be superfluous if the outward appearance of things coincided with their essence."[10] Thus we must detach the phenomena from the form in which they are immediately given and discover the intervening links which connect them to their core, their essence. In so doing, we shall arrive at an understanding of their apparent form and see it as the form in which the inner core necessarily appears. It is necessary because of the historical character of the facts, because they have grown in the soil of capitalist society. This twofold character, the simultaneous recognition and transcendence of immediate appearances is precisely the dialectical nexus.

In this respect, superficial readers imprisoned in the modes of thought created by capitalism, experienced the gravest difficulties in comprehending the structure of thought in *Capital*. For on the one hand, Marx's account pushes the capitalist nature of all economic forms to their furthest limits, he creates an intellectual milieu where they can exist in their purest form by positing a society "corresponding to the theory," i.e. capitalist through and through, consisting of none but capitalists and proletarians. But conversely, no sooner does this strategy produce results, no sooner does this world of phenomena seem to be on the point of crystallizing out into theory than it dissolves into a mere illusion, a distorted situation appears as in a distorting mirror which is, however, "only the conscious expression of an imaginary movement."

Only in this context which sees the isolated facts of social life as aspects of the historical process and integrates them in a *totality*, can knowledge of the facts hope to become knowledge of *reality*. This knowledge starts from the simple (and to the capitalist world), pure, immediate, natural determinants described above. It progresses from them to the knowledge of the concrete totality, i.e. to the conceptual reproduction of reality. This concrete totality is by no means an unmediated datum for thought. "The concrete is concrete," Marx says,[11] "because it is a synthesis of many particular determinants, i.e. a unity of diverse elements."

Idealism succumbs here to the delusion of confusing the intellectual reproduction of reality with the actual structure of reality itself. For "in thought, reality appears as the process of synthesis, not as starting-point, but as outcome, although it is the real starting-point and hence the starting-point for perception and ideas."

Conversely, the vulgar materialists, even in the modern guise donned by Bernstein and others, do not go beyond the reproduction of the immediate, simple determinants of social life. They imagine that they are being quite extraordinarily "exact" when they simply take over these determinants without either analyzing them further or welding them into a concrete totality. They take the facts in abstract isolation, explaining them only in terms of abstract laws unrelated to the concrete totality. As Marx observes: "Crudeness and conceptual nullity consist in the tendency to forge arbitrary unmediated connections between things that belong together in an organic union."[12]

The crudeness and conceptual nullity of such thought lies primarily in the fact that it obscures the historical, transitory nature of capitalist society. Its determinants take on the appearance of timeless, eternal categories valid for all social formations.

This could be seen at its crassest in the vulgar bourgeois economists, but the vulgar Marxists soon followed in their footsteps. The dialectical method was overthrown and with it the methodological supremacy of the totality over the individual aspects; the parts were prevented from finding their definition within the whole and, instead, the whole was dismissed as unscientific or else it degenerated into the mere "idea" or "sum" of the parts. With the totality out of the way, the fetishistic relations of the isolated parts appeared as a timeless law valid for every human society.

Marx's dictum: "The relations of production of every society form a whole"[13] is the methodological point of departure and the key to the *historical* understanding of social relations. All the isolated partial categories can be thought of and treated – in isolation – as something that is always present in every society. (If it cannot be found in a given society this is put down to "chance" as the exception that proves the rule.) But the changes to which these individual aspects are subject give no clear and unambiguous picture of the real differences in the various stages of the evolution of society. These can really only be discerned in the context of the total historical process of their relation to society as a whole.

III

This dialectical conception of totality seems to have put a great distance between itself and reality, it appears to construct reality very "unscientifically." But it is the only method capable of understanding and reproducing reality. Concrete totality is, therefore, the category that governs reality.[14] The rightness of this view only emerges with complete clarity when we direct our attention to the real, material substratum of our method, viz. capitalist society with its internal antagonism between the forces and the relations of production. The methodology of the natural sciences which forms the methodological ideal of every fetishistic science and every kind of Revisionism rejects the idea of contradiction and antagonism in its subject matter. If, despite this, contradictions do spring up between particular theories, this only proves that our knowledge is as yet imperfect. Contradictions between theories show that these theories have reached their natural limits; they must therefore be transformed and subsumed under even wider theories in which the contradictions finally disappear.

But we maintain that in the case of social reality these contradictions are not a sign of the imperfect understanding of society; on the contrary, they belong to *the nature of reality itself and to the nature of capitalism*. When the totality is known they will not be transcended and *cease* to be contradictions. Quite the reverse, they will be seen to be necessary contradictions arising out of the antagonisms of this system of production. When theory (as the knowledge of the whole) opens up the way to resolving these contradictions it does so by revealing the *real tendencies* of social evolution. For these are destined to effect a *real* resolution of the contradictions that have emerged in the course of history....

Thus the objective forms of all social phenomena change constantly in the course of their ceaseless dialectical interactions with each other. The intelligibility of objects develops in proportion as we grasp their function in the totality to which they belong. This is why only the dialectical conception of totality can enable us to understand *reality as a social process*. For only this conception dissolves the fetishistic forms necessarily produced by the capitalist mode of production and enables us to see them as mere illusions which are not less illusory for being seen to be necessary. These unmediated concepts, these "laws" sprout just as inevitably from the soil of capitalism and veil the real relations between objects. They can all be seen as ideas necessarily held by the agents of the capitalist system of production. They are, therefore, objects of knowledge, but the object which is known through them is not the capitalist system of production itself, but the ideology of its ruling class.

Only when this veil is torn aside does historical knowledge become possible. For the function of these unmediated concepts that have been derived from the fetishistic forms of objectivity is to make the phenomena of capitalist society appear as suprahistorical essences. The knowledge of the real, objective nature of a phenomenon, the knowledge of its historical character and the knowledge of its actual function in the totality of society form, therefore, a single, undivided act of cognition. This unity is shattered by the pseudo–scientific method. Thus only through the dialectical method could the distinction between constant and variable capital, crucial to economics, be understood. Classical economics was unable to go beyond the distinction between fixed and circulating capital. This was not accidental. For "variable capital is only a particular historical manifestation of the fund for providing the necessaries of life, or the labor-fund which the laborer requires for the maintenance of himself and his family, and which whatever be the system of social production, he must himself produce and reproduce. If the labor-fund constantly flows to him in the form of money that pays for his labor, it is because the product he has created moves constantly away from him in the form of capital.... The transaction is veiled by the fact that the product appears as a commodity and the commodity as money."[15]

The fetishistic illusions enveloping all phenomena in capitalist society succeed in concealing reality, but more is concealed than the historical, i.e. transitory, ephemeral nature of phenomena. *This* concealment is made possible by the fact that in capitalist society man's environment, and especially the categories of economics, appear to him immediately and necessarily in forms of objectivity which conceal the fact that they are the categories of the *relations of men with each other*. Instead they appear as things and the relations of things with each other. Therefore, when the dialectical method destroys the fiction of the immortality of the categories it also destroys their reified character and clears the way to a knowledge of reality. According to Engels in his discussion of Marx's *Critique of Political Economy*, "economics does not treat of things, but of the relations between persons and, in the last analysis, between classes; however, these relations are always *bound to things* and *appear as things*."[16]

It is by virtue of this insight that the dialectical method and its concept of totality can be seen to provide real knowledge of what goes on in society. It might appear as if the dialectic relations between parts and whole were no more than a construct of thought as remote from the true categories of social reality as the unmediated formulae of bourgeois economics. If so, the superiority of dialectics would be purely methodological. The real difference, however, is deeper and more fundamental....

V

The premise of dialectical materialism is, we recall: "It is not men's consciousness that determines their existence, but on the contrary, their social existence that determines their consciousness." Only in the context sketched above can this premise point beyond mere theory and become a question of praxis. Only when the core of existence stands revealed as a social process can existence be seen as the product, albeit the hitherto unconscious product, of human activity. This activity will be seen in its turn as the element crucial for the transformation of existence. Man finds himself confronted by purely natural relations or social forms mystified into natural relations. They appear to be fixed, complete, and immutable entities which can be manipulated and even comprehended, but never overthrown. But also this situation creates the possibility of praxis in the individual consciousness. Praxis becomes the form of action appropriate to the isolated individual, it becomes his ethics. Feuerbach's attempt to supersede Hegel foundered on this reef: like the German idealists, and to a much greater extent than Hegel, he stopped short at the isolated individual of "civil society."

Marx urged us to understand "the sensuous world," the object, reality, as human sensuous activity.[17] This means that man must become conscious of himself as a social being, as simultaneously the subject and object of the sociohistorical process. In feudal society man could not yet see himself as a social being because his social relations were still mainly natural. Society was far too unorganized and had far too little control over the totality of relations between men for it to appear to consciousness as *the* reality of man. (The question of the structure and unity of feudal society cannot be considered in any detail here.) Bourgeois society carried out the process of socializing society. Capitalism destroyed both the spatiotemporal barriers between different lands and territories and also the legal partitions between the different "estates" (Stände). In its universe there is a formal equality for all men; the economic relations that directly determined the metabolic exchange between men and nature progressively disappear. Man becomes, in the true sense of the word, a social being. Society becomes *the* reality for man.

Thus the recognition that society is reality becomes possible only under capitalism, in bourgeois society. But the class which carried out this revolution did so without consciousness of its function; the social forces it unleashed, the very forces that carried it to supremacy seemed to be opposed to it like a second nature, but a more soulless, impenetrable nature than feudalism ever was.[18] It was necessary for the proletariat to be born for social reality to become fully conscious. The reason for this is that the discovery of the class-outlook of the proletariat provided a vantage point from which to survey the whole of society. With the emergence of historical materialism there arose the theory of the "conditions for the liberation of the proletariat" and the doctrine of reality understood as the total process of social evolution. This was only possible because for the proletariat the total knowledge of its class-situation was a vital necessity, a matter of life and death; because its class situation becomes comprehensible only if the whole of society can be understood; and because this understanding is the inescapable precondition of its actions. Thus the unity of theory and practice is only the reverse side of the social and historical position of the proletariat. From its own point of view self-knowledge coincides with knowledge of the whole so that the proletariat is at one and the same time the subject and object of its own knowledge.

The mission of raising humanity to a higher level is based, as Hegel rightly observed[19] (although he was still concerned with nations), on the fact that these "stages of evolution exist as *immediate, natural principles*" and it devolves upon every nation (i.e. class) "endowed with such a *natural* principle to put it into practice." Marx concretizes this idea with great clarity by applying it to social development:[20] "If socialist writers attribute this world-historical role to the proletariat it is not because they believe ... that the proletariat are gods. Far from it. The proletariat can and must liberate itself because when the proletariat is fully developed, its humanity and even the appearance of its humanity has become totally abstract; because in the conditions of its life all the conditions of life of contemporary society find their most inhuman consummation; because in the proletariat man is lost to himself but at the same time he has acquired a theoretical consciousness of this loss, and is driven by the absolutely imperious dictates of his misery – the practical expression of this necessity – which can no longer be ignored or whitewashed, to rebel against this inhumanity. However, the proletariat cannot liberate itself without destroying the conditions of its own life. But it cannot do that without destroying *all* the inhuman conditions of life in contemporary society which exist in the proletariat in a concentrated form."

Thus the essence of the method of historical materialism is inseparable from the "practical and critical" activity of the proletariat: both are aspects of the same process of social evolution. So, too, the knowledge of reality provided by the dialectical method is likewise inseparable from the class standpoint of the proletariat. The question raised by the Austrian Marxists of the methodological separation of the "pure" science of Marxism from socialism is a pseudo-problem.[21] For, the Marxist method, the dialectical materialist knowledge of reality, can arise only from the point of view of a class, from the point of view of the struggle of the proletariat. To abandon this point of view is to move away from historical materialism, just as to adopt it leads directly into the thick of the struggle of the proletariat.

Historical materialism grows out of the "immediate, natural" life-principle of the proletariat; it means the acquisition of total knowledge of reality from this one point of view. But it does not follow from this that this knowledge or this methodological attitude is the inherent or natural possession of the proletariat as a class (let alone of proletarian individuals). On the contrary. It is true that the proletariat is the conscious subject of total social reality. But the conscious subject is not defined here as in Kant, where "subject" is defined as that which can never be an object. The "subject" here is not a detached spectator of the process. The proletariat is more than just the active and passive part of this process: the rise and evolution of its knowledge and its actual rise and evolution in the course of history are just the two different sides of the same real process. It is not simply the case that the working class arose in the course of spontaneous, unconscious actions born of immediate, direct despair (the Luddite destruction of machines can serve as a primitive illustration of this), and then advanced gradually through incessant social struggle to the point where it "formed itself into a class." But it is no less true that proletarian consciousness of social reality, of its own class situation, of its own historical vocation and the materialist view of history are all products of this self-same process of evolution which historical materialism understands adequately and for what it really is for the first time in history.

Thus the Marxist method is equally as much the product of class warfare as any other political or economic product. In the same way, the evolution of the proletariat reflects the inner structure of the society which it was the first to understand. "Its result, therefore, appears just as constantly presupposed by it as its presuppositions appear as its results."[22] The idea of totality which we have come to recognize as the presupposition necessary to comprehend reality is the product of history in a double sense.

First, historical materialism became a formal, objective possibility only because economic factors created the proletariat, because the proletariat did emerge (i.e. at a particular stage of historical development), and because the subject and object of the knowledge of social reality were transformed. Second, this formal possibility became a real one only in the course of the evolution of the proletariat. If the meaning of history is to be found in the process of history itself and not, as formerly, in a transcendental, mythological, or ethical meaning foisted on to recalcitrant material, this presupposes a proletariat with a relatively advanced awareness of its own position, i.e. a relatively advanced proletariat, and, therefore, a long preceding period of evolution. The path taken by this evolution leads from utopia to the knowledge of reality; from transcendental goals fixed by the first great leaders of the workers' movement to the clear perception by the Commune of 1871 that the working class has "no ideals to realize," but wishes only "to liberate the elements of the new society." It is the path leading from the "class opposed to capitalism" to the class "for itself."

Seen in this light the revisionist separation of movement and ultimate goal represents a regression to the most primitive stage of the working-class movement. For the ultimate goal is not a "state of the future" awaiting the proletariat somewhere independent of the movement and the path leading up to it. It is not a condition which can be happily forgotten in the stress of daily life and recalled only in Sunday sermons as a stirring contrast to workaday cares. Nor is it a "duty," an "idea" designed to regulate the "real" process. The ultimate goal is rather that *relation to the totality* (to the whole of society seen as a process), through which every aspect of the struggle acquires its revolutionary significance. This relation informs every aspect in its simple and sober ordinariness, but only consciousness makes it real and so confers reality on the day-to-day struggle by manifesting its relation to the whole. Thus it elevates mere existence to reality. Do not let us forget either that every attempt to rescue the "ultimate goal" or the "essence" of the proletariat from every impure contact with – capitalist – existence leads ultimately to the same remoteness from reality, from "practical, critical activity" and to the same relapse into the utopian dualism of subject and object, of theory and practice to which Revisionism has succumbed.[23]

The practical danger of every such dualism shows itself in the loss of any directive for *action*.

As soon as you abandon the ground of reality that has been conquered and reconquered by dialectical materialism, as soon as you decide to remain on the "natural" ground of existence, of the empirical in its stark, naked brutality, you create a gulf between the subject of an action and the milieux of the "facts" in which the action unfolds so that they stand opposed to each other as harsh, irreconcilable principles. It then becomes impossible to impose the subjective will, wish, or decision upon the facts or to discover in them any directive for action. A situation in which the "facts" speak out unmistakably for or against a definite course of action has never existed, and neither can or will exist. The more conscientiously the facts are explored – in their isolation, i.e. in their unmediated relations – the less compellingly will they point in any one direction. It is self-evident that a merely subjective decision will be shattered by the pressure of uncomprehended facts acting automatically "according to laws."

Thus dialectical materialism is seen to offer the only approach to reality which can give action a direction. The self-knowledge, both subjective and objective, of the proletariat at a given point in its evolution is at the same time knowledge of the stage of development achieved by the whole society. The facts no longer appear strange when they are comprehended in their coherent reality, in the relation of all partial aspects to their inherent, but hitherto unelucidated roots in the whole: we then perceive the tendencies which strive towards the centre of reality, to what we are wont to call the ultimate goal. This ultimate goal is not an abstract ideal opposed to the process, but an aspect of truth and reality. It is the concrete meaning of each stage reached and an integral part of the concrete moment. Because of this, to comprehend it is to recognize the direction taken (unconsciously) by events and tendencies towards the totality. It is to know the direction that determines concretely the correct course of action at any given moment – in terms of the interest of the total process, viz. the emancipation of the proletariat.

However, the evolution of society constantly heightens the tension between the partial aspects and the whole. Just because the inherent meaning of reality shines forth with an ever more resplendent light, the meaning of the process is embedded ever more deeply in day-to-day events, and totality permeates the spatiotemporal character of phenomena. The path to consciousness throughout the course of history does not become smoother but on the contrary ever more arduous and exacting. For this reason the task of orthodox Marxism, its victory over Revisionism and utopianism can never mean the defeat, once and for all, of false tendencies. It is an ever-renewed struggle against the insidious effects of bourgeois ideology on the thought of the proletariat. Marxist orthodoxy is no guardian of traditions, it is the eternally vigilant prophet proclaiming the relation between the tasks of the immediate present and the totality of the historical process. Hence the words of the *Communist Manifesto* on the tasks of orthodoxy and of its

representatives, the Communists, have lost neither their relevance nor their value: "The Communists are distinguished from the other working-class parties *by this only*: 1. In the national struggles of the proletarians of the different countries, they point out and bring to the front the common interests of the *entire* proletariat, independent of nationality. 2. In the various stages of development which the struggle of the working class against the bourgeoisie has to pass through, they always and everywhere represent the interests of *the movement as a whole*."

Notes

1 *The Critique of Hegel's Philosophy of Right*, in *Early Writings* edited by T. B. Bottomore, London, 1963, p. 52.

2 Ibid., p. 54.

3 *Nachlass* I, pp. 382–3. [*Correspondence of 1843*].

4 Ibid., p. 398. See also the essay on Class Consciousness.

5 *Feuerbach and the End of Classical German Philosophy*, in Marx/Engels, *Selected Works* (2 vols), Lawrence and Wishart, London, 1950; henceforth cited as: S.W. II, p. 350.

6 *A Contribution to the Critique of Political Economy*, translated by N. I. Stone, London, 1904 (my italics). It is of the first importance to realize that the method is limited here to the realms of history and society. The misunderstandings that arise from Engels' account of dialectics can in the main be put down to the fact that Engels – following Hegel's mistaken lead – extended the method to apply also to nature. However, the crucial determinants of dialectics – the interaction of subject and object, the unity of theory and practice, the historical changes in the reality underlying the categories as the root cause of changes in thought, etc. – are absent from our knowledge of nature. Unfortunately it is not possible to undertake a detailed analysis of these questions here.

7 Ibid., pp. 298–9.

8 Introduction to *The Class Struggles in France* in S.W. I, p. 110. But it must be borne in mind that "scientific exactitude" presupposes that the elements remain "constant." This had been postulated as far back as Galileo.

9 *Capital* III, p. 205. Similarly also pp. 47–8 and 307. The distinction between existence (which is divided into appearance, phenomenon, and essence) and reality derives from Hegel's *Logic*. It is unfortunately not

possible here to discuss the degree to which the conceptual framework of *Capital* is based on these distinctions. Similarly, the distinction between idea (*Vorstellung*) and concept (*Begriff*) is also to be found in Hegel.

10 *Capital* III, p. 797.

11 *A Contribution to Political Economy*, p. 293.

12 Ibid., p. 273. The category of reflective connection also derives from Hegel's *Logic*. [See Explanatory Notes for this concept].

13 *The Poverty of Philosophy*, Moscow, n.d., p. 123.

14 We would draw the attention of readers with a greater interest in questions of methodology to the fact that in Hegel's logic, too, the relation of the parts to the whole forms the dialectical transition from existence to reality. It must be noted in this context that the question of the relation of internal and external also treated there is likewise concerned with the problem of totality. Hegel, *Werke* IV, pp. 156 ff. (The quotations from the *Logic* are all taken from the 2nd edition.)

15 *Capital* I, p. 568.

16 Cf. the essay on *Reification and the Consciousness of the Proletariat*.

17 *Theses on Feuerbach*, in S.W. II, pp. 364–7.

18 See the essay *Class Consciousness* for an explanation of this situation.

19 *The Philosophy of Right*, § 346–7.

20 *Nachlass* II, p. 133. [*The Holy Family*, chapter 4].

21 Hilferding, *Finanzkapital*, pp. viii–ix.

22 *Capital* III.

23 Cf. Zinoviev's polemics against Guesde and his attitude to the war in Stuttgart. *Gegen den Strom*, pp. 470–1. Likewise Lenin's book, *"Left-Wing" Communism – an Infantile Disorder*.

Select Bibliography

The Destruction of Reason. Translated by Peter Palmer. Atlantic Highlands, NJ: Humanities Press, 1981.

Georg Lukács: Theory, Culture, and Politics. Edited by Judith Marcus and Zoltan Tarr. New Brunswick, NJ: Transaction Publishers, 1989.

German Realists in the Nineteenth Century. Edited by Rodney Livingstone. Translated by Jeremy Gaines and Paul Keast. Cambridge, Mass.: MIT Press, 1993.

The Historical Novel. Translated by Hannah Mitchell and Stanley Mitchell. Lincoln: University of Nebraska Press, 1983.

History and Class Consciousness. Translated by Rodney Livingstone. Cambridge, Mass.: MIT Press, 1986.

Marxism and Human Liberation: Essays on History, Culture and Revolution. Edited by E. San Juan, Jr. New York: Dell Publishing, 1973.

The Process of Democratization. Translated by Susanne Bernhardt and Norman Levine. Albany: State University of New York Press, 1991.

Realism in Our Time: Literature and the Class Struggle. Translated by John Mander and Necke Mander. New York: Harper and Row, 1971.

Soul and Form. Translated by Anna Bostock. Cambridge, Mass.: MIT Press, 1974.

The Theory of the Novel: A Historico-Philosophical Essay on the Forms of Great Epic Literature. Translated by Anna Bostock. Cambridge, Mass.: MIT Press, 1971.

Writer and Critic, and Other Essays. Edited and translated by Arthur D. Kahn. New York: Grosset and Dunlap, 1971.

5

Antonio Gramsci

Italian socialist Antonio Gramsci (1891–1937), a founder of the Italian Communist Party in 1921, was imprisoned by the Fascists in 1926 until shortly before his death. His prison writings comprise some thirty-two notebooks, plus various reviews, newspaper articles, and letters. For Gramsci, philosophy is not something that could be realized in revolutionary action such as to disappear or become unnecessary. Rather, philosophical thought is important as involving the ability to criticize one's own way of conceiving the world; like human existence itself, philosophy is never simply an accomplishment, but a task. In the following short essay from *The Modern Prince* (first published in 1957), Gramsci reflects on the historical nature of human existence and on the role of philosophical knowledge in shaping and realizing political action. The true philosopher, in gaining consciousness of the complex nexus of relationships that historically constitute human society, thereby changes himself and his relationships to others; in this sense, argues Gramsci, he cannot avoid being political.

What is Man?

This is the primary and main question in philosophy. How can it be answered? The definition is to be found in man himself, and therefore in each single man. But is this correct? In each single man, we will discover what each "single man" is. But we are not interested in what each single man is, which, after all, signifies what each single man is at each single moment. When we consider it, we find that by putting the question "What is man?" we really mean; "What can man become?", that is, whether or not man can control his own destiny, can "make himself," can create a life for himself. Therefore we say that man is a process, and precisely the process of his actions. When we consider it, the question "What is man?" is not an abstract or "objective" question. It stems from what we have thought about ourselves and others, and, relative to what we have thought and seen, we seek to know what we are and what we can become, whether it is

From *The Modern Prince and Other Writings*, translated by Louis Marks (New York: International Publishers, 1987), pp. 76–81. Copyright © 1957. Reprinted by permission of International Publishers Co.

true and within what limits that we do "make ourselves," create our own lives and our own destinies. We want to know this "now," in the given conditions of the present and of our "daily" life, and not about any life and about any man.

The question arises and derives its content from special, or rather, determined patterns of considering the life of man; the most important of these patterns is the "religious" one and a given religious one – Catholicism. Actually when we ask ourselves "what is man, how important is his will and his concrete activity in the creation of himself and the life he lives?" what we mean is: "Is Catholicism a true concept of man and of life? In being a Catholic, in making Catholicism a way of life, are we mistaken or right?" Everyone has the vague intuition that to make Catholicism a way of life is a mistake, because no one completely embraces Catholicism as a way of life even while declaring himself a Catholic. A strict Catholic who applied Catholic rules to every act of his life would appear as a monster; and this, when one thinks about it, is the strongest, most irrefutable criticism of Catholicism itself.

Catholics will reply by saying that no concepts are rigidly followed, and they are right. But this only proves that there does not in fact exist historically one rule and no other for thinking and functioning that applies equally to all men. It is no argument for Catholicism, even though this way of thinking and acting has for centuries been organized to this end – something which has not yet happened with any other religion with the same means at its disposal, the same spirit of system, the same continuity and centralization. From the "philosophical" point of view, Catholicism's failure to satisfy rests in the fact that despite everything, it roots the cause of all evil in man himself, that is, it conceives of man as a clearly defined and limited individual. It can be said that all philosophies up to the present repeat this position taken by the Catholics; man is conceived of as limited by his individuality, and his spirit as well. It is precisely on this point that a change in the conception of man is required. That is, it is essential to conceive of man as a series of active relationships (a process) in which individuality, while of the greatest importance, is not the sole element to be considered. The humanity reflected in every individual consists of various elements: (1) the individual, (2) other men, (3) nature. The second and third elements are not as simple as they seem. The individual does not enter into relations with other men in opposition to

them but through an organic unity with them, because he becomes part of social organisms of all kinds from the simplest to the most complex. Thus man does not enter into relationship with nature simply because he is himself part of nature, but actively, through work and through techniques. More. These relationships are not mechanical. They are active and conscious, and they correspond to the lesser or greater intelligence which the individual man possesses; therefore one can say that man changes himself, modifies himself, to the same extent that he changes and modifies the whole complex of relationships of which he is the nexus. In this sense the true philosopher is, and cannot avoid being political – that is, man active, who changes his environment – environment being understood to include the relationships into which each individual enters. If individuality is the whole mass of these relationships, the acquiring of a personality means the acquiring of consciousness of these relationships, and changing the personality means changing the whole mass of these relationships.

But, as stated earlier, these relationships are not simple. Moreover, some are involuntary and some voluntary. Furthermore, the very fact of being more or less profoundly conscious (knowing more or less of the way in which these relationships can be modified) already modifies them. Once recognized as necessary, these same necessary relationships change in aspect and importance. In this sense, recognition is power. But this problem is complicated in still another aspect; it is not enough to know the totality of the relations as they exist in a given moment within a given pattern; it is important to know their genesis, the impulse of their formation, because each individual is not only the synthesis of existing relations but also the history of these relations, the sum of all of the past. It will be said that what each individual is able to change is very little indeed. But considering that each individual is able to associate himself with all others who desire the same changes as himself, and provided the change is a rational one, the single individual is able to multiply himself by an impressive number and can thus obtain a far more radical change than would first appear.

The number of societies in which an individual can participate is very great (more than one thinks). It is through these "societies" that the individual plays a part in the human species. Thus the ways in which the individual enters into relations with nature are multiple, because by techniques we mean not only the totality of scientific ideas applied to industry in the usual meaning of the word, but also "mental" instruments, philosophic knowledge.

It is a commonplace that it is impossible to conceive of man otherwise than as existing in a society, but not all the necessary conclusions, even those applying to individuals, are always drawn. It is also a commonplace that for a given society there must be a given society of things, and that human society is only possible insofar as there exists a given society of things. These organisms apart from individual cases, have up to now been given a mechanist and determinist significance (both *societas hominum* and *societas rerum*); hence the reaction. It is essential to evolve a theory in which all these relationships are seen as active and in motion, establishing clearly that the source of this activity is man's individual consciousness which knows, wills, strives, creates because he already knows, desires, strives, creates, etc., and conceives of himself not as an isolated individual but rich in the potentialities offered by other men and by the society of things of which he must have some knowledge (because each man is a philosopher, a scientist, etc.).

Feuerbach's thesis: "Man is what he eats," if taken by itself, can be interpreted in various ways. Interpreted narrowly and foolishly, one could say: "Man is alternately what he eats materially," or – foods have an immediate determining influence on modes of thinking. It calls to mind Amadea Mordiga's statement, for instance, that if one knew what a man had eaten before he made a speech one could better interpret the speech itself – a childish statement and actually one that is alien even to positive science, because the brain is not nourished by beans and truffles but by foods which are transformed into homogeneous assimilable material and which unite to form the cells of the brain; that is, foods have potentially a "similar nature" to cerebral cells. If this statement were true, the matrix of history would be found in the kitchen, and revolutions would coincide with radical changes in the diet of the masses. Historical truth proves the contrary. It is revolutionary and complex historical development which has changed feeding habits and created successive "tastes" in the selection of food. It was not the regular sowing of grain which brought nomadism to a halt but vice versa, it was the conditions developing out of nomad life which forced regular cultivation, etc.

However, since diet is one expression of complex social relationships and each social regrouping has a basic food pattern, there is some truth in the saying "man is what he eats," but in the same way one could say "man is the clothing he wears," man is his habitation, man is his particular way of reproducing himself, or "he is his family," because food, dress, housing, and reproducing are elements of social life in which, in point of fact, the whole complex of social relations are most obviously and most widely manifested.

Thus the problem of what man is is always posed as the problem of so-called "human nature," or of "man in general," the attempt to create a science of man (a philosophy) whose point of departure is primarily based on a "unitary" idea, on an abstraction designed to contain all that is "human." But is "humanity," as a reality and as an idea, a point of departure – or a point of arrival? Or isn't it rather that when posed as a point of departure, the attempt is reduced to a survival of theology and metaphysics? Philosophy cannot be reduced to naturalistic anthropology; unity in mankind is not a quality of man's biological nature; the differences in man which matter in history are not the biological differences (of race, skull formation, skin color, etc.), from which is deduced the theory that man is what he eats. In Europe man eats grain, in Asia, rice, etc. – which can then be reduced to the other statement: "Man is the country he inhabits," because diet is generally related to the country inhabited. And not even "biological unity" has counted for much in history (man is the animal who devoured his own kind when he was closest to the "natural state," before he was able "artificially" to multiply production of natural benefits). Nor did the "faculty of reasoning" or "spirit" create unity; it cannot be recognized as a "unifying" fact because it is a categorical formal concept. It is not "thought" but what is actually thought which unites and differentiates men.

The most satisfying answer is that "human nature" is a "complex of human relations," because this answer includes the idea of "becoming" (man becomes, changes himself continually with the changing of social relations), and because it denies "man in general." In reality social relations are expressed by diverse groups of men which are presupposed and the unity of which is dialectical and not formal. Man is aristocratic because he is the servant of the soil, etc. It can also be said that man's nature is "history" (and in this sense, history equals spirit, the nature of man is the spirit), if history is given the meaning of "becoming" in a *concordia discors* which does not destroy unity but contains within itself grounds for a possible unity. Therefore "human nature" is not to be found in any one particular man but in the whole history of mankind (and the fact that we naturally use the word "kind" is significant), while in each single individual are found characteristics made distinct through their difference from the characteristics of other individuals. The concept of "spirit" in traditional philosophy and the concept of "human nature" in biology also, should be defined as "scientific utopias" which are substitutes for the greater utopia "human nature" sought for in God (and in man, the son of God), and which indicate the travail of history, rational and emotional hopes, etc. It is true, of course, that the religions which preached the equality of men as the sons of God, as well as those philosophies which affirmed man's equality on the basis of his reasoning faculty, were the expressions of complex revolutionary movements (the transformation of the classical world, the transformation of the medieval world), and that these forged the strongest links in the chain of historical development.

The basis of the latest utopian philosophies, like that of Croce, is that Hegelian dialectics was the last reflection of these great historical links, and that dialectics, the expression of social contradictions, will develop into a pure conceptual dialectic when these contradictions disappear.

In history, real "equality," that is the degree of "spirituality" achieved through the historical development of "human nature," is identified in the system of "public and private," "explicit and implicit" associations that are linked in the "state" and in the world political system; the "equality" here meant is that which is felt as such between the members of an association and the "inequality" felt between different associations; equality and inequality which are of value because there is both individual and group understanding of them. Thus one arrives at the equality or equation between "philosophy and politics," between thought and action, Marxism. All is politics, philosophy as well as the philosophies, and the only "philosophy" is history in action, life itself. It is in this sense that one can interpret the theory of the German proletariat, heir to German classical philosophy, and that it can be affirmed that the theory and elaboration of hegemony by Lenin was also a great "metaphysical" event.

Select Bibliography

An Antonio Gramsci Reader: Selected Writings, 1916–1935. Edited by David Forgacs. New York: Schocken Books, 1988.

Antonio Gramsci: Pre-Prison Writings. Edited by Richard Bellamy. Translated by Virginia Cox. Cambridge: Cambridge University Press, 1994.

Antonio Gramsci: Selections from Political Writings, 1910–1920. Edited by Quintin Hoare. Translated by John Mathews. Minneapolis: University of Minnesota Press, 1990.

Further Selections from the Prison Notebooks. Edited and translated by Derek Boothman. Minneapolis: University of Minnesota Press, 1995.

History, Philosophy and Culture in the Young Gramsci. Edited by Pedro Cavalcanti and Paul Piccone. Translated by Pierluigi Molajoni and others. St Louis: Telos Press, 1975.

Letters from Prison, 2 vols. Edited by Frank Rosengarten. Translated by Raymond Rosenthal. New York: Columbia University Press, 1994.

The Modern Prince and Other Writings. Translated by Louis Marks. New York: International Publishers, 1967.

Prison Notebooks, 2 vols. Edited by Joseph A. Buttigieg. Translated by Joseph A. Buttigieg and Antonio Callari. New York: Columbia University Press, 1991.

Selections from Cultural Writings. Edited by David Forgacs and Geoffrey Nowell-Smith. Translated by William Boelhower. Cambridge, Mass.: Harvard University Press, 1985.

Selections from Political Writings (1921–1926). Edited and translated by Quintin Hoare. Minneapolis: University of Minnesota Press, 1990.

6

Walter Benjamin

Philosopher and literary critic Walter Benjamin (1892–1940) was born in Berlin, and acquired genuine fame only posthumously, following the publication of a two-volume edition of his writings some fifteen years after his death. Influenced by Marxism, and by his Jewish heritage, Benjamin's work encompasses a variety of literary styles, including short philosophical essays, extended literary commentary, autobiographical writings, and aphorisms. Although he never held an academic position, Benjamin was associated with the Frankfurt School of critical theory inspired by Adorno and Horkheimer, who supported his work.

Although he is sometimes thought of as a Marxist philosopher, Benjamin's work resists convenient categorization; his writings on history, for example, are not easily aligned with the conventional view of dialectical materialism. The following excerpts from "The Work of Art in the Age of Mechanical Reproduction" (1936) present some of Benjamin's most influential reflections on the contemporary age. In this essay, Benjamin ponders the breakdown of the "aura" of the work of art, a breakdown resulting from demands and possibilities created by the technologies of mechanical reproduction.

The Work of Art in the Age of Mechanical Reproduction

Our fine arts were developed, their types and uses were established, in times very different from the present, by men whose power of action upon things was insignificant in comparison with ours. But the amazing growth of our techniques, the adaptability and preci-

From "The Work of Art in the Age of Mechanical Reproduction," in *Illuminations*, edited by Hannah Arendt and translated by Harry Zohn (New York: Schocken Books, 1969), pp. 217, 220–5, 230–7, 239–42.

sion they have attained, the ideas and habits they are creating, make it a certainty that profound changes are impending in the ancient craft of the Beautiful. In all the arts there is a physical component which can no longer be considered or treated as it used to be, which cannot remain unaffected by our modern knowledge and power. For the last twenty years neither matter nor space nor time has been what it was from time immemorial. We must expect great innovations to transform the entire technique of the arts, thereby affecting artistic invention itself and perhaps even bringing about an amazing change in our very notion of art.[1]

Paul Valéry, Pièces sur l'art, "La Conquête de l'ubiquité," Paris

II

Even the most perfect reproduction of a work of art is lacking in one element: its presence in time and space, its unique existence at the place where it happens to be. This unique existence of the work of art determined the history to which it was subject throughout the time of its existence. This includes the changes which it may have suffered in physical condition over the years as well as the various changes in its ownership.[2] The traces of the first can be revealed only by chemical or physical analyses which it is impossible to perform on a reproduction; changes of ownership are subject to a tradition which must be traced from the situation of the original.

The presence of the original is the prerequisite to the concept of authenticity. Chemical analyses of the patina of a bronze can help to establish this, as does the proof that a given manuscript of the Middle Ages stems from an archive of the fifteenth century. The whole sphere of authenticity is outside technical – and, of course, not only technical – reproducibility.[3] Confronted with its manual reproduction, which was usually branded as a forgery, the original preserved all its authority; not so *vis-à-vis* technical reproduction. The reason is twofold. First, process reproduction is more independent of the original than manual reproduction. For example, in photography, process reproduction can bring out those aspects of the original that are unattainable to the naked eye yet accessible to the lens, which is adjustable and chooses its angle at will. And photographic reproduction, with the aid of certain processes, such as enlargement or slow motion, can capture images which escape natural vision. Secondly, technical reproduction can put the copy of the original into situations which would be out of reach for the original itself. Above all, it enables the original to meet the beholder halfway, be it in the form of a photograph or a phonograph record. The cathedral leaves its locale to be received in the studio of a lover of art; the choral production, performed in an auditorium or in the open air, resounds in the drawing room.

The situations into which the product of mechanical reproduction can be brought may not touch the actual work of art, yet the quality of its presence is always depreciated. This holds not only for the art work but also, for instance, for a landscape which passes in review before the spectator in a movie. In the case of the art object, a most sensitive nucleus – namely, its authenticity – is interfered with whereas no natural object is vulnerable on that score. The authenticity of a thing is the essence of all that is transmissible from its beginning, ranging from its substantive duration to its testimony to the history which it has experienced. Since the historical testimony rests on the authenticity, the former, too, is jeopardized by reproduction when substantive duration ceases to matter. And what is really jeopardized when the historical testimony is affected is the authority of the object.[4]

One might subsume the eliminated element in the term "aura" and go on to say: that which withers in the age of mechanical reproduction is the aura of the work of art. This is a symptomatic process whose significance points beyond the realm of art. One might generalize by saying: the technique of reproduction detaches the reproduced object from the domain of tradition. By making many reproductions it substitutes a plurality of copies for a unique existence. And in permitting the reproduction to meet the beholder or listener in his own particular situation, it reactivates the object reproduced. These two processes lead to a tremendous shattering of tradition which is the obverse of the contemporary crisis and renewal of mankind. Both processes are intimately connected with the contemporary mass movements. Their most powerful agent is the film. Its social significance, particularly in its most positive form, is inconceivable without its destructive, cathartic aspect, that is, the liquidation of the traditional value of the cultural heritage. This phenomenon is most palpable in the great historical films. It extends to ever new positions. In 1927 Abel Gance exclaimed enthusiastically: "Shakespeare, Rembrandt, Beethoven will make films . . . all legends, all mythologies and all myths, all founders of religion, and the very religions . . . await their exposed resurrection, and the heroes crowd each other at the gate."[5] Presumably without intending it, he issued an invitation to a far-reaching liquidation.

III

. . . The concept of aura which was proposed above with reference to historical objects may usefully be illustrated with reference to the aura of natural ones. We define the aura of the latter as the unique phenomenon of a distance, however close it may be. If, while resting on a summer afternoon, you follow with your eyes a mountain range on the horizon or a branch which casts its shadow over you, you experience the aura of those mountains, of that branch. This image makes it easy to comprehend the social bases of the contemporary decay of the aura. It rests on two circumstances, both of which are related to the increasing significance of the masses in contemporary life. Namely, the desire of contemporary masses to bring things "closer" spatially and humanly, which is just as ardent as their bent toward overcoming the uniqueness of every reality by accepting its reproduction.[6] Every day the urge grows stronger to get hold of an object at very close range by way of its likeness, its reproduction. Unmistakably, reproduction as offered by picture magazines and newsreels differs from the image seen by the unarmed eye. Uniqueness and permanence are as closely linked in the latter as are transitoriness and reproducibility in the former. To pry an object from its shell, to destroy its aura, is the mark of a perception whose "sense of the universal equality of things" has increased to such a degree that it extracts it even from a unique object by means of reproduction. Thus is manifested in the field of perception what in the theoretical sphere is noticeable in the increasing importance of statistics. The adjustment of reality to the masses and of the masses to reality is a process of unlimited scope, as much for thinking as for perception.

IV

The uniqueness of a work of art is inseparable from its being embedded in the fabric of tradition. This tradition itself is thoroughly alive and extremely changeable. An ancient statue of Venus, for example, stood in a different traditional context with the Greeks, who made it an object of veneration, than with the clerics of the Middle Ages, who viewed it as an ominous idol. Both of them, however, were equally confronted with its uniqueness, that is, its aura. Originally the contextual integration of art in tradition found its expression in the cult. We know that the earliest art works originated in the service of a ritual – first the magical, then the religious kind. It is significant that the existence of the work of art with reference to its aura is never entirely separated from its ritual function.[7] In other words, the unique value of the "authentic" work of art has its basis in ritual, the location of its original use value. This ritualistic basis, however remote, is still recognizable as secularized ritual even in the most profane forms of the cult of beauty.[8] The secular cult of beauty, developed during the Renaissance and prevailing for three centuries, clearly showed that ritualistic basis in its decline and the first deep crisis which befell it. With the advent of the first truly revolutionary means of reproduction, photography, simultaneously with the rise of socialism, art sensed the approaching crisis which has become evident a century later. At the time, art reacted with the doctrine of *l'art pour l'art*, that is, with a theology of art. This gave rise to what might be called a negative theology in the form of the idea of "pure" art, which not only denied any social function of art but also any categorizing by subject matter. (In poetry, Mallarmé was the first to take this position.)

An analysis of art in the age of mechanical reproduction must do justice to these relationships, for they lead us to an all-important insight: for the first time in world history, mechanical reproduction emancipates the work of art from its parasitical dependence on ritual. To an ever greater degree the work of art reproduced becomes the work of art designed for reproducibility.[9] From a photographic negative, for example, one can make any number of prints; to ask for the "authentic" print makes no sense. But the instant the criterion of authenticity ceases to be applicable to artistic production, the total function of art is reversed. Instead of being based on ritual, it begins to be based on another practice – politics.

V

Works of art are received and valued on different planes. Two polar types stand out: with one, the accent is on the cult value; with the other, on the exhibition value of the work. Artistic production begins with ceremonial objects destined to serve in a cult. One may assume that what mattered was their existence, not their being on view. The elk portrayed by the man of the Stone Age on the walls of his cave was an instrument of magic. He did expose it to his fellow men, but in the main it was meant for the spirits. Today the cult value would seem to demand that the work of art remain hidden. Certain statues of gods are accessible only to the priest in the cella; certain Madonnas remain covered nearly all year round; certain sculptures on medieval cathedrals are invisible to the spectator on ground level. With the emancipation of the various art practices from ritual go increasing opportunities for the exhibition of their products. It is easier to exhibit a portrait bust that can be sent here and there than to exhibit the statue of a divinity that has its fixed place in the interior of a temple. The same holds for the painting as against the mosaic or fresco that preceded it. And even though the public presentability of a mass originally may have been just as great as that of a symphony, the latter originated at the moment when its public presentability promised to surpass that of the mass.

With the different methods of technical reproduction of a work of art, its fitness for exhibition increased to such an extent that the quantitative shift between its two poles turned into a qualitative transformation of its nature. This is comparable to the situation of the work of art in prehistoric times when, by the absolute emphasis on its cult value, it was, first and foremost, an instrument of magic. Only later did it come to be recognized as a work of art. In the same way today, by the absolute emphasis on its exhibition value the work of art becomes a creation with entirely new functions, among which the one we are conscious of, the artistic function, later may be recognized as incidental.[10] This much is certain: today photography and the film are the most serviceable exemplifications of this new function. . . .

X

The feeling of strangeness that overcomes the actor before the camera, as Pirandello describes it, is basically of the same kind as the estrangement felt before one's own image in the mirror. But now the reflected image has become separable, transportable. And where is it transported? Before the public.[11] Never for a moment does the screen actor cease to be conscious of this fact. While facing the camera he knows that ultimately he will face the public, the consumers who constitute the market. This market, where he offers not only his labor but also his whole self, his heart and soul, is beyond his reach. During the shooting he has as little contact with it as any article made in a factory. This may contribute to that oppression, that new anxiety which, according to Pirandello, grips the actor before the camera. The film responds to the shriveling of the aura with an artificial build-up of the

"personality" outside the studio. The cult of the movie star, fostered by the money of the film industry, preserves not the unique aura of the person but the "spell of the personality," the phony spell of a commodity. So long as the moviemakers' capital sets the fashion, as a rule no other revolutionary merit can be accredited to today's film than the promotion of a revolutionary criticism of traditional concepts of art. We do not deny that in some cases today's films can also promote revolutionary criticism of social conditions, even of the distribution of property. However, our present study is no more specifically concerned with this than is the film production of Western Europe. . . .

XI

The shooting of a film, especially of a sound film, affords a spectacle unimaginable anywhere at any time before this. It presents a process in which it is impossible to assign to a spectator a viewpoint which would exclude from the actual scene such extraneous accessories as camera equipment, lighting machinery, staff assistants, etc. – unless his eye were on a line parallel with the lens. This circumstance, more than any other, renders superficial and insignificant any possible similarity between a scene in the studio and one on the stage. In the theater one is well aware of the place from which the play cannot immediately be detected as illusionary. There is no such place for the movie scene that is being shot. Its illusionary nature is that of the second degree, the result of cutting. That is to say, in the studio the mechanical equipment has penetrated so deeply into reality that its pure aspect freed from the foreign substance of equipment is the result of a special procedure, namely, the shooting by the specially adjusted camera and the mounting of the shot together with other similar ones. The equipment-free aspect of reality here has become the height of artifice; the sight of immediate reality has become an orchid in the land of technology.

Even more revealing is the comparison of these circumstances, which differ so much from those of the theater, with the situation in painting. Here the question is: How does the cameraman compare with the painter? To answer this we take recourse to an analogy with a surgical operation. The surgeon represents the polar opposite of the magician. The magician heals a sick person by the laying on of hands; the surgeon cuts into the patient's body. The magician maintains the natural distance between the patient and himself; though he reduces it very slightly by the laying on of hands, he greatly increases it by virtue of his authority. The surgeon does exactly the reverse; he greatly diminishes the distance between himself and the patient by penetrating into the patient's body, and increases it but little by the caution with which his hand moves among the organs. In short, in contrast to the magician – who is still hidden in the medical practitioner – the surgeon at the decisive moment abstains from facing the patient man to man; rather, it is through the operation that he penetrates into him.

Magician and surgeon compare to painter and cameraman. The painter maintains in his work a natural distance from reality, the cameraman penetrates deeply into its web.[12] There is a tremendous difference between the pictures they obtain. That of the painter is a total one, that of the cameraman consists of multiple fragments which are assembled under a new law. Thus, for contemporary man the representation of reality by the film is incomparably more significant than that of the painter, since it offers, precisely because of the thoroughgoing permeation of reality with mechanical equipment, an aspect of reality which is free of all equipment. And that is what one is entitled to ask from a work of art. . . .

XIII

The characteristics of the film lie not only in the manner in which man presents himself to mechanical equipment but also in the manner in which, by means of this apparatus, man can represent his environment. A glance at occupational psychology illustrates the testing capacity of the equipment. Psychoanalysis illustrates it in a different perspective. The film has enriched our field of perception with methods which can be illustrated by those of Freudian theory. Fifty years ago, a slip of the tongue passed more or less unnoticed. Only exceptionally may such a slip have revealed dimensions of depth in a conversation which had seemed to be taking its course on the surface. Since the *Psychopathology of Everyday Life* things have changed. This book isolated and made analyzable things which had heretofore floated along unnoticed in the broad stream of perception. For the entire spectrum of optical, and now also acoustical, perception the film has brought about a similar deepening of apperception. It is only an obverse of this fact that

behavior items shown in a movie can be analyzed much more precisely and from more points of view than those presented on paintings or on the stage. As compared with painting, filmed behavior lends itself more readily to analysis because of its incomparably more precise statements of the situation. In comparison with the stage scene, the filmed behavior item lends itself more readily to analysis because it can be isolated more easily. This circumstance derives its chief importance from its tendency to promote the mutual penetration of art and science. Actually, of a screened behavior item which is neatly brought out in a certain situation, like a muscle of a body, it is difficult to say which is more fascinating, its artistic value or its value for science. To demonstrate the identity of the artistic and scientific uses of photography which heretofore usually were separated will be one of the revolutionary functions of the film.[13]

By close-ups of the things around us, by focusing on hidden details of familiar objects, by exploring commonplace milieux under the ingenious guidance of the camera, the film, on the one hand, extends our comprehension of the necessities which rule our lives; on the other hand, it manages to assure us of an immense and unexpected field of action. Our taverns and our metropolitan streets, our offices and furnished rooms, our railroad stations and our factories appeared to have us locked up hopelessly. Then came the film and burst this prison-world asunder by the dynamite of the tenth of a second, so that now, in the midst of its far-flung ruins and debris, we calmly and adventurously go traveling. With the close-up, space expands; with slow motion, movement is extended. The enlargement of a snapshot does not simply render more precise what in any case was visible, though unclear: it reveals entirely new structural formations of the subject. So, too, slow motion not only presents familiar qualities of movement but reveals in them entirely unknown ones "which, far from looking like retarded rapid movements, give the effect of singularly gliding, floating, supernatural motions."[14] Evidently a different nature opens itself to the camera than opens to the naked eye – if only because an unconsciously penetrated space is substituted for a space consciously explored by man. Even if one has a general knowledge of the way people walk, one knows nothing of a person's posture during the fractional second of a stride. The act of reaching for a lighter or a spoon is familiar routine, yet we hardly know what really goes on between hand and metal, not to mention how this fluctuates with our moods. Here the camera intervenes with the resources of its lowerings and liftings, its interruptions and isolations, its extensions and accelerations, its enlargements and reductions. The camera introduces us to unconscious optics as does psychoanalysis to unconscious impulses. . . .

XV

The mass is a matrix from which all traditional behavior toward works of art issues today in a new form. Quantity has been transmuted into quality. The greatly increased mass of participants has produced a change in the mode of participation. The fact that the new mode of participation first appeared in a disreputable form must not confuse the spectator. Yet some people have launched spirited attacks against precisely this superficial aspect. Among these, Duhamel has expressed himself in the most radical manner. What he objects to most is the kind of participation which the movie elicits from the masses. Duhamel calls the movie "a pastime for helots, a diversion for uneducated, wretched, worn-out creatures who are consumed by their worries . . ., a spectacle which requires no concentration and presupposes no intelligence . . ., which kindles no light in the heart and awakens no hope other than the ridiculous one of someday becoming a 'star' in Los Angeles."[15] Clearly, this is at bottom the same ancient lament that the masses seek distraction whereas art demands concentration from the spectator. That is a commonplace. The question remains whether it provides a platform for the analysis of the film. A closer look is needed here. Distraction and concentration form polar opposites which may be stated as follows: A man who concentrates before a work of art is absorbed by it. He enters into this work of art the way legend tells of the Chinese painter when he viewed his finished painting. In contrast, the distracted mass absorbs the work of art. This is most obvious with regard to buildings. Architecture has always represented the prototype of a work of art the reception of which is consummated by a collectivity in a state of distraction. The laws of its reception are most instructive.

Buildings have been man's companions since primeval times. Many art forms have developed and perished. Tragedy begins with the Greeks, is extinguished with them, and after centuries its "rules" only are revived. The epic poem, which had its origin in the youth of nations, expires in Europe at the end of the Renaissance. Panel painting is a creation of the Middle Ages, and nothing guarantees its uninterrupted existence. But the human need for shelter is lasting. Architecture has never been idle. Its history is more ancient than that of any other art, and its claim to being a living force has significance in every attempt to comprehend the relationship of the masses to art. Buildings are appropriated in a twofold manner: by use and by perception – or rather, by touch and sight. Such appropriation cannot be understood in terms of the attentive concentration of a tourist before a famous building. On the tactile side there is no counterpart to contemplation on the optical side. Tactile appropriation is accomplished not so much by attention as by habit. As regards architecture, habit determines to a large extent even optical reception. The latter, too, occurs much less through rapt attention than by noticing the object in incidental fashion. This mode of appropriation, developed with reference to architecture, in certain circumstances acquires canonical value. For the tasks which face the human apparatus of perception at the turning points of history cannot be solved by optical means, that is, by contemplation, alone. They are mastered gradually by habit, under the guidance of tactile appropriation.

The distracted person, too, can form habits. More, the ability to master certain tasks in a state of distraction proves that their solution has become a matter of habit. Distraction as provided by art presents a covert control of the extent to which new tasks have become soluble by apperception. Since, moreover, individuals are tempted to avoid such tasks, art will tackle the most difficult and most important ones where it is able to mobilize the masses. Today it does so in the film. Reception in a state of distraction, which is increasing noticeably in all fields of art and is symptomatic of profound changes in apperception, finds in the film its true means of exercise. The film with its shock effect meets this mode of reception halfway. The film makes the cult value recede into the background not only by putting the public in the position of the critic, but also by the fact that at the movies this position requires no attention. The public is an examiner, but an absent-minded one.

Epilogue

The growing proletarianization of modern man and the increasing formation of masses are two aspects of the same process. Fascism attempts to organize the newly created proletarian masses without affecting the property structure which the masses strive to eliminate. Fascism sees its salvation in giving these masses not their right, but instead a chance to express themselves.[16] The masses have a right to change property relations; Fascism seeks to give them an expression while preserving property. The logical result of Fascism is the introduction of aesthetics into political life. The violation of the masses, whom Fascism, with its *Führer* cult, forces to their knees, has its counterpart in the violation of an apparatus which is pressed into the production of ritual values.

All efforts to render politics aesthetic culminate in one thing: war. War and war only can set a goal for mass movements on the largest scale while respecting the traditional property system. This is the political formula for the situation. The technological formula may be stated as follows: Only war makes it possible to mobilize all of today's technical resources while maintaining the property system. It goes without saying that the Fascist apotheosis of war does not employ such arguments. Still, Marinetti says in his manifesto on the Ethiopian colonial war: "For twenty-seven years we Futurists have rebelled against the branding of war as anti-aesthetic. . . . Accordingly we state: . . . War is beautiful because it establishes man's dominion over the subjugated machinery by means of gas masks, terrifying megaphones, flame throwers, and small tanks. War is beautiful because it initiates the dreamt-of metalization of the human body. War is beautiful because it enriches a flowering meadow with the fiery orchids of machine guns. War is beautiful because it combines the gunfire, the cannonades, the cease-fire, the scents, and the stench of putrefaction into a symphony. War is beautiful because it creates new architecture, like that of the big tanks, the geometrical formation flights, the smoke spirals from burning villages, and many

others. . . . Poets and artists of Futurism! . . . remember these principles of an aesthetics of war so that your struggle for a new literature and a new graphic art . . . may be illumined by them!"

This manifesto has the virtue of clarity. Its formulations deserve to be accepted by dialecticians. To the latter, the aesthetics of today's war appears as follows: If the natural utilization of productive forces is impeded by the property system, the increase in technical devices, in speed, and in the sources of energy will press for an unnatural utilization, and this is found in war. The destructiveness of war furnishes proof that society has not been mature enough to incorporate technology as its organ, that technology has not been sufficiently developed to cope with the elemental forces of society. The horrible features of imperialistic warfare are attributable to the discrepancy between the tremendous means of production and their inadequate utilization in the process of production – in other words, to unemployment and the lack of markets. Imperialistic war is a rebellion of technology which collects, in the form of "human material," the claims to which society has denied its natural material. Instead of draining rivers, society directs a human stream into a bed of trenches; instead of dropping seeds from airplanes, it drops incendiary bombs over cities; and through gas warfare the aura is abolished in a new way.

"*Fiat ars – pereat mundus*," says Fascism, and, as Marinetti admits, expects war to supply the artistic gratification of a sense perception that has been changed by technology. This is evidently the consummation of "*l'art pour l'art*." Mankind, which in Homer's time was an object of contemplation for the Olympian gods, now is one for itself. Its self-alienation has reached such a degree that it can experience its own destruction as an aesthetic pleasure of the first order. This is the situation of politics which Fascism is rendering aesthetic. Communism responds by politicizing art.

Notes

1 Quoted from Paul Valéry, *Aesthetics*, "The Conquest of Ubiquity," translated by Ralph Manheim, p. 225. Pantheon Books, Bollingen Series, New York, 1964. (Original ed.)

2 Of course, the history of a work of art encompasses more than this. The history of the *Mona Lisa*, for instance, encompasses the kind and number of its copies made in the seventeenth, eighteenth and nineteenth centuries.

3 Precisely because authenticity is not reproducible, the intensive penetration of certain (mechanical) processes of reproduction was instrumental in differentiating and grading authenticity. To develop such differentiations was an important function of the trade in works of art. The invention of the woodcut may be said to have struck at the root of the quality of authenticity even before its late flowering. To be sure, at the time of its origin a medieval picture of the

Madonna could not yet be said to be "authentic." It became "authentic" only during the succeeding centuries and perhaps most strikingly so during the last one.

4   The poorest provincial staging of *Faust* is superior to a Faust film in that, ideally, it competes with the first performance at Weimar. Before the screen it is unprofitable to remember traditional contents which might come to mind before the stage – for instance, that Goethe's friend Johann Heinrich Merck is hidden in Mephisto, and the like.

5   Abel Gance, "Le Temps de l'image est venu," *L'Art cinématographique*, vol. 2, pp. 94 ff., Paris, 1927. (Original ed.)

6   To satisfy the human interest of the masses may mean to have one's social function removed from the field of vision. Nothing guarantees that a portraitist of today, when painting a famous surgeon at the breakfast table in the midst of his family, depicts his social function more precisely than a painter of the seventeenth century who portrayed his medical doctors as representing this profession, like Rembrandt in his *Anatomy Lesson*.

7   The definition of the aura as a "unique phenomenon of a distance however close it may be" represents nothing but the formulation of the cult value of the work of art in categories of space and time perception. Distance is the opposite of closeness. The essentially distant object is the unapproachable one. Unapproachability is indeed a major quality of the cult image. True to its nature, it remains "distant, however close it may be." The closeness which one may gain from its subject matter does not impair the distance which it retains in its appearance.

8   To the extent to which the cult value of the painting is secularized the ideas of its fundamental uniqueness lose distinctness. In the imagination of the beholder the uniqueness of the phenomena which hold sway in the cult image is more and more displaced by the empirical uniqueness of the creator or of his creative achievement. To be sure, never completely so; the concept of authenticity always transcends mere genuineness. (This is particularly apparent in the collector who always retains some traces of the fetishist and who, by owning the work of art, shares in its ritual power.) Nevertheless, the function of the concept of authenticity remains determinate in the evaluation of art; with the secularization of art, authenticity displaces the cult value of the work.

9   In the case of films, mechanical reproduction is not, as with literature and painting, an external condition for mass distribution. Mechanical reproduction is inherent in the very technique of film production. This technique not only permits in the most direct way but virtually causes mass distribution. It enforces distribution because the production of a film is so expensive that an individual who, for instance, might afford to buy a painting no longer can afford to buy a film. In

1927 it was calculated that a major film, in order to pay its way, had to reach an audience of nine million. With the sound film, to be sure, a setback in its international distribution occurred at first: audiences became limited by language barriers. This coincided with the Fascist emphasis on national interests. It is more important to focus on this connection with Fascism than on this setback, which was soon minimized by synchronization. The simultaneity of both phenomena is attributable to the depression. The same disturbances which, on a larger scale, led to an attempt to maintain the existing property structure by sheer force led the endangered film capital to speed up the development of the sound film. The introduction of the sound film brought about a temporary relief, not only because it again brought the masses into the theaters but also because it merged new capital from the electrical industry with that of the film industry. Thus, viewed from the outside, the sound film promoted national interests, but seen from the inside it helped to internationalize film production even more than previously.

10 Bertolt Brecht, on a different level, engaged in analogous reflections: "If the concept of 'work of art' can no longer be applied to the thing that emerges once the work is transformed into a commodity, we have to eliminate this concept with cautious care but without fear, lest we liquidate the function of the very thing as well. For it has to go through this phase without mental reservation, and not as noncommittal deviation from the straight path; rather, what happens here with the work of art will change it fundamentally and erase its past to such an extent that should the old concept be taken up again – and it will, why not? – it will no longer stir any memory of the thing it once designated."

11 The change noted here in the method of exhibition caused by mechanical reproduction applies to politics as well. The present crisis of the bourgeois democracies comprises a crisis of the conditions which determine the public presentation of the rulers. Democracies exhibit a member of government directly and personally before the nation's representatives. Parliament is his public. Since the innovations of camera and recording equipment make it possible for the orator to become audible and visible to an unlimited number of persons, the presentation of the man of politics before camera and recording equipment becomes paramount. Parliaments, as much as theaters, are deserted. Radio and film not only affect the function of the professional actor but likewise the function of those who also exhibit themselves before this mechanical equipment, those who govern. Though their tasks may be different, the change affects equally the actor and the ruler. The trend is toward establishing controllable and transferrable skills under certain social

251

conditions. This results in a new selection, a selection before the equipment from which the star and the dictator emerge victorious.

12   The boldness of the cameraman is indeed comparable to that of the surgeon. Luc Durtain lists among specific technical sleights of hand those "which are required in surgery in the case of certain difficult operations. I choose as an example a case from oto-rhinolaryngology;...the so-called endonasal perspective procedure; or I refer to the acrobatic tricks of larynx surgery which have to be performed following the reversed picture in the laryngoscope. I might also speak of ear surgery which suggests the precision work of watchmakers. What range of the most subtle muscular acrobatics is required from the man who wants to repair or save the human body! We have only to think of the couching of a cataract where there is virtually a debate of steel with nearly fluid tissue, or of the major abdominal operations (laparotomy)."

13   Renaissance painting offers a revealing analogy to this situation. The incomparable development of this art and its significance rested not least on the integration of a number of new sciences, or at least of new scientific data. Renaissance painting made use of anatomy and perspective, of mathematics, meteorology, and chromatology. Valéry writes: "What could be further from us than the strange claim of a Leonardo to whom painting was a supreme goal and the ultimate demonstration of knowledge? Leonardo was convinced that painting demanded universal knowledge, and he did not even shrink from a theoretical analysis which to us is stunning because of its very depth and precision...." – Paul Valéry, *Pièces sur l'art*, "Autour de Corot," Paris, p. 191.

14   Rudolf Arnheim, *Film als Kunst*, Berlin, 1932, p. 138. (Original ed.)

15   Duhamel, *Scènes de la vie future*, Paris, 1930, p. 58. (Original ed.).

16   One technical feature is significant here, especially with regard to newsreels, the propagandist importance of which can hardly be overestimated. Mass reproduction is aided especially by the reproduction of masses. In big parades and monster rallies, in sports events, and in war, all of which nowadays are captured by camera and sound recording, the masses are brought face to face with themselves. This process, whose significance need not be stressed, is intimately connected with the development of the techniques of reproduction and photography. Mass movements are usually discerned more clearly by a camera than by the naked eye. A bird's-eye view best captures gatherings of hundreds of thousands. And even though such a view may be as accessible to the human eye as it is to the camera, the image received by the eye cannot be enlarged the way a negative is enlarged. This means that mass movements, including war, constitute a form of human behavior which particularly favors mechanical equipment.

Select Bibliography

Charles Baudelaire: A Lyric Poet in the Era of High Capitalism. Translated by Harry Zohn. London: Verso, 1983.

Illuminations. Edited by Hannah Arendt. Translated by Harry Zohn. New York: Schocken Books, 1968.

Moscow Diary. Edited by Gary Smith. Translated by Richard Sieburth. Cambridge, Mass.: Harvard University Press, 1986.

One-Way Street and Other Writings. Translated by Edmund Jephcott and Kingsley Shorter. London: Verso, 1985.

The Origin of German Tragic Drama. Translated by John Osborne. London: Verso, 1985.

Reflections: Essays, Aphorisms, Autobiographical Writings. Edited by Peter Demetz. Translated by Edmund Jephcott. New York: Schocken Books, 1986.

Selected Writings. Edited by Marcus Bullock and Michael W. Jennings. Cambridge: Belknap Press, 1996.

Understanding Brecht. Translated by Anna Bostock. London: Verso, 1983.

7

Theodor Adorno and Max Horkheimer

Theodor Adorno (1903–69) and Max Horkheimer (1895–1973) were central figures at the Institute of Social Research in Frankfurt, Germany. The Institute was the birthplace of the so-called Frankfurt School of Critical Theory, a form of Marxist cultural criticism influenced as well by Freud and phenomenology. Adorno, a musicologist and cultural critic who had also studied philosophy and sociology, was attracted early on by the atonal music of Arnold Schönberg, in which he saw an expression of human autonomy that offered resistance to the phenomena of mass culture and mass media. Horkheimer was head of the Institute for Social Research for several decades, including the Nazi period during which the Institute fled to Geneva and then to New York. Together, Adorno and Horkheimer wrote the influential *Dialectic of Enlightenment* (1947), in which, as the following selection illustrates, the Enlightenment, technology, and "the culture industry" as a whole are seen as inextricably bound to domination and the thwarting of individuality.

Dialectic of Enlightenment

The Culture Industry: Enlightenment as Mass Deception

The sociological theory that the loss of the support of objectively established religion, the dissolution of the last remnants of precapitalism, together with technological and social differentiation or specialization, have led to cultural chaos is disproved every

day; for culture now impresses the same stamp on everything. Films, radio, and magazines make up a system which is uniform as a whole and in every part. Even the aesthetic activities of political opposites are one in their enthusiastic obedience to the rhythm of the iron system. The decorative industrial management buildings and exhibition centers in authoritarian countries are much the same as anywhere else. The huge gleaming towers that shoot up everywhere are outward signs of the ingenious planning of international concerns, toward which the unleashed entrepreneurial system (whose monuments are a mass of gloomy houses and business premises in grimy, spiritless cities) was already hastening. Even now the older houses just outside the concrete city centers look like slums, and the new bungalows on the outskirts are at one with the flimsy structures of world fairs in their praise of technical progress and their built-in demand to be discarded after a short while like empty food cans. Yet the city housing projects designed to perpetuate the individual as a supposedly independent unit in a small hygienic dwelling make him all the more subservient to his adversary – the absolute power of capitalism. Because the inhabitants, as producers and as consumers, are drawn into the center in search of work and pleasure, all the living units crystallize into well-organized complexes. The striking unity of microcosm and macrocosm presents men with a model of their culture: the false identity of the general and the particular. Under monopoly all mass culture is identical, and the lines of its artificial framework begin to show through. The people at the top are no longer so interested in concealing monopoly: as its violence becomes more open, so its power grows. Movies and radio need no longer pretend to be art. The truth that they are just business is made into an ideology in order to justify the rubbish they deliberately produce. They call themselves industries; and when their directors' incomes are published, any doubt about the social utility of the finished products is removed.

Interested parties explain the culture industry in technological terms. It is alleged that because millions participate in it, certain reproduction processes are necessary that inevitably require identical needs in innumerable places to be satisfied with identical goods. The technical contrast between the few production centers and the large number of widely dispersed consumption points is said to demand organization and planning by management. Furthermore, it is claimed that standards were based in the first place on consumers' needs, and for that reason were accepted with so little resistance. The result is the circle of manipulation and retroactive need in which the unity of the system grows ever stronger. No mention is made of the fact that the basis on which technology acquires power over society is the power of those whose economic hold over society is greatest. A technological rationale is the rationale of domination itself. It is the coercive nature of society alienated from itself. Automobiles, bombs, and movies keep the whole thing together until their leveling element shows its strength in the very wrong which

it furthered. It has made the technology of the culture industry no more than the achievement of standardization and mass production, sacrificing whatever involved a distinction between the logic of the work and that of the social system. This is the result not of a law of movement in technology as such but of its function in today's economy. The need which might resist central control has already been suppressed by the control of the individual consciousness. The step from the telephone to the radio has clearly distinguished the roles. The former still allowed the subscriber to play the role of subject, and was liberal. The latter is democratic: it turns all participants into listeners and authoritatively subjects them to broadcast programs which are all exactly the same. No machinery of rejoinder has been devised, and private broadcasters are denied any freedom. They are confined to the apocryphal field of the "amateur," and also have to accept organization from above. But any trace of spontaneity from the public in official broadcasting is controlled and absorbed by talent scouts, studio competitions, and official programs of every kind selected by professionals. Talented performers belong to the industry long before it displays them; otherwise they would not be so eager to fit in. The attitude of the public, which ostensibly and actually favors the system of the culture industry, is a part of the system and not an excuse for it. If one branch of art follows the same formula as one with a very different medium and content; if the dramatic intrigue of broadcast soap operas becomes no more than useful material for showing how to master technical problems at both ends of the scale of musical experience – real jazz or a cheap imitation; or if a movement from a Beethoven symphony is crudely "adapted" for a film soundtrack in the same way as a Tolstoy novel is garbled in a film script: then the claim that this is done to satisfy the spontaneous wishes of the public is no more than hot air. We are closer to the facts if we explain these phenomena as inherent in the technical and personnel apparatus which, down to its last cog, itself forms part of the economic mechanism of selection. In addition there is the agreement – or at least the determination – of all executive authorities not to produce or sanction anything that in any way differs from their own rules, their own ideas about consumers, or above all themselves.

In our age the objective social tendency is incarnate in the hidden subjective purposes of company directors, the foremost among whom are in the most powerful sectors of industry – steel, petroleum, electricity, and chemicals. Culture monopolies are weak and dependent in comparison. They cannot afford to neglect their appeasement of the real holders of power if their sphere of activity in mass society (a sphere producing a specific type of commodity which anyhow is still too closely bound up with easygoing liberalism and Jewish intellectuals) is not to undergo a series of purges. The dependence of the most powerful broadcasting company on the electrical industry, or of the motion picture industry on the banks, is characteristic of the whole sphere, whose individual branches are themselves economically interwoven. All are in such close contact that the extreme concentration of mental forces allows demarcation lines between different firms and technical branches to be ignored. The ruthless unity in the culture industry is evidence of what will happen in politics. Marked differentiations such as those of A and B films, or of stories in magazines in different price ranges, depend not so much on subject matter as on classifying, organizing, and labeling consumers. Something is provided for all so that none may escape; the distinctions are emphasized and extended. The public is catered for with a hierarchical range of mass-produced products of varying quality, thus advancing the rule of complete quantification. Everybody must behave (as if spontaneously) in accordance with his previously determined and indexed level, and choose the category of mass product turned out for his type. Consumers appear as statistics on research organization charts, and are divided by income groups into red, green, and blue areas; the technique is that used for any type of propaganda.

How formalized the procedure is can be seen when the mechanically differentiated products prove to be all alike in the end. That the difference between the Chrysler range and General Motors products is basically illusory strikes every child with a keen interest in varieties. What connoisseurs discuss as good or bad points serve only to perpetuate the semblance of competition and range of choice. The same applies to the Warner Brothers and Metro Goldwyn Mayer productions. But even the differences between the more expensive and cheaper models put out by the same firm steadily diminish: for automobiles, there are such differences as the number of cylinders, cubic capacity, details of patented gadgets; and for films there are the number of stars, the extravagant use of technology, labor, and equipment, and the introduction of the latest psychological formulas. The universal criterion of merit is the amount of "conspicuous production," of blatant cash investment. The varying budgets in the culture industry do not bear the slightest relation to factual values, to the meaning of the products themselves. Even the technical media are relentlessly forced into uniformity. Television aims at a synthesis of radio and film, and is held up only because the interested parties have not yet reached agreement, but its consequences will be quite enormous and promise to intensify the impoverishment of aesthetic matter so drastically, that by tomorrow the thinly veiled identity of all industrial culture products can come triumphantly out into the open, derisively fulfilling the Wagnerian dream of the *Gesamtkunstwerk* – the fusion of all the arts in one work. The alliance of word, image, and music is all the more perfect than in *Tristan* because the sensuous elements which all approvingly reflect the surface of social reality are in principle embodied in the same technical process, the unity of which becomes its distinctive content. This process integrates all the elements of the production, from the novel (shaped with an eye to the film) to the last sound effect. It is the triumph of invested capital, whose title as absolute master is etched deep into the hearts of the dispossessed in the employment line; it is the meaningful content of every film, whatever plot the production team may have selected. . . .

In the culture industry the individual is an illusion not merely because of the standardization of the means of production. He is tolerated only so long as his complete identification with the generality is unquestioned. Pseudo individuality is rife: from the standardized jazz improvization to the exceptional film star whose hair curls over her eye to demonstrate her originality. What is individual is no more than the generality's power to stamp the accidental detail so firmly that it is accepted as such. The defiant reserve or elegant appearance of the individual on show is mass-produced like Yale locks, whose only difference can be measured in fractions of millimeters. The peculiarity of the self is a monopoly commodity determined by society; it is falsely represented as natural. It is no more than the moustache, the French accent, the deep voice of the woman of the world, the Lubitsch touch: finger prints on identity cards which are otherwise exactly the same, and into which the lives and faces of every single person are transformed by the power of the generality. Pseudo individuality is the prerequisite for comprehending

255

tragedy and removing its poison: only because individuals have ceased to be themselves and are now merely centers where the general tendencies meet, is it possible to receive them again, whole and entire, into the generality. In this way mass culture discloses the fictitious character of the "individual" in the bourgeois era, and is merely unjust in boasting on account of this dreary harmony of general and particular. The principle of individuality was always full of contradiction. Individuation has never really been achieved. Self-preservation in the shape of class has kept everyone at the stage of a mere species being. Every bourgeois characteristic, in spite of its deviation and indeed because of it, expressed the same thing: the harshness of the competitive society. The individual who supported society bore its disfiguring mark: seemingly free, he was actually the product of its economic and social apparatus. Power based itself on the prevailing conditions of power when it sought the approval of persons affected by it. As it progressed, bourgeois society did also develop the individual. Against the will of its leaders, technology has changed human beings from children into persons. However, every advance in individuation of this kind took place at the expense of the individuality in whose name it occurred, so that nothing was left but the resolve to pursue one's own particular purpose. The bourgeois whose existence is split into a business and a private life, whose private life is split into keeping up his public image and intimacy, whose intimacy is split into the surly partnership of marriage and the bitter comfort of being quite alone, at odds with himself and everybody else, is already virtually a Nazi, replete both with enthusiasm and abuse; or a modern city-dweller who can now only imagine friendship as a "social contact": that is, as being in social contact with others with whom he has no inward contact. The only reason why the culture industry can deal so successfully with individuality is that the latter has always reproduced the fragility of society. On the faces of private individuals and movie heroes put together according to the patterns on magazine covers vanishes a pretense in which no one now believes; the popularity of the hero models comes partly from a secret satisfaction that the effort to achieve individuation has at last been replaced by the effort to imitate, which is admittedly more breathless. It is idle to hope that this self-contradictory, disintegrating "person" will not last for generations, that the system must collapse because of such a psychological split, or that the deceitful

substitution of the stereotype for the individual will of itself become unbearable for mankind. Since Shakespeare's *Hamlet*, the unity of the personality has been seen through as a pretense. Synthetically produced physiognomies show that the people of today have already forgotten that there was ever a notion of what human life was. For centuries society has been preparing for Victor Mature and Mickey Rooney. By destroying they come to fulfill. . . .

Culture is a paradoxical commodity. So completely is it subject to the law of exchange that it is no longer exchanged; it is so blindly consumed in use that it can no longer be used. Therefore it amalgamates with advertising. The more meaningless the latter seems to be under a monopoly, the more omnipotent it becomes. The motives are markedly economic. One could certainly live without the culture industry, therefore it necessarily creates too much satiation and apathy. In itself, it has few resources itself to correct this. Advertising is its elixir of life. But as its product never fails to reduce to a mere promise the enjoyment which it promises as a commodity, it eventually coincides with publicity, which it needs because it cannot be enjoyed. In a competitive society, advertising performed the social service of informing the buyer about the market; it made choice easier and helped the unknown but more efficient supplier to dispose of his goods. Far from costing time, it saved it. Today when the free market is coming to an end, those who control the system are entrenching themselves in it. It strengthens the firm bond between the consumers and the big combines. Only those who can pay the exorbitant rates charged by the advertising agencies, chief of which are the radio networks themselves; that is, only those who are already in a position to do so, or are coopted by the decision of the banks and industrial capital, can enter the pseudo-market as sellers. The costs of advertising, which finally flow back into the pockets of the combines, make it unnecessary to defeat unwelcome outsiders by laborious competition. They guarantee that power will remain in the same hands – not unlike those economic decisions by which the establishment and running of undertakings is controlled in a totalitarian state. Advertising today is a negative principle, a blocking device: everything that does not bear its stamp is economically suspect. Universal publicity is in no way necessary for people to get to know the kinds of goods – whose supply is restricted anyway. It helps sales only indirectly. For a particular firm, to phase out a current advertising practice constitutes a loss of prestige, and a breach of the discipline imposed by the influential clique on its members. In wartime, goods which are unobtainable are still advertised, merely to keep industrial power in view. Subsidizing ideological media is more important than the repetition of the name. Because the system obliges every product to use advertising, it has permeated the idiom – the "style" – of the culture industry. Its victory is so complete that it is no longer evident in the key positions: the huge buildings of the top men, floodlit stone advertisements, are free of advertising; at most they exhibit on the rooftops, in monumental brilliance and without any self-glorification, the firm's initials. But, in contrast, the nineteenth-century houses, whose architecture still shamefully indicates that they can be used as a consumption commodity and are intended to be lived in, are covered with posters and inscriptions from the ground right up to and beyond the roof: until they become no more than backgrounds for bills and sign-boards. Advertising becomes art and nothing else, just as Goebbels – with foresight – combines them: *l'art pour l'art*, advertising for its own sake, a pure representation of social power. In the most influential American magazines, *Life* and *Fortune*, a quick glance can now scarcely distinguish advertising from editorial picture and text. The latter features an enthusiastic and gratuitous account of the great man (with illustrations of his life and grooming habits) which will bring him new fans, while the advertisement pages use so many factual photographs and details that they represent the ideal of information which the editorial part has only begun to try to achieve. The assembly-line character of the culture industry, the synthetic, planned method of turning out its products (factory-like not only in the studio but, more or less, in the compilation of cheap biographies, pseudo-documentary novels, and hit songs) is very suited to advertising: the important individual points, by becoming detachable, interchangeable, and even technically alienated from any connected meaning, lend themselves to ends external to the work. The effect, the trick, the isolated repeatable device, have always been used to exhibit goods for advertising purposes, and today every monster close-up of a star is an advertisement for her name, and every hit song a plug for its tune. Advertising and the culture industry merge technically as well as economically. In both cases the same thing can be seen in innumerable places, and the mechanical repetition of the same culture product has come to be the same as that of the propaganda slogan. In both cases the insistent demand for effectiveness makes technology into psychotechnology, into a procedure for manipulating men. In both cases the standards are the striking yet familiar, the easy yet catchy, the skillful yet simple; the object is to overpower the customer, who is conceived as absent-minded or resistant.

By the language he speaks, he makes his own contribution to culture as publicity. The more completely language is lost in the announcement, the more words are debased as substantial vehicles of meaning and become signs devoid of quality; the more purely and transparently words communicate what is intended, the more impenetrable they become. The demythologization of language, taken as an element of the whole process of enlightenment, is a relapse into magic. Word and essential content were distinct yet inseparable from one another. Concepts like melancholy and history, even life, were recognized in the word, which separated them out and preserved them. Its form simultaneously constituted and reflected them. The absolute separation, which makes the moving accidental and its relation to the object arbitrary, puts an end to the superstitious fusion of word and thing. Anything in a determined literal sequence which goes beyond the correlation to the event is rejected as unclear and as verbal metaphysics. But the result is that the word, which can now be only a sign without any meaning, becomes so fixed to the thing that it is just a petrified formula. This affects language and object alike. Instead of making the object experiential, the purified word treats it as an abstract instance, and everything else (now excluded by the demand for ruthless clarity from expression – itself now banished) fades away in reality. A left-half at football, a black-shirt, a member of the Hitler Youth, and so on, are no more than names. If before its rationalization the word had given rise to lies as well as to longing, now, after its rationalization, it is a straitjacket for longing more even than for lies. The blindness and dumbness of the data to which positivism reduces the world pass over into language itself, which restricts itself to recording those data. Terms themselves become impenetrable; they obtain a striking force, a power of adhesion and repulsion which makes them like their extreme opposite, incantations. They come to be a kind of trick, because the name of the prima donna is cooked up in the studio on a statistical basis, or because a welfare state is anathematized by using taboo terms such as "bureaucrats" or "intellectuals," or because base practice uses the name of the country as a charm. In general, the name – to which magic most easily attaches – is undergoing a chemical change: a metamorphosis into capricious, manipulable designations, whose effect is admittedly now calculable, but which for that very reason is just as despotic as that of the archaic name. First names, those archaic remnants, have been brought up to date either by stylization as advertising trademarks (film stars' surnames have become first names), or by collective standardization. In comparison, the bourgeois family name which, instead of being a trademark, once individualized its bearer by relating him to his own past history, seems antiquated. It arouses a strange embarrassment in Americans. In order to hide the awkward distance between individuals, they call one another "Bob" and "Harry," as interchangeable team members. This practice reduces relations between human beings to the good fellowship of the sporting community and is a defense against the true kind of relationship. Signification, which is the only function of a word admitted by semantics, reaches perfection in the sign. Whether folksongs were rightly or wrongly called upper-class culture in decay, their elements have only acquired their popular form through a long process of repeated transmission. The spread of popular songs, on the other hand, takes place at lightning speed. The American expression "fad," used for fashions which appear like epidemics – that is, inflamed by highly-concentrated economic forces – designated this phenomenon long before totalitarian advertising bosses enforced the general lines of culture. When the German Fascists decide one day to launch a word – say, "intolerable" – over the loudspeakers the next day the whole nation is saying "intolerable." By the same pattern, the nations against whom the weight of the German "blitzkrieg" was thrown took the word into their own jargon. The general repetition of names for measures to be taken by the authorities makes them, so to speak, familiar, just as the brand name on everybody's lips increased sales in the era of the free market. The blind and rapidly spreading repetition of words with special designations links advertising with the totalitarian watchword. The layer of experience which created the words for their speakers has been removed; in this swift appropriation language acquires the coldness which until now it had only on billboards and in the advertisement columns of newspapers. Innumerable people use words and expressions which they have either ceased to understand or employ only because they trigger off conditioned reflexes; in this sense, words are trademarks which are finally all the more firmly linked to the things they denote, the less their linguistic sense is grasped. The minister for mass education talks incomprehendingly of "dynamic forces," and the hit songs unceasingly celebrate "reverie" and "rhapsody," yet base their popularity precisely on the magic of the unintelligible as creating the thrill of a more exalted life. Other stereotypes, such as memory, are still partly comprehended, but escape from the experience which might allow them content. They appear like enclaves in the spoken language. On the radio of Flesch and Hitler they may be recognized from the affected pronunciation of the announcer when he says to the nation, "Good night, everybody!" or "This is the Hitler Youth," and even intones "the Führer" in a way imitated by millions. In such clichés the last bond between sedimentary experience and language is severed which still had a reconciling effect in dialect in the nineteenth century. But in the prose of the journalist whose adaptable attitude led to his appointment as an all-German editor, the German words become petrified, alien terms. Every word shows how far it has been debased by the Fascist pseudo-folk community. By now, of course, this kind of language is already universal, totalitarian. All the violence done to words is so vile that one can hardly bear to hear them any longer. The announcer does not need to speak pompously; he would indeed be impossible if his inflection were different from that of his particular audience. But, as against that, the language and gestures of the audience and spectators are colored more strongly than ever before by the culture industry, even in fine nuances which cannot yet be explained experimentally. Today the culture industry has taken over the civilizing inheritance of the entrepreneurial and frontier democracy – whose appreciation of intellectual deviations was never very finely attuned. All are free to dance and enjoy themselves, just as they have been free, since the historical neutralization of religion, to join any of the innumerable sects. But freedom to choose an ideology – since ideology always reflects economic coercion – everywhere proves to be freedom to choose what is always the same. The way in which a girl accepts and keeps the obligatory date, the inflection on the telephone or in the most intimate situation, the choice of words in conversation, and the whole inner life as classified by the now somewhat devalued depth psychology, bear witness to man's attempt to make himself a proficient apparatus, similar (even in emotions) to the model served up by the culture industry. The most intimate reactions of human beings have been so thoroughly reified that the idea of anything specific to themselves now persists only as an utterly abstract notion: personality scarcely signifies anything more than shining white teeth and freedom from body odor and emotions. The triumph of advertising in the culture industry is that consumers feel compelled to buy and use its products even though they see through them.

Select Bibliography

Adorno: The Stars Down to Earth, and Other Essays on the Irrational in Culture. (Adorno.) Edited by Stephen Crook. London: Routledge, 1994.

Aesthetic Theory. (Adorno.) London: Routledge and Kegan Paul, 1984.

Against Epistemology: A Metacritique: Studies in Husserl and the Phenomenological Antinomies. (Adorno.) Translated by Willis Domingo. Cambridge, Mass.: MIT Press, 1983.

The Authoritarian Personality. (Adorno and other authors.) New York: Norton, 1982.

Between Philosophy and Social Science: Selected Early Writings. (Horkheimer.) Translated by G. Frederick Hunter, Matthew S. Kramer, and John Torpey. Cambridge, Mass.: MIT Press, 1993.

Critical Theory: Selected Essays. (Horkheimer.) Translated by Matthew J. O'Connell and others. New York: Continuum, 1982.

Critique of Instrumental Reason: Lectures and Essays since the End of World War II. (Horkheimer.) Translated by Matthew J. O'Connell and others. New York: Continuum, 1974.

Dawn and Decline: Notes 1926–1931 and 1950–1969. (Horkheimer.) Translated by Michael Shaw. New York: Seabury Press, 1978.

Dialectic of Enlightenment. (Adorno and Horkheimer.) Translated by John Cumming. London: Verso, 1989.

Eclipse of Reason. (Horkheimer.) New York: Continuum, 1985.

Introduction to the Sociology of Music. (Adorno.) Translated by E. B. Ashton. New York: Seabury Press, 1976.

Minima Moralia: Reflections from a Damaged Life. (Adorno.) Translated by E. F. N. Jephcott. London: NLB, 1978.

Negative Dialectics. (Adorno.) Translated by E. B. Ashton. New York: Continuum, 1983.

Philosophy of Modern Music. (Adorno.) Translated by Anne G. Mitchell and Wesley V. Blomster. New York: Continuum, 1984.

Prisms. (Adorno.) Translated by Samuel Weber and Shierry Weber. Cambridge, Mass.: MIT Press, 1981.

Quasi Una Fantasia: Essays on Modern Music. (Adorno.) Translated by Rodney Livingstone. London: Verso, 1992.

8

Hannah Arendt

Hannah Arendt (1906–75) was born in Germany and studied under Husserl, Heidegger, and Jaspers. Of Jewish descent, she left Germany in 1933, eventually settling in the United States. Although Arendt is not a Marxist thinker (she indeed is critical of Marx), her work is concentrated primarily in the field of political philosophy and cultural critique, where she attempts to address the meaning of the political in the modern age by reference to the beginnings of our political tradition in Greek philosophy and civilization. Much of Arendt's thought is concerned with regaining a lost appreciation of political praxis and of the plurality of human affairs, concerns that (she argues) are largely erased today by the overwhelming dominance of economic interests and the consequent breakdown of the distinction between public and private. Questions of justice and of the nature of political judgment lie at the heart of her work. *The Human Condition* (1958), from which the following excerpt is taken, is a sustained meditation on the distinction of political action from labor, work, and contemplation.

The Human Condition

Prologue

In 1957, an earth-born object made by man was launched into the universe, where for some weeks it circled the earth according to the same laws of gravitation that swing and keep in motion the celestial bodies – the sun, the moon, and the stars. To be sure, the man-made satellite was no

From *The Human Condition* (Chicago: University of Chicago Press, 1958), pp. 1–21. Reprinted by permission of the publisher.

moon or star, no heavenly body which could follow its circling path for a time span that to us mortals, bound by earthly time, lasts from eternity to eternity. Yet, for a time it managed to stay in the skies; it dwelt and moved in the proximity of the heavenly bodies as though it had been admitted tentatively to their sublime company.

This event, second in importance to no other, not even to the splitting of the atom, would have been greeted with unmitigated joy if it had not been for the uncomfortable military and political circumstances attending it. But, curiously enough, this joy was not triumphal; it was not pride or awe at the tremendousness of human power and mastery which filled the hearts of men, who now, when they looked up from the earth toward the skies, could behold there a thing of their own making. The immediate reaction, expressed on the spur of the moment, was relief about the first "step toward escape from men's imprisonment to the earth." And this strange statement, far from being the accidental slip of some American reporter, unwittingly echoed the extraordinary line which, more than twenty years ago, had been carved on the funeral obelisk for one of Russia's great scientists: "Mankind will not remain bound to the earth forever."

Such feelings have been commonplace for some time. They show that men everywhere are by no means slow to catch up and adjust to scientific discoveries and technical developments, but that, on the contrary, they have outsped them by decades. Here, as in other respects, science has realized and affirmed what men anticipated in dreams that were neither wild nor idle. What is new is only that one of this country's most respectable newspapers finally brought to its front page what up to then had been buried in the highly nonrespectable literature of science fiction (to which, unfortunately, nobody yet has paid the attention it deserves as a vehicle of mass sentiments and mass desires). The banality of the statement should not make us overlook how extraordinary in fact it was; for although Christians have spoken of the earth as a vale of tears and philosophers have looked upon their body as a prison of mind or soul, nobody in the history of mankind has ever conceived of the earth as a prison for men's bodies or shown such eagerness to go literally from here to the moon. Should the emancipation and secularization of the modern age, which began with a turning-away, not necessarily from God, but from a god who was the Father of men in heaven, end with an even more fateful repudiation of an Earth who was the Mother of all living creatures under the sky?

The earth is the very quintessence of the human condition, and earthly nature, for all we know, may be unique in the universe in providing human beings with a habitat in which they can move and breathe without effort and without artifice. The human artifice of the world separates human existence from all mere animal environment, but life itself is outside this artificial world, and through life man remains related to all other living organisms. For some time now, a great many scientific endeavors have been directed toward making life also "artificial," toward cutting the last tie through which even man belongs among the children of nature. It is the same desire to escape from imprisonment to the earth that is manifest in the attempt to create life in the test tube, in the desire to mix "frozen germ plasm from people of demonstrated ability under the microscope to produce superior human beings" and "to alter [their] size, shape and function"; and the wish to escape the human condition, I suspect, also underlies the hope to extend man's life-span far beyond the hundred-year limit.

This future man, whom the scientists tell us they will produce in no more than a hundred years, seems to be possessed by a rebellion against human existence as it has been given, a free gift from nowhere (secularly speaking), which he wishes to exchange, as it were, for something he has made himself. There is no reason to doubt our abilities to accomplish such an exchange, just as there is no reason to doubt our present ability to destroy all organic life on earth. The question is only whether we wish to use our new scientific and technical knowledge in this direction, and this question cannot be decided by scientific means; it is a political question of the first order and therefore can hardly be left to the decision of professional scientists or professional politicians.

While such possibilities still may lie in a distant future, the first boomerang effects of science's great triumphs have made themselves felt in a crisis within the natural sciences themselves. The trouble concerns the fact that the "truths" of the modern scientific world view, though they can be demonstrated in mathematical formulas and proved technologically, will no longer lend themselves to normal expression in speech and thought. The moment these "truths" are spoken of conceptually and coherently, the resulting statements will be "not perhaps as meaningless as a 'triangular circle,' but much more so than a 'winged lion'" (Erwin Schrödinger). We do not yet know whether this situation is final. But it could be that we, who are earth-bound creatures and have begun to act as though we were dwellers of the universe, will forever be unable to understand, that is, to think and speak about the things which nevertheless we are able to do. In this case, it would be as though our brain, which constitutes the physical, material condition of our thoughts, were unable to follow what we do, so that from now on we would indeed need artificial machines to do our thinking and speaking. If it should turn out to be true that knowledge (in the modern sense of know-how) and thought have parted company for good, then we would indeed become the helpless slaves, not so much of our machines as of our know-how, thoughtless creatures at the mercy of every gadget which is technically possible, no matter how murderous it is.

However, even apart from these last and yet uncertain consequences, the situation created by the sciences is of great political significance. Wherever the relevance of speech is at stake, matters become political by definition, for speech is what makes man a political being. If we would follow the advice, so frequently urged upon us, to adjust our cultural attitudes to the present status of scientific achievement, we would in all earnest adopt a way of life in which speech is no longer meaningful. For the sciences today have been forced to adopt a "language" of mathematical symbols which, though it was originally meant only as an abbreviation for spoken statements, now contains statements that in no way can be translated back into speech. The reason why it may be wise to distrust the political judgment of scientists *qua* scientists is not primarily their lack of "character" – that they did not refuse to develop atomic weapons – or their naïveté – that they did not understand that once these weapons were developed they would be the last to be consulted about their use – but precisely the fact that they move in a world where speech has lost its power. And whatever men do or know or experience can make sense only to the extent that it can be spoken about. There may be truths beyond speech, and they may be of great relevance to man in the singular, that is, to man insofar as he is not a political being, whatever else he may be. Men in the plural, that is, men insofar as they live and move and act in this world, can experience meaningfulness only because they can talk with and make sense to each other and to themselves.

Closer at hand and perhaps equally decisive is another no less threatening event. This is the advent of automation, which in a few decades probably will empty the factories and liberate mankind from its oldest and most natural burden, the burden of laboring and the bondage to necessity. Here, too, a fundamental aspect of the human condition is at stake, but the rebellion against it, the wish to be liberated from labor's "toil and trouble," is not modern but as old as recorded history. Freedom from labor itself is not new; it once belonged among the most firmly established privileges of the few. In this instance, it seems as though scientific progress and technical develop-

ments had been only taken advantage of to achieve something about which all former ages dreamed but which none had been able to realize.

However, this is so only in appearance. The modern age has carried with it a theoretical glorification of labor and has resulted in a factual transformation of the whole of society into a laboring society. The fulfillment of the wish, therefore, like the fulfillment of wishes in fairy tales, comes at a moment when it can only be self-defeating. It is a society of laborers which is about to be liberated from the fetters of labor, and this society does no longer know of those other higher and more meaningful activities for the sake of which this freedom would deserve to be won. Within this society, which is egalitarian because this is labor's way of making men live together, there is no class left, no aristocracy of either a political or spiritual nature from which a restoration of the other capacities of man could start anew. Even presidents, kings, and prime ministers think of their offices in terms of a job necessary for the life of society, and among the intellectuals, only solitary individuals are left who consider what they are doing in terms of work and not in terms of making a living. What we are confronted with is the prospect of a society of laborers without labor, that is, without the only activity left to them. Surely, nothing could be worse.

To these preoccupations and perplexities, this book does not offer an answer. Such answers are given every day, and they are matters of practical politics, subject to the agreement of many; they can never lie in theoretical considerations or the opinion of one person, as though we dealt here with problems for which only one solution is possible. What I propose in the following is a reconsideration of the human condition from the vantage point of our newest experiences and our most recent fears. This, obviously, is a matter of thought, and thoughtlessness – the heedless recklessness or hopeless confusion or complacent repetition of "truths" which have become trivial and empty – seems to me among the outstanding characteristics of our time. What I propose, therefore, is very simple: it is nothing more than to think what we are doing.

"What we are doing" is indeed the central theme of this book. It deals only with the most elementary articulations of the human condition, with those activities that traditionally, as well as according to current opinion, are within the range of every human being. For this and other reasons, the highest and perhaps purest activity of which men are capable, the activity of thinking, is left out of these present considerations. Systematically, therefore, the book is limited to a discussion of labor, work, and action, which forms its three central chapters. Historically, I deal in a last chapter with the modern age, and throughout the book with the various constellations within the hierarchy of activities as we know them from Western history.

However, the modern age is not the same as the modern world. Scientifically, the modern age which began in the seventeenth century came to an end at the beginning of the twentieth century; politically, the modern world, in which we live today, was born with the first atomic explosions. I do not discuss this modern world, against whose background this book was written. I confine myself, on the one hand, to an analysis of those general human capacities which grow out of the human condition and are permanent, that is, which cannot be irretrievably lost so long as the human condition itself is not changed. The purpose of the historical analysis, on the other hand, is to trace back modern world alienation, its twofold flight from the earth into the universe and from the world into the self, to its origins, in order to arrive at an understanding of the nature of society as it had developed and presented itself at the very moment when it was overcome by the advent of a new and yet unknown age.

1 *Vita Activa* and the Human Condition

With the term *vita activa*, I propose to designate three fundamental human activities: labor, work, and action. They are fundamental because each corresponds to one of the basic conditions under which life on earth has been given to man.

Labor is the activity which corresponds to the biological process of the human body, whose spontaneous growth, metabolism, and eventual decay are bound to the vital necessities produced and fed into the life process by labor. The human condition of labor is life itself.

Work is the activity which corresponds to the unnaturalness of human existence, which is not embedded in, and whose mortality is not compensated by, the species' ever-recurring life cycle. Work provides an "artificial" world of things, distinctly different from all natural surroundings. Within its borders each individual life is housed, while this world itself is meant to outlast and

transcend them all. The human condition of work is worldliness.

Action, the only activity that goes on directly between men without the intermediary of things or matter, corresponds to the human condition of plurality, to the fact that men, not Man, live on the earth and inhabit the world. While all aspects of the human condition are somehow related to politics, this plurality is specifically *the* condition – not only the *conditio sine qua non*, but the *conditio per quam* – of all political life. Thus the language of the Romans, perhaps the most political people we have known, used the words "to live" and "to be among men" (*inter homines esse*) or "to die" and "to cease to be among men" (*inter homines esse desinere*) as synonyms. But in its most elementary form, the human condition of action is implicit even in Genesis ("Male and female created He *them*"), if we understand that this story of man's creation is distinguished in principle from the one according to which God originally created Man (*adam*), "him" and not "them," so that the multitude of human beings becomes the result of multiplication.[1] Action would be an unnecessary luxury, a capricious interference with general laws of behavior, if men were endlessly reproducible repetitions of the same model, whose nature or essence was the same for all and as predictable as the nature or essence of any other thing. Plurality is the condition of human action because we are all the same, that is, human, in such a way that nobody is ever the same as anyone else who ever lived, lives, or will live.

All three activities and their corresponding conditions are intimately connected with the most general condition of human existence: birth and death, natality and mortality. Labor assures not only individual survival, but the life of the species. Work and its product, the human artifact, bestow a measure of permanence and durability upon the futility of mortal life and the fleeting character of human time. Action, insofar as it engages in founding and preserving political bodies, creates the condition for remembrance, that is, for history. Labor and work, as well as action, are also rooted in natality insofar as they have the task to provide and preserve the world for, to foresee and reckon with, the constant influx of newcomers who are born into the world as strangers. However, of the three, action has the closest connection with the human condition of natality; the new beginning inherent in birth can make itself felt in the world only because the newcomer possesses the capacity of beginning something anew, that is, of acting. In this sense of initiative, an element of action, and therefore of natality, is inherent in all human activities. Moreover, since action is the political activity *par excellence*, natality, and not mortality, may be the central category of political, as distinguished from metaphysical, thought.

The human condition comprehends more than the conditions under which life has been given to man. Men are conditioned beings because everything they come in contact with turns immediately into a condition of their existence. The world in which the *vita activa* spends itself consists of things produced by human activities; but the things that owe their existence exclusively to men nevertheless constantly condition their human makers. In addition to the conditions under which life is given to man on earth, and partly out of them, men constantly create their own, self-made conditions, which, their human origin and their variability notwithstanding, possess the same conditioning power as natural things. Whatever touches or enters into a sustained relationship with human life immediately assumes the character of a condition of human existence. This is why men, no matter what they do, are always conditioned beings. Whatever enters the human world of its own accord or is drawn into it by human effort becomes part of the human condition. The impact of the world's reality upon human existence is felt and received as a conditioning force. The objectivity of the world – its object- or thing-character – and the human condition supplement each other; because human existence is conditioned existence, it would be impossible without things, and things would be a heap of unrelated articles, a nonworld, if they were not the conditioners of human existence.

To avoid misunderstanding: the human condition is not the same as human nature, and the sum total of human activities and capabilities which correspond to the human condition does not constitute anything like human nature. For neither those we discuss here nor those we leave out, like thought and reason, and not even the most meticulous enumeration of them all, constitute essential characteristics of human existence in the sense that without them this existence would no longer be human. The most radical change in the human condition we can imagine would be an emigration of men from the earth to some other planet. Such an event, no longer totally impossible, would imply that man would have to live under man-made conditions, radically different from those the earth offers him. Neither labor nor work nor action nor, indeed, thought as we know it would then make sense any longer. Yet even these hypothetical wanderers from the earth would still be human; but the only statement we could make regarding their "nature" is that they still are conditioned beings, even though their condition is now self-made to a considerable extent.

The problem of human nature, the Augustinian *quaestio mihi factus sum* ("a question have I become for myself"), seems unanswerable in both its individual psychological sense and its general philosophical sense. It is highly unlikely that we, who can know, determine, and define the natural essences of all things surrounding us, which we are not, should ever be able to do the same for ourselves – this would be like jumping over our own shadows. Moreover, nothing entitles us to assume that man has a nature or essence in the same sense as other things. In other words, if we have a nature or essence, then surely only a god could know and define it, and the first prerequisite would be that he be able to speak about a "who" as though it were a "what."[2] The perplexity is that the modes of human cognition applicable to things with "natural" qualities, including ourselves to the limited extent that we are specimens of the most highly developed species of organic life, fail us when we raise the question: And *who* are we? This is why attempts to define human nature almost invariably end with some construction of a deity, that is, with the god of the philosophers, who, since Plato, has revealed himself upon closer inspection to be a kind of Platonic idea of man. Of course, to demask such philosophic concepts of the divine as conceptualizations of human capabilities and qualities is not a demonstration of, not even an argument for, the nonexistence of God; but the fact that attempts to define the nature of man lead so easily into an idea which definitely strikes us as "superhuman" and therefore is identified with the divine may cast suspicion upon the very concept of "human nature."

On the other hand, the conditions of human existence – life itself, natality and mortality, worldliness, plurality, and the earth – can never "explain" what we are or answer the question of who we are for the simple reason that they never condition us absolutely. This has always been the opinion of philosophy, in distinction from the sciences – anthropology, psychology, biology, etc. – which also concern themselves with man. But today we may almost say that we have demonstrated even scientifically that, though we live now, and probably always will, under the earth's conditions, we are not mere earth-bound creatures. Modern natural science owes its great triumphs to having looked upon and treated earth-bound nature from a truly universal viewpoint, that is, from an Archimedean standpoint taken, wilfully and explicitly, outside the earth.

2 The Term *Vita Activa*

The term *vita activa* is loaded and overloaded with tradition. It is as old as (but not older than) our tradition of political thought. And this tradition, far from comprehending and conceptualizing all the political experiences of Western mankind, grew out of a specific historical constellation: the trial of Socrates and the conflict between the philosopher and the *polis*. It eliminated many experiences of an earlier past that were irrelevant to its immediate political purposes and proceeded until its end, in the work of Karl Marx, in a highly selective manner. The term itself, in medieval philosophy the standard translation of the Aristotelian *bios politikos*, already occurs in Augustine, where, as *vita negotiosa* or *actuosa*, it still reflects its original meaning: a life devoted to public–political matters.[3]

Aristotle distinguished three ways of life (*bioi*) which men might choose in freedom, that is, in full independence of the necessities of life and the relationships they originated. This prerequisite of freedom ruled out all ways of life chiefly devoted to keeping one's self alive – not only labor, which was the way of life of the slave, who was coerced by the necessity to stay alive and by the rule of his master, but also the working life of the free craftsman and the acquisitive life of the merchant. In short, it excluded everybody who involuntarily or voluntarily, for his whole life or temporarily, had lost the free disposition of his movements and activities.[4] The remaining three ways of life have in common that they were concerned with the "beautiful," that is, with things neither necessary nor merely useful: the life of enjoying bodily pleasures in which the beautiful, as it is given, is consumed; the life devoted to the matters of the *polis*, in which excellence produces beautiful deeds; and the life of the philosopher devoted to inquiry into, and contemplation of, things eternal, whose everlasting beauty can neither be brought about through the producing interference of man nor be changed through his consumption of them.[5]

The chief difference between the Aristotelian and the later medieval use of the term is that the *bios politikos* denoted explicitly only the realm of human affairs, stressing the action, *praxis*, needed to establish and sustain it. Neither labor nor work was considered to possess sufficient dignity to constitute a *bios* at all, an autonomous and authentically human way of life; since they served and produced what was necessary and useful, they could not be free, independent of human needs and wants.[6] That the political way of life escaped this verdict is due to the Greek understanding of *polis* life, which to them denoted a very special and freely chosen form of political organization and by no means just any form of action necessary to keep men together in an orderly fashion. Not that the Greeks or Aristotle were ignorant of the fact that human life always demands some form of political organization and that ruling over subjects might constitute a distinct way of life; but the despot's way of life, because it was "merely" a necessity, could not be considered free and had no relationship with the *bios politikos*.[7]

With the disappearance of the ancient city-state – Augustine seems to have been the last to know at least what it once meant to be a citizen – the term *vita activa* lost its specifically political meaning and denoted all kinds of active engagement in the things of this world. To be sure, it does not follow that work and labor had risen in the hierarchy of human activities and were now equal in dignity with a life devoted to politics.[8] It was, rather, the other way round: action was now also reckoned among the necessities of earthly life, so that contemplation (the *bios theoretikos*, translated into the *vita contemplativa*) was left as the only truly free way of life.[9]

However, the enormous superiority of contemplation over activity of any kind, action not excluded, is not Christian in origin. We find it in Plato's political philosophy, where the whole utopian reorganization of *polis* life is not only directed by the superior insight of the philosopher but has no aim other than to make possible the philosopher's way of life. Aristotle's very articulation of the different ways of life, in whose order the life of pleasure plays a minor role, is clearly guided by the ideal of contemplation (*theōria*). To the ancient freedom from the necessities of life and from compulsion by others, the philosophers added freedom and surcease from political activity (*skholē*),[10] so that the later Christian claim to be free from entanglement in worldly affairs, from all the business of this world, was preceded by and originated in the philosophic *apolitia* of late antiquity. What had been demanded only by the few was now considered to be a right of all.

The term *vita activa*, comprehending all human activities and defined from the viewpoint of the absolute quiet of contemplation, therefore corresponds more closely to the Greek *askholia* ("unquiet"), with which Aristotle designated all activity, than to the Greek *bios politikos*. As early as Aristotle the distinction between quiet and unquiet, between an almost breathless abstention from external physical movement and activity of every kind, is more decisive than the distinction between the political and the theoretical way of life, because it can eventually be found within each of the three ways of life. It is like the distinction between war and peace: just as war takes place for the sake of peace, thus every kind of activity, even the processes of mere thought, must culminate in the absolute quiet of contemplation.[11] Every movement, the movements of body and soul as well as of speech and reasoning, must cease before truth. Truth, be it the ancient truth of Being or the Christian truth of the living God, can reveal itself only in complete human stillness.[12]

Traditionally and up to the beginning of the modern age, the term *vita activa* never lost its negative connotation of "unquiet," *nec-otium*, *a-skholia*. As such it remained intimately related to the even more fundamental Greek distinction between things that are by themselves whatever they are and things which owe their existence to man, between things that are *physei* and things that are *nomō*. The primacy of contemplation over activity rests on the conviction that no work of human hands can equal in beauty and truth the physical *kosmos*, which swings in itself in changeless eternity without any interference or assistance from outside, from man or god. This eternity discloses itself to mortal eyes only when all human movements and activities are at perfect rest. Compared with this attitude of quiet, all distinctions and articulations within the *vita activa* disappear. Seen from the viewpoint of contemplation, it does not matter what disturbs the necessary quiet, as long as it is disturbed.

Traditionally, therefore, the term *vita activa* receives its meaning from the *vita contemplativa*; its very restricted dignity is bestowed upon it because it serves the needs and wants of contemplation in a living body.[13] Christianity, with its belief in a hereafter whose joys announce themselves in the delights of contemplation,[14] conferred a religious sanction upon the abasement of the *vita activa* to its derivative, secondary position; but the determination of the order itself coincided with the very discovery of contemplation (*theōria*) as a human faculty, distinctly different from thought and reasoning, which occurred in the Socratic school and from then on has ruled metaphysical and political thought throughout our tradition.[15] It seems unnecessary to my present purpose to discuss the reasons for this tradition. Obviously they are deeper than the historical occasion which gave rise to the conflict between the *polis* and the philosopher and thereby, almost incidentally, also led to the discovery of contemplation as the philosopher's way of life. They must lie in an altogether different aspect of the human condition, whose diversity is not exhausted in the various articulations of the *vita activa* and, we may suspect, would not be exhausted even if thought and the movement of reasoning were included in it.

If, therefore, the use of the term *vita activa*, as I propose it here, is in manifest contradiction to the tradition, it is because I doubt not the validity of the experience underlying the distinction but rather the hierarchical order inherent in it from its inception. This does not mean that I wish to contest or even to discuss, for that matter, the traditional concept of truth as revelation and therefore something essentially given to man, or that I prefer the modern age's pragmatic assertion that man can know only what he makes himself. My contention is simply that the enormous weight of contemplation in the traditional hierarchy has blurred the distinctions and articulations within the *vita activa* itself and that, appearances notwithstanding, this condition has not been changed essentially by the modern break with the tradition and the eventual reversal of its hierarchical order in Marx and Nietzsche. It lies in the very nature of the famous "turning upside down" of philosophic systems or currently accepted values, that is, in the nature of the operation itself, that the conceptual framework is left more or less intact.

The modern reversal shares with the traditional hierarchy the assumption that the same central human preoccupation must prevail in all activities of men, since without one comprehensive principle no order could be established. This assumption is not a matter of course, and my use of the term *vita activa* presupposes that the concern underlying all its activities is not the same as and is neither superior nor inferior to the central concern of the *vita contemplativa*.

3 Eternity versus Immortality

That the various modes of active engagement in the things of this world, on one side, and pure thought culminating in contemplation, on the other, might correspond to two altogether different central human concerns has in one way or another been manifest ever since "the men of thought and the men of action began to take different paths,"[16] that is, since the rise of political thought in the Socratic school. However, when the philosophers discovered – and it is probable, though unprovable, that this discovery was made by Socrates himself – that the political realm did not as a matter of course provide for all of man's higher activities, they assumed at once, not that they had found something different in addition to what was already known, but that they had found a higher principle to replace the principle that ruled the *polis*. The shortest, albeit somewhat superficial, way to indicate these two different and to an extent even conflicting principles is to recall the distinction between immortality and eternity.

Immortality means endurance in time, deathless life on this earth and in this world as it was given, according to Greek understanding, to nature and the Olympian gods. Against this background of nature's ever-recurring life and the gods' deathless and ageless lives stood mortal men, the only mortals in an immortal but not eternal universe, confronted with the immortal lives of their gods but not under the rule of an eternal God. If we trust Herodotus, the difference between the two seems to have been striking to Greek self-understanding prior to the conceptual articulation of the philosophers, and therefore prior to the specifically Greek experiences of the eternal which underlie this articulation. Herodotus, discussing Asiatic forms of worship and beliefs in an invisible God, mentions explicitly that compared with this transcendent God (as we would say today) who is beyond time and life and the universe, the Greek gods are *anthrōpophyeis*, have the same nature, not simply the same shape, as man.[17] The Greeks' concern with immortality grew out of their experience of an immortal nature and immortal gods which together surrounded the individual lives of mortal men. Embedded in a cosmos where everything was immortal, mortality became the hallmark of human existence. Men are "the mortals," the only mortal things in existence, because unlike animals they do not exist only as members of a species whose immortal life is guaranteed through procreation.[18] The mortality of men lies in the fact that individual life, with a recognizable life-story from birth to death, rises out of biological life. This individual life is distinguished from all other things by the rectilinear course of its movement, which, so to speak, cuts through the circular movement of biological life. This is mortality: to move along a rectilinear line in a universe where everything, if it moves at all, moves in a cyclical order.

The task and potential greatness of mortals lie in their ability to produce things – works and deeds and words[19] – which would deserve to be and, at least to a degree, are at home in everlastingness, so that through them mortals could find their place in a cosmos where everything is immortal except themselves. By their capacity for the immortal deed, by their ability to leave nonperishable traces behind, men, their individual mortality notwithstanding, attain an immortality of their own and prove themselves to be of a "divine" nature. The distinction between man and animal runs right through the human species itself: only the best (*aristoi*), who constantly prove themselves to be the best (*aristeuein*, a verb for which there is no equivalent in any other language) and who "prefer immortal fame to mortal things," are really human; the others, content with whatever pleasures nature will yield them, live and die like animals. This was still the opinion of Heraclitus,[20] an opinion whose equivalent one will find in hardly any philosopher after Socrates.

In our context it is of no great importance whether Socrates himself or Plato discovered the eternal as the true center of strictly metaphysical thought. It weighs heavily in favor of Socrates that he alone among the great thinkers – unique in this as in many other respects – never cared to write down his thoughts; for it is obvious that, no matter how concerned a thinker may be with eternity, the moment he sits down to write his thoughts he ceases to be concerned primarily with eternity and shifts his attention to leaving some trace of them. He has entered the *vita activa* and chosen its way of permanence and potential immortality. One thing is certain: it is only in Plato that concern with the eternal and the life of the philosopher are seen as inherently contradictory and in conflict with the striving for immortality, the way of life of the citizen, the *bios politikos*.

The philosopher's experience of the eternal, which to Plato was *arrhēton* ("unspeakable"), and to Aristotle *aneu logou* ("without word"), and which later was conceptualized in the paradoxical *nunc stans* ("the standing now"), can occur only outside the realm of human affairs and outside the plurality of men, as we know from the Cave parable in Plato's *Republic*, where the philosopher, having liberated himself from the fetters that bound him to his fellow men, leaves the cave in perfect "singularity," as it were, neither accompanied nor followed by others. Politically speaking, if to die is the same as "to cease to be among men," experience of the eternal is a kind of death, and the only thing that separates it from real death is that it is not final because no living creature can endure it for any length of time. And this is precisely what separates the *vita contemplativa* from the *vita activa* in medieval thought.[21] Yet it is decisive that the experience of the eternal, in contradistinction to that of the immortal, has no correspondence with and cannot be transformed into any activity whatsoever, since even the activity of thought, which goes on within one's self by means of words, is obviously not only inadequate to render it but would interrupt and ruin the experience itself.

Theōria, or "contemplation," is the word given to the experience of the eternal, as distinguished from all other attitudes, which at most may pertain to immortality. It may be that the philosophers' discovery of the eternal was helped by their very justified doubt of the chances of the *polis* for immortality or even permanence, and it may be that the shock of this discovery was so overwhelming that they could not but look down upon all striving for immortality as vanity and vainglory, certainly placing themselves thereby into open opposition to the ancient city-state and the religion which inspired it. However, the eventual victory of the concern with eternity over all kinds of aspirations toward immortality is not due to philosophic thought. The fall of the Roman Empire plainly demonstrated that no work of mortal hands can be immortal, and it was accompanied by the rise of the Christian gospel of an everlasting individual life to its position as the exclusive religion of Western mankind. Both together made any striving for an earthly immortality futile and unnecessary. And they succeeded so well in making the *vita activa* and the *bios politikos* the handmaidens of contemplation that not even the rise of the secular in the modern age and the concomitant reversal of the traditional hierarchy between action and contemplation sufficed to save from oblivion the striving for immortality which originally had been the spring and center of the *vita activa*.

Notes

1 In the analysis of postclassical political thought, it is often quite illuminating to find out which of the two biblical versions of the creation story is cited. Thus it is highly characteristic of the difference between the teaching of Jesus of Nazareth and of Paul that Jesus, discussing the relationship between man and wife, refers to Genesis 1:27: "Have ye not read, that he which made *them* at the beginning made them male and female" (Matt. 19:4), whereas Paul on a similar occasion insists that the woman was created "of the man" and hence "for the man," even though he then somewhat attenuates the dependence: "neither is the man without the woman, neither the woman without the man" (I Cor. 11: 8–12). The difference indicates much more than a different attitude to the role of woman. For Jesus, faith was closely related to action (cf. § 33 below); for Paul, faith was primarily related to salvation. Especially interesting in this respect is Augustine (*De civitate Dei* xii. 21), who not only ignores Genesis 1:27 altogether but sees the difference between man and animal in that man was created *unum ac singulum*, whereas all animals were ordered "to come into being several at once" (*plura simul iussit exsistere*). To Augustine, the creation story offers a welcome opportunity to stress the species character of animal life as distinguished from the singularity of human existence.

2 Augustine, who is usually credited with having been the first to raise the so-called anthropological question in philosophy, knew this quite well. He distinguishes between the questions of "Who am I?" and "What am I?" the first being directed by man at himself ("And I directed myself at myself and said to me: You, who are you? And I answered: A man" – *tu, quis es?* [*Confessiones* x. 6]) and the second being addressed to God ("What then am I, my God? What is my nature?" – *Quid ergo sum, Deus meus? Quae natura sum?* [x. 17]). For in the "great mystery," the *grande profundum*, which man is (iv. 14), there is "something of man [*aliquid hominis*] which the spirit of man which is in him itself knoweth not. But Thou, Lord, who has made him [*fecisti eum*] knowest everything of him [*eius omnia*]" (x. 5). Thus, the most familiar of these phrases which I quoted in the text, the *quaestio mihi factus sum*, is a question raised in the presence of God, "in whose eyes I have become a question for myself".

(x. 33). In brief, the answer to the question "Who am I?" is simply: "You are a man – whatever that may be"; and the answer to the question "What am I?" can be given only by God who made man. The question about the nature of man is no less a theological question than the question about the nature of God; both can be settled only within the framework of a divinely revealed answer.

3 See Augustine *De civitate Dei* xix. 2, 19.

4 William L. Westermann ("Between Slavery and Freedom," *American Historical Review*, vol. L [1945]) holds that the "statement of Aristotle . . . that craftsmen live in a condition of limited slavery meant that the artisan, when he made a work contract, disposed of two of the four elements of his free status [viz., of freedom of economic activity and right of unrestricted movement], but by his own volition and for a temporary period"; evidence quoted by Westermann shows that freedom was then understood to consist of "status, personal inviolability, freedom of economic activity, right of unrestricted movement," and slavery consequently "was the lack of these four attributes." Aristotle, in his enumeration of "ways of life" in the *Nicomachean Ethics* (i. 5) and the *Eudemian Ethics* (1215a35 ff.), does not even mention a craftsman's way of life; to him it is obvious that a *banausos* is not free (cf. *Politics* 1337b5). He mentions, however, "the life of money-making" and rejects it because it too is "undertaken under compulsion" (*Nic. Eth.* 1096a5). That the criterion is freedom is stressed in the *Eudemian Ethics*: he enumerates only those lives that are chosen *ep' exousian*.

5 For the opposition of the beautiful to the necessary and the useful see *Politics* 1333a30 ff., 1332b32.

6 For the opposition of the free to the necessary and the useful see ibid. 1332b2.

7 See ibid. 1277b8 for the distinction between despotic rule and politics. For the argument that the life of the despot is not equal to the life of a free man because the former is concerned with "necessary things," see ibid. 1325a24.

8 On the widespread opinion that the modern estimate of labor is Christian in origin, see below, § 44.

9 See Aquinas *Summa theologica* ii. 2. 179, esp. art. 2, where the *vita activa* arises out of the *necessitas vitae praesentis*, and *Expositio in Psalmos* 45.3, where the body politic is assigned the task of finding all that is necessary for life: *in civitate oportet invenire omnia necessaria ad vitam.*

10 The Greek word *skholē*, like the Latin *otium*, means primarily freedom from political activity and not simply leisure time, although both words are also used to indicate freedom from labor and life's necessities. In any event, they always indicate a condition free from worries and cares. An excellent description of the everyday life of an ordinary Athenian citizen, who enjoys full freedom from labor and work, can be found in Fustel de Coulanges, *The Ancient City*

(Anchor ed., 1956), pp. 334–6; it will convince everybody how time-consuming political activity was under the conditions of the city-state. One can easily guess how full of worry this ordinary political life was if one remembers that Athenian law did not permit remaining neutral and punished those who did not want to take sides in factional strife with loss of citizenship.

11 See Aristotle *Politics* 1333a30–33. Aquinas defines contemplation as *quies ab exterioribus motibus* (*Summa theologica* ii. 2. 179. 1).

12 Aquinas stresses the stillness of the soul and recommends the *vita activa* because it exhausts and therefore "quietens interior passions" and prepares for contemplation (*Summa theologica* ii. 2. 182. 3).

13 Aquinas is quite explicit on the connection between the *vita activa* and the wants and needs of the human body which men and animals have in common (*Summa theologica* ii. 2. 182. 1).

14 Augustine speaks of the "burden" (*sarcina*) of active life imposed by the duty of charity, which would be unbearable without the "sweetness" (*suavitas*) and the "delight of truth" given in contemplation (*De civitate Dei* xix. 19).

15 The time-honored resentment of the philosopher against the human condition of having a body is not identical with the ancient contempt for the necessities of life; to be subject to necessity was only one aspect of bodily existence, and the body, once freed of this necessity, was capable of that pure appearance the Greeks called beauty. The philosophers since Plato added to the resentment of being forced by bodily wants the resentment of movement of any kind. It is because the philosopher lives in complete quiet that it is only his body which, according to Plato, inhabits the city. Here lies also the origin of the early reproach of busy-bodiness (*polypragmosynē*) leveled against those who spent their lives in politics.

16 See F. M. Cornford, "Plato's Commonwealth," in *Unwritten Philosophy* (1950), p. 54: "The death of Pericles and the Peloponnesian War mark the moment when the men of thought and the men of action began to take different paths, destined to diverge more and more widely till the Stoic sage ceased to be a citizen of his own country and became a citizen of the universe."

17 Herodotus (i. 131), after reporting that the Persians have "no images of the gods, no temples nor altars, but consider these doings to be foolish," goes on to explain that this shows that they "do not believe, as the Greeks do, that the gods are *anthrōpophyeis*, of human nature," or, we may add, that gods and men have the same nature. See also Pindar *Carmina Nemaea* vi.

18 See Ps. Aristotle *Economics* 1343b24: Nature guarantees to the species their being forever through recurrence (*periodos*), but cannot guarantee such being forever to the individual. The same thought,

"For living things, life is being," appears in *On the Soul* 415b13.

19 The Greek language does not distinguish between "works" and "deeds," but calls both *erga* if they are durable enough to last and great enough to be remembered. It is only when the philosophers, or rather the Sophists, began to draw their "endless distinctions" and to distinguish between making and acting (*poiein* and *prattein*) that the nouns *poiēmata* and *pragmata* received wider currency (see Plato's *Charmides* 163).

Homer does not yet know the word *pragmata*, which in Plato (*ta tōn anthrōpōn pragmata*) is best rendered by "human affairs" and has the connotations of trouble and futility. In Herodotus *pragmata* can have the same connotation (cf., for instance, i. 155).

20 Heraclitus, frag. B29 (Diels, *Fragmente der Vorsokratiker* [4th edn, 1922]).

21 *In vita activa fixi permanere possumus; in contemplativa autem intenta mente manere nullo modo valemus* (Aquinas *Summa theologica* ii. 2. 181. 4).

Select Bibliography

Between Past and Future: Eight Exercises in Political Thought. New York: Penguin Books, 1978.

Eichmann in Jerusalem: A Report on the Banality of Evil. New York: Penguin Books, 1994.

Essays in Understanding, 1930–1954. Edited by Jerome Kohn. New York: Harcourt, Brace, 1994.

The Human Condition. Chicago: University of Chicago Press, 1958.

The Jew as Pariah: Jewish Identity and Politics in the Modern Age. Edited by Ron H. Feldman. New York: Grove Press, 1978.

Lectures on Kant's Political Philosophy. Edited by Ronald Beiner. Chicago: University of Chicago Press, 1982.

The Life of the Mind. New York: Harcourt Brace Jovanovich, 1981.

Love and Saint Augustine. Edited by Joanna Vecchiarelli Scott and Judith Chelius Stark. Chicago: University of Chicago Press, 1996.

Men in Dark Times. New York: Harcourt, Brace and World, 1968.

On Revolution. London: Penguin Books, 1990.

On Violence. New York: Harcourt, Brace and World, 1970.

The Origins of Totalitarianism. San Diego: Harcourt Brace Jovanovich, 1985.

9

Louis Althusser

A former member of the French Communist Party and philosopher at the École Normale in Paris, Louis Althusser (1918–90) is known as a structuralist and antihumanist Marxist thinker. His structuralist interpretation of Marx is influenced primarily by Marx's own emphasis on the priority of the social, economic, and ideological systems of capitalism over the individual. Althusser stresses the extent to which individual subjects are formed by the largely hidden and repressive operations of relatively autonomous systems of structural forces that produce and sustain a given social order. Here ideology, as "the locus of political struggle," plays a crucial role, and humanism itself is seen as one particular ideology. For Althusser, ideology is a system of representations that expresses the way in which human beings, at the level of "the imaginary," actually live out the relations between themselves and their conditions of existence; as such, ideology is in a continual and "overdetermined" tension with the "real" relation of human beings to their world. As the following selection from the essay "Marxism and Humanism" (first published in 1964) illustrates, Althusser finds this structuralist understanding of ideology in Marx's later, scientific conception of historical materialism which, he alleges, rejects the role of the human "subject" as the bearer of history.

For Marx

Marxism and Humanism

I

Today, Socialist "Humanism" is on the agenda.

From *For Marx*, translated by Ben Brewster (New York: Vintage Books, 1970), pp. 221–36. Copyright © 1969 by Allen Lane, The Penguin Press. Reprinted by permission of Pantheon Books, a division of Random House, Inc.

As it enters the period which will lead it from socialism (to each according to his labor) to communism (to each according to his needs), the Soviet Union has proclaimed the slogan: All for Man, and introduced new themes: the freedom of the individual, respect for legality, the dignity of the person. In workers' parties the achievements of socialist humanism are celebrated and justification for its theoretical claims is sought in *Capital*, and more and more frequently, in Marx's early works.

This is a historical event. I wonder even whether socialist humanism is not such a reassuring and attractive theme that it will allow a dialogue between Communists and Social Democrats, or even a wider exchange with those "men of good will" who are opposed to war and poverty. Today, even the high-road of Humanism seems to lead to socialism. . . .

II

To see beyond this event, to understand it, to know the meaning of socialist humanism, it is not enough just to register the event, nor to record the concepts (humanism, socialism) in which the event itself thinks itself. The theoretical claims of the concepts must be tested to insure that they really do provide us with a truly scientific knowledge of the event.

But precisely in the couple "humanism–socialism" there is a striking theoretical unevenness: in the framework of the Marxist conception, the concept "socialism" is indeed a scientific concept, but the concept "humanism" is no more than an *ideological* one.

Note that my purpose is not to dispute the reality that the concept of socialist humanism is supposed to designate, but to define the *theoretical* value of the concept. When I say that the concept of humanism is an ideological concept (not a scientific one), I mean that while it really does designate a set of existing relations, unlike a scientific concept, it does not provide us with a means of knowing them. In a particular (ideological) mode, it designates some existents, but it does not give us their essences. If we were to confuse these two orders we should cut ourselves off from all knowledge, uphold a confusion and risk falling into error.

To show this clearly, I shall briefly invoke Marx's own experience, for he only arrived at a scientific theory of history at the price of a radical critique of the philosophy of man that had served as his theoretical basis during the years of his youth (1840–5). I use the words "theoretical basis" in their strict sense. For the young Marx, "Man" was not just a cry denouncing poverty and slavery. It was the theoretical principle of his world outlook and of his practical attitude. The "Essence of Man" (whether freedom–reason or community) was the basis both for a rigorous theory of history and for a consistent political practice.

This can be seen in the two stages of Marx's humanist period.

The First Stage was dominated by a liberal–rationalist humanism closer to Kant and Fichte than to Hegel. In his conflict with censorship, Rhenish feudal laws, Prussian despotism, Marx's political struggle and the theory of history sustaining it were based theoretically on a philosophy of man. Only the essence of man makes history, and this essence is freedom and reason. *Freedom*: it is the essence of man just as weight is the essence of bodies. Man is destined to freedom, it is his very being. Whether he rejects it or negates it, he remains in it for ever: "*So much is freedom the essence of Man that even its adversaries are realizing it when they fight against its reality. . . . So freedom has always existed, in one way or another, sometimes only as a particular privilege, sometimes as a general right.*"[1] This distinction illuminates the whole of history: thus, feudalism is freedom, but in the "nonrational" form of privilege; the modern state is freedom, but in the rational form of a universal right. *Reason*: man is only freedom as reason. Human freedom is neither caprice, nor the determinism of interest, but, as Kant and Fichte meant it, autonomy, obedience to the inner law of reason. This reason, which has "*always existed though not always in a rational form*"[2] (e.g. feudalism), in modern times does at least exist in the form of reason in the state, the state of law and right. "*Philosophy regards the State as the great organism in which legal, moral and political freedom should find their realization and in which the individual citizen, when he obeys the State's laws, is only obeying the natural laws of his own reason, of human reason.*"[3] Hence the task of philosophy: "*Philosophy demands that the State be the State of human nature.*"[4] This injunction is addressed to the state itself: if it would recognize its essence it would become reason, the true freedom of man, through its own reform of itself. Therefore, politico-philosophical criticism (which reminds the state of its duty to itself) sums up the whole of politics: the free press, the free reason of humanity, becomes politics itself. This political practice – summed up in *public theoretical criticism*, that is, in public criticism by way of the press – which demands as its absolute precondition the *freedom of the press* is the one Marx adopted in the *Rheinische Zeitung*. Marx's development of his theory of history was the basis and justification for his own *practice*: the journalist's public criticism that he saw as political action *par excellence*. This Enlightenment Philosophy was completely rigorous.

The Second Stage (1842–5) was dominated by a new form of humanism: Feuerbach's "communalist" humanism. The Reason-state had remained deaf to reason: there was no reform of the Prussian state. History itself delivered this judgment on the illusions of the humanism of reason: the young German radicals had been expecting that when he was king the heir to the throne would keep the liberal promises he had made before his coronation. But the throne soon changed the liberal into a despot – the state, which should at last have become reason, since it was in itself reason, gave birth merely to unreason once again. From this enormous disappointment, lived by the young radicals as a true historical and theoretical crisis, Marx drew the conclusion: "*The political State ... encapsulates the demands of reason precisely in its modern forms. But it does not stop there. Everywhere it presupposes realized reason. But everywhere it also slides into the contradiction between its theoretical definition and its real hypotheses.*" A decisive step had been taken: the state's abuses were no longer conceived as misappropriations of the state *vis-à-vis* its essence, but as a real contradiction between its essence (reason) and its existence (unreason). Feuerbach's humanism made it possible to think just this contradiction by showing in unreason the alienation of reason, and in this alienation the history of man, that is, his realization.[5]

Marx still professes a philosophy of man: "To be radical is to grasp things by the root; but for man the root is man himself" (1843). But then man is only freedom–reason because he is first of all "*Gemeinwesen*," "communal being," a being that is only consummated theoretically (science) and practically (politics) in universal human relations, with men and with his objects (external nature "humanized" by labor). Here also the essence of man is the basis for history and politics.

History is the alienation and production of reason in unreason, of the true man in the alienated man. Without knowing it, man realizes the essence of man in the alienated products of his labor (commodities, state, religion). The loss of man that produces history and man must presuppose a definite pre-existing essence. At the end of history, this man, having become in human objectivity, has merely to regrasp as subject his own essence alienated in property, religion, and the state to become total man, true man.

This new theory of man is the basis for a new type of political action: the politics of *practical* reappropriation. The appeal to the simple reason of the state disappears. Politics is no longer simply theoretical criticism, the enlightenment of reason through the free press, but man's practical reappropriation of his essence. For the state, like religion, may well be man, but man dispossessed: man is split into citizen (state) and civil man, two abstractions. In the heaven of the state, in "the citizen's rights," man lives in imagination the human community he is deprived of on the earth of the "rights of man." So the revolution must no longer be merely *political* (rational liberal reform of the state), but "*human*" ("communist"), if man is to be restored his nature, alienated in the fantastic forms of money, power, and gods. From this point on, this practical revolution must be the common work of philosophy and of the proletariat, for, in philosophy, man is theoretically affirmed; in the proletariat he is practically negated. The penetration of philosophy into the proletariat will be the conscious revolt of the affirmation against its own negation, the revolt of man against his inhuman conditions. Then the proletariat will negate its own negation and take possession of itself in communism. The revolution is the very *practice* of the logic immanent in alienation: it is the moment in which criticism, hitherto unarmed, recognizes its arms in the proletariat. It gives the proletariat the theory of what it is; in return, the proletariat gives it its armed force, a single unique force in which no one is allied except to himself. So the revolutionary alliance of the proletariat and of philosophy is once again sealed in the essence of man.

III

In 1845, Marx broke radically with every theory that based history and politics on an essence of man. This unique rupture contained three indissociable elements.

(1) The formation of a theory of history and politics based on radically new concepts: the concepts of social formation, productive forces, relations of production, superstructure, ideologies, determination in the last instance by the economy, specific determination of the other levels, etc.

(2) A radical critique of the *theoretical* pretensions of every philosophical humanism.

(3) The definition of humanism as an *ideology*.

This new conception is completely rigorous as well, but it is a new rigor: the essence criticized (2) is defined as an ideology (3), a category belonging to the new theory of society and history (1).

This rupture with every *philosophical* anthropology or humanism is no secondary detail; it is Marx's scientific discovery.

It means that Marx rejected the problematic of the earlier philosophy and adopted a new problematic in one and the same act. The earlier idealist ("bourgeois") philosophy depended in all its domains and arguments (its "theory of knowledge," its conception of history, its political economy, its ethics, its aesthetics, etc.) on a problematic of *human nature* (or the essence of man). For centuries, this problematic had been transparency itself, and no one had thought of questioning it even in its internal modifications.

This problematic was neither vague nor loose; on the contrary, it was constituted by a coherent system of precise concepts tightly articulated together. When Marx confronted it, it implied the two complementary postulates he defined in the Sixth Thesis on Feuerbach:

(1) that there is a universal essence of man;
(2) that this essence is the attribute of *"each single individual"* who is its real subject.

These two postulates are complementary and indissociable. But their existence and their unity presuppose a whole empiricist–idealist world outlook. If the essence of man is to be a universal attribute, it is essential that *concrete subjects* exist as absolute givens; this implies an *empiricism of the subject*. If these empirical individuals are to be men, it is essential that each carries in himself the whole human essence, if not in fact, at least in principle; this implies an *idealism of the essence*. So empiricism of the subject implies idealism of the essence and vice versa. This relation can be inverted into its "opposite" – empiricism of the concept/idealism of the subject. But the inversion respects the basic structure of the problematic, which remains fixed.

In this type-structure it is possible to recognize not only the principle of theories of society (from Hobbes to Rousseau), of political economy (from Petty to Ricardo), of ethics (from Descartes to Kant), but also the very principle of the (pre-Marxist) idealist and materialist "theory of knowledge" (from Locke to Feuerbach, via Kant). The content of the human essence or of the empirical subjects may vary (as can be seen from Descartes to Feuerbach); the subject may change from empiricism to idealism (as can be seen from Locke to Kant): the terms presented and their relations only vary within the invariant type-structure which constitutes this very problematic: *an empiricism of the subject always corresponds to an idealism of the essence (or an empiricism of the essence to an idealism of the subject)*.

By rejecting the essence of man as his theoretical basis, Marx rejected the whole of this organic system of postulates. He drove the philosophical categories of the *subject*, of *empiricism*, of the *ideal essence*, etc., from all the domains in which they had been supreme. Not only from political economy (rejection of the myth of *homo oeconomicus*, that is, of the individual with definite faculties and needs as the *subject* of the classical economy); not just from history (rejection of social atomism and ethico-political idealism); not just from ethics (rejection of the Kantian ethical idea); but also from philosophy itself: for Marx's materialism excludes the empiricism of the subject (and its inverse: the transcendental subject) and the idealism of the concept (and its inverse: the empiricism of the concept).

This total theoretical revolution was only empowered to reject the old concepts because it replaced them by new concepts. In fact Marx established a new problematic, a new systematic way of asking questions of the world, new principles and a new method. This discovery is immediately contained in the theory of historical materialism, in which Marx did not only propose a new theory of the history of societies, but at the same time implicitly, but necessarily, a new "philosophy," infinite in its implications. Thus, when Marx replaced the old couple individuals/human essence in the theory of history by new concepts (forces of production, relations of production, etc.), he was, in fact, simultaneously proposing a new conception of "philosophy." He replaced the old postulates (empiricism/idealism of the subject, empiricism/idealism of the essence) which were the basis not only for idealism but also for pre-Marxist materialism, by a historico-dialectical materialism of *praxis*: that is, by a theory of the different specific *levels of human practice* (economic practice, political practice, ideological practice, scientific practice) in their characteristic articulations, based on the specific articulations of the unity of human society. In a word, Marx substituted for the "ideological" and universal concept of Feuerbachian "practice" a concrete conception of the specific differences that enables us to situate each particular practice in the specific differences of the social structure.

So, to understand what was radically new in Marx's contribution, we must become aware not only of the novelty of the concepts of historical materialism, but also of the depth of the theoretical revolution they imply and inaugurate. On this condition it is possible to define humanism's status, and reject its *theoretical* pretensions while recognizing its practical function as an ideology.

Strictly in respect to theory, therefore, one can and must speak openly of *Marx's theoretical antihumanism*, and see in this *theoretical antihumanism* the absolute (negative) precondition of the (positive) knowledge of the human world itself, and of its practical transformation. It is impossible to *know* anything about men except on the absolute precondition that the philosophical (theoretical) myth of man is reduced to ashes. So any thought that appeals to Marx for any kind of restoration of a theoretical anthropology or humanism is no more than ashes, *theoretically*. But in practice it could pile up a monument of pre-Marxist ideology that would weigh down on real history and threaten to lead it into blind alleys.

For the corollary of theoretical Marxist antihumanism is the recognition and knowledge of humanism itself: as an *ideology*. Marx never fell into the idealist illusion of believing that the knowledge of an object might ultimately replace the object or dissipate its existence. Cartesians, knowing that the sun was two thousand leagues away, were astonished that this distance only looked like two hundred paces: they could not even find enough of God to fill in this gap. Marx never believed that a knowledge of the nature of *money* (a social relation) could destroy its *appearance*, its form of existence – a thing, for this appearance was its very being, as necessary as the existing mode of production.[6] Marx never believed that an ideology might be dissipated by a knowledge of it: for the knowledge of this ideology, as the knowledge of its conditions of possibility, of its structure, of its specific logic and of its practical role, within a given society, is simultaneously knowledge of the conditions of its necessity. So Marx's theoretical *antihumanism* does not suppress anything in the historical *existence* of humanism. In the real world philosophies of man are found after Marx as often as before, and today even some Marxists are tempted to develop the themes of a new theoretical humanism. Furthermore, Marx's theoretical antihumanism, by relating it to its conditions of existence, recognizes a necessity for humanism as an *ideology*, a conditional necessity. The recognition of this necessity is not purely speculative. On it alone can Marxism base a policy in relation to the existing ideological forms, of every kind: religion, ethics, art, philosophy, law – and in the very front rank, humanism. When (eventually) a Marxist policy of humanist ideology, that is, a political attitude to humanism, is achieved – a policy which may be either a rejection or a critique, or a use, or a support, or a development, or a humanist renewal of contemporary forms of ideology in the *ethico-political* domain – this policy will only have been possible on the absolute condition that it is based on Marxist philosophy, and a precondition for this is theoretical *antihumanism*.

IV

So everything depends on the knowledge of the nature of humanism as an ideology.

There can be no question of attempting a profound definition of ideology here. It will suffice to know very schematically that an ideology is a system (with its own logic and rigor) of representations (images, myths, ideas, or concepts, depending on the case) endowed with a historical existence and role within a given society. Without embarking on the problem of the relations between a science and its (ideological) past, we can say that ideology, as a system of representations, is distinguished from science in that in it the practico-social function is more important than the theoretical function (function as knowledge).

What is the nature of this social function? To understand it we must refer to the Marxist theory of history. The "subjects" of history are given human societies. They present themselves as totalities whose unity is constituted by a certain specific type of *complexity*, which introduces instances, that, following Engels, we can, very schematically, reduce to three: the economy, politics, and ideology. So in every society we can posit, in forms which are sometimes very paradoxical, the existence of an economic activity as the base, a political organization and "ideological" forms (religion, ethics, philosophy, etc.). *So ideology is as such an organic part of every social totality.* It is as if human societies could not survive without these *specific formations*, these systems of representations (at various levels), their ideologies. Human societies secrete ideology as the very element and atmosphere indispensable to their historical respiration and life. Only an ideological world outlook could have imagined societies *without ideology* and accepted the utopian idea of a world in which ideology (not just one of its historical forms) would disappear without trace, to be replaced by *science*. For example, this utopia is the principle behind the idea that ethics, which is in its essence ideology, could be replaced by science or become scientific through and through; or that religion could be destroyed by science which would in some way take its place; that *art* could merge with knowledge or become "everyday life," etc.

And I am not going to steer clear of the crucial question: *historical materialism cannot conceive that even a communist society could ever do without ideology*, be it ethics, art, or "world outlook." Obviously it is possible to foresee important modifications in its ideological forms and their relations and even the disappearance of certain existing forms or a shift of their functions to neighboring forms; it is also possible (on the premise of already acquired experience) to foresee the development of new ideological forms (e.g. the ideologies of "the scientific world outlook" and "communist humanism") but in the present state of Marxist theory strictly conceived, it is not conceivable that communism, a new mode of production implying determinate forces of production and relations of production, could do without a social organization of production, and corresponding ideological forms.

So ideology is not an aberration or a contingent excrescence of History: it is a structure essential to the historical life of societies. Further, only the existence and the recognition of its necessity enable us to act on ideology and transform ideology into an instrument of deliberate action on history.

It is customary to suggest that ideology belongs to the region of "consciousness." We must not be misled by this appellation which is still contaminated by the idealist problematic that preceded Marx. In truth, ideology has very little to do with "consciousness," even supposing this term to have an unambiguous meaning. It is profoundly *unconscious*, even when it presents itself in a reflected form (as in pre- Marxist "philosophy"). Ideology is indeed a system of representations, but in the majority of cases these representations have nothing to do with "consciousness": they are usually images and occasionally concepts, but it is above all as *structures* that they impose on the vast majority of men, not via their "consciousness." They are perceived–accepted–suffered cultural objects and they act functionally on men via a process that escapes them. Men "live" their ideologies as the Cartesian "saw" or did not see – if he was not looking at it – the moon two hundred paces away:

not at all as a form of consciousness, but as an object of their "world" – as their "*world*" itself. But what do we mean, then, when we say that ideology is a matter of men's "consciousness"? First, that ideology is distinct from other social instances, but also that men *live* their actions, usually referred to freedom and "consciousness" by the classical tradition, in ideology, *by and through ideology*; in short, that the "lived" relation between men and the world, including History (in political action or inaction), passes through ideology, or better, *is ideology itself*. This is the sense in which Marx said that it is in ideology (as the locus of political struggle) that men *become conscious* of their place in the world and in history, it is within this ideological unconsciousness that men succeed in altering the "lived" relation between them and the world and acquiring that new form of specific unconsciousness called "consciousness."

So ideology is a matter of the *lived* relation between men and their world. This relation, that only appears as "*conscious*" on condition that it is *unconscious*, in the same way only seems to be simple on condition that it is complex, that it is not a simple relation but a relation between relations, a second degree relation. In ideology men do indeed express, not the relation between them and their conditions of existence, but *the way* they live the relation between them and their conditions of existence: this presupposes both a real relation and an "*imaginary*", "*lived*" relation. Ideology, then, is the expression of the relation between men and their "world," that is, the (overdetermined) unity of the real relation and the imaginary relation between them and their real conditions of existence. In ideology the real relation is inevitably invested in the imaginary relation, a relation that *expresses a will* (conservative, conformist, reformist, or revolutionary), a hope, or a nostalgia, rather than describing a reality.

It is in this overdetermination of the real by the imaginary and of the imaginary by the real that ideology is *active* in principle, that it reinforces or modifies the relation between men and their conditions of existence, in the imaginary relation itself. It follows that this action can never be purely *instrumental*; the men who would use an ideology purely as a means of action, as a tool, find that they have been caught by it, implicated by it, just when they are using it and believe themselves to be absolute masters of it.

This is perfectly clear in the case of a *class society*. The ruling ideology is then the ideology of the ruling *class*. But the ruling class does not maintain with the ruling ideology, which is its own ideology, an external and lucid relation of pure utility and cunning. When, during the eighteenth century, the "rising class," the bourgeoisie, developed a humanist ideology of equality, freedom, and reason, it gave its own demands the form of universality, since it hoped thereby to enroll at its side, by their education to this end, the very men it would liberate only for their exploitation. This is the Rousseauan myth of the origins of inequality: the rich holding forth to the poor in "the most deliberate discourse" ever conceived, so as to persuade them to live their slavery as their freedom. In reality, the bourgeoisie has to believe in its own myth before it can convince others, and not only so as to convince others, since what it lives in its ideology is *the very relation* between it and its real conditions of existence which allows it simultaneously to act on itself (provide itself with a legal and ethical consciousness, and the legal and ethical conditions of economic liberalism) and on others (those it exploits and is going to exploit in the future: the "free laborers") so as to take up, occupy, and maintain its historical role as a ruling class. Thus, in a very exact sense, the bourgeoisie *lives* in the ideology of *freedom* the relation between it and its conditions of existence: that is, *its* real relation (the law of a liberal capitalist economy) *but invested in an imaginary relation* (all men are free, including the free laborers). Its ideology consists of this play on the word *freedom*, which betrays the bourgeois wish to mystify those ("free men"!) it exploits, blackmailing them with freedom so as to keep them in harness, as much as the bourgeoisie's need to *live* its own class rule as the freedom of those it is exploiting. Just as a people that exploits another cannot be free, so a class that *uses* an ideology is its captive too. So when we speak of the class function of an ideology it must be understood that the ruling ideology is indeed the ideology of the ruling class and that the former serves the latter not only in its rule over the exploited class, *but in its own constitution of itself as the ruling class*, by making it accept the lived relation between itself and the world as real and justified.

But, we must go further and ask what becomes of *ideology* in a society in which classes have disappeared. What we have just said allows us to answer this question. If the whole social function of ideology could be summed up cynically as a myth (such as Plato's "beautiful lies" or the techniques of modern advertising) fabricated and manipulated from the outside by the ruling class to fool those it is exploiting, then ideology would disappear with classes. But as we have seen that even in the case of a class society ideology is active on the ruling class itself and contributes to its molding, to the modification of its attitudes to adapt it to its real conditions of existence (for example, legal freedom) – it is clear that *ideology (as a system of mass representations) is indispensable in any society if men are to be formed, transformed, and equipped to respond to the demands of their conditions of existence*. If, as Marx said, history is a perpetual transformation of men's conditions of existence, and if this is equally true of a socialist society, then men must be ceaselessly transformed so as to adapt them to these conditions; if this "adaptation" cannot be left to spontaneity but must be constantly assumed, dominated, and controlled, it is in ideology that this demand is expressed, that this distance is measured, that this contradiction is lived and that its resolution is "activated." It is in ideology that the classless society *lives* the inadequacy/adequacy of the relation between it and the world, it is in it and by it that it transforms men's "consciousness," that is, their attitudes and behavior so as to raise them to the level of their tasks and the conditions of their existence.

In a class society ideology is the relay whereby, and the element in which, the relation between men and their conditions of existence is settled to the profit of the ruling class. In a classless society ideology is the relay whereby, and the element in which, the relation between men and their conditions of existence is lived to the profit of all men. . . .

Notes

1 *Die Rheinische Zeitung*, "The Freedom of the Press," May 12, 1842.
2 Letter to Ruge, September 1843 – an admirable formulation, the key to Marx's early philosophy.
3 *Die Rheinische Zeitung*, "On the leading article in no. 179 of the *Kölnische Zeitung*", July 14, 1842.
4 Ibid.
5 This confluence of Feuerbach and the theoretical crisis in which history had thrown the young German

radicals explains their enthusiasm for the author of the *Provisional Theses*, of the *Essence of Christianity*, and of the *Principles of the Philosophy of the Future*. Indeed, Feuerbach represented the *theoretical* solution to the young intellectuals' theoretical crisis. In his humanism of alienation, he gave them the theoretical concepts that enabled them to think the alienation of the human essence as an indispensable moment in the realization of the human essence, unreason (the irrational *reality* of the state) as a necessary moment in the realization of reason (the idea of the state). It thus enabled them to *think* what they would otherwise have suffered as irrationality itself: the necessary *connexion* between reason and unreason. Of course, this relation remained trapped in a philosophical anthropology, its basis, with this theoretical proviso: the remanipulation of the concept of man, indispensable to think the historical relation between historical reason and unreason. Man ceases to be defined by reason and freedom: he becomes, in his very principle, "communalist," concrete intersubjectivity, love, fraternity, "species being."

6 The whole, fashionable, theory of "reification" depends on a projection of the theory of alienation found in the early texts, particularly the *1844 Manuscripts*, on to the theory of "fetishism" in *Capital*. In the *1844 Manuscripts*, the objectification of the human essence is claimed as the indispensable preliminary to the reappropriation of the human essence by man. Throughout the process of objectification, man only exists in the form of an objectivity in which he meets his own essence in the appearance of a foreign, nonhuman, essence. This "objectification" is not called "reification" even though it is called *inhuman*. Inhumanity is not represented *par excellence* by the model of a "thing": but sometimes by the model of animality (or even of pre-animality – the man who no longer even has simple animal relations with nature), sometimes by the model of the omnipotence and fascination of transcendence (God, the state) and of money, which is, of course, a "thing." In *Capital* the only social relation that is presented in the form of a *thing* (this piece of metal) is *money*. But the conception of money as a *thing* (that is, the confusion of value with use-value in money) does not correspond to the reality of this "thing": it is not the brutality of a simple "thing" that man is faced with when he is in direct relation with money; it is a *power* (or a *lack* of it) over things and men. An ideology of reification that sees "things" everywhere in human relations confuses in this category "thing" (a category more foreign to Marx cannot be imagined) every social relation, conceived according to the model of a money-thing ideology.

Select Bibliography

Essays in Self-Criticism. Translated by Grahame Lock. London: NLB, 1976.

Essays on Ideology. London: Verso, 1984.

For Marx. Translated by Ben Brewster. London: Verso, 1990.

Lenin and Philosophy, and Other Essays. Translated by Ben Brewster. New York: Monthly Review Press, 1972.

Philosophy and the Spontaneous Philosophy of the Scientists, and Other Essays. Edited by Gregory Elliott. Translated by Ben Brewster. London: Verso, 1990.

Politics and History: Montesquieu, Rousseau, Marx. Translated by Ben Brewster. London: NLB, 1982.

Reading "Capital" (with Etienne Balibar). Translated by Ben Brewster. London: Verso, 1977.

The Spectre of Hegel: Early Writings. Edited by François Matheron. Translated by G.M. Goshgarian. London: Verso, 1997.

Writings on Psychoanalysis: Freud and Lacan. Edited by Olivier Corpet and François Matheron. Translated by Jeffrey Mehlman. New York: Columbia University Press, 1996.

10

Herbert Marcuse

Herbert Marcuse (1898–1979) was one of the central philosophers and social critics of the Frankfurt School. Schooled in Hegel, Marx, and Heidegger, Marcuse in his later period also assimilated many of the insights of Nietzsche and Freud in order to provide a comprehensive critique of modern political reality under capitalism. Marcuse's critiques of Western society emphasize the overarching promotion of homogenization and conformism that stifle individual freedom and expression; the extension of utilitarian and productionist attitudes to all aspects of life; and the insidious oppression that occurs via technological forms of social control. The following excerpt from *One-Dimensional Man* (1964) examines some of the forms of ideological manipulation imposed by technological rationality.

One-Dimensional Man

The New Forms of Control

A comfortable, smooth, reasonable, democratic unfreedom prevails in advanced industrial civilization, a token of technical progress. Indeed, what could be more rational than the suppression of individuality in the mechanization of socially necessary but painful performances; the concentration of individual enterprises in more effective, more productive corporations; the regulation of free competition among unequally equipped economic subjects; the curtailment of prerogatives and national sovereignties which impede the international organization of resources. That this technological order also involves a political and intellectual coordination may be a regrettable and yet promising development.

The rights and liberties which were such vital factors in the origins and earlier stages of industrial society yield to a higher stage of this society: they are losing their traditional rationale and content. Freedom of thought, speech, and conscience were – just as free enterprise, which they served to promote and protect – essentially *critical* ideas, designed to replace an obsolescent material and intellectual culture by a more productive and rational one. Once institutionalized, these rights

From *One-Dimensional Man: Studies in the Ideology of Advanced Industrial Society* (Boston: Beacon Press, 1966), pp. 1–12, 14–18. © 1964 by Herbert Marcuse. Reprinted by permission of Beacon Press, Boston.

and liberties shared the fate of the society of which they had become an integral part. The achievement cancels the premises.

To the degree to which freedom from want, the concrete substance of all freedom, is becoming a real possibility, the liberties which pertain to a state of lower productivity are losing their former content. Independence of thought, autonomy, and the right to political opposition are being deprived of their basic critical function in a society which seems increasingly capable of satisfying the needs of the individuals through the way in which it is organized. Such a society may justly demand acceptance of its principles and institutions, and reduce the opposition to the discussion and promotion of alternative policies *within* the status quo. In this respect, it seems to make little difference whether the increasing satisfaction of needs is accomplished by an authoritarian or a nonauthoritarian system. Under the conditions of a rising standard of living, nonconformity with the system itself appears to be socially useless, and the more so when it entails tangible economic and political disadvantages and threatens the smooth operation of the whole. Indeed, at least insofar as the necessities of life are involved, there seems to be no reason why the production and distribution of goods and services should proceed through the competitive concurrence of individual liberties.

Freedom of enterprise was from the beginning not altogether a blessing. As the liberty to work or to starve, it spelled toil, insecurity, and fear for the vast majority of the population. If the individual were no longer compelled to prove himself on the market, as a free economic subject, the disappearance of this kind of freedom would be one of the greatest achievements of civilization. The technological processes of mechanization and standardization might release individual energy into a yet uncharted realm of freedom beyond necessity. The very structure of human existence would be altered; the individual would be liberated from the work world's imposing upon him alien needs and alien possibilities. The individual would be free to exert autonomy over a life that would be his own. If the productive apparatus could be organized and directed toward the satisfaction of the vital needs, its control might well be centralized; such control would not prevent individual autonomy, but render it possible.

This is a goal within the capabilities of advanced industrial civilization, the "end" of technological rationality. In actual fact, however, the contrary trend operates: the apparatus imposes its economic and political requirements for defense and expansion on labor time and free time, on the material and intellectual culture. By virtue of the way it has organized its technological base, contemporary industrial society tends to be totalitarian. For "totalitarian" is not only a terroristic political coordination of society, but also a nonterroristic economic–technical coordination which operates through the manipulation of needs by vested interests. It thus precludes the emergence of an effective opposition against the whole. Not only a specific form of government or party rule makes for totalitarianism, but also a specific system of production and distribution which may well be compatible with a "pluralism" of parties, newspapers, "countervailing powers," etc.

Today political power asserts itself through its power over the machine process and over the technical organization of the apparatus. The government of advanced and advancing industrial societies can maintain and secure itself only when it succeeds in mobilizing, organizing, and exploiting the technical, scientific, and mechanical productivity available to industrial civilization. And this productivity mobilizes society as a whole, above and beyond any particular individual or group interests. The brute fact that the machine's physical (only physical?) power surpasses that of the individual, and of any particular group of individuals, makes the machine the most effective political instrument in any society whose basic organization is that of the machine process. But the political trend may be reversed; essentially the power of the machine is only the stored-up and projected power of man. To the extent to which the work world is conceived of as a machine and mechanized accordingly, it becomes the *potential* basis of a new freedom for man.

Contemporary industrial civilization demonstrates that it has reached the stage at which "the free society" can no longer be adequately defined in the traditional terms of economic, political, and intellectual liberties, not because these liberties have become insignificant, but because they are too significant to be confined within the traditional forms. New modes of realization are needed, corresponding to the new capabilities of society.

Such new modes can be indicated only in negative terms because they would amount to the negation of the prevailing modes. Thus economic freedom would mean freedom *from* the economy – from being controlled by economic forces and relationships; freedom from the daily struggle for existence, from earning a living. Political freedom would mean liberation of the individuals *from* politics over which they have no effective control. Similarly, intellectual freedom would mean the restoration of individual thought now absorbed by mass communication and indoctrination, abolition of "public opinion" together with its makers. The unrealistic sound of these propositions is indicative, not of their utopian character, but of the strength of the forces which prevent their realization. The most effective and enduring form of warfare against liberation is the implanting of material and intellectual needs that perpetuate obsolete forms of the struggle for existence.

The intensity, the satisfaction and even the character of human needs, beyond the biological level, have always been preconditioned. Whether or not the possibility of doing or leaving, enjoying or destroying, possessing or rejecting something is seized as a *need* depends on whether or not it can be seen as desirable and necessary for the prevailing societal institutions and interests. In this sense, human needs are historical needs and, to the extent to which the society demands the repressive development of the individual, his needs themselves and their claim for satisfaction are subject to overriding critical standards.

We may distinguish both true and false needs. "False" are those which are superimposed upon the individual by particular social interests in his repression: the needs which perpetuate toil, aggressiveness, misery, and injustice. Their satisfaction might be most gratifying to the individual, but this happiness is not a condition which has to be maintained and protected if it serves to arrest the development of the ability (his own and others) to recognize the disease of the whole and grasp the chances of curing the disease. The result then is euphoria in unhappiness. Most of the prevailing needs to relax, to have fun, to behave and consume in accordance with the advertisements, to love and hate what others love and hate, belong to this category of false needs.

Such needs have a societal content and function which are determined by external powers over which the individual has no control; the development and satisfaction of these needs is heteronomous. No matter how much such needs may have become the individual's own, reproduced and fortified by the conditions of his existence; no matter how much he identifies himself with them and finds himself in their satisfaction, they continue to be what they were from the beginning – products of a society whose dominant interest demands repression.

The prevalence of repressive needs is an accomplished fact, accepted in ignorance and defeat, but a fact that must be undone in the interest of the happy individual as well as all those whose misery is the price of his satisfaction. The only needs that have an unqualified claim for satisfaction are the vital ones – nourishment, clothing, lodging at the attainable level of culture. The satisfaction of these needs is the prerequisite for the realization of *all* needs, of the unsublimated as well as the sublimated ones.

For any consciousness and conscience, for any experience which does not accept the prevailing societal interest as the supreme law of thought and behavior, the established universe of needs and satisfactions is a fact to be questioned – questioned in terms of truth and falsehood. These terms are historical throughout, and their objectivity is historical. The judgment of needs and their satisfaction, under the given conditions, involves standards of *priority* – standards which refer to the optimal development of the individual, of all individuals, under the optimal utilization of the material and intellectual resources available to man. The resources are calculable. "Truth" and "falsehood" of needs designate objective conditions to the extent to which the universal satisfaction of vital needs and, beyond it, the progressive alleviation of toil and poverty, are universally valid standards. But as historical standards, they do not only vary according to area and stage of development, they also can be defined only in (greater or lesser) *contradiction* to the prevailing ones. What tribunal can possibly claim the authority of decision?

In the last analysis, the question of what are true and false needs must be answered by the individuals themselves, but only in the last analysis; that is, if and when they are free to give their own answer. As long as they are kept incapable of being autonomous, as long as they are indoctrinated and manipulated (down to their very instincts), their answer to this question cannot be taken as their own. By the same token, however, no tribunal can justly arrogate to itself the right to decide which needs should be developed and satisfied. Any such tribunal is reprehensible, although our revulsion does not do away with the question: how can the people who have been the object of effective and productive domination by themselves create the conditions of freedom?

The more rational, productive, technical, and total the repressive administration of society becomes, the more unimaginable the means and ways by which the administered individuals might break their servitude and seize their own liberation. To be sure, to impose Reason upon an entire society is a paradoxical and scandalous idea – although one might dispute the righteousness of a society which ridicules this idea while making its own population into objects of total administration. All liberation depends on the consciousness of servitude, and the emergence of this consciousness is always hampered by the predominance of needs and satisfactions which, to a great extent, have become the individual's own. The process always replaces one system of preconditioning by another; the optimal goal is the replacement of false needs by true ones, the abandonment of repressive satisfaction.

The distinguishing feature of advanced industrial society is its effective suffocation of those needs which demand liberation – liberation also from that which is tolerable and rewarding and comfortable – while it sustains and absolves the destructive power and repressive function of the affluent society. Here, the social controls exact the overwhelming need for the production and consumption of waste; the need for stupefying work where it is no longer a real necessity; the need for modes of relaxation which soothe and prolong this stupefication; the need for maintaining such deceptive liberties as free competition at administered prices, a free press which censors itself, free choice between brands and gadgets.

Under the rule of a repressive whole, liberty can be made into a powerful instrument of domination. The range of choice open to the individual is not the decisive factor in determining the degree of human freedom, but *what* can be chosen and what *is* chosen by the individual. The criterion for free choice can never be an absolute one, but neither is it entirely relative. Free election of masters does not abolish the masters or the slaves. Free choice among a wide variety of goods and services does not signify freedom if these goods and services sustain social controls over a life of toil and fear – that is, if they sustain alienation. And the spontaneous reproduction of superimposed needs by the individual does not establish autonomy; it only testifies to the efficacy of the controls.

Our insistence on the depth and efficacy of these controls is open to the objection that we overrate greatly the indoctrinating power of the "media,"

and that by themselves the people would feel and satisfy the needs which are now imposed upon them. The objection misses the point. The preconditioning does not start with the mass production of radio and television and with the centralization of their control. The people enter this stage as preconditioned receptacles of long standing; the decisive difference is in the flattening out of the contrast (or conflict) between the given and the possible, between the satisfied and the unsatisfied needs. Here, the so-called equalization of class distinctions reveals its ideological function. If the worker and his boss enjoy the same television program and visit the same resort places, if the typist is as attractively made up as the daughter of her employer, if the Negro owns a Cadillac, if they all read the same newspaper, then this assimilation indicates not the disappearance of classes, but the extent to which the needs and satisfactions that serve the preservation of the Establishment are shared by the underlying population.

Indeed, in the most highly developed areas of contemporary society, the transplantation of social into individual needs is so effective that the difference between them seems to be purely theoretical. Can one really distinguish between the mass media as instruments of information and entertainment, and as agents of manipulation and indoctrination? Between the automobile as nuisance and as convenience? Between the horrors and the comforts of functional architecture? Between the work for national defense and the work for corporate gain? Between the private pleasure and the commercial and political utility involved in increasing the birth rate?

We are again confronted with one of the most vexing aspects of advanced industrial civilization: the rational character of its irrationality. Its productivity and efficiency, its capacity to increase and spread comforts, to turn waste into need, and destruction into construction, the extent to which this civilization transforms the object world into an extension of man's mind and body makes the very notion of alienation questionable. The people recognize themselves in their commodities; they find their soul in their automobile, hi-fi set, split-level home, kitchen equipment. The very mechanism which ties the individual to his society has changed, and social control is anchored in the new needs which it has produced.

The prevailing forms of social control are technological in a new sense. To be sure, the technical structure and efficacy of the productive and destructive apparatus has been a major instrumentality for subjecting the population to the established social division of labor throughout the modern period. Moreover, such integration has always been accompanied by more obvious forms of compulsion: loss of livelihood, the administration of justice, the police, the armed forces. It still is. But in the contemporary period, the technological controls appear to be the very embodiment of Reason for the benefit of all social groups and interests – to such an extent that all contradiction seems irrational and all counteraction impossible.

No wonder then that, in the most advanced areas of this civilization, the social controls have been introjected to the point where even individual protest is affected at its roots. The intellectual and emotional refusal "to go along" appears neurotic and impotent. This is the sociopsychological aspect of the political event that marks the contemporary period: the passing of the historical forces which, at the preceding stage of industrial society, seemed to represent the possibility of new forms of existence.

But the term "introjection" perhaps no longer describes the way in which the individual by himself reproduces and perpetuates the external controls exercised by his society. Introjection suggests a variety of relatively spontaneous processes by which a Self (Ego) transposes the "outer" into the "inner." Thus introjection implies the existence of an inner dimension distinguished from and even antagonistic to the external exigencies – an individual consciousness and an individual unconscious *apart from* public opinion and behavior.[1] The idea of "inner freedom" here has its reality: it designates the private space in which man may become and remain "himself."

Today this private space has been invaded and whittled down by technological reality. Mass production and mass distribution claim the *entire* individual, and industrial psychology has long since ceased to be confined to the factory. The manifold processes of introjection seem to be ossified in almost mechanical reactions. The result is, not adjustment but *mimesis:* an immediate identification of the individual with *his* society and, through it, with the society as a whole.

This immediate, automatic identification (which may have been characteristic of primitive forms of association) reappears in high industrial civilization; its new "immediacy," however, is the product of a sophisticated, scientific management and organization. In this process, the "inner" dimension of the mind in which opposition to the status quo can take root is whittled down. The loss of this dimension, in which the power of negative thinking – the critical power of Reason – is at home, is the ideological counterpart to the very material process in which advanced industrial society silences and reconciles the opposition. The impact of progress turns Reason into submission to the facts of life, and to the dynamic capability of producing more and bigger facts of the same sort of life. The efficiency of the system blunts the individuals' recognition that it contains no facts which do not communicate the repressive power of the whole. If the individuals find themselves in the things which shape their life, they do so, not by giving, but by accepting the law of things – not the law of physics but the law of their society.

I have just suggested that the concept of alienation seems to become questionable when the individuals identify themselves with the existence which is imposed upon them and have in it their own development and satisfaction. This identification is not illusion but reality. However, the reality constitutes a more progressive stage of alienation. The latter has become entirely objective; the subject which is alienated is swallowed up by its alienated existence. There is only one dimension, and it is everywhere and in all forms. The achievements of progress defy ideological indictment as well as justification; before their tribunal, the "false consciousness" of their rationality becomes the true consciousness.

This absorption of ideology into reality does not, however, signify the "end of ideology." On the contrary, in a specific sense advanced industrial culture is *more* ideological than its predecessor, inasmuch as today the ideology is in the process of production itself.[2] In a provocative form, this proposition reveals the political aspects of the prevailing technological rationality. The productive apparatus and the goods and services which it produces "sell" or impose the social system as a whole. The means of mass transportation and communication, the commodities of lodging, food, and clothing, the irresistible output of the entertainment and information industry carry with them prescribed attitudes and habits, certain intellectual and emotional reactions which bind the consumers more or less pleasantly to the producers and, through the latter, to the whole. The products indoctrinate and manipulate; they promote a false consciousness which is immune against its falsehood. And as these beneficial products become available to more individuals in more social classes, the indoctrination they carry ceases to be publicity; it becomes a way of life. It is a good way of life – much better than before – and as a good way of life, it militates against qualitative change. Thus emerges a pattern of *one-dimensional thought and behavior* in which ideas, aspirations, and objectives that, by their content, transcend the established universe of discourse and action are either repelled or reduced to terms of this universe. They are redefined by the rationality of the given system and of its quantitative extension. . . .

One-dimensional thought is systematically promoted by the makers of politics and their purveyors of mass information. Their universe of discourse is populated by self-validating hypotheses which, incessantly and monopolistically repeated, become hypnotic definitions or dictations. For example, "free" are the institutions which operate (and are operated on) in the countries of the Free World; other transcending modes of freedom are by definition either anarchism, communism, or propaganda. "Socialistic" are all encroachments on private enterprises not undertaken by private enterprise itself (or by government contracts), such as universal and comprehensive health insurance, or the protection of nature from all too sweeping commercialization, or the establishment of public services which may hurt private profit. This totalitarian logic of accomplished facts has its Eastern counterpart. There, freedom is the way of life instituted by a communist regime, and all other transcending modes of freedom are either capitalistic, or revisionist, or leftist sectarianism. In both camps, nonoperational ideas are nonbehavioral and subversive. The movement of thought is stopped at barriers which appear as the limits of Reason itself. . . .

With the gradual closing of this dimension by the society, the self-limitation of thought assumes a larger significance. The interrelation between scientific–philosophical and societal processes, between theoretical and practical Reason, asserts itself "behind the back" of the scientists and philosophers. The society bars a whole type of oppositional operations and behavior; consequently, the concepts pertaining to them are rendered illusory or meaningless. Historical transcendence appears as metaphysical transcendence, not acceptable to science and scientific thought. The operational and behavioral point of view, practiced as a "habit of thought" at large, becomes the view of the established universe of discourse and action, needs and

aspirations. The "cunning of Reason" works, as it so often did, in the interest of the powers that be. The insistence on operational and behavioral concepts turns against the efforts to free thought and behavior *from* the given reality and *for* the suppressed alternatives. Theoretical and practical Reason, academic and social behaviorism meet on common ground: that of an advanced society which makes scientific and technical progress into an instrument of domination.

"Progress" is not a neutral term; it moves toward specific ends, and these ends are defined by the possibilities of ameliorating the human condition. Advanced industrial society is approaching the stage where continued progress would demand the radical subversion of the prevailing direction and organization of progress. This stage would be reached when material production (including the necessary services) becomes automated to the extent that all vital needs can be satisfied while necessary labor time is reduced to marginal time. From this point on, technical progress would transcend the realm of necessity, where it served as the instrument of domination and exploitation which thereby limited its rationality; technology would become subject to the free play of faculties in the struggle for the pacification of nature and of society.

Such a state is envisioned in Marx's notion of the "abolition of labor." The term "pacification of existence" seems better suited to designate the historical alternative of a world which – through an international conflict which transforms and suspends the contradictions within the established societies – advances on the brink of a global war. "Pacification of existence" means the development of man's struggle with man and with nature, under conditions where the competing needs, desires, and aspirations are no longer organized by vested interests in domination and scarcity – an organization which perpetuates the destructive forms of this struggle.

Today's fight against this historical alternative finds a firm mass basis in the underlying population, and finds its ideology in the rigid orientation of thought and behavior to the given universe of facts. Validated by the accomplishments of science and technology, justified by its growing productivity, the status quo defies all transcendence. Faced with the possibility of pacification on the grounds of its technical and intellectual achievements, the mature industrial society closes itself against this alternative. Operationalism, in theory and practice, becomes the theory and practice of *containment*.

Underneath its obvious dynamics, this society is a thoroughly static system of life: self-propelling in its oppressive productivity and in its beneficial coordination. Containment of technical progress goes hand in hand with its growth in the established direction. In spite of the political fetters imposed by the status quo, the more technology appears capable of creating the conditions for pacification, the more are the minds and bodies of man organized against this alternative.

The most advanced areas of industrial society exhibit throughout these two features: a trend toward consummation of technological rationality, and intensive efforts to contain this trend within the established institutions. Here is the internal contradiction of this civilization: the irrational element in its rationality. It is the token of its achievements. The industrial society which makes technology and science its own is organized for the ever-more-effective domination of man and nature, for the ever-more-effective utilization of its resources. It becomes irrational when the success of these efforts opens new dimensions of human realization. Organization for peace is different from organization for war; the institutions which served the struggle for existence cannot serve the pacification of existence. Life as an end is qualitatively different from life as a means.

Such a qualitatively new mode of existence can never be envisaged as the mere by-product of economic and political changes, as the more or less spontaneous effect of the new institutions which constitute the necessary prerequisite. Qualitative change also involves a change in the *technical* basis on which this society rests – one which sustains the economic and political institutions through which the "second nature" of man as an aggressive object of administration is stabilized. The techniques of industrialization are political techniques; as such, they prejudge the possibilities of Reason and Freedom.

To be sure, labor must precede the reduction of labor, and industrialization must precede the development of human needs and satisfactions. But as all freedom depends on the conquest of alien necessity, the realization of freedom depends on the *techniques* of this conquest. The highest productivity of labor can be used for the perpetuation of labor, and the most efficient industrialization can serve the restriction and manipulation of needs.

When this point is reached, domination – in the guise of affluence and liberty – extends to all spheres of private and public existence, integrates all authentic opposition, absorbs all alternatives. Technological rationality reveals its political character as it becomes the great vehicle of better domination, creating a truly totalitarian universe in which society and nature, mind and body are kept in a state of permanent mobilization for the defense of this universe.

Notes

1 The change in the function of the family here plays a decisive role: its "socializing" functions are increasingly taken over by outside groups and media. See my *Eros and Civilization* (Boston: Beacon Press, 1955), p. 96 ff.

2 Theodor W. Adorno, *Prismen. Kulturkritik und Gesellschaft* (Frankfurt: Suhrkamp, 1955), p. 24 ff.

Select Bibliography

The Aesthetic Dimension: Toward a Critique of Marxist Aesthetics. Boston: Beacon Press, 1978.

Counterrevolution and Revolt. Boston: Beacon Press, 1972.

A Critique of Pure Tolerance (with Robert Paul Wolff and Barrington Moore, Jr). Boston: Beacon Press, 1969.

Eros and Civilization: A Philosophical Inquiry into Freud. Boston: Beacon Press, 1974.

An Essay on Liberation. Boston: Beacon Press, 1969.

Five Lectures: Psychoanalysis, Politics, and Utopia. Translated by Jeremy J. Shapiro and Shierry M. Weber. Boston: Beacon Press, 1970.

Hegel's Ontology and the Theory of Historicity. Translated by Seyla Benhabib. Cambridge, Mass.: MIT Press, 1987.

Negations: Essays in Critical Theory. London: Free Association Books, 1988.

One-Dimensional Man: Studies in the Ideology of Advanced Industrial Society. Boston: Beacon Press, 1966.

Reason and Revolution: Hegel and the Rise of Social Theory. Atlantic Highlands, NJ: Humanities Press, 1989.

Soviet Marxism: A Critical Analysis. Harmondsworth: Penguin Books, 1971.

Studies in Critical Philosophy. Translated by Joris De Bres. Boston: Beacon Press, 1973.

11

Jürgen Habermas

German philosopher Jürgen Habermas (1929–) is known as a second-generation representative of the Frankfurt School and exponent of critical theory. For Habermas, critical social theory aims at the overcoming of oppressive power relations and at the achievement of transparent and uncoerced understanding among human beings, which would permit a rational and informed organization of society on the basis of freely attained consensus. This task entails developing a "theory of communicative action" (Habermas published a major study under this title in 1982) that would provide a normative and rational foundation for social critique. As the following essay, published as an Appendix to *Knowledge and Human Interests* (1968), explains, however, the emancipatory interest that underlies critical theory entails that such "theory" cannot be objective and disinterested, or share the value-neutral status claimed by the positive sciences; it presupposes, rather, an interest in autonomy and responsibility.

Knowledge and Human Interests: *A General Perspective*

I

In 1802, during the summer semester at Jena, Schelling gave his Lectures on the Method of Academic Study. In the language of German idealism he emphatically renewed the concept of theory

From *Knowledge and Human Interests*, translated by Jeremy J. Shapiro (Cambridge: Polity Press, 1987), pp. 301–17. Copyright © 1987. © Suhrkamp Verlag, Frankfurt am Main, 1968, 1973. Reprinted by permission of Blackwell Publishers and Suhrkamp Verlag.

that has defined the tradition of great philosophy since its beginnings.

> The fear of speculation, the ostensible rush from the theoretical to the practical, brings about the same shallowness in action that it does in knowledge. It is by studying a strictly theoretical philosophy that we become most immediately acquainted with Ideas, and only Ideas provide action with energy and ethical significance.[1]

The *only* knowledge that can truly orient action is knowledge that frees itself from mere human interests and is based on Ideas – in other words, knowledge that has taken a theoretical attitude.

The word "theory" has religious origins. The *theoros* was the representative sent by Greek cities to public celebrations.[2] Through *theoria*, that is through looking on, he abandoned himself to the sacred events. In philosophical language, *theoria* was transferred to contemplation of the cosmos. In this form, theory already presupposed the demarcation between Being and time that is the foundation of ontology. This separation is first found in the poem of Parmenides and returns in Plato's *Timaeus*. It reserves to *logos* a realm of Being purged of inconstancy and uncertainty and leaves to *doxa* the realm of the mutable and perishable. When the philosopher views the immortal order, he cannot help bringing himself into accord with the proportions of the cosmos and reproducing them internally. He manifests these proportions, which he sees in the motions of nature and the harmonic series of music, within himself; he forms himself through mimesis. Through the soul's likening itself to the ordered motion of the cosmos, theory enters the conduct of life. In *ethos* theory molds life to its form and is reflected in the conduct of those who subject themselves to its discipline.

This concept of theory and of life in theory has defined philosophy since its beginnings. The distinction between theory in this traditional sense and theory in the sense of critique was the object of one of Max Horkheimer's most important studies.[3] Today, a generation later, I should like to re-examine this theme,[4] starting with Husserl's *The Crisis of the European Sciences*, which appeared at about the same time as Horkheimer's.[5] Husserl used as his frame of reference the very concept of theory that Horkheimer was countering with that of critical theory. Husserl was concerned with crisis: not with crisis in the sciences, but with their crisis as science. For "in our vital state of need this science has nothing to say to us." Like almost all philosophers before him, Husserl, without second thought, took as the norm of his critique an idea of knowledge that preserves the Platonic connection of pure theory with the conduct of life. What ultimately produces a scientific culture is not the information content of theories but the formation among theorists themselves of a thoughtful and enlightened mode of life. The evolution of the European mind seemed to be aiming at the creation of a scientific culture of this sort. After 1933, however, Husserl saw this historical tendency endan-

gered. He was convinced that the danger was threatening not from without but from within. He attributed the crisis to the circumstance that the most advanced disciplines, especially physics, had degenerated from the status of true theory.

II

Let us consider this thesis. There is a real connection between the positivistic self-understanding of the sciences and traditional ontology. The *empirical–analytic* sciences develop their theories in a self-understanding that automatically generates continuity with the beginnings of philosophical thought. For both are committed to a theoretical attitude that frees those who take it from dogmatic association with the natural interests of life and their irritating influence; and both share the cosmological intention of describing the universe theoretically in its lawlike order, just as it is. In contrast, the *historical–hermeneutic* sciences, which are concerned with the sphere of transitory things and mere opinion, cannot be linked up so smoothly with this tradition – they have nothing to do with cosmology. But they, too, comprise a *scientistic consciousness*, based on the model of science. For even the symbolic meanings of tradition seem capable of being brought together in a cosmos of facts in ideal simultaneity. Much as the cultural sciences may comprehend their facts through understanding and little though they may be concerned with discovering general laws, they nevertheless share with the empirical–analytic sciences the methodological consciousness of describing a structured reality within the horizon of the theoretical attitude. Historicism has become the positivism of the cultural and social sciences.

Positivism has also permeated the self-understanding of the *social sciences*, whether they obey the methodological demands of an empirical–analytic behavioral science or orient themselves to the pattern of normative–analytic sciences, based on presuppositions about maxims of action.[6] In this field of inquiry, which is so close to practice, the concept of value-freedom (or ethical neutrality) has simply reaffirmed the ethos that modern science owes to the beginnings of theoretical thought in Greek philosophy: psychologically an unconditional commitment to theory and epistemologically the severance of knowledge from interest. This is represented in logic by the distinction between descriptive and prescriptive statements, which makes grammatically obligatory the filtering out of merely emotive from cognitive contents.

Yet the very term "value freedom" reminds us that the postulates associated with it no longer correspond to the classical meaning of theory. To dissociate values from facts means counterposing an abstract Ought to pure Being. Values are the nominalistic by-products of a centuries-long critique of the emphatic concept of Being to which theory was once exclusively oriented. The very term "values," which neo-Kantianism brought into philosophical currency, and in relation to which science is supposed to preserve neutrality, renounces the connection between the two that theory originally intended.

Thus, although the sciences share the concept of theory with the major tradition of philosophy, they destroy its classical claim. They borrow two elements from the philosophical heritage: the methodological meaning of the theoretical attitude and the basic ontological assumption of a structure of the world independent of the knower. On the other hand, however, they have abandoned the connection of *theoria* and *kosmos*, of *mimesis* and *bios theoretikos* that was assumed from Plato through Husserl. What was once supposed to comprise the practical efficacy of theory has now fallen prey to methodological prohibitions. The conception of theory as a process of cultivation of the person has become apocryphal. Today it appears to us that the mimetic conformity of the soul to the proportions of the universe, which seemed accessible to contemplation, had only taken theoretical knowledge into the service of the internalization of norms and thus estranged it from its legitimate task.

III

In fact the sciences had to lose the specific significance for life that Husserl would like to regenerate through the renovation of pure theory. I shall reconstruct his critique in three steps. It is directed in the first place against the objectivism of the sciences, for which the world appears objectively as a universe of facts whose lawlike connection can be grasped descriptively. In truth, however, knowledge of the apparently objective world of facts has its transcendental basis in the prescientific world. The possible objects of scientific analysis are constituted *a priori* in the self-evidence of our primary life-world. In this layer phenomenology discloses

the products of a meaning-generative subjectivity. Second, Husserl would like to show that this productive subjectivity disappears under the cover of an objectivistic self-understanding, because the sciences have not radically freed themselves from interests rooted in the primary life-world. Only phenomenology breaks with the naive attitude in favor of a rigorously contemplative one and definitively frees knowledge from interest. Third, Husserl identifies transcendental self-reflection, to which he accords the name of phenomenological description, with theory in the traditional sense. The philosopher owes the theoretical attitude to a transposition that liberates him from the fabric of empirical interests. In this regard theory is "unpractical." But this does not cut it off from practical life. For, according to the traditional concept, it is precisely the consistent abstinence of theory that produces action-orienting culture. Once the theoretical attitude has been adopted, it is capable in turn of being mediated with the practical attitude:

> This occurs in the form of a novel practice . . . , whose aim is to elevate mankind to all forms of veridical norms through universal scientific reason, to transform it into a fundamentally new humanity, capable of absolute self-responsibility on the basis of absolute theoretical insight.

If we recall the situation of thirty years ago, the prospect of rising barbarism, we can respect this invocation of the therapeutic power of phenomenological description; but it is unfounded. At best, phenomenology grasps transcendental norms in accordance with which consciousness necessarily operates. It describes (in Kantian terms) laws of pure reason, but not norms of a universal legislation derived from practical reason, which a free will could obey. Why, then, does Husserl believe that he can claim practical efficacy for phenomenology as pure theory? He errs because he does not discern the connection of positivism, which he justifiably criticizes, with the ontology from which he unconsciously borrows the traditional concept of theory.

Husserl rightly criticizes the objectivist illusion that deludes the sciences with the image of a reality-in-itself consisting of facts structured in a lawlike manner; it conceals the constitution of these facts, and thereby prevents consciousness of the interlocking of knowledge with interests from the life-world. Because phenomenology brings this to consciousness, it is itself, in Husserl's view, free of such interests. It thus earns the title of pure theory unjustly claimed by the sciences. It is to this freeing of knowledge from interest that Husserl attaches the expectation of practical efficacy. But the error is clear. Theory in the sense of the classical tradition only had an impact on life because it was thought to have discovered in the cosmic order an ideal world structure, including the prototype for the order of the human world. Only as cosmology was *theoria* also capable of orienting human action. Thus Husserl cannot expect self-formative processes to originate in a phenomenology that, as transcendental philosophy, purifies the classical theory of its cosmological contents, conserving something like the theoretical attitude only in an abstract manner. Theory had educational and cultural implications not because it had freed knowledge from interest. To the contrary, it did so because it derived *pseudo-normative power* from *the concealment of its actual interest*. While criticizing the objectivist self-understanding of the sciences, Husserl succumbs to another objectivism, which was always attached to the traditional concept of theory.

IV

In the Greek tradition, the same forces that philosophy reduces to powers of the soul still appeared as gods and superhuman powers. Philosophy domesticated them and banished them to the realm of the soul as internalized demons. If from this point of view we regard the drives and affects that enmesh man in the empirical interests of his inconstant and contingent activity, then the attitude of pure theory, which promises *purification* from these very affects, takes on a new meaning: disinterested contemplation then obviously signifies emancipation. The release of knowledge from interest was not supposed to purify theory from the obfuscations of subjectivity but inversely to provide the subject with an ecstatic purification from the passions. What indicates the new stage of emancipation is that catharsis is now no longer attained through mystery cults but established in the will of individuals themselves by means of theory. In the communication structure of the polis, individuation has progressed to the point where the identity of the individual ego as a stable entity can only be developed through identification with abstract laws of cosmic order. Consciousness, emancipated from archaic powers, now anchors

itself in the unity of a stable cosmos and the identity of immutable Being.

Thus it was only by means of ontological distinctions that theory originally could take cognizance of a self-subsistent world purged of demons. At the same time, the illusion of pure theory served as a protection against regression to an earlier stage that had been surpassed. Had it been possible to detect that the identity of pure Being was an objectivistic illusion, ego identity would not have been able to take shape on its basis. The repression of interest appertained to this interest itself.

If this interpretation is valid, then the two most influential aspects of the Greek tradition, the theoretical attitude and the basic ontological assumption of a structured, self-subsistent world, appear in a connection that they explicitly prohibit: the connection of knowledge with human interests. Hence we return to Husserl's critique of the objectivism of the sciences. But this connection turns *against* Husserl. Our reason for suspecting the presence of an unacknowledged connection between knowledge and interest is not that the sciences have abandoned the classical concept of theory, but that they have not completely abandoned it. The suspicion of objectivism exists because of the *ontological illusion of pure theory* that the sciences still deceptively share with the philosophical tradition *after casting off its practical content*.

With Husserl we shall designate as objectivistic an attitude that naively correlates theoretical propositions with matters of fact. This attitude presumes that the relations between empirical variables represented in theoretical propositions are self-existent. At the same time, it suppresses the transcendental framework that is the precondition of the meaning of the validity of such propositions. As soon as these statements are understood in relation to the prior frame of reference to which they are affixed, the objectivist illusion dissolves and makes visible a knowledge-constitutive interest.

There are three categories of processes of inquiry for which a specific connection between logical-methodological rules and knowledge-constitutive interests can be demonstrated. This demonstration is the task of a critical philosophy of science that escapes the snares of positivism.[7] The approach of the empirical–analytic sciences incorporates a *technical* cognitive interest; that of the historical–hermeneutic sciences incorporates a *practical* one; and the approach of critically oriented sciences incorporates the *emancipatory* cognitive interest that, as we saw, was at the root of traditional theories. I should like to clarify this thesis by means of a few examples.

V

In the *empirical–analytic sciences* the frame of reference that prejudges the meaning of possible statements establishes rules both for the construction of theories and for their critical testing.[8] Theories comprise hypothetico–deductive connections of propositions, which permit the deduction of lawlike hypotheses with empirical content. The latter can be interpreted as statements about the covariance of observable events; given a set of initial conditions, they make predictions possible. Empirical–analytic knowledge is thus possible predictive knowledge. However, the *meaning* of such predictions, that is their technical exploitability, is established only by the rules according to which we apply theories to reality.

In controlled observation, which often takes the form of an experiment, we generate initial conditions and measure the results of operations carried out under these conditions. Empiricism attempts to ground the objectivist illusion in observations expressed in basic statements. These observations are supposed to be reliable in providing immediate evidence without the admixture of subjectivity. In reality basic statements are not simple representations of facts in themselves, but express the success or failure of our operations. We can say that facts and the relations between them are apprehended descriptively. But this way of talking must not conceal that as such the facts relevant to the empirical sciences are first constituted through an *a priori* organization of our experience in the behavioral system of instrumental action.

Taken together, these two factors, that is the logical structure of admissible systems of propositions and the type of conditions for corroboration, suggest that theories of the empirical sciences disclose reality subject to the constitutive interest in the possible securing and expansion, through information, of feedback-monitored action. This is the cognitive interest in technical control over objectified processes.

The *historical–hermeneutic sciences* gain knowledge in a different methodological framework. Here the meaning of the validity of propositions is not constituted in the frame of reference of technical control. The levels of formalized language and objectified experience have not yet

been divorced. For theories are not constructed deductively and experience is not organized with regard to the success of operations. Access to the facts is provided by the understanding of meaning, not observation. The verification of lawlike hypotheses in the empirical–analytic sciences has its counterpart here in the interpretation of texts. Thus the rules of hermeneutics determine the possible meaning of the validity of statements of the cultural sciences.[9]

Historicism has taken the understanding of meaning, in which mental facts are supposed to be given in direct evidence, and grafted onto it the objectivist illusion of pure theory. It appears as though the interpreter transposes himself into the horizon of the world or language from which a text derives its meaning. But here, too, the facts are first constituted in relation to the standards that establish them. Just as positivist self-understanding does not take into account explicitly the connection between measurement operations and feedback control, so it eliminates from consideration the interpreter's pre-understanding. Hermeneutic knowledge is always mediated through this pre-understanding, which is derived from the interpreter's initial situation. The world of traditional meaning discloses itself to the interpreter only to the extent that his own world becomes clarified at the same time. The subject of understanding establishes communication between both worlds. He comprehends the substantive content of tradition by *applying* tradition to himself and his situation.

If, however, methodological rules unite interpretation and application in this way, then this suggests that hermeneutic inquiry discloses reality subject to a constitutive interest in the preservation and expansion of the intersubjectivity of possible action-orienting mutual understanding. The understanding of meaning is directed in its very structure toward the attainment of possible consensus among actors in the framework of a self-understanding derived from tradition. This we shall call the *practical* cognitive interest, in contrast to the technical.

The systematic *sciences of social action*, that is economics, sociology, and political science, have the goal, as do the empirical–analytic sciences, of producing nomological knowledge.[10] A critical social science, however, will not remain satisfied with this. It is concerned with going beyond this goal to determine when theoretical statements grasp invariant regularities of social action as such and when they express ideologically frozen relations of dependence that can in principle be transformed. To the extent that this is the case, the *critique of ideology*, as well, moreover, as *psychoanalysis*, take into account that information about lawlike connections sets off a process of reflection in the consciousness of those whom the laws are about. Thus the level of unreflected consciousness, which is one of the initial conditions of such laws, can be transformed. Of course, to this end a critically mediated knowledge of laws cannot through reflection alone render a law itself inoperative, but it can render it inapplicable.

The methodological framework that determines the meaning of the validity of critical propositions of this category is established by the concept of *self-reflection*. The latter releases the subject from dependence on hypostatized powers. Self-reflection is determined by an emancipatory cognitive interest. Critically oriented sciences share this interest with philosophy.

However, as long as philosophy remains caught in ontology, it is itself subject to an objectivism that disguises the connection of its knowledge with the human interest in autonomy and responsibility (*Mündigkeit*). There is only one way in which it can acquire the power that it vainly claims for itself in virtue of its seeming freedom from presuppositions: by acknowledging its dependence on this interest and turning against its own illusion of pure theory the critique it directs at the objectivism of the sciences.[11]

VI

The concept of knowledge-constitutive human interests already conjoins the two elements whose relation still has to be explained: knowledge and interest. From everyday experience we know that ideas serve often enough to furnish our actions with justifying motives in place of the real ones. What is called rationalization at this level is called ideology at the level of collective action. In both cases the manifest content of statements is falsified by consciousness's unreflected tie to interests, despite its illusion of autonomy. The discipline of trained thought thus correctly aims at excluding such interests. In all the sciences routines have been developed that guard against the subjectivity of opinion, and a new discipline, the sociology of knowledge, has emerged to counter the uncontrolled influence of interests on a deeper level,

which derive less from the individual than from the objective situation of social groups. But this accounts for only one side of the problem. Because science must secure the objectivity of its statements against the pressure and seduction of particular interests, it deludes itself about the fundamental interests to which it owes not only its impetus but *the conditions of possible objectivity* themselves.

Orientation toward technical control, toward mutual understanding in the conduct of life, and toward emancipation from seemingly "natural" constraint establish the specific viewpoints from which we can apprehend reality as such in any way whatsoever. By becoming aware of the impossibility of getting beyond these transcendental limits, a part of nature acquires, through us, autonomy in nature. If knowledge could ever outwit its innate human interest, it would be by comprehending that the mediation of subject and object that philosophical consciousness attributes exclusively to *its own* synthesis is produced originally by interests. The mind can become aware of this natural basis reflexively. Nevertheless, its power extends into the very logic of inquiry.

Representations and descriptions are never independent of standards. And the choice of these standards is based on attitudes that require critical consideration by means of arguments, because they cannot be either logically deduced or empirically demonstrated. Fundamental methodological decisions, for example such basic distinctions as those between categorial and noncategorial being, between analytic and synthetic statements, or between descriptive and emotive meaning, have the singular character of being neither arbitrary nor compelling.[12] They prove appropriate or inappropriate. For their criterion is the metalogical necessity of interests that we can neither prescribe nor represent, but with which we must instead *come to terms*. Therefore my first thesis is this: *The achievements of the transcendental subject have their basis in the natural history of the human species.*

Taken by itself this thesis could lead to the misunderstanding that reason is an organ of adaptation for men just as claws and teeth are for animals. True, it does serve this function. But the human interests that have emerged in man's natural history, to which we have traced back the three knowledge-constitutive interests, derive both from nature and *from the cultural break* with nature. Along with the tendency to realize natural drives they have incorporated the tendency toward release from the constraint of nature. Even the interest in self-preservation, natural as it seems, is represented by a social system that compensates for the lacks in man's organic equipment and secures his historical existence *against* the force of nature threatening from without. But society is not only a system of self-preservation. An enticing natural force, present in the individual as libido, has detached itself from the behavioral system of self-preservation and urges toward utopian fulfillment. These individual demands, which do not initially accord with the requirement of collective self-preservation, are also absorbed by the social system. That is why the cognitive processes to which social life is indissolubly linked function not only as means to the reproduction of life; for in equal measure they themselves determine the definitions of this life. What may appear as naked survival is always in its roots a historical phenomenon. For it is subject to the criterion of what a society intends for itself as *the good life*. My *second thesis* is thus that *knowledge equally serves as an instrument and transcends mere self-preservation.*

The specific viewpoints from which, with transcendental necessity, we apprehend reality ground three categories of possible knowledge: information that expands our power of technical control; interpretations that make possible the orientation of action within common traditions; and analyses that free consciousness from its dependence on hypostatized powers. These viewpoints originate in the interest structure of a species that is linked in its roots to definite means of social organization: work, language, and power. The human species secures its existence in systems of social labor and self-assertion through violence, through tradition-bound social life in ordinary-language communication, and with the aid of ego identities that at every level of individuation reconsolidate the consciousness of the individual in relation to the norms of the group. Accordingly the interests constitutive of knowledge are linked to the functions of an ego that adapts itself to its external conditions through learning processes, is initiated into the communication system of a social life-world by means of self-formative processes, and constructs an identity in the conflict between instinctual aims and social constraints. In turn these achievements become part of the productive forces accumulated by a society, the cultural tradition through which a society interprets itself, and the legitimations that a society accepts or criticizes. My *third thesis* is thus that *knowledge-constitutive interests take form in the medium of work, language, and power.*

However, the configuration of knowledge and interest is not the same in all categories. It is true that at this level it is always illusory to suppose an autonomy, free of presuppositions, in which knowing first grasps reality theoretically, only to be taken subsequently into the service of interests alien to it. But the mind can always reflect back upon the interest structure that joins subject and object *a priori*: this is reserved to self-reflection. If the latter cannot cancel out interest, it can to a certain extent make up for it.

It is no accident that the standards of self-reflection are exempted from the singular state of suspension in which those of all other cognitive processes require critical evaluation. They possess theoretical certainty. The human interest in autonomy and responsibility is not mere fancy, for it can be apprehended *a priori*. What raises us out of nature is the only thing whose nature we can know: *language*. Through its structure, autonomy and responsibility are posited for us. Our first sentence expresses unequivocally the intention of universal and unconstrained consensus. Taken together, autonomy and responsibility constitute the only Idea that we possess *a priori* in the sense of the philosophical tradition. Perhaps that is why the language of German idealism, according to which "reason" contains both will and consciousness as its elements, is not quite obsolete. Reason also means the will to reason. In self-reflection knowledge for the sake of knowledge attains congruence with the interest in autonomy and responsibility. The emancipatory cognitive interest aims at the pursuit of reflection as such. My *fourth thesis* is thus that *in the power of self-reflection, knowledge and interest are one.*

However, only in an emancipated society, whose members' autonomy and responsibility had been realized, would communication have developed into the nonauthoritarian and universally practiced dialogue from which both our model of reciprocally constituted ego identity and our idea of true consensus are always implicitly derived. To this extent the truth of statements is based on anticipating the realization of the good life. The ontological illusion of pure theory behind which knowledge-constitutive interests become invisible promotes the fiction that Socratic dialogue is possible everywhere and at any time. From the beginning philosophy has presumed that the autonomy and responsibility posited with the structure of language are not only anticipated but real. It is pure theory, wanting to derive everything from itself, that succumbs to unacknowledged external conditions and becomes ideological. Only when philosophy discovers in the dialectical course of history the traces of violence that deform repeated attempts at dialogue and recurrently close off the path to unconstrained communication does it further the process whose suspension it otherwise legitimates: mankind's evolution toward autonomy and responsibility. My *fifth thesis* is thus that *the unity of knowledge and interest proves itself in a dialectic that takes the historical traces of suppressed dialogue and reconstructs what has been suppressed.*

VII

The sciences have retained one characteristic of philosophy: the illusion of pure theory. This illusion does not determine the practice of scientific research but only its self-understanding. And to the extent that this self-understanding reacts back upon scientific practice, it even has its point.

The glory of the sciences is their unswerving application of their methods without reflecting on knowledge-constitutive interests. From knowing not what they do methodologically, they are that much surer of their discipline, that is of methodical progress within an unproblematic framework. False consciousness has a protective function. For the sciences lack the means of dealing with the risks that appear once the connection of knowledge and human interest has been comprehended on the level of self-reflection. It was possible for Fascism to give birth to the freak of a national physics and Stalinism to that of a Soviet Marxist genetics (which deserves to be taken more seriously than the former) only because the illusion of objectivism was lacking. It would have been able to provide immunity against the more dangerous bewitchments of misguided reflection.

But the praise of objectivism has its limits. Husserl's critique was right to attack it, if not with the right means. As soon as the objectivist illusion is turned into an affirmative *Weltanschauung*, methodologically unconscious necessity is perverted to the dubious virtue of a scientific profession of faith. Objectivism in no way prevents the sciences from intervening in the conduct of life, as Husserl thought it did. They are integrated into it in any case. But they do not of themselves develop their practical efficacy in the direction of a growing rationality of action.

Instead, the positivist self-understanding of the *nomological sciences* lends countenance to the sub-

stitution of technology for enlightened action. It directs the utilization of scientific information from an illusory viewpoint, namely that the practical mastery of history can be reduced to technical control of objectified processes. The objectivist self-understanding of the *hermeneutic sciences* is of no lesser consequence. It defends sterilized knowledge against the reflected appropriation of active traditions and locks up history in a museum. Guided by the objectivist attitude of theory as the image of facts, the nomological and hermeneutical sciences reinforce each other with regard to their practical consequences. The latter displace our connection with tradition into the realm of the arbitrary, while the former, on the levelled-off basis of the repression of history, squeeze the conduct of life into the behavioral system of instrumental action. The dimension in which acting subjects could arrive rationally at agreement about goals and purposes is surrendered to the obscure area of mere decision among reified value systems and irrational beliefs.[13] When this dimension, abandoned by all men of good will, is subjected to reflection that relates to history objectivistically, as did the philosophical tradition, then positivism triumphs at the highest level of thought, as with Comte. This happens when critique uncritically abdicates its own connection with the emancipatory knowledge-constitutive interest in favor of pure theory. This sort of high-flown critique projects the undecided process of the evolution of the human species onto the level of a philosophy of history that dogmatically issues instructions for action. *A delusive philosophy of history, however, is only the obverse of deluded decisionism.* Bureaucratically prescribed partisanship goes only too well with contemplatively misunderstood value freedom.

These practical consequences of a restricted, scientistic consciousness of the sciences[14] can be countered by a critique that destroys the illusion of objectivism. Contrary to Husserl's expectations, objectivism is eliminated not through the power of renewed *theoria* but through demonstrating what it conceals: the connection of knowledge and interest. Philosophy remains true to its classic tradition by renouncing it. The insight that the truth of statements is linked in the last analysis to the intention of the good and true life can be preserved today only on the ruins of ontology. However even this philosophy remains a specialty alongside of the sciences and outside public consciousness as long as the heritage that it has critically abandoned lives on in the positivistic self-understanding of the sciences.

Notes

1 Friedrich W. J. von Schelling, *Werke*, edited by Manfred Schröter (Munich: Beck, 1958–9), vol. 3, p. 299.

2 Bruno Snell, "Theorie und Praxis," in *Die Entdeckung des Geistes*, 3rd edn (Hamburg: Claassen, 1955), p. 401 ff.; Georg Picht, "Der Sinn der Unterscheidung von Theorie und Praxis in der griechischen Philosophie," in *Evangelische Ethik* (1964), vol. 8, p. 321ff.

3 "Traditionelle und kritische Theorie," in *Zeitschrift für Sozialforschung*, vol. 6, p. 245 ff. Reprinted in Max Horkheimer, *Kritische Theorie*, edited by Alfred Schmidt (Frankfurt am Main: Fischer, 1968), pp. 137–91.

4 The appendix was the basis of my inaugural lecture at the University of Frankfurt am Main on June 28, 1965. Bibliographical notes are restricted to a few references.

5 *Die Krisis der europäischen Wissenschaften und die transzendentale Phänomenologie* in *Gesammelte Werke* (The Hague: Martinus Nijhoff, 1950), vol. 6.

6 See Gérard Gäfgen, *Theorie der wirtschaftlichen Entscheidung* (Tübingen: Mohr, 1963).

7 This path has been marked out by Karl-Otto Apel. See chapter 10, n. 1, above.

8 See Popper's *The Logic of Scientific Discovery*, and my paper "Analytische Wissenschaftstheorie," in *Zeugnisse* (Frankfurt am Main: Europäische Verlagsanstalt, 1963), p. 473 ff.

9 I concur with the analyses in Part II of Hans-Georg Gadamer, *Wahrheit und Methode*.

10 Ernst Topitsch (ed.), *Logik der Sozialwissenschaften* (Cologne: 1965).

11 Theodor W. Adorno, *Zur Metakritik der Erkenntnistheorie*.

12 Morton White, *Toward Reunion in Philosophy* (Cambridge, Mass.: Harvard University Press, 1956).

13 See my essay "Dogmatismus, Vernunft und Entscheidung" (Dogmatism, Reason, and Decision) in *Theorie und Praxis*.

14 In *One-Dimensional Man* (Boston: Beacon Press, 1964) Herbert Marcuse has analyzed the dangers of the reduction of reason to technical rationality and the reduction of society to the dimension of technical control. In another context, Helmut Schelsky has made the same diagnosis:

With a scientific civilization that man himself creates according to plan, a new peril has entered the world: the danger that man will develop himself only in external actions of altering the environment, and keep and deal with everything, himself and other human beings, at this object level of constructive action. This new self-alienation of man, which can rob him of his own and others' identity . . . is the danger of the creator losing himself in his work, the constructor in his construction. Man may recoil from completely transcending himself toward self-produced objectivity, toward constructed being; yet he works incessantly at extending this process of scientific self-objectification.

See Schelsky's *Einsamkeit und Freiheit* (Hamburg: 1963), p. 299.

Select Bibliography

Autonomy and Solidarity: Interviews with Jürgen Habermas. Edited by Peter Dews. London: Verso, 1992.

Communication and the Evolution of Society. Translated by Thomas McCarthy. Boston: Beacon Press, 1979.

Jürgen Habermas on Society and Politics: A Reader. Edited by Steven Seidman. Boston: Beacon Press, 1989.

Knowledge and Human Interests. Translated by Jeremy J. Shapiro. Cambridge: Polity Press, 1987.

Legitimation Crisis. Translated by Thomas McCarthy. Boston: Beacon Press, 1975.

Moral Consciousness and Communicative Action. Translated by Christian Lenhardt and Shierry Weber Nicholsen. Cambridge, Mass.: MIT Press, 1990.

The New Conservatism: Cultural Criticism and the Historians' Debate. Edited and translated by Shierry Weber Nicholsen. Cambridge, Mass.: MIT Press, 1989.

On the Logic of the Social Sciences. Translated by Shierry Weber Nicholsen and Jerry A. Stark. Cambridge, Mass.: MIT Press, 1988.

The Philosophical Discourse of Modernity: Twelve Lectures. Translated by Frederick G. Lawrence. Cambridge, Mass.: MIT Press, 1987.

Philosophical–Political Profiles. Translated by Frederick G. Lawrence. Cambridge, Mass.: MIT Press, 1983.

Postmetaphysical Thinking: Philosophical Essays. Translated by William Mark Hohengarten. Cambridge, Mass.: MIT Press, 1992.

Theory and Practice. Translated by John Viertel. Boston: Beacon Press, 1973.

The Theory of Communicative Action, 2 vols. Translated by Thomas McCarthy. Boston: Beacon Press, 1984–7.

PART IV

Structuralism and Psychoanalysis

1

Ferdinand de Saussure

The Swiss thinker Ferdinand de Saussure (1857–1913) is widely regarded as the founder of modern linguistics. His *Course in General Linguistics* was reconstructed in text form on the basis of lectures held at the University of Geneva from 1906–11. Here Saussure develops a structuralist theory of language and proposes the new science of "semiology," whose task is to investigate the operation of signs within society. The following selection from the *Course* presents some of Saussure's most fun-

damental insights into the nature of the linguistic sign, which he analyzes in terms of the relation between the "signifier" (or sound-image) and "signified" (or concept). This relation, Saussure points out, is arbitrary, that is, there is no necessary or natural connection between the two, but only a connection established by convention and tradition. The arbitrary nature of the sign, as Saussure goes on to indicate, carries profound implications for human existence as invested in language.

Course in General Linguistics

Nature of the Linguistic Sign

1 Sign, signified, signifier

Some people regard language, when reduced to its elements, as a naming-process only – a list of words, each corresponding to the thing that it names. For example:

From *Course in General Linguistics*, edited by Charles Bally and Albert Sechehaye in collaboration with Albert Reidlinger, translated by Wade Baskin (New York: Fontana/Collins, 1974), pp. 65–78. Copyright © 1959. Reprinted by permission.

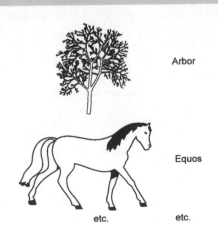

Arbor

Equos

etc.   etc.

This conception is open to criticism at several points. It assumes that ready-made ideas exist before words; it does not tell us whether a name is vocal or psychological in nature (*arbor*, for instance, can be considered from either viewpoint); finally, it lets us assume that the linking of a name and a thing is a very simple operation – an assumption that is anything but true. But this rather naive approach can bring us near the truth by showing us that the linguistic unit is a double entity, one formed by the associating of two terms.

We have seen in considering the speaking-circuit that both terms involved in the linguistic sign are psychological and are united in the brain by an associative bond. This point must be emphasized.

The linguistic sign unites, not a thing and a name, but a concept and a sound-image.[1] The latter is not the material sound, a purely physical thing, but the psychological imprint of the sound, the impression that it makes on our senses. The sound-image is sensory, and if I happen to call it "material," it is only in that sense, and by way of opposing it to the other term of the association, the concept, which is generally more abstract.

The psychological character of our sound-images becomes apparent when we observe our own speech. Without moving our lips or tongue, we can talk to ourselves or recite mentally a selection of verse. Because we regard the words of our language as sound-images, we must avoid speaking of the "phonemes" that make up the words. This term, which suggests vocal activity, is applicable to the spoken word only, to the realization of the inner image in discourse. We can avoid that misunderstanding by speaking of the *sounds* and *syllables* of a word provided we remember that the names refer to the sound-image.

The linguistic sign is then a two-sided psychological entity that can be represented by the drawing:

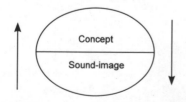

The two elements are intimately united, and each recalls the other. Whether we try to find the meaning of the Latin word *arbor* or the word that Latin uses to designate the concept "tree," it is clear that only the associations sanctioned by that language appear to us to conform to reality, and we disregard whatever others might be imagined.

Our definition of the linguistic sign poses an important question of terminology. I call the combination of a concept and a sound-image a *sign*, but in current usage the term generally designates only a sound-image, a word, for example (*arbor*, etc.). One tends to forget that *arbor* is called a sign only because it carries the concept "tree," with the result that the idea of the sensory part implies the idea of the whole.

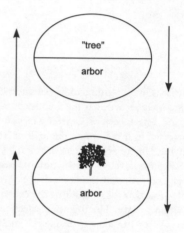

Ambiguity would disappear if the three notions involved here were designated by three names, each suggesting and opposing the others. I propose to retain the word *sign* [*signe*] to designate the whole and to replace *concept* and *sound-image* respectively by *signified* [*signifié*] and *signifier* [*signifiant*]; the last two terms have the advantage of indicating the opposition that separates them from each other and from the whole of which they are parts. As regards *sign*, if I am satisfied with it, this is simply because I do not know of any word to replace it, the ordinary language suggesting no other.

The linguistic sign, as defined, has two primordial characteristics. In enunciating them I am also positing the basic principles of any study of this type.

2 *Principle I: the arbitrary nature of the sign*

The bond between the signifier and the signified is arbitrary. Since I mean by sign the whole that results from the associating of the signifier with the signified, I can simply say: *the linguistic sign is arbitrary*.

The idea of "sister" is not linked by any inner relationship to the succession of sounds *s-ö-r* which serves as its signifier in French; that it could be represented equally by just any other sequence is proved by differences among languages and by the very existence of different languages: the signified "ox" has as its signifier *b-ö-f* on one side of the border and *o-k-s* (*Ochs*) on the other.

No one disputes the principle of the arbitrary nature of the sign, but it is often easier to discover a truth than to assign to it its proper place. Principle I dominates all the linguistics of language; its consequences are numberless. It is true that not all of them are equally obvious at first glance; only after many detours does one discover them, and with them the primordial importance of the principle.

One remark in passing: when semiology becomes organized as a science, the question will arise whether or not it properly includes modes of expression based on completely natural signs, such as pantomime. Supposing that the new science welcomes them, its main concern will still be the whole group of systems grounded on the arbitrariness of the sign. In fact, every means of expression used in society is based, in principle, on collective behavior or – what amounts to the same thing – on convention. Polite formulas, for instance, though often imbued with a certain natural expressiveness (as in the case of a Chinese who greets his emperor by bowing down to the ground nine times), are nonetheless fixed by rule; it is this rule and not the intrinsic value of the gestures that obliges one to use them. Signs that are wholly arbitrary realize better than the others the ideal of the semiological process; that is why language, the most complex and universal of all systems of expression, is also the most characteristic; in this sense linguistics can become the master-pattern for all branches of semiology although language is only one particular semiological system.

The word *symbol* has been used to designate the linguistic sign, or more specifically, what is here called the signifier. Principle I in particular weighs against the use of this term. One characteristic of the symbol is that it is never wholly arbitrary; it is not empty, for there is the rudiment of a natural bond between the signifier and the signified. The symbol of justice, a pair of scales, could not be replaced by just any other symbol, such as a chariot.

The word *arbitrary* also calls for comment. The term should not imply that the choice of the signifier is left entirely to the speaker (we shall see below that the individual does not have the power to change a sign in any way once it has become established in the linguistic community); I mean that it is unmotivated, i.e. arbitrary in that it actually has no natural connection with the signified.

In concluding let us consider two objections that might be raised to the establishment of Principle I:

(1) *Onomatopoeia* might be used to prove that the choice of the signifier is not always arbitrary. But onomatopoeic formations are never organic elements of a linguistic system. Besides, their number is much smaller than is generally supposed. Words like French *fouet* "whip" or *glas* "knell" may strike certain ears with suggestive sonority, but to see that they have not always had this property we need only examine their Latin forms (*fouet* is derived from *fāgus* "beech-tree," *glas* from *classicum* "sound of a trumpet"). The quality of their present sounds, or rather the quality that is attributed to them, is a fortuitous result of phonetic evolution.

As for authentic onomatopoeic words (e.g. *glug-glug*, *tick-tock*, etc.), not only are they limited in number, but also they are chosen somewhat arbitrarily, for they are only approximate and more or less conventional imitations of certain sounds (cf. English *bow-wow* and French *ouaoua*). In addition, once these words have been introduced into the language, they are to a certain extent subjected to the same evolution – phonetic, morphological, etc. – that other words undergo (cf. *pigeon*, ultimately from Vulgar Latin *pīpiō*, derived in turn from an onomatopoeic formation): obvious proof that they lose something of their original character in order to assume that of the linguistic sign in general, which is unmotivated.

(2) *Interjections*, closely related to onomatopoeia, can be attacked on the same grounds and come no closer to refuting our thesis. One is tempted to see in them spontaneous expressions of reality dictated, so to speak, by natural forces. But for most interjections we can show that there is no fixed bond between their signified and their signifier. We need only compare two languages on this point to see how much such expressions differ from one language to the next (e.g. the English equivalent of French *aïe!* is *ouch!*). We know, moreover, that many interjections were once words with specific meanings (cf. French *diable!* "darn!" *mordieu!* "golly!" from *mort Dieu* "God's death," etc.).[2]

Onomatopoeic formations and interjections are of secondary importance, and their symbolic origin is in part open to dispute.

3 Principle II: the linear nature of the signifier

The signifier, being auditory, is unfolded solely in time from which it gets the following characteristics: (a) it represents a span, and (b) the span is measurable in a single dimension; it is a line.

While Principle II is obvious, apparently linguists have always neglected to state it, doubtless because they found it too simple; nevertheless, it is fundamental, and its consequences are incalculable. Its importance equals that of Principle I; the whole mechanism of language depends upon it. In contrast to visual signifiers (nautical signals, etc.) which can offer simultaneous groupings in several dimensions, auditory signifiers have at their command only the dimension of time. Their elements are presented in succession; they form a chain. This feature becomes readily apparent when they are represented in writing and the spatial line of graphic marks is substituted for succession in time.

Sometimes the linear nature of the signifier is not obvious. When I accent a syllable, for instance, it seems that I am concentrating more than one significant element on the same point. But this is an illusion; the syllable and its accent constitute only one phonational act. There is no duality within the act but only different oppositions to what precedes and what follows.

Immutability and Mutability of the Sign

1 Immutability

The signifier, though to all appearances freely chosen with respect to the idea that it represents, is fixed, not free, with respect to the linguistic community that uses it. The masses have no voice in the matter, and the signifier chosen by language could be replaced by no other. This fact, which seems to embody a contradiction, might be called colloquially "the stacked deck." We say to language: "Choose!" but we add: "It must be this sign and no other." No individual, even if he willed it, could modify in any way at all the choice that has been made; and what is more, the community itself cannot control so much as a single word; it is bound to the existing language.

No longer can language be identified with a contract pure and simple, and it is precisely from this viewpoint that the linguistic sign is a particularly interesting object of study; for language furnishes the best proof that a law accepted by a community is a thing that is tolerated and not a rule to which all freely consent.

Let us first see why we cannot control the linguistic sign and then draw together the important consequences that issue from the phenomenon.

No matter what period we choose or how far back we go, language always appears as a heritage of the preceding period. We might conceive of an act by which, at a given moment, names were assigned to things and a contract was formed between concepts and sound-images; but such an act has never been recorded. The notion that things might have happened like that was prompted by our acute awareness of the arbitrary nature of the sign.

No society, in fact, knows or has ever known language other than as a product inherited from preceding generations, and one to be accepted as such. That is why the question of the origin of speech is not so important as it is generally assumed to be. The question is not even worth asking; the only real object of linguistics is the normal, regular life of an existing idiom. A particular language-state is always the product of historical forces, and these forces explain why the sign is unchangeable, i.e. why it resists any arbitrary substitution.

Nothing is explained by saying that language is something inherited and leaving it at that. Can not existing and inherited laws be modified from one moment to the next?

To meet that objection, we must put language into its social setting and frame the question just as we would for any other social institution. How are other social institutions transmitted? This more general question includes the question of immutability. We must first determine the greater or lesser amounts of freedom that the other institutions enjoy; in each instance it will be seen that a different proportion exists between fixed tradition and the free action of society. The next step is to discover why in a given category, the forces of the first type carry more weight or less weight than those of the second. Finally, coming back to language, we must ask why the historical factor of transmission dominates it entirely and prohibits any sudden widespread change.

There are many possible answers to the question. For example, one might point to the fact that succeeding generations are not superimposed on one another like the drawers of a piece of furniture, but fuse and interpenetrate, each generation embracing individuals of all ages – with the result that modifications of language are not tied to the succession of generations. One might also recall the sum of the efforts required for learning the mother language and conclude that a general change would be impossible. Again, it might be added that reflection does not enter into the active use of an idiom – speakers are largely unconscious of the laws of language; and if they are unaware of them, how could they modify them? Even if they were aware of these laws, we may be sure that their awareness would seldom lead to criticism, for people are generally satisfied with the language they have received.

The foregoing considerations are important but not specifically to the point. The following are more basic and direct, and all the others depend on them.

(1) *The arbitrary nature of the sign.* Above, we had to accept the theoretical possibility of change; further reflection suggests that the arbitrary nature of the sign is really what protects language from any attempt to modify it. Even if people were more conscious of language than they are, they would still not know how to discuss it. The reason is simply that any subject in order to be discussed must have a reasonable basis. It is possible, for instance, to discuss whether the monogamous form of marriage is more reasonable than the polygamous form and to advance arguments to support either side. One could also argue about a system of symbols, for the symbol has a rational relationship with the thing signified (see above); but language is a system of arbitrary signs and lacks the necessary basis, the solid ground for discussion. There is no reason for preferring *soeur* to *sister*, *Ochs* to *boeuf*, etc.

(2) *The multiplicity of signs necessary to form any language.* Another important deterrent to linguistic change is the great number of signs that must go into the making of any language. A system of writing comprising twenty to forty letters can in case of need be replaced by another system. The same would be true of language if it contained a limited number of elements; but linguistic signs are numberless.

(3) *The over-complexity of the system.* A language constitutes a system. In this one respect (as we shall see later) language is not completely arbitrary but is ruled to some extent by logic; it is here

also, however, that the inability of the masses to transform it becomes apparent. The system is a complex mechanism that can be grasped only through reflection; the very ones who use it daily are ignorant of it. We can conceive of a change only through the intervention of specialists, grammarians, logicians, etc.; but experience shows us that all such meddlings have failed.

(4) *Collective inertia toward innovation.* Language – and this consideration surpasses all the others – is at every moment everybody's concern; spread throughout society and manipulated by it, language is something used daily by all. Here we are unable to set up any comparison between it and other institutions. The prescriptions of codes, religious rites, nautical signals, etc., involve only a certain number of individuals simultaneously and then only during a limited period of time; in language, on the contrary, everyone participated at all times, and that is why it is constantly being influenced by all. This capital fact suffices to show the impossibility of revolution. Of all social institutions, language is least amenable to initiative. It blends with the life of society, and the latter, inert by nature, is a prime conservative force.

But to say that language is a product of social forces does not suffice to show clearly that it is unfree; remembering that it is always the heritage of the preceding period, we must add that these social forces are linked with time. Language is checked not only by the weight of the collectivity but also by time. These two are inseparable. At every moment solidarity with the past checks freedom of choice. We say *man* and *dog* because our predecessors said *man* and *dog*. This does not prevent the existence in the total phenomenon of a bond between the two antithetical forces – arbitrary convention by virtue of which choice is free and time which causes choice to be fixed. Because the sign is arbitrary, it follows no law other than that of tradition, and because it is based on tradition, it is arbitrary.

2 Mutability

Time, which insures the continuity of language, wields another influence apparently contradictory to the first: the more or less rapid change of linguistic signs. In a certain sense, therefore, we can speak of both the immutability and the mutability of the sign.[3]

In the last analysis, the two facts are interdependent: the sign is exposed to alteration because it perpetuates itself. What predominates in all change is the persistence of the old substance; disregard for the past is only relative. That is why the principle of change is based on the principle of continuity.

Change in time takes many forms, on any one of which an important chapter in linguistics might be written. Without entering into detail, let us see what things need to be delineated.

First, let there be no mistake about the meaning that we attach to the word change. One might think that it deals especially with phonetic changes undergone by the signifier, or perhaps changes in meaning which affect the signified concept. That view would be inadequate. Regardless of what the forces of change are, whether in isolation or in combination, they always result in a *shift in the relationship between the signified and the signifier*.

Here are some examples. Latin *necāre* "kill" became *noyer* "drown" in French. Both the sound-image and the concept changed; but it is useless to separate the two parts of the phenomenon; it is sufficient to state with respect to the whole that the bond between the idea and the sign was loosened, and that there was a shift in their relationship. If instead of comparing Classical Latin *necāre* with French *noyer*, we contrast the former term with *necare* of Vulgar Latin of the fourth or fifth century meaning "drown" the case is a little different; but here again, although there is no appreciable change in the signifier, there is a shift in the relationship between the idea and the sign.[4]

Old German *dritteil* "one-third" became *Drittel* in Modern German. Here, although the concept remained the same, the relationship was changed in two ways: the signifier was changed not only in its material aspect but also in its grammatical form; the idea of *Teil* "part" is no longer implied; *Drittel* is a simple word. In one way or another there is always a shift in the relationship.

In Anglo-Saxon the preliterary form *fot* "foot" remained while its plural **fōti* became *fēt* (Modern English *feet*). Regardless of the other changes that are implied, one thing is certain: there was a shift in their relationship; other correspondences between the phonetic substance and the idea emerged.

Language is radically powerless to defend itself against the forces which from one moment to the next are shifting the relationship between the signified and the signifier. This is one of the consequences of the arbitrary nature of the sign.

Unlike language, other human institutions – customs, laws, etc. – are all based in varying degrees on the natural relations of things; all have of necessity adapted the means employed to the ends pursued. Even fashion in dress is not entirely arbitrary; we can deviate only slightly from the conditions dictated by the human body. Language is limited by nothing in the choice of means, for apparently nothing would prevent the associating of any idea whatsoever with just any sequence of sounds.

To emphasize the fact that language is a genuine institution, Whitney quite justly insisted upon the arbitrary nature of signs; and by so doing, he placed linguistics on its true axis. But he did not follow through and see that the arbitrariness of language radically separates it from all other institutions. This is apparent from the way in which language evolves. Nothing could be more complex. As it is a product of both the social force and time, no one can change anything in it, and on the other hand, the arbitrariness of its signs theoretically entails the freedom of establishing just any relationship between phonetic substance and ideas. The result is that each of the two elements united in the sign maintains its own life to a degree unknown elsewhere, and that language changes, or rather evolves, under the influence of all the forces which can affect either sounds or meanings. The evolution is inevitable; there is no example of a single language that resists it. After a certain period of time, some obvious shifts can always be recorded.

Mutability is so inescapable that it even holds true for artificial languages. Whoever creates a language controls it only so long as it is not in circulation; from the moment when it fulfills its mission and becomes the property of everyone, control is lost. Take Esperanto as an example; if it succeeds, will it escape the inexorable law? Once launched, it is quite likely that Esperanto will enter upon a fully semiological life; it will be transmitted according to laws which have nothing in common with those of its logical creation, and there will be no turning backwards. A man proposing a fixed language that posterity would have to accept for what it is would be like a hen hatching a duck's egg: the language created by him would be borne along, willy-nilly, by the current that engulfs all languages.

Signs are governed by a principle of general semiology: continuity in time is coupled to change in time; this is confirmed by orthographic systems, the speech of deaf-mutes, etc.

But what supports the necessity for change? I might be reproached for not having been as explicit on this point as on the principle of immutability. This is because I failed to distinguish between the different forces of change. We must consider their great variety in order to understand the extent to which they are necessary.

The causes of continuity are *a priori* within the scope of the observer, but the causes of change in time are not. It is better not to attempt giving an exact account at this point, but to restrict discussion to the shifting of relationships in general. Time changes all things; there is no reason why language should escape this universal law.

Let us review the main points of our discussion and relate them to the principles set up in the Introduction.

(1) Avoiding sterile word definitions, within the total phenomenon represented by speech we first singled out two parts: language and speaking. Language is speech less speaking. It is the whole set of linguistic habits which allow an individual to understand and to be understood.

(2) But this definition still leaves language outside its social context; it makes language something artificial since it includes only the individual part of reality; for the realization of language, a community of speakers [*masse parlante*] is necessary. Contrary to all appearances, language never exists apart from the social fact, for it is a semiological phenomenon. Its social nature is one of its inner characteristics. Its complete definition confronts us with two inseparable entities, as shown in this drawing:

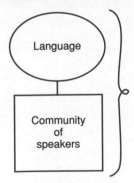

But under the conditions described language is not living – it has only potential life; we have considered only the social, not the historical, fact.

(3) The linguistic sign is arbitrary; language, as defined, would therefore seem to be a system which, because it depends solely on a rational principle, is free and can be organized at will. Its social nature, considered independently, does not definitely rule out this viewpoint. Doubtless it is not on a purely logical basis that group psychology operates; one must consider everything that deflects reason in actual contacts between individuals. But the thing which keeps language from being a simple convention that can be modified at the whim of interested parties is not its social nature; it is rather the action of time combined with the social force. If time is left out, the linguistic facts are incomplete and no conclusion is possible.

If we considered language in time, without the community of speakers – imagine an isolated individual living for several centuries – we probably would notice no change; time would not influence language. Conversely, if we considered the community of speakers without considering time, we would not see the effect of the social forces that influence language. To represent the actual facts, we must then add to our first drawing a sign to indicate passage of time:

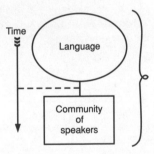

Language is no longer free, for time will allow the social forces at work on it to carry out their effects. This brings us back to the principle of continuity, which cancels freedom. But continuity necessarily implies change, varying degrees of shifts in the relationship between the signified and the signifier.

Notes

1   The term sound-image may seem to be too restricted inasmuch as beside the representation of the sounds of a word there is also that of its articulation, the muscular image of the phonational act. But for F. de

Saussure language is essentially a depository, a thing received from without. The sound-image is *par excellence* the natural representation of the word as a fact of potential language, outside any actual use of it in speaking. The motor side is thus implied or, in any event, occupies only a subordinate role with respect to the sound-image. (Original ed.)

2 Cf. English *goodness!* and *zounds!* (from *God's wounds*). (Trans.)

3 It would be wrong to reproach F. de Saussure for being illogical or paradoxical in attributing two contradictory qualities to language. By opposing two striking terms, he wanted only to emphasize the fact that language changes in spite of the inability of speakers to change it. One can also say that it is intangible but not unchangeable. (Original ed.)

4 From May to July of 1911, Saussure used interchangeably the old terminology (*idea* and *sign*) and the new (*signified* and *signifier*). (Trans.)

Select Bibliography

Course in General Linguistics. Edited by Charles Bally and Albert Sechehaye with Albert Riedlinger. Translated by Wade Baskin. New York: Fontana/Collins, 1974.

2

Claude Lévi-Strauss

The French social anthropologist Claude Lévi-Strauss (1908–) became famous for introducing structuralist techniques of analysis, adopted from Saussure's linguistic analysis, into the study of culture and society. Lévi-Strauss's approach emphasizes the fundamental symbolic structures that underlie cultural and social manifestations, and that display a large degree of universality and homogeneity across different peoples, cultures, and ages. Much of his work is concerned with the study of so-called primitive societies, with a view to discovering paradigmatic structures of human signification. The following excerpt from his pioneering study *The Elementary Structures of Kinship* (1949) highlights the proximity of structuralist analysis of society to the science of linguistics. Here Lévi-Strauss argues that the artificial rules of social exchange (of which marriage is the "archetype") have the same fundamental function as language, namely enabling social organization and communication; in this sense, he concludes, linguists and sociologists study "the same thing."

The Elementary Structures of Kinship

The Principles of Kinship

I

... It is always a system of exchange that we find at the origin of rules of marriage, even of those of

From *The Elementary Structures of Kinship*, edited by Rodney Needham, translated by James Harle Bell, John Richard von Sturmer, and Rodney Needham (Boston, Beacon Press, 1969), pp. 478–83, 492–7. Translation © 1969 by Beacon Press. Reprinted by permission of Beacon Press, Boston.

which the apparent singularity would seem to allow only a special and arbitrary interpretation. In the course of this work, we have seen the notion of exchange become complicated and diversified; it has constantly appeared to us in different forms. Sometimes exchange appears as direct (the case of marriage with the bilateral cousin), sometimes as indirect (and in this case it can comply with two formulas, one continuous, the other discontinuous, corresponding to two different rules of marriage with the unilateral cousin). Sometimes it functions within a total system (this is the theoretically common characteristic of bilateral marriage and of matrilateral marriage), and at others it instigates the formation of an unlimited number of special systems and short cycles, unconnected among themselves (and in this form it represents a permanent threat to moiety systems, and as an inevitable weakness attacks patrilateral systems). Sometimes exchange appears as a cash or short-term transaction (with the exchange of sisters and daughters, and avuncular marriage), and at other times more as a long-term transaction (as in the case where the prohibited degrees include first, and occasionally second, cousins). Sometimes the exchange is explicit and at other times it is implicit (as seen in the example of so-called marriage by purchase). Sometimes the exchange is closed (when marriage must satisfy a special rule of alliance between marriage classes or a special rule for the observance of preferential degrees), while sometimes it is open (when the rule of exogamy is merely a collection of negative stipulations, which, beyond the prohibited degrees, leaves a free choice). Sometimes it is secured by a sort of mortgage on reserved categories (classes or degrees); sometimes (as in the case of the simple prohibition of incest, as found in our society) it rests on a wider fiduciary guarantee, viz., the theoretical freedom to claim any woman of the group, in return for the renunciation of certain designated women in the family circle, a freedom insured by the extension of a prohibition, similar to that affecting each man in particular, to all men in general. But no matter what form it takes, whether direct or indirect, general or special, immediate or deferred, explicit or implicit, closed or open, concrete or symbolic, it is exchange, always exchange, that emerges as the fundamental and common basis of all modalities of the institution of marriage. If these modalities can be subsumed under the general term of exogamy (for, as we have seen in Part I, endogamy is not opposed to exogamy, but presupposes it), this is conditional upon the apperception, behind the superficially negative expression of the rule of exogamy, of the final principle which, through the prohibition of marriage within prohibited degrees, tends to insure the total and continuous circulation of the group's most important assets, its wives and its daughters....

The value of exchange is not simply that of the goods exchanged. Exchange – and consequently the rule of exogamy which expresses it – has in itself a social value. It provides the means of binding men together, and of superimposing upon the natural links of kinship the henceforth artificial links – artificial in the sense that they are removed from chance encounters or the promiscuity of family life – of alliance governed by rule. In this connexion, marriage serves as model for that artificial and temporary "conjugality" between young people of the same sex in some schools and on which Balzac makes the profound remark that it is never superimposed upon blood ties but replaces them: "It is strange, but never in my time did I know brothers who were 'Activists.' If man lives only by his feelings, he thinks perhaps that he will make his life the poorer if he merges an affection of his own choosing in a natural tie.". . .[1]

No relationship can be arbitrarily isolated from all other relationships. It is likewise impossible to remain on this or that side of the world of relationships. The social environment should not be conceived of as an empty framework within which beings and things can be linked, or simply juxtaposed. It is inseparable from the things which people it. Together they constitute a field of gravitation in which the weights and distances form a coordinated whole, and in which a change in any element produces a change in the total equilibrium of the system. We have given a partial illustration at least of this principle in our analysis of cross-cousin marriage. However, it can be seen how its field of application must be extended to all the rules of kinship, and above all, to that universal and fundamental rule, the prohibition of incest. Every kinship system (and no human society is without one) has a total character, and it is because of this that the mother, sister, and daughter are perpetually coupled, as it were, with elements of the system which, in relation to them, are neither son, nor brother, nor father, because the latter are themselves coupled with other women, or other classes of women, or feminine elements defined by a relationship of a different order. Because marriage is exchange, because marriage is the archetype of exchange, the analysis of exchange can help in the understanding of the solidarity which unites the gift and the counter-gift, and one marriage with other marriages....

V

Despite these presentiments, only one social science has reached the point at which synchronic and diachronic explanation have merged, because synchronic explanation allows the reconstitution of the origin of systems and their synthesis, while diachronic explanation reveals their internal logic and perceives the evolution which directs them towards an end. This social science is linguistics, regarded as a phonological study.[2] When we consider its methods, and even more its object, we may ask ourselves whether the sociology of the family, as conceived of in this work, involves as different a reality as might be believed, and consequently whether it has not the same possibilities at its disposal.

The diversity of the historical and geographical modalities of the rules of kinship and marriage have appeared to us to exhaust all possible methods for insuring the integration of biological families within the social group. We have thus established that superficially complicated and arbitrary rules may be reduced to a small number. There are only three possible elementary kinship structures; these three structures are constructed by means of two forms of exchange; and these two forms of exchange themselves depend upon a single differential characteristic, namely the harmonic or disharmonic character of the regime considered. Ultimately, the whole imposing apparatus of prescriptions and prohibitions could be reconstructed *a priori* from one question, and one alone: in the society concerned, what is the relationship between the rule of residence and the rule of descent? Every disharmonic regime leads to restricted exchange, just as every harmonic regime announces generalized exchange.

The progress of our analysis is thus close to that of the phonological linguist. What is more, if the incest prohibition and exogamy have an essentially positive function, if the reason for their existence is to establish a tie between men which the latter cannot do without if they are to raise themselves from a biological to a social organization, it must be recognized that linguists and sociologists do not merely apply the same methods but are studying the same thing. Indeed, from this point of view, "exogamy and language . . . have fundamentally the same function – communication and integration with others."[3] It is to be regretted that after this profound remark its author makes off in another direction, and assimilates the incest prohibition to other taboos, such as the prohibition on sexual relations with an uncircumcised boy among the Wachagga, or the inversion of the hypergamous rule in India.[4] The incest prohibition is not a prohibition like the others. It is *the* prohibition in the most general form, the one perhaps to which all others – beginning with those cited above – are related as particular cases. The incest prohibition is universal like language, and if it is true that we are better informed on the nature of the latter than on the origin of the former, it is only by pursuing the comparison to its conclusion that we can hope to get to the meaning of the institution.

Modern civilization has acquired such a mastery of the linguistic instrument and of means of communication, and makes such a diversified use of them, that we have, as it were, immunized ourselves against language, or at least so we believe. We see language as no more than an inert medium, in itself ineffective, the passive bearer of ideas on which the fact of expression confers no additional characteristic. For most men, language represents without falsifying. But modern psychology has refuted this simplistic conception: "Language does not enter into a world of accomplished objective perceptions merely to give purely external and arbitrary signs or 'names' to individual given objects which are clearly delimited from one another; but it is itself a mediator in the formation of objects. It is in one sense the supreme denominator."[5] This more accurate view of linguistic fact is not a discovery or a new invention. It merely places the narrow perspectives of the civilized white adult in a vaster, and consequently more valid, human experience, in which "the naming mania" of the child, and the study of the profound upheaval produced in backward subjects by the sudden discovery of the function of language, corroborate observations made in the field; from which it emerges that the conception of the spoken word as communication, as power, and as action represents a universal feature of human thought.[6]

Certain facts taken from psychopathology already tend to suggest that the relations between the sexes can be conceived as one of the modalities of a great "communication function" which also includes language. For certain sufferers from obsessions, noisy conversation seems to have the same significance as an unbridled sexual activity. They themselves speak only in a low voice and in a murmur, as if the human voice were unconsciously interpreted as a sort of substitute for sexual power.[7] But, even if one is prepared to accept and use these facts only with reservation (and here we call upon psychopathology only because, like infantile psychology and social anthropology, it allows a more comprehensive way of experiencing the social universe), it must be acknowledged that they receive striking confirmation from certain observations on primitive customs and attitudes. One need only recall that in New Caledonia "the evil word" is adultery, for "word" should probably be interpreted as meaning "act."[8] More significant evidence is also available. For several very primitive peoples in the Malay Archipelago, the supreme sin, unleashing storm and tempest, comprises a series of superficially incongruous acts which informants list higgledy-piggledy as follows: marriage with near kin; father and daughter or mother and son sleeping too close to one another; incorrect speech between kin; ill-considered conversation; for children, noisy play, and, for adults, demonstrative happiness shown at social reunions; imitating the calls of certain insects or birds; laughing at one's own face in the mirror; and finally, teasing animals, and in particular, dressing a monkey as a man, and making fun of him.[9] What possible connexion could there be between such a bizarre collection of acts?

Let us make a short digression. In a neighboring region, Radcliffe-Brown came across only one of these prohibitions. The Andaman Islanders believe that the tempest is provoked by killing a cicada, or by making a noise when it sings. As the prohibition seems to exist in isolation, and since he avoids all comparative study, in the name of the principle that every custom is explainable by an immediately apparent function, the English anthropologist treated this example on a purely empirical basis: the prohibition, he argues, proceeds from the myth of the ancestor who killed a cicada; it cried out, and night appeared. Consequently, according to Radcliffe-Brown, this myth expresses the difference in value between night and day in native thought. Night creates fear, this fear is reflected in a prohibition, and, as night cannot be acted upon, it is the cicada which becomes the object of the taboo.[10]

If this method were to be applied to the complete system of prohibitions as listed above, each prohibition would require a different explanation. But why then does native thought group them under the one heading? Either native thought must be accused of being incoherent, or we must search for the common characteristic which, in a certain respect, makes these apparently heterogeneous acts express an identical situation.

A native remark puts us on the track. The Pygmies of the Malay Peninsula consider it a sin to laugh at one's own face in a mirror, but they add that it is not a sin to ridicule a real human being since he can defend himself. This interpretation obviously also applies to the dressed-up monkey which is treated as a human being when it is teased, and looks like a human being (just as does the face in the mirror), although it is not really one. This

interpretation can also be extended to the imitation of the calls of certain insects or birds, "singing" creatures, no doubt, like the Andamanese cicada. By imitating them, one is treating an emission of sound which "sounds" like a word as a human manifestation when it is not. Thus, we find two categories of acts definable as an immoderate use of language: the first, from a quantitative point of view, to play noisily, to laugh too loudly, or to make an excessive show of one's feelings; the second, from a qualitative point of view, to answer sounds which are not words, or to converse with something (mirror or monkey) which is human only in appearance.[11] These prohibitions are all thus reduced to a single common denominator: they all constitute a *misuse of language*, and on this ground they are grouped together with the incest prohibition, or with acts evocative of incest. What does this mean, except that women themselves are treated as signs, which are *misused* when not put to the use reserved to signs, which is to be communicated?

In this way, language and exogamy represent two solutions to one and the same fundamental situation. Language has achieved a high degree of perfection, while exogamy has remained approximate and precarious. This disparity, however, is not without its counterpart. The very nature of the linguistic symbol prevented it from remaining for long in the stage which was ended by Babel, when words were still the essential property of each particular group: values as much as signs, jealously preserved, reflectively uttered, and exchanged for other words the meaning of which, once revealed, would bind the stranger, as one put oneself in his power by initiating him, something of oneself and acquires some power over the other. The respective attitudes of two individuals in communication acquire a meaning of which they would otherwise be devoid. Henceforth, acts and thoughts become mutually solidary. The freedom to be mistaken has been lost. But, to the extent that words have become common property, and their signifying function has supplanted their character as values, language, along with scientific civilization,[12] has helped to impoverish perception and to strip it of its affective, aesthetic, and magical implications, as well as to schematize thought.

Passing from speech to alliance, i.e. to the other field of communication, the situation is reversed. The emergence of symbolic thought must have required that women, like words, should be things that were exchanged. In this new case, indeed, this was the only means of overcoming the contradiction by which the same woman was seen under two incompatible aspects: on the one hand, as the object of personal desire, thus exciting sexual and proprietorial instincts; and, on the other, as the subject of the desire of others, and seen as such, i.e. as the means of binding others through alliance with them. But woman could never become just a sign and nothing more, since even in a man's world she is still a person, and since insofar as she is defined as a sign she must be recognized as a generator of signs. In the matrimonial dialogue of men, woman is never purely what is spoken about; for if women in general represent a certain category of signs, destined to a certain kind of communication, each woman preserves a particular value arising from her talent, before and after marriage, for taking her part in a duet. In contrast to words, which have wholly become signs, woman has remained at once a sign and a value. This explains why the relations between the sexes have preserved that affective richness, ardor and mystery which

doubtless originally permeated the entire universe of human communications.

But that atmosphere of feverish excitement and sensitivity which engendered symbolic thought, and social life, which is its collective form, can still with its far-off vision kindle our dreams. To this very day, mankind has always dreamed of seizing and fixing that fleeting moment when it was permissible to believe that the law of exchange could be evaded, that one could gain without losing, enjoy without sharing. At either end of the earth and at both extremes of time, the Sumerian myth of the golden age and the Andaman myth of the future life correspond, the former placing the end of primitive happiness at a time when the confusion of languages made words into common property, the latter describing the bliss of the hereafter as a heaven where women will no longer be exchanged, i.e. removing to an equally unattainable past or future the joys, eternally denied to social man, of a world in which one might *keep to oneself.*

Notes

1 "The conjugal regard that united us as boys, and which we used to express by calling ourselves 'Activists'." Balzac, *Oeuvres Complètes*, vol. X (Paris, 1937), pp. 366, 382.

2 Trubetzkoy, E. N. "La Phonologie actuelle." *Psychologie du langage*, pp. 227–46 (1933); *Grundzüge der Phonologie* (Prague, 1939).

3 Thomas, W. I. *Primitive Behaviour* (New York, 1937), p. 182.

4 Ibid. p. 197.

5 Cassirer, E. "Le Langage et la construction du monde des objets." *Psychologie du langage*, pp. 18–44 (1933), p. 23.

6 Ibid. p. 25; *An Essay on Man* (New Haven, 1944), p. 31 et seq.; Leenhardt, "Ethnologie de la parole." *Cahiers Internationaux de Sociologie*, vol. I, 1946; Firth, *Primitive Polynesian Economy* (London, 1939), p. 317.

7 Reik, T. *Ritual* (London, 1931), p. 263.

8 Leenhardt, 1946, p. 87.

9 Skeat, W. W. and Blagden, C.O., *Pagan Races of the Malay Peninsula*. 2 vols (London, 1906), vol. II, p. 223; Schebesta, P., *Among the Forest Dwarfs of Malaya* (London, 1929), *passim*; Evans, I. H. N., *Studies in Religion, Folk-lore, and Customs in British North Borneo and the Malay Peninsula* (Cambridge, 1923), pp. 199–200 and *The Negritos of Malaya* (Cambridge, 1937), p. 175.

10 Radcliffe-Brown, A. R., *The Andaman Islanders* (Cambridge, 1933), pp. 155–6, 333.

11 The same definition can be made to include all actions classified by the Dayak as *djeadjea* or forbidden, viz., " 'giving a man or animal a name that is not his or its . . . or to say something about him that is contrary to his nature; for example, that a louse dances, or a rat sings, or a fly goes to war . . .; or to say of a man that he had a cat or some other animal for a mother or wife.' To bury any living animal and say 'I am burying a man'." (Hardeland, 1859, s.v.; cf. Caillois, R., *Man and the Sacred* (Glencoe, Ill., 1959).) However, we believe that these acts relate to the positive interpretation which we propose, rather than Caillois's interpretation based on disorder, or "counter-order" (ibid. ch. III). "Mystic homosexuality" appears to us a false category since homosexuality is not the prototype of "the misuse of communications," but is one of its particular cases, for the same reason (but in a different sense) as are incest and all the other acts just enumerated.

12 "Our scientific civilization . . . tends to impoverish our perception" (Köhler, W., "Psychological Remarks on Some Questions of Anthropology." *American Journal of Psychology*, Vol. I (1937), p. 277).

Claude Lévi-Strauss

Select Bibliography

Anthropology and Myth: Lectures, 1951–1982. Translated by Roy Willis. Oxford: Blackwell Publishers, 1987.

Conversations with Claude Lévi-Strauss. Translated by Paula Wissing. Chicago: University of Chicago Press, 1991.

The Elementary Structures of Kinship. Edited by Rodney Needham. Translated by James Harle Bell, John Richard von Sturmer, and Rodney Needham. Boston: Beacon Press, 1969.

From Honey to Ashes. Translated by John Weightman and Doreen Weightman. Chicago: University of Chicago Press, 1983.

Myth and Meaning. New York: Schocken Books, 1995.

The Naked Man. Translated by John Weightman and Doreen Weightman. Chicago: University of Chicago Press, 1990.

The Raw and the Cooked. Translated by John Weightman and Doreen Weightman. Chicago: University of Chicago Press, 1990.

The Savage Mind. Chicago: University of Chicago Press, 1966.

The Scope of Anthropology. Translated by Sherry Ortner Paul and Robert A. Paul. London: Cape, 1967.

Structural Anthropology, 2 vols. Translated by Monique Layton. Chicago: University of Chicago Press, 1983.

Totemism. Translated by Rodney Needham. Boston: Beacon Press, 1963.

Tristes Tropiques. Translated by John Weightman and Doreen Weightman. New York: Penguin Books, 1992.

The View from Afar. Translated by Joachim Neugroschel and Phoebe Hoss. Chicago: University of Chicago Press, 1992.

Roland Barthes

Cultural critic, writer, and literary theorist, the French thinker Roland Barthes (1915–80) extends Saussure's conception of the semiological analysis of meaning to the realm of political and cultural critique. According to Barthes, the structuralist analysis of linguistic signification reveals that cultural phenomena in general are embedded in contexts of complex and hidden meanings that are often unacknowledged by the dominant forms of ideology, but nonetheless operate in accordance with certain rules. In the following essay *The Structuralist Activity* (1963), Barthes describes his conception of structuralism as a creative "activity" (rather than a school of thought), whose task is to discover the hidden rules governing how linguistic units signify in a given context.

The Structuralist Activity

What is structuralism? Not a school, nor even a movement (at least, not yet), for most of the authors ordinarily labeled with this word are unaware of being united by any solidarity of doctrine or commitment. Nor is it a vocabulary. *Structure* is already an old word (of anatomical and grammatical provenance), today quite overworked: all the social sciences resort to it abundantly, and its use can distinguish no one, except to polemicize about the content assigned to it; *functions, forms, signs,* and

From *Critical Essays,* translated by Richard Howard (Evanston, Ill.: Northwestern University Press, 1979), pp. 213–20. Copyright © 1972 by Northwestern University Press. Reprinted by permission of the publisher.

significations are scarcely more pertinent: they are, today, words in common use from which one asks (and obtains) whatever one wants, notably the camouflage of the old determinist schema of cause and product; we must doubtless resort to pairings like those of *signifier/signified* and *synchronic/diachronic* in order to approach what distinguishes structuralism from other modes of thought: the first because it refers to the linguistic model as originated by Saussure and because, along with economics, linguistics is, in the present state of affairs, the true science of structure; the second, more decisively, because it seems to imply a certain revision of the notion of history, insofar as the idea of synchrony (although in Saussure this is a preeminently operational concept) accredits a certain immobilization of time, and insofar as diachrony tends to represent the historical process as a pure succession of forms. This second pairing is all the more distinctive in that the chief resistance to structuralism today seems to be of Marxist origin and in that it focuses on the notion of history (and not of structure); whatever the case, it is probably the serious recourse to the nomenclature of signification (and not to the word itself, which is, paradoxically, not at all distinctive) which we must ultimately take as structuralism's spoken sign: watch who uses *signifier* and *signified, synchrony* and *diachrony*, and you will know whether the structuralist vision is constituted.

This is valid for the intellectual metalanguage, which explicitly employs methodological concepts. But since structuralism is neither a school nor a movement, there is no reason to reduce it *a priori*, even in a problematical way, to the activity of philosophers; it would be better to try and find its broadest description (if not its definition) on another level than that of reflexive language. We can in fact presume that there exist certain writers, painters, musicians in whose eyes a certain exercise of structure (and no longer merely its thought) represents a distinctive experience, and that both analysts and creators must be placed under the common sign of what we might call *structural man*, defined not by his ideas or his languages, but by his imagination – in other words, by the way in which he mentally experiences structure.

So the first thing to be said is that in relation to all its users, structuralism is essentially an *activity*, i.e. the controlled succession of a certain number of mental operations: we might speak of structuralist activity as we once spoke of surrealist activity (surrealism, moreover, may well have produced the first experience of structural literature, a possibility which must some day be explored). But before seeing what these operations are, we must say a word about their goal.

The goal of all structuralist activity, whether reflexive or poetic, is to reconstruct an "object" in such a way as to manifest thereby the rules of functioning (the "functions") of this object. Structure is therefore actually a *simulacrum* of the object, but a directed, *interested* simulacrum, since the imitated object makes something appear which remained invisible or, if one prefers, unintelligible in the natural object. Structural man takes the real, decomposes it, then recomposes it; this appears to be little enough (which makes some say that the structuralist enterprise is "meaningless," "uninteresting," "useless," etc.). Yet from another point of view, this "little enough" is decisive: for between the two objects, or the two tenses, of structuralist activity, there occurs something new, and what is new is nothing less than the generally intelligible: the simulacrum is intellect added to object, and this addition has an anthropological value, in that it is man himself, his history, his situation, his freedom, and the very resistance which nature offers to his mind.

We see, then, why we must speak of a structuralist *activity*: creation or reflection are not, here, an original "impression" of the world, but a veritable fabrication of a world which resembles the primary one, not in order to copy it but to render it intelligible. Hence one might say that structuralism is essentially *an activity of imitation*, which is also why there is, strictly speaking, no *technical* difference between structuralism as an intellectual activity, on the one hand, and literature in particular, art in general, on the other: both derive from a *mimesis*, based not on the analogy of substances (as in so-called realist art), but on the analogy of functions (what Lévi-Strauss calls *homology*). When Troubetskoy reconstructs the phonetic object as a system of variations; when Dumézil elaborates a functional mythology; when Propp constructs a folk tale resulting by structuration from all the Slavic tales he has previously decomposed; when Lévi-Strauss discovers the homologic functioning of the totemic imagination, or Granger the formal rules of economic thought, or Gardin the pertinent features of prehistoric bronzes; when Richard decomposes a poem by Mallarmé into its distinctive vibrations – they are all doing nothing different from what Mondrian, Boulez, or Butor are doing when they articulate a certain object – what will be called, precisely, a *composition* – by the controlled manifestation of certain units and certain associations of these units. It is of little consequence whether the initial object submitted to the simulacrum activity is given by the world in an already assembled fashion (in the case of the structural analysis made of a constituted language or society or work) or is still dispersed (in the case of the structural "composition"); whether this initial object is drawn from a social reality or an imaginary reality. It is not the nature of the copied object which defines an art (though this is a tenacious prejudice in all realism), it is the fact that man adds to it in reconstructing it: technique is the very being of all creation. It is therefore to the degree that the goals of structuralist activity are indissolubly linked to a certain technique that structuralism exists in a distinctive fashion in relation to other modes of analysis or creation: we recompose the object in order to make certain functions appear, and it is, so to speak, the way that makes the work; this is why we must speak of the structuralist activity rather than the structuralist work.

The structuralist activity involves two typical operations: dissection and articulation. To dissect the first object, the one which is given to the simulacrum-activity, is to find in it certain mobile fragments whose differential situation engenders a certain meaning; the fragment has no meaning in itself, but it is nonetheless such that the slightest variation wrought in its configuration produces a change in the whole; a *square* by Mondrian, a *series* by Pousseur, a *versicle* of Butor's *Mobile*, the "mytheme" in Lévi-Strauss, the phoneme in the work of the phonologists, the "theme" in certain literary criticism – all these units (whatever their inner structure and their extent, quite different according to cases) have no significant existence except by their frontiers: those which separate them from other actual units of the discourse (but this is a problem of articulation) and also those which distinguish them from other virtual units, with which they form a certain class (which linguistics calls a *paradigm*); this notion of a paradigm is essential, apparently, if we are to understand the structuralist vision: the paradigm is a group, a reservoir – as limited as possible – of objects (of units) from which we summon, by an act of citation, the object or unit we wish to endow with an actual meaning; what characterizes the paradigmatic object is that it is, *vis-à-vis* other objects of its class, in a certain relation of affinity and of dissimilarity: two units of the same paradigm must resemble each other somewhat *in order* that the difference which separates them be indeed evident: *s* and *z* must have both a common feature (dentality) and a distinctive feature (presence or absence of sonority) so that we cannot, in French, attribute the same meaning to *poisson* and *poison*; Mondrian's squares must have both certain affinities by their shape as squares, and certain dissimilarities by their proportion and color; the American automobiles (in Butor's *Mobile*) must be constantly regarded in the same way, yet they must differ each time by both their make and color; the episodes of the Oedipus myth (in Lévi-Strauss's analysis) must be both identical and varied – in order that all these languages, these works may be intelligible. The dissection-operation thus produces an initial dispersed state of the simulacrum, but the units of the structure are not at all anarchic: before being distributed and fixed in the continuity of the composition, each one forms with its own virtual group or reservoir an intelligent organism, subject to a sovereign motor principle: that of the least difference.

Once the units are posited, structural man must discover in them or establish for them certain rules of association: this is the activity of articulation, which succeeds the summoning activity. The syntax of the arts and of discourse is, as we know, extremely varied; but what we discover in every work of structural enterprise is the submission to regular constraints whose formalism, improperly indicted, is much less important than their stability; for what is happening, at this second stage of the simulacrum-activity, is a kind of battle against chance; this is why the constraint of recurrence of the units has an almost demiurgic value: it is by the regular return of the units and of the associations of units that the work appears constructed, i.e. endowed with meaning; linguistics calls these rules of combination *forms*, and it would be advantageous to retain this rigorous sense of an overtaxed word: form, it has been said, is what keeps the contiguity of units from appearing as a pure effect of chance: the work of art is what man wrests from chance. This perhaps allows us to understand on the one hand why so-called nonfigurative works are nonetheless to the highest degree works of art, human thought being established not by the analogy of copies and models but by the regularity of assemblages; and on the other hand why these same works appear, precisely, fortuitous and thereby useless to those who discern in them no form: in front of an abstract painting, Khrushchev is certainly wrong to see only the traces of a donkey's tail whisked across the canvas; at least he knows in his way, though, that art is a certain conquest of chance (he simply forgets that every rule must be learned, whether one wants to apply or interpret it).

The simulacrum, thus constructed, does not render the world as it has found it, and it is here that structuralism is important. First of all, it manifests a new category of the object, which is neither the real nor the rational, but the *functional*, thereby joining a whole scientific complex which is being developed around information theory and research. Subsequently and especially, it highlights the strictly human process by which men give meaning to things. Is this new? To a certain degree, yes; of course the world has never stopped looking for the meaning of what is given it and of what it produces; what is new is a mode of thought (or a "poetics") which seeks less to assign completed meanings to the objects it discovers than to know how meaning is possible, at what cost and by what means. Ultimately, one might say that the object of structuralism is not man endowed with meanings but man fabricating meanings, as if it could not be the *content* of meanings which exhausted the semantic goals of humanity, but only the act by which these meanings, historical and contingent variables, are produced. *Homo significans*: such would be the new man of structural inquiry.

According to Hegel, the ancient Greek was amazed by the natural in nature; he constantly listened to it, questioned the meaning of mountains, springs, forests, storms; without knowing what all these objects were telling him by name, he perceived in the vegetal or cosmic order a tremendous shudder of meaning, to which he gave the name of a god: *Pan*. Subsequently, nature has changed, has become social: everything given to man is already human, down to the forest and the river which we cross when we travel. But confronted with this social nature, which is quite simply culture, structural man is no different from the ancient Greek: he too listens for the natural in culture, and constantly perceives in it not so much stable, finite, "true" meanings as the shudder of an enormous machine which is humanity tirelessly undertaking to create meaning, without which it would no longer be human. And it is because this fabrication of meaning is more important, to its view, than the meanings themselves, it is because the function is extensive with the works, that structuralism constitutes itself as an activity, and refers the exercise of the work and the work itself to a single identity: a

serial composition or an analysis by Lévi-Strauss are not objects except insofar as they have been made: their present being *is* their past act: they are *having-been-mades*; the artist, the analyst recreates the course taken by meaning, he need not designate it: his function, to return to Hegel's example, is a *manteia*; like the ancient soothsayer, he speaks the locus of meaning but does not name it. And it is because literature, in particular, is a mantic activity that it is both intelligible and interrogating, speaking and silent, engaged in the world by the course of the meaning which it remakes with the world, but disengaged from the contingent meanings which the world elaborates: an answer to the man who consumes it yet always a question to nature, an answer which questions and a question which answers.

How then does structural man deal with the accusation of "unreality" which is sometimes flung at him? Are not forms in the world? are not forms responsible? Was it really his Marxism that was revolutionary in Brecht? Was it not rather the decision to link to Marxism, in the theater, the placing of a spotlight or the deliberate fraying of a costume? Structuralism does not withdraw history from the world: it seeks to link to history not only certain contents (this has been done a thousand times) but also certain forms, not only the material but also the intelligible, not only the ideological but also the aesthetic. And precisely because all thought about the historically intelligible is also a participation in that intelligibility, structural man is scarcely concerned to last; he knows that structuralism, too, is a certain form of the world, which will change with the world; and just as he experiences his validity (but not his truth) in his power to speak the old languages of the world in a new way, so he knows that it will suffice that a new language rise out of history, a new language which speaks *him* in his turn, for his task to be done.

Select Bibliography

A Barthes Reader. Edited by Susan Sontag. New York: Hill and Wang, 1982.

Critical Essays. Translated by Richard Howard. Evanston Ill.: Northwestern University Press, 1979.

Criticism and Truth. Translated and edited by Katrine Pilcher Keuneman. Minneapolis: University of Minnesota Press, 1987.

Elements of Semiology. Translated by Annette Lavers and Colin Smith. New York: Hill and Wang, 1968.

Empire of Signs. Translated by Richard Howard. New York: Hill and Wang, 1982.

The Fashion System. Translated by Matthew Ward and Richard Howard. Berkeley: University of California Press, 1990.

Image, Music, Text. Translated by Stephen Heath. New York: Hill and Wang, 1977.

Mythologies. Translated by Annette Lavers. New York: Hill and Wang, 1972.

The Pleasure of the Text. Translated by Richard Miller. New York: Hill and Wang, 1975.

The Responsibility of Forms: Critical Essays on Music, Art and Representation. Translated by Richard Howard. Berkeley: University of California Press, 1991.

S/Z. Translated by Richard Miller. New York: Hill and Wang, 1974.

The Semiotic Challenge. Translated by Richard Howard. Berkeley: University of California Press, 1994.

Writing Degree Zero. Translated by Annette Lavers and Colin Smith. New York: Hill and Wang, 1968.

4

Sigmund Freud

Sigmund Freud (1856–1939) is the most famous figure in modern psychology, and the founder of psychoanalysis. Originally a student of medicine at the University of Vienna, Freud's work in neurology and on the treatment of hysteria led him to ascribe sexual origins to particular symptoms of his patients. Eventually Freud came to believe that sexuality and its repression were the source of much of human behavior and of cultural phenomena in general. Here the notion of the unconscious is crucial; only by claiming the existence of a sphere of the forgotten, repressed, and denied could Freud argue that early childhood and forgotten or repressed traumas exert a lasting effect upon a person's behavior. Freud's accounts of early male and female development are controversial in that they emphasize the boy's valuation of his penis and the consequences of this for the so-called Oedipal phase, whereas, according to Freud, the girl's lack of this organ is a source of envy and renders her development potentially more complicated. The following selection from *Beyond the Pleasure Principle* (1920) contains some of Freud's most compelling speculations on the phenomenon of life as a series of "detours" taken by the death-drive; while the excerpts from the lecture *Femininity* (1933) address "the riddle of femininity" in relation to the Oedipus complex.

Beyond the Pleasure Principle

IV

What follows is speculation, often far-fetched speculation, which the reader will consider or dis-

From *Beyond the Pleasure Principle*, edited and translated by James Strachey (New York: W. W. Norton, 1961), pp. 18–22, 28–37. Translation copyright © 1961 by, James Strachey. Reprinted by permission of Liveright Publishing Corporation, and The Hogarth Press.

miss according to his individual predilection. It is further an attempt to follow out an idea consistently, out of curiosity to see where it will lead.

Psychoanalytic speculation takes as its point of departure the impression, derived from examining unconscious processes, that consciousness may be, not the most universal attribute of mental processes, but only a particular function of them. Speaking in metapsychological terms, it asserts that consciousness is a function of a particular system which it describes as $Cs.$[1] What conscious-ness yields consists essentially of perceptions of excitations coming from the external world and of feelings of pleasure and unpleasure which can only arise from within the mental apparatus; it is there-fore possible to assign to the system $Pcpt.-Cs.$[2] a position in space. It must lie on the borderline between outside and inside; it must be turned towards the external world and must envelop the other psychical systems. It will be seen that there is nothing daringly new in these assumptions; we have merely adopted the views on localization held by cerebral anatomy, which locates the "seat" of consciousness in the cerebral cortex – the outermost, enveloping layer of the central organ. Cerebral anatomy has no need to consider why, speaking anatomically, consciousness should be lodged on the surface of the brain instead of being safely housed somewhere in its inmost inter-ior. Perhaps *we* shall be more successful in account-ing for this situation in the case of our system $Pcpt.-Cs.$

Consciousness is not the only distinctive char-acter which we ascribe to the processes in that system. On the basis of impressions derived from our psychoanalytic experience, we assume that all excitatory processes that occur in the *other* systems leave permanent traces behind in them which form the foundation of memory. Such memory-traces, then, have nothing to do with the fact of becoming conscious; indeed they are often most powerful and most enduring when the process which left them behind was one which never entered conscious-ness. We find it hard to believe, however, that permanent traces of excitation such as these are also left in the system $Pcpt.-Cs.$ If they remained constantly conscious, they would very soon set limits to the system's aptitude for receiving fresh excitations.[3] If, on the other hand, they were unconscious, we should be faced with the problem of explaining the existence of unconscious pro-cesses in a system whose functioning was otherwise accompanied by the phenomenon of consciousness. We should, so to say, have altered nothing and gained nothing by our hypothesis relegating the process of becoming conscious to a special system. Though this consideration is not absolutely con-clusive, it nevertheless leads us to suspect that becoming conscious and leaving behind a mem-ory-trace are processes incompatible with each other within one and the same system. Thus we should be able to say that the excitatory process becomes conscious in the system $Cs.$ but leaves no

permanent trace behind there; but that the excita-tion is transmitted to the systems lying next within and that it is in *them* that its traces are left. I followed these same lines in the schematic picture which I included in the speculative section of my *Interpretation of Dreams*. It must be borne in mind that little enough is known from other sources of the origin of consciousness; when, therefore, we lay down the proposition that *consciousness arises instead of a memory-trace*, the assertion deserves consideration, at all events on the ground of its being framed in fairly precise terms.

If this is so, then, the system $Cs.$ is characterized by the peculiarity that in it (in contrast to what happens in the other psychical systems) excitatory processes do not leave behind any permanent change in its elements but expire, as it were, in the phenomenon of becoming conscious. An exception of this sort to the general rule requires to be explained by some factor that applies exclus-ively to that one system. Such a factor, which is absent in the other systems, might well be the exposed situation of the system $Cs.$, immediately abutting as it does on the external world.

Let us picture a living organism in its most simplified possible form as an undifferentiated vesicle of a substance that is susceptible to stimula-tion. Then the surface turned towards the external world will from its very situation be differentiated and will serve as an organ for receiving stimuli. Indeed embryology, in its capacity as a recapitula-tion of developmental history, actually shows us that the central nervous system originates from the ectoderm; the gray matter of the cortex remains a derivative of the primitive superficial layer of the organism and may have inherited some of its essen-tial properties. It would be easy to suppose, then, that as a result of the ceaseless impact of external stimuli on the surface of the vesicle, its substance to a certain depth may have become permanently modified, so that excitatory processes run a differ-ent course in it from what they run in the deeper layers. A crust would thus be formed which would at last have been so thoroughly "baked through" by stimulation that it would present the most favor-able possible conditions for the reception of stimuli and become incapable of any further modification. In terms of the system $Cs.$, this would mean that its elements could undergo no further permanent modification from the passage of excitation, because they had already been modified in the respect in question to the greatest possible extent: now, however, they would have become capable of giving rise to consciousness. Various ideas may be formed which cannot at present be verified as to the nature of this modification of the substance and of the excitatory process. It may be supposed that, in passing from one element to another, an excitation has to overcome a resistance, and that the diminution of resistance thus effected is what lays down a permanent trace of the excitation, that is, a facilitation. In the system *Cs.*, then, resistance of this kind to passage from one element to another would no longer exist. This picture can be brought into relation with Breuer's distinction between quiescent (or bound) and mobile cathectic energy in the elements of the psychical systems;[4] the elements of the system *Cs.* would carry no bound energy but only energy capable of free discharge. It seems best, however, to express oneself as cautiously as possible on these points. Nonetheless, this speculation will have enabled us to bring the origin of consciousness into some sort of connection with the situation of the system *Cs.* and with the peculiarities that must be ascribed to the excitatory processes taking place in it.

But we have more to say of the living vesicle with its receptive cortical layer. This little fragment of living substance is suspended in the middle of an external world charged with the most powerful energies; and it would be killed by the stimulation emanating from these if it were not provided with a protective shield against stimuli. It acquires the shield in this way: its outermost surface ceases to have the structure proper to living matter, becomes to some degree inorganic and thenceforward functions as a special envelope or membrane resistant to stimuli. In consequence, the energies of the external world are able to pass into the next underlying layers, which have remained living, with only a fragment of their original intensity; and these layers can devote themselves, behind the protective shield, to the reception of the amounts of stimulus which have been allowed through it. By its death, the outer layer has saved all the deeper ones from a similar fate – unless, that is to say, stimuli reach it which are so strong that they break through the protective shield. *Protection against* stimuli is an almost more important function for the living organism than *reception* of stimuli. The protective shield is supplied with its own store of energy and must above all endeavor to preserve the special modes of transformation of energy operating in it against the effects threatened by the enormous energies at work in the external world – effects which tend towards a leveling out of them and

hence towards destruction. The main purpose of the *reception* of stimuli is to discover the direction and nature of the external stimuli; and for that it is enough to take small specimens of the external world, to sample it in small quantities. In highly developed organisms the receptive cortical layer of the former vesicle has long been withdrawn into the depths of the interior of the body, though portions of it have been left behind on the surface immediately beneath the general shield against stimuli. These are the sense organs, which consist essentially of apparatus for the reception of certain specific effects of stimulation, but which also include special arrangements for further protection against excessive amounts of stimulation and for excluding unsuitable kinds of stimuli. It is characteristic of them that they deal only with very small quantities of external stimulation and only take in *samples* of the external world. They may perhaps be compared with feelers which are all the time making tentative advances towards the external world and then drawing back from it. . . .

V

The fact that the cortical layer which receives stimuli is without any protective shield against excitations from within must have as its result that these latter transmissions of stimulus have a preponderance in economic importance and often occasion economic disturbances comparable with traumatic neuroses. The most abundant sources of this internal excitation are what are described as the organism's "instincts" – the representatives of all the forces originating in the interior of the body and transmitted to the mental apparatus – at once the most important and the most obscure element of psychological research.

It will perhaps not be thought too rash to suppose that the impulses arising from the instincts do not belong to the type of *bound* nervous processes but of *freely mobile* processes which press towards discharge. The best part of what we know of these processes is derived from our study of the dreamwork. We there discovered that the processes in the unconscious systems were fundamentally different from those in the preconscious (or conscious) systems. In the unconscious, cathexes can easily be completely transferred, displaced, and condensed. Such treatment, however, could produce only invalid results if it were applied to preconscious material; and this accounts for the familiar peculiarities exhibited by manifest dreams after the preconscious residues of the preceding day have been worked over in accordance with the laws operating in the unconscious. I described the type of process found in the unconscious as the "primary" psychical process, in contradistinction to the "secondary" process which is the one obtaining in our normal waking life. Since all instinctual impulses have the unconscious systems as their point of impact, it is hardly an innovation to say that they obey the primary process. Again, it is easy to identify the primary psychical process with Breuer's freely mobile cathexis and the secondary process with changes in his bound or tonic cathexis.[5] If so, it would be the task of the higher strata of the mental apparatus to bind the instinctual excitation reaching the primary process. A failure to effect this binding would provoke a disturbance analogous to a traumatic neurosis; and only after the binding has been accomplished would it be possible for the dominance of the pleasure principle (and of its modification, the reality principle) to proceed unhindered. Till then the other task of the mental apparatus, the task of mastering or binding excitations, would have precedence – not, indeed, in *opposition* to the pleasure principle, but independently of it and to some extent in disregard of it.

The manifestations of a compulsion to repeat (which we have described as occurring in the early activities of infantile mental life as well as among the events of psychoanalytic treatment) exhibit to a high degree an instinctual character and, when they act in opposition to the pleasure principle, give the appearance of some "daemonic" force at work. In the case of children's play we seemed to see that children repeat unpleasurable experiences for the additional reason that they can master a powerful impression far more thoroughly by being active than they could by merely experiencing it passively. Each fresh repetition seems to strengthen the mastery they are in search of. Nor can children have their *pleasurable* experiences repeated often enough, and they are inexorable in their insistence that the repetition shall be an identical one. This character trait disappears later on. If a joke is heard for a second time it produces almost no effect; a theatrical production never creates so great an impression the second time as the first; indeed, it is hardly possible to persuade an adult who has very much enjoyed reading a book to reread it immediately. Novelty is always the condition of enjoyment. But children will never tire of asking an adult to repeat a game that he has shown

them or played with them, till he is too exhausted to go on. And if a child has been told a nice story, he will insist on hearing it over and over again rather than a new one; and he will remorselessly stipulate that the repetition shall be an identical one and will correct any alterations of which the narrator may be guilty – though they may actually have been made in the hope of gaining fresh approval. None of this contradicts the pleasure principle; repetition, the re-experiencing of something identical, is clearly in itself a source of pleasure. In the case of a person in analysis, on the contrary, the compulsion to repeat the events of his childhood in the transference evidently disregards the pleasure principle in every way. The patient behaves in a purely infantile fashion and thus shows us that the repressed memory-traces of his primeval experiences are not present in him in a bound state and are indeed in a sense incapable of obeying the secondary process. It is to this fact of not being bound, moreover, that they owe their capacity for forming, in conjunction with the residues of the previous day, a wishful phantasy that emerges in a dream. This same compulsion to repeat frequently meets us as an obstacle to our treatment when at the end of an analysis we try to induce the patient to detach himself completely from his physician. It may be presumed, too, that when people unfamiliar with analysis feel an obscure fear – a dread of rousing something that, so they feel, is better left sleeping – what they are afraid of at bottom is the emergence of this compulsion with its hint of possession by some "daemonic" power.

But how is the predicate of being "instinctual" related to the compulsion to repeat? At this point we cannot escape a suspicion that we may have come upon the track of a universal attribute of instincts and perhaps of organic life in general which has not hitherto been clearly recognized or at least not explicitly stressed. *It seems, then, that an instinct is an urge inherent in organic life to restore an earlier state of things* which the living entity has been obliged to abandon under the pressure of external disturbing forces; that is, it is a kind of organic elasticity, or, to put it another way, the expression of the inertia inherent in organic life.[6]

This view of instincts strikes us as strange because we have become used to see in them a factor impelling towards change and development, whereas we are now asked to recognize in them the precise contrary – an expression of the *conservative* nature of living substance. On the other hand we soon call to mind examples from animal life which seem to confirm the view that instincts are historically determined. Certain fishes, for instance, undertake laborious migrations at spawning-time in order to deposit their spawn in particular waters far removed from their customary haunts. In the opinion of many biologists what they are doing is merely to seek out the localities in which their species formerly resided but which in the course of time they have exchanged for others. The same explanation is believed to apply to the migratory flights of birds of passage – but we are quickly relieved of the necessity for seeking for further examples by the reflection that the most impressive proofs of there being an organic compulsion to repeat lie in the phenomena of heredity and the facts of embryology. We see how the germ of a living animal is obliged in the course of its development to recapitulate (even if only in a transient and abbreviated fashion) the structures of all the forms from which it is sprung, instead of proceeding quickly by the shortest path to its final shape. This behavior is only to a very slight degree attributable to mechanical causes, and the historical explanation cannot accordingly be neglected. So too the power of regenerating a lost organ by growing afresh a precisely similar one extends far up into the animal kingdom.

We shall be met by the plausible objection that it may very well be that, in addition to the conservative instincts which impel towards repetition, there may be others which push forward towards progress and the production of new forms. This argument must certainly not be overlooked, and it will be taken into account at a later stage. But for the moment it is tempting to pursue to its logical conclusion the hypothesis that all instincts tend towards the restoration of an earlier state of things. The outcome may give an impression of mysticism or of sham profundity; but we can feel quite innocent of having had any such purpose in view. We seek only for the sober results of research or of reflection based on it; and we have no wish to find in those results any quality other than certainty.

Let us suppose, then, that all the organic instincts are conservative, are acquired historically and tend towards the restoration of an earlier state of things. It follows that the phenomena of organic development must be attributed to external disturbing and diverting influences. The elementary living entity would from its very beginning have had no wish to change; if conditions remained the same, it would do no more than constantly repeat the same course of life. In the last resort, what has left its mark on the development of organisms must be the history of the earth we live in and of its relation to the sun. Every modification which is thus imposed upon the course of the organism's life is accepted by the conservative organic instincts and stored up for further repetition. Those instincts are therefore bound to give a deceptive appearance of being forces tending towards change and progress, whilst in fact they are merely seeking to reach an ancient goal by paths alike old and new. Moreover it is possible to specify this final goal of all organic striving. It would be in contradiction to the conservative nature of the instincts if the goal of life were a state of things which had never yet been attained. On the contrary, it must be an *old* state of things, an initial state from which the living entity has at one time or other departed and to which it is striving to return by the circuitous paths along which its development leads. If we are to take it as a truth that knows no exception that everything living dies for *internal* reasons – becomes inorganic once again – then we shall be compelled to say that "*the aim of all life is death*" and, looking backwards, that "*inanimate things existed before living ones.*"

The attributes of life were at some time evoked in inanimate matter by the action of a force of whose nature we can form no conception. It may perhaps have been a process similar in type to that which later caused the development of consciousness in a particular stratum of living matter. The tension which then arose in what had hitherto been an inanimate substance endeavored to cancel itself out. In this way the first instinct came into being: the instinct to return to the inanimate state. It was still an easy matter at that time for a living substance to die; the course of its life was probably only a brief one, whose direction was determined by the chemical structure of the young life. For a long time, perhaps, living substance was thus being constantly created afresh and easily dying, till decisive external influences altered in such a way as to oblige the still surviving substance to diverge ever more widely from its original course of life and to make ever more complicated *détours* before reaching its aim of death. These circuitous paths to death, faithfully kept to by the conservative instincts, would thus present us today with the picture of the phenomena of life. If we firmly maintain the exclusively conservative nature of instincts, we cannot arrive at any other notions as to the origin and aim of life.

The implications in regard to the great groups of instincts which, as we believe, lie behind the phenomena of life in organisms must appear no less bewildering. The hypothesis of self-preservative instincts, such as we attribute to all living beings, stands in marked opposition to the idea that instinctual life as a whole serves to bring about death. Seen in this light, the theoretical importance of the instincts of self-preservation, of self-assertion, and of mastery greatly diminishes. They are component instincts whose function it is to assure that the organism shall follow its own path to death, and to ward off any possible ways of returning to inorganic existence other than those which are immanent in the organism itself. We have no longer to reckon with the organism's puzzling determination (so hard to fit into any context) to maintain its own existence in the face of every obstacle. What we are left with is the fact that the organism wishes to die only in its own fashion. Thus these guardians of life, too, were originally the myrmidons of death. Hence arises the paradoxical situation that the living organism struggles most energetically against events (dangers, in fact) which might help it to attain its life's aim rapidly – by a kind of short-circuit. Such behavior is, however, precisely what characterizes purely instinctual as contrasted with intelligent efforts.

But let us pause for a moment and reflect. It cannot be so. The sexual instincts, to which the theory of the neuroses gives a quite special place, appear under a very different aspect.

The external pressure which provokes a constantly increasing extent of development has not imposed itself upon *every* organism. Many have succeeded in remaining up to the present time at their lowly level. Many, though not all, such creatures, which must resemble the earliest stages of the higher animals and plants, are, indeed, living today. In the same way, the whole path of development to natural death is not trodden by *all* the elementary entities which compose the complicated body of one of the higher organisms. Some of them, the germ-cells, probably retain the original structure of living matter and, after a certain time, with their full complement of inherited and freshly acquired instinctual dispositions, separate themselves from the organism as a whole. These two characteristics may be precisely what enables them to have an independent existence. Under favorable conditions, they begin to develop – that is, to repeat the performance to which they owe their existence; and in the end once again one portion of their substance pursues its development to a finish, while another portion harks back once again as a fresh residual germ to the beginning of the process of development. These germ-cells, therefore, work against the death of the living substance and succeed in winning for it what we can only regard as potential immortality, though that may mean no more than a lengthening of the road to death. We must regard as in the highest degree significant the fact that this function of the germ-cell is reinforced, or only made possible, if it coalesces with another cell similar to itself and yet differing from it.

The instincts which watch over the destinies of these elementary organisms that survive the whole individual, which provide them with a safe shelter while they are defenceless against the stimuli of the external world, which bring about their meeting with other germ-cells, and so on – these constitute the group of the sexual instincts. They are conservative in the same sense as the other instincts in that they bring back earlier states of living substance; but they are conservative to a higher degree in that they are peculiarly resistant to external influences; and they are conservative too in another sense in that they preserve life itself for a comparatively long period.[7] They are the true life instincts. They operate against the purpose of the other instincts, which leads, by reason of their function, to death; and this fact indicates that there is an opposition between them and the other instincts, an opposition whose importance was long ago recognized by the theory of the neuroses. It is as though the life of the organism moved with a vacillating rhythm. One group of instincts rushes forward so as to reach the final aim of life as swiftly as possible; but when a particular stage in the advance has been reached, the other group jerks back to a certain point to make a fresh start and so prolong the journey. And even though it is certain that sexuality and the distinction between the sexes did not exist when life began, the possibility remains that the instincts which were later to be described as sexual may have been in operation from the very first, and it may not be true that it was only at a later time that they started upon their work of opposing the activities of the "ego-instincts."[8]

Let us now hark back for a moment ourselves and consider whether there is any basis at all for these speculations. Is it really the case that, *apart from the sexual instincts*, there are no instincts that do not seek to restore an earlier state of things? that there are none that aim at a state of things which has never yet been attained? I know of no certain example from the organic world that would contradict the characterization I have thus proposed. There is unquestionably no universal instinct towards higher development observable in the animal or plant world, even though it is undeniable that development does in fact occur in that direction. But on the one hand it is often merely a matter of opinion when we declare that one stage of development is higher than another, and on the other hand biology teaches us that higher development in one respect is very frequently balanced or outweighed by involution in another. Moreover there are plenty of animal forms from whose early stages we can infer that their development has, on the contrary, assumed a retrograde character. Both higher development and involution might well be the consequences of adaptation to the pressure of external forces; and in both cases the part played by instincts might be limited to the retention (in the form of an internal source of pleasure) of an obligatory modification.[9]

It may be difficult, too, for many of us, to abandon the belief that there is an instinct towards perfection at work in human beings, which has brought them to their present high level of intellectual achievement and ethical sublimation and which may be expected to watch over their development into supermen. I have no faith, however, in the existence of any such internal instinct and I cannot see how this benevolent illusion is to be preserved. The present development of human beings requires, as it seems to me, no different explanation from that of animals. What appears in a minority of human individuals as an untiring impulsion towards further perfection can easily be understood as a result of the instinctual repression upon which is based all that is most precious in human civilization. The repressed instinct never ceases to strive for complete satisfaction, which would consist in the repetition of a primary experience of satisfaction. No substitutive or reactive formations and no sublimations will suffice to remove the repressed instinct's persisting tension; and it is the difference in amount between the pleasure of satisfaction which is *demanded* and that which is actually *achieved* that provides the driving factor which will permit of no halting at any position attained, but, in the poet's words, "*ungebändigt immer vorwärts dringt.*"[10] The backward path that leads to complete satisfaction is as a rule obstructed by the resistance which maintain the repressions. So there is no alternative but to advance in the direction in which growth is still free – though with no prospect of bringing the process to a conclusion or of being able to reach the goal. The processes involved in the formation of a neurotic phobia, which is nothing else than an attempt at flight from the satisfaction of an instinct, present us with a model of the manner of origin of this supposititious "instinct towards perfection" – an instinct which cannot possibly be attributed to *every* human being. The *dynamic* conditions for its development are, indeed, universally present; but it is only in rare cases that the *economic* situation appears to favor the production of the phenomenon.

I will add only a word to suggest that the efforts of Eros to combine organic substances into ever larger unities probably provide a substitute for this "instinct towards perfection" whose existence we cannot admit. The phenomena that are attributed to it seem capable of explanation by these efforts of Eros taken in conjunction with the results of repression.

Femininity

Ladies and Gentlemen...

Today's lecture... should have no place in an introduction; but it may serve to give you an example of a detailed piece of analytic work, and I can say two things to recommend it. It brings forward nothing but observed facts, almost without any speculative additions, and it deals with a subject which has a claim on your interest second almost to no other. Throughout history people have knocked their heads against the riddle of the nature of femininity –

> Häupter in Hieroglyphenmützen,
> Häupter in Turban und schwarzem Barett,
> Perückenhäupter und tausend andre
> Arme, schwitzende Menschenhäupter....[11]

Nor will *you* have escaped worrying over this problem – those of you who are men; to those of you who are women this will not apply – you are yourselves the problem. When you meet a human being, the first distinction you make is "male or female?" and you are accustomed to make the distinction with unhesitating certainty. Anatomical science shares your certainty at one point and not much further. The male sexual product, the spermatozoon, and its vehicle are male; the ovum and the organism that harbors it are female. In both sexes organs have been formed which serve exclusively for the sexual functions; they were probably developed from the same [innate] disposition into two different forms. Besides this, in both sexes the other organs, the bodily shapes and tissues, show the influence of the individual's sex, but this is inconstant and its amount variable; these are what are known as the secondary sexual characters. Science next tells you something that runs counter to your expectations and is probably calculated to

confuse your feelings. It draws your attention to the fact that portions of the male sexual apparatus also appear in women's bodies, though in an atrophied state, and vice versa in the alternative case. It regards their occurrence as indications of *bisexuality*, as though an individual is not a man or a woman but always both – merely a certain amount more the one than the other. You will then be asked to make yourselves familiar with the idea that the proportion in which masculine and feminine are mixed in an individual is subject to quite considerable fluctuations. Since, however, apart from the very rarest cases, only one kind of sexual product – ova or semen – is nevertheless present in one person, you are bound to have doubts as to the decisive significance of those elements and must conclude that what constitutes masculinity or femininity is an unknown characteristic which anatomy cannot lay hold of....

And now you are already prepared to hear that psychology too is unable to solve the riddle of femininity. The explanation must no doubt come from elsewhere, and cannot come till we have learnt how in general the differentiation of living organisms into two sexes came about. We know nothing about it, yet the existence of two sexes is a most striking characteristic of organic life which distinguishes it sharply from inanimate nature. However, we find enough to study in those human individuals who, through the possession of female genitals, are characterized as manifestly or predominantly feminine. In conformity with its peculiar nature, psychoanalysis does not try to describe what a woman is – that would be a task it could scarcely perform – but sets about inquiring how she comes into being, how a woman develops out of a child with a bisexual disposition. In recent times we have begun to learn a little about this, thanks to the circumstance that several of our excellent women colleagues in analysis have begun to work at the question. The discussion of this has gained special attractiveness from the distinction between the sexes. For the ladies, whenever some comparison seemed to turn out unfavorable to their sex, were able to utter a suspicion

From "Femininity," in *New Introductory Lectures on Psychoanalysis*, translated and edited by James Strachey (New York: W. W. Norton, 1965), pp. 99–105, 110–17, 119. Translation copyright © 1965, 1964 by James Strachey. Reprinted by permission of W. W. Norton and The Hogarth Press.

that we, the male analysts, had been unable to overcome certain deeply rooted prejudices against what was feminine, and that this was being paid for in the partiality of our researches. We, on the other hand, standing on the ground of bisexuality, had no difficulty in avoiding impoliteness. We had only to say: "This doesn't apply to *you*. You're the exception; on this point you're more masculine than feminine."

We approach the investigation of the sexual development of women with two expectations. The first is that here once more the constitution will not adapt itself to its function without a struggle. The second is that the decisive turning-points will already have been prepared for or completed before puberty. Both expectations are promptly confirmed. Furthermore, a comparison with what happens with boys tells us that the development of a little girl into a normal woman is more difficult and more complicated, since it includes two extra tasks, to which there is nothing corresponding in the development of a man. Let us follow the parallel lines from their beginning. . . .

Both sexes seem to pass through the early phases of libidinal development in the same manner. It might have been expected that in girls there would already have been some lag in aggressiveness in the sadistic-anal phase, but such is not the case. Analysis of children's play has shown our women analysts that the aggressive impulses of little girls leave nothing to be desired in the way of abundance and violence. With their entry into the phallic phase the differences between the sexes are completely eclipsed by their agreements. We are now obliged to recognize that the little girl is a little man. In boys, as we know, this phase is marked by the fact that they have learnt how to derive pleasurable sensations from their small penis and connect its excited state with their ideas of sexual intercourse. Little girls do the same thing with their still smaller clitoris. It seems that with them all their masturbatory acts are carried out on this penis-equivalent, and that the truly feminine vagina is still undiscovered by both sexes. It is true that there are a few isolated reports of early vaginal sensations as well, but it could not be easy to distinguish these from sensations in the anus or vestibulum; in any case they cannot play a great part. We are entitled to keep to our view that in the phallic phase of girls the clitoris is the leading erotogenic zone. But it is not, of course, going to remain so. With the change to femininity the clitoris should wholly or in part

hand over its sensitivity, and at the same time its importance, to the vagina. This would be one of the two tasks which a woman has to perform in the course of her development, whereas the more fortunate man has only to continue at the time of his sexual maturity the activity that he has previously carried out at the period of the early efflorescence of his sexuality.

We shall return to the part played by the clitoris; let us now turn to the second task with which a girl's development is burdened. A boy's mother is the first object of his love, and she remains so too during the formation of his Oedipus complex and, in essence, all through his life. For a girl too her first object must be her mother (and the figures of wet-nurses and foster-mothers that merge into her). The first object-cathexes occur in attachment to the satisfaction of the major and simple vital needs, and the circumstances of the care of children are the same for both sexes. But in the Oedipus situation the girl's father has become her love-object, and we expect that in the normal course of development she will find her way from this paternal object to her final choice of an object. In the course of time, therefore, a girl has to change her erotogenic zone and her object – both of which a boy retains. The question then arises of how this happens: in particular, how does a girl pass from her mother to an attachment to her father? or, in other words, how does she pass from her masculine phase to the feminine one to which she is biologically destined?

It would be a solution of ideal simplicity if we could suppose that from a particular age onwards the elementary influence of the mutual attraction between the sexes makes itself felt and impels the small woman towards men, while the same law allows the boy to continue with his mother. We might suppose in addition that in this the children are following the pointer given them by the sexual preference of their parents. But we are not going to find things so easy; we scarcely know whether we are to believe seriously in the power of which poets talk so much and with such enthusiasm but which cannot be further dissected analytically. We have found an answer of quite another sort by means of laborious investigations... Unless we can find something that is specific for girls and is not present or not in the same way present in boys, we shall not have explained the termination of the attachment of girls to their mother.

I believe we have found this specific factor, and indeed where we expected to find it, even though in a surprising form. Where we expected to find it, I say, for it lies in the castration complex. After all, the anatomical distinction [between the sexes] must express itself in psychical consequences. It was, however, a surprise to learn from analyses that girls hold their mother responsible for their lack of a penis and do not forgive her for their being thus put at a disadvantage.

As you hear, then, we ascribe a castration complex to women as well. And for good reasons, though its content cannot be the same as with boys. In the latter the castration complex arises after they have learnt from the sight of the female genitals that the organ which they value so highly need not necessarily accompany the body. At this the boy recalls to mind the threats he brought on himself by his doings with that organ, he begins to give credence to them and falls under the influence of fear of castration, which will be the most powerful motive force in his subsequent development. The castration complex of girls is also started by the sight of the genitals of the other sex. They at once notice the difference and, it must be admitted, its significance too. They feel seriously wronged, often declare that they want to "have something like it too," and fall a victim to "envy for the penis," which will leave ineradicable traces on their development and the formation of their character and which will not be surmounted in even the most favorable cases without a severe expenditure of psychical energy. The girl's recognition of the fact of her being without a penis does not by any means imply that she submits to the fact easily. On the contrary, she continues to hold on for a long time to the wish to get something like it herself and she believes in that possibility for improbably long years; and analysis can show that, at a period when knowledge of reality has long since rejected the fulfillment of the wish as unattainable, it persists in the unconscious and retains a considerable cathexis of energy. The wish to get the longed-for penis eventually in spite of everything may contribute to the motives that drive a mature woman to analysis, and what she may reasonably expect from analysis – a capacity, for instance, to carry on an intellectual profession – may often be recognized as a sublimated modification of this repressed wish.

One cannot very well doubt the importance of envy for the penis. You may take it as an instance of male injustice if I assert that envy and jealousy play an even greater part in the mental life of women than of men. It is not that I think these characteristics are absent in men or that I think they have no other roots in women than envy for the penis; but I am inclined to attribute their greater amount in women to this latter influence....

The discovery that she is castrated is a turning-point in a girl's growth. Three possible lines of development start from it: one leads to sexual inhibition or to neurosis, the second to change of character in the sense of a masculinity complex, the third, finally, to normal femininity. We have learnt a fair amount, though not everything, about all three.

The essential content of the first is as follows: the little girl has hitherto lived in a masculine way, has been able to get pleasure by the excitation of her clitoris and has brought this activity into relation with her sexual wishes directed towards her mother, which are often active ones; now, owing to the influence of her penis-envy, she loses her enjoyment in her phallic sexuality. Her self-love is mortified by the comparison with the boy's far superior equipment and in consequence she renounces her masturbatory satisfaction from her clitoris, repudiates her love for her mother and at the same time not infrequently represses a good part of her sexual trends in general. No doubt her turning away from her mother does not occur all at once, for to begin with the girl regards her castration as an individual misfortune, and only gradually extends it to other females and finally to her mother as well. Her love was directed to her *phallic* mother; with the discovery that her mother is castrated it becomes possible to drop her as an object, so that the motives for hostility, which have long been accumulating, gain the upper hand. This means, therefore, that as a result of the discovery of women's lack of a penis they are debased in value for girls just as they are for boys and later perhaps for men....

Along with the abandonment of clitoridal masturbation a certain amount of activity is renounced. Passivity now has the upper hand, and the girl's turning to her father is accomplished principally with the help of passive instinctual impulses. You can see that a wave of development like this, which clears the phallic activity out of the way, smooths the ground for femininity. If too much is not lost in the course of it through repression, this femininity may turn out to be normal. The wish with which the girl turns to her father is no doubt originally the wish for the penis which her mother has refused her and which she now expects from her father.

The feminine situation is only established, however, if the wish for a penis is replaced by one for a baby, if, that is, a baby takes the place of a penis in accordance with an ancient symbolic equivalence. It has not escaped us that the girl has wished for a baby earlier, in the undisturbed phallic phase: that, of course, was the meaning of her playing with dolls. But that play was not in fact an expression of her femininity; it served as an identification with her mother with the intention of substituting activity for passivity. *She* was playing the part of her mother and the doll was herself: now she could do with the baby everything that her mother used to do with her. Not until the emergence of the wish for a penis does the doll-baby become a baby from the girl's father, and thereafter the aim of the most powerful feminine wish. Her happiness is great if later on this wish for a baby finds fulfillment in reality, and quite especially so if the baby is a little boy who brings the longed-for penis with him. Often enough in her combined picture of "a baby from her father" the emphasis is laid on the baby and her father left unstressed. In this way the ancient masculine wish for the possession of a penis is still faintly visible through the femininity now achieved. But perhaps we ought rather to recognize this wish for a penis as being *par excellence* a feminine one.

With the transference of the wish for a penis-baby on to her father, the girl has entered the situation of the Oedipus complex. Her hostility to her mother, which did not need to be freshly created, is now greatly intensified, for she becomes the girl's rival, who receives from her father everything that she desires from him. For a long time the girl's Oedipus complex concealed her pre-Oedipus attachment to her mother from our view, though it is nevertheless so important and leaves such lasting fixations behind it. For girls the Oedipus situation is the outcome of a long and difficult development; it is a kind of preliminary solution, a position of rest which is not soon abandoned, especially as the beginning of the latency period is not far distant. And we are now struck by a difference between the two sexes, which is probably momentous, in regard to the relation of the Oedipus complex to the castration complex. In a boy the Oedipus complex, in which he desires his mother and would like to get rid of his father as being a rival, develops naturally from the phase of his phallic sexuality. The threat of castration compels him, however, to give up that attitude. Under the impression of the danger of losing his penis, the

Oedipus complex is abandoned, repressed and, in the most normal cases, entirely destroyed, and a severe super-ego is set up as its heir. What happens with a girl is almost the opposite. The castration complex prepares for the Oedipus complex instead of destroying it; the girl is driven out of her attachment to her mother through the influence of her envy for the penis and she enters the Oedipus situation as though into a haven of refuge. In the absence of fear of castration the chief motive is lacking which leads boys to surmount the Oedipus complex. Girls remain in it for an indeterminate length of time; they demolish it late and, even so, incompletely. In these circumstances the formation of the super-ego must suffer; it cannot attain the strength and independence which give it its cultural significance, and feminists are not pleased when we point out to them the effects of this factor upon the average feminine character....

What I have been telling you here may be described as the prehistory of women. It is a product of the very last few years and may have been of interest to you as an example of detailed analytic work. Since its subject is woman, I will venture on this occasion to mention by name a few of the women who have made valuable contributions to this investigation. Dr Ruth Mack Brunswick [1928] was the first to describe a case of neurosis which went back to a fixation in the pre-Oedipus stage and had never reached the Oedipus situation at all. The case took the form of jealous paranoia and proved accessible to therapy. Dr Jeanne Lampl-de Groot [1927] has established the incredible phallic activity of girls towards their mother by some assured observations, and Dr Helene Deutsch [1932] has shown that the erotic actions of homosexual women reproduce the relations between mother and baby.

It is not my intention to pursue the further behavior of femininity through puberty to the period of maturity. Our knowledge, moreover, would be insufficient for the purpose. But I will bring a few features together in what follows. Taking its prehistory as a starting point, I will only emphasize here that the development of femininity remains exposed to disturbance by the residual phenomena of the early masculine period. Regressions to the fixations of the pre-Oedipus phases very frequently occur; in the course of some women's lives there is a repeated alternation between periods in which masculinity or femininity gains the upper hand. Some portion of what we men call "the enigma of women" may perhaps be derived from this expression of bisexuality in women's lives. But another question seems to have become ripe for judgment in the course of these researches. We have called the motive force of sexual life "the libido." Sexual life is dominated by the polarity of masculine–feminine; thus the notion suggests itself of considering the relation of the libido to this antithesis. It would not be surprising if it were to turn out that each sexuality had its own special libido appropriated to it, so that one sort of libido would pursue the aims of a masculine sexual life and another sort those of a feminine one. But nothing of the kind is true. There is only one libido, which serves both the masculine and the feminine sexual functions. To it itself we cannot assign any sex; if, following the conventional equation of activity and masculinity, we are inclined to describe it as masculine, we must not forget that it also covers trends with a passive aim. Nevertheless the juxtaposition "feminine libido" is without any justification. Furthermore, it is our impression that more constraint has been applied to the libido when it is pressed into the service of the feminine function, and that – to speak teleologically – Nature takes less careful account of its [that function's] demands than in the case of masculinity. And the reason for this may lie – thinking once again teleologically – in the fact that the accomplishment of the aim of biology has been entrusted to the aggressiveness of men and has been made to some extent independent of women's consent....

I have promised to tell you of a few more psychical peculiarities of mature femininity, as we come across them in analytic observation. We do not lay claim to more than an average validity for these assertions; nor is it always easy to distinguish what should be ascribed to the influence of the sexual function and what to social breeding. Thus, we attribute a larger amount of narcissism to femininity, which also affects women's choice of object, so that to be loved is a stronger need for them than to love. The effect of penis-envy has a share, further, in the physical vanity of women, since they are bound to value their charms more highly as a late compensation for their original sexual inferiority. Shame, which is considered to be a feminine characteristic *par excellence* but is far more a matter of convention than might be supposed, has as its purpose, we believe, concealment of genital deficiency. We are not forgetting that at a later time shame takes on other functions. It seems that women have made few contributions to the

discoveries and inventions in the history of civilization; there is, however, one technique which they may have invented – that of plaiting and weaving. If that is so, we should be tempted to guess the unconscious motive for the achievement. Nature herself would seem to have given the model which this achievement imitates by causing the growth at maturity of the pubic hair that conceals the genitals. The step that remained to be taken lay in making the threads adhere to one another, while on the body they stick into the skin and are only matted together. If you reject this idea as fantastic and regard my belief in the influence of lack of a penis on the configuration of femininity as an *idée fixe*, I am of course defenceless. . . .

The fact that women must be regarded as having little sense of justice is no doubt related to the predominance of envy in their mental life; for the demand for justice is a modification of envy and lays down the condition subject to which one can put envy aside. We also regard women as weaker in their social interests and as having less capacity for sublimating their instincts than men. The former is no doubt derived from the dissocial quality which unquestionably characterizes all sexual relations. Lovers find sufficiency in each other, and families too resist inclusion in more comprehensive associations. The aptitude for sublimation is subject to the greatest individual variations. On the other hand I cannot help mentioning an impression that we are constantly receiving during analytic practice. A man of about thirty strikes us as a youthful, somewhat unformed individual, whom we expect to make powerful use of the possibilities for development opened up to him by analysis. A woman of the same age, however, often frightens us by her psychical rigidity and unchangeability. Her libido has taken up final positions and seems incapable of exchanging them for others. There are no paths open to further development; it is as though the whole process had already run its course and remains thenceforward insusceptible to influence – as though, indeed, the difficult development to femininity had exhausted the possibilities of the person concerned. As therapists we lament this state of things, even if we succeed in putting an end to our patient's ailment by doing away with her neurotic conflict.

That is all I had to say to you about femininity. It is certainly incomplete and fragmentary and does not always sound friendly. But do not forget that I have only been describing women insofar as their nature is determined by their sexual function. It is true that that influence extends very far; but we do not overlook the fact that an individual woman may be a human being in other respects as well. If you want to know more about femininity, inquire from your own experiences of life, or turn to the poets, or wait until science can give you deeper and more coherent information.

Notes

1 An abbreviation for "consciousness." (Eds)
2 An abbreviation for "perceptual consciousness." (Eds)
3 What follows is based throughout on Breuer's views in [the second section of his theoretical contribution to] *Studies on Hysteria* (Breuer and Freud, 1895).
4 Breuer and Freud, 1895.
5 Cf. my *Interpretation of Dreams*, chapter VII.
6 I have no doubt that similar notions as to the nature of "instincts" have already been put forward repeatedly.
7 [Footnote added 1923:] Yet it is to them alone that we can attribute an internal impulse towards "progress" and towards higher development!
8 [Footnote added 1925:] It should be understood from the context that the term "ego-instincts" is used here as a provisional description and derives from the earliest psychoanalytical terminology.
9 Ferenczi (1913, 137) has reached the same conclusion along different lines: "If this thought is pursued to its logical conclusion, one must make oneself familiar with the idea of a tendency to perseveration or regression dominating organic life as well, while the tendency to further development, to adaptation, etc., would become active only as a result of external stimuli."
10 ["Presses ever forward unsubdued."] Mephistopheles in *Faust*, Part I [Scene 4].
11 Heads in hieroglyphic bonnets,
Heads in turbans and black birettas,
Heads in wigs and thousand other
Wretched, sweating heads of humans....
(Heine, *Nordsee* [Second Cycle, VII, "Fragen"].)

Select Bibliography

Beyond the Pleasure Principle. Edited and translated by James Strachey. New York: W. W. Norton, 1965.

Civilization and Its Discontents. Edited and translated by Joan Riviere. New York: Dover Publications, 1994.

The Ego and the Id. Edited by James Strachey. Translated by Joan Riviere. New York: W. W. Norton, 1989.

The Freud Reader. Edited by Peter Gay. New York: W. W. Norton, 1989.

The Future of an Illusion. Translated by James Strachey. New York: Norton, 1975.

General Psychological Theory: Papers on Metapsychology. Edited by Philip Rieff. New York: Collier Books, 1963.

Inhibitions, Symptoms and Anxiety. Edited by James Strachey. Translated by Alix Strachey. New York: Norton, 1989.

The Interpretation of Dreams. Translated by A. A. Brill. New York: Gramercy Books, 1996.

Jokes and Their Relation to the Unconscious. Edited and translated by James Strachey. New York: Norton, 1989.

New Introductory Lectures on Psycho-Analysis. Edited and translated by James Strachey. New York: W. W. Norton, 1965.

An Outline of Psycho-Analysis. Edited and translated by James Strachey. New York: W. W. Norton, 1989.

The Psychopathology of Everyday Life. Edited by James Strachey. Translated by Alan Tyson. New York: Norton, 1989.

Three Essays on the Theory of Sexuality. Edited and translated by James Strachey. New York: Basic Books, 1975.

Totem and Taboo. Edited and translated by James Strachey. New York: W. W. Norton, 1989.

5

Jacques Lacan

Influenced by Saussure's structural conception of language, French psychoanalyst Jacques Lacan (1901–81) came to prominence through his adaptation of structuralist insights to the field of psychoanalysis. Lacan's interpretation of psychoanalysis is built around his fundamental thesis that the unconscious (whose workings Freud attributes to the libidinal structures of drives) is structured like a language. Lacan's early work focuses on the level of what he calls the imaginary, and most famously on the constitution of the ego via the "mirror stage," in which the young child of six to eighteen months, whose experience of its own body has hitherto been fragmented, is said to identify with an image of itself as other. From the early 1950s on, Lacan progressively distinguishes the imaginary from the symbolic. As in Saussure, the symbolic

order can be divided into language and speech. Psychoanalytic practice operates at the level of speech. According to Lacan, if imaginary relations or identifications are articulated in speech, psychoanalytic practice aims at unveiling the signifiers that determine the patient's symptoms and that were covered up by these imaginary relations. The following selections present Lacan's classic discussion of the mirror stage (from 1949) and the important essay "The signification of the phallus" (1958), which begins by discussing Freud's theory of the castration complex and proceeds to consider the relation between signification and what Lacan calls "the phallus," which is not to be understood as the penis, but as signifier of the desire of "the Other."

The Mirror Stage as Formative of the Function of the I as Revealed in Psychoanalytic Experience

Delivered at the 16th International Congress of Psychoanalysis, Zürich, July 17, 1949

The conception of the mirror stage that I introduced at our last congress, thirteen years ago, has since become more or less established in the practice of the French group. However, I think it worthwhile to bring it again to your attention, especially today, for the light it sheds on the formation of the *I* as we experience it in psychoanalysis. It is an experience that leads us to oppose any philosophy directly issuing from the *Cogito*.

Some of you may recall that this conception originated in a feature of human behavior illuminated by a fact of comparative psychology. The child, at an age when he is for a time, however short, outdone by the chimpanzee in instrumental intelligence, can nevertheless already recognize as such his own image in a mirror. This recognition is indicated in the illuminative mimicry of the *Aha-Erlebnis*, which Köhler sees as the expression of situational apperception, an essential stage of the act of intelligence.

This act, far from exhausting itself, as in the case of the monkey, once the image has been mastered and found empty, immediately rebounds in the case of the child in a series of gestures in which he experiences in play the relation between the movements assumed in the image and the reflected environment, and between this virtual complex and the reality it reduplicates – the child's own body, and the persons and things, around him.

This event can take place, as we have known since Baldwin, from the age of six months, and its repetition has often made me reflect upon the startling spectacle of the infant in front of the

mirror. Unable as yet to walk, or even to stand up, and held tightly as he is by some support, human or artificial (what, in France, we call a *"trotte-bébé"*), he nevertheless overcomes, in a flutter of jubilant activity, the obstructions of his support and, fixing his attitude in a slightly leaning-forward position, in order to hold it in his gaze, brings back an instantaneous aspect of the image.

For me, this activity retains the meaning I have given it up to the age of eighteen months. This meaning discloses a libidinal dynamism, which has hitherto remained problematic, as well as an ontological structure of the human world that accords with my reflections on paranoiac knowledge.

We have only to understand the mirror stage *as an identification*, in the full sense that analysis gives to the term: namely, the transformation that takes place in the subject when he assumes an image – whose predestination to this phase-effect is sufficiently indicated by the use, in analytic theory, of the ancient term *imago*.

This jubilant assumption of his specular image by the child at the *infans* stage, still sunk in his motor incapacity and nursing dependence, would seem to exhibit in an exemplary situation the symbolic matrix in which the *I* is precipitated in a primordial form, before it is objectified in the dialectic of identification with the other, and before language restores to it, in the universal, its function as subject.

This form would have to be called the Ideal-I,[1] if we wished to incorporate it into our usual register, in the sense that it will also be the source of secondary identifications, under which term I would place the functions of libidinal normalization. But the important point is that this form situates the agency of the ego, before its social determination, in a fictional direction, which will always remain irreducible for the individual alone, or rather, which will only rejoin the coming-into-being (*le devenir*) of the subject asymptotically, whatever the success of the dialectical syntheses by which he must resolve as *I* his discordance with his own reality.

The fact is that the total form of the body by which the subject anticipates in a mirage the maturation of his power is given to him only as *Gestalt*, that is to say, in an exteriority in which this form is certainly more constituent than constituted, but in which it appears to him above all in a contrasting size (*un relief de stature*) that fixes it and in a symmetry that inverts it, in contrast with the turbulent movements that the subject feels are animating him. Thus, this *Gestalt* – whose pregnancy should be regarded as bound up with the species, though its motor style remains scarcely recognizable – by these two aspects of its appearance, symbolizes the mental permanence of the *I*, at the same time as it prefigures its alienating destination; it is still pregnant with the correspondences that unite the *I* with the statue in which man projects himself, with the phantoms that dominate him, or with the automaton in which, in an ambiguous relation, the world of his own making tends to find completion.

Indeed, for the *imagos* – whose veiled faces it is our privilege to see in outline in our daily experience and in the penumbra of symbolic efficacity[2] – the mirror-image would seem to be the threshold of the visible world, if we go by the mirror disposition that the *imago of one's own body* presents in hallucinations or dreams, whether it concerns its individual features, or even its infirmities, or its object-projections; or if we observe the role of the mirror apparatus in the appearances of the *double*, in which psychical realities, however heterogeneous, are manifested.

That a *Gestalt* should be capable of formative effects in the organism is attested by a piece of biological experimentation that is itself so alien to the idea of psychical causality that it cannot bring itself to formulate its results in these terms. It nevertheless recognizes that it is a necessary condition for the maturation of the gonad of the female pigeon that it should see another member of its species, of either sex; so sufficient in itself is this condition that the desired effect may be obtained merely by placing the individual within reach of the field of reflection of a mirror. Similarly, in the case of the migratory locust, the transition within a generation from the solitary to the gregarious form can be obtained by exposing the individual, at a certain stage, to the exclusively visual action of a similar image, provided it is animated by movements of a style sufficiently close to that character-istic of the species. Such facts are inscribed in an order of homeomorphic identification that would itself fall within the larger question of the meaning of beauty as both formative and erogenic.

But the facts of mimicry are no less instructive when conceived as cases of heteromorphic identification, in as much as they raise the problem of the signification of space for the living organism – psychological concepts hardly seem less appropriate for shedding light on these matters than ridiculous attempts to reduce them to the supposedly supreme law of adaptation. We have only to recall how Roger Caillois (who was then very young, and still fresh from his breach with the sociological school in which he was trained) illuminated the subject by using the term "*legendary psychasthenia*" to classify morphological mimicry as an obsession with space in its derealizing effect.

I have myself shown in the social dialectic that structures human knowledge as paranoiac[3] why human knowledge has greater autonomy than animal knowledge in relation to the field of force of desire, but also why human knowledge is determined in that "little reality" (*ce peu de réalité*), which the Surrealists, in their restless way, saw as its limitation. These reflections lead me to recognize in the spatial captation manifested in the mirror-stage, even before the social dialectic, the effect in man of an organic insufficiency in his natural reality – insofar as any meaning can be given to the word "nature."

I am led, therefore, to regard the function of the mirror-stage as a particular case of the function of the *imago*, which is to establish a relation between the organism and its reality – or, as they say, between the *Innenwelt* and the *Umwelt*.

In man, however, this relation to nature is altered by a certain dehiscence at the heart of the organism, a primordial Discord betrayed by the signs of uneasiness and motor unco-ordination of the neonatal months. The objective notion of the anatomical incompleteness of the pyramidal system and likewise the presence of certain humoral residues of the maternal organism confirm the view I have formulated as the fact of a real *specific prematurity of birth* in man.

It is worth noting, incidentally, that this is a fact recognized as such by embryologists, by the term *foetalization*, which determines the prevalence of the so-called superior apparatus of the neurax, and especially of the cortex, which psychosurgical operations lead us to regard as the intraorganic mirror.

This development is experienced as a temporal dialectic that decisively projects the formation of the individual into history. The *mirror stage* is a drama whose internal thrust is precipitated from insufficiency to anticipation – and which manufactures for the subject, caught up in the lure of spatial identification, the succession of phantasies that extends from a fragmented body-image to a form of its totality that I shall call orthopaedic – and, lastly, to the assumption of the armor of an alienating identity, which will mark with its rigid structure the subject's entire mental development. Thus, to break out of the circle of the *Innenwelt* into the *Umwelt* generates the inexhaustible quadrature of the ego's verifications.

This fragmented body – which term I have also introduced into our system of theoretical references – usually manifests itself in dreams when the movement of the analysis encounters a certain level of aggressive disintegration in the individual. It then appears in the form of disjointed limbs, or of those organs represented in exoscopy, growing wings and taking up arms for intestinal persecutions – the very same that the visionary Hieronymus Bosch has fixed, for all time, in painting, in their ascent from the fifteenth century to the imaginary zenith of modern man. But this form is even tangibly revealed at the organic level, in the lines of "fragilization" that define the anatomy of phantasy, as exhibited in the schizoid and spasmodic symptoms of hysteria.

Correlatively, the formation of the *I* is symbolized in dreams by a fortress, or a stadium – its inner arena and enclosure, surrounded by marshes and rubbish-tips, dividing it into two opposed fields of contest where the subject flounders in quest of the lofty, remote inner castle whose form (sometimes juxtaposed in the same scenario) symbolizes the id in a quite startling way. Similarly, on the mental plane, we find realized the structures of fortified works, the metaphor of which arises spontaneously, as if issuing from the symptoms themselves, to designate the mechanisms of obsessional neurosis – inversion, isolation, reduplication, cancellation, and displacement.

But if we were to build on these subjective givens alone – however little we free them from the condition of experience that makes us see them as partaking of the nature of a linguistic technique – our theoretical attempts would remain exposed to the charge of projecting themselves into the unthinkable of an absolute subject. This is why I have sought in the present hypothesis, grounded in a conjunction of objective data, the guiding grid for a *method of symbolic reduction*.

It establishes in the *defenses of the ego* a genetic order, in accordance with the wish formulated by Miss Anna Freud, in the first part of her great work, and situates (as against a frequently expressed prejudice) hysterical repression and its returns at a more archaic stage than obsessional inversion and its isolating processes, and the latter in turn as preliminary to paranoic alienation, which dates from the deflection of the specular *I* into the social *I*.

This moment in which the mirror-stage comes to an end inaugurates, by the identification with the *imago* of the counterpart and the drama of primordial jealousy (so well brought out by the school of Charlotte Bühler in the phenomenon of infantile *transitivism*), the dialectic that will henceforth link the *I* to socially elaborated situations.

It is this moment that decisively tips the whole of human knowledge into mediatization through the desire of the other, constitutes its objects in an abstract equivalence by the cooperation of others, and turns the *I* into that apparatus for which every instinctual thrust constitutes a danger, even though it should correspond to a natural maturation – the very normalization of this maturation being henceforth dependent, in man, on a cultural mediation as exemplified, in the case of the sexual object, by the Oedipus complex.

In the light of this conception, the term primary narcissism, by which analytic doctrine designates the libidinal investment characteristic of that moment, reveals in those who invented it the most profound awareness of semantic latencies. But it also throws light on the dynamic opposition between this libido and the sexual libido, which the first analysts tried to define when they invoked destructive and, indeed, death instincts, in order to explain the evident connection between the narcissistic libido and the alienating function of the *I*, the aggressivity it releases in any relation to the other, even in a relation involving the most Samaritan of aid.

In fact, they were encountering that existential negativity whose reality is so vigorously proclaimed by the contemporary philosophy of being and nothingness.

But unfortunately that philosophy grasps negativity only within the limits of a self-sufficiency of consciousness, which, as one of its premises, links to the *méconnaissances* that constitute the ego, the illusion of autonomy to which it entrusts itself.

This flight of fancy, for all that it draws, to an unusual extent, on borrowings from psychoanalytic experience, culminates in the pretention of providing an existential psychoanalysis.

At the culmination of the historical effort of a society to refuse to recognize that it has any function other than the utilitarian one, and in the anxiety of the individual confronting the "concentrational"[4] form of the social bond that seems to arise to crown this effort, existentialism must be judged by the explanations it gives of the subjective impasses that have indeed resulted from it; a freedom that is never more authentic than when it is within the walls of a prison; a demand for commitment, expressing the impotence of a pure consciousness to master any situation; a voyeuristic–sadistic idealization of the sexual relation; a personality that realizes itself only in suicide; a consciousness of the other than can be satisfied only by Hegelian murder.

These propositions are opposed by all our experience, insofar as it teaches us not to regard the ego as centered on the *perception-consciousness system*, or as organized by the "reality principle" – a principle that is the expression of a scientific prejudice most hostile to the dialectic of knowledge. Our experience shows that we should start instead from the *function of méconnaissance* that characterizes the ego in all its structures, so markedly articulated by Miss Anna Freud. For, if the *Verneinung* represents the patent form of that function, its effects will, for the most part, remain latent, so long as they are not illuminated by some light reflected on to the level of fatality, which is where the id manifests itself.

We can thus understand the inertia characteristic of the formations of the *I*, and find there the most extensive definition of neurosis – just as the captation of the subject by the situation gives us the most general formula for madness, not only the madness that lies behind the walls of asylums, but also the madness that deafens the world with its sound and fury.

The sufferings of neurosis and psychosis are for us a schooling in the passions of the soul, just as the beam of the psychoanalytic scales, when we calculate the tilt of its threat to entire communities, provides us with an indication of the deadening of the passions in society.

At this junction of nature and culture, so persistently examined by modern anthropology, psychoanalysis alone recognizes this knot of imaginary servitude that love must always undo again, or sever.

For such a task, we place no trust in altruistic feeling, we who lay bare the aggressivity that underlies the activity of the philanthropist, the idealist, the pedagogue, and even the reformer.

In the recourse of subject to subject that we preserve, psychoanalysis may accompany the patient to the ecstatic limit of the *"Thou art that,"* in which is revealed to him the cipher of his mortal destiny, but it is not in our mere power as practitioners to bring him to that point where the real journey begins.

The Signification of the Phallus

The following is the original, unaltered text of a lecture that I delivered in German on May 9, 1958, at the Max-Planck Institute, Munich, where Professor Paul Matussek had invited me to speak.

If one has any notion of the state of mind then prevalent in even the least unaware circles, one will appreciate the effect that my use of such terms as, for example, "the other scene," which I was the first to extract from Freud's work, must have had.

From *Écrits*, translated by Alan Sheridan (New York: W. W. Norton, 1977), pp. 281–91.

If "deferred action" (Nachtrag), to rescue another of these terms from the facility into which they have since fallen, renders this effort impracticable, it should be known that they were unheard of at that time.

We know that the unconscious castration complex has the function of a knot:

1 in the dynamic structuring of symptoms in the analytic sense of the term, that is to say, in that which is analyzable in the neuroses, perversions, and psychoses;

2 in a regulation of the development that gives its *ratio* to this first role: namely, the installation in the subject of an unconscious position without which he would be unable to identify himself with the ideal type of his sex, or to respond without grave risk to the needs of his partner in the sexual relation, or even to accept in a satisfactory way the needs of the child who may be produced by this relation.

There is an antinomy, here, that is internal to the assumption by man (*Mensch*) of his sex: why must he assume the attributes of that sex only through a threat – the threat, indeed, of their privation? In *Civilization and its Discontents* Freud, as we know, went so far as to suggest a disturbance of human sexuality, not of a contingent, but of an essential kind, and one of his last articles concerns the irreducibility in any finite (*endliche*) analysis of the sequellae resulting from the castration complex in the masculine unconscious and from *Penisneid* in the unconscious of women.

This is not the only aporia, but it is the first that the Freudian experience and the metapsychology that resulted from it introduced into our experience of man. It is insoluble by any reduction to biological givens: the very necessity of the myth subjacent to the structuring of the Oedipus complex demonstrates this sufficiently.

It would be mere trickery to invoke in this case some hereditary amnesic trait, not only because such a trait is in itself debatable, but because it leaves the problem unsolved: namely, what is the link between the murder of the father and the pact of the primordial law, if it is included in that law that castration should be the punishment for incest?

It is only on the basis of the clinical facts that any discussion can be fruitful. These facts reveal a relation of the subject to the phallus that is established without regard to the anatomical difference of the sexes, and which, by this very fact, makes any interpretation of this relation especially difficult in the case of women. This problem may be treated under the following four headings:

1 from this "why," the little girl considers herself, if only momentarily, as castrated, in the sense of deprived of the phallus, by someone, in the first instance by her mother, an important point, and then by her father, but in such a way that one must recognize in it a transference in the analytic sense of the term;

2 from this "why," in a more primordial sense, the mother is considered, by both sexes, as possessing the phallus, as the phallic mother;

3 from this "why," correlatively, the signification of castration in fact takes on its (clinically manifest) full weight as far as the formation of symptoms is concerned, only on the basis of its discovery as castration of the mother;

4 these three problems lead, finally, to the question of the reason, in development, for the phallic stage. We know that in this term Freud specifies the first genital maturation: on the one hand, it would seem to be characterized by the imaginary dominance of the phallic attribute and by masturbatory *jouissance* and, on the other, it localizes this *jouissance* for the woman in the clitoris, which is thus raised to the function of the phallus. It therefore seems to exclude in both sexes, until the end of this stage, that is, to the decline of the Oedipal stage, all instinctual mapping of the vagina as locus of genital penetration.

This ignorance is suspiciously like *méconnaissance* in the technical sense of the term – all the more so in that it is sometimes quite false. . . .

It might be a good idea to re-examine the question by asking what could have necessitated for Freud the evident paradox of his position. For one has to admit that he was better guided than anyone in his recognition of the order of unconscious phenomena, of which he was the inventor, and that, failing an adequate articulation of the nature of these phenomena, his followers were doomed to lose their way to a greater or lesser degree.

It is on the basis of the following bet – which I lay down as the principle of a commentary of Freud's work that I have pursued during the past seven years – that I have been led to certain results: essentially, to promulgate as necessary to any articulation of analytic phenomena the notion of the signifier, as opposed to that of the signified, in modern linguistic analysis. Freud could not take this notion, which postdates him, into account, but I would claim that Freud's discovery stands out precisely because, although it set out from a domain in which one could not expect to recognize its reign, it could not fail to anticipate its formulas. Conversely, it is Freud's discovery that gives to the signifier/signified opposition the full extent of its implications: namely, that the signifier has an active function in determining certain effects in which the signifiable appears as submitting to its mark, by becoming through that passion the signified.

This passion of the signifier now becomes a new dimension of the human condition in that it is not only man who speaks, but that in man and through man *it* speaks (*ça parle*), that his nature is woven by effects in which is to be found the structure of language, of which he becomes the material, and that therefore there resounds in him, beyond what could be conceived of by a psychology of ideas, the relation of speech.

In this sense one can say that the consequences of the discovery of the unconscious have not yet been so much as glimpsed in theory, although its effects have been felt in praxis to a greater degree than perhaps we are aware of, if only in the form of effects of retreat.

It should be made clear that this advocacy of man's relation to the signifier as such has nothing to do with a "culturalist" position in the ordinary sense of the term, the position in which Karen Horney, for example, was anticipated in the dispute concerning the phallus by a position described by Freud himself as a feminist one. It is not a question of the relation between man and language as a social phenomenon, there being no question even of something resembling the ideological psychogenesis with which we are familiar, and which is not superseded by peremptory recourse to the quite metaphysical notion, which lurks beneath its question-begging appeal to the concrete, conveyed so pitifully by the term "affect."

It is a question of rediscovering in the laws that govern that other scene (*ein anderer Schauplatz*), which Freud, on the subject of dreams, designates as being that of the unconscious, the effects that are discovered at the level of the chain of materially unstable elements that constitutes language: effects determined by the double play of combination and substitution in the signifier, according to the two aspects that generate the signified, metonymy and metaphor; determining effects for the institution of the subject. From this test, a topology, in the mathematical sense of the term, appears, without which one soon realizes that it is impossible simply to note the structure of a symptom in the analytic sense of the term.

It speaks in the Other, I say, designating by the Other the very locus evoked by the recourse to speech in any relation in which the Other intervenes. If *it* speaks in the Other, whether or not the subject hears it with his ear, it is because it is there

that the subject, by means of a logic anterior to any awakening of the signified, finds its signifying place. The discovery of what it articulates in that place, that is to say, in the unconscious, enables us to grasp at the price of what splitting (*Spaltung*) it has thus been constituted.

The phallus reveals its function here. In Freudian doctrine, the phallus is not a phantasy, if by that we mean an imaginary effect. Nor is it as such an object (part-, internal, good, bad, etc.) in the sense that this term tends to accentuate the reality pertaining in a relation. It is even less the organ, penis or clitoris, that it symbolizes. And it is not without reason that Freud used the reference to the simulacrum that it represented for the Ancients.

For the phallus is a signifier, a signifier whose function, in the intrasubjective economy of the analysis, lifts the veil perhaps from the function it performed in the mysteries. For it is the signifier intended to designate as a whole the effects of the signified, in that the signifier conditions them by its presence as a signifier.

Let us now examine the effects of this presence. In the first instance, they proceed from a deviation of man's needs from the fact that he speaks, in the sense that insofar as his needs are subjected to demand, they return to him alienated. This is not the effect of his real dependence (one should not expect to find here the parasitic conception represented by the notion of dependence in the theory of neurosis), but rather the turning into signifying form as such, from the fact that it is from the locus of the Other that its message is emitted.

That which is thus alienated in needs constitutes an *Urverdrängung* (primal repression), an inability, it is supposed, to be articulated in demand, but it reappears in something it gives rise to that presents itself in man as desire (*das Begehren*). The phenomenology that emerges from analytic experience is certainly of a kind to demonstrate in desire the paradoxical, deviant, erratic, eccentric, even scandalous character by which it is distinguished from need. This fact has been too often affirmed not to have been always obvious to moralists worthy of the name. The Freudianism of earlier days seemed to owe its status to this fact. Paradoxically, however, psychoanalysis is to be found at the head of an ever-present obscurantism that is still more boring when it denies the fact in an ideal of theoretical and practical reduction of desire to need.

This is why we must articulate this status here, beginning with *demand*, whose proper characteristics are eluded in the notion of frustration (which Freud never used).

Demand in itself bears on something other than the satisfactions it calls for. It is demand of a presence or of an absence – which is what is manifested in the primordial relation to the mother, pregnant with that Other to be situated *within* the needs that it can satisfy. Demand constitutes the Other as already possessing the "privilege" of satisfying needs, that is to say, the power of depriving them of that alone by which they are satisfied. This privilege of the Other thus outlines the radical form of the gift of that which the Other does not have, namely, its love.

In this way, demand annuls (*aufhebt*) the particularity of everything that can be granted by transmuting it into a proof of love, and the very satisfactions that it obtains for need are reduced (*sich erniedrigt*) to the level of being no more than the crushing of the demand for love (all of which is perfectly apparent in the psychology of child-rearing, to which our analyst-nurses are so attached).

It is necessary, then, that the particularity thus abolished should reappear *beyond* demand. It does, in fact, reappear there, but preserving the structure contained in the unconditional element of the demand for love. By a reversal that is not simply a negation of the negation, the power of pure loss emerges from the residue of an obliteration. For the unconditional element of demand, desire substitutes the "absolute" condition: this condition unties the knot of that element in the proof of love that is resistant to the satisfaction of a need. Thus desire is neither the appetite for satisfaction, nor the demand for love, but the difference that results from the subtraction of the first from the second, the phenomenon of their splitting (*Spaltung*).

One can see how the sexual relation occupies this closed field of desire, in which it will play out its fate. This is because it is the field made for the production of the enigma that this relation arouses in the subject by doubly "signifying" it to him: the return of the demand that it gives rise to, as a demand on the subject of the need – an ambiguity made present on to the Other in question in the proof of love demanded. The gap in this enigma betrays what determines it, namely, to put it in the simplest possible way, that for both partners in the relation, both the subject and the Other, it is not enough to be subjects of need, or objects of love, but that they must stand for the cause of desire.

This truth lies at the heart of all the distortions that have appeared in the field of psychoanalysis on the subject of the sexual life. It also constitutes the condition of the happiness of the subject: and to disguise the gap it creates by leaving it to the virtue of the "genital" to resolve it through the maturation of tenderness (that is to say, solely by recourse to the Other as reality), however well intentioned, is fraudulent nonetheless. It has to be said here that the French analysts, with their hypocritical notion of genital oblativity, opened the way to the moralizing tendency, which, to the accompaniment of its Salvationist choirs, is now to be found everywhere.

In any case, man cannot aim at being whole (the "total personality" is another of the deviant premises of modern psychotherapy), while ever the play of displacement and condensation to which he is doomed in the exercise of his functions marks his relation as a subject to the signifier.

The phallus is the privileged signifier of that mark in which the role of the logos is joined with the advent of desire.

It can be said that this signifier is chosen because it is the most tangible element in the real of sexual copulation, and also the most symbolic in the literal (typographical) sense of the term, since it is equivalent there to the (logical) copula. It might also be said that, by virtue of its turgidity, it is the image of the vital flow as it is transmitted in generation.

All these propositions merely conceal the fact that it can play its role only when veiled, that is to say, as itself a sign of the latency with which any signifiable is struck, when it is raised (*aufgehoben*) to the function of signifier.

The phallus is the signifier of this *Aufhebung* itself, which it inaugurates (initiates) by its disappearance. That is why the demon of Αἰδώς (*Scham*, shame) arises at the very moment when, in the ancient mysteries, the phallus is unveiled (cf. the famous painting in the Villa di Pompei).

It then becomes the bar which, at the hands of this demon, strikes the signified, marking it as the bastard offspring of this signifying concatenation.

Thus a condition of complementarity is produced in the establishment of the subject by the signifier – which explains the *Spaltung* in the subject and the movement of intervention in which that "splitting" is completed.

Namely:

1 that the subject designates his being only by barring everything he signifies, as it appears in

the fact that he wants to be loved for himself, a mirage that cannot be dismissed as merely grammatical (since it abolishes discourse);

2   that the living part of that being in the *urverdrängt* (primally repressed) finds its signifier by receiving the mark of the *Verdrängung* (repression) of the phallus (by virtue of which the unconscious is language).

The phallus as signifier gives the ratio of desire (in the sense in which the term is used in music in the "mean and extreme ratio" of harmonic division).

I shall also be using the phallus as an algorithm, so if I am to help you to grasp this use of the term I shall have to rely on the echoes of the experience that we share – otherwise, my account of the problem could go on indefinitely.

The fact that the phallus is a signifier means that it is in the place of the Other that the subject has access to it. But since this signifier is only veiled, as ratio of the Other's desire, it is this desire of the Other as such that the subject must recognize, that is to say, the other insofar as he is himself a subject divided by the signifying *Spaltung*.

The emergences that appear in psychological genesis confirm this signifying function of the phallus.

Thus, to begin with, the Kleinian fact that the child apprehends from the outset that the mother "contains" the phallus may be formulated more correctly.

But it is in the dialectic of the demand for love and the test of desire that development is ordered.

The demand for love can only suffer from a desire whose signifier is alien to it. If the desire of the mother *is* the phallus, the child wishes to be the phallus in order to satisfy that desire. Thus the division immanent in desire is already felt to be experienced in the desire of the Other, in that it is already opposed to the fact that the subject is content to present to the Other what in reality he may *have* that corresponds to this phallus, for what he has is worth no more than what he does not have, as far as his demand for love is concerned because that demand requires that he be the phallus.

Clinical experience has shown us that this test of the desire of the Other is decisive not in the sense that the subject learns by it whether or not he has a real phallus, but in the sense that he learns that the mother does not have it. This is the moment of the experience without which no symptomatic consequence (phobia) or structural consequence (*Penis-*

neid) relating to the castration complex can take effect. Here is signed the conjunction of desire, in that the phallic signifier is its mark, with the threat or nostalgia of lacking it.

Of course, its future depends on the law introduced by the father into this sequence.

But one may, simply by reference to the function of the phallus, indicate the structures that will govern the relations between the sexes.

Let us say that these relations will turn around a "to be" and a "to have," which, by referring to a signifier, the phallus, have the opposed effect, on the one hand, of giving reality to the subject in this signifier, and, on the other, of derealizing the relations to be signified.

This is brought about by the intervention of a "to seem" that replaces the "to have," in order to protect it on the one side, and to mask its lack in the other, and which has the effect of projecting in their entirety the ideal or typical manifestations of the behavior of each sex, including the act of copulation itself, into the comedy.

These ideals take on new vigor from the demand that they are capable of satisfying, which is always a demand for love, with its complement of the reduction of desire to demand.

Paradoxical as this formulation may seem, I am saying that it is in order to be the phallus, that is to say, the signifier of the desire of the Other, that a woman will reject an essential part of femininity, namely, all her attributes in the masquerade. It is for that which she is not that she wishes to be desired as well as loved. But she finds the signifier of her own desire in the body of him to whom she addresses her demand for love. Perhaps it should not be forgotten that the organ that assumes this signifying function takes on the value of a fetish. But the result for the woman remains that an experience of love, which, as such (cf. above), deprives her ideally of that which the object gives, and a desire which finds its signifier in this object, converge on the same object. That is why one can observe that a lack in the satisfaction proper to sexual need, in other words, frigidity, is relatively well tolerated in women, whereas the *Verdrängung* (repression) inherent in desire is less present in women than in men.

In the case of men, on the other hand, the dialectic of demand and desire engenders the effects – and one must once more admire the sureness with which Freud situated them at the precise articulations on which they depended – of a specific depreciation (*Erniedrigung*) of love.

If, in effect, the man finds satisfaction for his demand for love in the relation with the woman, in as much as the signifier of the phallus constitutes her as giving in love what she does not have – conversely, his own desire for the phallus will make its signifier emerge in its persistent divergence towards "another woman" who may signify this phallus in various ways, either as a virgin or as a prostitute. There results from this a centrifugal tendency of the genital drive in love life, which makes impotence much more difficult to bear for him, while the *Verdrängung* inherent in desire is more important.

Yet it should not be thought that the sort of infidelity that would appear to be constitutive of the male function is proper to it. For if one looks more closely, the same redoubling is to be found in the woman, except that the Other of Love as such, that is to say, insofar as he is deprived of what he gives, finds it difficult to see himself in the retreat in which he is substituted for the being of the very man whose attributes she cherishes.

One might add here that male homosexuality, in accordance with the phallic mark that constitutes desire, is constituted on the side of desire, while female homosexuality, on the other hand, as observation shows, is orientated on a disappointment that reinforces the side of the demand for love. These remarks should really be examined in greater detail, from the point of view of a return to the function of the mask insofar as it dominates the identifications in which refusals of demand are resolved.

The fact that femininity finds its refuge in this mask, by virtue of the fact of the *Verdrängung* inherent in the phallic mark of desire, has the curious consequence of making virile display in the human being itself seem feminine.

Correlatively, one can glimpse the reason for a characteristic that had never before been elucidated, and which shows once again the depth of Freud's intuition: namely, why he advances the view that there is only one *libido*, his text showing that he conceives it as masculine in nature. The function of the phallic signifier touches here on its most profound relation: that in which the Ancients embodied the Νοῦς and the Λογὸς.

Notes

1 Throughout this article I leave in its peculiarity the translation I have adopted for Freud's *Ideal-Ich* [i.e. "je-idéal"], without further comment, other than to say that I have not maintained it since.

2 Cf. Claude Lévi-Strauss, *Structural Anthropology*, chapter X.

3 Cf. "Aggressivity in Psychoanalysis," p. 8 and *Écrits*, p. 180.

4 "*Concentrationnaire*," an adjective coined after World War II (this article was written in 1949) to describe the life of the concentration-camp. In the hands of certain writers it became, by extension, applicable to many aspects of "modern" life. (Trans.)

Select Bibliography

Écrits: A Selection. Translated by Alan Sheridan. New York: W. W. Norton, 1977.

The Ego in Freud's Theory and in the Technique of Psychoanalysis, 1954–1955. Translated by Sylvana Tomaselli. New York: W. W. Norton, 1988.

The Ethics of Psychoanalysis, 1959–60. Translated by Dennis Porter. New York: Norton, 1992.

Feminine Sexuality: Jacques Lacan and the École Freudienne. Edited by Juliet Mitchell and Jacqueline Rose. Translated by Jacqueline Rose. New York: W. W. Norton, 1982.

The Four Fundamental Concepts of Psycho-Analysis. Edited by Jacques-Alain Miller. Translated by Alan Sheridan. New York: W. W. Norton, 1981.

Freud's Papers on Technique, 1953–1954. Translated by John Forrester. New York: W. W. Norton, 1988.

The Psychoses. Translated by Russell Grigg. New York: W. W. Norton, 1993.

Speech and Language in Psychoanalysis. Translated by Anthony Wilden. Baltimore: Johns Hopkins University Press, 1981.

Television. Translated by Denis Hollier, Rosalind Krauss, and Annette Michelson. New York: Norton, 1990.

PART V

Deconstruction, Feminism, and Postmodernism

1

Georges Bataille

French thinker Georges Bataille (1897–1962) was the author of a number of novels, philosophical essays, and poetry on the themes of excess, excrement, heterogeneity, transgression, sacrifice, and eroticism. Trained as a medievalist librarian, Bataille was variously associated with the French surrealists and for a short time with the Communist Party; as founder of the journal *Acéphale* and as one of the founders of the College of Sociology, a short-lived (1937–9) avant-garde group of intellectuals and social scientists, Bataille conspired to rekindle the antihumanistic power of myth and experiences of the sacred in contemporary society. The Nietzschean themes of the death of God and the transvaluation of values are apparent in Bataille's work, as is a fascination with the conflation of eroticism, sacrifice, and suffering notorious in the writings of the Marquis de Sade. In each case, Bataille's work operates on and at a limit, whether a limit of the physical body, the social body, the limit between literature and philosophy, or the limit between mortality and divinity. As the following selections from the essay *The Use Value of D. A. F. de Sade* (written 1929–30, first published 1970) illustrate, Bataille's limit-philosophy concerns itself with remains, with excess, the unassimilable, and the heterogeneous.

The Use Value of D. A. F. de Sade

Appropriation and Excretion

1   The division of social facts into religious facts (prohibitions, obligations, and the realization of

From "The Use Value of D. A. F. de Sade," in *Visions of Excess: Selected Writings, 1927–1939*, edited by Allan Stoekl (Minneapolis: University of Minnesota Press, 1986), pp. 94–102. English translation copyright © 1985 by the University of Minnesota. Reprinted by permission of the publisher.

sacred action) on the one hand and profane facts (civil, political, juridical, industrial, and commercial organization) on the other, even though it is not easily applied to primitive societies and lends itself in general to a certain number of confusions, can nevertheless serve as the basis for the determination of two polarized human impulses: EXCRETION and APPROPRIATION. In other words, during a period in which the religious organization of a given country *is developing*, this organization represents the freest opening for excremental collective impulses (orgiastic impulses) established in opposition to political, juridical, and economic institutions.

2   Sexual activity, whether perverted or not; the behavior of one sex before the other; defecation; urination; death and the cult of cadavers (above all, insofar as it involves the stinking decomposition of bodies); the different taboos; ritual cannibalism; the sacrifice of animal-gods; omophagia; the laughter of exclusion; sobbing (which in general has death as its object); religious ecstasy; the identical attitude toward shit, gods, and cadavers; the terror that so often accompanies involuntary defecation; the custom of making women both brilliant and lubricious with makeup, gems, and gleaming jewels; gambling; heedless expenditure and certain fanciful uses of money, etc. together present a common character in that the object of the activity (excrement, shameful parts, cadavers, etc.) is found each time treated as a foreign body (*das ganz Andere*); in other words, it can just as well be expelled following a brutal rupture as reabsorbed through the desire to put one's body and mind entirely in a more or less violent state of expulsion (or projection). The notion of the (heterogeneous) *foreign body* permits one to note the elementary *subjective* identity between types of excrement (sperm, menstrual blood, urine, fecal matter) and everything that can be seen as sacred, divine, or marvelous: a half-decomposed cadaver fleeing through the night in a luminous shroud can be seen as characteristic of this unity.[1]

3   The process of simple appropriation is normally presented within the process of composite excretion, insofar as it is necessary for the production of an alternating rhythm, for example, in the following passage from Sade:

> Verneuil makes someone shit, he eats the turd, and then he demands that someone eat his. The one who eats his shit vomits; he devours her puke.

The elementary form of appropriation is oral consumption, considered as communion (participation, identification, incorporation, or assimilation). Consumption is either sacramental (sacrificial) or not depending on whether the heterogeneous character of food is heightened or conventionally destroyed. In the latter case, the

identification takes place first in the preparation of foods, which must be given an appearance of striking homogeneity, based on strict conventions. Eating as such then intervenes in the process as a complex phenomenon in that the very fact of swallowing presents itself as a partial rupture of physical equilibrium and is accompanied by, among other things, a sudden liberation of great quantities of saliva. Nevertheless, the element of appropriation, in moderate and rational form, in fact dominates, because cases in which eating's principal goal is physiological tumult (gluttony or drunkenness followed by vomiting) are no doubt unusual.

The process of appropriation is thus characterized by a homogeneity (static equilibrium) of the author of the appropriation, and of objects as final result, whereas excretion presents itself as the result of a heterogeneity, and can move in the direction of an ever greater heterogeneity, liberating impulses whose ambivalence is more and more pronounced. The latter case is represented by, for example, sacrificial consumption in the elementary form of the orgy, which has no other goal than the incorporation in the person of irreducibly heterogeneous elements, insofar as such elements risk provoking an increase of force (or more exactly an increase of *mana*).

4   Man does not only appropriate his food, but also the different products of his activity: clothes, furniture, dwellings, and instruments of production. Finally, he appropriates land divided into parcels. Such appropriations take place by means of a more or less conventional homogeneity (identity) established between the possessor and the object possessed. It involves sometimes a personal homogeneity that in primitive times could only be solemnly destroyed with the aid of an excretory rite, and sometimes a general homogeneity, such as that established by the architect between a city and its inhabitants.

In this respect, production can be seen as the excretory phase of a process of appropriation, and the same is true of selling.

5   The homogeneity of the kind realized in cities between men and that which surrounds them is only a subsidiary form of a much more consistent homogeneity, which man has established throughout the external world by everywhere replacing *a priori* inconceivable objects with classified series of conceptions or ideas. The identification of all the elements of which the world is composed has been

pursued with a constant obstinacy, so that scientific conceptions, as well as the popular conceptions of the world, seem to have voluntarily led to a representation as different from what could have been imagined *a priori* as the public square of a capital is from a region of high mountains.

This last appropriation – the work of philosophy as well as of science or common sense – has included phases of revolt and scandal, but it has always had as its goal the establishment of the homogeneity of the world, and it will only be able to lead to a terminal phase in the sense of excretion when the irreducible waste products of the operation are determined.

Philosophy, Religion, and Poetry in Relation to Heterology

6   The interest of philosophy resides in the fact that, in opposition to science or common sense, it must positively envisage the waste products of intellectual appropriation. Nevertheless, it most often envisages these waste products only in abstract forms of totality (nothingness, infinity, the absolute), to which it itself cannot give a positive content; it can thus freely proceed in speculations that more or less have as a goal, all things considered, the *sufficient* identification of an endless world with a finite world, an unknowable (noumenal) world with the known (phenomenal) world.

Only an intellectual elaboration in a religious form can, in its periods of autonomous development, put forward the waste products of appropriative thought as the definitively heterogeneous (sacred) object of speculation. But in general one must take into account the fact that religions bring about a profound separation within the sacred domain, dividing it into a superior world (celestial and divine) and an inferior world (demoniacal, a world of decomposition); now such a division necessarily leads to a progressive homogeneity of the entire superior domain (only the inferior domain resists all efforts at appropriation). God rapidly and almost entirely loses his terrifying features, his appearance as a decomposing cadaver, in order to become, at the final stage of degradation, the simple (paternal) sign of universal homogeneity.

7   In practice, one must understand by religion not really that which answers the need for the unlimited projection (expulsion or excretion) of human nature, but the totality of prohibitions, obligations, and partial freedom that socially channel and regularize this projection. Religion thus differs from a practical and theoretical *heterology*[2] (even though both are equally concerned with sacred or excremental facts), not only in that the former excludes the scientific rigor proper to the latter (which generally appears as different from religion as chemistry is from alchemy), but also in that, under normal conditions, it betrays the needs that it was not only supposed to regulate, but satisfy.

8   Poetry at first glance seems to remain valuable as a method of mental projection (in that it permits one to accede to an entirely heterogeneous world). But it is only too easy to see that it is hardly less debased than religion. It has almost always been at the mercy of the great historical systems of appropriation. And insofar as it can be developed autonomously, this autonomy leads it onto the path of a total poetic conception of the world, which ends at any one of a number of aesthetic homogeneities. The practical unreality of the heterogeneous elements it sets in motion is, in fact, an indispensable condition for the continuation of heterogeneity: starting from the moment when this unreality immediately constitutes itself as a superior reality, whose mission is to eliminate (or degrade) inferior vulgar reality, poetry is reduced to playing the role of the standard of things, and, in opposition, the worst vulgarity takes on an ever stronger excremental value.

The Heterological Theory of Knowledge

9   When one says that heterology scientifically considers questions of heterogeneity, one does not mean that heterology is, in the usual sense of such a formula, the science of the heterogeneous. The heterogeneous is even resolutely placed outside the reach of scientific knowledge, which by definition is only applicable to homogeneous elements. Above all, heterology is opposed to any homogeneous representation of the world, in other words, to any philosophical system. The goal of such representations is always the deprivation of our universe's sources of excitation and the development of a servile human species, fit only for the fabrication, rational consumption, and conservation of products. But the intellectual process automatically limits itself by producing of its own

accord its own waste products, thus liberating in a disordered way the heterogeneous excremental element. Heterology is restricted to taking up again, consciously and resolutely, this terminal process which up until now has been seen as the abortion and the shame of human thought.

In that way it [heterology] leads to the complete reversal of the philosophical process, which ceases to be the instrument of appropriation, and now serves excretion; it introduces the demand for the violent gratifications implied by social life.

10   Only, on the one hand, the process of limitation and, on the other, the study of the violently alternating reactions of antagonism (expulsion) and love (reabsorption) obtained by positing the heterogeneous element, lie within the province of heterology as science. This element itself remains indefinable and can only be determined through negation. The specific character of fecal matter or of the specter, as well as of unlimited time or space, can only be the object of a series of negations, such as the absence of any possible common denominator, irrationality, etc. It must even be added that there is no way of placing such elements in the immediate objective human domain, in the sense that the pure and simple objectification of their specific character would lead to their incorporation in a homogeneous intellectual system, in other words, to a hypocritical cancellation of their excremental character.

The objectivity of heterogeneous elements thus is of only purely theoretical interest, since one can only attain it on the condition that one envisage *waste products* in the total form of the infinite obtained by negation (in other words, objective heterogeneity's shortcoming is that it can only be envisaged in an abstract form, whereas the subjective heterogeneity of particular elements is, in practice, alone concrete).

11   Scientific data – in other words, the result of appropriation – alone retains an immediate and appreciable objective character, since immediate objectivity is defined by the possibilities of intellectual appropriation. If one defines real exterior objects it is necessary to introduce at the same time the possibility of a relation of scientific appropriation. And if such a relation is impossible, the element envisaged remains in practice unreal, and can only abstractly be made objective. All questions posed beyond this represent the persistence of a dominant need for appropriation, the sickly obstin-

acy of a will seeking to represent, in spite of everything, and through simple cowardice, a homogeneous and servile world.

12   It is useless to try to deny that one finds there – much more than in the difficulty (less embarrassing than facility) met with in the analysis of the process of excretion and appropriation – the weak point (in practice) of these conceptions, for one must generally take into account the unconscious obstinacy furnished by defections and complacency. It would be too easy to find in objective nature a large number of phenomena that in a crude way correspond to the human model of excretion and appropriation, in order to attain *once again* the notion of the unity of being, for example, in a dialectical form. One can attain it more generally through animals, plants, matter, nature, and being, without meeting really consistent obstacles. Nevertheless, it can already be indicated that as one moves away from man, the opposition loses its importance to the point where it is only a superimposed form that one obviously could not have discovered in the facts considered if it had not been borrowed from a different order of facts. The only way to resist this dilution lies in the practical part of heterology, which leads to an action that resolutely goes against this regression to homogeneous nature.

As soon as the effort at rational comprehension ends in contradiction, the practice of intellectual scatology requires the excretion of unassimilable elements, which is another way of stating vulgarly that a burst of laughter is the only imaginable and definitively terminal result – and not the means – of philosophical speculation. And then one must indicate that a reaction as *insignificant* as a burst of laughter derives from the extremely vague and distant character of the intellectual domain, and that it suffices to go from a speculation resting on abstract facts to a practice whose mechanism is not different, but which immediately reaches concrete heterogeneity, in order to arrive at ecstatic trances and orgasm.

Principles of Practical Heterology

13   Excretion is not simply a middle term between two appropriations, just as decay is not simply a middle term between the grain and the ear of wheat. The inability to consider in this latter case decay as an end in itself is the result not precisely of the human viewpoint but of the speci-

fically intellectual viewpoint (to the extent that this viewpoint is in practice subordinate to a process of appropriation). The human viewpoint, independent of official declarations, in other words as it results from, among other things, the analysis of dreams, on the contrary represents appropriation as a means of excretion. In the final analysis it is clear that a worker works in order to obtain the violent pleasures of coitus (in other words, he accumulates in order to spend). On the other hand, the conception according to which the worker must have coitus in order to provide for the future necessities of work is linked to the unconscious identification of the worker with the slave. In fact, to the extent that the various functions are distributed among the various social categories, appropriation in its most overwhelming form historically devolves on slaves: thus in the past serfs had to accumulate products for knights and clerks, who barely took part in the labor of appropriation, and then only through the establishment of a morality that regularized for their own profit the circulation of goods. But as soon as one attacks the accursed exploitation of man by man, it becomes time to leave to the exploiters this abominable appropriative morality, which for such a long time has permitted their own orgies of wealth. To the extent that man no longer thinks of crushing his comrades under the yoke of morality, he acquires the capacity to link overtly not only his intellect and his virtue but his *raison d'être* to the violence and incongruity of his excretory organs, as well as to his ability to become excited and entranced by heterogeneous elements, commonly starting in debauchery.

14 The need – before being able to go on to radical demands and to the violent practice of a rigorous moral liberty – to abolish all exploitation of man by man is not the only motive that links the practical development of heterology to the overturning of the established order.

In that they are manifested in a social milieu, the urges that heterology identifies *in practice* with the *raison d'être* of man can be seen in a certain sense as antisocial (to the same degree that sexual corruption or even pleasure is seen by certain individuals as a waste of strength, like, for example, the great ritual destructions of goods in British Columbia, or, among civilized peoples, the pleasure of crowds watching great fires at night). Nevertheless, the impulses that go against the interests of a society in a state of stagnation (during a phase of appro-

priation) have, on the contrary, social revolution (the phase of excretion) as their end: thus they can find, through the historical movements by means of which humanity spends its own strength freely and limitlessly, both total gratification and use in the very sense of general conscious benefit. Besides, whatever the reality of this ulterior benefit might be, it is no less true that if one considers the submerged masses, doomed to an obscure and impotent life, the revolution by which these masses liberate force with a long-restrained violence is as much the practical *raison d'être* of societies as it is their means of development.

15 Of course the term *excretion* applied to the Revolution must first be understood in the strictly mechanical – and moreover etymological – sense of the word. The first phase of a revolution is *separation*, in other words, a process leading to the position of two groups of forces, each one characterized by the necessity of excluding the other. The second phase is the violent *expulsion* of the group that has possessed power by the revolutionary group.

But one also notes that each of the groups, by its very constitution, gives the opposing group an almost exclusively negative excremental character, and it is only because of this negativity that the sacrificial character of a revolution remains profoundly unconscious. The revolutionary impulse of the proletarian masses is, moreover, sometimes implicitly and sometimes openly treated as sacred, and that is why it is possible to use the word *Revolution* entirely stripped of its utilitarian meaning without, however, giving it an idealist meaning.

16 *Participation* – in the purely psychological sense as well as in the active sense of the word – does not only commit revolutionaries to a particular politics, for example, to the establishment of socialism throughout the world. It is also – and necessarily – presented as moral participation: immediate participation in the destructive action of the revolution (expulsion realized through the total shattering of the equilibrium of the social edifice), indirect participation in all equivalent destructive action. It is the very character of the revolutionary will to link such actions – not, as in the Christian apocalypse, to punishment – but to the enjoyment or the utility of human beings, and it is obvious that all destruction that is neither useful nor inevitable can only be the achievement of an exploiter and, consequently, of morality as the principle of all exploitation.[3] But then it is easy to

ascertain that the reality of such *participation* is at the very basis of the separation of the socialist parties, divided into reformists and revolutionaries.

Without a profound complicity with natural forces such as violent death, gushing blood, sudden catastrophes and the horrible cries of pain that accompany them, terrifying ruptures of what had seemed to be immutable, the fall into stinking filth of what had been elevated – without a sadistic understanding of an incontestably thundering and torrential nature, there could be no revolutionaries, there could only be a revolting utopian sentimentality.

17   The *participation* in everything that, among men, is horrible and allegedly sacred can take place in a limited and unconscious form, but this limitation and this unconsciousness obviously have only a provisional value, and nothing can stop the movement that leads human beings toward an ever more shameless awareness of the erotic bond that links them to death, to cadavers, and to horrible physical pain. It is high time that human nature cease being subjected to the autocrat's vile repression and to the morality that authorizes exploitation. Since it is true that one of a man's attributes is the derivation of pleasure from the suffering of others, and that erotic pleasure is not only the negation of an agony that takes place at the same instant, but also a lubricious participation in that agony, it is time to choose between the conduct of cowards afraid of their own joyful excesses, and the conduct of those who judge that any given man need not cower like a hunted animal, but instead can see all the moralistic buffoons as so many dogs.

18   As a result of these elementary considerations, it is necessary from now on to envisage two distinct phases in human emancipation, as undertaken successively by the different revolutionary surges, from Jacobinism to bolshevism.

During the revolutionary phase, the current phase that will only end with the world triumph of socialism, only the social Revolution can serve as an outlet for collective impulses, and no other activity can be envisaged in practice.

But the postrevolutionary phase implies the necessity of a division between the economic and political organization of society on one hand, and on the other, an antireligious and asocial organization having as its goal orgiastic participation in different forms of destruction, in other words, the collective satisfaction of needs that correspond to the necessity of provoking the violent excitation that results from the expulsion of heterogeneous elements.

Such an organization can have no other conception of morality than the one scandalously affirmed for the first time by the Marquis de Sade.

19   When it is a question of the means of realizing this orgiastic participation, [such] an organization will find itself as close to religions anterior *to the formations of autocratic states* as it is distant from religions such as Christianity or Buddhism.

One must broadly take into account, in such a forecast, the probable intervention of blacks in the general culture. To the extent that blacks participate in revolutionary emancipation, the attainment of socialism will bring them the possibility of all kinds of exchanges with white people, but in conditions radically different from those currently experienced by the civilized blacks of America. Now black communities, once liberated from all superstition as from all oppression, represent in relation to heterology not only the possibility but the necessity of an adequate organization. All organizations that have ecstasy and frenzy as their goal (the spectacular death of animals, partial tortures, orgiastic dances, etc.) will have no reason to disappear when a heterological conception of human life is substituted for the primitive conception; they can only transform themselves while they spread, under the violent impetus of a moral doctrine of white origin, taught to blacks by all those whites who have become aware of the abominable inhibitions paralyzing their race's communities. It is only starting from this collusion of European scientific theory with black practice that institutions can develop which will serve as the final outlets (with no other limitations than those of human strength) for the urges that today require worldwide society's fiery and bloody Revolution.

Notes

1   The identical nature, from the psychological point of view, of God and excrement should not shock the intellect of anyone familiar with the problems posed by the history of religions. The cadaver is not much

more repugnant than shit, and the specter that projects its horror is *sacred* even in the eyes of modern theologians. The following passage from Frazer very nearly sums up the basic historical aspect of the question: " ... These different categories of people differ, in our eyes, by virtue of their character and their condition: we should say that one group is sacred, the other filthy or impure. This is not the case for the savage, for his mind is much too crude to understand clearly what a sacred being is, and what an impure being is."

2 The science of what is completely other. The term *agiology* would perhaps be more precise, but one would have to catch the double meaning of *agio* (analogous to the double meaning of *sacer*), *soiled* as well as *holy*. But it is above all the term *scatology* (the science of excrement) that retains in the present circumstances (the specialization of the sacred) an incontestable expressive value as the doublet of an abstract term such as *heterology*.

3 For example, imperialist war.

Select Bibliography

The Absence of Myth: Writings on Surrealism. Edited and translated by Michael Richardson. London: Verso, 1994.

The Accursed Share: An Essay on General Economy. Three volumes in two books. Translated by Robert Hurley. New York: Zone Books, 1988–91.

The Bataille Reader. Edited by Fred Botting and Scott Wilson. Oxford: Blackwell Publishers, 1997.

Blue of Noon. Translated by Harry Mathews. London: M. Boyars, 1986.

Erotism: Death and Sensuality. Translated by Mary Dalwood. San Francisco: City Lights Books, 1986.

Inner Experience. Translated by Leslie Anne Boldt. Albany: State University of New York Press, 1988.

Literature and Evil. Translated by Alastair Hamilton. New York: M. Boyars, 1985.

On Nietzsche. Translated by Bruce Boone. New York: Paragon House, 1992.

Story of the Eye. Translated by Joachim Neugroschel. San Francisco: City Lights Books, 1987.

The Tears of Eros. Translated by Peter Connor. San Francisco: City Lights Books, 1989.

Theory of Religion. Translated by Robert Hurley. New York: Zone Books, 1989.

Visions of Excess: Selected Writings, 1927–1939. Edited by Allan Stoekl. Translated by Allan Stoekl, with Carl L. Lovitt and Donald M. Leslie, Jr. Minneapolis: University of Minnesota Press, 1986.

2

Maurice Blanchot

The writings of French novelist and critic Maurice Blanchot (1907–) have been influenced by a broad spectrum of philosophical thought, including that of Hegel, Heidegger, and Levinas, as well as by the literary and poetic work of Hölderlin, Kafka, Rilke, and Mallarmé. Blanchot's literary *oeuvre* may be regarded as a sustained meditation on and encounter with the limits of writing, its possibilities and impossibilities. In philosophical terms, the being of language and its relation to mortality is Blanchot's central concern. The theme of death appears as the enduring locus of his work, articulating the possible and impossible relations between the artist and writer as creator, and the work that comes to exceed its presumed author. The following selection from *The Space of Literature* (1955) reflects on the distance and "void" intrinsic to the communicative potential of the literary work.

The Space of Literature

Communication

What most threatens reading is this: the reader's reality, his personality, his immodesty, his stubborn insistence upon remaining himself in the face of what he reads – a man who knows in general how to read. To read a poem is not to read yet another poem; it is not even to enter, via this poem, into the essence of poetry. The reading of a poem is the

From *The Space of Literature*, translated by Ann Smock (Lincoln: University of Nebraska Press, 1989), pp. 198–207. By permission of the University of Nebraska Press. English-language translation © 1982 by the University of Nebraska Press. © Editions Gallimard, 1955.

poem itself, affirming itself in the reading as a work. It is the poem giving birth, in the space held open by the reader, to the reading that welcomes it; it is the poem becoming power to read, becoming communication opened between *power* and *impossibility*, between the power linked to the moment of reading and the impossibility linked to the moment of writing.

Communication of the work lies not in the fact that it has become communicable, through reading, to a reader. The work is itself communication. It is intimacy shared in struggle by reading's demand and writing's: by the work as form and measure, constituting itself as power, and the same work's measureless excess, tending toward impossibility. It is intimate strife shared moreover by the form where the work takes its shape and the limitlessness where it is all refusal, by the resolution which is the being of beginning and the indecision which is the being of beginning over. This violence lasts as long as the work is a work. It is violence that is never pacified, but it is also the calm of an accord; it is rivalry, and also the reconciliation – an understanding. But it breaks off as soon as it ceases to be the approach toward what rules out any understanding.

To read is thus not to obtain communication from the work, but to "make" the work communicate itself. And, if we may employ an inadequate image, to read is to be one of the two poles between which, through mutual attraction and repulsion, the illuminating violence of communication erupts – one of the two poles between which that event comes to pass and which it constitutes by the very passage. But of course this comparison is inadequate. At most it indicates that the antagonism, which in the work opposes its two moments, reading and writing (or, more exactly, which makes of the work a tension where its moments seem to oppose each other two by two), opens the work by means of this radical disjunction to the freedom of its communication. But we should not so simply represent this antagonism as that of fixed poles opposing each other like two powers determined once and for all, called reading and writing. It must at least be added that this antagonistic exaltation, which eventually takes the personified form of the reader and the author, has never ceased to develop in the course of the work's genesis. Although, in the end, the work seems to have become a dialogue between two persons in whom two stabilized demands have been incarnated, this "dialogue" is primarily the more original combat of more indistinct demands, the torn intimacy of irreconcilable and inseparable moments which we call measure and measurelessness, form and infinitude, resolution and indecision. Beneath their successive oppositions, these moments steadily give reality to the same violence. To the violence, that is, of what tends to open and tends to close, tends to cohere in the contours of a clear figure that limits, and yet tends to err without end, to lose itself in an ever restless migration, that of the *other* night which never comes but comes back again. In this communication it is obscurity that must reveal itself and night that must dawn. This is revelation where nothing appears, but where concealment becomes appearance.

The Reader Yet to Come

It is sometimes said that every author writes in the presence of some reader or that he writes in order to be read. This is a rather careless way of speaking. One ought to say that the reader's role, or that which will become, once the work is complete, the power or the possibility of reading, is already present, in changing forms, in the genesis of the work. To the extent that to write is to snatch oneself back from the impossibility where writing becomes possible, writing assumes the characteristics of reading's demand, and the writer becomes the nascent intimacy of the still infinitely future reader. But it goes without saying that this power is nonetheless power to write, only because of the opposition to itself which it becomes in the experience of impossibility. There is not power on one side, impossibility on the other; there is no such clash of these contraries. There is, in the event of the fact of writing, the tension which, through the intimacy into which the writing gathers them, demands of the opposites what they are in their extreme opposition, but demands also that they come into their own by quitting themselves, by detaining each other together outside themselves in the restless unity of their common belonging. The power in question is power only by comparison with impossibility, the impossibility which is affirmed as power.

The writer, inasmuch as he remains a real person and believes himself to be this real person who is writing, also believes that he willingly shelters in himself the reader of what he writes. He feels within himself, vital and demanding, the role of the reader still to be born. And very often, through a usurpation which he barely escapes, it is the reader, prematurely and falsely engendered, who begins to write in him. (Hence, to give only a simplistic example, those choice passages, those fine phrases which come to the surface and which cannot be said to have been written, but only to be readable.) This illusion, as we can now understand, comes from the fact that the moments which prefigure reading's demand pass through the writer in the course of the work's genesis. But these moments must, precisely, fall outside of him when they are gathered together in the final decisiveness of the reading – in the liberty of the welcome and of the sojourn near the work which alone constitutes an authentic reading.

The writer can never read his work for the very same reason which gives him the illusion that he does. "He is," says René Char, "the genesis of being who projects and of a being who contains." But in order for the "being who contains" – the being who gives form and measure, the form-giver, the "Beginner" – to attain the ultimate metamorphosis which would turn him into "the reader," the finished work has to escape from him. It has to escape from the one who makes it, complete itself by putting him at a distance, culminate in this "distancing" which dispossesses him conclusively, this distancing which then, precisely, takes the form of the reading (and in which the reading takes form).

The moment when that which is glorified in the work *is* the work, when the work ceases in some way to have been made, to refer back to someone who made it, but gathers all the essence of the work in the fact that now there is a work – a beginning and initial decision – this moment which cancels the author is also the moment when, as the book opens to itself, the reading finds its origin in this opening.

Reading is born, therefore, at this moment when the work's distance from itself changes its sign. In the course of the book's genesis this "void" marked the work's unfinished quality, but also the intimacy of its progression, the first precipitous advances of the "being who projects." This emptiness changes its sign, and the reading is born at the moment when the distance of the work with respect to itself no longer indicates incompletion but perfection, no longer signifies that the work is not yet done, but that it never needed to be done.

In general the reader, unlike the writer, naively feels superfluous. He does not think that he fashions the work. Even if the work overwhelms him, and all the more so if it becomes his sole concern, he feels that he does not exhaust it, that it remains altogether outside his most intimate approach. He does not penetrate it; it is free of him, and this freedom makes for the profundity of his relation to the work, the intimacy of his yes. But in this very yes, the work's freedom still keeps him at a distance. It re-establishes the distance which alone assures the freedom of the welcome and which is constantly reborn from the passion of the reading that abolishes it.

This distance is what perfects the work – if, that is, the reader keeps it pure, and inasmuch as it is, moreover, the measure of his intimacy with the work. For he is close to the work to the degree that he recognizes it as a work regardless of him. By removing it from any author and from all consideration of having been made, this distance gives the work for what it is. And so it would seem that reading's effacement, which renders it innocent of the work's making and exempts it from this responsibility, is, for that very reason, nearer to the accomplished work, to the essence of its creation, than is the author who always believes himself to have made everything and created all.

Abhorrence of a Vacuum

But this *distance*, which evokes the yes of the finished work (given as complete in the moment when, for the movement that completed it, is substituted the affirmation that it is) – this distance of the work with respect to itself, to the reader, to the world's doings, to other works – this distance which, precisely, constitutes reading's innocence also defines its responsibility and its risk. It seems to be very difficult to preserve such an interval. Here the natural abhorrence of a vacuum is expressed in the need to fill it up with a judgment of value. The work is said to be good or bad with respect to morality, laws, various systems of values, etc. It is declared to be successful or not with respect to rules (very precarious at present) which may constitute instances of an aesthetic, that is to say the simple impressions of a more or less refined taste or of a more or less vigorous absence of taste. The work is judged to be rich or poor with respect to culture, which compares it to other works, which does or does not draw from it an increase in knowledge, which adds it to the national, to the human treasury or yet again sees in it only a pretext to talk or to teach.

It is possible that the more a work is esteemed, the more it is imperiled. For when it is designated as a good work, it is assigned a place on the side of the good which uses it, rendering it utilitarian. A work which is judged bad sometimes finds room in this judgment to preserve itself. It is put aside, condemned to the nether regions of libraries, or burned, or forgotten; but in a sense this exile, this disappearance in the midst of flames or in tepid forgetfulness also extends the proper distance of the work. It corresponds to the force of the work's remove. This does not mean that a century later the work will necessarily find the readers it lacked. Posterity is promised to no one, and no book would consider it a happy ending. The work does not endure over the ages; it is. This being can inaugurate a new age, for it is an appeal to the beginning, recalling that nothing is affirmed except through the fecundity of an initial decisiveness. But the work's very coming to be is revealed by the flash of its disappearance at least as well as by the false light shed by survival from mere habit. The feeling that works escape time originates in the work's "distance," and expresses, by disguising it, the remove which always comes from the work's presence. Our impression that works are ageless expresses, by forgetting it, what makes the work always accede to presence for the first time in its reading – its unique reading, each time the first and each time the only.

The risk which this reading entails, however, is no mere matter of chance. If the work's "void," which is its presence to itself in its reading, is difficult to preserve, this is not only because it is in itself hard to sustain, but also because it remembers, as it were, the void which, in the course of the work's genesis, marked the incompletion of the work and was the tension of its antagonist moments. That is why reading draws whoever reads the work into the remembrance of that profound genesis. Not that the reader necessarily perceives afresh the manner in which the work was produced – not that he is in attendance at the real experience of its creation. But he partakes of the work as the unfolding of something in the making, the intimacy of the void which comes to be. If this progression takes on the aspect of a temporal unfolding, it founds the essence of the literary genre called the novel.

This kind of reading – this presence to the work as a genesis – changes, and thus produces the critical reading: the reader, now the specialist, interrogates the work in order to know how it was fashioned. He asks it the secrets and the conditions of its creation, and examines it closely to see whether it answers adequately to these conditions, etc. The reader, having become the specialist, becomes an author in reverse. The true reader does not rewrite the book, but he is apt to return, drawn by an imperceptible pull, toward the various prefigurations of the reader which have caused him to be present in advance at the hazardous experience of the book. It ceases, then, to appear necessary to him and again becomes a possibility among others. It regains the indecisiveness of something uncertain, something altogether still to be achieved. And the work thus regains its disquietude, the wealth of its indigence, the insecurity of its void, while reading, joining in this disquietude and espousing this poverty, comes to resemble the desire, the anguish, and the levity of a movement of passion.

All these metamorphoses belong to the authentic essence of reading. Its task is to keep what we call the work's distance pure, but no less to keep it alive: to make it communicate with the work's intimacy, to keep this intimacy from congealing and protecting itself in the vain solitude of the ideal. The "vacuum" which, in the course of the work's genesis, belongs to the torn intimacy of the work, seems, in the end, to fall out of it. While opening it altogether to itself, rendering it absolutely present, the emptiness seems nevertheless to make of this presence the remove which preserves its approach, giving us the impression that the painting is always behind the painting and also that the poem, the temple, and the statue escape the vicissitudes of time, whose mark, however, they bear.

It is as if this divisive void which, in the course of the genesis, is now the abyss where the work subsides, now the soaring energy by which it comes to light, now that empty violence where everything repeats eternally but then again the search from which everything begins – it is as if this "distant interior," as Michaux calls it, passed, at the moment of completion, altogether outside, isolating the work, forming around it that halo of absence so characteristic of the presence of masterpieces, which is like their aura of glory and which shelters them beneath a veil of empty majesty, unexpressive indifference. Thus are works immobilized in a lifeless distance. Isolated, preserved by a void which is no longer a reading but a cult of admiration, they cease to be works. The work of art is never connected to repose, it has nothing to do with the tranquil certitude which makes masterpieces familiar; it does not take shelter in museums. In this sense it never is. And if, clumsily transposing the idea that it is not an object someone has perfected, we say of it that its perfection is everlasting, at least this reminds us that the work never ceases to be related to its origin: that the incessant experience of the origin is the condition of its being, and also that the antagonistic violence due to which it was, in the course of its genesis, the opposition of its contrary moments, is not just a feature of this genesis, but belongs to the character of agonistic struggle which is the character of the work's very being. The work is the *violent liberty* by which it is communicated, and by which the *origin*

– the empty and indecisive depth of the origin – is *communicated* through the work to form the brimming resolution, the definiteness of the beginning. That is why the work tends ever increasingly to manifest the experience of the work: the experience which is not exactly that of its creation and which is not that of its technical fashioning either. This experience leads the work ceaselessly back from the clarity of the beginning to the obscurity of the origin and subjects its brilliant apparition, the moment of its opening, to the disquietude of the dissimulation into which it withdraws.

The reading which takes form in the work's distance – the reading which is the form of this void and the moment when it seems to fall out of the work – must thus also be a profound return to its intimacy, to what seems its eternal birth. Reading is not an angel flying about the work and, with winged feet, making this sphere turn. It is not the look which from without, from behind the window, captures what is happening within a foreign world. It is connected to the life of the work. It is present at all the work's moments. It is one of them, and it is by turns and at the same time each of them. It is not only their remembrance, their ultimate transfiguration; it retains in itself everything that is really at stake in the work. That is why in the end it alone bears all the weight of communication.

The Work and History

It is not surprising then, that, strengthened by such intimacy, reading, incarnated in the reader, should naturally proceed to take over the work, wanting to "grasp" it, reducing and eliminating all distance from it. Nor is it surprising that reading should make of this distance, this sign of the work's completion, the principle of a new genesis: the realization of the work's historical destiny. In the world of culture, the work becomes the guarantor of truths and the repository of meaning. None of this is surprising; this movement is inevitable. But it does not simply mean that the artistic work follows the course of works in general and obeys the law that moves them through their successive transformations. For this movement is also encouraged by the work's own nature. It comes from the profound distance of the work from itself, the remove due to which it always escapes what it is – seems, for example, definitively finished and yet incomplete; seems, in the restlessness that steals it from every grasp, to enter into complicity with the in-

finite variations of becoming. The distance which puts the work beyond our reach and beyond time's – where it perishes in glorious immobility – also exposes it to all the contingencies of time, showing it ceaselessly in search of a new form, of another culmination, acquiescing in all the metamorphoses which, attaching it to history, seem to make of its remove the promise of an unlimited future.

Thus the reading which initially projected itself into the intimacy of the work, only to fall out of it the better to maintain it and to fix it in a monumental immobility, finally projects itself outside and makes of the work's intimate life something which can no longer be realized unless it is displayed in the world and filled with the world's life and with history's.

This transformation is produced to the extent that the "empty" movement takes on content, while the work, momentarily or definitively losing the force and the intimacy of its constant genesis, unfolds as a newborn world where values are at stake and where these values call for arbitration by some criterion or contribute to the advent of such a standard, such a truth.

So: that which, in the work, was communication of the work to itself, *the origin blossoming into a beginning*, becomes the communication of a given thing. That which, opening it, made the work the advent and the brilliance of what opens becomes an opened place, in the image of this world of stable things and in imitation of this subsisting reality where, from a need to subsist, we live. And that which had neither sense nor truth nor value, but in which everything seemed to take on sense, becomes the language which says true things, says false things, and which one reads for instruction, for increased self-knowledge, or to cultivate the mind.

Through this realization then, the work is realized outside of itself and also on the model of exterior things, at their invitation. Through this movement – determined, so to speak, by gravity – instead of being the force of the beginning, the work becomes a thing beginning. Instead of getting all its reality from the pure, contentless affirmation that it is, it becomes an enduring reality, containing many meanings which it acquires from the movement of time or which are perceived variously according to culture's forms and the exigencies of history. And through all this, through all that makes it graspable – makes of it no longer the being of the work but the work functioning in the productive fashion of works of the world – it puts itself at the reader's service. It takes part in the public dialogue. It expresses or it refutes what is generally said; it consoles, it entertains, it bores, not by virtue of itself or by virtue of a relation with the void and the cutting edge of its being, but via its content, and then finally thanks to its reflection of the common language and the current truth. At this juncture what is read is surely no longer the work; rather, these are the thoughts of everyone rethought, our common habits rendered more habitual still, everyday routines continuing to weave the fabric of our days. And this movement is in itself very important, one which it is not fitting to discredit. But neither the work of art nor its reading is present here.

This transformation is not definitive; it is not even an evil or a good for the work. Disappearance, even when it is disguised as useful presence, belongs to the work's essence; and we should add that it is also related to the dialectic of art. This movement leads from the hymn – where the work, art, and the world are absent – to the work where men and the world seek to make themselves present, and from there to the work where the very experience of the work – art, the communication of the origin as a beginning – is affirmed in a presence which is also disappearance.

It is sometimes said regretfully that the work of art will never again speak the language it spoke when it was born, the language of its birth, which only those who belonged to the same world heard and received. Never again will the Eumenides speak to the Greeks, and we will never know what was said in that language. This is true. But it is also true that the Eumenides have still never spoken, and that each time they speak it is the unique birth of their language that they announce. Long ago they spoke as enraged and appeased divinities before withdrawing into the temple of night – and this is unknown to us and will ever remain foreign. Later they spoke as symbols of the dark forces that must be combated in order for there to be justice and culture – and this is only too well known to us. Finally, one day, perhaps they will speak as the work in which language is always original, in which it is the language of the origin. And this is unknown to us, but not foreign. And not withstanding all this, reading and vision each time recollect, from the weight of a given content and along the ramifications of an evolving world, the unique intimacy of the work, the wonder of its constant genesis and the swell of its unfurling.

Select Bibliography

Death Sentence. Translated by Lydia Davis. Barrytown, NY: Station Hill Press, 1978.

Friendship. Translated by Elizabeth Rottenberg. Stanford: Stanford University Press, 1997.

The Gaze of Orpheus, and Other Literary Essays. Edited by P. Adams Sitney. Translated by Lydia Davis. Barrytown, NY: Station Hill Press, 1981.

The Infinite Conversation. Translated by Susan Hanson. Minneapolis: University of Minnesota Press, 1993.

The Most High/ Le Tres haut. Translated by Allan Stoekl. Lincoln: University of Nebraska Press, 1996.

The One Who Was Standing Apart from Me. Translated by Lydia Davis. Barrytown, NY: Station Hill Press, 1993.

The Sirens' Song: Selected Essays. Edited by Gabriel Josipovici. Translated by Sacha Ravinovitch. Bloomington: Indiana University Press, 1982.

The Space of Literature. Translated by Ann Smock. Lincoln: University of Nebraska Press, 1989.

The Step Not Beyond. Translated by Lycette Nelson. Albany: State University of New York Press, 1992.

Thomas the Obscure. Translated by Robert Lamberton. Barrytown, NY: Station Hill Press, 1988.

The Unavowable Community. Translated by Pierre Joris. Barrytown, NY: Station Hill Press, 1988.

The Work of Fire. Translated by Charlotte Mandell. Stanford: Stanford University Press, 1995.

The Writing of the Disaster/ L'Ecriture du désastre. Translated by Ann Smock. Lincoln: University of Nebraska Press, 1995.

3

Jacques Derrida

Jacques Derrida (1930–) was born in Algeria but studied in Paris where he currently teaches at the École des Hautes Études en Sciences Sociales. Widely known as the leading exponent of "deconstruction," Derrida's work has had immense influence across a range of disciplines including philosophy, literary theory and criticism, social and political thought, feminism, and psychoanalysis. Broadly speaking, a "deconstructionist" approach is critical of traditional metaphysics as tending to privilege presence, the self-presence of thought, and the desire for fully constituted meaning and grounds. Deconstruction as practiced by

Derrida thereby undermines the stability of traditional philosophical hierarchies, such as those between soul and body, the invisible and the visible, and masculine and feminine. Derrida's early interest in phenomenology, with emphasis on Husserl, Heidegger, and Levinas, continues to be seen throughout his most recent work, which has increasingly focused on ethical and political questions. The following excerpt from *Of Grammatology* (1967) takes up the critique of presence in attempting to problematize the traditional privileging of what Derrida identifies as "phono-" and "logocentrism."

Of Grammatology

Exergue: Writing Before the Letter

1 The one who will shine in the science of writing will shine like the sun. A scribe (*EP*, p. 87)

From *Of Grammatology*, translated by Gayatri Chakravorty Spivak (Baltimore: Johns Hopkins University Press, 1984), pp. 3–18. © 1976 the Johns Hopkins University Press.

O Samas (sun-god), by your light you scan the totality of lands as if they were cuneiform signs (ibid.).

2 These three ways of writing correspond almost exactly to three different stages according to which one can consider men gathered into a nation. The depicting of objects is appropriate to a savage people; signs of words and of propositions, to a barbaric people; and the alphabet to civilized people. J.-J. Rousseau, *Essai sur l'origine des langues*.

3   Alphabetic script is in itself and for itself the most intelligent. Hegel, *Enzyklopädie*.

This triple exergue is intended not only to focus attention on the *ethnocentrism* which, everywhere and always, had controlled the concept of writing. Nor merely to focus attention on what I shall call *logocentrism*: the metaphysics of phonetic writing (for example, of the alphabet) which was fundamentally – for enigmatic yet essential reasons that are inaccessible to a simple historical relativism – nothing but the most original and powerful ethnocentrism, in the process of imposing itself upon the world, controlling in one and the same *order*:

1 *the concept of writing* in a world where the phoneticization of writing must dissimulate its own history as it is produced;

2 *the history of* (the only) *metaphysics*, which has, in spite of all differences, not only from Plato to Hegel (even including Leibniz) but also, beyond these apparent limits, from the pre-Socratics to Heidegger, always assigned the origin of truth in general to the logos: the history of truth, of the truth of truth, has always been – except for a metaphysical diversion that we shall have to explain – the debasement of writing, and its repression outside "full" speech.

3 *the concept of science* or the scientificity of science – what has always been determined as *logic* – a concept that has always been a philosophical concept, even if the practice of science has constantly challenged its imperialism of the logos, by invoking, for example, from the beginning and ever increasingly, nonphonetic writing. No doubt this subversion has always been contained within a system of direct address [*système allocutoire*] which gave birth to the project of science and to the conventions of all nonphonetic characteristics.[1] It could not have been otherwise. Nonetheless, it is a peculiarity of our epoch that, at the moment when the phoneticization of writing – the historical origin and structural possibility of philosophy as of science, the condition of the *epistémè* – begins to lay hold on world culture,[2] science, in its advancements, can no longer be satisfied with it. This inadequation had always already begun to make its presence felt. But today something lets it appear as such, allows it a kind of takeover without our being able to translate this novelty into clear cut notions of mutation, explicitation, accumulation, revolution, or tradition. These values belong no doubt to the system whose dislocation is today presented as such, they describe the styles of an

historical movement which was meaningful – like the concept of history itself – only within a logocentric epoch.

By alluding to a science of writing reined in by metaphor, metaphysics, and theology,[3] this exergue must not only announce that the science of writing – *grammatology*[4] – shows signs of liberation all over the world, as a result of decisive efforts. These efforts are necessarily discreet, dispersed, almost imperceptible; that is a quality of their meaning and of the milieu within which they produce their operation. I would like to suggest above all that, however fecund and necessary the undertaking might be, and even if, given the most favorable hypothesis, it did overcome all technical and epistemological obstacles as well as all the theological and metaphysical impediments that have limited it hitherto, such a science of writing runs the risk of never being established as such and with that name. Of never being able to define the unity of its project or its object. Of not being able either to write its discourse on method or to describe the limits of its field. For essential reasons: the unity of all that allows itself to be attempted today through the most diverse concepts of science and of writing, is, in principle, more or less covertly yet always, determined by an historico-metaphysical epoch of which we merely glimpse the *closure*. I do not say the *end*. The idea of science and the idea of writing – therefore also of the science of writing – is meaningful for us only in terms of an origin and within a world to which a certain concept of the sign (later I shall call it *the* concept of sign) and a certain concept of the relationships between speech and writing, have *already* been assigned. A most determined relationship, in spite of its privilege, its necessity, and the field of vision that it has controlled for a few millennia, especially in the West, to the point of being now able to produce its own dislocation and itself proclaim its limits.

Perhaps patient meditation and painstaking investigation on and around what is still provisionally called writing, far from falling short of a science of writing or of hastily dismissing it by some obscurantist reaction, letting it rather develop its positivity as far as possible, are the wanderings of a way of thinking that is faithful and attentive to the ineluctable world of the future which proclaims itself at present, beyond the closure of knowledge. The future can only be anticipated in the form of an absolute danger. It is that which breaks absolutely with constituted normality and can only be proclaimed, *presented*, as a sort of monstrosity. For that future world and for that within it which will have put into question the values of sign, word, and writing, for that which guides our future anterior, there is as yet no exergue.

1   The End of the Book and the Beginning of Writing

Socrates, he who does not write[5] – Nietzsche

However the topic is considered, the *problem of language* has never been simply one problem among others. But never as much as at present has it invaded, *as such*, the global horizon of the most diverse researches and the most heterogeneous discourses, diverse and heterogeneous in their intention, method, and ideology. The devaluation of the word "language" itself, and how, in the very hold it has upon us, it betrays a loose vocabulary, the temptation of a cheap seduction, the passive yielding to fashion, the consciousness of the avant-garde, in other words – ignorance – are evidences of this effect. This inflation of the sign "language" is the inflation of the sign itself, absolute inflation, inflation itself. Yet, by one of its aspects or shadows, it is itself still a sign: this crisis is also a symptom. It indicates, as if in spite of itself, that a historico–metaphysical epoch *must* finally determine as language the totality of its problematic horizon. It must do so not only because all that desire had wished to wrest from the play of language finds itself recaptured within that play but also because, for the same reason, language itself is menaced in its very life, helpless, adrift in the threat of limitlessness, brought back to its own finitude at the very moment when its limits seem to disappear, when it ceases to be self-assured, contained, and *guaranteed* by the infinite signified which seemed to exceed it.

The program

By a slow movement whose necessity is hardly perceptible, everything that for at least some twenty centuries tended toward and finally succeeded in being gathered under the name of language is beginning to let itself be transferred to, or at least summarized under, the name of writing. By a hardly perceptible necessity, it seems as though the concept of writing – no longer indicating a particular, derivative, auxiliary form of language in general (whether understood as communication, relation, expression, signification, constitution of meaning or thought, etc.), no longer designating the exterior surface, the insubstantial double of a major signifier, *the signifier of the signifier* – is beginning to go beyond the extension of language. In all senses of the word, writing thus *comprehends* language. Not that the word "writing" has ceased to designate the signifier of the signifier, but it appears, strange as it may seem, that "signifier of the signifier" no longer defines accidental doubling and fallen secondarity. "Signifier of the signifier" describes on the contrary the movement of language in its origin, to be sure, but one can already suspect that an origin whose structure can be expressed as "signifier of the signifier" conceals and erases itself in its own production. There the signified always already functions as a signifier. The secondarity that it seemed possible to ascribe to writing alone affects all signifieds in general, affects them always already, the moment they *enter the game*. There is not a single signified that escapes, even if recaptured, the play of signifying references that constitute language. The advent of writing is the advent of this play; today such a play is coming into its own, effacing the limit starting from which one had thought to regulate the circulation of signs, drawing along with it all the reassuring signifieds, reducing all the strongholds, all the out-of-bounds shelters that watched over the field of language. This, strictly speaking, amounts to destroying the concept of "sign" and its entire logic. Undoubtedly it is not by chance that this *overwhelming* supervenes at the moment when the extension of the concept of language effaces all its limits. We shall see that this overwhelming and this effacement have the same meaning, are one and the same phenomenon. It is as if the Western concept of language (in terms of what, beyond its plurivocity and beyond the strict and problematic opposition of speech [*parole*] and language [*langue*], attaches it *in general* to phonematic or glossematic production, to language, to voice, to hearing, to sound and breadth, to speech) were revealed today as the guise or disguise of a primary writing:[6] more fundamental than that which, before this conversion, passed for the simple "supplement to the spoken word" (Rousseau). Either writing was never a simple "supplement," or it is urgently necessary to construct a new logic of the "supplement." It is this urgency which will guide us further in reading Rousseau.

These disguises are not historical contingencies that one might admire or regret. Their movement was absolutely necessary, with a necessity which cannot be judged by any other tribunal. The privilege of the *phonè* does not depend upon a choice that could have been avoided. It responds to a moment of *economy* (let us say of the "life" of "history" or of "being as self-relationship"). The system of "hearing (understanding)-oneself-speak" through the phonic substance – which *presents itself* as the nonexterior, nonmundane, therefore nonempirical or noncontingent signifier – has necessarily dominated the history of the world during an entire epoch, and has even produced the idea of the world, the idea of world-origin, that arises from the difference between the worldly and the nonworldly the outside and the inside, ideality and nonideality, universal and nonuniversal, transcendental and empirical, etc.[7]

With an irregular and essentially precarious success, this movement would apparently have tended, as toward its *telos*, to confine writing to a secondary and instrumental function: translator of a full speech that was fully *present* (present to itself, to its signified, to the other, the very condition of the theme of presence in general), technics in the service of language, *spokesman*, interpreter of an originary speech itself shielded from interpretation.

Technics in the service of language: I am not invoking a general essence of technics which would be already familiar to us and would help us in *understanding* the narrow and historically determined concept of writing as an example. I believe on the contrary that a certain sort of question about the meaning and origin of writing precedes, or at least merges with, a certain type of question about the meaning and origin of technics. That is why the notion of technique can never simply clarify the notion of writing.

It is therefore as if what we call language could have been in its origin and in its end only a moment, an essential but determined mode, a phenomenon, an aspect, a species of writing. And as if it had succeeded in making us forget this, and *in wilfully misleading us*, only in the course of an adventure: as that adventure itself. All in all a short enough adventure. It merges with the history that has associated technics and logocentric metaphysics for nearly three millennia. And it now seems to be approaching what is really its own *exhaustion*; under the circumstances – and this is no more than one example among others – of this death of the civilization of the book, of which so much is said and which manifests itself particularly through a convulsive proliferation of libraries. All

appearances to the contrary, this death of the book undoubtedly announces (and in a certain sense always has announced) nothing but a death of speech (of a *so-called* full speech) and a new mutation in the history of writing, in history as writing. Announces it at a distance of a few centuries. It is on that scale that we must reckon it here, being careful not to neglect the quality of a very heterogeneous historical duration: the acceleration is such, and such its qualitative meaning, that one would be equally wrong in making a careful evaluation according to past rhythms. "Death of speech" is of course a metaphor here: before we speak of disappearance, we must think of a new situation for speech, of its subordination within a structure of which it will no longer be the archon.

To affirm in this way that the concept of writing exceeds and comprehends that of language, presupposes of course a certain definition of language and of writing. If we do not attempt to justify it, we shall be giving in to the movement of inflation that we have just mentioned, which has also taken over the word "writing," and that not fortuitously. For some time now, as a matter of fact, here and there, by a gesture and for motives that are profoundly necessary, whose degradation is easier to denounce than it is to disclose their origin, one says "language" for action, movement, thought, reflection, consciousness, unconsciousness, experience, affectivity, etc. Now we tend to say "writing" for all that and more: to designate not only the physical gestures of literal pictographic or ideographic inscription, but also the totality of what makes it possible; and also, beyond the signifying face, the signified face itself. And thus we say "writing" for all that gives rise to an inscription in general, whether it is literal or not and even if what it distributes in space is alien to the order of the voice: cinematography, choreography, of course, but also pictorial, musical, sculptural "writing." One might also speak of athletic writing, and with even greater certainty of military or political writing in view of the techniques that govern those domains today. All this to describe not only the system of notation secondarily connected with these activities but the essence and the content of these activities themselves. It is also in this sense that the contemporary biologist speaks of writing and *pro-gram* in relation to the most elementary processes of information within the living cell. And, finally, whether it has essential limits or not, the entire field covered by the cybernetic *program* will be the field of writing. If the theory of cybernetics is by itself to oust all metaphysical concepts – including the concepts of soul, of life, of value, of choice, of memory – which until recently served to separate the machine from man,[8] it must conserve the notion of writing, trace, grammè [written mark], or grapheme, until its own historico-metaphysical character is also exposed. Even before being determined as human (with all the distinctive characteristics that have always been attributed to man and the entire system of significations that they imply) or nonhuman, the *grammè* – or the *grapheme* – would thus name the element. An element without simplicity. An element, whether it is understood as the medium or as the irreducible atom, of the arche-synthesis in general, of what one must forbid oneself to define within the system of oppositions of metaphysics, of what consequently one should not even call *experience* in general, that is to say the origin of *meaning* in general.

This situation has always already been announced. Why is it today in the process of making itself known *as such* and *after the fact*? This question would call forth an interminable analysis. Let us simply choose some points of departure in order to introduce the limited remarks to which I shall confine myself. I have already alluded to *theoretical* mathematics; its writing – whether understood as a sensible *graphie* [manner of writing] (and that already presupposes an identity, therefore an ideality, of its form, which in principle renders absurd the so easily admitted notion of the "sensible signifier"), or understood as the ideal synthesis of signifieds or a trace operative on another level, or whether it is understood, more profoundly, as the *passage* of the one to the other – has never been absolutely linked with a phonetic production. Within cultures practicing so-called phonetic writing, mathematics is not just an enclave. That is mentioned by all historians of writing; they recall at the same time the imperfections of alphabetic writing, which passed for so long as the most convenient and "the most intelligent"[9] writing. This enclave is also the place where the practice of scientific language challenges intrinsically and with increasing profundity the ideal of phonetic writing and all its implicit metaphysics (metaphysics *itself*), particularly, that is, the philosophical idea of the *epistémè*; also of *istoria*, a concept profoundly related to it in spite of the dissociation or opposition which has distinguished one from the other during one phase of their common progress. History and knowledge, *istoria* and *epistémè* have always been determined (and not only

etymologically or philosophically) as detours *for the purpose* of the reappropriation of presence.

But beyond theoretical mathematics, the development of the *practical methods* of information retrieval extends the possibilities of the "message" vastly, to the point where it is no longer the "written" translation of a language, the transporting of a signified which could remain spoken in its integrity. It goes hand in hand with an extension of phonography and of all the means of conserving the spoken language, of making it function without the presence of the speaking subject. This development, coupled with that of anthropology and of the history of writing, teaches us that phonetic writing, the medium of the great metaphysical, scientific, technical, and economic adventure of the West, is limited in space and time and limits itself even as it is in the process of imposing its laws upon the cultural areas that had escaped it. But this nonfortuitous conjunction of cybernetics and the "human sciences" of writing leads to a more profound reversal.

The signifier and truth

The "rationality" – but perhaps that word should be abandoned for reasons that will appear at the end of this sentence – which governs a writing thus enlarged and radicalized, no longer issues from a logos. Further, it inaugurates the destruction, not the demolition but the de-sedimentation, the deconstruction, of all the significations that have their source in that of the logos. Particularly the signification of *truth*. All the metaphysical determinations of truth, and even the one beyond metaphysical ontotheology that Heidegger reminds us of, are more or less immediately inseparable from the instance of the logos, or of a reason thought within the lineage of the logos, in whatever sense it is understood: in the pre-Socratic or the philosophical sense, in the sense of God's infinite understanding or in the anthropological sense, in the pre-Hegelian or the post-Hegelian sense. Within this logos, the original and essential link to the *phonè* has never been broken. It would be easy to demonstrate this and I shall attempt such a demonstration later. As has been more or less implicitly determined, the essence of the *phonè* would be immediately proximate to that which within "thought" as logos relates to "meaning," produces it, receives it, speaks it, "composes" it. If, for Aristotle, for example, "spoken words (ta en tē phonē) are the symbols of mental experience (pathēmata tes psychēs) and written words are the symbols of spoken words" (*De interpretatione*, 1, 16a 3) it is because the voice, producer of *the first symbols*, has a relationship of essential and immediate proximity with the mind. Producer of the first signifier, it is not just a simple signifier among others. It signifies "mental experiences" which themselves reflect or mirror things by natural resemblance. Between being and mind, things and feelings, there would be a relationship of translation or natural signification; between mind and logos, a relationship of conventional symbolization. And the *first* convention, which would relate immediately to the order of natural and universal signification, would be produced as spoken language. Written language would establish the conventions, interlinking other conventions with them.

> Just as all men have not the same writing so all men have not the same speech sounds, but mental experiences, of which these are the *primary symbols* (*semeîa prótos*), are the same for all, as also are those things of which our experiences are the images. (*De interpretatione*, 1, 16a; italics added)

The feelings of the mind, expressing things naturally, constitute a sort of universal language which can then efface itself. It is the stage of transparence. Aristotle can sometimes omit it without risk.[10] In every case, the voice is closest to the signified, whether it is determined strictly as sense (thought or lived) or more loosely as thing. All signifiers, and first and foremost the written signifier, are derivative with regard to what would wed the voice indissolubly to the mind or to the thought of the signified sense, indeed to the thing itself (whether it is done in the Aristotelian manner that we have just indicated or in the manner of medieval theology, determining the *res* as a thing created from its *eidos*, from its sense thought in the logos or in the infinite understanding of God). The written signifier is always technical and representative. It has no constitutive meaning. This derivation is the very origin of the notion of the "signifier." The notion of the sign always implies within itself the distinction between signifier and signified, even if, as Saussure argues, they are distinguished simply as the two faces of one and the same leaf. This notion remains therefore within the heritage of that logocentrism which is also a phonocentrism: absolute proximity of voice and being, of voice and the meaning of being, of voice and the ideality of mean-

ing. Hegel demonstrates very clearly the strange privilege of sound in idealization, the production of the concept and the self-presence of the subject.

> This ideal motion, in which through the sound what is as it were the simple subjectivity [*Subjektivität*], the soul of the material thing expresses itself, the ear receives also in a theoretical [*theoretisch*] way, just as the eye shape and color, thus allowing the interiority of the object to become interiority itself [*läßt dadurch das Innere der Gegenstände für das Innere selbst werden*] (*Esthétique*, III. I tr. fr. p. 16).[11] ... The ear, on the contrary, perceives [*vernimmt*] the result of that interior vibration of material substance without placing itself in a practical relation toward the objects, a result by means of which it is no longer the material form [*Gestalt*] in its repose, but the first, more ideal activity of the soul itself which is manifested [*zum Vorschein kommt*] (p. 296).[12]

What is said of sound in general is *a fortiori* valid for the *phonè* by which, by virtue of hearing (understanding) oneself-speak – an indissociable system – the subject affects itself and is related to itself in the element of ideality.

We already have a foreboding that phonocentrism merges with the historical determination of the meaning of being in general as *presence* with all the subdeterminations which depend on this general form and which organize within it their system and their historical sequence (presence of the thing to the sight as *eidos*, presence as substance/essence/existence [*ousia*], temporal presence as point [*stigmè*] of the now or of the moment [*nun*], the self-presence of the *cogito*, consciousness, subjectivity, the co-presence of the other and of the self, intersubjectivity as the intentional phenomenon of the ego, and so forth). Logocentrism would thus support the determination of the being of the entity as presence. To the extent that such a logocentrism is not totally absent from Heidegger's thought, perhaps it still holds that thought within the epoch of ontotheology, within the philosophy of presence, that is to say within philosophy *itself*. This would perhaps mean that one does not leave the epoch whose closure one can outline. The movements of belonging or not belonging to the epoch are too subtle, the illusions in that regard are too easy, for us to make a definite judgment.

The epoch of the logos thus debases writing considered as mediation of mediation and as a fall into the exteriority of meaning. To this epoch belongs the difference between signified and signifier, or at least the strange separation of their "parallelism," and the exteriority, however extenuated, of the one to the other. This appurtenance is organized and hierarchized in a history. The difference between signified and signifier belongs in a profound and implicit way to the totality of the great epoch covered by the history of metaphysics, and in a more explicit and more systematically articulated way to the narrower epoch of Christian creationism and infinitism when these appropriate the resources of Greek conceptuality. This appurtenance is essential and irreducible; one cannot retain the convenience or the "scientific truth" of the Stoic and later medieval opposition between *signans* and *signatum* without also bringing with it all its metaphysico-theological roots. To these roots adheres not only the distinction between the sensible and the intelligible – already a great deal – with all that it controls, namely, metaphysics in its totality. And this distinction is generally accepted as self-evident by the most careful linguists and semiologists, even by those who believe that the scientificity of their work begins where metaphysics ends. Thus, for example:

As modern structural thought has clearly realized, language is a system of signs and linguistics is part and parcel of the science of signs, or *semiotics* (Saussure's *sémiologie*). The medieval definition of sign – "*aliquid stat pro aliquo*" – has been resurrected and put forward as still valid and productive. Thus the constitutive mark of any sign in general and of any linguistic sign in particular is its twofold character: every linguistic unit is bipartite and involves both aspects – one sensible and the other intelligible, or in other words, both the *signans* "signifier" (Saussure's *signifiant*) and the *signatum* "signified" (*signifié*). These two constituents of a linguistic sign (and of sign in general) necessarily suppose and require each other.[13]

But to these metaphysico-theological roots many other hidden sediments cling. The semiological or, more specifically, linguistic "science" cannot therefore hold on to the difference between signifier and signified – the very idea of the sign – without the difference between sensible and intelligible, certainly, but also not without retaining, more profoundly and more implicitly, and by the same token the reference to a signified able to "take place" in

its intelligibility, before its "fall," before any expulsion into the exteriority of the sensible here below. As the face of pure intelligibility, it refers to an absolute logos to which it is immediately united. This absolute logos was an infinite creative subjectivity in medieval theology: the intelligible face of the sign remains turned toward the word and the face of God.

Of course, it is not a question of "rejecting" these notions; they are necessary and, at least at present, nothing is conceivable for us without them. It is a question at first of demonstrating the systematic and historical solidarity of the concepts and gestures of thought that one often believes can be innocently separated. The sign and divinity have the same place and time of birth. The age of the sign is essentially theological. Perhaps it will never *end*. Its historical *closure* is, however, outlined.

Since these concepts are indispensable for unsettling the heritage to which they belong, we should be even less prone to renounce them. Within the closure, by an oblique and always perilous movement, constantly risking falling back within what is being deconstructed, it is necessary to surround the critical concepts with a careful and thorough discourse – to mark the conditions, the medium, and the limits of their effectiveness and to designate rigorously their intimate relationship to the machine whose deconstruction they permit; and, in the same process, designate the crevice through which the yet unnameable glimmer beyond the closure can be glimpsed. The concept of the sign is here exemplary. We have just marked its metaphysical appurtenance. We know, however, that the thematics of the sign have been for about a century the agonized labor of a tradition that professed to withdraw meaning, truth, presence, being, etc., from the movement of signification. Treating as suspect, as I just have, the difference between signified and signifier, or the idea of the sign in general, I must state explicitly that it is not a question of doing so in terms of the instance of the present truth, anterior, exterior, or superior to the sign, or in terms of the place of the effaced difference. Quite the contrary. We are disturbed by that which, in the concept of the sign – which has never existed or functioned outside the history of (the) philosophy (of presence) – remains systematically and genealogically determined by that history. It is there that the concept and above all the work of deconstruction, its "style," remain by nature exposed to misunderstanding and nonrecognition.

The exteriority of the signifier is the exteriority of writing in general, and I shall try to show later that there is no linguistic sign before writing. Without that exteriority, the very idea of the sign falls into decay. Since our entire world and language would collapse with it, and since its evidence and its value keep, to a certain point of derivation, an indestructible solidity, it would be silly to conclude from its placement within an epoch that it is necessary to "move on to something else," to dispose of the sign, of the term and the notion. For a proper understanding of the gesture that we are sketching here, one must understand the expressions "epoch," "closure of an epoch," "historical genealogy" in a new way; and must first remove them from all relativism.

Thus, within this epoch, reading and writing, the production or interpretation of signs, the text in general as fabric of signs, allow themselves to be confined within secondariness. They are preceded by a truth, or a meaning already constituted by and within the element of the logos. Even when the thing, the "referent," is not immediately related to the logos of a creator God where it began by being the spoken/thought sense, the signified has at any rate an immediate relationship with the logos in general (finite or infinite), and a mediated one with the signifier, that is to say with the exteriority of writing. When it seems to go otherwise, it is because a metaphoric mediation has insinuated itself into the relationship and has simulated immediacy; the writing of truth in the soul, opposed by *Phaedrus* (278a) to bad writing (writing in the "literal" [*propre*] and ordinary sense, "sensible" writing, "in space"), the book of Nature and God's writing, especially in the Middle Ages; all that functions as *metaphor* in these discourses confirms the privilege of the logos and founds the "literal" meaning then given to writing: a sign signifying a signifier itself signifying an eternal verity, eternally thought and spoken in the proximity of a present logos. The paradox to which attention must be paid is this: natural and universal writing, intelligible and nontemporal writing, is thus named by metaphor. A writing that is sensible, finite, and so on, is designated as writing in the literal sense; it is thus thought on the side of culture, technique, and artifice; a human procedure, the ruse of a being accidentally incarnated or of a finite creature. Of course, this metaphor remains enigmatic and refers to a "literal" meaning of writing as the first metaphor. This "literal" meaning is yet unthought by the adherents of this discourse. It is not, there-fore, a matter of inverting the literal meaning and the figurative meaning but of determining the "literal" meaning of writing as metaphoricity itself.

In "The Symbolism of the Book," that excellent chapter of *European Literature and the Latin Middle Ages*, E. R. Curtius describes with great wealth of examples the evolution that led from the *Phaedrus* to Calderon, until it seemed to be "precisely the reverse" (tr. fr. p. 372)[14] by the "newly attained position of the book" (p. 374) [p. 306]. But it seems that this modification, however important in fact it might be, conceals a fundamental continuity. As was the case with the Platonic writing of the truth in the soul, in the Middle Ages too it is a writing understood in the metaphoric sense, that is to say a *natural*, eternal, and universal writing, the system of signified truth, which is recognized in its dignity. As in the *Phaedrus*, a certain fallen writing continues to be opposed to it. There remains to be written a history of this metaphor, a metaphor that systematically contrasts divine or natural writing and the human and laborious, finite and artificial inscription. It remains to articulate rigorously the stages of that history, as marked by the quotations below, and to follow the theme of God's book (nature or law, indeed natural law) through all its modifications.

Rabbi Eliezer said: "If all the seas were of ink, and all ponds planted with reeds, if the sky and the earth were parchments and if all human beings practised the art of writing – they would not exhaust the Torah I have learned, just as the Torah itself would not be diminished any more than is the sea by the water removed by a paint brush dipped in it."[15]

Galileo: "It [the book of Nature] is written in a mathematical language."[16]

Descartes: "... to read in the great book of Nature..."[17]

Demea, in the name of natural religion, in the *Dialogues* of Hume: "And this volume of nature contains a great and inexplicable riddle, more than any intelligible discourse or reasoning."[18]

Bonnet: "It would seem more philosophical to me to presume that our earth is a book that God has given to intelligences far superior to ours to read, and where they study in depth the infinitely multiplied and varied characters of His adorable wisdom."

G. H. von Schubert: "This language made of images and hieroglyphs, which supreme Wisdom uses in all its revelations to humanity – which is found in the inferior [*nieder*] language of poetry – and which, in the most inferior and imperfect way [*auf der allerniedrigsten und unvollkommensten*], is more like the metaphorical expression of the dream than the prose of wakefulness, . . . we may wonder if this language is not the true and wakeful language of the superior regions. If, when we consider ourselves awakened, we are not plunged in a millennial slumber, or at least in the echo of its dreams, where we only perceive a few isolated and obscure words of God's language, as a sleeper perceives the conversation of the people around him."[19]

Jaspers: "The world is the manuscript of an other, inaccessible to a universal reading, which only existence deciphers."[20]

Above all, the profound differences distinguishing all these treatments of the same metaphor must not be ignored. In the history of this treatment, the most decisive separation appears at the moment when, at the same time as the science of nature, the determination of absolute presence is constituted as self-presence, as subjectivity. It is the moment of the great rationalisms of the seventeenth century. From then on, the condemnation of fallen and finite writing will take another form, within which we still live: it is non-self-presence that will be denounced. Thus the exemplariness of the "Rousseauist" moment, which we shall deal with later, begins to be explained. Rousseau repeats the Platonic gesture by referring to another model of presence: self-presence in the senses, in the sensible *cogito*, which simultaneously carries in itself the inscription of divine law. On the one hand, *representative*, fallen, secondary, instituted writing, writing in the literal and strict sense, is condemned in *The Essay on the Origin of Languages* (it "enervates" speech; to "judge genius" from books is like "painting a man's portrait from his corpse," etc.). Writing in the common sense is the dead letter, it is the carrier of death. It exhausts life. On the other hand, on the other face of the same proposition, writing in the metaphoric sense, natural, divine, and living writing, is venerated; it is equal in dignity to the origin of value, to the voice of conscience as divine law, to the heart, to sentiment, and so forth.

The Bible is the most sublime of all books, . . . but it is after all a book. . . . It is not at all in a few sparse pages that one should look for God's law, but in the human heart where His hand deigned to write (*Lettre à Vernes*).[21]

If the natural law had been written only in the human reason, it would be little capable of directing most of our actions. But it is also engraved in the heart of man in ineffacable characters. . . . There it cries to him (*L'État de guerre*.)[22]

Natural writing is immediately united to the voice and to breath. Its nature is not grammatological but pneumatological. It is hieratic, very close to the interior holy voice of the *Profession of Faith*, to the voice one hears upon retreating into oneself: full and truthful presence of the divine voice to our inner sense: "The more I retreat into myself, the more I consult myself, the more plainly do I read these words written in my soul: be just and you will be happy. . . . I do not derive these rules from the principles of the higher philosophy, I find them in the depths of my heart written by nature in characters which nothing can efface."[23]

There is much to say about the fact that the native unity of the voice and writing is *prescriptive*. Arche-speech is writing because it is a law. A natural law. The beginning word is understood, in the intimacy of self-presence, as the voice of the other and as commandment.

There is therefore a good and a bad writing: the good and natural is the divine inscription in the heart and the soul; the perverse and artful is technique, exiled in the exteriority of the body. A modification well within the Platonic diagram: writing of the soul and of the body, writing of the interior and of the exterior, writing of conscience and of the passions, as there is a voice of the soul and a voice of the body. "Conscience is the voice of the soul, the passions are the voice of the body" [p. 249]. One must constantly go back toward the "voice of nature," the "holy voice of nature," that merges with the divine inscription and prescription; one must encounter oneself within it, enter into a dialogue within its signs, speak and respond to oneself in its pages.

It was as if nature had spread out all her magnificence in front of our eyes to offer its text for our consideration. . . . I have therefore closed all the books. Only one is open to all eyes. It is the book of Nature. In this great and sublime book I learn to serve and adore its author.

The good writing has therefore always been *comprehended*. Comprehended as that which had to be comprehended: within a nature or a natural law, created or not, but first thought within an eternal presence. Comprehended, therefore, within a totality, and enveloped in a volume or a book. The idea of the book is the idea of a totality, finite or infinite, of the signifier; this totality of the signifier cannot be a totality, unless a totality constituted by the signified pre-exists it, supervises its

inscriptions and its signs, and is independent of it in its ideality. The idea of the book, which always refers to a natural totality, is profoundly alien to the sense of writing. It is the encyclopedic protection of theology and of logocentrism against the disruption of writing, against its aphoristic energy, and, as I shall specify later, against difference in general. If I distinguish the text from the book, I shall say that the destruction of the book, as it is now under way in all domains, denudes the surface of the text. That necessary violence responds to a violence that was no less necessary.

Notes

1 Cf. for example, the notions of "secondary elaboration" or "symbolism of second intention" in Edmond Ortigues, *Le Discours et le symbole* (Aubier, 1962) pp. 62 and 171. "Mathematical symbolism is a convention of writing, a scriptual symbolism. It is only by an abuse of vocabulary or by analogy that one speaks of a 'mathematical language.' Algorithm is actually a 'characteristics,' it is composed of written characters. It does not speak, except through the intermediary of a language which furnishes not only the phonetic expression of the characters, but also the formulation of axioms permitting the determination of the value of these characters. It is true that at a pinch one could decipher unknown characters, but that always supposes an acquired knowledge, a thought already formed by the usage of speech. Therefore, in all hypothesis, mathematical symbolism is the fruit of a secondary elaboration, supposing preliminarily the usage of discourse and the possibility of conceiving explicit conventions. It is nevertheless true that mathematical algorithm will express the formal laws of symbolization, of syntactic structures, independent of particular means of expression." On these problems, cf. also Gilles Gaston Granger, *Pensée formelle et sciences de l'homme* (Paris, 1960), pp. 38 ff. and particularly pp. 43 and 50 ff. (on the "Reversal of Relationships between the Spoken Language and Writing").

2 All works on the history of writing devote space to the problem of the introduction of phonetic writing in the cultures that did not practice it previously. Cf. e.g. *EP*, pp. 44 ff. or "La Reforme de l'écriture chinoise," *Linguistique, Recherches internationales à la lumière du marxisme* 7 (May–June 1958).

3 Here I do not merely mean those "theological prejudices" which, at an identifiable time and place, inflected or repressed the theory of the written sign in the seventeenth and eighteenth centuries. I shall speak of them later in connection with Madeleine V.-David's book. These prejudices are nothing but

the most clearsighted and best circumscribed, historically determined manifestation of a constitutive and permanent presupposition essential to the history of the West, therefore to metaphysics in its entirety, even when it professes to be atheist.

4 *Grammatology*: "A treatise upon Letters, upon the alphabet, syllabation, reading, and writing," Littré. To my knowledge and in our time, this word has only been used by I. J. Gelb to designate the project of a modern science in *A Study of Writing: The Foundations of Grammatology* [Chicago], 1952 (the subtitle disappears in the 1963 edition). In spite of a concern for systematic or simplified classification, and in spite of the controversial hypotheses on the monogenesis or polygenesis of scripts, this book follows the classical model of histories of writing.

5 "Aus dem Gedankenkreise der Geburt der Tragödie," I. 3. *Nietzsche Werke* (Leipzig, 1903), vol. 9, part 2, i, p. 66. (Trans.)

6 To speak of a primary writing here does not amount to affirming a chronological priority of fact. That debate is well known; is writing, as affirmed, for example, by Metchaninov and Marr, then Loukotka, "anterior to phonetic language?" (A conclusion assumed by the first edition of the Great Soviet Encyclopedia, later contradicted by Stalin. On this debate, cf. V. Istrine, "Langue et écriture," *Linguistique*, pp. 35, 60. This debate also forms around the theses advanced by P. van Ginneken. On the discussion of these propositions, cf. James Février, *Histoire de l'écriture* [Payot, 1948–59], pp. 5 ff.). I shall try to show below why the terms and premises of such a debate are suspicious.

7 I shall deal with this problem more directly in *La Voix et le phénomène* (Paris, 1967) [*Speech and Phenomenon*]. (Evanston, Ill.: Northwestern University Press, 1973).

8 Wiener, for example, while abandoning "semantics," and the opposition, judged by him as too crude and

363

too general, between animate and inanimate etc., nevertheless continues to use expressions like "organs of sense," "motor organs," etc. to qualify the parts of the machine.

9   Cf., e.g., *EP*, pp. 126, 148, 355, etc. From another point of view, cf. Roman Jakobson, *Essais de linguistique générale* (tr. fr. [Nicolas Ruwet, Paris, 1963], p. 116) [Jakobson and Morris Halle, *Fundamentals of Language* (the Hague, 1956), p. 16].

10 This is shown by Pierre Aubenque (*Le Problème de l'être chez Aristote* [Paris, 1966], pp. 106 ff.). In the course of a provocative analysis, to which I am here indebted, Aubenque remarks: "In other texts, to be sure, Aristotle designates as symbol the relationship between language and things: 'It is not possible to bring the things themselves to the discussion, but, instead of things, we can use their names as symbols.' The intermediary constituted by the mental experience is here suppressed or at least neglected, but this suppression is legitimate, since, mental experiences behaving like things, things can be substituted for them immediately. On the other hand, one cannot by any means substitute names for things" (pp. 107–8).

11 Georg Wilhelm Friedrich Hegel, *Werke*, Suhrkamp edition (Frankfurt am Main, 1970), vol. 14, p. 256; translated as *The Philosophy of Fine Art* by F. P. Osmaston (London, 1920), vol. 3, pp. 15–16. (Trans.)

12 Hegel, p. 134; Osmaston, p. 341. (Trans.)

13 Roman Jakobson, *Essais de linguistique générale*, tr. fr., p. 162 ["The Phonemic and Grammatical Aspects of Language in their Interrelations," *Proceedings of the Sixth International Congress of Linguistics* (Paris, 1949), p. 6]. On this problem, on

the tradition of the concept of the sign, and on the originality of Saussure's contribution within this continuity, cf. Ortigues, *Les Discours*, pp. 54ff.

14 Ernst Robert Curtius, "Das Buch als Symbol," *Europäische Literatur und lateinisches Mittelalter* (Bern, 1948), p. 307. French translation by Jean Bréjoux (Paris, 1956): translated as *European Literature and the Latin Middle Ages*, by Willard R. Trask, Harper Torchbooks edition (New York, 1963), pp. 305, 306. (Trans.)

15 Cited by Emmanuel Levinas, in *Difficile liberté* [Paris, 1963], p. 44.

16 Quoted in Curtius, "Das Buch" (German), p. 326, (English), p. 324; Galileo's word is "philosophy" rather than "nature." (Trans.)

17 Ibid. (German) p. 324, (English) p. 322. (Trans.)

18 David Hume, *Dialogues Concerning Natural Religion*, ed. Norman Kemp Smith (Oxford, 1935), p. 193. (Trans.)

19 Gotthilf Heinrich von Schubert, *Die Symbolik des Traumes* (Leipzig, 1862), pp. 23–4. (Trans.)

20 Quoted in Paul Ricoeur, *Gabriel Marcel et Karl Jaspers* (Paris, 1947), p. 45. (Trans.)

21 *Correspondance complète de Jean Jacques Rousseau*, ed. R. A. Leigh (Geneva, 1967), vol. V, pp. 65–6. The original reads "l'évangile" rather than "la Bible." (Trans.)

22 Rousseau, *Oeuvres complètes*, Pléiade edition, vol. III, p. 602. (Trans.)

23 Derrida's reference is *Emile*, Pléiade edition, vol. 4, pp. 589, 594. My reference is *Emile*, tr. Barbara Foxley (London, 1911), pp. 245, 249. Subsequent references to this translation are placed within brackets. (Trans.)

Select Bibliography

Aporias. Translated by Thomas Dutoit. Stanford: Stanford University Press, 1993.

A Derrida Reader: Between the Blinds. Edited by Peggy Kamuf. New York: Columbia University Press, 1991.

Edmund Husserl's Origin of Geometry: An Introduction. Translated by John P. Leavey, Jr. Lincoln: University of Nebraska Press, 1989.

Margins of Philosophy. Translated by Alan Bass. Chicago: University of Chicago Press, 1982.

Memoires: For Paul de Man. Translated by Cecile Lindsay, Jonathan Culler, and Eduardo Cadava. New York: Columbia University Press, 1989.

Memoirs of the Blind: The Self-Portrait and Other Ruins. Translated by Pascale-Anne Brault and Michael Naas. Chicago: University of Chicago Press, 1993.

Of Grammatology. Translated by Gayatri Chakravorty Spivak. Baltimore: Johns Hopkins University Press, 1984.

Of Spirit: Heidegger and the Question. Translated by Geoffrey Bennington and Rachel Bowlby. Chicago: University of Chicago Press, 1989.

The Other Heading: Reflections on Today's Europe. Translated by Pascale-Anne Brault and Michael Naas. Bloomington: Indiana University Press, 1992.

The Post Card: From Socrates to Freud and Beyond. Translated by Alan Bass. Chicago: University of Chicago Press, 1987.

Specters of Marx: The State of the Debt, the Work of Mourning, and the New International. Translated by Peggy Kamuf. New York: Routledge, 1994.

Speech and Phenomena, and Other Essays on Husserl's Theory of Signs. Translated by David B. Allison. Evanston, Ill.: Northwestern University Press, 1973.

Spurs: Nietzsche's Styles/ Eperons: Les Styles de Nietzsche. Translated by Barbara Harlow. Chicago: University of Chicago Press, 1979.

Writing and Difference. Translated by Alan Bass. Chicago: University of Chicago Press, 1978.

4

Gilles Deleuze and Félix Guattari

French philosopher Gilles Deleuze (1925–95) and psychoanalyst Félix Guattari (1930–92) collaborated on a number of texts in addition to individually authored books and articles. In their most famous work, *Anti-Oedipus*, they attack the representational structures of psychoanalysis and capitalism that appeal to a "Platonic logic of desire" formulated in terms of lack. By contrast, Deleuze and Guattari emphasize the essential productivity and dynamism of desire. In the following selections from *Anti-Oedipus*, their critique is directed toward the representations of ego and self in psychoanalysis, which aims at the restoration of the healthy ego-subject. In place of such representations, Deleuze and Guattari take the schizophrenic as a model of "desiring-production," and the notion of a "desiring machine" is set against a traditional psychoanalytic view of desire as presupposing an ego-subject and constituted by lack.

Anti-Oedipus: Capitalism and Schizophrenia

The Desiring-Machines

1 Desiring-Production

It is at work everywhere, functioning smoothly at times, at other times in fits and starts. It breathes, it heats, it eats. It shits and fucks. What a mistake to

From *Anti-Oedipus: Capitalism and Schizophrenia*, translated by Robert Hurley, Mark Seem, and Helen R. Lane (London: Athlone Press, 1984), pp. 1–8, 23–4, 25–7, 28–9, 35. Translation copyright © 1977 by Viking Penguin Inc., English language translation © University of Minnesota Press, 1983. Used by permission of Viking Penguin, a division of Penguin Books USA Inc., and the Athlone Press.

have ever said *the* id. Everywhere *it* is machines – real ones, not figurative ones: machines driving other machines, machines being driven by other machines, with all the necessary couplings and connections. An organ-machine is plugged into an energy-source-machine: the one produces a flow that the other interrupts. The breast is a machine that produces milk, and the mouth a machine coupled to it. The mouth of the anorexic wavers between several functions: its possessor is uncertain as to whether it is an eating-machine, an anal-machine, a talking-machine, or a breathing-machine (asthma attacks). Hence we are all handymen: each with his little machines. For every organ-machine, an energy-machine: all the time, flows and interruptions. Judge Schreber[1] has sunbeams in his ass. *A solar anus.* And rest assured that it works: Judge Schreber feels something, produces something, and is capable of explaining the process theoretically. Something is produced: the effects of a machine, not mere metaphors.

A schizophrenic out for a walk is a better model than a neurotic lying on the analyst's couch. A breath of fresh air, a relationship with the outside world. Lenz's stroll, for example, as reconstructed by Büchner. This walk outdoors is different from the moments when Lenz finds himself closeted with his pastor, who forces him to situate himself socially, in relationship to the God of established religion, in relationship to his father, to his mother. While taking a stroll outdoors, on the other hand, he is in the mountains, amid falling snowflakes, with other gods or without any gods at all, without a family, without a father or a mother, with nature. "What does my father want? Can he offer me more than that? Impossible. Leave me in peace."[2] Everything is a machine. Celestial machines, the stars or rainbows in the sky, alpine machines – all of them connected to those of his body. The continual whirr of machines. "He thought that it must be a feeling of endless bliss to be in contact with the profound life of every form, to have a soul for rocks, metals, water, and plants, to take into himself, as in a dream, every element of nature, like flowers that breathe with the waxing and waning of the moon."[3] To be a chlorophyll- or a photosynthesis-machine, or at least slip his body into such machines as one part among the others. Lenz has projected himself back to a time before the man–nature dichotomy, before all the coordinates based on this fundamental dichotomy have been laid down. He does not live nature as nature, but as a process of production. There is no such thing as either man or nature now, only a process that produces the one within the other and couples the machines together. Producing-machines, desiring-machines everywhere, schizophrenic machines, all of species life: the self and the nonself, outside and inside, no longer have any meaning whatsoever.

Now that we have had a look at this stroll of a schizo, let us compare what happens when Samuel Beckett's characters decide to venture outdoors. Their various gaits and methods of self-locomotion constitute, in and of themselves, a finely tuned machine. And then there is the function of the bicycle in Beckett's works: what relationship does the bicycle-horn machine have with the mother-anus machine? "What a rest to speak of bicycles and horns. Unfortunately it is not of them I have to speak, but of her who brought me into the world, through the hole in her arse if my memory is correct."[4] It is often thought that Oedipus[5] is an easy subject to deal with, something perfectly obvious, a "given" that is there from the very beginning. But that is not so at all: Oedipus presupposes a fantastic repression of desiring-machines. And why are they repressed? To what end? Is it really necessary or desirable to submit to such repression? And what means are to be used to accomplish this? What ought to go inside the Oedipal triangle, what sort of thing is required to construct it? Are a bicycle horn and my mother's arse sufficient to do the job? Aren't there more important questions than these, however? Given a certain effect, what machine is capable of producing it? And given a certain machine, what can it be used for? Can we possibly guess, for instance, what a knife rest is used for if all we are given is a geometrical description of it? Or yet another example: on being confronted with a complete machine made up of six stones in the right-hand pocket of my coat (the pocket that serves as the source of the stones), five stones in the right-hand pocket of my trousers, and five in the left-hand pocket (transmission pockets), with the remaining pocket of my coat receiving the stones that have already been handled, as each of the stones moves forward one pocket, how can we determine the effect of this circuit of distribution in which the mouth, too, plays a role as a stone-sucking machine? Where in this entire circuit do we find the production of sexual pleasure? At the end of *Malone Dies*, Lady Pedal takes the schizophrenics out for a ride in a van and a rowboat, and on a picnic in the midst of nature: an infernal machine is being assembled. "Under the skin the body is an over-heated factory,/ and outside,/ the invalid shines,/ glows,/ from every burst pore."[6]

This does not mean that we are attempting to make nature one of the poles of schizophrenia. What the schizophrenic experiences, both as an individual and as a member of the human species, is not at all any one specific aspect of nature, but nature as a process of production. What do we mean here by process? It is probable that at a certain level nature and industry are two separate and distinct things: from one point of view, industry is the opposite of nature; from another, industry extracts its raw materials from nature; from yet another, it returns its refuse to nature; and so on.

Even within society, this characteristic man–nature, industry–nature, society–nature relationship is responsible for the distinction of relatively autonomous spheres that are called production, distribution, consumption. But in general this entire level of distinctions, examined from the point of view of its formal developed structures, presupposes (as Marx has demonstrated) not only the existence of capital and the division of labor, but also the false consciousness that the capitalist being necessarily acquires, both of itself and of the supposedly fixed elements within an overall process. For the real truth of the matter – the glaring, sober truth that resides in delirium – is that there is no such thing as relatively independent spheres or circuits: production is immediately consumption and a recording process (*enregistrement*[7]), without any sort of mediation, and the recording process and consumption directly determine production, though they do so within the production process itself. Hence everything is production: *production of productions*, of actions and of passions; *productions of recording processes*, of distributions and of coordinates that serve as points of reference; *productions of consumptions*, of sensual pleasures, of anxieties, and of pain. Everything is production, since the recording processes are immediately consumed, immediately consummated, and these consumptions directly reproduced.[8] This is the first meaning of process as we use the term: incorporating recording and consumption within production itself, thus making them the productions of one and the same process.

Second, we make no distinction between man and nature: the human essence of nature and the natural essence of man become one within nature in the form of production or industry, just as they do within the life of man as a species. Industry is then no longer considered from the extrinsic point of view of utility, but rather from the point of view of its fundamental identity with nature as production of man and by man.[9] Not man as the king of creation, but rather as the being who is in intimate contact with the profound life of all forms or all types of beings, who is responsible for even the stars and animal life, and who ceaselessly plugs an organ-machine into an energy-machine, a tree into his body, a breast into his mouth, the sun into his asshole: the eternal custodian of the machines of the universe. This is the second meaning of process as we use the term: man and nature are not like two opposite terms confronting each other – not even in the sense of bipolar opposites within a relationship

of causation, ideation, or expression (cause and effect, subject and object, etc.); rather, they are one and the same essential reality, the producer-product. Production as process overtakes all idealistic categories and constitutes a cycle whose relationship to desire is that of an immanent principle. That is why desiring-production is the principal concern of a materialist psychiatry, which conceives of and deals with the schizo as *Homo natura*. This will be the case, however, only on one condition, which in fact constitutes the third meaning of process as we use the term: it must not be viewed as a goal or an end in itself, nor must it be confused with an infinite perpetuation of itself. Putting an end to the process or prolonging it indefinitely – which, strictly speaking, is tantamount to ending it abruptly and prematurely – is what creates the artificial schizophrenic found in mental institutions: a limp rag forced into autistic behavior, produced as an entirely separate and independent entity. D. H. Lawrence says of love: "We have pushed a process into a goal. The aim of any process is not the perpetuation of that process, but the completion thereof.... The process should work to a completion, not to some horror of intensification and extremity wherein the soul and body ultimately perish."[10] Schizophrenia is like love: there is no specifically schizophrenic phenomenon or entity; schizophrenia is the universe of productive and reproductive desiring-machines, universal primary production as "the essential reality of man and nature."

Desiring-machines are binary machines, obeying a binary law or set of rules governing associations: one machine is always coupled with another. The productive synthesis, the production of production, is inherently connective in nature: "and..." "and then..." This is because there is always a flow-producing machine, and another machine connected to it that interrupts or draws off part of this flow (the breast – the mouth). And because the first machine is in turn connected to another whose flow it interrupts or partially drains off, the binary series is linear in every direction. Desire constantly couples continuous flows and partial objects that are by nature fragmentary and fragmented. Desire causes the current to flow, itself flows in turn, and breaks the flows. "I love everything that flows, even the menstrual flow that carries away the seed unfecund."[11] Amniotic fluid spilling out of the sac and kidney stones; flowing hair; a flow of spittle, a flow of sperm, shit, or urine that are produced by partial objects and constantly cut off by other partial objects, which in turn produce other flows, interrupted by other partial objects. Every "object" presupposes the continuity of a flow; every flow, the fragmentation of the object. Doubtless each organ-machine interprets the entire world from the perspective of its own flux, from the point of view of the energy that flows from it: the eye interprets everything – speaking, understanding, shitting, fucking – in terms of seeing. But a connection with another machine is always established, along a transverse path, so that one machine interrupts the current of the other or "sees" its own current interrupted.

Hence the coupling that takes place within the partial object-flow connective synthesis also has another form: product/producing. Producing is always something "grafted onto" the product; and for that reason desiring-production is production of production, just as every machine is a machine connected to another machine. We cannot accept the idealist category of "expression" as a satisfactory or sufficient explanation of this phenomenon. We cannot, we must not attempt to describe the schizophrenic object without relating it to the process of production. The *Cahiers de l'art brut*[12] are a striking confirmation of this principle, since by taking such an approach they deny that there is any such thing as a specific, identifiable schizophrenic entity. Or to take another example, Henri Michaux describes a schizophrenic table in terms of a process of production which is that of desire: "Once noticed, it continued to occupy one's mind. It even persisted, as it were, in going about its own business.... The striking thing was that it was neither simple nor really complex, initially or intentionally complex, or constructed according to a complicated plan. Instead, it had been desimplified in the course of its carpentering.... As it stood, it was a table of additions, much like certain schizophrenics' drawings, described as 'over-stuffed,' and if finished it was only insofar as there was no way of adding anything more to it, the table having become more and more an accumulation, less and less a table.... It was not intended for any specific purpose, for anything one expects of a table. Heavy, cumbersome, it was virtually immovable. One didn't know how to handle it (mentally or physically). Its top surface, the useful part of the table, having been gradually reduced, was disappearing, with so little relation to the clumsy framework that the thing did not strike one as a table, but as some freak piece of furniture, an unfamiliar instrument ... for which

there was no purpose. A dehumanized table, nothing cozy about it, nothing 'middle class,' nothing rustic, nothing countrified, not a kitchen table or a work table. A table which lent itself to no function, self-protective, denying itself to service and communication alike. There was something stunned about it, something petrified. Perhaps it suggested a stalled engine."[13]

The schizophrenic is the universal producer. There is no need to distinguish here between producing and its product. We need merely note that the pure "thisness" of the object produced is carried over into a new act of producing. The table continues to "go about its business." The surface of the table, however, is eaten up by the supporting framework. The nontermination of the table is a necessary consequence of its mode of production. When Claude Lévi-Strauss defines *bricolage*,[14] he does so in terms of a set of closely related characteristics: the possession of a stock of materials or of rules of thumb that are fairly extensive, though more or less a hodgepodge – multiple and at the same time limited; the ability to rearrange fragments continually in new and different patterns or configurations; and as a consequence, an indifference toward the act of producing and toward the product, toward the set of instruments to be used and toward the overall result to be achieved.[15] The satisfaction the handyman experiences when he plugs something into an electric socket or diverts a stream of water can scarcely be explained in terms of "playing mommy and daddy," or by the pleasure of violating a taboo. The rule of continually producing production, of grafting producing onto the product, is a characteristic of desiring-machines or of primary production: the production of production. A painting by Richard Lindner, *Boy with Machine*, shows a huge, pudgy, bloated boy working one of his little desiring-machines, after having hooked it up to a vast technical social machine – which, as we shall see, is what even the very young child does.

Producing, a product: a producing/product identity. It is this identity that constitutes a third term in the linear series: an enormous undifferentiated object. Everything stops dead for a moment, everything freezes in place – and then the whole process will begin all over again. From a certain point of view it would be much better if nothing worked, if nothing functioned. Never being born, escaping the wheel of continual birth and rebirth, no mouth to suck with, no anus to shit through. Will the machines run so badly, their component pieces fall apart to such a point that they will return to nothingness and thus allow us to return to nothingness? It would seem, however, that the flows of energy are still too closely connected, the partial objects still too organic, for this to happen. What would be required is a pure fluid in a free state, flowing without interruption, streaming over the surface of a full body. Desiring-machines make us an organism; but at the very heart of this production, within the very production of this production, the body suffers from being organized in this way, from not having some other sort of organization, or no organization at all. "An incomprehensible, absolutely rigid stasis" in the very midst of process, as a third stage: "*No mouth. No tongue. No teeth. No larynx. No esophagus. No belly. No anus.*" The automata stop dead and set free the unorganized mass they once served to articulate. The full body without organs is the unproductive, the sterile, the unengendered, the unconsumable. Antonin Artaud discovered this one day, finding himself with no shape or form whatsoever, right there where he was at that moment. The death instinct: that is its name, and death is not without a model. For desire desires death also, because the full body of death is its motor, just as it desires life, because the organs of life are the *working machine*. We shall not inquire how all this fits together so that the machine will run: the question itself is the result of a process of abstraction.

Desiring-machines work only when they break down, and by continually breaking down. Judge Schreber "lived for a long time without a stomach, without intestines, almost without lungs, with a torn esophagus, without a bladder, and with shattered ribs; he used sometimes to swallow part of his own larynx with his food, etc."[16] The body without organs is nonproductive; nonetheless it is produced, at a certain place and a certain time in the connective synthesis, as the identity of producing and the product: the schizophrenic table is a body without organs. The body without organs is not the proof of an original nothingness, nor is it what remains of a lost totality. Above all, it is not a projection; it has nothing whatsoever to do with the body itself, or with an image of the body. It is the body without an image. This imageless, organless body, the nonproductive, exists right there where it is produced, in the third stage of the binary-linear series. It is perpetually reinserted into the process of production. The catatonic body is produced in the water of the hydrotherapy tub. The full body without organs belongs to the realm

of antiproduction; but yet another characteristic of the connective or productive synthesis is the fact that it couples production with antiproduction, with an element of antiproduction....

A Materialist Psychiatry

... The question as to how to deal analytically with the relationship between drives (*pulsions*) and symptoms, between the symbol and what is symbolized, has arisen again and again. Is this relationship to be considered *causal?* Or is it a relationship of *comprehension?* A mode of *expression?* The question, however, has been posed too theoretically. The fact is, from the moment that we are placed within the framework of Oedipus – from the moment that we are measured in terms of Oedipus – the cards are stacked against us, and the only real relationship, that of production, has been done away with. The great discovery of psychoanalysis was that of the production of desire, of the productions of the unconscious. But once Oedipus entered the picture, this discovery was soon buried beneath a new brand of idealism: a classical theater was substituted for the unconscious as a factory; representation was substituted for the units of production of the unconscious; and an unconscious that was capable of nothing but expressing itself – in myth, tragedy, dreams – was substituted for the productive unconscious....

To a certain degree, the traditional logic of desire is all wrong from the very outset: from the very first step that the Platonic logic of desire forces us to take, making us choose between *production* and *acquisition*. From the moment that we place desire on the side of acquisition, we make desire an idealistic (dialectical, nihilistic) conception, which causes us to look upon it as primarily a lack: a lack of an object, a lack of the real object....

In point of fact, if desire is the lack of the real object, its very nature as a real entity depends upon an "essence of lack" that produces the fantasized object. Desire thus conceived of as production, though merely the production of fantasies, has been explained perfectly by psychoanalysis. On the very lowest level of interpretation, this means that the real object that desire lacks is related to an extrinsic natural or social production, whereas desire intrinsically produces an imaginary object that functions as a double of reality, as though there were a "dreamed-of object behind every real object," or a mental production behind all real productions. This conception does not necessarily compel psychoanalysis to engage in a study of gadgets and markets, in the form of an utterly dreary and dull psychoanalysis of the object: psychoanalytic studies of packages of noodles, cars, or "thingumajigs." But even when the fantasy is interpreted in depth, not simply as an object, but as a specific machine that brings desire itself front and center, this machine is merely theatrical, and the complementarity of what it sets apart still remains: it is now need that is defined in terms of a relative lack and determined by its own object, whereas desire is regarded as what produces the fantasy and produces itself by detaching itself from the object, though at the same time it intensifies the lack by making it absolute: an "incurable insufficiency of being," an "inability-to-be that is life itself." Hence the presentation of desire as something *supported* by needs, while these needs, and their relationship to the object as something that is lacking or missing, continue to be the basis of the productivity of desire (theory of an underlying support). In a word, when the theoretician reduces desiring-production to a production of fantasy, he is content to exploit to the fullest the idealist principle that defines desire as a lack, rather than a process of production, of "industrial" production. Clément Rosset puts it very well: every time the emphasis is put on a lack that desire supposedly suffers from as a way of defining its object, "the world acquires as its double some other sort of world, in accordance with the following line of argument: there is an object that desire feels the lack of; hence the world does not contain each and every object that exists; there is at least one object missing, the one that desire feels the lack of; hence there exists some other place that contains the key to desire (missing in this world)."[17]

If desire produces, its product is real. If desire is productive, it can be productive only in the real world and can produce only reality. Desire is the set of *passive syntheses* that engineer partial objects, flows, and bodies, and that function as units of production. The real is the end product, the result of the passive syntheses of desire as autoproduction of the unconscious. Desire does not lack anything; it does not lack its object. It is, rather, the *subject* that is missing in desire, or desire that lacks a fixed subject; there is no fixed subject unless there is repression. Desire and its object are one and the same thing: the machine, as a machine of a machine. Desire is a machine, and the object of desire is another machine connected to it. Hence

the product is something removed or deducted from the process of producing: between the act of producing and the product, something becomes detached, thus giving the vagabond, nomad subject a residuum. The objective being of desire is the Real in and of itself.[18] There is no particular form of existence that can be labeled "psychic reality." As Marx notes, what exists in fact is not lack, but passion, as a "natural and sensuous object." Desire is not bolstered by needs, but rather the contrary; needs are derived from desire: they are counterproducts within the real that desire produces. Lack is a countereffect of desire; it is deposited, distributed, vacuolized within a real that is natural and social. Desire always remains in close touch with the conditions of objective existence; it embraces them and follows them, shifts when they shift, and does not outlive them. For that reason it so often becomes the desire to die, whereas need is a measure of the withdrawal of a subject that has lost its desire at the same time that it loses the passive syntheses of these conditions. This is precisely the significance of need as a search in a void: hunting about, trying to capture or become a parasite of passive syntheses in whatever vague world they may happen to exist in. It is no use saying: We are not green plants; we have long since been unable to synthesize chlorophyll, so it's necessary to eat.... Desire then becomes this abject fear of lacking something. But it should be noted that this is not a phrase uttered by the poor or the dispossessed. On the contrary, such people know that they are close to grass, almost akin to it, and that desire "needs" very few things – *not those leftovers that chance to come their way, but the very things that are continually taken from them* – and that what is missing is not things a subject feels the lack of somewhere deep down inside himself, but rather the objectivity of man, the objective being of man, for whom to desire is to produce, to produce within the realm of the real. ...

We know very well where lack – and its subjective correlative – come from. Lack (*manque*)[19] is created, planned, and organized in and through social production. It is counterproduced as a result of the pressure of antiproduction; the latter falls back on (*se rabat sur*) the forces of production and appropriates them. It is never primary; production is never organized on the basis of a pre-existing need or lack (*manque*). It is lack that infiltrates itself, creates empty spaces or vacuoles, and propagates itself in accordance with the organization of an already existing organization of production.[20]

The deliberate creation of lack as a function of market economy is the art of a dominant class. This involves deliberately organizing wants and needs (*manque*) amid an abundance of production; making all of desire teeter and fall victim to the great fear of not having one's needs satisfied; and making the object dependent upon a real production that is supposedly exterior to desire (the demands of rationality), while at the same time the production of desire is categorized as fantasy and nothing but fantasy.

There is no such thing as the social production of reality on the one hand, and a desiring-production that is mere fantasy on the other. The only connections that could be established between these two productions would be secondary ones of introjection and projection, as though all social practices had their precise counterpart in introjected or internal mental practices, or as though mental practices were projected upon social systems, without either of the two sets of practices ever having any real or concrete effect upon the other. As long as we are content to establish a perfect parallel between money, gold, capital, and the capitalist triangle on the one hand, and the libido, the anus, the phallus, and the family triangle on the other, we are engaging in an enjoyable pastime, but the mechanisms of money remain totally unaffected by the anal projections of those who manipulate money. The Marx–Freud parallelism between the two remains utterly sterile and insignificant as long as it is expressed in terms that make them introjections or projections of each other without ceasing to be utterly alien to each other, as in the famous equation money = shit. The truth of the matter is that *social production is purely and simply desiring-production itself under determinate conditions*. We maintain that the social field is immediately invested by desire, that it is the historically determined product of desire, and that libido has no need of any mediation or sublimation, any psychic operation, any transformation, in order to invade and invest the productive forces and the relations of production. *There is only desire and the social, and nothing else.*

Even the most repressive and the most deadly forms of social reproduction are produced by desire within the organization that is the consequence of such production under various conditions that we must analyze. That is why the fundamental problem of political philosophy is still precisely the one that Spinoza saw so clearly, and that Wilhelm Reich rediscovered: "Why do men fight *for* their servitude as stubbornly as though it were their salvation?" How can people possibly reach the point of shouting: "More taxes! Less bread!"? As Reich remarks, the astonishing thing is not that some people steal or that others occasionally go out on strike, but rather that all those who are starving do not steal as a regular practice, and all those who are exploited are not continually out on strike: after centuries of exploitation, why do people still tolerate being humiliated and enslaved, to such a point, indeed, that they *actually want* humiliation and slavery not only for others but for themselves? Reich is at his profoundest as a thinker when he refuses to accept ignorance or illusion on the part of the masses as an explanation of fascism, and demands an explanation that will take their desires into account, an explanation formulated in terms of desire: no, the masses were not innocent dupes; at a certain point, under a certain set of conditions, they *wanted* fascism, and it is this perversion of the desire of the masses that needs to be accounted for....[21]

There is no doubt that at this point in history the neurotic, the pervert, and the psychotic cannot be adequately defined in terms of drives, for drives are simply the desiring-machines themselves. They must be defined in terms of modern territorialities. The neurotic is trapped within the residual or artificial territorialities of our society, and reduces all of them (*les rabat toutes*) to Oedipus as the ultimate territoriality – as reconstructed in the analyst's office and projected upon the full body of the psychoanalyst (yes, my boss is my father, and so is the Chief of State, and so are you, Doctor). The pervert is someone who takes the artifice seriously and plays the game to the hilt: if you want them, you can have them – territorialities infinitely more artificial than the ones that society offers us, totally artificial new families, secret lunar societies. As for the schizo, continually wandering about, migrating here, there, and everywhere as best he can, he plunges further and further into the realm of deterritorialization, reaching the furthest limits of the decomposition of the socius on the surface of his own body without organs. It may well be that these peregrinations are the schizo's own particular way of rediscovering the earth. The schizophrenic deliberately seeks out the very limit of capitalism: he is its inherent tendency brought to fulfillment, its surplus product, its proletariat, and its exterminating angel. He scrambles all the codes and is the transmitter of the decoded flows of desire. The real continues to flow. In the schizo, the two aspects of *process* are conjoined: the metaphysical process that puts us in contact with the "demoniacal" element in nature or within the heart of the earth, and the historical process of social production that restores the autonomy of desiring-machines in relation to the deterritorialized social machine. Schizophrenia is desiring-production as the limit of social production. Desiring-production, and its difference in régime as compared to social production, are thus end points, not points of departure. Between the two there is nothing but an ongoing process of becoming that is the becoming of reality. And if materialist psychiatry may be defined as the psychiatry that introduces the concept of production into consideration of the problem of desire, it cannot avoid posing in eschatological terms the problem of the ultimate relationship between the analytic machine, the revolutionary machine, and desiring-machines.

Notes

1 Daniel Paul Schreber was a German judge who began psychiatric treatment in 1884 at the age of forty-two, and spent the remaining twenty-seven years of his life in and out of mental institutions. In 1903, at the age of sixty-one, he published his *Denkwürdigkeiten eines Nervenkranken (Memoirs of a Nervous Illness)*, which Freud used as the basis of his influential 1911 study on paranoia, "Psycho-Analytic Notes" (reference note 16, below). pp. 390–472. (Trans.)

2 See Georg Büchner, *Lenz*, in *Complete Plays and Prose*, trans. Carl Richard Mueller (New York: Hill & Wang, 1963), p. 141.

3 Ibid.

4 Samuel Beckett, *Molloy*, in *Three Novels by Samuel Beckett* (New York: Grove Press, 1959), p. 16. *Molloy* was translated from the French by Patrick Bowles in collaboration with the author. (Trans.)

5 As will be seen below, the term Oedipus has many widely varying connotations in this volume. It refers, for instance, not only to the Greek myth of Oedipus and to the Oedipus complex as defined by classical psychoanalysis, but also to Oedipal mechanisms, processes, and structures. The translators follow the authors' use and employ the word "Oedipus" by itself, using the more traditional term "Oedipus complex" only when the authors do so. (Trans.)

6 Antonin Artaud, *Van Gogh, the Man Suicided by Society*, trans. Mary Beach and Lawrence Ferlinghetti, in *Artaud Anthology* (San Francisco: City Lights Books, 1965), p. 158.

7 The French term *enregistrement* has a number of meanings, among them the process of making a recording to be played back by a mechanical device (e.g. a phonograph), the recording so made (e.g. a phonograph record or a magnetic tape), and the entering of births, deaths, deeds, marriages, and so on, in an official register. (Trans.)

8 When Georges Bataille speaks of sumptuary, nonproductive expenditures or consumptions in connection with the energy of nature, these are expenditures or consumptions that are not part of the supposedly independent sphere of human production, insofar as the latter is determined by "the useful." They therefore have to do with what we call the production of consumption. See Georges Bataille, *La Part maudite, précédé de La notion de dépense* (Paris: Editions de Minuit).

9 On the identity of nature and production, and species life in general, according to Marx, see the commentaries of Gérard Granel, "L'Ontologie marxiste de 1844 et la question de la coupure," in *L'Endurance de la pensée* (Paris: Plon, 1968), pp. 301–10.

10 D. H. Lawrence, *Aaron's Rod* (New York: Penguin, 1976), pp. 200–1.

11 Henry Miller, *Tropic of Cancer*, ch. 13. See in this same chapter the celebration of desire-as-flux expressed in the phrase "and my guts spilled out in a grand schizophrenic rush, an evacuation that leaves me face to face with the Absolute."

12 A series of monographs, issued periodically, containing reproductions of art works created by inmates of the psychiatric asylums of Europe. *L'Art brut* is edited by Jean Dubuffet.

13 Henri Michaux, *The Major Ordeals of the Mind*, trans. Richard Howard (New York: Harcourt Brace Jovanovich, 1974), pp. 125–7.

14 *bricolage*: The tinkering about of the *bricoleur*, or amateur handyman. The art of making do with what's at hand. (Trans.)

15 Claude Lévi-Strauss, *The Savage Mind* (Chicago: University of Chicago Press, 1966), p. 17: "The 'bricoleur' is adept at performing a large number of diverse tasks; but unlike the engineer, he does not subordinate each of them to the availability of raw materials and tools conceived and procured for the purpose of the project. His universe of instruments is closed and the rules of his game are always to make do with 'whatever is at hand,' that is to say with a set of tools and materials which is always finite and is also heterogeneous because what it contains bears no relation to the current project, or indeed to any particular project, but is the contingent result of all the occasions there have been to renew or enrich the

stock or to maintain it with the remains of previous constructions or destructions."

16 Sigmund Freud, "Psycho-Analytic Notes upon an Autobiographical Case of Paranoia (Dementia Paranoides)," *Collected Papers: Authorized Translation under the Supervision of Joan Rivière* (New York: Basic Books, 1959), vol. 3, p. 396.

17 Clément Rosset, *Logique du pire* (Paris: Presses Universitaires de France, 1970), p. 37.

18 "Lacan's admirable theory of desire appears to us to have two poles: one related to 'the object small *a*' as a desiring-machine, which defines desire in terms of a real production, thus going beyond both any idea of need and any idea of fantasy; and the other related to the 'great Other' as a signifier, which reintroduces a certain notion of lack. In Serge Leclaire's article "La Réalité du désir" (ch. 4, reference note 26), the oscillation between these two poles can be seen quite clearly.

19 The French word *manque* may mean both lack and need in a psychological sense, as well as want or

privation or scarcity in an economic sense. Depending upon the context, it will hence be translated in various ways below. (Trans.)

20 Maurice Clavel remarks, apropos of Jean-Paul Sartre, that a Marxist philosophy cannot allow itself to introduce the notion of scarcity as its initial premise: "Such a scarcity antedating exploitation makes of the law of supply and demand a reality that will remain forever independent, since it is situated at a primordial level. Hence it is no longer a question of including or deducing this law within Marxism, since it is immediately evident at a prior stage, at a level from which Marxism itself derives. Being a rigorous thinker, Marx refuses to employ the notion of scarcity, and is quite correct to do so, for this category would be his undoing." In *Qui est aliéné?* (Paris: Flammarion, 1970), p. 330.

21 Wilhelm Reich, *The Mass Psychology of Fascism*, trans. Vincent R. Carfagno (London: Souvenir Press, 1970).

Select Bibliography

Anti-Oedipus: Capitalism and Schizophrenia. (Deleuze and Guattari.) Translated by Robert Hurley, Mark Seem, and Helen R. Lane. Minneapolis: University of Minnesota Press, 1983.

Bergsonism. (Deleuze.) Translated by Hugh Tomlinson and Barbara Habberjam. New York: Zone Books, 1988.

Chaosmosis: An Ethico-Aesthetic Paradigm. (Guattari.) Translated by Paul Bains and Julian Pefanis. Bloomington: Indiana University Press, 1995.

Cinema 1: The Movement-Image. (Deleuze.) Translated by Hugh Tomlinson and Barbara Habberjam. London: Athlone Press, 1986.

Cinema 2: The Time-Image. (Deleuze.) Translated by Hugh Tomlinson and Robert Galeta. London: Athlone Press, 1989.

Communists like Us: New Spaces of Liberty, New Lines of Alliance (Guattari, with Toni Negri.) Translated by Michael Ryan. New York: Semiotext(e), 1990.

The Deleuze Reader. (Deleuze.) Edited by Constantin V. Boundas. New York: Columbia University Press, 1993.

Difference and Repetition. (Deleuze.) Translated by Paul Patton. New York: Columbia University Press, 1994.

The Guattari Reader. Edited by Gary Genosko. Oxford: Blackwell Publishers, 1996.

Kant's Critical Philosophy: The Doctrine of the Faculties. (Deleuze.) Translated by Hugh Tomlinson and Barbara Habberjam. Minneapolis: University of Minnesota Press, 1984.

The Logic of Sense. (Deleuze.) Edited by Constantin V. Boundas. Translated by Mark Lester with Charles Stivale. New York: Columbia University Press, 1990.

Negotiations 1972–1990. (Deleuze.) Translated by Martin Joughin. New York: Columbia University Press, 1995.

Nietzsche and Philosophy. (Deleuze.) Translated by Hugh Tomlinson. New York: Columbia University Press, 1983.

Nomadology: The War Machine. (Deleuze and Guattari.) Translated by Brian Massumi. New York: Semiotext(e), 1986.

A Thousand Plateaus: Capitalism and Schizophrenia. (Deleuze and Guattari.) Translated by Brian Massumi. Minneapolis: University of Minnesota Press, 1987.

What is Philosophy? (Deleuze and Guattari.) Translated by Hugh Tomlinson and Graham Burchell. New York: Columbia University Press, 1994.

5

Hélène Cixous

Algerian-born author Hélène Cixous (1937–) is professor of literature at the University of Paris VIII–Vincennes at Saint Denis, a school which she helped to found following the student unrest of May 1968. Known for her work in a broad range of genres including fiction, poetry, and literary criticism, Cixous was also (in 1974) founder of the Women's Studies program at Vincennes, and has achieved philosophical prominence through her work on woman and femininity. Key writings include the essay "The Laugh of the Medusa" (1975) and (from the same year) *The Newly Born Woman*, written with Catherine Clément. In the following selection from her essay "Sorties..." in *The Newly Born Woman*, Cixous attempts to expose the economies of logocentrism and phallocentrism that appropriate and repress woman, and promotes the practice of a feminine writing that exceeds and disrupts the logic of sameness.

Sorties: Out and Out: Attacks/Ways Out/Forays

Where is she?
Activity/passivity
Sun/Moon
Culture/Nature

From "Sorties: Out and Out: Attacks/Ways Out/Forays," in *The Newly Born Woman*, by Hélène Cixous and Catherine Clément, translated by Betsy Wing (Minneapolis, University of Minnesota Press, 1986), pp. 63–8, 87–97. Originally published in France as *La Jeune née*, copyright © 1975 by Union Générale d'Éditions, Paris. English translation and Introduction copyright © 1986 by the University of Minnesota. Reprinted by permission of the publishers, the University of Minnesota Press, and I. B. Taurius & Co. Ltd.

Day/Night

Father/Mother
Head/Heart
Intelligible/Palpable
Logos/Pathos.
Form, convex, step, advance, semen, progress.
Matter, concave, ground – where steps are taken, holding- and dumping-ground.

Man
Woman

Always the same metaphor: we follow it, it carries us, beneath all its figures, wherever discourse is organized. If we read or speak, the same thread or double braid is leading us throughout literature, philosophy, criticism, centuries of representation and reflection.

Thought has always worked through opposition,
Speaking/Writing
Parole/Écriture
High/Low

Through dual, hierarchical oppositions. Superior/Inferior. Myths, legends, books. Philosophical systems. Everywhere (where) ordering intervenes, where a law organizes what is thinkable by oppositions (dual, irreconcilable; or sublatable, dialectical). And all these pairs of oppositions are *couples*. Does that mean something? Is the fact that Logocentrism subjects thought – all concepts, codes and values – to a binary system, related to "the" couple, man/woman?

Nature/History
Nature/Art
Nature/Mind
Passion/Action

Theory of culture, theory of society, symbolic systems in general – art, religion, family, language – it is all developed while bringing the same schemes to light. And the movement whereby each opposition is set up to make sense is the movement through which the couple is destroyed. A universal battlefield. Each time, a war is let loose. Death is always at work.
Father/son Relations of authority, privilege, force.
The Word/Writing Relations: opposition, conflict, sublation, return.
Master/slave Violence. Repression.

We see that "victory" always comes down to the same thing: things get hierarchical. Organization by hierarchy makes all conceptual organization subject to man. Male privilege, shown in the opposition between *activity* and *passivity*, which he uses to sustain himself. Traditionally, the question of sexual difference is treated by coupling it with the opposition: activity/passivity.

There are repercussions. Consulting the history of philosophy – since philosophical discourse both orders and reproduces all thought – one notices[1] that it is marked by an absolute *constant* which orders values and which is precisely this opposition, activity/passivity.

Moreover, woman is always associated with passivity in philosophy. Whenever it is a question of woman, when one examines kinship structures, when a family model is brought into play. In fact, as soon as the question of ontology raises its head, as soon as one asks oneself "what is it?," as soon as there is intended meaning. Intention: desire, authority – examine them and you are led right back... to the father. It is even possible not to notice that there is no place whatsoever for woman in the calculations. Ultimately the world of "being" can function while precluding the mother. No need for a mother, as long as there is some motherliness: and it is the father, then, who acts the part, who is the mother. Either woman is passive or she does not exist. What is left of her is unthinkable, unthought. Which certainly means that she is not thought, that she does not enter into the oppositions, that she does not make a couple with the father (who makes a couple with the son)....

And if we consult literary history, it is the same story. It all comes back to man – to *his* torment, his desire to be (at) the origin. Back to the father. There is an intrinsic connection between the philosophical and the literary (to the extent that it conveys meaning, literature is under the command of the philosophical) and the phallocentric. Philosophy is constructed on the premise of woman's abasement. Subordination of the feminine to the masculine order, which gives the appearance of being the condition for the machinery's functioning.

Now it has become rather urgent to question this solidarity between logocentrism and phallocentrism – bringing to light the fate dealt to woman, her burial – to threaten the stability of the masculine structure that passed itself off as eternal–natural, by conjuring up from femininity the reflections and hypotheses that are necessarily ruinous for the stronghold still in possession of authority. What would happen to logocentrism, to the great philosophical systems, to the order of the world in general if the rock upon which they founded this church should crumble?

If some fine day it suddenly came out that the logocentric plan had always, inadmissibly, been to create a foundation for (to found and fund) phallocentrism, to guarantee the masculine order a rationale equal to history itself.

So all the history, all the stories would be there to retell differently; the future would be incalculable; the historic forces would and will change hands and change body – another thought which is yet unthinkable – will transform the functioning of all society. We are living in an age where the conceptual foundation of an ancient culture is in the process of being undermined by millions of a species of mole (Topoi, ground mines) never known before. . . .

Night to his day – that has forever been the fantasy. Black to his white. Shut out of his system's space, she is the repressed that insures the system's functioning.

Kept at a distance so that he can enjoy the ambiguous advantages of the distance, so that she, who is distance and postponement, will keep alive the enigma, the dangerous delight of seduction, in suspense, in the role of "eloper," she is Helen, somehow "outside." But she cannot appropriate this "outside" (it is rare that she even wants it); it is his outside: outside on the condition that it not be entirely outside, the unfamiliar stranger that would escape him. So she stays inside a domesticated outside.

Eloper: carried away with herself and carried off from herself.

– Not only is she the portion of strangeness – *inside* his universe where she revives his restlessness and desire. Within his economy, she is the strangeness he likes to appropriate. . . .

Today, still, the masculine return to the Selfsame is narrower and more restricted than femininity's. It all happens as if man were more directly threatened in his being by the nonselfsame than woman. Ordinarily, this is exactly the cultural product described by psychoanalysis: someone who still has something to lose. And in the development of desire, of exchange, he is the en-grossing party: loss and expense are stuck in the commercial deal that always turns the gift into a gift-that-takes. The gift brings in a return. Loss, at the end of a curved line, is turned into its opposite and comes back to him as profit.

But does woman escape this law of return? Can one speak of another spending? Really, there is no "free" gift. You never give something for nothing. But all the difference lies in the why and how of the gift, in the values that the gesture of giving affirms, causes to circulate; in the type of profit the giver draws from the gift and the use to which he or she puts it. Why, how, is there this difference?

When one gives, what does one give oneself?

What does he want in return – the traditional man? And she? At first what *he* wants, whether on the level of cultural or of personal exchanges, whether it is a question of capital or of affectivity (or of love, of *jouissance*) – is that he gain more

masculinity: plus-value of virility, authority, power, money, or pleasure, all of which reenforce his phallocentric narcissism at the same time. Moreover, that is what society is made for – how it is made; and men can hardly get out of it. An unenviable fate they've made for themselves. A man is always proving something; he has to "show off," show up the others. Masculine profit is almost always mixed up with a success that is socially defined.

How does she give? What are her dealings with saving or squandering, reserve, life, death? She too gives *for*. She too, with open hands, gives herself – pleasure, happiness, increased value, enhanced self-image. But she doesn't try to "recover her expenses." She is able not to return to herself, never settling down, pouring out, going everywhere to the other. She does not flee extremes; she is not the being-of-the-end (the goal), but she is how-far-being-reaches.

If there is a self proper to woman, paradoxically it is her capacity to depropriate herself without self-interest: endless body, without "end," without principal "parts"; if she is a whole, it is a whole made up of parts that are wholes, not simple, partial objects but varied entirely, moving and boundless change, a cosmos where eros never stops traveling, vast astral space. She doesn't revolve around a sun that is more star than the stars.

That doesn't mean that she is undifferentiated magma; it means that she doesn't create a monarchy of her body or her desire. Let masculine sexuality gravitate around the penis, engendering this centralized body (political anatomy) under the party dictatorship. Woman does not perform on herself this regionalization that profits the couple head-sex, that only inscribes itself within frontiers. Her libido is cosmic, just as her unconscious is worldwide: her writing also can only go on and on, without ever inscribing or distinguishing contours, daring these dizzying passages in other, fleeting and passionate dwellings within him, within the hims and hers whom she inhabits just long enough to watch them, as close as possible to the unconscious from the moment they arise; to love them, as close as possible to instinctual drives, and then, further, all filled with these brief identifying hugs and kisses, she goes and goes on infinitely. She alone dares and wants to know from within where she, the one excluded, has never ceased to hear what-comes-before-language reverberating. She lets the other tongue of a thousand tongues speak – the tongue, sound without barrier or death. She refuses life nothing. Her tongue doesn't hold back but holds forth, doesn't keep in but keeps on enabling. Where the wonder of being several and turmoil is expressed, she does not protect herself against these unknown feminines; she surprises herself at seeing, being, pleasuring in her gift of changeability. I am spacious singing Flesh: onto which is grafted no one knows which I – which masculine or feminine, more or less human but above all living, because changing I. . . .

There is a bond between woman's libidinal economy – her *jouissance*, the feminine Imaginary – and her way of self-constituting a subjectivity that splits apart without regret, and without this regretlessness being the equivalent of dying, of the exhaustion described by Valéry as the Young Fate – answering herself with anomalies, without the ceaseless summoning of the authority called Ego.

Unleashed and raging, she belongs to the race of waves. She arises, she approaches, she lifts up, she reaches, covers over, washes a shore, flows embracing the cliff's least undulation, already she is another, arising again, throwing the fringed vastness of her body up high, follows herself, and covers over, uncovers, polishes, makes the stone body shine with the gentle undeserting ebbs, which return to the shoreless nonorigin, as if she recalled herself in order to come again as never before. . . .

She has never "held still"; explosion, diffusion, effervescence, abundance, she takes pleasure in being boundless, outside self, outside same, far from a "center," from any capital of her "dark continent," very far from the "hearth" to which man[2] brings her so that she will tend his fire, which always threatens to go out. She watches for him, but he has to keep an eye on her; for she can be his storm as well: "will I die by a storm? Or will I go out like a light that doesn't wait to be blown out by the wind, but which dies tired and self-satisfied? . . . or: will I extinguish my own self in order not to burn down to the end?"[3] Masculine energy, with its limited oil reserves, questions itself. Whereas, the fact that feminine energy has vast resources is not without consequences – still very rarely analyzed – for exchange in general, for love-life, and for the fate created for woman's desire. Exasperating: he's afraid she "goes too far." And the irony of her fate has her either be this "nothing," which punctuates the Dora case – ("You know my wife is nothing to me") – or this too-much, too-much reversed into not-enough, the "not how it should

be" that reminds her that her master is on the limited side.

She doesn't hold still, she overflows. An outpouring that can be agonizing, since she may fear, and make the other fear, endless aberration and madness in her release. Yet, vertiginous, it can also be intoxicating – as long as the personal, the permanence of identity is not fetishized – a "where-am-I," a "who-enjoys-there," a "who-I-where-delight": questions that drive reason, the principle of unity, mad, and that are not asked, that ask for no answer, that open up the space where woman is wandering, roaming (a rogue wave), flying (thieving).

This power to be errant is strength; it is also what makes her vulnerable to those who champion the Selfsame, acknowledgment, and attribution. No matter how submissive and docile she may be in relation to the masculine order, she still remains the threatening possibility of savagery, the unknown quantity in the household whole. "Mysterious"[4] – the incalculable with which they must be counted. – Mysterious, yes – but she is blamed for that even if pleasure is derived from always wanting to expose her. And mysterious to herself, something she has been disturbed by for a long time, made to feel guilty for "not understanding herself" (taking herself in) or knowing herself (cunt-born), because all around her they valorized a "knowledge" (cunt-birth) as ordained, as a mastery, a "control" (cunt-role) (of knowings! cunt-births!) established on repression and on "capture," arrest, sub-poenis, confinement.

Writing femininity transformation:

And there is a link between the economy of femininity – the open, extravagant subjectivity, that relationship to the other in which the gift doesn't calculate its influence – and the possibility of love; and a link today between this "libido of the other" and writing.

At the present time, *defining* a feminine practice of writing is impossible with an impossibility that will continue; for this practice will never be able to be *theorized*, enclosed, coded, which does not mean it does not exist. But it will always exceed the discourse governing the phallocentric system; it takes place and will take place somewhere other than in the territories subordinated to philosophical–theoretical domination. It will not let itself think except through subjects that break automatic functions, border runners never subjugated by any authority. But one can begin to speak. Begin to point out some effects, some elements of unconscious drives, some relations of the feminine Imaginary to the Real, to writing.

What I have to say about it is also only a beginning, because right from the start these features affect me powerfully.

First I sense femininity in writing by: a privilege of *voice: writing and voice* are entwined and interwoven and writing's continuity/voice's rhythm take each other's breath away through interchanging, make the text gasp or form it out of suspenses and silences, make it lose its voice or rend it with cries.

In a way, feminine writing never stops reverberating from the wrench that the acquisition of speech, speaking out loud, is for her – "acquisition" that is experienced more as tearing away, dizzying flight and flinging oneself, diving. Listen to woman speak in a gathering (if she is not painfully out of breath): she doesn't "speak," she throws her trembling body into the air, she lets herself go, she flies, she goes completely into her voice, she vitally defends the "logic" of her discourse with her body; her flesh speaks true. She exposes herself. Really she makes what she thinks materialize carnally, she conveys meaning with her body. She *inscribes* what she is saying because she does not deny unconscious drives the unmanageable part they play in speech. . . .

We have turned away from our bodies. Shamefully we have been taught to be unaware of them, to lash them with stupid modesty; we've been tricked into a fool's bargain: each one is to love the other sex. I'll give you your body and you will give me mine. But which men give women the body that they blindly hand over to him? Why so few texts? Because there are still so few women winning back their bodies. Woman must write her body, must make up the unimpeded tongue that bursts partitions, classes, and rhetorics, orders and codes, must inundate, run through, go beyond the discourse with its last reserves, including the one of laughing off the word "silence" that has to be said, the one that, aiming for the impossible, stops dead before the word "impossible" and writes it as "end."

In body/Still more: woman is body more than man is. Because he is invited to social success, to sublimation. More body hence more writing. For a long time, still, bodily, within her body she has answered the harassment, the familial conjugal venture of domestication, the repeated attempts to castrate her. Woman, who has run her tongue ten thousand times seven times around her mouth before not speaking, either dies of it or knows her

tongue and her mouth better than anyone. Now, I-woman am going to blow up the Law: a possible and inescapable explosion from now on; let it happen, right now, in language.

When "*The* Repressed" of their culture and their society come back, it is an explosive return, which is *absolutely* shattering, staggering, overturning, with a force never let loose before, on the scale of the most tremendous repressions: for at the end of the Age of the Phallus, women will have been either wiped out or heated to the highest, most violent, white-hot fire. Throughout their deafening dumb history, they have lived in dreams, embodied but still deadly silent, in silences, in voiceless rebellions. . . .

If woman has always functioned "within" man's discourse, a signifier referring always to the opposing signifier that annihilates its particular energy, puts down or stifles its very different sounds, now it is time for her to displace this "within," explode it, overturn it, grab it, make it hers, take it in, take it into her women's mouth, bite its tongue with her women's teeth, make up her own tongue to get inside of it. And you will see how easily she will well up, from this "within" where she was hidden and dormant, to the lips where her foams will overflow.

It is not a question of appropriating their instruments, their concepts, their places for oneself or of wishing oneself in their position of mastery. Our knowing that there is a danger of identification does not mean we should give in. Leave that to the worriers, to masculine anxiety and its obsessional relationship to workings they must control – knowing "how it runs" in order to "make it run." Not taking possession to internalize or manipulate but to shoot through and smash the walls. . . .

A feminine text cannot not be more than subversive: if it writes itself it is in volcanic heaving of the old "real" property crust. In ceaseless displacement. She must write herself because, when the time comes for her liberation, it is the invention of a *new*, *insurgent* writing that will allow her to put the breaks and indispensable changes into effect in her history. At first, individually, on two inseparable levels: – woman, writing herself, will go back to this body that has been worse than confiscated, a body replaced with a disturbing stranger, sick or dead, who so often is a bad influence, the cause and place of inhibitions. By censuring the body, breath and speech are censored at the same time.

To write – the act that will "realize" the uncensored relationship of woman to her sexuality, to her woman-being giving her back access to her own forces; that will return her goods, her pleasures, her organs, her vast bodily territories kept under seal; that will tear her out of the superegoed, over-Mosesed structure where the same position of guilt is always reserved for her (guilty of everything, every time: of having desires, of not having any; of being frigid, of being "too" hot; of not being both at once; of being too much of a mother and not enough; of nurturing and of not nurturing . . .). Write yourself: your body must make itself heard. Then the huge resources of the unconscious will burst out. Finally the inexhaustible feminine Imaginary is going to be deployed. Without gold or black dollars, our naphtha will spread values over the world, un-quoted values that will change the rules of the old game.

Notes

1 All Derrida's work traversing–detecting the history of philosophy is devoted to bringing this to light. In Plato, Hegel, and Nietzsche, the same process continues: repression, repudiation, distancing of woman; a murder that is mixed up with history as the manifestation and representation of masculine power.
2 The home manager, according to the definition of the English word "husband," is the "servant of the house," called the "mari."
3 Nietzsche, Aphorism 315, *The Gay Science*.
4 Is it just chance that it is something of woman, a dismembering feminine, which torments the I/Me who is not/is born only to pursue itself, split by Valéry, infinitely dispersed, never really put back together again in the Young Fate?

Select Bibliography

Angst. Translated by Jo Levy. New York: Riverrun Press, 1985.
The Book of Promethea/ Le Livre de Promethea. Translated by Betsy Wing. Lincoln: University of Nebraska Press, 1991.
"Coming to Writing" and Other Essays. Edited by Deborah Jenson. Translated by Sarah Cornell et al. Cambridge, Mass.: Harvard University Press, 1991.
The Hélène Cixous Reader. Edited by Susan Sellers. New York: Routledge, 1994.
Inside. Translated by Carol Barko. New York: Schocken Books, 1986.
The Newly Born Woman (with Catherine Clément). Translated by Betsy Wing. Minneapolis: University of Minnesota Press, 1986.

Portrait of Dora. Translated by Anita Barrows. Dallas: Riverrun Press, 1979. Published in one volume with Simone Benmussa, *The Singular Life of Albert Nobbs*.
Reading with Clarice Lispector. Edited and translated by Verena Andermatt Conley. Minneapolis: University of Minnesota Press, 1990.
Readings: The Poetics of Blanchot, Joyce, Kafka, Kleist, Lispector, and Tsvetayeva. Edited and translated by Verena Andermatt Conley. Minneapolis: University of Minnesota Press, 1991.
Three Steps on the Ladder of Writing. Translated by Sarah Cornell and Susan Sellers. New York: Columbia University Press, 1993.
Writing Differences: Readings from the Seminar of Hélène Cixous. Edited by Susan Sellers. Milton Keynes: Open University Press, 1988.

6

Michel Foucault

The work of French philosopher Michel Foucault (1926–84) may in general be characterized as an attempt to provide a critical history of the present, that is, to understand how we have come to be who we are at the present time. Foucault's early work concentrates initially on the field of mental illness and psychology (investigating the historical constitution of "madness" in the emergence of modern rationality), and then on the constitution of modern "man" as the object of the human sciences. This "archeological" phase of his work is followed by a more "genealogical" focus (inspired in part by Nietzsche) on the role played by institutional, nondiscursive practices through which power is exercised and brought to bear on the constitution of individual lives. Here Foucault argues that the exercise of power, which can never be separated from knowledge, occurs for the most part through concealed and subtle operations by which individual human "subjects" are formed, manipulated, and subjected to "disciplinary" norms and standards that are thoroughly historical and have no intrinsic necessity or truth. In the final phase of his work, Foucault examines the historical constitution of various ascetic practices of the self in relation to "sexuality." The following selection, from *The History of Sexuality*, Volume One (1976), examines how "sex" comes to be constituted as an object of discursive and social practices presupposing a conception of power that Foucault problematizes under the rubric of "the repressive hypothesis."

The History of Sexuality

We "Other Victorians"

For a long time, the story goes, we supported a Victorian regime, and we continue to be dominated by it even today. Thus the image of the imperial prude is emblazoned on our restrained, mute, and hypocritical sexuality.

At the beginning of the seventeenth century a certain frankness was still common, it would seem. Sexual practices had little need of secrecy; words were said without undue reticence, and things were done without too much concealment; one had a tolerant familiarity with the illicit. Codes regulating the coarse, the obscene, and the indecent were quite lax compared to those of the nineteenth century. It was a time of direct gestures, shameless discourse, and open transgressions, when anatomies were shown and intermingled at will, and knowing children hung about amid the laughter of adults: it was a period when bodies "made a display of themselves."

But twilight soon fell upon this bright day, followed by the monotonous nights of the Victorian bourgeoisie. Sexuality was carefully confined; it moved into the home. The conjugal family took custody of it and absorbed it into the serious function of reproduction. On the subject of sex, silence became the rule. The legitimate and procreative couple laid down the law. The couple imposed itself as model, enforced the norm, safeguarded the truth, and reserved the right to speak while retaining the principle of secrecy. A single locus of sexuality was acknowledged in social space as well as at the heart of every household, but it was a utilitarian and fertile one: the parents' bedroom. The rest had only to remain vague; proper demeanor avoided contact with other bodies, and verbal decency sanitized one's speech. And sterile behavior carried the taint of abnormality; if it insisted

From *The History of Sexuality*, Volume One, translated by Robert Hurley (New York: Vintage Books, 1990), pp. 3–9, 17–21, 34–5, 81–6, 90–6. Copyright © 1976 by Éditions Gallimard. Reprinted by permission of Georges Borchardt, Inc.

on making itself too visible, it would be designated accordingly and would have to pay the penalty. . . .

This discourse on modern sexual repression holds up well, owing no doubt to how easy it is to uphold. A solemn historical and political guarantee protects it. By placing the advent of the age of repression in the seventeenth century, after hundreds of years of open spaces and free expression, one adjusts it to coincide with the development of capitalism: it becomes an integral part of the bourgeois order. The minor chronicle of sex and its trials is transposed into the ceremonious history of the modes of production; its trifling aspect fades from view. A principle of explanation emerges after the fact: if sex is so rigorously repressed, this is because it is incompatible with a general and intensive work imperative. At a time when labor capacity was being systematically exploited, how could this capacity be allowed to dissipate itself in pleasurable pursuits, except in those – reduced to a minimum – that enabled it to reproduce itself? Sex and its effects are perhaps not so easily deciphered; on the other hand, their repression, thus reconstructed, is easily analyzed. And the sexual cause – the demand for sexual freedom, but also for the knowledge to be gained from sex and the right to speak about it – becomes legitimately associated with the honor of a political cause: sex too is placed on the agenda for the future. A suspicious mind might wonder if taking so many precautions in order to give the history of sex such an impressive filiation does not bear traces of the same old prudishness: as if those valorizing correlations were necessary before such a discourse could be formulated or accepted.

But there may be another reason that makes it so gratifying for us to define the relationship between sex and power in terms of repression: something that one might call the speaker's benefit. If sex is repressed, that is, condemned to prohibition, nonexistence, and silence, then the mere fact that one is speaking about it has the appearance of a deliberate transgression. A person who holds forth in such language places himself to a certain extent outside the reach of power; he upsets established law; he somehow anticipates the coming freedom. This explains the solemnity with which one speaks of sex nowadays. When they had to allude to it, the first demographers and psychiatrists of the nineteenth century thought it advisable to excuse themselves for asking their readers to dwell on matters so trivial and base. But for decades now, we have found it difficult to speak on the subject without striking a different pose: we are conscious of defying established power, our tone of voice shows that we know we are being subversive, and we ardently conjure away the present and appeal to the future, whose day will be hastened by the contribution we believe we are making. Something that smacks of revolt, of promised freedom, of the coming age of a different law, slips easily into this discourse on sexual oppression. Some of the ancient functions of prophecy are reactivated therein. Tomorrow sex will be good again. Because this repression is affirmed, one can discreetly bring into coexistence concepts which the fear of ridicule or the bitterness of history prevents most of us from putting side by side: revolution and happiness; or revolution and a different body, one that is newer and more beautiful; or indeed, revolution and pleasure. What sustains our eagerness to speak of sex in terms of repression is doubtless this opportunity to speak out against the powers that be, to utter truths and promise bliss, to link together enlightenment, liberation, and manifold pleasures; to pronounce a discourse that combines the fervor of knowledge, the determination to change the laws, and the longing for the garden of earthly delights. This is perhaps what also explains the market value attributed not only to what is said about sexual repression, but also to the mere fact of lending an ear to those who would eliminate the effects of repression. Ours is, after all, the only civilization in which officials are paid to listen to all and sundry impart the secrets of their sex: as if the urge to talk about it, and the interest one hopes to arouse by doing so, have far surpassed the possibilities of being heard, so that some individuals have even offered their ears for hire.

But it appears to me that the essential thing is not this economic factor, but rather the existence in our era of a discourse in which sex, the revelation of truth, the overturning of global laws, the proclamation of a new day to come, and the promise of a certain felicity are linked together. Today it is sex that serves as a support for the ancient form – so familiar and important in the West – of preaching. A great sexual sermon – which has had its subtle theologians and its popular voices – has swept through our societies over the last decades; it has chastised the old order, denounced hypocrisy, and praised the rights of the immediate and the real; it has made people dream of a New City. The Franciscans are called to mind. And we might wonder how it is possible that the lyricism and religiosity that long accompanied the revolutionary project have, in Western industrial societies, been largely carried over to sex.

The notion of repressed sex is not, therefore, only a theoretical matter. The affirmation of a sexuality that has never been more rigorously subjugated than during the age of the hypocritical, bustling, and responsible bourgeoisie is coupled with the grandiloquence of a discourse purporting to reveal the truth about sex, modify its economy within reality, subvert the law that governs it, and change its future. The statement of oppression and the form of the sermon refer back to one another; they are mutually reinforcing. To say that sex is not repressed, or rather that the relationship between sex and power is not characterized by repression, is to risk falling into a sterile paradox. It not only runs counter to a well-accepted argument, it goes against the whole economy and all the discursive "interests" that underlie this argument.

This is the point at which I would like to situate the series of historical analyses that will follow, the present volume being at the same time an introduction and a first attempt at an overview: it surveys a few historically significant points and outlines certain theoretical problems. Briefly, my aim is to examine the case of a society which has been loudly castigating itself for its hypocrisy for more than a century, which speaks verbosely of its own silence, takes great pains to relate in detail the things it does not say, denounces the powers it exercises, and promises to liberate itself from the very laws that have made it function. I would like to explore not only these discourses but also the will that sustains them and the strategic intention that supports them. The question I would like to pose is not, Why are we repressed? but rather, Why do we say, with so much passion and so much resentment against our most recent past, against our present, and against ourselves, that we are repressed? By what spiral did we come to affirm that sex is negated? What led us to show, ostentatiously, that sex is something we hide, to say it is something we silence? And we do all this by formulating the matter in the most explicit terms, by trying to reveal it in its most naked reality, by affirming it in the positivity of its power and its effects. It is certainly legitimate to ask why sex was associated with sin for such a long time – although it would remain to be discovered how this association was formed, and one would have to be careful not to state in a summary and hasty fashion that sex was "condemned" – but we must also ask why we burden ourselves today with so much guilt for having once made sex a sin. What paths have brought us to the point where we are "at fault" with respect to our own sex? And how have we come to be a civilization so peculiar as to tell itself that, through an abuse of power which has not ended, it has long "sinned" against sex? How does one account for the displacement which, while claiming to free us from the sinful nature of sex, taxes us with a great historical wrong which consists precisely in imagining that nature to be blameworthy and in drawing disastrous consequences from that belief? ...

The Repressive Hypothesis

The incitement to discourse

The seventeenth century, then, was the beginning of an age of repression emblematic of what we call the bourgeois societies, an age which perhaps we still have not completely left behind. Calling sex by its name thereafter became more difficult and more costly. As if in order to gain mastery over it in reality, it had first been necessary to subjugate it at the level of language, control its free circulation in speech, expunge it from the things that were said, and extinguish the words that rendered it too visibly present. And even these prohibitions, it seems, were afraid to name it. Without even having to pronounce the word, modern prudishness was able to insure that one did not speak of sex, merely through the interplay of prohibitions that referred back to one another: instances of muteness which, by dint of saying nothing, imposed silence. Censorship.

Yet when one looks back over these last three centuries with their continual transformations, things appear in a very different light: around and apropos of sex, one sees a veritable discursive explosion. We must be clear on this point, however. It is quite possible that there was an expurgation – and a very rigorous one – of the authorized vocabulary. It may indeed be true that a whole rhetoric of allusion and metaphor was codified.

Without question, new rules of propriety screened out some words: there was a policing of statements. A control over enunciations as well: where and when it was not possible to talk about such things became much more strictly defined; in which circumstances, among which speakers, and within which social relationships. Areas were thus established, if not of utter silence, at least of tact and discretion: between parents and children, for instance, or teachers and pupils, or masters and domestic servants. This almost certainly constituted a whole restrictive economy, one that was incorporated into that politics of language and speech – spontaneous on the one hand, concerted on the other – which accompanied the social redistributions of the classical period.

At the level of discourses and their domains, however, practically the opposite phenomenon occurred. There was a steady proliferation of discourses concerned with sex – specific discourses, different from one another both by their form and by their object: a discursive ferment that gathered momentum from the eighteenth century onward. Here I am thinking not so much of the probable increase in "illicit" discourses, that is, discourses of infraction that crudely named sex by way of insult or mockery of the new code of decency; the tightening up of the rules of decorum likely did produce, as a countereffect, a valorization and intensification of indecent speech. But more important was the multiplication of discourses concerning sex in the field of exercise of power itself: an institutional incitement to speak about it, and to do so more and more; a determination on the part of the agencies of power to hear it spoken about, and to cause *it* to speak through explicit articulation and endlessly accumulated detail.

Consider the evolution of the Catholic pastoral and the sacrament of penance after the Council of Trent. Little by little, the nakedness of the questions formulated by the confession manuals of the Middle Ages, and a good number of those still in use in the seventeenth century, was veiled. One avoided entering into that degree of detail which some authors, such as Sanchez or Tamburini, had for a long time believed indispensable for the confession to be complete: description of the respective positions of the partners, the postures assumed, gestures, places touched, caresses, the precise moment of pleasure – an entire painstaking review of the sexual act in its very unfolding. Discretion was advised, with increasing emphasis. The greatest reserve was counseled when dealing with sins against purity: "This matter is similar to pitch, for, however one might handle it, even to cast it far from oneself, it sticks nonetheless, and always soils."[1] And later, Alfonso de' Liguori prescribed starting – and possibly going no further, especially when dealing with children – with questions that were "roundabout and vague."[2]

But while the language may have been refined, the scope of the confession – the confession of the flesh – continually increased. This was partly because the Counter Reformation busied itself with stepping up the rhythm of the yearly confession in the Catholic countries, and because it tried to impose meticulous rules of self-examination; but above all, because it attributed more and more importance in penance – and perhaps at the expense of some other sins – to all the insinuations of the flesh: thoughts, desires, voluptuous imaginings, delectations, combined movements of the body and the soul; henceforth all this had to enter, in detail, into the process of confession and guidance. According to the new pastoral, sex must not be named imprudently, but its aspects, its correlations, and its effects must be pursued down to their slenderest ramifications: a shadow in a daydream, an image too slowly dispelled, a badly exorcised complicity between the body's mechanics and the mind's complacency: everything had to be told. A twofold evolution tended to make the flesh into the root of all evil, shifting the most important moment of transgression from the act itself to the stirrings – so difficult to perceive and formulate – of desire. For this was an evil that afflicted the whole man, and in the most secret of forms: "Examine diligently, therefore, all the faculties of your soul: memory, understanding, and will. Examine with precision all your senses as well. . . . Examine, moreover, all your thoughts, every word you speak, and all your actions. Examine even unto your dreams, to know if, once awakened, you did not give them your consent. And finally, do not think that in so sensitive and perilous a matter as this, there is anything trivial or insignificant."[3] Discourse, therefore, had to trace the meeting line of the body and the soul, following all its meanderings: beneath the surface of the sins, it would lay bare the unbroken nervure of the flesh. Under the authority of a language that had been carefully expurgated so that it was no longer directly named, sex was taken charge of, tracked down as it were, by a discourse that aimed to allow it no obscurity, no respite.

It was here, perhaps, that the injunction, so peculiar to the West, was laid down for the first time, in the form of a general constraint. I am not talking about the obligation to admit to violations of the laws of sex, as required by traditional penance; but of the nearly infinite task of telling – telling oneself and another, as often as possible, everything that might concern the interplay of innumerable pleasures, sensations, and thoughts which, through the body and the soul, had some affinity with sex. This scheme for transforming sex into discourse had been devised long before in an ascetic and monastic setting. The seventeenth century made it into a rule for everyone. It would seem in actual fact that it could scarcely have applied to any but a tiny elite; the great majority of the faithful who only went to confession on rare occasions in the course of the year escaped such complex prescriptions. But the important point no doubt is that this obligation was decreed, as an ideal at least, for every good Christian. An imperative was established: Not only will you confess to acts contravening the law, but you will seek to transform your desire, your every desire, into discourse. Insofar as possible, nothing was meant to elude this dictum, even if the words it employed had to be carefully neutralized. The Christian pastoral prescribed as a fundamental duty the task of passing everything having to do with sex through the endless mill of speech.[4] The forbidding of certain words, the decency of expressions, all the censorings of vocabulary, might well have been only secondary devices compared to that great subjugation: ways of rendering it morally acceptable and technically useful. . . .

The objection will doubtless be raised that if so many stimulations and constraining mechanisms were necessary in order to speak of sex, this was because there reigned over everyone a certain fundamental prohibition; only definite necessities – economic pressures, political requirements – were able to lift this prohibition and open a few approaches to the discourse on sex, but these were limited and carefully coded; so much talk about sex, so many insistent devices contrived for causing it to be talked about – but under strict conditions: does this not prove that it was an object of secrecy, and more important, that there is still an attempt to keep it that way? But this often-stated theme, that sex is outside of discourse and that only the removing of an obstacle, the breaking of a secret, can clear the way leading to it, is precisely what needs to be examined. Does it not partake of the injunction by which discourse is provoked? Is it not with the aim of inciting people to speak of sex that it is made to mirror, at the outer limit of every actual discourse, something akin to a secret whose discovery is imperative, a thing abusively reduced to silence, and at the same time difficult and necessary, dangerous and precious to divulge? We must not forget that by making sex into that which, above all else, had to be confessed, the Christian pastoral always presented it as the disquieting enigma: not a thing which stubbornly shows itself, but one which always hides, the insidious presence that speaks in a voice so muted and often disguised that one risks remaining deaf to it. Doubtless the secret does not reside in that basic reality in relation to which all the incitements to speak of sex are situated – whether they try to force the secret, or whether in some obscure way they reinforce it by the manner in which they speak of it. It is a question rather of a theme that forms part of the very mechanics of these incitements: a way of giving shape to the requirement to speak about the matter, a fable that is indispensable to the endlessly proliferating economy of the discourse on sex. What is peculiar to modern societies, in fact, is not that they consigned sex to a shadow existence, but that they dedicated themselves to speaking of it *ad infinitum*, while exploiting it as *the* secret.

The Deployment of Sexuality

Objective

Why these investigations? I am well aware that an uncertainty runs through the sketches I have drawn thus far, one that threatens to invalidate the more detailed inquiries that I have projected. I have repeatedly stressed that the history of the last centuries in Western societies did not manifest the movement of a power that was essentially repressive. I based my argument on the disqualification of that notion while feigning ignorance of the fact that a critique has been mounted from another quarter and doubtless in a more radical fashion: a critique conducted at the level of the theory of desire. In point of fact, the assertion that sex is not "repressed" is not altogether new. Psychoanalysts have been saying the same thing for some time. They have challenged the simple little machinery that comes to mind when one speaks of repression; the idea of a rebellious energy that must be throttled has appeared to them inadequate for deciphering the manner in which power and desire are joined to one another; they consider them to be linked in a more complex and primary way than through the interplay of a primitive, natural, and living energy welling up from below, and a higher order seeking to stand in its way; thus one should not think that desire is repressed, for the simple reason that the law is what constitutes both desire and the lack on which it is predicated. Where there is desire, the power relation is already present: an illusion, then, to denounce this relation for a repression exerted after the event; but vanity as well, to go questing after a desire that is beyond the reach of power.

But, in an obstinately confused way, I sometimes spoke, as though I were dealing with equivalent notions, of *repression*, and sometimes of *law*, of prohibition or censorship. Through stubbornness or neglect, I failed to consider everything that can distinguish their theoretical implications. And I grant that one might justifiably say to me: By constantly referring to positive technologies of power, you are playing a double game where you hope to win on all counts; you confuse your adversaries by appearing to take the weaker position, and, discussing repression alone, you would have us believe, wrongly, that you have rid yourself of the problem of law; and yet you keep the essential practical consequence of the principle of power-as-law, namely the fact that there is no escaping from power, that it is always-already present, constituting that very thing which one attempts to counter it with. As to the idea of a power-repression, you have retained its most fragile theoretical element, and this in order to criticize it; you have retained the most sterilizing political consequence of the idea of power-law, but only in order to preserve it for your own use.

The aim of the inquiries that will follow is to move less toward a "theory" of power than toward an "analytics" of power: that is, toward a definition of the specific domain formed by relations of power, and toward a determination of the instruments that will make possible its analysis. However, it seems to me that this analytics can be constituted only if it frees itself completely from a certain representation of power that I would term – it will be seen later why – "juridico-discursive." It is this conception that governs both the thematics of repression and the theory of the law as constitutive of desire. In other words, what distinguishes the analysis made in terms of the repression of instincts from that made in terms of the law of desire is clearly the way in which they each conceive of the nature and dynamics of the drives, not the way in which they conceive of power. They both rely on a common representation of power which, depending on the use made of it and the position it is accorded with respect to desire, leads to two contrary results: either to the promise of a "liberation," if power is seen as having only an external hold on desire, or, if it is constitutive of desire itself, to the affirmation: you are always-already trapped. Moreover, one must not imagine that this representation is peculiar to those who are concerned with the problem of the relations of power with sex. In fact it is much more general; one frequently encounters it in political analyses of power, and it is deeply rooted in the history of the West.

These are some of its principal features:

The negative relation. It never establishes any connection between power and sex that is not negative: rejection, exclusion, refusal, blockage, concealment, or mask. Where sex and pleasure are concerned, power can "do" nothing but say no to them; what it produces, if anything, is absences and gaps; it overlooks elements, introduces discontinuities, separates what is joined, and marks off boundaries. Its effects take the general form of limit and lack.

The insistence of the rule. Power is essentially what dictates its law to sex. Which means first of all that sex is placed by power in a binary system: licit and illicit, permitted and forbidden. Secondly, power prescribes an "order" for sex that operates at the same time as a form of intelligibility: sex is to be deciphered on the basis of its relation to the law. And finally, power acts by laying down the rule: power's hold on sex is maintained through language, or rather through the act of discourse that creates, from the very fact that it is articulated, a rule of law. It speaks, and that is the rule. The pure form of power resides in the function of the legislator; and its mode of action with regard to sex is of a juridico-discursive character.

The cycle of prohibition: thou shalt not go near, thou shalt not touch, thou shalt not consume, thou shalt not experience pleasure, thou shalt not speak, thou shalt not show thyself; ultimately thou shalt not exist, except in darkness and secrecy. To deal with sex, power employs nothing more than a law of prohibition. Its objective: that sex renounce itself. Its instrument: the threat of a punishment that is nothing other than the suppression of sex. Renounce yourself or suffer the penalty of being suppressed; do not appear if you do not want to

disappear. Your existence will be maintained only at the cost of your nullification. Power constrains sex only through a taboo that plays on the alternative between two nonexistences.

The logic of censorship. This interdiction is thought to take three forms: affirming that such a thing is not permitted, preventing it from being said, denying that it exists. Forms that are difficult to reconcile. But it is here that one imagines a sort of logical sequence that characterizes censorship mechanisms: it links the inexistent, the illicit, and the inexpressible in such a way that each is at the same time the principle and the effect of the others: one must not talk about what is forbidden until it is annulled in reality; what is inexistent has no right to show itself, even in the order of speech where its inexistence is declared; and that which one must keep silent about is banished from reality as the thing that is tabooed above all else. The logic of power exerted on sex is the paradoxical logic of a law that might be expressed as an injunction of nonexistence, nonmanifestation, and silence.

The uniformity of the apparatus. Power over sex is exercised in the same way at all levels. From top to bottom, in its overall decisions and its capillary interventions alike, whatever the devices or institutions on which it relies, it acts in a uniform and comprehensive manner; it operates according to the simple and endlessly reproduced mechanisms of law, taboo, and censorship: from state to family, from prince to father, from the tribunal to the small change of everyday punishments, from the agencies of social domination to the structures that constitute the subject himself, one finds a general form of power, varying in scale alone. This form is the law of transgression and punishment, with its interplay of licit and illicit. Whether one attributes to it the form of the prince who formulates rights, of the father who forbids, of the censor who enforces silence, or of the master who states the law, in any case one schematizes power in a juridical form, and one defines its effects as obedience. Confronted by a power that is law, the subject who is constituted as subject – who is "subjected" – is he who obeys. To the formal homogeneity of power in these various instances corresponds the general form of submission in the one who is constrained by it – whether the individual in question is the subject opposite the monarch, the citizen opposite the state, the child opposite the parent, or the disciple opposite the master. A legislative power on one side, and an obedient subject on the other.

Underlying both the general theme that power represses sex and the idea that the law constitutes desire, one encounters the same putative mechanics of power. It is defined in a strangely restrictive way, in that, to begin with, this power is poor in resources, sparing of its methods, monotonous in the tactics it utilizes, incapable of invention, and seemingly doomed always to repeat itself. Further, it is a power that only has the force of the negative on its side, a power to say no; in no condition to produce, capable only of posting limits, it is basically anti-energy. This is the paradox of its effectiveness: it is incapable of doing anything, except to render what it dominates incapable of doing anything either, except for what this power allows it to do. And finally, it is a power whose model is essentially juridical, centered on nothing more than the statement of the law and the operation of taboos. All the modes of domination, submission, and subjugation are ultimately reduced to an effect of obedience.

Why is this juridical notion of power, involving as it does the neglect of everything that makes for its productive effectiveness, its strategic resourcefulness, its positivity, so readily accepted? In a society such as ours, where the devices of power are so numerous, its rituals so visible, and its instruments ultimately so reliable, in this society that has been more imaginative, probably, than any other in creating devious and supple mechanisms of power, what explains this tendency not to recognize the latter except in the negative and emaciated form of prohibition? Why are the deployments of power reduced simply to the procedure of the law of interdiction?

Let me offer a general and tactical reason that seems self-evident: power is tolerable only on condition that it mask a substantial part of itself. Its success is proportional to its ability to hide its own mechanisms. Would power be accepted if it were entirely cynical? For it, secrecy is not in the nature of an abuse; it is indispensable to its operation. Not only because power imposes secrecy on those whom it dominates, but because it is perhaps just as indispensable to the latter: would they accept it if they did not see it as a mere limit placed on their desire, leaving a measure of freedom – however slight – intact? Power as a pure limit set on freedom is, at least in our society, the general form of its acceptability....

This history of sexuality, or rather this series of studies concerning the historical relationships of power and the discourse on sex, is, I realize, a circular project in the sense that it involves two endeavors that refer back to one another. We shall try to rid ourselves of a juridical and negative representation of power, and cease to conceive of it in terms of law, prohibition, liberty, and sovereignty. But how then do we analyze what has occurred in recent history with regard to this thing – seemingly one of the most forbidden areas of our lives and bodies – that is sex? How, if not by way of prohibition and blockage, does power gain access to it? Through which mechanisms, or tactics, or devices? But let us assume in turn that a somewhat careful scrutiny will show that power in modern societies has not in fact governed sexuality through law and sovereignty; let us suppose that historical analysis has revealed the presence of a veritable "technology" of sex, one that is much more complex and above all much more positive than the mere effect of a "defense" could be; this being the case, does this example – which can only be considered a privileged one, since power seemed in this instance, more than anywhere else, to function as prohibition – not compel one to discover principles for analyzing power which do not derive from the system of right and the form of law? Hence it is a question of forming a different grid of historical decipherment by starting from a different theory of power; and, at the same time, of advancing little by little toward a different conception of power through a closer examination of an entire historical material. We must at the same time conceive of sex without the law, and power without the king.

Method

Hence the objective is to analyze a certain form of knowledge regarding sex, not in terms of repression or law, but in terms of power. But the word *power* is apt to lead to a number of misunderstandings – misunderstandings with respect to its nature, its form, and its unity. By power, I do not mean "Power" as a group of institutions and mechanisms that insure the subservience of the citizens of a given state. By power, I do not mean, either, a mode of subjugation which, in contrast to violence, has the form of the rule. Finally, I do not have in mind a general system of domination exerted by one group over another, a system whose effects, through successive derivations, pervade the entire social body. The analysis, made in terms of power, must not assume that the sovereignty of the state, the form of the law, or the overall unity of a domination are given at the outset; rather, these are only the terminal forms power takes. It seems to me that power must be understood in the first instance as the multiplicity of force relations immanent in the sphere in which they operate and which constitute their own organization; as the process which, through ceaseless struggles and confrontations, transforms, strengthens, or reverses them; as the support which these force relations find in one another, thus forming a chain or a system, or on the contrary, the disjunctions and contradictions which isolate them from one another; and lastly, as the strategies in which they take effect, whose general design or institutional crystallization is embodied in the state apparatus, in the formulation of the law, in the various social hegemonies. Power's condition of possibility, or in any case the viewpoint which permits one to understand its exercise, even in its more "peripheral" effects, and which also makes it possible to use its mechanisms as a grid of intelligibility of the social order, must not be sought in the primary existence of a central point, in a unique source of sovereignty from which secondary and descendent forms would emanate; it is the moving substrate of force relations which, by virtue of their inequality, constantly engender states of power, but the latter are always local and unstable. The omnipresence of power: not because it has the privilege of consolidating everything under its invincible unity, but because it is produced from one moment to the next, at every point, or rather in every relation from one point to another. Power is everywhere; not because it embraces everything, but because it comes from everywhere. And "Power," insofar as it is permanent, repetitious, inert, and self-reproducing, is simply the overall effect that emerges from all these mobilities, the concatenation that rests on each of them and seeks in turn to arrest their movement. One needs to be nominalistic, no doubt: power is not an institution, and not a structure; neither is it a certain strength we are endowed with; it is the name that one attributes to a complex strategical situation in a particular society.

Should we turn the expression around, then, and say that politics is war pursued by other means? If we still wish to maintain a separation between war and politics, perhaps we should postulate rather that this multiplicity of force relations can be coded – in part but never totally – either in the form of "war," or in the form of "politics"; this would imply two different strategies (but the one always liable to switch into the other) for integrating these unbalanced, heterogeneous, unstable, and tense force relations.

Continuing this line of discussion, we can advance a certain number of propositions:

— Power is not something that is acquired, seized, or shared, something that one holds on to or allows to slip away; power is exercised from innumerable points, in the interplay of non-egalitarian and mobile relations.

— Relations of power are not in a position of exteriority with respect to other types of relationships (economic processes, knowledge relationships, sexual relations), but are immanent in the latter; they are the immediate effects of the divisions, inequalities, and disequilibriums which occur in the latter, and conversely they are the internal conditions of these differentiations; relations of power are not in superstructural positions, with merely a role of prohibition or accompaniment; they have a directly productive role, wherever they come into play.

— Power comes from below; that is, there is no binary and all-encompassing opposition between rulers and ruled at the root of power relations, and serving as a general matrix – no such duality extending from the top down and reacting on more and more limited groups to the very depths of the social body. One must suppose rather that the manifold relationships of force that take shape and come into play in the machinery of production, in families, limited groups, and institutions, are the basis for wide-ranging effects of cleavage that run through the social body as a whole. These then form a general line of force that traverses the local oppositions and links them together; to be sure, they also bring about redistributions, realignments, homogenizations, serial arrangements, and convergences of the force relations. Major dominations are the hegemonic effects that are sustained by all these confrontations.

— Power relations are both intentional and non-subjective. If in fact they are intelligible, this is not because they are the effect of another instance that "explains" them, but rather because they are imbued, through and through, with calculation: there is no power that is exercised without a series of aims and objectives. But this does not mean that it results from the choice or decision of an individual subject; let us not look for the headquarters that presides over its rationality; neither the caste which governs, nor the groups which control the state apparatus, nor those who make the most important economic decisions direct the entire network of power that functions in a society (and makes *it* function); the rationality of power is characterized by tactics that are often quite explicit at the restricted level where they are inscribed (the local cynicism of power), tactics which, becoming connected to one another, attracting and propagating one another, but finding their base of support and their condition elsewhere, end by forming comprehensive systems: the logic is perfectly clear, the aims decipherable, and yet it is often the case that no one is there to have invented them, and few who can be said to have formulated them: an implicit characteristic of the great anonymous, almost unspoken strategies which coordinate the loquacious tactics whose "inventors" or decisionmakers are often without hypocrisy.

— Where there is power, there is resistance, and yet, or rather consequently, this resistance is never in a position of exteriority in relation to power. Should it be said that one is always "inside" power, there is no "escaping" it, there is no absolute outside where it is concerned, because one is subject to the law in any case? Or that, history being the ruse of reason, power is the ruse of history, always emerging the winner? This would be to misunderstand the strictly relational character of power relationships. Their existence depends on a multiplicity of points of resistance: these play the role of adversary, target, support, or handle in power relations. These points of resistance are present everywhere in the power network. Hence there is no single locus of great Refusal, no soul of revolt, source of all rebellions, or pure law of the revolutionary. Instead there is a plurality of resistances, each of them a special case: resistances that are possible, necessary, improbable; others that are spontaneous, savage, solitary, concerted, rampant, or violent; still others that are quick to compromise, interested, or sacrificial; by definition, they can only exist in the strategic field of power relations. But this does not mean that they are only a reaction or rebound, forming with respect to the basic domination an underside that is in the end always passive, doomed to perpetual defeat. Resistances do not derive from a few heterogeneous principles; but neither are they a lure or a promise that is of necessity betrayed. They are the odd term in relations of power; they are inscribed in the latter as an irreducible opposite. Hence they too are distributed in irregular fashion: the points, knots, or focuses of resistance are spread over time and space at varying densities, at times mobilizing groups or individuals in a definitive way, inflaming certain points of the body, certain moments in life, certain types of behavior. Are there no great radical ruptures, massive binary divisions, then? Occasionally, yes. But more often one is dealing with mobile and transitory points of resistance, producing cleavages in a society that shift about, fracturing unities and effecting regroupings, furrowing across individuals themselves, cutting them up and remolding them, marking off irreducible regions in them, in their bodies and minds. Just as the network of power relations ends by forming a dense web that passes through apparatuses and institutions, without being exactly localized in them, so too the swarm of points of resistance traverses social stratifications and individual unities. And it is doubtless the strategic codification of these points of resistance that makes a revolution possible, somewhat similar to the way in which the state relies on the institutional integration of power relationships.

Notes

1 Paolo Segneri, *L'Instruction du pénitent* (French trans. 1695), p. 301.

2 Alfonso de' Liguori, *Pratique des confesseurs* (French trans. 1854), p. 140.

3 Segneri, *L'Instruction du pénitent*, pp. 301–2.

4 The reformed pastoral also laid down rules, albeit in a more discreet way, for putting sex into discourse. This notion will be developed in the next volume, *The Body and the Flesh*.

Michel Foucault

Select Bibliography

The Archaeology of Knowledge. Translated by A. M. Sheridan Smith. New York: Pantheon Books, 1982.

The Birth of the Clinic: An Archaeology of Medical Perception. Translated by A. M. Sheridan Smith. New York: Vintage Books, 1994.

The Care of the Self: Volume 3 of the History of Sexuality. Translated by Robert Hurley. New York: Pantheon Books, 1986.

Discipline and Punish: The Birth of the Prison. Translated by Alan Sheridan. New York: Vintage Books, 1995.

The Foucault Reader. Edited by Paul Rabinow. New York: Pantheon Books, 1984.

The History of Sexuality, Volume I: An Introduction. Translated by Robert Hurley. New York: Vintage Books, 1990.

Language, Counter-Memory, Practice: Selected Essays and Interviews. Edited by Donald F. Bouchard. Translated by Donald F. Bouchard and Sherry Simon. Ithaca, NY: Cornell University Press, 1977.

Madness and Civilization: A History of Insanity in the Age of Reason. Translated by Richard Howard. New York: Vintage Books, 1988.

Mental Illness and Psychology. Translated by Alan Sheridan. Berkeley: University of California Press, 1987.

The Order of Things: An Archaeology of the Human Sciences. New York: Vintage Books, 1994.

Politics, Philosophy, Culture: Interviews and Other Writings, 1977–1984. Edited by Lawrence D. Kritzman. Translated by Alan Sheridan and others. New York: Routledge, 1988.

Power/Knowledge: Selected Interviews and Other Writings, 1972–1977. Edited by Colin Gordon. Translated by Colin Gordon et al. New York: Pantheon Books, 1980.

Remarks on Marx: Conversations with Duccio Trombadori. Translated by R. James Goldstein and James Cascaito. New York: Semiotext(e), 1991.

The Use of Pleasure: Volume 2 of the History of Sexuality. Translated by Robert Hurley. New York: Pantheon Books, 1985.

7

Jean-François Lyotard

Jean-François Lyotard (1924–), professor of philosophy at the University of Paris at Vincennes, and later at the Collège International de Philosophie, is known for his wide-ranging work in the fields of psychoanalysis, Marxism and political thought, and aesthetics, as well as his famous philosophical appraisal of what constitutes "postmodernism." The following excerpt is taken from *The Postmodern Condition: A Report on Knowledge*, a study originally published in 1979 and undertaken as a report to the Conseil des Universités of the government of Quebec. The topic of the report is the status of knowledge in the most highly developed modern societies. In his discussion, Lyotard defines postmodernism in terms of what he calls an "incredulity toward metanarratives," that is, toward any grand overarching theories or systems of thought (whether religious, political, philosophical, or cultural) that would constitute an objective and binding basis for legitimation and truth.

The Postmodern Condition: A Report on Knowledge

Introduction

The object of this study is the condition of knowledge in the most highly developed societies. I have decided to use the word *postmodern* to describe that

From *The Postmodern Condition: A Report on Knowledge*, translated by Geoff Bennington and Brian Massumi (Manchester: Manchester University Press, 1991), pp. xxiii–xxv, 3–17. Originally published in France as *La Condition postmoderne*, copyright © 1979 by Les Editions de Minuit. English translation © 1984 by the University of Minnesota. All rights reserved. Reprinted by permission of the University of Minnesota Press.

condition. The word is in current use on the American continent among sociologists and critics; it designates the state of our culture following the transformations which, since the end of the nineteenth century, have altered the game rules for science, literature, and the arts. The present study will place these transformations in the context of the crisis of narratives.

Science has always been in conflict with narratives. Judged by the yardstick of science, the majority of them prove to be fables. But to the extent that science does not restrict itself to stating useful regularities and seeks the truth, it is obliged to legitimate the rules of its own game. It then

391

produces a discourse of legitimation with respect to its own status, a discourse called philosophy. I will use the term *modern* to designate any science that legitimates itself with reference to a metadiscourse of this kind making an explicit appeal to some grand narrative, such as the dialectics of Spirit, the hermeneutics of meaning, the emancipation of the rational or working subject, or the creation of wealth. For example, the rule of consensus between the sender and addressee of a statement with truth-value is deemed acceptable if it is cast in terms of a possible unanimity between rational minds: this is the Enlightenment narrative, in which the hero of knowledge works toward a good ethico-political end – universal peace. As can be seen from this example, if a metanarrative implying a philosophy of history is used to legitimate knowledge, questions are raised concerning the validity of the institutions governing the social bond: these must be legitimated as well. Thus justice is consigned to the grand narrative in the same way as truth.

Simplifying to the extreme, I define *postmodern* as incredulity toward metanarratives. This incredulity is undoubtedly a product of progress in the sciences: but that progress in turn presupposes it. To the obsolescence of the metanarrative apparatus of legitimation corresponds, most notably, the crisis of metaphysical philosophy and of the university institution which in the past relied on it. The narrative function is losing its functors, its great hero, its great dangers, its great voyages, its great goal. It is being dispersed in clouds of narrative language elements – narrative, but also denotative, prescriptive, descriptive, and so on. Conveyed within each cloud are pragmatic valencies specific to its kind. Each of us lives at the intersection of many of these. However, we do not necessarily establish stable language combinations, and the properties of the ones we do establish are not necessarily communicable.

Thus the society of the future falls less within the province of a Newtonian anthropology (such as stucturalism or systems theory) than a pragmatics of language particles. There are many different language games – a heterogeneity of elements. They only give rise to institutions in patches – local determinism.

The decision-makers, however, attempt to manage these clouds of sociality according to input/output matrices, following a logic which implies that their elements are commensurable and that the whole is determinable. They allocate our lives for the growth of power. In matters of social justice and of scientific truth alike, the legitimation of that power is based on its optimizing the system's performance – efficiency. The application of this criterion to all of our games necessarily entails a certain level of terror, whether soft or hard: be operational (that is, commensurable) or disappear.

The logic of maximum performance is no doubt inconsistent in many ways, particularly with respect to contradiction in the socio-economic field: it demands both less work (to lower production costs) and more (to lessen the social burden of the idle population). But our incredulity is now such that we no longer expect salvation to rise from these inconsistencies, as did Marx.

Still, the postmodern condition is as much a stranger to disenchantment as it is to the blind positivity of delegitimation. Where, after the metanarratives, can legitimacy reside? The operativity criterion is technological; it has no relevance for judging what is true or just. Is legitimacy to be found in consensus obtained through discussion, as Jürgen Habermas thinks? Such consensus does violence to the heterogeneity of language games. And invention is always born of dissension. Postmodern knowledge is not simply a tool of the authorities; it refines our sensitivity to differences and reinforces our ability to tolerate the incommensurable. Its principle is not the expert's homology, but the inventor's paralogy.

Here is the question: is a legitimation of the social bond, a just society, feasible in terms of a paradox analogous to that of scientific activity? What would such a paradox be?

The text that follows is an occasional one. It is a report on knowledge in the most highly developed societies and was presented to the Conseil des Universités of the government of Quebec at the request of its president. I would like to thank him for his kindness in allowing its publication.

It remains to be said that the author of the report is a philosopher, not an expert. The latter knows what he knows and what he does not know: the former does not. One concludes, the other questions – two very different language games. I combine them here with the result that neither quite succeeds.

The philosopher at least can console himself with the thought that the formal and pragmatic analysis of certain philosophical and ethico-political discourses of legitimation, which underlies the report, will subsequently see the light of day. The report will have served to introduce that analysis from a somewhat sociologizing slant, one that truncates but at the same time situates it.

Such as it is, I dedicate this report to the Institut Polytechnique de Philosophie of the Université de Paris VIII (Vincennes) – at this very postmodern moment that finds the University nearing what may be its end, while the Institute may just be beginning.

1 The field: knowledge in computerized societies

Our working hypothesis is that the status of knowledge is altered as societies enter what is known as the postindustrial age and cultures enter what is known as the postmodern age.[1] This transition has been under way since at least the end of the 1950s, which for Europe marks the completion of reconstruction. The pace is faster or slower depending on the country, and within countries it varies according to the sector of activity: the general situation is one of temporal disjunction which makes sketching an overview difficult.[2] A portion of the description would necessarily be conjectural. At any rate, we know that it is unwise to put too much faith in futurology.[3]

Rather than painting a picture that would inevitably remain incomplete, I will take as my point of departure a single feature, one that immediately defines our object of study. Scientific knowledge is a kind of discourse. And it is fair to say that for the last forty years the "leading" sciences and technologies have had to do with language: phonology and theories of linguistics,[4] problems of communication and cybernetics,[5] modern theories of algebra and informatics,[6] computers and their languages,[7] problems of translation and the search for areas of compatibility among computer languages,[8] problems of information storage and data banks,[9] telematics and the perfection of intelligent terminals,[10] paradoxology.[11] The facts speak for themselves (and this list is not exhaustive).

These technological transformations can be expected to have a considerable impact on knowledge. Its two principal functions – research and the transmission of acquired learning – are already feeling the effect, or will in the future. With respect to the first function, genetics provides an example that is accessible to the layman: it owes its theoretical paradigm to cybernetics. Many other examples could be cited. As for the second function, it is common knowledge that the miniaturization and commercialization of machines is already changing the way in which learning is acquired, classified, made available, and exploited.[12] It is reasonable to suppose that the proliferation of information-processing machines is having, and will continue to have, as much of an effect on the circulation of learning as did advancements in human circulation (transportation systems) and later, in the circulation of sounds and visual images (the media).[13]

The nature of knowledge cannot survive unchanged within this context of general transformation. It can fit into the new channels, and become operational, only if learning is translated into quantities of information.[14] We can predict that anything in the constituted body of knowledge that is not translatable in this way will be abandoned and that the direction of new research will be dictated by the possibility of its eventual results being translatable into computer language. The "producers" and users of knowledge must now, and will have to, possess the means of translating into these languages whatever they want to invent or learn. Research on translating machines is already well advanced.[15] Along with the hegemony of computers comes a certain logic, and therefore a certain set of prescriptions determining which statements are accepted as "knowledge" statements.

We may thus expect a thorough exteriorization of knowledge with respect to the "knower," at whatever point he or she may occupy in the knowledge process. The old principle that the acquisition of knowledge is indissociable from the training (*Bildung*) of minds, or even of individuals, is becoming obsolete and will become ever more so. The relationship of the suppliers and users of knowledge to the knowledge they supply and use is now tending, and will increasingly tend, to assume the form already taken by the relationship of commodity producers and consumers to the commodities they produce and consume – that is, the form of value. Knowledge is and will be produced in order to be sold, it is and will be consumed in order to be valorized in a new production: in both cases, the goal is exchange. Knowledge ceases to be an end in itself, it loses its "use-value."[16]

It is widely accepted that knowledge has become the principal force of production over the last few decades;[17] this has already had a noticeable effect on the composition of the work force of the most highly developed countries[18] and constitutes the major bottleneck for the developing countries. In the postindustrial and postmodern age, science will maintain and no doubt strengthen its pre-eminence in the arsenal of productive capacities of the nation-states. Indeed, this situation is one of the reasons leading to the conclusion that the gap between developed and developing countries will grow ever wider in the future.[19]

But this aspect of the problem should not be allowed to over-shadow the other, which is complementary to it. Knowledge in the form of an informational commodity indispensable to productive power is already, and will continue to be, a major – perhaps *the* major – stake in the worldwide competition for power. It is conceivable that the nation-states will one day fight for control of information, just as they battled in the past for control over territory, and afterwards for control of access to and exploitation of raw materials and cheap labor. A new field is opened for industrial and commercial strategies on the one hand, and political and military strategies on the other.[20]

However, the perspective I have outlined above is not as simple as I have made it appear. For the mercantilization of knowledge is bound to affect the privilege the nation-states have enjoyed, and still enjoy, with respect to the production and distribution of learning. The notion that learning falls within the purview of the state, as the brain or mind of society, will become more and more outdated with the increasing strength of the opposing principle, according to which society exists and progresses only if the messages circulating within it are rich in information and easy to decode. The ideology of communicational "transparency," which goes hand in hand with the commercialization of knowledge, will begin to perceive the state as a factor of opacity and "noise." It is from this point of view that the problem of the relationship between economic and state powers threatens to arise with a new urgency.

Already in the last few decades, economic powers have reached the point of imperiling the stability of the state through new forms of the circulation of capital that go by the generic name of *multinational corporations*. These new forms of circulation imply that investment decisions have, at least in part, passed beyond the control of the nation-states.[21] The question threatens to become even more thorny with the development of computer technology and telematics. Suppose, for example, that a firm such as IBM is authorized to occupy a belt in the earth's orbital field and launch communications satellites or satellites housing data banks. Who will have access to them? Who will determine which channels or data are forbidden?

The state? Or will the state simply be one user among others? New legal issues will be raised, and with them the question: "who will know?"

Transformation in the nature of knowledge, then, could well have repercussions on the existing public powers, forcing them to reconsider their relations (both de jure and de facto) with the large corporations and, more generally, with civil society. The reopening of the world market, a return to vigorous economic competition, the breakdown of the hegemony of American capitalism, the decline of the socialist alternative, a probable opening of the Chinese market – these and many other factors are already, at the end of the 1970s, preparing states for a serious reappraisal of the role they have been accustomed to playing since the 1930s: that of guiding, or even directing investments.[22] In this light, the new technologies can only increase the urgency of such a re-examination, since they make the information used in decision-making (and therefore the means of control) even more mobile and subject to piracy.

It is not hard to visualize learning circulating along the same lines as money, instead of for its "educational" value or political (administrative, diplomatic, military) importance; the pertinent distinction would no longer be between knowledge and ignorance, but rather, as is the case with money, between "payment knowledge" and "investment knowledge" – in other words, between units of knowledge exchanged in a daily maintenance framework (the reconstitution of the work force, "survival") versus funds of knowledge dedicated to optimizing the performance of a project.

If this were the case, communicational transparency would be similar to liberalism. Liberalism does not preclude an organization of the flow of money in which some channels are used in decision-making while others are only good for the payment of debts. One could similarly imagine flows of knowledge traveling along identical channels of identical nature, some of which would be reserved for the "decision-makers," while the others would be used to repay each person's perpetual debt with respect to the social bond.

2 The problem: legitimation

That is the working hypothesis defining the field within which I intend to consider the question of the status of knowledge. This scenario, akin to the one that goes by the name "the computerization of society" (although ours is advanced in an entirely different spirit), makes no claims of being original, or even true. What is required of a working hypothesis is a fine capacity for discrimination. The scenario of the computerization of the most highly developed societies allows us to spotlight (though with the risk of excessive magnification) certain aspects of the transformation of knowledge and its effects on public power and civil institutions – effects it would be difficult to perceive from other points of view. Our hypothesis, therefore, should not be accorded predictive value in relation to reality, but strategic value in relation to the question raised.

Nevertheless, it has strong credibility, and in that sense our choice of this hypothesis is not arbitrary. It has been described extensively by the experts[23] and is already guiding certain decisions by the governmental agencies and private firms most directly concerned, such as those managing the telecommunications industry. To some extent, then, it is already a part of observable reality. Finally, barring economic stagnation or a general recession (resulting, for example, from a continued failure to solve the world's energy problems), there is a good chance that this scenario will come to pass: it is hard to see what other direction contemporary technology could take as an alternative to the computerization of society.

This is as much as to say that the hypothesis is banal. But only to the extent that it fails to challenge the general paradigm of progress in science and technology, to which economic growth and the expansion of sociopolitical power seem to be natural complements. That scientific and technical knowledge is cumulative is never questioned. At most, what is debated is the form that accumulation takes – some picture it as regular, continuous, and unanimous, others as periodic, discontinuous, and conflictual.[24]

But these truisms are fallacious. In the first place, scientific knowledge does not represent the totality of knowledge; it has always existed in addition to, and in competition and conflict with, another kind of knowledge, which I will call narrative in the interests of simplicity (its characteristics will be described later). I do not mean to say that narrative knowledge can prevail over science, but its model is related to ideas of internal equilibrium and conviviality[25] next to which contemporary scientific knowledge cuts a poor figure, especially if it is to undergo an exteriorization with respect to the "knower" and an alienation from its user even greater than has previously been the case. The

resulting demoralization of researchers and teachers is far from negligible; it is well known that during the 1960s, in all of the most highly developed societies, it reached such explosive dimensions among those preparing to practice these professions – the students – that there was noticeable decrease in productivity at laboratories and universities unable to protect themselves from its contamination.[26] Expecting this, with hope or fear, to lead to a revolution (as was then often the case) is out of the question: it will not change the order of things in postindustrial society overnight. But this doubt on the part of scientists must be taken into account as a major factor in evaluating the present and future status of scientific knowledge.

It is all the more necessary to take it into consideration since – and this is the second point – the scientists' demoralization has an impact on the central problem of legitimation. I use the word in a broader sense than do contemporary German theorists in their discussions of the question of authority.[27] Take any civil law as an example: it states that a given category of citizens must perform a specific kind of action. Legitimation is the process by which a legislator is authorized to promulgate such a law as a norm. Now take the example of a scientific statement: it is subject to the rule that a statement must fulfill a given set of conditions in order to be accepted as scientific. In this case, legitimation is the process by which a "legislator" dealing with scientific discourse is authorized to prescribe the stated conditions (in general, conditions of internal consistency and experimental verification) determining whether a statement is to be included in that discourse for consideration by the scientific community.

The parallel may appear forced. But as we will see, it is not. The question of the legitimacy of science has been indissociably linked to that of the legitimation of the legislator since the time of Plato. From this point of view, the right to decide what is true is not independent of the right to decide what is just, even if the statements consigned to these two authorities differ in nature. The point is that there is a strict interlinkage between the kind of language called science and the kind called ethics and politics: they both stem from the same perspective, the same "choice" if you will – the choice called the Occident.

When we examine the current status of scientific knowledge – at a time when science seems more completely subordinated to the prevailing powers than ever before and, along with the new technologies, is in danger of becoming a major stake in their conflicts – the question of double legitimation, far from receding into the background, necessarily comes to the fore. For it appears in its most complete form, that of reversion, revealing that knowledge and power are simply two sides of the same question: who decides what knowledge is, and who knows what needs to be decided? In the computer age, the question of knowledge is now more than ever a question of government.

3   The method: language games

The reader will already have noticed that in analyzing this problem within the framework set forth I have favored a certain procedure: emphasizing facts of language and in particular their pragmatic aspect.[28] To help clarify what follows it would be useful to summarize, however briefly, what is meant here by the term *pragmatic*.

A denotative utterance[29] such as "The university is sick," made in the context of a conversation or an interview, positions its sender (the person who utters the statement), its addressee (the person who receives it), and its referent (what the statement deals with) in a specific way: the utterance places (and exposes) the sender in the position of "knower" (he knows what the situation is with the university), the addressee is put in the position of having to give or refuse his assent, and the referent itself is handled in a way unique to denotatives, as something that demands to be correctly identified and expressed by the statement that refers to it.

If we consider a declaration such as "The university is open," pronounced by a dean or rector at convocation, it is clear that the previous specifications no longer apply. Of course, the meaning of the utterance has to be understood, but that is a general condition of communication and does not aid us in distinguishing the different kinds of utterances or their specific effects. The distinctive feature of this second, "performative,"[30] utterance is that its effect upon the referent coincides with its enunciation. The university is open because it has been declared open in the above-mentioned circumstances. That this is so is not subject to discussion or verification on the part of the addressee, who is immediately placed within the new context created by the utterance. As for the sender, he must be invested with the authority to make such a statement. Actually, we could say it the other way around: the sender is dean or rector – that is, he is invested with the authority to make this kind of statement – only insofar as he

can directly affect both the referent (the university) and the addressee (the university staff) in the manner I have indicated.

A different case involves utterances of the type, "Give money to the university"; these are prescriptions. They can be modulated as orders, commands, instructions, recommendations, requests, prayers, pleas, etc. Here, the sender is clearly placed in a position of authority, using the term broadly (including the authority of a sinner over a god who claims to be merciful): that is, he expects the addressee to perform the action referred to. The pragmatics of prescription entail concomitant changes in the posts of addressee and referent.[31]

Of a different order again is the efficiency of a question, a promise, a literary description, a narration, etc. I am summarizing. Wittgenstein, taking up the study of language again from scratch, focuses his attention on the effects of different modes of discourse; he calls the various types of utterances he identifies along the way (a few of which I have listed) *language games*.[32] What he means by this term is that each of the various categories of utterance can be defined in terms of rules specifying their properties and the uses to which they can be put – in exactly the same way as the game of chess is defined by a set of rules determining the properties of each of the pieces, in other words, the proper way to move them.

It is useful to make the following three observations about language games. The first is that their rules do not carry within themselves their own legitimation, but are the object of a contract, explicit or not, between players (which is not to say that the players invent the rules). The second is that if there are no rules, there is no game,[33] that even an infinitesimal modification of one rule alters the nature of the game, that a "move" or utterance that does not satisfy the rules does not belong to the game they define. The third remark is suggested by what has just been said: every utterance should be thought of as a "move" in a game.

This last observation brings us to the first principle underlying our method as a whole: to speak is to fight, in the sense of playing, and speech acts[34] fall within the domain of a general agonistics.[35] This does not necessarily mean that one plays in order to win. A move can be made for the sheer pleasure of its invention: what else is involved in that labor of language harassment undertaken by popular speech and by literature? Great joy is had in the endless invention of turns of phrase, of words and meanings, the process behind the evolution of language on the level of *parole*. But undoubtedly even this pleasure depends on a feeling of success won at the expense of an adversary – at least one adversary, and a formidable one: the accepted language, or connotation.[36]

This idea of an agonistics of language should not make us lose sight of the second principle, which stands as a complement to it and governs our analysis: that the observable social bond is composed of language "moves." An elucidation of this proposition will take us to the heart of the matter at hand.

4   The nature of the social bond: the modern alternative

If we wish to discuss knowledge in the most highly developed contemporary society, we must answer the preliminary question of what methodological representation to apply to that society. Simplifying to the extreme, it is fair to say that in principle there have been, at least over the last half-century, two basic representational models for society: either society forms a functional whole, or it is divided in two. An illustration of the first model is suggested by Talcott Parsons (at least the post-war Parsons) and his school, and of the second, by the Marxist current (all of its component schools, whatever differences they may have, accept both the principle of class struggle and dialectics as a duality operating within society).[37]

This methodological split, which defines two major kinds of discourse on society, has been handed down from the nineteenth century. The idea that society forms an organic whole, in the absence of which it ceases to be a society (and sociology ceases to have an object of study), dominated the minds of the founders of the French school. Added detail was supplied by functionalism; it took yet another turn in the 1950s with Parsons's conception of society as a self-regulating system. The theoretical and even material model is no longer the living organism; it is provided by cybernetics, which, during and after World War II, expanded the model's applications.

In Parsons's work, the principle behind the system is still, if I may say so, optimistic: it corresponds to the stabilization of the growth economies and societies of abundance under the aegis of a moderate welfare state.[38] In the work of contemporary German theorists, *systemtheorie* is technocratic, even cynical, not to mention despairing: the harmony between the needs and hopes of indi-

viduals or groups and the functions guaranteed by the system is now only a secondary component of its functioning. The true goal of the system, the reason it programs itself like a computer, is the optimization of the global relationship between input and output – in other words, performativity. Even when its rules are in the process of changing and innovations are occurring, even when its dysfunctions (such as strikes, crises, unemployment, or political revolutions) inspire hope and lead to belief in an alternative, even then what is actually taking place is only an internal readjustment, and its result can be no more than an increase in the system's "viability." The only alternative to this kind of performance improvement is entropy, or decline.[39]

Here again, while avoiding the simplifications inherent in a sociology of social theory, it is difficult to deny at least a parallel between this "hard" technocratic version of society and the ascetic effort that was demanded (the fact that it was done in name of "advanced liberalism" is beside the point) of the most highly developed industrial societies in order to make them competitive – and thus optimize their "rationality" – within the framework of the resumption of economic world war in the 1960s.

Even taking into account the massive displacement intervening between the thought of a man like Comte and the thought of Luhmann, we can discern a common conception of the social: society is a unified totality, a "unicity." Parsons formulates this clearly: "The most essential condition of successful dynamic analysis is a continual and systematic reference of every problem to the state of the system as a whole.... A process or set of conditions either 'contributes' to the maintenance (or development) of the system or it is 'dysfunctional' in that it detracts from the integration, effectiveness, etc., of the system."[40] The "technocrats"[41] also subscribe to this idea. Whence its credibility: it has the means to become a reality, and that is all the proof it needs. This is what Horkheimer called the "paranoia" of reason.[42]

But this realism of systemic self-regulation, and this perfectly sealed circle of facts and interpretations, can be judged paranoid only if one has, or claims to have, at one's disposal a viewpoint that is in principle immune from their allure. This is the function of the principle of class struggle in theories of society based on the work of Marx.

"Traditional" theory is always in danger of being incorporated into the programming of the social whole as a simple tool for the optimization of its performance; this is because its desire for a unitary and totalizing truth lends itself to the unitary and totalizing practice of the system's managers. "Critical" theory,[43] based on a principle of dualism and wary of syntheses and reconciliations, should be in a position to avoid this fate. What guides Marxism, then, is a different model of society, and a different conception of the function of the knowledge that can be produced by society and acquired from it. This model was born of the struggles accompanying the process of capitalism's encroachment upon traditional civil societies. There is insufficient space here to chart the vicissitudes of these struggles, which fill more than a century of social, political, and ideological history. We will have to content ourselves with a glance at the balance sheet, which is possible for us to tally today now that their fate is known: in countries with liberal or advanced liberal management, the struggles and their instruments have been transformed into regulators of the system; in communist countries, the totalizing model and its totalitarian effect have made a comeback in the name of Marxism itself, and the struggles in question have simply been deprived of the right to exist.[44] Everywhere, the Critique of political economy (the subtitle of Marx's *Capital*) and its correlate, the critique of alienated society, are used in one way or another as aids in programming the system.[45]

Of course, certain minorities, such as the Frankfurt School or the group *Socialisme ou barbarie*,[46] preserved and refined the critical model in opposition to this process. But the social foundation of the principle of division, or class struggle, was blurred to the point of losing all of its radicality; we cannot conceal the fact that the critical model in the end lost its theoretical standing and was reduced to the status of a "utopia" or "hope,"[47] a token protest raised in the name of man or reason or creativity, or again of some social category – such as the Third World or the students[48] – on which is conferred in extremis the henceforth improbable function of critical subject.

The sole purpose of this schematic (or skeletal) reminder has been to specify the problematic in which I intend to frame the question of knowledge in advanced industrial societies. For it is impossible to know what the state of knowledge is – in other words, the problems its development and distribution are facing today – without knowing something of the society within which it is situated. And today more than ever, knowing about that society

involves first of all choosing what approach the inquiry will take, and that necessarily means choosing how society can answer. One can decide that the principal role of knowledge is as an indispensable element in the functioning of society, and act in accordance with that decision, only if one has already decided that society is a giant machine.[49]

Conversely, one can count on its critical function, and orient its development and distribution in that direction, only after it has been decided that society does not form an integrated whole, but remains haunted by a principle of opposition.[50] The alternative seems clear: it is a choice between the homogeneity and the intrinsic duality of the social, between functional and critical knowledge. But the decision seems difficult, or arbitrary.

It is tempting to avoid the decision altogether by distinguishing two kinds of knowledge. One, the positivist kind, would be directly applicable to technologies bearing on men and materials, and would lend itself to operating as an indispensable productive force within the system. The other – the critical, reflexive, or hermeneutic kind – by reflecting directly or indirectly on values or aims, would resist any such "recuperation."[51]

5   The nature of the social bond: the postmodern perspective

I find this partition solution unacceptable. I suggest that the alternative it attempts to resolve, but only reproduces, is no longer relevant for the societies with which we are concerned and that the solution itself is still caught within a type of oppositional thinking that is out of step with the most vital modes of postmodern knowledge. As I have already said, economic "redeployment" in the current phase of capitalism, aided by a shift in techniques and technology, goes hand in hand with a change in the function of the state: the image of society this syndrome suggests necessitates a serious revision of the alternate approaches considered. For brevity's sake, suffice it to say that functions of regulation, and therefore of reproduction, are being and will be further withdrawn from administrators and entrusted to machines. Increasingly, the central question is becoming who will have access to the information these machines must have in storage to guarantee that the right decisions are made. Access to data is, and will continue to be, the prerogative of experts of all stripes. The ruling class is and will continue to be the class of decision-makers. Even now it is no longer composed of the traditional political class, but of a composite layer of corporate leaders, high-level administrators, and the heads of the major professional, labor, political, and religious organizations.[52]

What is new in all of this is that the old poles of attraction represented by nation-states, parties, professions, institutions, and historical traditions are losing their attraction. And it does not look as though they will be replaced, at least not on their former scale. The Trilateral Commission is not a popular pole of attraction. "Identifying" with the great names, the heroes of contemporary history, is becoming more and more difficult.[53] Dedicating oneself to "catching up with Germany," the life goal the French president [Giscard d'Estaing at the time this book was published in France] seems to be offering his countrymen, is not exactly exciting. But then again, it is not exactly a life goal. It depends on each individual's industriousness. Each individual is referred to himself. And each of us knows that our *self* does not amount to much.[54]

This breaking up of the grand Narratives (discussed below, sections 9 and 10) leads to what some authors analyze in terms of the dissolution of the social bond and the disintegration of social aggregates into a mass of individual atoms thrown into the absurdity of Brownian motion.[55] Nothing of the kind is happening: this point of view, it seems to me, is haunted by the paradisaic representation of a lost "organic" society.

A *self* does not amount to much, but no self is an island; each exists in a fabric of relations that is now more complex and mobile than ever before. Young or old, man or woman, rich or poor, a person is always located at "nodal points" of specific communication circuits, however tiny these may be.[56] Or better: one is always located at a post through which various kinds of messages pass. No one, not even the least privileged among us, is ever entirely powerless over the messages that traverse and position him at the post of sender, addressee, or referent. One's mobility in relation to these language game effects (language games, of course, are what this is all about) is tolerable, at least within certain limits (and the limits are vague); it is even solicited by regulatory mechanisms, and in particular by the self-adjustments the system undertakes in order to improve its performance. It may even be said that the system can and must encourage such movement to the extent that it combats its own entropy; the novelty of an unexpected "move," with its correlative displacement of a partner or group of partners, can supply the system with that increased performativity it forever demands and consumes.[57]

It should now be clear from which perspective I chose language games as my general methodological approach. I am not claiming that the *entirety* of social relations is of this nature – that will remain an open question. But there is no need to resort to some fiction of social origins to establish that language games are the minimum relation required for society to exist: even before he is born, if only by virtue of the name he is given, the human child is already positioned as the referent in the story recounted by those around him, in relation to which he will inevitably chart his course.[58] Or more simply still, the question of the social bond, insofar as it is a question, is itself a language game, the game of inquiry. It immediately positions the person who asks, as well as the addressee and the referent asked about: it is already the social bond.

On the other hand, in a society whose communication component is becoming more prominent day by day, both as a reality and as an issue,[59] it is clear that language assumes a new importance. It would be superficial to reduce its significance to the traditional alternative between manipulatory speech and the unilateral transmission of messages on the one hand, and free expression and dialogue on the other.

A word on this last point. If the problem is described simply in terms of communication theory, two things are overlooked: first, messages have quite different forms and effects depending on whether they are, for example, denotatives, prescriptives, evaluatives, performatives, etc. It is clear that what is important is not simply the fact that they communicate information. Reducing them to this function is to adopt an outlook which unduly privileges the system's own interests and point of view. A cybernetic machine does indeed run on information, but the goals programmed into it, for example, originate in prescriptive and evaluative statements it has no way to correct in the course of its functioning – for example, maximizing its own performance. How can one guarantee that performance maximization is the best goal for the social system in every case? In any case the "atoms" forming its matter are competent to handle statements such as these – and this question in particular.

Second, the trivial cybernetic version of information theory misses something of decisive importance, to which I have already called attention: the agonistic aspect of society. The atoms are placed at the crossroads of pragmatic relationships, but they are also displaced by the messages that traverse them, in perpetual motion. Each language partner, when a "move" pertaining to him is made, undergoes a "displacement," an alteration of some kind that not only affects him in his capacity as addressee and referent, but also as sender. These "moves" necessarily provoke "countermoves" – and everyone knows that a countermove that is merely reactional is not a "good" move. Reactional countermoves are no more than programmed effects in the opponent's strategy; they play into his hands and thus have no effect on the balance of power. That is why it is important to increase displacement in the games, and even to disorient it, in such a way as to make an unexpected "move" (a new statement).

What is needed if we are to understand social relations in this manner, on whatever scale we choose, is not only a theory of communication, but a theory of games which accepts agonistics as a founding principle. In this context, it is easy to see that the essential element of newness is not simply "innovation." Support for this approach can be found in the work of a number of contemporary sociologists,[60] in addition to linguists and philosophers of language.

This "atomization" of the social into flexible networks of language games may seem far removed from the modern reality, which is depicted, on the contrary, as afflicted with bureaucratic paralysis.[61] The objection will be made, at least, that the weight of certain institutions imposes limits on the games, and thus restricts the inventiveness of the players in making their moves. But I think this can be taken into account without causing any particular difficulty.

In the ordinary use of discourse – for example, in a discussion between two friends – the interlocutors use any available ammunition, changing games from one utterance to the next: questions, requests, assertions, and narratives are launched pell-mell into battle. The war is not without rules,[62] but the rules allow and encourage the greatest possible flexibility of utterance.

From this point of view, an institution differs from a conversation in that it always requires supplementary constraints for statements to be declared admissible within its bounds. The constraints function to filter discursive potentials, interrupting possible connections in the communication networks: there are things that should not be said. They also privilege certain classes of statements (sometimes only one) whose predominance characterizes the discourse of the particular institution: there are things that should be said, and there are ways of saying them. Thus: orders in the army, prayer in church, denotation in the schools, narration in families, questions in philosophy, performativity in businesses. Bureaucratization is the outer limit of this tendency.

However, this hypothesis about the institution is still too "unwieldy": its point of departure is an overly "reifying" view of what is institutionalized. We know today that the limits the institution imposes on potential language "moves" are never established once and for all (even if they have been formally defined).[63] Rather, the limits are themselves the stakes and provisional results of language strategies, within the institution and without. Examples: Does the university have a place for language experiments (poetics)? Can you tell stories in a cabinet meeting? Advocate a cause in the barracks? The answers are clear: yes, if the university opens creative workshops; yes, if the cabinet works with prospective scenarios; yes, if the limits of the old institution are displaced.[64] Reciprocally, it can be said that the boundaries only stabilize when they cease to be stakes in the game.

This, I think, is the appropriate approach to contemporary institutions of knowledge.

Notes

1 Alain Touraine, *La Société postindustrielle* (Paris: Denoël, 1969) [Eng. trans. Leonard Mayhew, *The Post-Industrial Society* (London: Wildwood House, 1974)]; Daniel Bell, *The Coming of Post-Industrial Society* (New York: Basic Books, 1973); Ihab Hassan, *The Dismemberment of Orpheus: Toward a Post Modern Literature* (New York: Oxford University Press, 1971); Michel Benamou and Charles Caramello, eds, *Performance in Postmodern Culture* (Wisconsin: Center for Twentieth Century Studies & Coda Press, 1977); M. Köhler, "Postmodernismus: ein begriffgeschichtlicher Überblick," *Amerikastudien* 22, 1 (1977).

2 An already classic literary expression of this is provided in Michel Butor, *Mobile: Etude pour une représentation des Etats-Unis* (Paris: Gallimard, 1962).

3   Jib Fowles, ed., *Handbook of Futures Research* (Westport, Conn.: Greenwood Press, 1978).

4   Nikolai S. Trubetskoi, *Grundzüge der Phonologie* (Prague: Travaux du cercle linguistique de Prague, vol. 7, 1939) [Eng. trans. Christiane Baltaxe, *Principles of Phonology* (Berkeley: University of California Press, 1969)].

5   Norbert Wiener, *Cybernetics and Society: The Human Use of Human Beings* (Boston: Houghton Mifflin, 1949); William Ross Ashby, *An Introduction to Cybernetics* (London: Chapman & Hall, 1956).

6   See the work of Johannes von Neumann (1903–57).

7   S. Bellert, "La Formalisation des systèmes cybernétiques," in *Le Concept d'information dans la science contemporaine* (Paris: Minuit, 1965).

8   Georges Mounin, *Les Problèmes théoriques de la traduction* (Paris: Gallimard, 1963). The computer revolution dates from 1965, with the new generation of IBM 360s: R. Moch, "Le Tournant informatique," *Documents contributifs*, Annex 4, *L'Informatisation de la société* (Paris: La Documentation française, 1978); R. M. Ashby, "La Seconde Génération de la micro-électronique," *La Recherche* 2 (June 1970), pp. 127 ff.

9   C. L. Gaudfernan and A. Taïb, "Glossaire," in P. Nora and A. Minc, *L'Informatisation de la société* (Paris: La Documentation française, 1978); R. Béca, "Les Banques de données," *Nouvelle informatique et nouvelle croissance*, Annex 1, *L'Informatisation de la société*.

10 L. Joyeux, "Les Applications avancées de l'informatique," *Documents contributifs*. Home terminals (Integrated Video Terminals) will be commercialized before 1984 and will cost about $1,400, according to a report of the International Resource Development: *The Home Terminal* (Conn.: I.R.D. Press, 1979).

11 Paul Watzlawick, Janet Helmick-Beavin, Don D. Jackson, *Pragmatics of Human Communication: A Study of Interactional Patterns, Pathologies, and Paradoxes* (New York: Norton, 1967).

12 J. M. Treille, of the Groupe d'analyse et de prospective des systèmes économiques et technologiques (GAPSET), states that, "Not enough has been said about the new possibilities for disseminating stored information, in particular, using semiconductor and laser technology.... Soon everyone will be able to store information cheaply wherever he wishes, and, further, will be able to process it autonomously" (*La Semaine media* 16, February 16, 1979). According to a study by the National Science Foundation, more than one high school student in two has ready access to the services of a computer, and all schools will have one in the early 1980s (*La Semaine media* 13, January 25, 1979).

13 L. Brunel, *Des Machines et des hommes* (Montréal: Québec Science, 1978): Jean-Louis Missika and Dominique Wolton, *Les Réseaux pensants* (Librairie

technique et documentaire, 1978). The use of videoconferences between the province of Quebec and France is becoming routine: in November and December 1978 the fourth series of videoconferences (relayed by the satellite "Symphonie") took place between Quebec and Montreal on the one hand, and Paris (Université Paris Nord and the Beaubourg Center) on the other (*La Semaine media* 5, November 30, 1978). Another example is provided by electronic journalism. The three big American networks (ABC, NBC, and CBS) have increased the number of production studios around the world to the extent that almost all the events that occur can now be processed electronically and transmitted to the United States by satellite. Only the Moscow offices still work on film, which is sent to Frankfurt for satellite transmission. London has become the great "packing point" (*La Semaine media* 20, March 15, 1979).

14 The unit of information is the bit. For these definitions see Gaudfernan and Taïb, "Glossaire." This is discussed in René Thom, "Un protée de la sémantique: l'information" (1973), in *Modèles mathématiques de la morphogenèse* (Paris: Union Générale d'Edition, 1974). In particular, the transcription of messages into code allows ambiguities to be eliminated: see Watzlawick et al., *Pragmatics of Human Communication*, p. 98.

15 The firms Craig and Lexicon have announced the commercial production of pocket translators: four modules for four different languages with simultaneous reception, each containing 1,500 words, with memory. Weidner Communication Systems Inc. produces a *Multilingual Word Processor* that allows the capacity of an average translator to be increased from 600 to 2,400 words per hour. It includes a triple memory: bilingual dictionary, dictionary of synonyms, grammatical index (*La Semaine media* 6, December 6, 1978, 5).

16 Jürgen Habermas, *Erkenntnis und Interesse* (Frankfurt: Suhrkamp, 1968) [Eng. trans. Jeremy Shapiro, *Knowledge and Human Interests* (Boston: Beacon, 1971)].

17 "Man's understanding of nature and his mastery over it by virtue of his presence as a social body ... - appears as the great foundation-stone [*Grundpfeiler*] of production and of wealth," so that "general social knowledge becomes a *direct force of production*," writes Marx in the *Grundrisse* (1857–8) [(Berlin: Dietz Verlag, 1953), p. 593; Eng. trans. Martin Nicolaus (New York: Vintage, 1973), p. 705]. However, Marx concedes that it is not "only in the form of knowledge, but also as immediate organs of social practice" that learning becomes force, in other words, as machines: machines are *"organs of the human brain created by the human hand*; the power of knowledge, objectified" [p. 706]. See Paul Mattick, *Marx and Keynes: The Limits of the Mixed Economy* (Boston: Extending Horizons Books,

1969). This point is discussed in Lyotard, "La place de l'aliénation dans le retournement marxiste" (1969), in *Dérive à partir de Marx et Freud* (Paris: Union Générale d'Edition 1973), pp. 78–166.

18 The composition of the labor force in the United States changed as follows over a twenty-year period (1950–71):

	1950	1971
Factory, service sector, or agricultural workers	62.5%	51.4%
Professionals and technicians	7.5	14.2
White-collar	30.0	34.0

(*Statistical Abstracts*, 1971)

19 Because of the time required for the "fabrication" of a high-level technician or the average scientist in comparison to the time needed to extract raw materials and transfer money-capital. At the end of the 1960s, Mattick estimated the net rate of investment in underdeveloped countries at 3–5 percent of the GNP and at 10–15 percent in the developed countries [*Marx and Keynes*, p. 248.]

20 Nora and Minc, *L'Informatisation de la société*, especially pt. 1, "Les défis"; Y. Stourdzé, "Les Etats-Unis et la guerre des communications," *Le Monde*, December 13–15, 1978. In 1979, the value of the world market of telecommunications devices was $30 billion; it is estimated that in ten years it will reach $68 billion (*La Semaine media* 19, 8 March, 1979).

21 F. De Combret, "Le redéploiement industriel," *Le Monde*, April 1978; M. Lepage, *Demain le capitalisme* (Paris: Le Livre de Poche, 1978); Alain Cotta, *La France et l'impératif mondial* (Paris: Presses Universitaires de France, 1978).

22 It is a matter of "weakening the administration," of reaching the "minimal state." This is the decline of the Welfare State, which is accompanying the "crisis" that began in 1974.

23 "La Nouvelle Informatique et ses utilisateurs," Annex 3, *L'Informatisation de la société* (note 8).

24 B. P. Lécuyer, "Bilan et perspectives de la sociologie des sciences dans les pays occidentaux," *Archives européennes de sociologie* 19 (1978): 257–336 (bibliography). Good information on English and American currents: the hegemony of Merton's school until the beginning of the 1970s and the current dispersion, especially under the influence of Kuhn; not much information on German sociology of science.

25 The term has been given weight by Ivan Illich, *Tools for Conviviality* (New York, Harper & Row, 1973).

26 On this "demoralization", see A. Jaubert and J.-M. Lévy-Leblond, eds, *(Auto) critique de la science* (Paris: Seuil, 1973), Pt. 1.

27 Jürgen Habermas, *Legitimationsprobleme im Spätkapitalismus* (Frankfurt: Suhrkamp, 1973) [Eng. trans. Thomas McCarthy, *Legitimation Crisis* (Boston: Beacon Press, 1975)].

28 In the wake of Peirce's semiotics, the distinction of the syntactic, semantic, and pragmatic domains is made by Charles W. Morris, "Foundations of the Theory of Signs," in Otto Neurath, Rudolf Carnap, and Charles Morris, eds, *International Encyclopedia of Unified Science*, vol. 1, pt. 2 (1938), pp. 77–137. For the use of this term I refer especially to: Ludwig Wittgenstein, *Philosophical Investigations* [trans. G. E. M. Anscombe (New York: Macmillan, 1953)]; J. L. Austin, *How to Do Things with Words* (Oxford: Oxford University Press, 1962); J. R. Searle, *Speech Acts* (Cambridge: Cambridge University Press, 1969); Jürgen Habermas, "Unbereitende Bemerkungen zu einer Theorie der kommunikativen Kompetens," in Habermas and Luhmann, *Theorie der gesellschaft oder Sozialtechnologie* (Stuttgart: Suhrkamp, 1971); Oswald Ducrot, *Dire et ne pas dire* (Paris: Hermann, 1972); J. Poulain, "Vers une pragmatique nucléaire de la communication" (typescript, Université de Montréal, 1977). See too Watzlawick et al. *Pragmatics of Human Communication* (note 11).

29 "Denotation" corresponds here to "description" in the classical usage of logicians. Quine replaces "denotation" by "true of"; see W. V. Quine, *Word and Object* (Cambridge, Mass.: MIT Press, 1960). J. L. Austin, *How to Do Things with Words*, p. 39, prefers "constative" to "descriptive."

30 The term *performative* has taken on a precise meaning in language theory since Austin. Later in this book, the concept will reappear in association with the term *performativity* (in particular, of a system) in the new current sense of efficiency measured according to an input/output ratio. The two meanings are not far apart. Austin's performative realizes the optimal performance.

31 A recent analysis of these categories is to be found in Habermas, "Unbereitende Bemerkungen," and is discussed by J. Poulain, "Vers une pragmatique nucléaire."

32 *Philosophical Investigations*, sec. 23.

33 John Von Neumann and Oskar Morgenstern, *Theory of Games and Economic Behavior* (Princeton University Press, 1944), p. 49: "The *game* is simply the totality of the rules which describe it." This formulation is foreign to the spirit of Wittgenstein, for whom the concept of the game cannot be mastered by a definition, since definition is already a language game (*Philosophical Investigations*, especially secs. 65–84).

34 The term comes from Searle: "Speech acts ... are the basic or minimal units of linguistic communication" [*Speech Acts*, p. 16]. I place them within the domain of the *agon* (the joust) rather than that of communication.

35 Agonistics is the basis of Heraclitus's ontology and of the Sophists' dialectic, not to mention the early tragedians. A good part of Aristotle's reflections in the *Topics* and the *Sophistici Elenchi* is devoted to it.

See F. Nietzsche, "Homer's Contest" [trans. Maximilian A. Mügge, in *Complete Works*, vol. 2 (London: T. N. Fowlis, 1911; reprint, New York: Gordon Press, 1974)].

36 In the sense established by Louis Hjelmslev, in *Prolegomena to a Theory of Language* (Madison: University of Wisconsin Press, 1963), and taken up by Roland Barthes, *Eléments de sémiologie* (1964) (Paris: Seuil, 1966), 4:1 [Eng. trans. Annette Lavers and Colin Smith, *Elements of Semiology* (New York: Hill and Wang, 1968)].

37 See in particular Talcott Parsons, *The Social System* (Glencoe, Ill.: Free Press, 1967), and *Sociological Theory and Modern Society* (New York: Free Press, 1967). A bibliography of Marxist theory of contemporary society would fill more than fifty pages. The reader can consult the useful summary (dossiers and critical bibliography) provided by Pierre Souyri, *Le Marxisme après Marx* (Paris: Flammarion, 1970). An interesting view of the conflict between these two great currents of social theory and of their intermixing is given by A. W. Gouldner, *The Coming Crisis of Western Sociology* (New York: Basic Books, 1970). This conflict occupies an important place in the thought of Habermas, who is simultaneously the heir of the Frankfurt School and in a polemical relationship with the German theory of the social system, especially that of Luhmann.

38 This optimism appears clearly in the conclusions of Robert Lynd, *Knowledge for What?* (Princeton: Princeton University Press, 1939), p. 239; quoted by Max Horkheimer, *Eclipse of Reason* (Oxford: Oxford University Press, 1947): in modern society, science must replace religion ("worn threadbare") in defining the aims of life.

39 Helmut Schelsky, *Der Mensch in der Wissenschaftlichen Zivilisation* (Köln and Opladen: Arbeitsgemeinschaft für Forschung des Landes Nordrhein-Westfalen, Geisteswissenschaften Heft 96), pp. 24ff.: "The sovereignty of the State is no longer manifested by simple fact that it monopolizes the use of violence (Max Weber) or possesses emergency powers (Carl Schmitt), but primarily by the fact that the State determines the degree of effectiveness of all of the technical means existing within it, reserving their greatest effectiveness for itself, while at the same time exempting its own use of these instruments from the limitations it applies to their use by others." It will be said that this is a theory of the State, not of the system. But Schelsky adds: "In the process, the State's choice of goals is subordinated to the law that I have already mentioned as being the universal law of scientific civilization: namely that the means determine the ends, or rather, that the technical possibilities dictate what use is made of them." Habermas invokes against this law the fact that sets of technical means and systems of finalized rational action never develop autonomously: cf.

"Dogmatism, Reason, and Decision: On Theory and Practice in Our Scientific Civilization" [trans. John Viertel, in *Theory and Practice* (Boston: Beacon, 1973)]. See too Jacques Ellul, *La Technique ou l'enjeu du siècle* (Paris: Armand Colin, 1954), and *Le Système technicien* (Paris: Calmann-Lévy, 1977). That strikes, and in general the strong pressure brought to bear by powerful workers' organizations, produce a tension that is in the long run beneficial to the performance of the system is stated clearly by C. Levinson, a union leader; he attributes the technical and managerial advance of American industry to this tension (quoted by H.-F. de Virieu, *Le Matin*, special number, "Que veut Giscard?" December 1978).

40 Talcott Parsons, *Essays in Sociological Theory Pure and Applied*, revd edn (Glencoe, Ill.: Free Press, 1954), pp. 216–18.

41 I am using this word in the sense of John Kenneth Galbraith's term *technostructure* as presented in *The New Industrial State* (Boston: Houghton Mifflin, 1967), or Raymond Aron's term *technico-bureaucratic structure* in *Dix-huit leçons sur la société industrielle* (Paris: Gallimard, 1962) [Eng. trans. M. K. Bottomore, *Eighteen Lectures on Industrial Society* (London: Weidenfeld and Nicolson, 1967)], not in a sense associated with the term *bureaucracy*. The term *bureaucracy* is much "harder" because it is sociopolitical as much as it is economical, and because it descends from the critique of Bolshevik power by the worker's Opposition (Kollontaï) and the critique of Stalinism by the Trotskyist opposition. See on this subject Claude Lefort, *Eléments d'une critique de la bureaucratie* (Geneva: Droz, 1971), in which the critique is extended to bureaucratic society as a whole.

42 *Eclipse of Reason*, p. 183.

43 Max Horkheimer, "Traditionnelle und kritische Theorie" (1937) [Eng. trans. in J. O'Connell et al., trans., *Critical Theory: Selected Essays* (New York: Herder & Herder, 1972)].

44 See Claude Lefort, *Eléments d'une critique*, and *Un homme en trop* (Paris: Seuil, 1976); Cornelius Castoriadis, *La Société bureaucratique* (Paris: Union Générale d'Edition, 1973).

45 See for example J. P. Garnier, *Le Marxisme lénifiant* (Paris: Le Sycomore, 1979).

46 This was the title of the "organ of critique and revolutionary orientation" published between 1949 and 1965 by a group whose principal editors, under various pseudonyms, were C. de Beaumont, D. Blanchard, C. Castoriadis, S. de Diesbach, C. Lefort, J.-F. Lyotard, A. Maso, D. Mothé, P. Simon, P. Souyri.

47 Ernest Bloch, *Das Prinzip Hoffnung* (Frankfurt: Suhrkamp Verlag, 1959). See G. Raulet, ed., *Utopie-Marxisme selon E. Bloch* (Paris: Payot, 1976).

48 This is an allusion to the theoretical bunglings occasioned by the Algerian and Vietnam wars, and the

student movement of the 1960s. A historical survey of these is given by Alain Schapp and Pierre Vidal-Naquet in their introduction to the *Journal de la Commune étudiante* (Paris: Seuil, 1969) [Eng. trans. Maria Jolas, *The French Student Uprising, November 1967–June 1968* (Boston: Beacon, 1971)].

49 Lewis Mumford, *The Myth of the Machine: Technics and Human Development*, 2 vols (New York: Harcourt, Brace, 1967).

50 An appeal that was intended to secure intellectuals' participation in the system is nonetheless imbued with hesitation between these two hypotheses: P. Nemo, "La Nouvelle Responsabilité des clercs," *Le Monde*, September 8, 1978.

51 The origin of the theoretical opposition between *Naturwissenschaft* and *Geisteswissenschaft* is to be found in the work of Wilhelm Dilthey (1863–1911).

52 M. Albert, a commission member of the French Plan, writes: "The Plan is a governmental research department.... It is also a great meeting place where ideas ferment, where points of view clash and where change is prepared.... We must not be alone. Others must enlighten us...." (*L'Expansion*, November 1978). On the problem of decision, see G. Gafgen, *Theorie der wissenschaftlichen Entscheidung* (Tübingen, 1963); L. Sfez *Critique de la décision* (1973; Presses de la Fondation nationale des sciences politiques, 1976).

53 Think of the waning of names such as Stalin, Mao, and Castro as the eponyms of revolution over the last twenty years; consider the erosion of the image of the president in the United States since the Watergate affair.

54 This is a central theme in Robert Musil, *Der Mann ohne Eigenschaften* (1930–3; Hamburg: Rowolt, 1952) [Eng. trans. Eithne Wilkins and Ernest Kaiser, *The Man without Qualities* (London: Secker and Warburg, 1953–60)]. In a free commentary, J. Bouveresse underlines the affinity of this theme of the "dereliction" of the self with the "crisis" of science at the beginning of the twentieth century and with Mach's epistemology; he cites the following evidence: "Given the state of science in particular, a man is made only of what people say he is or of what is done with what he is.... The world is one in which lived events have become independent of man.... It is a world of happening, of what happens without its happening to anyone, and without anyone's being responsible" ("La problématique du sujet dans *L'Homme sans qualités*," *Noroît* (Arras) 234 and 235 (December 1978 and January 1979); the published text was not revised by the author.

55 Jean Baudrillard, *A l'ombre des majorités silencieuses, ou la fin du social* (Fontenay-sous-bois: Cahiers Utopie 4, 1978) [Eng. trans. *In the Shadow of the Silent Majority* (New York: Semiotexte, 1983)].

56 This is the vocabulary of systems theory. See for example P. Nemo, "La Nouvelle Responsabilité": "Think of society as a system, in the cybernetic sense. This system is a communication grid with intersections where messages converge and are redistributed...."

57 An example of this is given by J.-P. Garnier, *Le Marxisme lénifiant*, "The role of the Center for Information on Social Innovation, directed by H. Dougier and F. Bloch-Lainé, is to inventory, analyze, and distribute information on new experiences of daily life (education, health, justice, cultural activities, town planning and architecture, etc.). This data bank on 'alternative practices' lends its services to those state organs whose job it is to see to it that 'civil society' remains a civilized society: the Commissariat au Plan, the Secrétariat à l'action sociale, DATAR, etc."

58 Freud in particular stressed this form of "predestination." See Marthe Robert, *Roman des origines, origine du roman* (Paris: Grasset, 1972).

59 See the work of Michel Serres, especially *Hermès I–IV* (Paris: Editions de Minuit, 1969–77).

60 For example, Erving Goffman, *The Presentation of Self in Everyday Life* (Garden City, NY: Doubleday, 1959); Gouldner, *The Coming Crisis* (note 37), ch. 10; Alain Touraine et al., *Lutte étudiante* (Paris: Seuil, 1978); M. Callon, "Sociologie des techniques?" *Pandore* 2 (February 1979), pp. 28–32; Watzlawick et al., *Pragmatics of Human Communication* (note 11).

61 See note 41. The theme of general bureaucratization as the future of modern societies was first developed by B. Rizzi, *La Bureaucratisation du monde* (Paris: B. Rizzi, 1939).

62 See H. P. Grice, "Logic and Conversation" in Peter Cole and Jeremy Morgan, eds, *Speech Acts III, Syntax and Semantics* (New York: Academic Press, 1975), pp. 59–82.

63 For a phenomenological approach to the problem, see Maurice Merleau-Ponty, *Résumés de cours*, ed. Claude Lefort (Paris: Gallimard, 1968), the course for 1954–5. For a psychosociological approach, see R. Loureau, *L'Analyse institutionnelle* (Paris: Editions de Minuit, 1970).

64 M. Callon, "Sociologie des techniques?" p. 30: "Sociologics is the movement by which actors constitute and institute differences, or frontiers, between what is social and what is not, what is technical and what is not, what is imaginary and what is real: the outline of these frontiers is open to dispute, and no consensus can be achieved except in cases of total domination." Compare this with what Alain Touraine calls permanent sociology in *La Voix et le regard*.

Select Bibliography

The Differend: Phrases in Dispute. Translated by Georges Van Den Abbeele. Minneapolis: University of Minnesota Press, 1987.

Heidegger and "the jews." Translated by Andreas Michel and Mark S. Roberts. Minneapolis: University of Minnesota Press, 1990.

The Inhuman: Reflections on Time. Translated by Geoffrey Bennington and Rachel Bowlby. Stanford: Stanford University Press, 1991.

Just Gaming (with Jean-Loup Thebaud). Translated by Wlad Godzich. Minneapolis: University of Minnesota Press, 1985.

Lessons on the Analytic of the Sublime: Kant's Critique of Judgment, 23–29. Translated by Elizabeth Rottenberg. Stanford: Stanford University Press, 1994.

Libidinal Economy. Translated by Iain Hamilton Grant. Bloomington: Indiana University Press, 1993.

The Lyotard Reader. Edited by Andrew Benjamin. Oxford: Blackwell Publishers, 1989.

Peregrinations: Law, Form, Event. New York: Columbia University Press, 1988.

Phenomenology. Translated by Brian Beakley. Albany: State University of New York Press, 1991.

Political Writings. Translated by Bill Readings and Kevin Paul Geiman. Minneapolis: University of Minnesota Press, 1993.

The Postmodern Condition: A Report on Knowledge. Translated by Geoff Bennington and Brian Massumi. Manchester: Manchester University Press, 1991.

Toward the Postmodern. Edited by Robert Harvey and Mark S. Roberts. Atlantic Highlands, NJ: Humanities Press, 1993.

8

Julia Kristeva

Of Bulgarian origin, Julia Kristeva (1941–) now resides as a professor in Paris, where her work traverses the boundaries of philosophy, psychoanalysis, literary studies, linguistics, and feminism. Kristeva's early work uses linguistic and semiotic approaches to study poetic and literary language, emphasizing in particular the resources of such language to transcend totalizing or systematizing analyses. From the 1970s, her work increasingly turns to the way in which the "subject" (understood in a nonhypostasized, dynamic sense) is formed and situated in relation to language; here her approach is informed by both Freudian and Lacanian psychoanalysis. All of these diverse interests may be seen in the present essay "Women's Time" (1979), an important essay in feminist studies in which Kristeva argues against any essentialist theory of woman and investigates women's participation in what she calls the "sociosymbolic contract."

Women's Time

. . . The reader will find in the following pages, first, an attempt to situate the problematic of women in Europe within an inquiry on time: that time which the feminist movement both inherits and modifies. Secondly, I will attempt to distinguish two phases or two generations of women which, while immediately universalist and cosmopolitan in their demands, can nonetheless be differentiated by the fact that the first generation is more determined by the implications of a national problematic (in the sense suggested above), while the second, more determined by its place within the "symbolic denominator," is European *and* trans-European. Finally, I will try, both through the problems approached and through the type of analysis I propose, to present what I consider a viable stance for a European – or at least a European woman – within a domain which is henceforth worldwide in scope.

From *The Kristeva Reader*, edited by Toril Moi (New York: Columbia University Press, 1986), pp. 190–211. Copyright © 1986 by Columbia University Press. Reprinted with permission of the publisher.

Which Time?

"Father's time, mother's species," as Joyce put it; and indeed, when evoking the name and destiny of women, one thinks more of the *space* generating and forming the human species than of *time*, becoming or history. The modern sciences of subjectivity, of its genealogy and accidents, confirm in their own way this intuition, which is perhaps itself the result of a socio-historical conjuncture. Freud, listening to the dreams and fantasies of his patients, thought that "hysteria was linked to place."[1] Subsequent studies on the acquisition of the symbolic function by children show that the permanence and quality of maternal love condition the appearance of the first spatial references which induce the child's laugh and then induce the entire range of symbolic manifestations which lead eventually to sign and syntax.[2] Moreover, anti-psychiatry and psychoanalysis as applied to the treatment of psychoses, before attributing the capacity for transference and communication to the patient, proceed to the arrangement of new places, gratifying substitutes that repair old deficiencies in the maternal space. I could go on giving examples. But they all converge on the problematic of space, which innumerable religions of matriarchal (re)appearance attribute to "woman," and which Plato, recapitulating in his own system the atomists of antiquity, designated by the aporia of the *chora*, matrix space, nourishing, unnameable, anterior to the One, to God and, consequently, defying metaphysics.[3]

As for time, female[4] subjectivity would seem to provide a specific measure that essentially retains *repetition* and *eternity* from among the multiple modalities of time known through the history of civilizations. On the one hand, there are cycles, gestation, the eternal recurrence of a biological rhythm which conforms to that of nature and imposes a temporality whose stereotyping may shock, but whose regularity and unison with what is experienced as extra-subjective time, cosmic time, occasion vertiginous visions and unnameable *jouissance*.[5] On the other hand, and perhaps as a consequence, there is the massive presence of a monumental temporality, without cleavage or escape, which has so little to do with linear time (which passes) that the very word "temporality" hardly fits: all-encompassing and infinite like imaginary space, this temporality reminds one of Kronos in Hesiod's mythology, the incestuous son whose massive presence covered all of Gea in order to separate her from Ouranos, the father.[6] Or one is reminded of the various myths of resurrection which, in all religious beliefs, perpetuate the vestige of an anterior or concomitant maternal cult, right up to its most recent elaboration, Chris-

tianity, in which the body of the Virgin Mother does not die but moves from one spatiality to another within the same time via dormition (according to the Orthodox faith) or via assumption (the Catholic faith).[7]

The fact that these two types of temporality (cyclical and monumental) are traditionally linked to female subjectivity insofar as the latter is thought of as necessarily maternal should not make us forget that this repetition and this eternity are found to be the fundamental, if not the sole, conceptions of time in numerous civilizations and experiences, particularly mystical ones.[8] The fact that certain currents of modern feminism recognize themselves here does not render them fundamentally incompatible with "masculine" values.

In return, female subjectivity as it gives itself up to intuition becomes a problem with respect to a certain conception of time: time as project, teleology, linear and prospective unfolding: time as departure, progression and arrival – in other words, the time of history. It has already been abundantly demonstrated that this kind of temporality is inherent in the logical and ontological values of any given civilization, that this temporality renders explicit a rupture, an expectation or an anguish which other temporalities work to conceal. It might also be added that this linear time is that of language considered as the enunciation of sentences (noun + verb; topic–comment; beginning–ending), and that this time rests on its own stumbling block, which is also the stumbling block of that enunciation – death. A psychoanalyst would call this "obsessional time," recognizing in the mastery of time the true structure of the slave. The hysteric (either male or female) who suffers from reminiscences would, rather, recognize his or her self in the anterior temporal modalities: cyclical or monumental. This antimony, one perhaps embedded in psychic structures, becomes, nonetheless, within a given civilization, an antimony among social groups and ideologies in which the radical positions of certain feminists would rejoin the discourse of marginal groups of spiritual or mystical inspiration and, strangely enough, rejoin recent scientific preoccupations. Is it not true that the problematic of a time indissociable from space, of a space-time in infinite expansion, or rhythmed by accidents or catastrophes, preoccupies both space science and genetics? And, at another level, is it not true that the contemporary media revolution, which is manifest in the storage and reproduction of information, implies an idea of time as frozen or exploding according to the vagaries of demand, returning to its source but uncontrollable, utterly bypassing its subject and leaving only two preoccupations to those who approve of it: Who is to have power over the origin (the programming) and over the end (the use)?

It is for two precise reasons, within the framework of this article, that I have allowed myself this rapid excursion into a problematic of unheard-of complexity. The reader will undoubtedly have been struck by a fluctuation in the term of reference: mother, woman, hysteric . . . I think that the apparent coherence which the term "woman" assumes in contemporary ideology, apart from its "mass" or "shock" effect for activist purposes, essentially has the negative effect of effacing the differences among the diverse functions or structures which operate beneath this word. Indeed, the time has perhaps come to emphasize the multiplicity of female expressions and preoccupations so that from the intersection of these differences there might arise, more precisely, less commercially and more truthfully, the real *fundamental difference* between the two sexes: a difference that feminism has had the enormous merit of rendering painful, that is, productive of surprises and of symbolic life in a civilization which, outside the stock exchange and wars, is bored to death.

It is obvious, moreover, that one cannot speak of Europe or of "women in Europe" without suggesting the time in which this sociocultural distribution is situated. If it is true that a female sensibility emerged a century ago, the chances are great that by introducing *its own* notion of time, this sensibilty is not in agreement with the idea of an "eternal Europe" and perhaps not even with that of a "modern Europe." Rather, through and with the European past and present, as through and with the ensemble of "Europe," which is the repository of memory, this sensibility seeks its own trans-European temporality. There are, in any case, three attitudes on the part of European feminist movements towards this conception of linear temporality, which is readily labeled masculine and which is at once both civilizational and obsessional.

Two Generations

In its beginnings, the women's movement, as the struggle of suffragists and of existential feminists, aspired to gain a place in linear time as the time of project and history. In this sense, the movement, while immediately universalist, is also deeply rooted in the sociopolitical life of nations. The political demands of women; the struggles for equal pay for equal work, for taking power in social institutions on an equal footing with men; the rejection, when necessary, of the attributes traditionally considered feminine or maternal insofar as they are deemed incompatible with insertion in that history – all are part of the *logic of identification*[9] with certain values: not with the ideological (these are combated, and rightly so, as reactionary) but, rather, with the logical and ontological values of a rationality dominant in the nation-state. Here it is unnecessary to enumerate the benefits which this logic of identification and the ensuing struggle have achieved and continue to achieve for women (abortion, contraception, equal pay, professional recognition, etc.); these have already had or will soon have effects even more important than those of the Industrial Revolution. Universalist in its approach, this current in feminism *globalizes* the problems of women of different milieux, ages, civilizations or simply of varying psychic structures, under the label "Universal Woman." A consideration of *generations* of women can only be conceived of in this global way as a succession, as a progression in the accomplishment of the initial program mapped out by its founders.

In a second phase, linked, on the one hand, to the younger women who came to feminism after May 1968 and, on the other, to women who had an aesthetic or psychoanalytic experience, linear temporality has been almost totally refused, and as a consequence there has arisen an exacerbated distrust of the entire political dimension. If it is true that this more recent current of feminism refers to its predecessors and that the struggle for sociocultural recognition of women is necessarily its main concern, this current seems to think of itself as belonging to another generation – qualitatively different from the first one – in its conception of its own identity and, consequently, of temporality as such. Essentially interested in the specificity of female psychology and its symbolic realizations, these women seek to give a language to the intrasubjective and corporeal experiences left mute by culture in the past. Either as artists or writers, they have undertaken a veritable exploration of the *dynamic of signs*, an exploration which relates this tendency, at least at the level of its aspirations, to all major projects of aesthetic and religious upheaval. Ascribing this experience to a new generation does not only mean that other, more subtle problems have been added to the demands for sociopolitical identification made in the beginning. It also means that, by demanding recognition of an irreducible identity, without equal in the opposite sex and, as such, exploded, plural, fluid, in a certain way non-identical, this feminism situates itself outside the linear time of identities which communicate through projection and revindication. Such a feminism rejoins, on the one hand, the archaic (mythical) memory and, on the other, the cyclical or monumental temporality of marginal movements. It is certainly not by chance that the European and trans-European problematic has been poised as such at the same time as this new phase of feminism.

Finally, it is the mixture of the two attitudes – *insertion* into history and the radical *refusal* of the subjective limitations imposed by this history's time on an experiment carried out in the name of the irreducible difference – that seems to have broken loose over the past few years in European feminist movements, particularly in France and in Italy.

If we accept this meaning of the expression "a new generation of women," two kinds of questions might then be posed. What sociopolitical processes or events have provoked this mutation? What are its problems: its contributions as well as dangers?

Socialism and Freudianism

One could hypothesize that if this new generation of women shows itself to be more diffuse and perhaps less conscious in the United States and more massive in Western Europe, this is because of a veritable split in social relations and mentalities, a split produced by socialism and Freudianism. I mean by *socialism* that egalitarian doctrine which is increasingly broadly disseminated and accepted as based on common sense, as well as that social practice adopted by governments and political parties in democratic regimes which are forced to extend the zone of egalitarianism to include the distribution of goods as well as access to culture. By *Freudianism* I mean that lever, inside this egalitarian and socializing field, which once again poses the question of sexual difference and of the difference among subjects who themselves are not reducible one to the other.

Western socialism, shaken in its very beginnings by the egalitarian or differential demands of its women (e.g. Flora Tristan), quickly got rid of those women who aspired to recognition of a spe-

cificity of the female role in society and culture, only retaining from them, in the egalitarian and universalistic spirit of Enlightenment Humanism, the idea of a necessary identification between the two sexes as the only and unique means for liberating the "second sex." I shall not develop here the fact that this "ideal" is far from being applied in practice by these socialist-inspired movements and parties and that it was in part from the revolt against this situation that the new generation of women in Western Europe was born after May 1968. Let us just say that in theory, and as put into practice in Eastern Europe, socialist ideology, based on a conception of the human being as determined by its place in *production* and the *relations of production*, did not take into consideration this same human being according to its place in *reproduction*, on the one hand, or in the *symbolic order*, on the other. Consequently, the specific character of women could only appear as nonessential or even nonexistent to the totalizing and even totalitarian spirit of this ideology.[10] We begin to see that this same egalitarian and in fact censuring treatment has been imposed, from Enlightenment Humanism through socialism, on religious specificities and, in particular, on Jews.[11]

What has been achieved by this attitude remains nonetheless of capital importance for women, and I shall take as an example the change in the destiny of women in the socialist countries of Eastern Europe. It could be said, with only slight exaggeration, that the demands of the suffragists and existential feminists have, to a great extent, been met in these countries, since three of the main egalitarian demands of early feminism have been or are now being implemented despite vagaries and blunders: economic, political, and professional equality. The fourth, sexual equality, which implies permissiveness in sexual relations (including homosexual relations), abortions, and contraception, remains stricken by taboo in Marxian ethics as well as for reasons of state. It is, then, this fourth equality which is the problem and which therefore appears *essential* in the struggle of a new generation. But simultaneously and as a consequence of these socialist accomplishments – which are in fact a total deception – the struggle is no longer concerned with the quest for equality but, rather, with difference and specificity. It is precisely at this point that the new generation encounters what might be called the *symbolic* question.[12] Sexual difference – which is at once biological, physiological, and relative to reproduction – is translated by and translates a difference in the relationship of subjects to the symbolic contract which *is* the social contract: a difference, then, in the relationship to power, language, and meaning. The sharpest and most subtle point of feminist subversion brought about by the new generation will henceforth be situated on the terrain of the inseparable conjunction of the sexual and the symbolic, in order to try to discover, first, the specificity of the female, and then, in the end, that of each individual woman.

A certain saturation of socialist ideology, a certain exhaustion of its potential as a program for a new social contract (it is obvious that the effective realization of this program is far from being accomplished, and I am here treating only its system of thought) makes way for ... Freudianism. I am, of course, aware that this term and this practice are somewhat shocking to the American intellectual consciousness (which rightly reacts to a muddled and normatizing form of psychoanalysis) and, above all, to the feminist consciousness. To restrict my remarks to the latter: Is it not true that Freud has been seen only as a denigrator or even an exploiter of women? as an irritating phallocrat in a Vienna which was at once puritan and decadent – a man who fantasized women as sub-men, castrated men?

Castrated and/or Subject to Language

Before going beyond Freud to propose a more just or more modern vision of women, let us try, first, to understand his notion of castration. It is, first of all, a question of an *anguish* or *fear* of castration, or of correlative penis *envy*; a question, therefore, of *imaginary* formations readily perceivable in the *discourse* of neurotics of both sexes, men and women. But, above all, a careful reading of Freud, going beyond his biologism and his mechanism, both characteristic of his time, brings out two things. First, as presupposition for the "primal scene," the castration fantasy and its correlative (penis envy) are hypotheses, *a priori* suppositions intrinsic to the theory itself, in the sense that these are not the ideological fantasies of their inventor but, rather, logical necessities to be placed at the "origin" in order to explain what unceasingly functions in neurotic discourse. In other words, neurotic discourse, in man and woman, can only be understood in terms of its own logic when its fundamental causes are admitted as the fantasies of the primal scene and castration, even if (as may be the case) nothing renders them present in reality

itself. Stated in still other terms, the reality of castration is no more real than the hypothesis of an explosion which, according to modern astrophysics, is at the origin of the universe: nothing proves it, in a sense it is an article of faith, the only difference being that numerous phenomena of life in this "big-bang" universe are explicable only through this initial hypothesis. But one is infinitely more jolted when this kind of intellectual method concerns inanimate matter than when it is applied to our own subjectivity and thus, perhaps, to the fundamental mechanism of our epistemophilic thought.

Moreover, certain texts written by Freud (*The Interpretation of Dreams*, but especially those of the second topology, in particular the *Metapsychology*) and their recent extensions (notably by Lacan),[13] imply that castration is, in sum, the imaginary construction of a radical operation which constitutes the symbolic field and all beings inscribed therein. This operation constitutes signs and syntax; that is, language, as a *separation* from a presumed state of nature, of pleasure fused with nature so that the introduction of an articulated network of differences, which refers to objects henceforth and only in this way separated from a subject, may constitute *meaning*. This logical operation of separation (confirmed by all psycholinguistic and child psychology) which preconditions the binding of language which is already syntactical, is therefore the common destiny of the two sexes, men and women. That certain biofamilial conditions and relationships cause women (and notably hysterics) to deny this separation and the language which ensues from it, whereas men (notably obsessionals) magnify both and, terrified, attempt to master them – this is what Freud's discovery has to tell us on this issue.

The analytic situation indeed shows that it is the penis which, becoming the major referent in this operation of separation, gives full meaning to the *lack* or to the *desire* which constitutes the subject during his or her insertion into the order of language. I should only like to indicate here that, in order for this operation constitutive of the symbolic and the social to appear in its full truth and for it to be understood by both sexes, it would be just to emphasize its extension to all that is privation of fulfillment and of totality; exclusion of a pleasing, natural and sound state: in short, the break indispensable to the advent of the symbolic.

It can now be seen how women, starting with this theoretical apparatus, might try to understand their sexual and symbolic difference in the framework of social, cultural, and professional realization, in order to try, by seeing their position therein, either to fulfill their own experience to a maximum or – but always starting from this point – to go further and call into question the very apparatus itself.

Living the Sacrifice

In any case, and for women in Europe today, whether or not they are conscious of the various mutations (socialist and Freudian) which have produced or simply accompanied their coming into their own, the urgent question on our agenda might be formulated as follows: *What can be our place in the symbolic contract?* If the social contract, far from being that of equal men, is based on an essentially sacrificial relationship of separation and articulation of differences which in this way produces communicable meaning, what is our place in this order of sacrifice and/or of language? No longer wishing to be excluded or no longer content with the function which has always been demanded of us (to maintain, arrange, and perpetuate this sociosymbolic contract as mothers, wives, nurses, doctors, teachers . . .), how can we reveal our place, first as it is bequeathed to us by tradition, and then as we want to transform it? . . .

Creatures and Creatresses

The desire to be a mother, considered alienating and even reactionary by the preceding generation of feminists, has obviously not become a standard for the present generation. But we have seen in the past few years an increasing number of women who not only consider their maternity compatible with their professional life or their feminist involvement (certain improvements in the quality of life are also at the origin of this: an increase in the number of daycare centers and nursery schools, more active participation of men in child care and domestic life, etc.), but also find it indispensable to their discovery, not of the plenitude, but of the complexity of the female experience, with all that this complexity comprises in joy and pain. This tendency has its extreme: in the refusal of the paternal function by lesbian and single mothers can be seen one of the most violent forms taken by the rejection of the symbolic outlined above, as well as one of the most

fervent divinizations of maternal power – all of which cannot help but trouble an entire legal and moral order without, however, proposing an alternative to it. Let us remember here that Hegel distinguished between female right (familial and religious) and male law (civil and political). If our societies know well the uses and abuses of male law, it must also be recognized that female right is designated, for the moment, by a blank. And if these practices of maternity, among others, were to be generalized, women themselves would be responsible for elaborating the appropriate legislation to check the violence to which, otherwise, both their children and men would be subject. But are they capable of doing so? This is one of the important questions that the new generation of women encounters, especially when the members of this new generation refuse to ask those questions seized by the same rage with which the dominant order originally victimized them.

Faced with this situation, it seems obvious – and feminist groups become more aware of this when they attempt to broaden their audience – that the refusal of maternity cannot be a mass policy and that the majority of women today see the possibility for fulfillment, if not entirely at least to a large degree, in bringing a child into the world. What does this desire for motherhood correspond to? This is one of the new questions for the new generation, a question the preceding generation had foreclosed. For want of an answer to this question, feminist ideology leaves the door open to the return of religion, whose discourse, tried and proved over thousands of years, provides the necessary ingredients for satisfying the anguish, the suffering and the hopes of mothers. If Freud's affirmation – that the desire for a child is the desire for a penis and, in this sense, a substitute for phallic and symbolic dominion – can be only partially accepted, what modern women have to say about this experience should nonetheless be listened to attentively. Pregnancy seems to be experienced as the radical ordeal of the splitting of the subject:[14] redoubling up of the body, separation and coexistence of the self and of an other, of nature and consciousness, of physiology and speech. This fundamental challenge to identity is then accompanied by a fantasy of totality – narcissistic completeness – a sort of instituted, socialized, natural psychosis. The arrival of the child, on the other hand, leads the mother into the labyrinths of an experience that, without the child, she would only rarely encounter: love for an other. Not for herself, nor for an identical being, and still less for another person with whom "I" fuse (love or sexual passion). But the slow, difficult, and delightful apprenticeship in attentiveness, gentleness, forgetting oneself. The ability to succeed in this path without masochism and without annihilating one's affective, intellectual, and professional personality – such would seem to be the stakes to be won through guiltless maternity. It then becomes a creation in the strong sense of the term. For this moment, utopian?

On the other hand, it is in the aspiration towards artistic and, in particular, literary creation that woman's desire for affirmation now manifests itself. Why literature?

Is it because, faced with social norms, literature reveals a certain knowledge and sometimes the truth itself about an otherwise repressed, nocturnal, secret, and unconscious universe? Because it thus redoubles the social contract by exposing the unsaid, the uncanny? And because it makes a game, a space of fantasy and pleasure, out of the abstract and frustrating order of social signs, the words of everyday communication? Flaubert said, "Madame Bovary, c'est moi." Today many women imagine, "Flaubert, c'est moi." This identification with the potency of the imaginary is not only an identification, an imaginary potency (a fetish, a belief in the maternal penis maintained at all costs), as a far too normative view of the social and symbolic relationship would have it. This identification also bears witness to women's desire to lift the weight of what is sacrificial in the social contract from their shoulders, to nourish our societies with a more flexible and free discourse, one able to name what has thus far never been an object of circulation in the community: the enigmas of the body, the dreams, secret joys, shames, hatreds of the second sex.

It is understandable from this that women's writing has lately attracted the maximum attention of both "specialists" and the media.[15] The pitfalls encountered along the way, however, are not to be minimized: for example, does one not read there a relentless belittling of male writers whose books, nevertheless, often serve as "models" for countless productions by women? Thanks to the feminist label, does one not sell numerous works whose naive whining or market-place romanticism would otherwise have been rejected as anachronistic? And does one not find the pen of many a female writer being devoted to phantasmic attacks against Language and Sign as the ultimate supports of phallocratic power, in the name of a semi-aphonic

corporality whose truth can only be found in that which is "gestural" or "tonal"?

And yet, no matter how dubious the results of these recent productions by women, the symptom is there – women are writing, and the air is heavy with expectation: What will they write that is new?

In the Name of the Father, the Son . . . and the Woman?

These few elements of the manifestations by the new generation of women in Europe seem to me to demonstrate that, beyond the sociopolitical level where it is generally inscribed (or inscribes itself), the women's movement – in its present stage, less aggressive but more artful – is situated within the very framework of the religious crisis of our civilization.

I call "religion" this phantasmic necessity on the part of speaking beings to provide themselves with a *representation* (animal, female, male, parental, etc.) in place of what constitutes them as such, in other words, symbolization – the double articulation and syntactic sequence of language, as well as its preconditions or substitutes (thoughts, affects, etc.). The elements of the current practice of feminism that we have just brought to light seem precisely to constitute such a representation which makes up for the frustrations imposed on women by the anterior code (Christianity or its lay humanist variant). The fact that this new ideology has affinities, often revindicated by its creators, with so-called matriarchal beliefs (in other words, those beliefs characterizing matrilinear societies) should not overshadow its radical novelty. This ideology seems to me to be part of the broader antisacrificial current which is animating our culture and which, in its protest against the constraints of the sociosymbolic contract, is no less exposed to the risks of violence and terrorism. At this level of radicalism, it is the very principle of sociality which is challenged.

Certain contemporary thinkers consider, as is well known, that modernity is characterized as the first epoch in human history in which human beings attempt to live without religion. In its present form, is not feminism in the process of becoming one?

Or is it, on the contrary and as avant-garde feminists hope, that having started with the idea of difference, feminism will be able to break free of its belief in Woman, Her power, Her writing, so as to channel this demand for difference into each and every element of the female whole, and, finally, to bring out the singularity of each woman, and beyond this, her multiplicities, her plural languages, beyond the horizon, beyond sight, beyond faith itself?

A factor for ultimate mobilization? Or a factor for analysis?

Imaginary support in a technocratic era where all narcissism is frustrated? Or instruments fitted to these times in which the cosmos, atoms, and cells – our true contemporaries – call for the constitution of a fluid and free subjectivity?

The question has been posed. Is to pose it already to answer it?

Another Generation is Another Space

If the preceding can be *said* – the question whether all this is *true* belongs to a different register – it is undoubtedly because it is now possible to gain some distance on these two preceding generations of women. This implies, of course, that a *third* generation is now forming, at least in Europe. I am not speaking of a new group of young women (though its importance should not be underestimated) or of another "mass feminist movement" taking the torch passed on from the second generation. My usage of the word "generation" implies less a chronology than a *signifying space*, a both corporeal and desiring mental space. So it can be argued that as of now a third attitude is possible, thus a third generation, which does not exclude – quite to the contrary – the *parallel* existence of all three in the same historical time, or even that they be interwoven one with the other.

In this third attitude, which I strongly advocate – which I imagine? – the very dichotomy man/ woman as an opposition between two rival entities may be understood as belonging to *metaphysics*. What can "identity," even "sexual identity," mean in a new theoretical and scientific space where the very notion of identity is challenged?[16] I am not simply suggesting a very hypothetical bisexuality which, even if it existed, would only, in fact, be the aspiration towards the totality of one of the sexes and thus an effacing of difference. What I mean is, first of all, the demassification of the problematic of *difference*, which would imply, in a first phase, an apparent de-dramatization of the "fight to the death" between rival groups and thus between the sexes. And this not in the name of

some reconciliation – feminism has at least had the merit of showing what is irreducible and even deadly in the social contract – but in order that the struggle, the implacable difference, the violence be conceived in the very place where it operates with the maximum intransigence, in other words, in personal and sexual identity itself, so as to make it disintegrate in its very nucleus.

It necessarily follows that this involves risks not only for what we understand today as "personal equilibrium" but also for social equilibrium itself, made up as it now is of the counterbalancing of aggressive and murderous forces massed in social, national, religious, and political groups. But is it not the insupportable situation of tension and explosive risk that the existing "equilibrium" presupposes which leads some of those who suffer from it to divest it of its economy, to detach themselves from it and to seek another means of regulating difference?

To restrict myself here to a personal level, as related to the question of women, I see arising, under the cover of a relative indifference towards the militance of the first and second generations, an attitude of retreat from sexism (male as well as female) and, gradually, from any kind of anthropomorphism. The fact that this might quickly become another form of spiritualism turning its back on social problems, or else a form of repression[17] ready to support all status quos, should not hide the radicalness of the process. This process could be summarized as an *interiorization of the founding separation of the sociosymbolic contract*, as an introduction of its cutting edge into the very interior of every identity whether subjective, sexual, ideological, or so forth. This in such a way that the habitual and increasingly explicit attempt to fabricate a scapegoat victim as foundress of a society or a countersociety may be replaced by the analysis of the potentialities of *victim/executioner* which characterize each identity, each subject, each sex.

What discourse, if not that of a religion, would be able to support this adventure which surfaces as a real possibility, after both the achievements and the impasses of the present ideological reworkings, in which feminism has participated? It seems to me that the role of what is usually called "aesthetic practices" must increase not only to counterbalance the storage and uniformity of information by present-day mass media, data-bank systems and, in particular, modern communications technology, but also to demystify the identity of the symbolic bond itself, to demystify, therefore, the *community* of language as a universal and unifying tool, one which totalizes and equalizes. In order to bring out – along with the *singularity* of each person and, even more, along with the multiplicity of every person's possible identifications (with atoms, e.g. stretching from the family to the stars) – the *relativity of his/her symbolic as well as biological existence*, according to the variation in his/her specific symbolic capacities. And in order to emphasize the *responsibility* which all will immediately face of putting this fluidity into play against the threats of death which are unavoidable whenever an inside and an outside, a self and an other, one group and another, are constituted. At this level of interiorization with its social as well as individual stakes, what I have called "aesthetic practices" are undoubtedly nothing other than the modern reply to the eternal question of morality. At least, this is how we might understand an ethics which, conscious of the fact that its order is sacrificial, reserves part of the burden for each of its adherents, therefore declaring them guilty while immediately affording them the possibility for *jouissance*, for various productions, for a life made up of both challenges and differences.

Spinoza's question can be taken up again here: Are women subject to ethics? If not to that ethics defined by classical philosophy – in relationship to which the ups and downs of feminist generations seem dangerously precarious – are women not already participating in the rapid dismantling that our age is experiencing at various levels (from wars to drugs to artificial insemination) and which poses the *demand* for a new ethics? The answer to Spinoza's question can be affirmative only at the cost of considering feminism as but a *moment* in the thought of that anthropomorphic identity which currently blocks the horizon of the discursive and scientific adventure of our species.

Notes

1 Sigmund Freud and Carl G. Jung, *Correspondance* (Paris: Gallimard, 1975), vol. I, p. 87.

2 R. Spitz, *La Première année de la vie de l'enfant* [First year of life: a psychoanalytic study of normal and deviant development of object relations] (Paris: PUF, 1958); D. Winnicott, *Jeu et réalité* [Playing and reality] (Paris: Gallimard, 1975); Julia Kristeva, "Noms de lieu", in *Polylogue* (Paris: Seuil, 1977), translated as "Place names" in Julia Kristeva, *Desire in Language: A Semiotic Approach to Literature and Art*, ed. Leon S. Roudiez, trans. Thomas Gora, Alice Jardine, and Leon Roudiez (New York: Columbia University Press, 1980).

3 Plato, *Timeus* 52: "Indefinitely a place; it cannot be destroyed, but provides a ground for all that can come into being; itself being perceptible, outside of all sensation, by means of a sort of bastard reasoning; barely assuming credibility, it is precisely that which makes us dream when we perceive it, and affirm that all that exists must be somewhere, in a determined place..." (author's translation).

4 As most readers of recent French theory in translation know, *le féminin* does not have the same pejorative connotations it has come to have in English. It is a term used to speak about women in general, but, as used most often in this article, it probably comes closest to our "female" as defined by Elaine Showalter in *A Literature of Their Own* (Princeton: Princeton University Press, 1977). I have therefore used either "women" or "female" according to the context. (Trans.)

5 I have retained *jouissance* – that word for pleasure which defies translation – as it is rapidly becoming a "believable neologism" in English (see the glossary in *Desire in Language*). (Trans.)

6 This particular mythology has important implications – equal only to those of the Oedipal myth – for current French thought. (Trans.)

7 See Julia Kristeva, "Stabat Mater," first published as "Héréthique de l'amour", *Tel Quel*, 74 (1977), pp. 30–49.

8 See H. C. Puech, *La Gnose et le temps* (Paris: Gallimard, 1977).

9 The term "identification" belongs to a wide semantic field ranging from everyday language to philosophy and psychoanalysis. While Kristeva is certainly referring in principle to its elaboration in Freudian and Lacanian psychoanalysis, it can be understood here as a logic, in its most general sense (see the entry on "identification" in Jean Laplanche and J. B. Pontalis, *Vocabulaire de la psychanalyse* [The language of psychoanalysis], Paris: Presses Universitaires de France, 1967; revd ed, 1976). (Trans.)

10 See D. Desanti, "L'autre sexe des bolcheviks", *Tel Quel*, 76 (1978); Julia Kristeva, *Des Chinoises* (Paris: des femmes, 1975), translated as *On Chinese Women*, trans. Anita Barrows (London: Marion Boyars, 1977).

11 See Arthur Hertzberg, *The French Enlightenment and the Jews* (New York: Columbia University Press, 1968); *Les Juifs et la révolution française*, ed. B. Blumenkranz and A. Seboul (Paris: Editions Privat, 1976).

12 Here, "symbolic" is being more strictly used in terms of that function defined by Kristeva in opposition to the semiotic: "it involves the thetic phase, the identification of subject and its distinction from objects, and the establishment of a sign system." (Trans.)

13 See, in general, Jacques Lacan, *Ecrits* (Paris: Seuil, 1966) and in particular, Jacques Lacan, *Le Séminaire XX: Encore* (Paris: Seuil, 1975). (Trans.)

14 The "split subject" (from *Spaltung* as both "splitting" and "cleavage"), as used in Freudian psychoanalysis, here refers directly to Kristeva's "subject in process/in question/on trial" as opposed to the unity of the transcendental ego. (Trans.)

15 Again a reference to *écriture féminine* as generically labeled in France over the past few years and not to women's writing in general. (Trans.)

16 See Seminar on *Identity* directed by Lévi-Strauss (Paris: Grasset & Fasquelle, 1977).

17 Repression (*le refoulement* or *Verdrängung*) as distinguished from the foreclosure (*la forclusion* or *Verwerfung*) evoked earlier in the article (see Laplanche and Pontalis). (Trans.)

Select Bibliography

About Chinese Women. Translated by Anita Barrows. London: Marion Boyars, 1986.

Black Sun: Depression and Melancholia. Translated by Leon S. Roudiez. New York: Columbia University Press, 1989.

Desire in Language: A Semiotic Approach to Literature and Art. Edited by Leon S. Roudiez. Translated by Thomas Gora, Alice Jardine, and Leon S. Roudiez. New York: Columbia University Press, 1980.

In the Beginning Was Love: Psychoanalysis and Faith. Translated by Arthur Goldhammer. New York: Columbia University Press, 1987.

The Kristeva Reader. Edited by Toril Moi. New York: Columbia University Press, 1986.

Language – the Unknown: An Initiation into Linguistics. Translated by Anne M. Menke. New York: Columbia University Press, 1989.

Nations Without Nationalism. Translated by Leon S. Roudiez. New York: Columbia University Press, 1993.

New Maladies of the Soul. Translated by Ross Guberman. New York: Columbia University Press, 1995.

Revolution in Poetic Language. Translated by Margaret Waller. New York: Columbia University Press, 1984.

Strangers to Ourselves. Translated by Leon S. Roudiez. New York: Columbia University Press, 1991.

Tales of Love. Translated by Leon S. Roudiez. New York: Columbia University Press, 1987.

9

Sarah Kofman

French philosopher Sarah Kofman (1934–94) is well known in contemporary French thought as a leading interpreter of Nietzsche and Freud. Kofman's doctoral thesis on "The Concept of Culture in Nietzsche and Freud," written at the Collège de France, and her subsequent appointment as lecturer at the Sorbonne in 1970 marked the beginnings of her rise to prominence in French philosophical circles. Kofman's work explores a large range of fields, from philosophy and psychoanalysis to aesthetics, literary criticism, and contemporary culture. The following selections from *The Enigma of Woman: Woman in Freud's Writings* (1980) discuss some of the tensions in Freud's analyses of femininity with respect to questions of truth and bisexuality.

The Enigma of Woman

The Battle of the Sexes

Didn't Freud himself predict it? Feminists would take to the warpath against his texts, which, on the subject of women, would be seen as rife with masculine prejudice. The woman question has indeed provoked opposition not only from without but from within the very heart of psychoanalysis, has unleashed a veritable internecine war: women analysts are turning psychoanalysis against its founder, accusing him of taking sides, of siding with his sex, because of his sex. In brief, they say, on the question of woman, a man, even a Freud, cannot produce objective, neutral, scientific discourse: he can only *speculate*, that is, philosophize, construct a system destined to justify an idée fixe, a tendentious view based not on observation but on self-perception. So he cannot help verging on madness, paranoia.

In his lecture "Femininity" ("Die Weiblichkeit"),[1] a text recently denigrated – to put it mildly – by a woman psychoanalyst,[2] speaking to men and women ("Ladies and Gentlemen," he says at the

From *The Enigma of Woman: Woman in Freud's Writings*, translated by Catherine Porter (Ithaca: Cornell University Press, 1985), pp. 11–15, 101–5. Published in France as *L'Enigme de la femme: La Femme dans les textes de Freud* by Editions Galilée. Copyright © 1980 by Editions Galilée. Translation copyright © 1985 by Cornell University. Used by permission of the publisher, Cornell University Press.

beginning of his talk, repeating an apparently banal formula in order to bring out all its enigmatic strangeness later on), Freud emphasizes – not without irony – that every time any point is made against women, female psychoanalysts suspect men of deeply rooted masculine prejudices that prevent them from being impartial.

Freud avails himself of various arguments in an effort to dispel such suspicions. He maintains that the use of psychoanalysis as a weapon in the controversy is not enough to decide the issue, does not make it possible to choose between himself and the women analysts. Psychoanalysis is a *two-edged* sword that may well be used against women's discourse, he argues, for it allows us to understand that the female sex cannot accept, or wish to accept, anything that runs counter to its strongest desires, anything that contradicts, for example, the equality with men that women so ardently seek. Psychoanalysis thus allows us to understand why "feminists" adamantly reject the Freudian concept of the feminine superego, for according to them this concept originates merely in man's "masculinity complex" and serves as a theoretical justification for men's innate tendency to belittle and repress women.[3]

Almost always, in fact, it is the concept of the *feminine superego* and its corollary, women's intellectual and cultural inferiority, that give rise to controversy. It takes real heroism for Freud to make his explosive conclusions public:

I cannot evade the notion (though I hesitate to give it expression) that for women the level of what is ethically normal is different from what it is in men. Their super-ego is never so inexorable, so impersonal, so independent of its emotional origins as we require it to be in men. Character-traits which critics of every epoch have brought up against women...would [all] be amply accounted for by the modification in the formation of their super-ego...We must not allow ourselves to be deflected from such conclusions by the denials of the feminists, who are anxious to force us to regard the two sexes as completely equal in position and worth.[4]

And with regard to the different outcomes of the Oedipus complex in girls and boys, outcomes responsible for the differences in their respective superegos, "here the feminist demand for equal rights for the sexes does not take us far."[5]

I, Freud, Truth, I speak, and Truth will soon be able to resist all pressures, all more or less hysterical "feminist" demands; for, O women, if you seek to use psychoanalysis against me, I shall be much better prepared to turn it back against you, even while I pretend to be granting you some concessions, agreeing to some compromises in order to put an end to the battle of the sexes between us, and to re-establish among male and female psychoanalysts a "polite agreement": in my lordly fashion I freely grant you that "pure femininity" and "pure masculinity" are purely theoretical constructions and that the content of such speculative constructions remains quite uncertain. I am prepared to grant, too, that most men fall far short of the masculine ideal, for "all human individuals, as a result of their bisexual disposition and of cross-inheritance, combine in themselves both masculine and feminine characteristics" ("Consequences," p. 258).

In this internecine war, the thesis of bisexuality is a weapon that is supposed to put an end to the accusations made by women psychoanalysts: Freud's injurious discourse on women no longer concerns *them*, for they are exceptions to the rule, more masculine than feminine.

The discussion of [femininity] has gained special attractiveness from the distinction between the sexes. For the ladies, whenever some comparison seemed to turn out unfavorable to their sex, were able to utter a suspicion that we, the male analysts, had been unable to overcome certain deeply rooted prejudices against what was feminine, and that this was being paid for in the partiality of our researches. We, on the other hand, standing on the ground of bisexuality, had no difficulty in avoiding impoliteness. We had only to say: "This doesn't apply to *you*. You're the exception; on this point you're more masculine than feminine." ["Femininity," pp. 116–17][6]

More masculine than feminine, if not homosexual. "The Psychogenesis of a Case of Homosexuality in a Woman" emphasizes that the patient "was in fact a feminist; she felt it to be unjust that girls should not enjoy the same freedom as boys, and rebelled against the lot of women in general."[7]

The thesis of bisexuality not only is the thesis that Freud is defending, it also serves as his defense against accusations of antifeminism; and it, too, is double-edged. It allows Freud to repeat the most tenacious, the most traditional, the most metaphysical phallocratic discourse: if you women are as intelligent as men, it is because you are really more masculine than feminine. Thus it allows him to shut women up, to put an end to their demands and accusations. But this thesis also makes it possible to displace the metaphysical categories that it renders problematic, since it proclaims the purely speculative character of the masculine/feminine opposition. The thesis of bisexuality thus implies that Sigmund Freud himself could not have been *purely and simply* a man (*vir*), that he could not have had (*purely*) masculine prejudices. That charge only reveals the metaphysical prejudices of those who press it.

Freud never appeals to this argument in his own defense, however, never exhibits his femininity as he indulges in exposing the masculinity of his female colleagues. The thesis of bisexuality, declared valid in principle for all humans, is in the last analysis used only as a strategic weapon in connection with women; we shall have the opportunity to verify this. And it is as though Freud were loudly proclaiming the universality of bisexuality in order better to disguise his silent disavowal of his own femininity, his paranoia.

The Interest in the Enigma of Woman

Freud pursues this investigation most particularly in his lecture "Femininity":[8] his inquiry is framed, at the beginning and end of the text, by a double appeal to poetry that warrants examination. After stating a general truth of the sort used to begin college essays – "Throughout history people have knocked their heads against the riddle of the nature of femininity" (p. 113) – Freud cites the poet Heine as a witness:

> Häupter in Hieroglyphenmützen,
> Häupter in Turban und schwarzem Barett,
> Perückenhäupter und tausend andre
> Arme, schwitzende Menschenhäupter[9]

At the end of the text the reader is referred back to poetry as if to a potential complement intended to make up for the deficiencies of the psychoanalytic investigation. In this supplementary role it is situated on the same level as (biological) science and personal experience: "If you want to know more about femininity, enquire from your own experiences of life, or turn to the poets [*Dichter*], or wait until science can give you deeper and more coherent information" (p. 135).

Psychoanalysis needs to be supplemented, for the results it offers are incomplete, fragmentary, and not always easy to accept. "That is all I had to say to you about femininity. It is certainly incomplete and fragmentary and does not always sound friendly [Es ist gewiss unvollständig und fragmentarisch, klingt auch nicht immer freundlich]" (p. 135). *Incomplete* since Freud has pursued his investigation from the starting point of observations gathered on the couch, basing his work on statements made by women who are more or less reserved, more or less sincere, more or less hysterical. *Fragmentary* since this investigation has dealt only with a theoretical object, female sexuality, which can by no means be all there is to the subject of woman.

Finally, these results are not always *easy to accept*, for they do not deal very gently with women, especially where their superego is concerned.

If, O women, you are not satisfied by the answers offered by psychoanalysis, which is seeking only to know the truth and not to please you, you can always console yourselves by reading the poets, who seek above all not to pursue knowledge but to give you pleasure.

Up till now we have left it to the creative writer to depict for us the "necessary conditions for loving" which govern people's choice of an object, and the way in which they bring the demands of their imagination into harmony with reality. The writer can indeed draw on certain qualities which fit him to carry out such a task: above all, on a sensitivity that enables him to perceive the hidden impulses in the minds of other people, and the courage to let his own unconscious speak. But there is one circumstance which lessens the evidential value of what he has to say. Writers are under the necessity to produce intellectual and aesthetic pleasure, as well as certain emotional effects. For this reason they cannot reproduce the stuff of reality unchanged, but must isolate portions of it, remove disturbing associations, tone down the whole and fill in what is missing. These are the privileges of what is known as "poetic licence".... In consequence it becomes inevitable that science should concern herself with the same materials whose treatment by artists has given enjoyment to mankind for thousands of years, though her touch must be clumsier and the yield of pleasure less. These observations will, it may be hoped, serve to justify us in extending a strictly scientific treatment to the field of human love. Science is, after all, the most complete renunciation of the pleasure principle of which our mental activity is capable. ["Object Choice," p. 165]

After all this, if poetry aims above all to please and not to speak the truth, how can it "make up for" the deficiencies of psychoanalysis? How can it fill in the gaps if it is basically seeking to camouflage and "remove disturbing associations"? Poetry cannot be "superior" to psychoanalysis and to its "scientific" treatment of amorous life except for those who seek not knowledge but pleasure and distractions – those who are ruled by the pleasure principle alone.

This means that the double appeal to poetry in "Femininity" has to be interpreted as part of a strategy: Freud is openly declaring the limits of psychoanalysis so as to gain the upper hand over the agencies that until then have claimed to hold the solution to the feminine enigma: above and beyond his declarations, what *the text does* shows, on the contrary, the insufficiencies of personal experience, of poetry, and of biology. The text reveals that poetry is basically a decoy force that "operates for knowledge" as long as it is reappropriated by psychoanalysis and subordinated to its truth. And though Freud states in all modesty that the results he is offering amount to very little (*Das ist alles*), that they are fragmentary and incomplete, he also shows that this fragmentary viewpoint, that of sexuality, has an enormous "influence" over all the rest, and that this remainder – which attaches woman to the human race – also depends, in the last analysis, on sexuality; the "fragment" indeed seems, in fact, to encompass the whole, and Freud's recourse to agencies destined to make up for the deficiencies of psychoanalysis seems to be superfluous, his modesty feigned and tactical: as always,[10] Freud only pretends to be giving way to the specialists (specialists in female sexuality, in this case) whose "truths" he exhibits the better to criticize or deconstruct them. Between these two purely strategic appeals to agencies external to psychoanalysis, Freud pursues his investigation, attempting to pose and to resolve the enigma of woman.

After stating that humanity in general (*die Menschen*) has always pondered the riddle (*die Rätsel*) of femininity, he distinguishes *men* (*die Männer*), who cannot help worrying over such an enigma (they have more than an intellectual interest in solving this problem), from *women* (*die Frauen*), who, because they themselves constitute this riddle, cannot help being interested in it: it is a matter of common knowledge that men and women alike are preoccupied with this puzzle, and that is why Freud, addressing himself to a mixed public – *Meine Damen und Herren!* – is sure of having the attention of his audience. Far from excluding part of this audience – women – at the outset in order to speak exclusively "among men," as Luce Irigaray claims, he is trying, on the contrary, to establish complicity with the women analysts so as to clear himself of the suspicion of "antifeminism." And if, as Freud shows, what is at stake is of more than theoretical interest, for men and women alike, it goes without saying that women could not be excluded. Finally, to exclude "women" would be to admit that they are simply the opposite of men, whereas the entire lecture aims at eradicating that opposition in favor of bisexuality, a bisexuality that presumably constitutes the whole enigma in what men call "the riddle of femininity": "some portion of what we men call 'the enigma of women' may perhaps be derived from this expression of bisexuality in women's lives" ("Femininity," p. 131).

Thus nothing in the text justifies Luce Irigaray's reading (according to which Freud, like Aristotle, deprives women of the right to the logos and to the phallus alike). We have seen that things are not that simple. And even supposing that Freud wished to speak "among men" of the enigma of femininity (which is not the case), that would not suffice to condemn him as a "metaphysician." One might interpret that gesture, indeed, in a Nietzschean sense: to speak of a riddle of femininity and to try to solve that riddle are a strictly masculine enterprise; women are not concerned with Truth, they are profoundly skeptical; they know perfectly well that there is no such thing as "truth," that behind their veils there is yet another veil, and that try as one may to remove them, one after another, truth in its "nudity," like a goddess, will never appear. Women who are truly women are perfectly "flat." *Mulier taceat de muliere!* For "truth," that metaphysical lure of depth, of a phallus concealed behind the veils, that lure is a fetishist illusion of man: a woman who gets involved with truth, with solving riddles, is a "degenerate" woman, reactive and hysterical. But the watchword *Mulier taceat de muliere* is not Freud's; *he* addresses himself to women, precisely because he knows that most of them are more or less hysterical, and for that reason complicitous with masculine discourse. And because he needs that complicity.

Notes

1 In *New Introductory Lectures on Psycho-Analysis*, in *The Standard Edition of the Complete Psychological Works of Sigmund Freud*, ed. James Strachey, 24 vols (London, 1953–74), 22: 112–135 (1933a [1932]). Unless otherwise noted, all excerpts from Freud's works are quoted from the *Standard Edition*; the volume number is followed by inclusive page numbers except when the text in question occupies the entire volume. The publication date indicated in the *Standard Edition* is shown in parentheses, with the letter assigned to the corresponding entry in the Freud bibliography (24: 47–82); the date of composition (when it differs) appears in brackets. Whenever possible, works identified in a previous note will be cited within the body of the text, identified by short titles as appropriate. (Trans.)

2 Luce Irigaray, *Speculum de l'autre femme* (Paris, 1974); published in English as *Speculum of the Other Woman*, trans. Gillian C. Gill (Ithaca, 1985).

3 Cf. "Female Sexuality," 21:223–43 (1931b), in which a comparison is made with Dostoevsky's "knife that cuts both ways" in *The Brothers Karamazov*. (Freud's English translator points out that "the actual simile used by Freud and in the Russian original is 'a stick with two ends'" [p. 230, n. 1]).

4 "Some Psychical Consequences of the Anatomical Distinction between the Sexes," 19:243–58 (1925j; hereafter cited as "Consequences"), pp. 257–58.

5 "The Dissolution of the Oedipus Complex," 19: 173–9 (1924d; hereafter cited as "Dissolution"), p. 178.

6 The French text here is retranslated directly from the German of *Gesammelte Werke*, 18 vols (Frankfurt and London, 1952–1968) (hereafter cited as *GW*), 15:124, as are most of the other excerpts from "Femininity": the existing French translation is quite dreadful, and it omits many passages. Indeed, in my view it is no accident that most of the criticisms leveled against Freud are based on this French "translation." Luce Irigaray claims that even the most meticulous translation would not have made much difference to the meaning of this discourse on "femininity" (*Speculum*, p. 9, n. 1). One may at least have one's doubts about this and wonder why, under the circumstances, Luce Irigaray almost always persists in using a translation that she knows is faulty – unless it is to further "the cause." That of Femininity? Going back to the German text is not a matter of trying to "save" Freud at all costs (I am no more likely to "save" him than she is), but only of manifesting the minimal intellectual honesty that consists in criticizing an author in terms of what he has said rather than what someone has managed to have him say: the critique will be all the stronger for it. When we turn to Freud's text, we note further that it is much more complex, more heterogeneous, than the French translation allows one to imagine. I shall return to this point. [As indicated in n. 1 above, English translations given here follow the *Standard Edition* except as otherwise noted. For a critique of the Strachey translations, however, and an analysis of their impact on Anglo-Saxon psychoanalytic thinking, see Bruno Bettelheim, *Freud and Man's Soul* (New York, 1982). (Trans.)]

7 18:147–72 (1920a; hereafter cited as "Psychogenesis"), p. 169.

8 Luce Irigaray was the first to draw attention to the phallocratic character of this text. I shall arrive at a similar conclusion while offering a quite different reading, one that emphasizes the complexity of the Freudian undertaking.

9 Heinrich Heine, *Nordsee* [Second Cycle, VII, "Fragen"], translated in "Femininity," p. 113, n. 1, as:

Heads in hieroglyphic bonnets,
Heads in turbans and black birettas,
Heads in wigs and thousand other
Wretched, sweating heads of humans...

10 I pointed out Freud's gesture with respect to art in *L'Enfance de l'art*.

Select Bibliography

The Childhood of Art: An Interpretation of Freud's Aesthetics. Translated by Winifred Woodhull. New York: Columbia University Press, 1988.

The Enigma of Woman: Woman in Freud's Writings. Translated by Catherine Porter. Ithaca: Cornell University Press, 1985.

Freud and Fiction. Translated by Sarah Wykes. Boston: Northeastern University Press, 1991.

Nietzsche and Metaphor. Translated by Duncan Large. Stanford: Stanford University Press, 1993.

10

Luce Irigaray

Of Belgian origin, Luce Irigaray (1930–) is a practicing psychoanalyst and philosopher now resident in Paris. Irigaray's work in feminist thought challenges the prioritizing of sameness over alterity and the homogenizing and totalizing effects of traditional male-oriented philosophical discourse, arguing that such discourse, which also pervades psychoanalysis in its Freudian and Lacanian forms, leaves no place for the feminine and occludes sexual difference. By contrast, Irigaray emphasizes the uniqueness and autonomy of the feminine and argues that womankind needs to be acknowledged in its own right, beyond the supposedly "neutral" categories of traditional philosophy. The following essay "Sexual Difference" (1984) argues the need for a "revolution in thought and ethics" that would accommodate such recognition and effect new economies of desire. This entails, according to Irigaray, a rethinking of time and space, and in particular of the place of the "maternal-feminine."

Sexual Difference

Sexual difference is one of the major philosophical issues, if not the issue, of our age. According to Heidegger, each age has one issue to think through, and one only. Sexual difference is probably the issue in our time which could be our "salvation" if we thought it through.

From *An Ethics of Sexual Difference*, translated by Carolyn Burke and Gillian C. Gill (Ithaca: Cornell University Press, 1993), pp. 5–19. Originally published in French under the title *Ethique de la différence sexuelle*, © 1984 by Les Editions de Minuit. Translation copyright © 1993 by Cornell University and the Athlone Press. Reprinted by permission of Cornell University Press and the Athlone Press.

But, whether I turn to philosophy, to science, or to religion, I find this underlying issue still cries out in vain for our attention. Think of it as an approach that would allow us to check the many forms that destruction takes in our world, to counteract a nihilism that merely affirms the reversal or the repetitive proliferation of status quo values – whether you call them the consumer society, the circularity of discourse, the more or less cancerous diseases of our age, the unreliability of words, the end of philosophy, religious despair or regression to religiosity, scientistic or technical imperialism that fails to consider the living subject.

Sexual difference would constitute the horizon of worlds more fecund than any known to date – at least in the West – and without reducing fecundity to the reproduction of bodies and flesh. For loving partners this would be a fecundity of birth and regeneration, but also the production of a new age of thought, art, poetry, and language: the creation of a new *poetics*.

Both in theory and in practice, everything resists the discovery and affirmation of such an advent or event. In theory, philosophy wants to be literature or rhetoric, wishing either to break with ontology or to regress to the ontological. Using the same ground and the same framework as "first philosophy," working toward its disintegration but without proposing any other goals that might assure new foundations and new works.

In politics, some overtures have been made to the world of women. But these overtures remain partial and local: some concessions have been made by those in power, but no new values have been established. Rarely have these measures been thought through and affirmed by women themselves, who consequently remain at the level of critical demands. Has a worldwide erosion of the gains won in women's struggles occurred because of the failure to lay foundations different from those on which the world of men is constructed? Psychoanalytic theory and therapy, the scenes of sexuality as such, are a long way from having effected their revolution. And with a few exceptions, sexual practice today is often divided between two parallel worlds: the world of men and the world of women. A nontraditional, fecund encounter between the sexes barely exists. It does not voice its demands publicly, except through certain kinds of silence and polemics.

A revolution in thought and ethics is needed if the work of sexual difference is to take place. We need to reinterpret everything concerning the relations between the subject and discourse, the subject and the world, the subject and the cosmic, the microcosmic and the macrocosmic. Everything, beginning with the way in which the subject has always been written in the masculine form, as *man*, even when it claimed to be universal or neutral. Despite the fact that *man* – at least in French – rather than being neutral, is sexed.

Man has been the subject of discourse, whether in theory, morality, or politics. And the gender of God, the guardian of every subject and every discourse, is always *masculine and paternal*, in the West. To women are left the so-called minor arts: cooking, knitting, embroidery, and sewing; and, in exceptional cases, poetry, painting, and music. Whatever their importance, these arts do not currently make the rules, at least not overtly.

Of course, we are witnessing a certain reversal of values: manual labor and art are being revalued. But the relation of these arts to sexual difference is never really thought through and properly apportioned. At best, it is related to the class struggle.

In order to make it possible to think through, and live, this difference, we must reconsider the whole problematic of *space* and *time*.

In the beginning there was space and the creation of space, as is said in all theogonies. The gods, God, first create *space*. And time is there, more or less in the service of space. On the first day, the first days, the gods, God, make a world by separating the elements. This world is then peopled, and a rhythm is established among its inhabitants. God would be time itself, lavishing or exteriorizing itself in its action in space, in places.

Philosophy then confirms the genealogy of the task of the gods or God. Time becomes the *interiority* of the subject itself, and space, its *exteriority* (this problematic is developed by Kant in the *Critique of Pure Reason*). The subject, the master of time, becomes the axis of the world's ordering, with its something beyond the moment and eternity: God. He effects the passage between time and space.

Which would be inverted in sexual difference? Where the feminine is experienced as space, but often with connotations of the abyss and night (God being space and light?), while the masculine is experienced as time.

The transition to a new age requires a change in our perception and conception of *space-time*, the *inhabiting of places*, and of *containers*, or *envelopes of identity*. It assumes and entails an evolution or a transformation of forms, of the relations of *matter* and *form* and of the interval *between*: the trilogy of the constitution of place. Each age inscribes a limit to this trinitary configuration: *matter, form, interval*, or *power [puissance], act, intermediary-interval*.

Desire occupies or designates the place of the *interval*. Giving it a permanent definition would amount to suppressing it as desire. Desire demands a sense of attraction: a change in the interval, the displacement of the subject or of the object in their relations of nearness or distance.

The transition to a new age comes at the same time as a change in the economy of desire. A new age signifies a different relation between:

– man and god(s),
– man and man,
– man and world,
– man and woman.

Our age, which is often thought to be one in which the problematic of desire has been brought forward, frequently theorizes this desire on the basis of observations of a moment of tension, or a moment in history, whereas desire ought to be thought of as a changing dynamic whose outlines can be described in the past, sometimes in the present, but never definitively predicted. Our age will have failed to realize the full dynamic reserve signified by desire if it is referred back to the economy of the *interval*, if it is situated in the attractions, tensions, and actions occurring between *form* and *matter*, but also in the *remainder* that subsists after each creation or work, *between* what has already been identified and what has still to be identified, and so on.

In order to imagine such an economy of desire, one must reinterpret what Freud implies by *sublimation* and observe that he does not speak of the sublimation of genitality (except in reproduction? But, if this were a successful form of sublimation, Freud would not be so pessimistic about parental childrearing practices) or of the sublimation of the *partial drives in relation to the feminine* but rather of their repression (little girls speak earlier and more skillfully than little boys; they have a better relationship to the social; and so on – qualities or aptitudes that disappear without leaving any creative achievements that capitalize on their energy, except for the task of becoming a woman: an object of attraction?)[1]

In this possible nonsublimation of herself, and by herself, woman always tends *toward* without any return to herself as the place where something positive can be elaborated. In terms of contemporary physics, it could be said that she remains on the side of the electron, with all that this implies for her, for man, for their encounter. If there is no double desire, the positive and negative poles divide themselves between the two sexes instead of establishing a chiasmus or a double loop in which each can go toward the other and come back to itself.

If these positive and negative poles are not found in both, the same one always attracts, while the other remains in motion but lacks a "proper" place. What is missing is the double pole of attraction and support, which excludes disintegration or

rejection, attraction and decomposition, but which instead insures the separation that articulates every encounter and makes possible speech, promises, alliances.

In order to distance oneself, must one be able to take? To speak? Which in a certain way comes to the same thing. Perhaps in order to take, one needs a fixed container or place? A soul? Or a spirit? Mourning nothing is the most difficult. Mourning the self in the other is almost impossible. I search for myself, as if I had been assimilated into maleness. I ought to reconstitute myself on the basis of a disassimilation. . . . [2] Rise again from the traces of a culture, of works already produced by the other. Searching through what is in them – for what is not there. What allowed them to be, for what is not there. Their conditions of possibility, for what is not there.

Woman ought to be able to find herself, among other things, through the images of herself already deposited in history and the conditions of production of the work of man, and not on the basis of his work, his genealogy.

If traditionally, and as a mother, woman represents *place* for man, such a limit means that she becomes *a thing*, with some possibility of change from one historical period to another. She finds herself delineated as a thing. Moreover, the maternal-feminine also serves as an *envelope*, a *container*, the starting point from which man limits his things. The *relationship between envelope and things* constitutes one of the aporias, or the aporia, of Aristotelianism and of the philosophical systems derived from it.

In our terminologies, which derive from this economy of thought but are impregnated with a psychologism unaware of its sources, it is said, for example, that the woman-mother is *castrating*. Which means that, since her status as envelope and as thing(s) has not been interpreted, she remains inseparable from the work or act of man, notably insofar as he defines her and creates *his* identity with her as his starting point or, correlatively, with this determination of her being. If after all this, she is still alive, she continuously undoes his work – distinguishing herself from both the envelope and the thing, ceaselessly creating there some interval, play, something in motion and unlimited which disturbs his perspective, his world, and his/its limits. But, because he fails to leave her a subjective life, and to be on occasion her place and her thing in an intersubjective dynamic, man remains within a master–slave dialectic. The slave, ultimately, of a God on whom he bestows the characteristics of an absolute master. Secretly or obscurely, a slave to the power of the maternal-feminine which he diminishes or destroys.

The maternal-feminine remains the *place separated from "its" own place*, deprived of "its" place. She is or ceaselessly becomes the place of the other who cannot separate himself from it. Without her knowing or willing it, she is then threatening because of what she lacks: a "proper" place. She would have to re-envelop herself with herself, and do so at least twice: as a woman and as a mother. Which would presuppose a change in the whole economy of space-time.

In the meantime, this ethical question comes into play in matters of *nudity* and *perversity*. Woman must be nude because she is not situated, does not situate herself in her place. Her clothes, her makeup, and her jewels are the things with which she tries to create her container(s), her envelope(s). She cannot make use of the envelope that she is, and must create artificial ones.

Freud's statement that woman is identified with orality is meaningful, but it still exiles her from her most archaic and constituent site. No doubt orality is an especially significant measure for her: morphologically, she has two mouths and two pairs of lips. But she can act on this morphology or make something of it only if she preserves her relation to *spatiality* and to the *fetal*. Although she needs these dimensions to create a space for herself (as well as to maintain a receptive place for the other), they are traditionally taken from her to constitute man's nostalgia and everything that he constructs in memory of this first and ultimate dwelling place. An obscure commemoration.... Centuries will perhaps have been needed for man to interpret the meaning of his work(s): the endless construction of a number of substitutes for his prenatal home. From the depths of the earth to the highest skies? Again and again, taking from the feminine the tissue or texture of spatiality. In exchange – but it isn't a real one – he buys her a house, even shuts her up in it, places limits on her that are the opposite of the unlimited site in which he unwittingly situates her. He contains or envelops her with walls while enveloping himself and his things with her flesh. The nature of these envelopes is not the same: on the one hand, invisibly alive, but with barely perceivable limits; on the other, visibly limiting or sheltering, but at the risk of being prison-like or murderous if the threshold is not left open.

We must, therefore, reconsider the whole question of our conception of place, both in order to move on to another age of difference (each age of thought corresponds to a particular time of meditation on difference), and in order to construct an ethics of the passions. We need to change the relations between form, matter, interval, and limit, an issue that has never been considered in a way that allows for a relationship between two loving subjects of different sexes.

Once there was the enveloping body and the enveloped body, the latter being the more mobile through what Aristotle termed *locomotion* (since maternity does not look much like "motion"). The one who offers or allows desire moves and envelops, engulfing the other. It is moreover a danger if no third term exists. Not only to serve as a limitation. This third term can occur within the one who contains as a relation of the latter to his or her own limit(s): relation to the divine, to death, to the social, to the cosmic. If a third term does not exist within and for the container, he or she becomes *all-powerful*.

Therefore, to deprive one pole of sexual difference, women, of a third term also amounts to putting them in the position of omnipotence: this is a danger for men, especially in that it suppresses an interval that is both entrance and space between.[3] A place for both to enter and exit the envelope (and on the same side, so as not to perforate the envelope or assimilate it into the digestive process); for both, a possibility of unhindered movement, of peaceful immobility without the risk of imprisonment.

To arrive at the constitution of an ethics of sexual difference, we must at least return to what is for Descartes the first passion: *wonder*. This passion has no opposite or contradiction and exists always as though for the first time. Thus man and woman, woman and man are always meeting as though for the first time because they cannot be substituted one for the other. I will never be in a man's place, never will a man be in mine. Whatever identifications are possible, one will never exactly occupy the place of the other – they are irreducible one to the other.

When the first encounter with some object surprises us, and we judge it to be new, or very different from what we formerly knew, or from what we supposed that it ought to be, that causes us to wonder and be surprised; and because that may happen before we in any way know whether this object is agreeable to us or is not so, it appears to me that wonder is the first of all the passions; and it has no opposite, because if the object which presents itself has nothing in it that surprises us, we are in nowise moved regarding it, and we consider it without passion.

(René Descartes, *The Passions of the Soul*, article 53).[4]

Who or what the other is, I never know. But the other who is forever unknowable is the one who differs from me sexually. This feeling of surprise, astonishment, and wonder in the face of the unknowable ought to be returned to its locus: that of sexual difference. The passions have either been repressed, stifled, or reduced, or reserved for God. Sometimes a space for wonder is left to works of art. But it is never found to reside in this locus: *between man and woman*. Into this place came attraction, greed, possession, consummation, disgust, and so on. But not that wonder which beholds what it sees always as if for the first time, never taking hold of the other as its object. It does not try to seize, possess, or reduce this object, but leaves it subjective, still free.

This has never existed between the sexes since wonder maintains their autonomy within their statutory difference, keeping a space of freedom and attraction between them, a possibility of separation and alliance.

This might take place at the time of the first meeting, even prior to the betrothal, and remain as a permanent proof of difference. The *interval* would never be *crossed*. Consummation would never take place, the idea itself being a delusion. One sex is not entirely consumable by the other. There is always a *remainder*.

Up until now this remainder has been entrusted to or reserved for *God*. Sometimes a portion was incarnated in the *child*. Or was thought of as being *neuter*. This neuter (in a different way, like the child or God?) suggests the possibility of an encounter but puts it off, deferring it until later, even when it is a question of a secondary revision [*après-coup*]. It always stays at an insurmountable distance, a respectful or deadly sort of no-man's-land:[5] no alliance is forged; nothing is celebrated. The immediacy of the encounter is annihilated or deferred to a future that never comes.

Of course, the neuter might signify an alchemical site of the sublimation of "genitality," and the possibility of generation, of the creation of and between different genders and genres. But it would still have

to be receptive to the advent of difference, and be understood as an anticipation from this side and not as a beyond, especially an ethical one. Generally the phrase *there is* upholds the present but defers celebration. There is not, there will not be the moment of wonder of the *wedding*, an ecstasy that remains *instant*.[6] The *there is* remains a present that may be subject to pressure by the god, but it does not form a foundation for the triumph of sexual fecundity. Only certain oriental traditions speak of the energizing, aesthetic, and religious fecundity of the sexual act: the two sexes give each other the seed of life and eternity, the growing generation of and between them both.

We must re-examine our own history thoroughly to understand why this sexual difference has not had its chance to develop, either empirically or transcendentally. Why it has failed to have its own ethics, aesthetic, logic, religion, or the micro- and macrocosmic realization of its coming into being or its destiny.

It is surely a question of the dissociation of body and soul, of sexuality and spirituality, of the lack of a passage for the spirit, for the god, between the inside and the outside, the outside and the inside, and of their distribution between the sexes in the sexual act. Everything is constructed in such a way that these realities remain separate, even opposed to one another. So that they neither mix, marry, nor form an alliance. Their wedding is always being put off to a beyond, a future life, or else devalued, felt and thought to be less worthy in comparison to the marriage between the mind and God in a transcendental realm where all ties to the world of sensation have been severed.

The consequences of the nonfulfillment of the sexual act remain, and there are many. To take up only the most beautiful, as yet to be made manifest in the realm of time and space, there are *angels*. These messengers who never remain enclosed in a place, who are also never immobile. Between God, as the perfectly immobile act, man, who is surrounded and enclosed by the world of his work, and woman, whose task would be to take care of nature and procreation, *angels* would circulate as mediators of that which has not yet happened, of what is still going to happen, of what is on the horizon. Endlessly reopening the enclosure of the universe, of universes, identities, the unfolding of actions, of history.

The angel is that which unceasingly *passes through the envelope(s)* or *container(s)*, goes from one side to the other, reworking every deadline, changing every decision, thwarting all repetition. Angels destroy the monstrous, that which hampers the possibility of a new age; they come to herald the arrival of a new birth, a new morning.

They are not unrelated to sex. There is of course Gabriel, the angel of the annunciation. But other angels announce the consummation of marriage, notably all the angels in the Apocalypse and many in the Old Testament. As if the angel were a representation of a sexuality that has never been incarnated. A light, divine gesture (or tale) of flesh that has not yet acted or flourished. Always fallen or still awaiting parousia. The fate of a love still torn between here and elsewhere. The work of a love that is the original sinner, since the first garden, the lost earthly paradise? The fate of all flesh which is, moreover, attributable to God![7]

These swift angelic messengers, who transgress all enclosures in their speed, tell of the passage between the envelope of God and that of the world as micro- or macrocosm. They proclaim that such a journey can be made by the body of man, and above all the body of woman. They represent and tell of another incarnation, another parousia of the body. Irreducible to philosophy, theology, morality, angels appear as the messengers of ethics evoked by art – sculpture, painting, or music – without its being possible to say anything more than the gesture that represents them.

They speak like messengers, but gesture seems to be their "nature." Movement, posture, the coming-and-going between the two. They move – or stir up? – the paralysis or *apatheia* of the body, or the soul, or the world. They set trances or convulsions to music, or give them harmony.

Their touch – when they touch – resembles that of gods. They are imperious in their grace even as they remain imperceptible.

One of the questions which arises about them is whether they can be found together in the same place. The traditional answer is no. This question, which is similar to and different from that of the co-location of bodies, comes back to the question of sexual ethics. The mucous should no doubt be pictured as related to the angel, whereas the inertia of the body deprived of its relation to the mucous and its gesture is linked to the fallen body or the corpse.

A sexual or carnal ethics would require that both angel and body be found together. This is a world that must be constructed or reconstructed. A genesis of love between the sexes has yet to come about

in all dimensions, from the smallest to the greatest, from the most intimate to the most political. A world that must be created or recreated so that man and woman may once again or at last live together, meet, and sometimes inhabit the same place.

The link uniting or reuniting masculine and feminine must be horizontal and vertical, terrestrial and heavenly. As Heidegger, among others, has written, it must forge an alliance between the divine and the mortal, such that the sexual encounter would be a festive celebration and not a disguised or polemical form of the master–slave relationship. Nor a meeting in the shadow or orbit of a Father-God who alone lays down the law, who is the immutable spokesman of a single sex.

Of course, the most extreme progression and regression goes under the name of God. I can only strive toward the absolute or regress to infinity under the guarantee of God's existence. This is what tradition has taught us, and its imperatives have not yet been overcome, since their destruction brings about terrible abandonments and pathological states, unless one has exceptional love partners. And even then...Unhappiness is sometimes all the more inescapable when it lacks the horizon of the divine, of the gods, of an opening onto a beyond, but also a *limit* that the other may or may not penetrate.

How can we mark this limit of a place, of place in general, if not through sexual difference? But, in order for an ethics of sexual difference to come into being, we must constitute a possible place for each sex, body, and flesh to inhabit. Which presupposes a memory of the past, a hope for the future, memory bridging the present and disconcerting the mirror symmetry that annihilates the difference of identity.

To do this requires time, both space and time. Perhaps we are passing through an era when *time must redeploy space*? A new morning of and for the world? A remaking of immanence and transcendence, notably through this *threshold* which has never been examined as such: the female sex. The threshold that gives access to the *mucous*. Beyond classical oppositions of love and hate, liquid and ice – a threshold that is always *half-open*. The threshold of the *lips*, which are strangers to dichotomy and oppositions. Gathered one against the other but without any possible suture, at least of a real kind. They do not absorb the world into or through themselves, provided they are not misused and reduced to a means of consumption or consummation. They offer a shape of welcome but do not assimilate, reduce, or swallow up. A sort of doorway to voluptuousness? They are not useful, except as that which designates a *place*, the very place of uselessness, at least as it is habitually understood. Strictly speaking, they serve neither conception nor *jouissance*. Is this the mystery of feminine identity? Of its self-contemplation, of this very strange word of silence? Both the threshold and reception of exchange, the sealed-up secret of wisdom, belief, and faith in all truths?

(Two sets of lips that, moreover, cross over each other like the arms of the cross, the prototype of the crossroads *between*. The mouth lips and the genital lips do not point in the same direction. In some way they point in the direction opposite from the one you would expect, with the "lower" ones forming the vertical.)

In this approach, where the borders of the body are wed in an embrace that transcends all limits – without, however, risking engulfment, thanks to the fecundity of the porous – in the most extreme experience of sensation, which is also always in the future, each one discovers the self in that experience which is inexpressible yet forms the supple grounding of life and language.

For this, "God" is necessary, or a love so attentive that it is divine. Which has never taken place? Love always postpones its transcendence beyond the here and now, except in certain experiences of God. And desire fails to act sufficiently on the porous nature of the body, omitting the communion that takes place through the most intimate mucous membranes. In this exchange, what is communicated is so subtle that one needs great perseverance to keep it from falling into oblivion, intermittency, deterioration, illness, or death.

This communion is often left to the child, as the symbol of the union. But there are other signs of union which precede the child – the space where the lovers give each other life or death? Regeneration or degeneration: both are possible. The intensity of desire and the filiation of both lovers are engaged.

And if the divine is present as the mystery that animates the copula, the *is* and the *being* in sexual difference, can the force of desire overcome the avatars of genealogical destiny? How does it manage this? With what power [*puissance*] does it reckon, while remaining nevertheless incarnate? Between the idealistic fluidity of an unborn body that is untrue to its birth and genetic determinism, how do we take the measure of a love that changes our condition from mortal to immortal? Certain figures of gods become men, of God become man, and of twice-born beings indicate the path of love.

Has something of the achievement of sexual difference still not been said or transmitted? Has something been held in reserve within the silence of a history in the feminine: an energy, a morphology, a growth and flourishing still to come from the female realm? An overture to a future that is still and always open? Given that the world has remained aporetic about this strange advent.

Notes

1 Cf. Luce Irigaray, *Speculum, de l'autre femme* (Paris: Minuit, 1984), pp. 9–162; trans. Gillian C. Gill, under the title *Speculum of the Other Woman* (Ithaca: Cornell University Press, 1985), pp. 11–129.

2 All ellipses occur in the original French text and do not indicate omissions in the translation. (Trans.)

3 Irigaray plays on the double sense of *entre*, meaning both "enter" and "between." (Trans.)

4 *The Philosophical Works of Descartes*, trans. E. S. Haldane and G. R. T. Ross (Cambridge: Cambridge University Press, 1931; reprinted Dover, 1955), I: 358.

5 In English in the original text. (Trans.)

6 *Instance* is rendered here as "in-stant" to underscore Irigaray's emphasis on the term's root meaning, standing within the self, as opposed to "ecstasy," standing outside the self. (Trans.)

7 See Luce Irigaray, "Epistle to the Last Christians," in *Marine Lover of Friedrich Nietzsche*, trans. Gillian C. Gill (New York: Columbia University Press, 1991).

Select Bibliography

An Ethics of Sexual Difference. Translated by Carolyn Burke and Gillian C. Gill. Ithaca: Cornell University Press: 1993.

Elemental Passions. Translated by Joanne Collie and Judith Still. New York: Routledge, 1992.

Luce Irigaray

I Love to You: Sketch for a Felicity within History. Translated by Alison Martin. New York: Routledge, 1996.

The Irigaray Reader. Edited by Margaret Whitford. Cambridge, Mass.: Blackwell Publishers, 1991.

Je, Tu, Nous: Toward a Culture of Difference. Translated by Alison Martin. New York: Routledge, 1993.

Marine Lover of Friedrich Nietzsche. Translated by Gillian C. Gill. New York: Columbia University Press, 1991.

Sexes and Genealogies. Translated by Gillian C. Gill. New York: Columbia University Press, 1993.

Speculum of the Other Woman. Translated by Gillian C. Gill. Ithaca: Cornell University Press, 1985.

Thinking the Difference: For a Peaceful Revolution. Translated by Karin Montin. New York: Routledge, 1994.

This Sex Which Is Not One. Translated by Catherine Porter with Carolyn Burke. Ithaca: Cornell University Press, 1985.

11

Jean-Luc Nancy

French philosopher Jean-Luc Nancy is professor of philosophy at the University of Human Sciences in Strasbourg. His work is broadly associated with a group of prominent contemporary French thinkers including Jacques Derrida, Sarah Kofman, and Jean-François Lyotard, who together participated in a range of philosophical initiatives including the formation of a research group on the teaching of philosophy, the founding of the Collège de Philosophie in Paris, and the establishment of a center for philosophical research on politics. As these activities suggest, much of Nancy's philosophical work is focused on the relation between philosophy and the political (although he has also written extensively on the history of philosophy), and in particular on the issue of community in the postmodern era. In the following selection, from *The Inoperative Community* (1986), Nancy argues against the immanentist notion of community as a fusion of identities, attempting instead to think it in terms of an "ecstatic" opening of consciousness that exceeds and interrupts notions of community based on the self-presence of consciousness.

The Inoperative Community

The gravest and most painful testimony of the modern world, the one that possibly involves all other testimonies to which this epoch must answer

(by virtue of some unknown decree or necessity, for we bear witness also to the exhaustion of thinking through History), is the testimony of the dissolution, the dislocation, or the conflagration of community. Communism, as Sartre said, is "the unsurpassable horizon of our time," and it is so in many senses – political, ideological, and strategic. But not least important among these senses is the following consideration, quite foreign to Sartre's intentions: the word "communism" stands as an emblem of the desire to discover or rediscover a place of community at once beyond social divisions and beyond subordination to technopolitical dominion, and thereby beyond such wasting away of liberty, of speech, or of simple happiness as comes about whenever these become subjugated to the exclusive order of privatization; and finally, more simply and even more decisively, a place from which to surmount the unraveling that occurs with the death of each one of us – that death that, when no longer anything more than the death of the individual, carries an unbearable burden and collapses into insignificance.

More or less consciously, more or less deliberately, and more or less politically, the word "communism" has constituted such an emblem – which no doubt amounted to something other than a concept, and even something other than the *meaning* of a word. This emblem is no longer in circulation, except in a belated way for a few; for still others, though very rare nowadays, it is an emblem capable of inferring a fierce but impotent resistance to the visible collapse of what it promised. If it is no longer in circulation, this is not only because the states that acclaimed it have appeared, for some time now, as the agents of its betrayal. (Bataille in 1933: "The Revolution's minimal hope has been described as the decline of the State: but it is in fact the revolutionary forces that the present world is seeing perish and, at the same time, every vital force today has assumed the form of the totalitarian State.")[1] The schema of betrayal, aimed at preserving an originary communist purity of doctrine or intention, has come to be seen as less and less tenable. Not that totalitarianism was already present, as such, in Marx: this would be a crude proposition, one that remains ignorant of the strident protest against the destruction of community that in Marx continuously parallels the Hegelian attempt to bring about a totality, and that thwarts or displaces this attempt.

But the schema of betrayal is seen to be untenable in that it was the very basis of the communist ideal that ended up appearing most problematic: namely, human beings defined as producers (one might even add: human beings *defined* at all), and fundamentally as the producers of their own essence in the form of their labor or their work.

That the justice and freedom – and the equality – included in the communist idea or ideal have in effect been betrayed in so-called real communism is something at once laden with the burden of an intolerable suffering (along with other, no less intolerable forms of suffering inflicted by our liberal societies) and at the same time politically deci-

sive (not only in that a political strategy must favor resistance to this betrayal, but because this strategy, as well as our thought in general, must reckon with the possibility that an entire society has been forged, docilely and despite more than one forum of revolt, in the mold of this betrayal – or more plainly, at the mercy of this abandonment: this would be Zinoviev's question, rather than Solzhenitsyn's). But these burdens are still perhaps only relative compared with the absolute weight that crushes or blocks all our "horizons": there is, namely, no form of communist opposition – or let us say rather "communitarian" opposition, in order to emphasize that the word should not be restricted in this context to strictly political references – that has not been or is not still profoundly subjugated to the goal of a *human* community, that is, to the goal of achieving a community of beings producing in essence their own essence as their work, and furthermore producing precisely this essence *as community*. An absolute immanence of man to man – a humanism – and of community to community – a communism – obstinately subtends, whatever be their merits or strengths, all forms of oppositional communism, all leftist and ultraleftist models, and all models based on the workers' council.[2] In a sense, all ventures adopting a communitarian opposition to "real communism" have by now run their course or been abandoned, but everything continues along its way as though, beyond these ventures, it were no longer even a question of thinking about community.

Yet it is precisely the immanence of man to man, or it is *man*, taken absolutely, considered as the immanent being *par excellence*, that constitutes the stumbling block to a thinking of community. A community presupposed as having to be one *of human beings* presupposes that it effect, or that it must effect, as such and integrally, its own essence, which is itself the accomplishment of the essence of humanness. ("What can be fashioned by man? Everything. Nature, human society, humanity," wrote Herder. We are stubbornly bound to this regulative idea, even when we consider that this "fashioning" is itself only a "regulative idea.") Consequently, economic ties, technological operations, and political fusion (into a *body* or under a *leader*) represent or rather present, expose, and realize this essence necessarily in themselves. Essence is set to work in them; through them, it becomes its own work. This is what we have called "totalitarianism," but it might be better named "immanentism," as long as we do not restrict the term to designating certain types of societies or regimes but rather see in it the general horizon of our time, encompassing both democracies and their fragile juridical parapets.

Is it really necessary to say something about the individual here? Some see in its invention and in the culture, if not in the cult built around the individual, Europe's incontrovertible merit of having shown the world the sole path to emancipation from tyranny, and the norm by which to measure all our collective or communitarian undertakings. But the individual is merely the residue of the experience of the dissolution of community. By its nature – as its name indicates, it is the atom, the indivisible – the individual reveals that it is the abstract result of a decomposition. It is another, and symmetrical, figure of immanence: the absolutely detached for-itself, taken as origin and as certainty.

But the experience through which this individual has passed, since Hegel at least (and through which he passes, it must be confessed, with staggering opinionatedness), is simply the experience of this: that the individual can be the origin and the certainty of nothing but its own death. And once immortality has passed into its works, an *operative* immortality remains its own alienation and renders its death still more strange than the irremediable strangeness that it already "is."

Still, one cannot make a world with simple atoms. There has to be a *clinamen*. There has to be an inclination or an inclining from one toward the other, of one by the other, or from one to the other. Community is at least the *clinamen* of the "individual." Yet there is no theory, ethics, politics, or metaphysics of the individual that is capable of envisaging this *clinamen*, this declination or decline of the individual within community. Neither "Personalism" nor Sartre ever managed to do anything more than coat the most classical individual-subject with a moral or sociological paste: they never *inclined* it, outside itself, over that edge that opens up its being-in-common.

An inconsequential atomism, individualism tends to forget that the atom is a world. This is why the question of community is so markedly absent from the metaphysics of the subject, that is to say, from the metaphysics of the absolute for-itself – be it in the form of the individual or the total State – which means also the metaphysics of the *absolute* in general, of being as ab-solute, as perfectly detached, distinct, and closed: being

without relation. This ab-solute can appear in the form of the Idea, History, the Individual, the State, Science, the Work of Art, and so on. Its logic will always be the same inasmuch as it is without relation. A simple and redoubtable logic will always imply that within its very separation the absolutely separate encloses, if we can say this, more than what is simply separated. Which is to say that the separation itself must be enclosed, that the closure must not only close around a territory (while still remaining exposed, at its outer edge, to another territory, with which it thereby communicates), but also, in order to complete the absoluteness of its separation, around the enclosure itself. The absolute must be the absolute of its own absoluteness, or not be at all. In other words: to be absolutely alone, it is not enough that I be so; I must also be alone being alone – and this of course is contradictory. The logic of the absolute violates the absolute. It implicates it in a relation that it refuses and precludes by its essence. This relation tears and forces open, from within and from without at the same time, and from an outside that is nothing other than the rejection of an impossible interiority, the "without relation" from which the absolute would constitute itself.

Excluded by the logic of the absolute-subject of metaphysics (Self, Will, Life, Spirit, etc.), community comes perforce *to cut into* this subject by virtue of this same logic. The logic of the absolute *sets it in relation*: but this, obviously, cannot make for a relation between two or several absolutes, no more than it can make an absolute of the relation. It undoes the absoluteness of the absolute. The relation (the community) is, if it *is*, nothing other than what undoes, in its very principle – and at its closure or on its limit – the autarchy of absolute immanence.

Bataille constantly experienced this violent logic of being-separated. For example:

But if the ensemble of men – or more simply their integral existence – WAS INCARNATED in a single being – obviously just as solitary and as abandoned as the ensemble – the head of the INCARNATED one would be the place of an unappeasable combat – and one so violent that sooner or later it would shatter into pieces. For it is difficult to see what degree of storming and unleashing the visions of the one incarnated would attain since it ought to see God but in the same instant kill him, then become God himself but only to rush straightway into nothingness: what would come about then would be a man just as deprived of meaning as the first passerby, but deprived of all possibility of rest. (*OC* 1:547)

Such an incarnation of humanity, aggregating its absolute being beyond relation and community, depicts the destiny willed by modern thought. We shall never escape the "unappeasable combat" as long as we remain unable to protect community from this destiny.

Carrying this logic into the sphere of knowledge, Bataille, in another text, asserts:

If I "mimic" absolute knowledge, I am at once, of necessity, God myself (in the system, there can be no knowledge, not even in God, which goes beyond absolute knowledge). The thought of this self – of *ipse* – could only make itself absolute by becoming everything. *The Phenomenology of Spirit* comprises two essential movements completing a circle: it is the completion by degrees of the consciousness of the self (of human *ipse*) and the becoming everything (the becoming God) of this *ipse* completing knowledge (and by this means destroying the particularity within it, thus completing the negation of oneself, becoming absolute knowledge). But if in this way, as if by contagion and by mime, I accomplish in myself Hegel's circular movement, I define – beyond the limits attained – no longer an unknown, but an unknowable. Unknowable not on account of the insufficiency of reason, but by its nature (and even, for Hegel, one could only have concern for this beyond for lack of possessing absolute knowledge . . .). Supposing then that I were to be God, that I were to have in the world the assurance of Hegel (suppressing shadow and doubt) – knowing everything and even why fulfilled knowledge required that man, the innumerable particularities of *selves*, and history produce themselves – at precisely that moment, the question is formulated which allows human, divine existence to enter . . . the deepest foray into darkness without return; why must there be *what I know?* Why is it a necessity? In this question is hidden – it doesn't appear at first – an extreme rupture, so deep that only the silence of ecstasy answers it.[3]

The rupture (*déchirure*) hidden in the question is occasioned by the question itself, which breaks up the totality of things that are – considered in terms

of the absolute, that is to say, separate from every other "thing" – and *Being* (which is not a "thing"), through which or in the name of which these things, in their totality, are. This rupture (analogous, if not identical, to Heidegger's distinction between the ontical and the ontological) defines a *relation* to the absolute, imposing on the absolute a relation *to* its own Being instead of making this Being immanent to the absolute totality of beings. And so, Being "itself" comes to be defined as relational, as nonabsoluteness, and, if you will – in any case this is what I am trying to argue – *as community*.

Ecstasy answers – if it is properly speaking an "answer" – to the impossibility of the absoluteness of the absolute, or to the "absolute" impossibility of complete immanence. Ecstasy, if we understand it according to a rigorous strain of thinking that would pass, were we to trace its philosophical history before Bataille and during his time, by way of Schelling and Heidegger, implies no effusion, and even less some form of effervescent illumination. Strictly speaking, it defines the impossibility, both ontological and gnosological, of absolute immanence (or of the absolute, and therefore of immanence) and consequently the impossibility either of an individuality, in the precise sense of the term, or of a pure collective totality. The theme of the individual and that of communism are closely bound up with (and bound together in) the general problematic of immanence.[4] They are bound together in their denial of ecstasy. And for us the question of the community is henceforth inseparable from a question of ecstasy – which is to say, as we are beginning to understand, from the question of Being considered as something other than the absoluteness of the totality of beings.

Community, or the being-ecstatic of Being itself? That would be the question.

I would like to introduce a qualification, to which I will return later: behind the theme of the individual, but beyond it, lurks the question of singularity. What is *a* body, *a* face, *a* voice, *a* death, *a* writing – not indivisible, but singular? What is their singular necessity in the sharing that divides and that puts in communication bodies, voices, and writings in general and in totality? In sum, this question would be exactly the reverse of the question of the absolute. In this respect, it is constitutive of the question of community, and it is in this context that it will have to be taken into account later on. But singularity never has the nature or the structure of individuality. Singularity never takes place at the level of atoms, those identifiable if not identical identities; rather it takes place at the level of the *clinamen*, which is unidentifiable. It is linked to ecstasy: one could not properly say that the singular being is the subject of ecstasy, for ecstasy has no "subject" – but one must say that ecstasy (community) happens *to* the singular being.

The solidarity of the individual with communism at the heart of a thinking of immanence, while neglecting ecstasy, does not however entail a simple symmetry. Communism – as, for example, in the generous exuberance that will not let Marx conclude without pointing to a reign of freedom, one beyond the collective regulation of necessity, in which surplus work would no longer be an exploitive *work*, but rather art and invention – communicates with an extremity of play, of sovereignty, even of ecstasy from which the individual as such remains definitively removed. But this link has remained distant, secret, and most often unknown to communism itself (let us say, to lend concreteness, unknown to Lenin, Stalin, and Trotsky), except in the fulgurating bursts of poetry, painting, and cinema at the very beginning of the Soviet revolution, or the motifs that Benjamin allowed as reasons for calling oneself a Marxist, or what Blanchot tried to bring across or propose (rather than signify) with the word "communism" ("Communism: that which excludes [and excludes itself from] every community already constituted").[5] But again even this proposal in the final analysis went unrecognized, not only by "real" communism, but also, on close inspection, by those singular "communists" themselves, who were perhaps never able to recognize (until now at least) either where the metaphor (or the hyperbole) began and ended in the usage they made of the word, or, especially, what other trope – supposing it were necessary to change words – or what effacement of tropes might have been appropriate to reveal what haunted their use of the word "communism."

By the usage to which this word was put, they were able to communicate with a thinking of art, of literature, and of thought itself – other figures or other exigencies of ecstasy – but they were not truly able to communicate, explicitly and thematically (even if "explicit" and "thematic" are only very fragile categories here), with a thinking of community. Or rather, their communication with such a thinking has remained secret, or suspended.

The ethics, the politics, the philosophies of community, when there were any (and there always are, even if they are reduced to chatter about fraternity or to laborious constructions around "intersubjectivity"), have pursued their paths or their humanist deadends without suspecting for an instant that these singular voices were speaking about community and were perhaps speaking about nothing else, without suspecting that what was taken for a "literary" or "aesthetic" experience was entrenched *in* the ordeal of community, was at grips with it. (Do we need to be reminded, to take a further example, what Barthes's first writings were about, and some of the later ones as well?)

Subsequently, these same voices that were unable to communicate what, perhaps without knowing it, they were saying, were exploited – and covered up again – by clamorous declarations brandishing the flag of the "cultural revolutions" and by all kinds of "communist writing" or "proletarian inscriptions." The professionals of society saw in them (and not without reason, even if their view was shortsighted) nothing more than a bourgeois Parisian (or Berliner) form of *Proletkult*, or else merely the unconscious return of a "republic of artists," the concept of which had been inaugurated two hundred years earlier by the Jena romantics. In one way or another, it was a matter of a simple, classical, and dogmatic system of truth: an art (or a thought) adequate to politics (to the form or the description of community), a politics adequate to art. The basic presupposition remained that of a community effectuating itself in the absolute of the work, or effectuating itself as work. For this reason, and whatever it may have claimed for itself, this "modernity" remained in its principle a humanism.

We will have to return to the question of what brought about – albeit at the cost of a certain naiveté or misconception – the exigency of a literary[6] experience of community or communism. This is even, in a sense, the only question. But the terms of this question all need to be transformed, to be put back into play in a space that would be distributed quite differently from one composed of all-too-facile relations (for example, solitude of the writer/collectivity, or culture/society, or elite/masses – whether these relations be proposed as oppositions, or, in the spirit of the "cultural revolutions," as equations). And for this to happen, the question of community must first of all be put back into play, for the necessary redistribution of space depends upon it. Before getting to this, and without rescinding any of the resistant generosity or the active restlessness of the word "communism" and without denying anything of the excesses to which it can lead, but also without forgetting either the burdensome mortgage that comes along with it or the usury it has (not accidentally) suffered, we must allow that *communism* can no longer be the unsurpassable horizon of our time. And if in fact it no longer is such a horizon, this is not because we have passed beyond any horizon. Rather, everything is inflected by resignation, as if the new unsurpassable horizon took form around the disappearance, the impossibility, or the condemnation of communism. Such reversals are customary; they have never altered anything. It is the *horizons* themselves that must be challenged. The ultimate limit of community, or the limit that is formed by community, as such, traces an entirely different line. This is why, even as we establish that communism is no longer our unsurpassable horizon, we must also establish, just as forcefully, that a communist exigency or demand communicates with the gesture by means of which we must go farther than all possible horizons.

The first task in understanding what is at stake here consists in focusing on the horizon *behind* us. This means questioning the breakdown in community that supposedly engendered the modern era. The consciousness of this ordeal belongs to Rousseau, who figured a *society* that experienced or acknowledged the loss or degradation of a communitarian (and communicative) intimacy – a society producing, of necessity, the solitary figure, but one whose desire and intention was to produce the citizen of a free sovereign community. Whereas political theoreticians preceding him had thought mainly in terms of the institution of a state, or the regulation of a society, Rousseau, although he borrowed a great deal from them, was perhaps the first thinker of community, or more exactly, the first to experience the question of society as an uneasiness directed toward the community, and as the consciousness of a (perhaps irreparable) rupture in this community. This consciousness would subsequently be inherited by the Romantics, and by Hegel in *The Phenomenology of Spirit*: the last figure of spirit, before the assumption of all the figures and of history into absolute knowledge, is that which cleaves community (which for Hegel figures the split in religion). Until this day history has been thought on the basis of a lost community – one to be regained or reconstituted.

The lost, or broken, community can be exemplified in all kinds of ways, by all kinds of para-

digms: the natural family, the Athenian city, the Roman Republic, the first Christian community, corporations, communes, or brotherhoods – always it is a matter of a lost age in which community was woven of tight, harmonious, and infrangible bonds and in which above all it played back to itself, through its institutions, its rituals, and its symbols, the representation, indeed the living offering, of its own immanent unity, intimacy, and autonomy. Distinct from society (which is a simple association and division of forces and needs) and opposed to emprise (which dissolves community by submitting its peoples to its arms and to its glory), community is not only intimate communication between its members, but also its organic communion with its own essence. It is constituted not only by a fair distribution of tasks and goods, or by a happy equilibrium of forces and authorities: it is made up principally of the sharing, diffusion, or impregnation of an identity by a plurality wherein each member identifies himself only through the supplementary mediation of his identification with the living body of the community. In the motto of the Republic, *fraternity* designates community: the model of the family and of love.

But it is here that we should become suspicious of the retrospective consciousness of the lost community and its identity (whether this consciousness conceives of itself as effectively retrospective or whether, disregarding the realities of the past, it constructs images of this past for the sake of an ideal or a prospective vision). We should be suspicious of this consciousness first of all because it seems to have accompanied the Western world from its very beginnings: at every moment in its history, the Occident has given itself over to the nostalgia for a more archaic community that has disappeared, and to deploring a loss of familiarity, fraternity, and conviviality. Our history begins with the departure of Ulysses and with the onset of rivalry, dissension, and conspiracy in his palace. Around Penelope, who reweaves the fabric of intimacy without ever managing to complete it, pretenders set up the warring and political scene of society – pure exteriority.

But the true consciousness of the loss of community is Christian: the community desired or pined for by Rousseau, Schlegel, Hegel, then Bak-ouine, Marx, Wagner, or Mallarmé is understood as communion, and communion takes place, in its principle as in its ends, at the heart of the mystical body of Christ. At the same time as it is the most ancient myth of the Western world, community might well be the altogether modern thought of humanity's partaking of divine life: the thought of a human being penetrating into pure immanence. (Christianity has had only two dimensions, antinomical to one another: that of the *deus absconditus*, in which the Western disappearance of the divine is still engulfed, and that of the god-man, *deus communis*, brother of humankind, invention of a familial immanence of humanity, then of history as the immanence of salvation.)

Thus, the thought of community or the desire for it might well be nothing other than a belated invention that tried to respond to the harsh reality of modern experience: namely, that divinity was withdrawing infinitely from immanence, that the god-brother was at bottom *himself* the *deus absconditus* (this was Hölderlin's insight), and that the divine essence of community – or community as the existence of a divine essence – was the impossible itself. One name for this has been the death of God: this expression remains pregnant with the possibility if not the necessity of a resurrection that restores both man and God to a common immanence. (Not only Hegel, but also Nietzsche himself, at least in part, bears witness to this.) The discourse of the "death of God" also misses the point that the "divine" is what it is (if it "is") only inasmuch as it is removed from immanence, or withdrawn from it – within it, one might say, yet withdrawn from it. And this, moreover, occurs in the very precise sense that it is not because there is a "divine" that its share would be subtracted from immanence, but on the contrary, it is only to the extent that immanence itself, here or there (but is it localizable? Is it not rather this that localizes, that spaces?), is subtracted from immanence that there can be something like the "divine." (And perhaps, in the end, it will no longer be necessary to speak of the "divine." Perhaps we will come to see that community, death, love, freedom, singularity are names for the "divine" not just because they substitute for it – and neither sublate nor resuscitate it under another form – but equally because this substitution is in no way anthropomorphic or anthropocentric and gives way to no becoming-human of the "divine." Community henceforth constitutes the limit of the human as well as of the divine. Through God or the gods communion – as substance and act, the act of communicated immanent substance – has been definitively withdrawn from community.)[7]

The modern, humanist Christian consciousness of the loss of community therefore gives every appearance of recuperating the transcendental illusion of reason when reason exceeds the bounds of all possible experience, which is basically the experience of concealed immanence. *Community has not taken place*, or rather, if it is indeed certain that humanity has known (or still knows, outside of the industrial world) social ties quite different from those familiar to us, community has never taken place along the lines of our projections of it according to these different social forms. It did not take place for the Guayaqui Indians, it did not take place in an age of huts; nor did it take place in the Hegelian "spirit of a people" or in the Christian agape. No *Gesellschaft* has come along to help the state, industry, and capital dissolve a prior *Gemeinschaft*. It would undoubtedly be more accurate to say, bypassing all the twists and turns taken by ethnological interpretation and all the mirages of an origin or of "bygone days," that *Gesellschaft* – "society," the dissociating association of forces, needs, and signs – has taken the place of something for which we have no name or concept, something that issued at once from a much more extensive communication than that of a mere social bond (a communication with the gods, the cosmos, animals, the dead, the unknown) *and* from much more piercing and dispersed segmentation of this same bond, often involving much harsher effects (solitude, rejection, admonition, helplessness) than what we expect from a communitarian minimum in the social bond. *Society* was not built on the ruins of a *community*. It emerged from the disappearance or the conservation of something – tribes or empires – perhaps just as unrelated to what we call "community" as to what we call "society." So that community, far from being what society has crushed or lost, is *what happens to us* – question, waiting, event, imperative – *in the wake of* society.

Nothing, therefore, has been lost, and for this reason nothing is lost. We alone are lost, we upon whom the "social bond" (relations, communication), our own invention, now descends heavily like the net of an economic, technical, political, and cultural snare. Entangled in its meshes, we have wrung for ourselves the phantasms of the lost community.

What this community has "lost" – the immanence and the intimacy of a communion – is lost only in the sense that such a "loss" is constitutive of "community" itself.

It is not a loss: on the contrary, immanence, if it were to come about, would instantly suppress community, or communication, as such. Death is not only the example of this, it is its truth. In death, at least if one considers in it what brings about immanence (decomposition leading back to nature – "everything returns to the ground and becomes part of the cycle" – or else the paradisal versions of the same "cycle") and if one forgets what makes it always irreducibly *singular*, there is no longer any community or communication: there is only the continuous identity of atoms.

This is why political or collective enterprises dominated by a will to absolute immanence have as their truth the truth of death. Immanence, communal fusion, contains no other logic than that of the suicide of the community that is governed by it. Thus the logic of Nazi Germany was not only that of the extermination of the other, of the subhuman deemed exterior to the communion of blood and soil, but also, effectively, the logic of sacrifice aimed at all those in the "Aryan" community who did not satisfy the criteria of *pure* immanence, so much so that – it being obviously impossible to set a limit on such criteria – the suicide of the German nation itself might have represented a plausible extrapolation of the process: moreover, it would not be false to say that this really took place, with regard to certain aspects of the spiritual reality of this nation.

The joint suicide or death of lovers is one of the mythico-literary figures of this logic of communion in immanence. Faced with this figure, one cannot tell which – the communion or the love – serves as a model for the other in death. In reality, with the immanence of the two lovers, death accomplishes the infinite reciprocity of two agencies: impassioned love conceived on the basis of Christian communion, and community thought according to the principle of love. The Hegelian state in its turn bears witness to this, for although it certainly is not established on the basis of love – for it belongs to the sphere of so-called objective spirit – it nonetheless has as its *principle* the reality of love, that is to say the fact "of having in another the moment of one's own subsistence." In this state, each member has his truth in the other, which is the state itself, whose reality is never more present than when its members give their lives in a war that the monarch – the effective presence-to-self of the subject-state – has alone and freely decided to wage.[8]

Doubtless such immolation for the sake of community – and by it, therefore – could and can be full of meaning, on the condition that this "mean-ing" be that of a community, and on the further condition that this community not be a "community of death" (as has been the case since at least World War I, thereby justifying all refusals to "die for one's country"). Now the community of human immanence, man made equal to himself or to God, to nature, and to his own works, is one such community of death – or of the dead. The fully realized person of individualistic or communistic humanism is the dead person. In other words, death, in such a community, is not the unmasterable excess of finitude, but the infinite fulfillment of an imman-ent life: it is death itself consigned to immanence; it is in the end that resorption of death that the Christian civilization, as though devouring its own transcendence, has come to minister to itself in the guise of a supreme work. Since Leibnitz there has been no death in our universe: in one way or another an absolute circulation of meaning (of values, of ends, of History) fills or reabsorbs all finite negativity, draws from each finite singular destiny a surplus value of humanity or an infinite superhumanity. But this presupposes, precisely, the death of each and all in the life of the infinite.

Generations of citizens and militants, of workers and servants of the states have imagined their death reabsorbed or sublated in a community, yet to come, that would attain immanence. But by now we have nothing more than the bitter conscious-ness of the increasing remoteness of such a com-munity, be it the people, the nation, or the society of producers. However, this consciousness, like that of the "loss" of community, is superficial. In truth, death is not sublated. The communion to come does not grow distant, it is not deferred: it was never to come; it would be incapable of coming about or forming a future. What forms a future, and consequently what truly comes about, is always the singular death – which does not mean that death does not come about in the community: on the contrary, I shall come to this. But communion is not what comes of death, no more than death is the simple perpetual past of community.

Millions of deaths, of course, are *justified* by the revolt of those who die: they are justified as a rejoinder to the intolerable, as insurrections against social, political, technical, military, religious oppression. But these deaths are not *sublated*: no dialectic, no salvation leads these deaths to any other immanence than that of . . . death (cessation, or decomposition, which forms only the parody or reverse of immanence). Yet the modern age has conceived the justification of death only in the guise of salvation or the dialectical sublation of history. The modern age has struggled to *close the circle* of the time of men and their communities in an immortal communion in which death, finally, loses the senseless meaning that it ought to have – and that it has, obstinately.

We are condemned, or rather reduced, to search for this meaning beyond meaning of death elsewhere than in community. But the enterprise is absurd (it is the absurdity of a thought derived from the individual). Death is indissociable from community, for it is through death that the community reveals itself – and reciprocally. It is not by chance that this motif of a reciprocal revelation has preoccupied thought informed by ethnology as well as the thinking of Freud and Heidegger, and at the same time Bataille, that is to say in the time leading from World War I to World War II.

The motif of the revelation, through death, of being-together or being-with, and of the crystallization of the community around the death of its members, *that is to say around the "loss" (the impossibility) of their immanence* and not around their fusional assumption in some collective hypostasis, leads to a space of thinking incommensurable with the problematics of sociality or intersubjectivity (including the Husserlian problematic of the alter ego) within which philosophy, despite its resistance, has remained captive. Death irremediably exceeds the resources of a metaphysics of the subject. The phantasm of this metaphysics, the phantasm that Descartes (almost) did not dare have but that was already proposed in Christian theology, is the phantasm of a dead man who says, like Villiers' Monsieur Waldemar, "I am dead" – *ego sum . . . mortuus*. If the *I* cannot say that it is dead, if the *I* disappears in effect in *its* death, in that death that is precisely what is most proper to it and most inalienably its own, it is because the *I* is something other than a subject. All of Heidegger's research into "being-for (or toward)-death" was nothing other than an attempt to state this: *I* is not – *am* not – a subject. (Although, when it came to the question of community as such, the same Heidegger also went astray with his vision of a people and a destiny conceived at least in part as a subject,[9] which proves no doubt that Dasein's "being-toward-death" was never radically implicated in its being-with – in *Mitsein* – and that it is this implication that remains to be thought.)

That which is not a subject opens up and opens onto a community whose conception, in turn, exceeds the resources of a metaphysics of the sub-

ject. Community does not weave a superior, immortal, or transmortal life between subjects (no more than it is itself woven of the inferior bonds of a consubstantiality of blood or of an association of needs), but it is constitutively, to the extent that it is a matter of a "constitution" here, calibrated on the death of those whom we call, perhaps wrongly, its "members" (inasmuch as it is not a question of an organism). But it does not make a work of this calibration. Community no more makes a work out of death than it is itself a work. The death upon which community is calibrated does not *operate* the dead being's passage into some communal intimacy, nor does community, for its part, *operate* the transfiguration of its dead into some substance or subject – be these homeland, native soil or blood, nation, a delivered or fulfilled humanity, absolute phalanstery, family, or mystical body. Community is calibrated on death as on that of which it is precisely impossible to *make a work* (other than a work of death, as soon as one tries to make a work of it). Community occurs in order to acknowledge this impossibility, or more exactly – for there is neither function nor finality here – the impossibility of making a work out of death is inscribed and acknowledged as "community."

Community is revealed in the death of others; hence it is always revealed to others. Community is what takes place always through others and for others. It is not the space of the *egos* – subjects and substances that are at bottom immortal – but of the *I*'s, who are always *others* (or else are nothing). If community is revealed in the death of others it is because death itself is the true community of *I*'s that are not *egos*. It is not a communion that fuses the *egos* into an *Ego* or a higher *We*. It is the community of *others*. The genuine community of mortal beings, or death as community, establishes their impossible communion. Community therefore occupies a singular place: it assumes the impossibility of its own immanence, the impossibility of a communitarian being in the form of a subject. In a certain sense community acknowledges and inscribes – this is its peculiar gesture – the impossibility of community. A community is not a project of fusion, or in some general way a productive or operative project – nor is it a *project* at all (once again, this is its radical difference from "the spirit of a people," which from Hegel to Heidegger has figured the collectivity as project, and figured the project, reciprocally, as collective – which does not mean that we can ignore the question of the singularity of a "people").

A community is the presentation to its members of their mortal truth (which amounts to saying that there is no community of immortal beings: one can imagine either a society or a communion of immortal beings, but not a community). It is the presentation of the finitude and the irredeemable excess that make up finite being: its death, but also its birth, and only the community can present me my birth, and along with it the impossibility of my reliving it, as well as the impossibility of my crossing over into my death.

If it sees its fellow-being die, a living being can subsist only *outside itself*. . . .
Each one of us is then driven out of the confines of his person and loses himself as much as possible in the community of his fellow creatures. It is for this reason that it is necessary for communal life to maintain itself at a level *equal to death*. The lot of a great number of private lives is pettiness. But a community cannot last except at the level of intensity of death – it decomposes as soon as it falls shy of danger's peculiar grandeur. It must take upon it what is "unappeasable" and "unappeased," and maintain a need that thirsts for glory. A man among thousands can have an intensity of life that is practically zero throughout the day: he behaves as though death did not exist and holds himself, without harm, beneath its level. (*OC* 7:245–6)

No doubt Bataille has gone farthest into the crucial experience of the modern destiny of community. Whatever the interest accorded his thought (and this remains, despite everything, a meager and all too often frivolous interest), what has not yet been sufficiently remarked[10] is the extent to which his thinking emerged out of a political exigency and uneasiness – or from an exigency and an uneasiness concerning the political that was itself guided by the thought of community. . . .
The reversal of the nostalgia for a lost community into the consciousness of an "immense failure" of the history of communities was linked for Bataille to the "inner experience," whose content, truth, or ultimate lesson is articulated thus: "Sovereignty is NOTHING." Which is to say that sovereignty is the sovereign exposure to an excess (to a transcendence) that does not present itself and does not let itself be appropriated (or simulated), that does not even *give* itself – but rather to which being is abandoned. The excess to which sovereignty is exposed and exposes us *is* not, in a sense

quite close to the sense in which Heideggerian Being "*is* not," that is, in the sense in which the Being of the finite being is less what makes it be than what leaves it abandoned to such an exposition. The Being of the finite being exposes it to the end of Being.

Thus, exposure to the NOTHING of sovereignty is the opposite of the movement of a subject who would reach the limit of nothingness (and this constitutes, at bottom, the permanent movement of the Subject, indefinitely devouring *in itself* the nothingness represented by everything that is not *for itself*; in the end, this is the autophagy of truth). "In" the "NOTHING" or in nothing – in sovereignty – being is "*outside itself*"; it is in an exteriority that is impossible to recapture, or perhaps we should say that it is *of* this exteriority, that it is of an outside that it cannot relate to *itself*, but with which it entertains an essential and incommensurable relation. This relation prescribes the place of the singular being. This is why the "inner experience" of which Bataille speaks is in no way "interior" or "subjective," but is indissociable from the experience of this relation to an incommensurable outside. Only community furnishes this relation its spacing, its rhythm.

In this sense, Bataille is without doubt the one who experienced first, or most acutely, the modern experience of community as neither a work to be produced, nor a lost communion, but rather as space itself, and the spacing of the experience of the outside, of the outside-of-self. The crucial point of this experience was the exigency, reversing all nostalgia and all communal metaphysics, of a "clear consciousness" of separation – that is to say of a "clear consciousness" (in fact the Hegelian *self-consciousness* itself, but *suspended* on the limit of its access to *self*) of the fact that immanence or intimacy cannot, nor are they ever to be, *regained*.

For this very reason, however, the exigency of "clear consciousness" is everything but that abandonment of community that would favor, for example, a reversion to the positions of the individual. The individual as such is only a thing,[11] and the *thing*, for Bataille, can be defined as the being without communication and without community. Clear consciousness of the communal *night* – this consciousness at the extremity of consciousness that is also the suspension of Hegelian desire (of consciousness's desire for recognition), the finite interruption of infinite desire, and the infinite syncope of finite desire (sovereignty itself: desire outside desire and mastery outside itself) – this "clear" consciousness, then, cannot take place elsewhere than in community, or rather it can only take place as the communication of community: both as what communicates within community, and as what community communicates.[12]

This consciousness – or this communication – is ecstasy: which is to say that such a consciousness is never *mine*, but to the contrary, I only have it in and through the community. This resembles, almost to the point that one might confuse it with, what in other contexts one might call a "collective unconscious" – a consciousness that perhaps more closely resembles what can be located throughout Freud as the ultimately collective essence of what he calls the unconscious. But it is not an unconscious – that is to say it is not the reverse side of a subject, nor its splitting. It has nothing to do with the subject's structure as *self*: it is clear consciousness at the extremity of its clarity, where consciousness *of* self turns out to be outside the self of consciousness.

Community, which is not a subject, and even less a subject (conscious or unconscious) greater than "myself," does not *have* or possess this consciousness: community *is* the ecstatic consciousness of the night of immanence, insofar as such a consciousness is the interruption of self-consciousness.

Notes

1 Georges Bataille, *Oeuvres Complètes*, vol. 1 (Paris: Gallimard, 1970), p. 332. Subsequent references to this work are indicated in the text as *OC*, volume and page number.

2 Considered in detail, taking into account the precise historical conjuncture of each instance, this is not rigorously exact as regards, for example, the Hungarian Council of '56, and even more so the left of Solidarity in Poland. Nor is it absolutely exact as regards all of the discourses held today: one might, in this respect alone, juxtapose the situationists of not so long ago with certain aspects of Hannah Arendt's thought and also, as strange or provocative as the mixture might appear, certain propositions advanced by Lyotard, Badiou, Ellul, Deleuze, Pasolini, and Rancière. These thoughts occur, although each one engages it in its own particular way (and sometimes whether they know it or not), in the wake of a Marxist event that I will try to characterize below and that signifies for us the bringing into question of communist or communitarian humanism (quite different from the questioning once undertaken by Althusser in the name of a Marxist science). This is also why such propositions communicate with what I shall name, tentatively and in spite of everything, "literary communism."

3 Georges Bataille, *Inner Experience*, trans. Leslie Anne Boldt (New York: State University of New York Press, 1988), pp. 108–9.

4 Michel Henry's reading of Marx, which is oriented around the conceptual reciprocity of the "individual" and "immanent life," bears witness to this. In this regard, "by principle the individual ecsapes the power of the dialectic" (Michel Henry, *Marx* [Paris: Gallimard, 1976], vol. 2, p. 46). This might permit me to preface everything I have to say with the following general remark: there are two ways of escaping the dialectic (that is to say mediation in a totality) – either by slipping away from it into immanence or by opening up its negativity to the point of rendering it "unworked" (*désoeuvré*), as Bataille puts it. In this latter case, there is no immanence of negativity: "there is" *ecstasy*, ecstasy of knowledge as well as of history and community.

5 "Le communisme sans héritage," revue *Comité*, 1968, in *Gramma* no. 3/4 (1976), p. 32.

6 For the moment, let us retain simply that "literature," here, must above all not be taken in the sense Bataille gave to the word when he wrote, for example (in his critique of *Inner Experience* and *Guilty*): "I have come to realize through experience that these books lead those who read them into complacency. They please most often those vague and impotent minds who want to flee and sleep and *satisfy* themselves with the escape provided by literature" (*OC* 8:583). He also spoke of the "sliding into impotence of thought that turns to literature" (ibid.).

7 See chapter 5, "Of Divine Places."

8 See J.-L. Nancy, "La juridiction du monarque hégélien," in *Rejouer le politique* (Paris: Galilée, 1981). Translation forthcoming in *The Birth to Presence* (Stanford: Stanford University Press).

9 See Philippe Lacoue-Labarthe, "Transcendence Ends in Politics," trans. P. Caws, in *Typography: Mimesis, Philosophy, Politics*, ed. C. Fynsk, Harvard University Press, 1989, pp. 267–300, and G. Granel, "Pourquoi avoir publié cela?" in *De l'université* (Toulouse: T.E.R., 1982).

10 Except for Denis Hollier, already in *La Prise de la Concorde* (Paris: Gallimard, 1974) and in particular with the publication of *Collège de sociologie* (Paris: Gallimard, 1979), English translation by Betsy Wing, *The College of Sociology* (Minneapolis: University of Minnesota Press, 1988). More recently, Francis Marmande has published a systematic examination of Bataille's political preoccupations. See *Georges Bataille politique* (Paris: Parenthèses, 1985).

11 See, for example, *OC* 7:312.

12 I employ the term "communication" in the manner of Bataille, that is to say, following the pattern of a permanent violence done to the word's meaning, both because it implies subjectivity or intersubjectivity and because it denotes the transmission of a message and a meaning. Rigorously, this word is untenable. I retain it because it resonates with "community," but I would superimpose upon it (which sometimes means substitute for it) the word "sharing." Bataille was aware that the violence he had inflicted upon the concept of "communication" was insufficient: "*To be isolated, communication,* have only one reality. Nowhere do there exist 'isolated beings' who do not communicate, nor is there a 'communication' independent of points of isolation. Let us be careful to set aside two poorly made concepts, the residue of puer-ile beliefs; by this means we will cut through the most poorly constructed problem" (*OC* 7:553). What this calls for, in short, is the deconstruction of the concept, such as Jacques Derrida has undertaken in "Signature, Event, Context," in *Margins of Philosophy*, trans. A. Bass (Chicago: University of Chicago Press, 1982), and such as it has been pursued, in another manner, by Gilles Deleuze and Félix Guattari ("Postulates of Linguistics," in *A Thousand Plateaux*, trans. B. Massumi [Minneapolis: University of Minnesota Press, 1987]). These operations necessarily entail a general re-evaluation of communication in and *of* the community (of speech, of literature, of exchange, of the image, etc.), in respect to which the current use of the term "communication" can only be provisional and preliminary.

Select Bibliography

The Birth to Presence. Translated by Brian Holmes and others. Stanford: Stanford University Press, 1993.

The Experience of Freedom. Translated by Bridget McDonald. Stanford: Stanford University Press, 1993.

The Inoperative Community. Edited by Peter Connor. Translated by Peter Connor, Lisa Garbus, Michael Holland, and Simona Sawhney. Minneapolis: University of Minnesota Press, 1991.

The Literary Absolute: The Theory of Literature in German Romanticism (with Philippe Lacoue-Labarthe). Translated by Philip Barnard and Cheryl Lester. Albany: State University of New York Press, 1988.

The Muses. Translated by Peggy Kamuf. Stanford: Stanford University Press, 1996.

The Title of the Letter: A Reading of Lacan (with Philippe Lacoue-Labarthe). Translated by David Pettigrew and Francois Raffoul. Albany: State University of New York Press, 1992.

12

Jean Baudrillard

French sociologist Jean Baudrillard (1929–) is best known for his influential analyses of contemporary technological society as a society in which reality apparently becomes indistinguishable in the end from its media presentation. Influenced by the work of Marshall McLuhan, Baudrillard argues that technological existence unfolds as the presentation of simulacra, that is, of images that correspond to no underlying reality or truth, but operate as a play of signification in which it becomes increasingly impossible to identify any original or uncontaminated reality. Where reality becomes virtualized in this manner, where the virtual and the real become fused, existence has been transformed into what Baudrillard calls "hyperreality." The following excerpt from *The Ecstasy of Communication* (1987) analyzes this hyperreality as an "ecstasy of communication" in which the very meaning of reality has been transformed.

The Ecstasy of Communication

Everything began with objects, yet there is no longer a system of objects. The critique of objects was based on signs saturated with meaning, along with their phantasies and unconscious logic as well as their prestigious differential logic. Behind this dual logic lies the anthropological dream: the dream of the object as existing beyond and above exchange and use, above and beyond equivalence; the dream of a sacrificial logic, of gift, expenditure,

From *The Ecstasy of Communication*, edited by Sylvère Lotringer, translated by Bernard and Caroline Schutze (New York: Semiotext(e), 1988), pp. 11–27, 103–4.

potlatch, "devil's share" consumption, symbolic exchange.[1]

All this still exists, and simultaneously it is disappearing. The description of this projective imaginary and symbolic universe was still the one of the object as the mirror of the subject. The opposition of the subject and the object was still significant, as was the profound imaginary of the mirror and the scene.[2] The scene of history as well as the scene of the everyday emerge in the shadow of history as it is progressively divested of politics. Today the scene and the mirror have given way to a screen and a network. There is no longer any transcendence or depth, but only the immanent surface of operations unfolding, the smooth and functional surface of communication. In the image of television, the most beautiful prototypical object of this new era, the surrounding universe and our very bodies are becoming monitoring screens.

We no longer invest our objects with the same emotions, the same dreams of possession, loss, mourning, jealousy; the psychological dimension has been blurred, even if one can still retrieve it in the particular.

Barthes already foresaw this for the car, where the logic of possession, from the projection inherent in strong subjective relation is substituted by a logic of driving. No more power, speed, appropriation phantasies linked to the object itself, but a potential tactic linked to its use – mastery, control and command, optimization of the game of possibilities, which the automobile offers as a vector, and no longer as a psychological sanctuary – resulting in the transformation of the subject himself into a driving computer, instead of the demi-urge drunk with power. The vehicle thus becomes a bubble, the dashboard a console, and the landscape all around unfolds as a television screen.

However, one can conceive of a subsequent stage to this one, where the car is still a performative instrument, the stage at which it becomes an informing network. That is, the car which speaks to you, which informs you spontaneously of its general state and yours (eventually refusing to function if you are not functioning well), the advising, the deliberating car, a partner in a general negotiation on life-styles; something (or some*one*, since at this stage there is no more difference) to which you are *wired*, the communication with the car becoming the fundamental stake, a perpetual test of the presence of the subject *vis-á-vis* his objects – an uninterrupted interface.

From here on neither speed nor traveling – not even the unconscious projection, competition, or prestige – count any longer. In fact the desacralization of the car has been going on for some time now in the sense that "Speed is out! Drive more and consume less." A kind of ecological ideal is taking over, an ideal of regulation, of moderate functionality, of solidarity between all the elements of one and the same system, of the control and global management of the whole. Each system (including the domestic universe) forms a kind of ecological niche, with a relational decor where all terms must remain in perpetual contact with one another, informed as to their respective strategies and that of the entire system because the failure of one term could lead to catastrophe.

Although this is no doubt only a discourse, one must take note that the analysis of consumption in the sixties and seventies originated in the advertising discourse or in the pseudo-conceptual discourse of professionals.[3] "Consumption," the "strategy of desire" were at first only a metadiscourse, the analysis of a projective myth whose real consequences were generally unknown.[4] Actually no more was known about the relation of people to their objects than about the reality of primitive societies. This is what allows one to build the myth, but it is also the reason why it is useless to try and objectively verify these hypotheses through statistics. As we know, the discourse of advertisers is for the use of professionals in the field, and who could say that the present discourse on computer science is not accessible strictly to professionals in computer science and communication (the discourse of intellectuals and sociologists, for that matter, raises the same question).

Private telematics: each individual sees himself promoted to the controls of a hypothetical machine, isolated in a position of perfect sovereignty, at an infinite distance from his original universe; that is to say, in the same position as the astronaut in his bubble, existing in a state of weightlessness which compels the individual to remain in perpetual orbital flight and to maintain sufficient speed in zero gravity to avoid crashing into his planet of origin.

The realization of the orbital satellite in the universe of the everyday corresponds to the elevation of the domestic universe to the celestial metaphor, with the orbiting of the two-room/kitchen/bathroom unit in the last lunar model; hence to the satellization of the real itself. The everydayness of the terrestrial habitat hypostatized in space marks the end of metaphysics, and signals the beginning of the era of hyperreality: that which was previously mentally projected, which was lived as a metaphor in the terrestrial habitat is from now on projected, entirely without metaphor, into the absolute space of simulation.

Our private sphere has ceased to be the stage where the drama of the subject at odds with his objects and with his image is played out: we no longer exist as playwrights or actors but as terminals of multiple networks. Television is the most direct prefiguration of this, and yet today one's private living space is conceived of as a receiving and operating area, as a monitoring screen endowed with telematic power, that is to say, with the capacity to regulate everything by remote control. Including the work process, within the prospects of telematic work performed at home, as well as consumption, play, social relations, leisure. One could conceive of simulating leisure or vacation situations in the same way that flight is simulated for pilots.

Is this science fiction? Yes, but up until now all environmental mutations derived from an irreversible tendency towards a formal abstraction of elements and functions, to their homogenization into a single process, as well as to the displacement of gestural behaviors: of bodies, of efforts, in electric or electronic commands, to the miniaturization in time and space. These are processes where the stage (which is no longer a stage) becomes that of the infinitesimal memory and the screen.

This is our problem, insofar as this electronic encephalization, this miniaturization of circuits and of energy, this transistorization of the environment condemn to futility, to obsolescence and almost to obscenity, all that which once constituted the stage of our lives. We know that the simple presence of television transforms our habitat into a kind of archaic, closed-off cell, into a vestige of human relations whose survival is highly questionable. From the moment that the actors and their phantasies have ceased to haunt this stage, as soon as behavior is focused on certain operational screens or terminals, the rest appears only as some vast useless body, which has been both abandoned and condemned. The real itself appears as a large, futile, body.

The era of miniaturization, of remote control, and of a microprocessing of time, bodies, and pleasure has come. There is no longer an ideal principle of these things on a human scale. All that remains are miniaturized, concentrated and immediately available effects. This change of scale is discernable everywhere: the human body, our body, seems superfluous in its proper expanse, in the complexity and multiplicity of its organs, of its tissue and functions, because today everything is concentrated in the brain and the genetic code, which alone sum up the operational definition of being. The landscape, the immense geographical landscape seems a vast, barren body whose very expanse is unnecessary (even off the highway it is boring to cross), from the moment that all events are concentrated in the cities, which are also being reduced to several extemely miniaturized high places. And what about time, this vast leisure time we are left with, and which engulfs us like an empty terrain; an expanse rendered futile in its unfolding from the moment that the instantaneousness of communication miniaturizes our exchanges into a series of instants?

The body as a stage, the landscape as a stage, and time as a stage are slowly disappearing. The same holds true for the public space: the theater of the social and of politics is progressively being reduced to a shapeless, multi-headed body. Advertising in its new version is no longer the baroque, utopian scenario ecstatic over objects and consumption, but rather the effect of the omnipresent visibility of corporations, trade marks, PR men, social dialogue, and the virtues of communication. With the disappearance of the public place, advertising invades everything (the street, the monument, the market, the stage, language). It determines architecture and the creation of super-objects such as Beaubourg, Les Halles, or La Villette[5] – which are literally advertising monuments (or anti-monuments) – not so much because they are centered on consumption, but because from the outset these monuments were meant to be a demonstration of the operation of culture, of the cultural operation of the commodity and that of the masses in movement. Today our only architecture is just that: huge screens upon which moving atoms, particles, and molecules are refracted. The public stage, the public place have been replaced by a gigantic circulation, ventilation, and ephemeral connecting space.

The private space undergoes the same fate. Its disappearance parallels the diminishing of the public space. Both have ceased to be either spectacle or secret. The distinction between an interior and an exterior, which was just what characterized the domestic stage of objects and that of a symbolic space of the object has been blurred in a *double obscenity*. The most intimate operation of your life becomes the potential grazing ground of the media (non-stop television on the Louds family in the USA,[6] endless "slice of life" and "psy" shows on French TV). The entire universe also unfolds unnecessarily on your home screen. This is a microscopic pornography, pornographic because it is forced, exaggerated, just like the close-up of sexual acts in a porno film. All this destroys the stage, once preserved through a minimal distance and which was based on a secret ritual known only to its actors.

The private universe was certainly alienating, insofar as it separated one from others, from the world in which it acted as a protective enclosure, as an imaginary protector. Yet it also contained the symbolic benefit of alienation (the fact that the other exists) and that otherness can be played out for better or for worse. Thus the consumer society was lived under the sign of alienation; it was a society of spectacle – but at least there was spectacle, and the spectacle, even if alienated, is never obscene.[7] Obscenity begins when there is no more spectacle, no more stage, no more theater, no more illusion, when everything becomes immediately transparent, visible, exposed in the raw and inexorable light of information and communication.

We no longer partake of the drama of alienation, but are in the ecstasy of communication. And this ecstasy is obscene. Obscene is that which eliminates the gaze, the image and every representation. Obscenity is not confined to sexuality, because today there is a pornography of information and communication, a pornography of circuits and networks, of functions and objects in their legibility, availability, regulation, forced signification, capacity to perform, connection, polyvalence, their free expression. . . .

It is no longer the obscenity of the hidden, the repressed, the obscure, but that of the visible, the all-too-visible, the more-visible-than-visible; it is the obscenity of that which no longer contains a secret and is entirely soluble in information and communication.

Marx already denounced the obscenity of the commodity, which is linked to the principle of its equivalence, to the abject principle of free circulation. The obscenity of the commodity derives from the fact that it is abstract, formal, and light in comparison with the weight, opacity, and substance of the object. The commodity is legible, as opposed to the object, which never quite reveals its secret, and it manifests its visible essence – its price. It is the locus of transcription of all possible objects: through it, objects communicate – the merchant form is the first great medium of the modern world. But the message which the objects deliver is radically simplified and is always the same – their exchange value. And so, deep down the message has already ceased to exist, it is the medium which imposes itself in its pure circulation. Let us call this ecstasy: the market is an ecstatic form of the circulation of goods, as prostitution and pornography are ecstatic forms of the circulation of sex.

One need only carry this analysis to its full potential to grasp what has happened to transparence and the obscenity of the universe of communication, which have long surpassed the obscenities still relative to the universe of the commodity.

Ecstasy is all functions abolished into one dimension, the dimension of communication. All events, all spaces, all memories are abolished in the sole dimension of information: this is obscene.

Hot, sexual obscenity is followed by cool communicational obscenity. The former implied a form of promiscuity, a clutter of objects accumulated in the private universe, or everything that remains unspoken and teeming in the silence of repression. However, this promiscuity is organic, visceral, carnal, while the promiscuity which reigns over the communication networks is one of a superficial saturation, an endless harassment, an extermination of interstitial space. When I pick up my telephone the marginal network hooks me up and keeps harping at me with the unbearable good will of that which seeks and claims to communicate. Deregulated radio speaks, sings, expresses itself.[8] All very well, but in terms of the medium the result is a space – that of the FM frequency – which is saturated with overlapping stations, so that what was once free by virtue of there having been space is no longer so. The word is free, but I am not; the space is so saturated, the pressure of all which wants to be heard so strong that I am no longer capable of knowing what I want. I plunge into the negative ecstasy of radio.

There is a state particular to fascination and giddiness. It is a singular form of pleasure, perhaps, but it is aleatory and dizzying. If one goes along with Roger Caillois' classification of games – mimicking, *agôn*, *alea*, *ilinx*: games of expression, games of competition, games of chance, games of giddiness[9] – then the movement of our entire culture will lead from a disappearance of the forms of expression and competition towards an extension of the forms of chance (*alea*) and giddiness.

These no longer imply any game of the scene, the mirror, challenge or otherness; they are rather, ecstatic, solitary, and narcissistic. Pleasure is no longer that of the scenic or aesthetic manifestation (*seductio*) but that of pure fascination, aleatory, and psychotropic (*subductio*). This does not necessarily imply a negative judgment, since the forms of pleasure and perception undoubtedly undergo a profound and original mutation. We can hardly assess the consequences of such a transformation. In applying our old criteria and the reflexes of a "scenic" sensibility, we run the risk of misconstruing the irruption of this new ecstatic and obscene form in our sensorial sphere.

One thing is for certain: if the scene seduced us, the obscene fascinates us. However, ecstacy is the opposite of passion. Desire, passion, seduction, or again, according to Caillois, expression and competition, are the games of the hot universe. Ecstasy, fascination, obscenity (Caillois' chance and giddiness), are games of the cold and cool universe (even giddiness is cold, especially the giddiness of drugs).

In any case we will suffer from this forced extraversion of all interiority, from this forced introjection of all exteriority which is implied by the categorical imperative of communication. Perhaps in this case one should apply metaphors drawn from pathology. If hysteria was the pathology of the exacerbated staging of the subject – of the theatrical and operational conversion of the body – and if paranoia was the pathology of organization – of the structuring of a rigid and jealous world – then today we have entered into a new form of schizophrenia – with the emergence of an immanent promiscuity and the perpetual interconnection of all information and communication networks. No more hysteria, or projective paranoia as such, but a state of terror which is characteristic of the schizophrenic, an over-proximity of all things, a foul promiscuity of all things which beleaguer and penetrate him, meeting with no resistance, and no halo, no aura, not even the aura of his own body protects him. In spite of himself the schizophrenic is open to everything and lives in the most extreme confusion. He is the obscene victim of the world's obscenity. The schizophrenic is not, as generally claimed, characterized by his loss of touch with reality, but by the absolute proximity to and total instantaneousness with things, this over-exposure to the transparency of the world. Stripped of a stage and crossed over without the least obstacle, the schizophrenic cannot produce the limits of his very being, he can no longer produce himself as a mirror. He becomes a pure screen, a pure absorption and resorption surface of the influent networks....

Conclusion

And what if reality dissolved before our very eyes? Not into nothingness, but into the more real than real (the triumph of simulacra)? What if the modern universe of communication, of hyper-communication, had plunged us, not into the senseless, but into a tremendous saturation of meaning entirely consumed by its success – without the game, the secret, or distance? If all publicity were the apology, not of a product, but of publicity? If information no longer had anything to do with an event, but were concerned with promoting information itself as the event? If history were only an accumulative, instantaneous memory without a past? If our society were no longer that of the "spectacle," as was said in '68, but, cynically, that of ceremony? If politics were increasingly a dated continent, replaced by the dizziness of terrorism, of a generalized hostage-taking, this very figure of the impossible exchange? If all this mutation did not arise out of a manipulation of subjects and opinions, as some believed, but out of a logic without a subject, a logic in which opinion has collapsed into fascination? If pornography signified the end of the sexual as such, from the instant that sex in its obscene form has invaded everything? If seduction followed desire and love, that is, once again the reign of the object and that of the subject? If, as a result, strategy replaced psychology? If it were no longer a question of setting truth against illusion, but of perceiving the prevalent illusion as truer than truth? If no other behavior were possible but to learn, ironically, to disappear? If there were no more fractures, no more vanishing lines, no more lines of rupture, but only a surface that is full and continuous, surface without depth, without interruption? And if all this were neither exciting, nor despairing – but fatal?

Notes

1 These concepts derive from Marcel Mauss and Georges Bataille, and were used extensively in Baudrillard's *L'Échange symbolique et la mort* (Paris: Gallimard, 1976). (Original ed.)

2 A reference to Jacques Lacan's celebrated "mirror phase," developed in *Écrits* (New York: Norton, 1977), and explored in Baudrillard's own *Mirror of Production* (St Louis: Telos, 1975). (Original ed.)

3 See Jean Baudrillard's *La Société de consommation* (Paris: Denoël, 1970). (Original ed.)

4 An allusion to Gilles Deleuze and Félix Guattari's *Anti-Oedipus* (New York: Viking, 1977). (Original ed.)

5 Three vast Parisian areas turned into public malls or museums. See Baudrillard's "The Beaubourg Effect," in *October*, no. 20, (spring, 1982). (Original ed.)

6 See Jean Baudrillard, *Simulations* (New York: Semi-
   otext(e), 1983). (Original ed.)

7 See Guy Debord's Situationist manifesto, *The Society
   of the Spectacle* (Detroit: Black and Red, 1977). (Original ed.)

8 *Radios libres*: a vast political attempt to reclaim the
   media at the end of the 1970s. (Original ed.)

9 Roger Caillois, *Les Jeux et les hommes* (Paris: Gallimard, 1967). (Original ed.)

Select Bibliography

America. Translated by Chris Turner. New York: Verso,
1989.

Baudrillard Live: Selected Interviews. Edited by Mike
Gane. London: Routledge, 1993.

The Ecstasy of Communication. Edited by Sylvère Lotringer. Translated by Bernard and Caroline Schutze. New
York: Semiotext(e), 1988.

For a Critique of the Political Economy of the Sign. Translated by Charles Levin. St Louis: Telos Press, 1981.

Forget Foucault. New York: Semiotext(e), 1987.

The Gulf War Did Not Take Place. Translated by Paul
Patton. Bloomington: Indiana University Press, 1995.

The Illusion of the End. Translated by Chris Turner.
Stanford: Stanford University Press, 1994.

*In the Shadow of the Silent Majorities – Or the End of the
Social, and Other Essays*. Translated by Paul Foss, Paul
Patton, and John Johnston. New York: Semiotext(e),
1983.

Jean Baudrillard: Selected Writings. Edited by Mark Pos-
ter. Stanford: Stanford University Press, 1988.

Seduction. Translated by Brian Singer. New York: St
Martin's Press, 1990.

Simulations. Translated by Paul Foss, Paul Patton, and
Philip Beitchman. New York: Semiotext(e), 1983.

Symbolic Exchange and Death. Translated by Iain Hamilton Grant. London: Sage Publications, 1993.

The Transparency of Evil: Essays on Extreme Phenomena.
Translated by James Benedict. London: Verso, 1993.

13

Slavoj Žižek

The Nation-Thing

A researcher at the Institute of Social Sciences at the University of Ljubljana in Yugoslavia, Slavoj Žižek has become known for his use of Lacanian psychoanalysis in analyzing contemporary social, political, and cultural phenomena. His studies address a wide range of issues in fields such as literature, film theory and media studies, contemporary philosophy, and political theory. In the following selection from *Looking Awry* (1991), Žižek employs the categories of Lacanian psycho-analysis to illuminate the limits and constitutive paradox of formal democracy. In addition to suggesting why and how this formal model of democracy is increasingly being questioned by contemporary social movements such as ecology and feminism, Žižek's analysis is particularly insightful with regard to the significance of the repeated resurgences of nationalism and ethnic tensions in the twentieth century.

The Democratic Abstraction

. . . We should begin with an elementary question: who is the subject of democracy? The Lacanian answer is unequivocal: the subject of democracy is not a human person, "man" in all the richness of his needs, interests, and beliefs. The subject of democracy, like the subject of psychoanalysis, is none other than the Cartesian subject in all its

From *Looking Awry: An Introduction to Jacques Lacan through Popular Culture* (Cambridge, Mass.: MIT Press, 1991), pp. 162–9. © 1991 Massachusetts Institute of Technology.

abstraction, the empty punctuality we reach after subtracting all its particular contents. In other words, there is a structural homology between the Cartesian procedure of radical doubt that produces the *cogito*, an empty point or reflective self-reference as a remainder, and the preamble of every democratic proclamation "all people *without regard to* (race, sex, religion, wealth, social status)." We should not fail to notice the violent act of abstraction at work in this "without regard to"; it is an abstraction of all positive features, a dissolution of all substantial, innate links, which produces an entity strictly correlative to the Cartesian *cogito* as a point of pure, nonsubstantial subjectivity. Lacan likened the subject of psychoanalysis to this entity, to the great surprise of those used to the "psycho-analytic image of man" as a wealth of "irrational" drives; he denotes the subject by a crossed-out S, indicating thereby a constitutive lack of any support that would offer the subject a positive, substantial identity. It is because of this lack of identity, that the concept of *identification* plays such a crucial role in psychoanalytic theory: the subject attempts to fill out its constitutive lack by means of identification, by identifying itself with some master-signifier guaranteeing its place in the symbolic network.

This violent act of abstraction does not express an ideologically overstretched image of democracy, an "exaggeration never met in real life," it pertains on the contrary to the very logic we follow as soon as we accept the principle of formal democracy: "democracy" is fundamentally "antihumanistic," it is not "made to the measure of (concrete, actual) men," but to the measure of a formal, heartless abstraction. There is in the very notion of democracy no place for the fullness of concrete human content, for the genuineness of community links: democracy *is* a formal link of abstract individuals. All attempts to fill out democracy with "concrete contents" succumb sooner or later to the totalitarian temptation, however sincere their motives may be.[1] Critics of democracy are thus correct in a way: democracy implies a split between the abstract *citoyen* and the *bourgeois* bearer of particular, "pathological" interests, and any reconciliation between the two is structurally impossible. Or, to refer to the traditional opposition between *Gesellschaft* (society, as a mechanical, external agglomeration of atomized individuals) and *Gemeinschaft* (society as a community held together by organic links): democracy is definitely bound up with *Gesellschaft*; it literally lives on the split between the "public" and "private," it is possible only within the framework of what was once, when the voice of Marxism was still heard, called "alienation."

Today, we can perceive this affinity of democracy with "alienated" *Gesellschaft* in the so-called "new social movements": ecology, feminism, the peace movement. They differ from traditional political movements (parties) by a certain self-limitation, the reverse side of which is a certain surplus; they want at the same time "less" and "more" than the traditional parties. That is to say, the "new social movements" are reluctant to enter the routine political struggle, they continually emphasize

their unwillingness to become political parties like the others, they exempt themselves from the sphere of the struggle for power. At the same time, however, they make it clear that their aim is much more radical than that of the ordinary political parties: what they are striving after is a fundamental transformation of the entire mode of action and belief, a change in the "life paradigm" affecting our most intimate attitudes. They offer, for example, a new attitude toward nature, which would no longer be that of domination but rather that of a dialogic interplay; against aggressive "masculine" reason, they stand for a pluralistic, "soft," "feminine" rationality, etc. In other words, it is not possible to be an ecologist or feminist in quite the same way as one can be a conservative or a social democrat in a Western formal democracy. What is at stake in the former case is not just a political belief but an entire life attitude. And such a project of radical change in the "life paradigm," once formulated as a political program, necessarily undermines the very foundations of formal democracy. The antagonism between formal democracy and the "new social movements" is irreducible, which is why this antagonism has to be fully assumed and not eluded by means of utopian projects for a "concrete democracy" which would absorb the whole diversity of the so-called "life-world."

The subject of democracy is thus a pure singularity, emptied of all content, freed from all substantial ties; and, according to Lacan, the problem with this subject does not lie where neoconservatism sees it. The problem is not that this abstraction proper to democracy dissolves all concrete substantial ties, but rather that *it can never dissolve them*. The subject of democracy is, in its very blankness, smeared with a certain "pathological" stain. The "democratic break" – the casting away of the wealth of particular contents constitutive of the democratic subject, homologous to the "epistemological break" through which science constitutes itself by freeing itself from the realm of ideological notions – never comes about without a certain remainder. This remainder is, however, not to be conceived as an empirical limitation, that which causes the break to fail. Instead this remainder possesses an *a priori* status, it is a positive condition of the "democratic break," its very support. Precisely insofar as it claims to be "pure," "formal," democracy remains forever tied to a contingent moment of positivity, of material "content": by losing this material support, the very form dissolves itself.

. . . And Its Leftover

This leftover to which formal democracy clings, that which renders possible the subtraction of all positive contents, is of course the ethnic moment conceived as "nation": democracy is always tied to the "pathological" fact of a nation-state. Every attempt to inaugurate a "planetary" democracy based upon the community of all people as "citizens of the world" soon attests its own impotence, fails to arouse political enthusiasm. Here we have again an exemplary case of the Lacanian logic of not-all where the universal function is founded upon an exception: the ideal leveling of all social differences, the production of the citizen, the subject of democracy, is possible only through an allegiance to some particular national Cause. If we apprehend this Cause as the Freudian Thing (*das Ding*), materialized enjoyment, it becomes clear why it is precisely "nationalism" that is the privileged domain of the eruption of enjoyment into the social field: the national Cause is ultimately the way subjects of a given nation organize their collective enjoyment through national myths. What is at stake in ethnic tensions is always the possession of the national Thing: the "other" wants to steal our enjoyment (by ruining our "way of life") and/or it has access to some secret, perverse enjoyment. In short, what gets on our nerves, what really bothers us about the "other," is the peculiar way he organizes his enjoyment (the smell of his food, his "noisy" songs and dances, his strange manners, his attitude to work – in the racist perspective, the "other" is either a workaholic stealing our jobs or an idler living on our labor). The basic paradox is that our Thing is conceived as something inaccessible to the other and at the same time threatened by him; this is similar to castration which, according to Freud, is experienced as something that "really cannot happen," but whose prospect nonetheless horrifies us.

The eruption of the national Thing in all its violence has always taken the devotees of international solidarity by surprise. Perhaps the most traumatic case of this was the debacle of the international workers' movement in the face of "patriotic" euphoria at the outbreak of World War I. Today, it is difficult to imagine what a traumatic shock it was to the leaders of all currents of social democracy, from Edouard Bernstein to Lenin, when the social democratic parties of all countries (with the exception of the Bolsheviks in Russia and Serbia) gave way to chauvinist outbursts and "patriotically" stood behind "their" respective governments, oblivious to the proclaimed solidarity of the working class "without country": this shock bears witness to an encounter of the real of enjoyment. Yet in some ways these chauvinist outbursts of "patriotic feeling" were far from unexpected: years before the actual outbreak of the war, social democracies drew the attention of workers to the fact that imperialist forces were preparing for a new world war, and warned against yielding to "patriotic" chauvinism. Even at the outbreak of the war, i.e. in the days following the Sarajevo assassination, the German social democrats cautioned workers that the ruling class would use the assassination as an excuse to declare war. Furthermore, the Socialist International adopted a formal resolution obliging all its members to vote against war credits in case of war – but with the outbreak of the war, internationalist solidarity vanished into thin air. This overnight reversal took Lenin by surprise: when he read in the daily newspaper that the social democratic deputies had voted for the war credits, he was at first convinced that this issue was fabricated by German police to lead workers astray!

Consequently, it is not sufficient to say that "pure" democracy is not possible: the crucial point is where we locate this impossibility. "Pure" democracy is not impossible because of some empirical inertia that prevents its full realization but which may be gradually abolished by democracy's further development; rather, democracy is possible only on the *basis* of its own impossibility; its limit, the irreducible "pathological" remainder, is its positive condition. At a certain level, this was already known to Marx (which is why, according to Lacan, the origin of the notion of the symptom is to be found in Marx): the "formal democracy" of the market, its equivalent exchange, implies "exploitation," appropriation of the surplus value, but this imbalance is not an indication of an "imperfect" realization of the principle of equivalent exchange, rather equivalent market exchange is *the very form of "exploitation,"* of the appropriation of surplus value. That is to say, formal equivalence is the form of a nonequivalence of contents. Herein lies the connection between the *objet petit a*, surplus enjoyment, and the Marxian notion of surplus value (Lacan himself coined the term *surplus enjoyment* on the model of *surplus value*): surplus value is the "material" remainder, the surplus contents, appropriated by the capitalist through the very form of the equivalent exchange between capital and the labor force.

One need not wait for Marx, however, to discover the imbalance, the paradoxes of the bourgeois principle of formal equality; difficulties had already arisen with the Marquis de Sade. His project for a "democracy of enjoyment" – as articulated in his pamphlet "Frenchmen, yet another effort if you want to be republicans...," included in *Philosophy in the Bedroom*[2] – stumbles upon the fact that democracy can only be a democracy of the subject (of the signifier): *there is no democracy of the object*. The respective domains of fantasy and symbolic law are radically incommensurable. That is to say, it is in the very nature of fantasy to resist universalization: fantasy is the absolutely particular way every one of us structures his/her "impossible" relation to the traumatic Thing. It is the way every one of us, by means of an imaginary scenario, dissolves and/or conceals the fundamental impasse of the inconsistent big Other, the symbolic order. The field of the law, of "rights" and "duties," on the other hand, pertains by its very nature to the dimension of universality, it is a field of universal equalization brought about by equivalent exchange and reciprocity. We could thus define *objet petit a*, the object-cause of desire embodying surplus enjoyment, precisely as the surplus that escapes the network of universal exchange, which is why the formula of fantasy as irreducible to the dimension of universality is $S \Diamond a$, i.e. the subject confronted with this "impossible" surplus.

The "heroism" of Sade's project consists in its impossible endeavor to confer upon the very field of enjoyment (of the fantasy structuring enjoyment) the bourgeois form of universal legality, of equivalent exchange, of the reciprocity of equal rights and duties. To the list of the "rights of man" proclaimed by the French revolution, Sade adds the "right to enjoyment," an embarrassing supplement that secretly subverts the universal field of rights in which it purports to place itself. Again we witness the logic of the not-all: the field of the universal "rights of man" is based upon the exclusion of a certain right (the right to enjoyment); as soon as we include this particular right, the very field of universal rights is thrown off balance. Sade starts from the statement that the French revolution got stuck halfway: in the domain of enjoyment, it remained prisoner of prerevolutionary, patriarchal, nonemancipated values. But as Lacan demonstrated in "Kant with Sade," any attempt to give to the "right to enjoyment" the

form of a universal norm in conformity with the "categorical imperative" necessarily ends in a deadlock. Such a Sadian norm would affirm that anybody – irrespective of his/her sex, age, social status, etc. – has a right to dispose freely of any part of my body in order to satisfy in any conceivable way his/her desires. In Lacan's fictional reconstruction, this reads: "I have the right of enjoyment over your body, anyone can say to me, and I will exercise this right, without any limit stopping me in the capriciousness of the exactions that I might have the taste to satiate."[3] Lacan points out that such a universal norm, although satisfying the criterion of Kant's categorical imperative, is self-defeating insofar as it excludes reciprocity: ultimately, one always gives more than one takes, i.e. everybody finds himself occupying the position of the victim. For that reason, it is not possible to sanction the right to enjoyment in the form "Everyone has a right to exert his/her particular fantasy!" Sooner or later, we entangle ourselves in a kind of self-obstruction; by definition, fantasies cannot coexist peacefully in some neutral medium. For example, since there is no sexual relationship, man can develop an endurable relation with a woman only insofar as she enters the frame of his peculiarly perverted fantasy. What can we say, then, about somebody with whom a sexual relation is possible only when the clitoris is cut out? Moreover, what can we say about *the woman* who accepts this and demands the right to undergo the painful ritual of cutting out her clitoris? Is this part of her "right to enjoyment," or are we supposed to liberate her in the name of Western values from this "barbaric" way of organizing her enjoyment? This point is, there is no way out: even if we say a woman can humiliate herself as long as she does so of her own free will, we can imagine the existence of a fantasy that consists in being humiliated *against* her will.

What to do, then, once we are confronted with this fundamental impasse of democracy? The "modernist" procedure (the one to which Marx is attached) would be to conclude – from such an "unmasking" of formal democracy, i.e. from the disclosure of the way the democratic form always conceals an imbalance of contents – that formal democracy as such has to be abolished, replaced by a superior form of concrete democracy. The "postmodernist" approach would require us, on the contrary, to assume this constitutive paradox of democracy. We must assume a kind of "active forgetfulness" by accepting the symbolic fiction even though we know that "in reality, things are not like that." The democratic attitude is always based upon a certain fetishistic split: *I know very well* (that the democratic form is just a form spoiled by stains of "pathological" imbalance), *but just the same* (I act as if democracy were possible). Far from indicating its fatal flaw, this split is the very source of the strength of democracy: democracy is able to take cognizance of the fact that its limit lies in itself, in its internal "antagonism." This is why it can avoid the fate of "totalitarianism," which is condemned ceaselessly to invent external "enemies" to account for its failures.

Freud's "Copernican turn," his subversion of the self-centered image of man, is thus not to be conceived as a renunciation of the Enlightenment, as a deconstruction of the notion of the autonomous subject, i.e. of the subject freed from the constraint of external authority. The point of Freud's "Copernican turn" is *not* to demonstrate that the subject is ultimately a puppet in the hands of unknown forces that escape his grasp (unconscious drives, etc.). It does not improve things to exchange this naive, naturalist notion of the unconscious for a more sophisticated notion of the unconscious as "discourse of the great Other" that makes the subject the place where language itself speaks, i.e. an agency subjected to decentered signifying mechanisms. Despite some Lacanian propositions that echo this structuralist notion,

this sort of "decentering" does not capture the objective of Lacan's "return to Freud." According to Lacan, Freud is far from proposing an image of man as a victim of "irrational" drives, proper to *Lebensphilosophie*; he assumes without restraint the fundamental gesture of the Enlightenment: a refusal of the external authority of tradition and a reduction of the subject to an empty, formal point of negative self-relation. The problem is that, by "circulating around itself," as its own sun, this autonomous subject encounters in itself something "more than itself," a strange body in its very center. This is what Lacan's neologism *extimité* aims at, the designation of a stranger in the midst of my intimacy. Precisely by "circulating only around itself," the subject circulates around something that is "in itself more than itself," the traumatic kernel of enjoyment that Lacan refers to by the German word *das Ding*. The subject is perhaps nothing but a name for this circular movement, for this distance toward the Thing which is "too hot" to be approached closely. It is because of this Thing that the subject resists universalization, that it cannot be reduced to a place – even if it is an empty place – in the symbolic order. It is because of this Thing that at a certain point, love for the neighbor necessarily turns into destructive hatred, in accordance with the Lacanian motto *I love you, but there is in you something more than you*, objet petit a, *which is why I mutilate you*.

Notes

1 The fate of Emmanuel Mounier, the founder of personalism, is here very suggestive. In theory, he strove for the recognition of the dignity and uniqueness of the human person against the double threat of liberal individualism and totalitarian collectivism; he is remembered above all as a hero of the French resistance. A crucial detail of his biography is, however, as a rule passed over in silence: after the French defeat in 1940, Mounier for a whole year placed his hope in Petain's corporativism, apprehending it as a unique opportunity to reinstate the spirit of organic community. Only afterward, disillusioned by Vichy's "excesses," did he turn to the resistance. In short, Mounier strove for "fascism with a human face," he wanted fascism without its dirty obverse, and he renounced it only on experiencing the illusiveness of this hope.

2 Cf. D. A. F. de Sade, *Philosophy in the Bedroom and Other Writings*, New York, Grove Press, 1966.

3 Lacan, *Écrits*, pp. 768–9.

Select Bibliography

Enjoy Your Symptom!: Jacques Lacan in Hollywood and Out. New York: Routledge, 1992.

Everything You Always Wanted to Know about Lacan (But Were Afraid to Ask Hitchcock). Edited by Slavoj Žižek. London: Verso, 1992.

For They Know Not What They Do: Enjoyment as a Political Factor. London: Verso, 1991.

The Indivisible Remainder: An Essay On Schelling and Related Matters. London: Verso, 1996.

Looking Awry: An Introduction to Jacques Lacan through Popular Culture. Cambridge, Mass.: MIT Press, 1991.

Mapping Ideology. Edited by Slavoj Žižek. London: Verso, 1994.

Slavoj Žižek

The Metastases of Enjoyment: Six Essays on Woman and Causality. London: Verso, 1994.

The Sublime Object of Ideology. London: Verso, 1989.

Tarrying with the Negative: Kant, Hegel, and the Critique of Ideology. Durham, NC: Duke University Press, 1993.

Index

Index

Index

Index